FROM OURS TO YOURS.

THE BEST CARS, SERVICE & RATES.

We offer the hottest cars for rent or lease.
Our fleet consists of any exotic, sport, convertible and prestige car available.

We offer free airport or local pickup, and with an advanced call, can have a car waiting for you at the hotel of your choice.

For business or pleasure, we fit right in your budget.

Beverly Hills CAR COLLECTION Budget

Treat yourself to the best.

For reservations and rate information, call toll-free
(800) 729-7350 or (310) 278-1273

An independent Budget System Licensee

FILM PRODUCERS, STUDIOS, AGENTS AND CASTING DIRECTORS

GUIDE

Third Edition

FILM PRODUCERS, STUDIOS, AGENTS AND CASTING DIRECTORS

GUIDE

Third Edition

Compiled and Edited by
David M. Kipen & Jack Lechner

LONE EAGLE

FILM PRODUCERS, STUDIOS, AGENTS AND CASTING DIRECTORS GUIDE
Third Edition

LONE EAGLE PUBLISHING CO.
2337 Roscomare Road, Suite Nine
Los Angeles, CA 90077
310/471-8066

Printed in the United States of America

Book design by Heidi Frieder and Liz Ridenour

This book was entirely typeset using an Apple Macintosh Plus, Apple Macintosh Two, LaserwriterPlus, Microsoft Word and Aldus Pagemaker.

Printed by McNaughton & Gunn, Saline, Michigan 48176

ISBN: 0-943728-44-4

NOTE: We have made every reasonable effort to ensure that the information contained herein is as accurate as possible. However, errors and omissions are sure to occur. We would appreciate your notifying us of any which you may find.

* Lone Eagle Publishing is a division of Lone Eagle Productions, Inc.

LONE EAGLE PUBLISHING STAFF
Publishers ....Joan V. Singleton
                                             Ralph S. Singleton
Editorial Director ....Bethann Wetzel
Advertising Director ....Lori Copeland
Editorial Assistant ....Steven A. LuKanic
Art Director ....Heidi Frieder
Computer Consultant ....Glenn Osako

iv

LETTER FROM THE PUBLISHERS

FILM
PRODUCERS,
STUDIOS,
AGENTS AND
CASTING
DIRECTORS
GUIDE

Producers, Studios, Agents and Casting Directors. When you think of it, a great deal of a movie's destiny is determined by these four groups.

As we enter 1992, the film industry is in a state of flux. The recession is being felt in a heretofore recession-proof industry. There is an actors' strike threatened for June and the big-budget pictures that were supposed to rescue the industry from the slump are not performing the way everyone had hoped.

Give up? Lock the doors? Change professions? Ask any producer worth his/her salt in phone logs and they will tell you, "Never!" Times like these are just ripe for opportunity, and the producers listed within these pages are the ones who will seize upon it. These are the people who can get films made, even in the worst of times. These are the people who will recognize that terrific script and then spend their lives on the phone negotiating the deal, convincing the director, the stars and finally the financing entity that their project should be made. These are the people who initiate the projects and then put them to bed years later.

Studios are changing, too. Overseas buyers now control many of the majors who have converted their love of movies into a love of movie studios. Time will be the judge as to how this new marriage works. But as always, the personnel changes so quickly that the daily trades have a hard time keeping up, let alone an annual directory. We hope that you will keep us posted of your new phone number and title when you are on the move.

Someone recently compared the agencies of today with the studios of the past. They have stables of talent, the ability to package, and many of them have the financing, too. All they lack is distribution which they then contract from the studios. In a recent entertainment publication, the most powerful person in Hollywood is not a director, not a producer, not a star...but an agent.

In the past we have listed casting directors—these powerful people with the Midas touch—but this year we add something new: their credits. So, for all you producers out there looking for the right casting director to find that special new face for your film, this should make it easier.

Let's see what 1992 brings for all of us. Hopefully a resurgence in the industry and a proliferation of new movies for us to enjoy, discuss and even argue about.

Again, our constant plea to you. Please keep us informed of your contact and credit information so that we may be as up-to-date as possible. And, let us know how we can improve our directories to make them even more useful to you.

We thank you for your continued support.

Joan V. Singleton and Ralph S. Singleton
Publishers

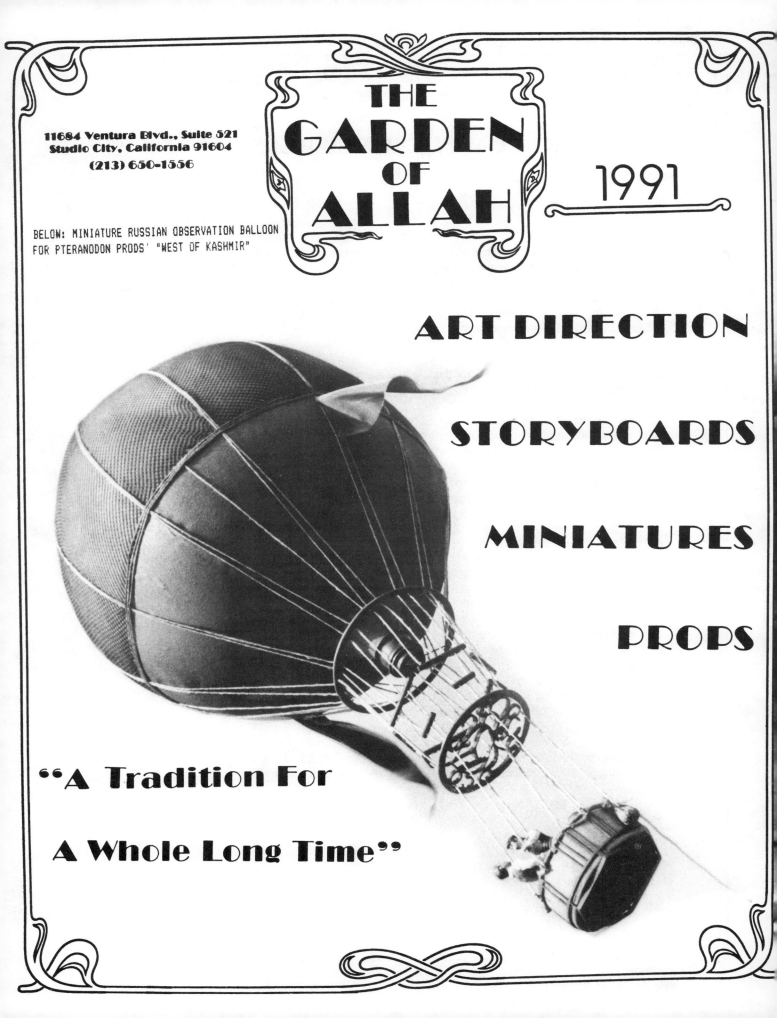

11684 Ventura Blvd., Suite 521
Studio City, California 91604
(213) 650-1556

THE GARDEN OF ALLAH

1991

BELOW: MINIATURE RUSSIAN OBSERVATION BALLOON
FOR PTERANODON PRODS' "WEST OF KASHMIR"

ART DIRECTION

STORYBOARDS

MINIATURES

PROPS

"A Tradition For

A Whole Long Time"

FILM
PRODUCERS,
STUDIOS,
AGENTS AND
CASTING
DIRECTORS
GUIDE

TABLE OF CONTENTS

FILM
PRODUCERS,
STUDIOS,
AGENTS AND
CASTING
DIRECTORS
GUIDE

KEY TO ABBREVIATIONS

EP = Executive Producer

CP = Co-Producer

SP = Supervising Producer

LP = Line Producer

AP = Associate Producer

FD = Feature Documentary

AF = Animated Feature

w/ = sharing the same credit with

KEY TO SYMBOLS

★ = after a film title denotes an Academy Award nomination

★★ = after a film titles denotes an Academy Award win.

† = denotes deceased person

* = credit not shared

INTRODUCTION

FILM
PRODUCERS,
STUDIOS,
AGENTS AND
CASTING
DIRECTORS
GUIDE

In Hollywood, a third film means you have a series, not just a movie and its sequel. So in the tradition of *ANOTHER THIN MAN, GOLDFINGER*, and *JAWS 3-D,* welcome to the third edition of the **FILM PRODUCERS, STUDIOS, AGENTS and CASTING DIRECTORS GUIDE.** In keeping up with the hundreds of new releases and personnel changes since our last edition, we sometimes feel like Alice in Wonderland; it takes all the running we can do to stay in the same place. This year, however, we've tried to run a little farther. The book now includes cross-referenced credits for casting directors — information not available in any other film sourcebook — and the producer listings are now complete from 1970 to the present.

The book consists of four sections:

FILM PRODUCERS lists credits for producers of feature films released in the United States over the last few decades. Not listed are most foreign films; short films; films made for television; films produced by people who have long since left the industry, or are deceased (unless co-produced with people who haven't and aren't); grade-Z exploitation films (unless the producer later graduated to at least grade-B); and films released directly on videocassette.

The section is organized alphabetically by producer, and indexed alphabetically by film title. We have omitted any names listed on a film's credits as "Presented By" or "In Association With," as well as Associate Producers who have no prior or subsequent credits in some other producing capacity. We realize this does a disservice to some significant producers, but we believe the minimum requirement for any book is that it be portable.

Alternate or foreign titles are listed in italics after the primary U.S. title. When a co-producer is listed in parentheses at the start of a producer entry, all credits *without* an asterisk are shared. (This does not necessarily mean that the two producers are business partners, either past or present.) Please refer to the KEY TO ABBREVIATIONS on page viii if you need help deciphering any of the symbols in the listings.

Films that have been nominated for a Best Picture Oscar are noted with one star (★), Best Picture winners with two stars (★★). Unlike the Academy, we have extended this recognition to every producer on each of the films. For a list of recent nominees and winners, see page two.

AGENTS lists talent agents and agencies serving the film industry, primarily in Los Angeles, New York and London. To the greatest extent possible, we have listed the names of agents who deal primarily with the film industry, i.e., theatrical agents.

STUDIOS lists current personnel and contact information for major studios, "mini-majors," independent distributors, and selected production companies. This information changes constantly, so please regard these listings as a snapshot of the way things were at the beginning of 1992. Many smaller production companies are not listed, but can be found under their principals' headings in the Producers Guide.

CASTING DIRECTORS lists credits and contact information for active film and television casting directors, chiefly in Los Angeles and New York. The accompanying index is alphabetical by film title.

FILM
PRODUCERS,
STUDIOS,
AGENTS AND
CASTING
DIRECTORS
GUIDE

Thanks as always to the wonderful team at Lone Eagle Publishing; Joan, Ralph, Katie and Elizabeth Singleton, Bethann Wetzel, Mike Green and Steve LuKanic. Another slaute to Michael Singer and our fellow Lone Eagle editors, whom we hope will raid this book for information as frequently as we raid their books. We're also indebted to the intrepid librarians at the Academy of Motion Picture Art and Sciences' Margaret Herrick Library, and the heroically fire-resistant Los Angeles Public Library at 433 S. Spring Street. And a toast to the people at agencies and production companies who helped us compile and confirm this information — may all your movies show a net profit.

David thanks Dick Adler for giving Miles Beller his first big break, and Miles for giving David his; Michael Canary, computer mahatma, for not having his phone number changed; Pat Raymond and Michael J. Wolfe, for their impeccable disk hygiene; Lisa Horowitz, for her help with the casting section; Meredith Kornfeld, for access to her capacious video library; Steven Amsterdam, for improbably trusting someone of my organizational skills with a valued reference book; my beloved new niece Sydney, and the looming figures she will come to recognize as her screwy family; Veronique de Turenne, for what not? and, of course, you Jack, for an ISBN number to call our own.

Jack thanks David, for taking over the care and feeding of this albatross; Susan Avallone, our partner in trivia; John Willis, a man I'd like to meet, whose annual *Screen World* books are the skeleton key to the film industry; the baffled clerks at several L.A. video stores, who were sure the guy in the corner scribbling names on a notepad was some kind of Federal agent; David Aukin and the very nice people at Channel Four; and my wife Sam Maser, who is always right.

In the tradition of *TARZAN FINDS A SON, ROAD TO UTOPIA*, and *POLICE ACADEMY 4: CITIZENS ON PATROL*, there will eventually be a fourth edition of this guide. Please do send us any comments, suggestions, updates, or corrections to keep us un our toes and off everybody else's. Meanwhile, enjoy the book, and support your local cinema!

Jack Lechner and David Kipen
London and Los Angeles

FILM PRODUCERS

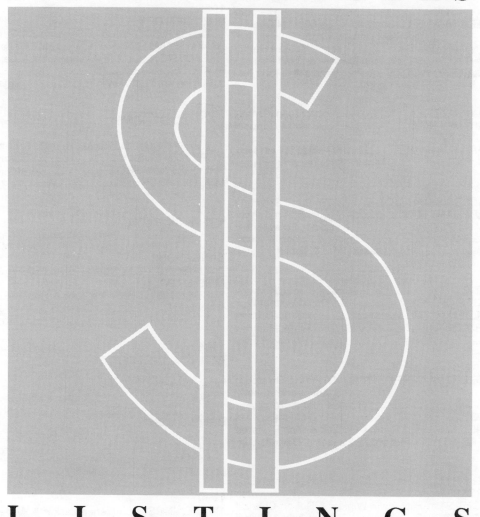

LISTINGS

Academy Awards & Nominations
1977-1990

★★ = Winner in the category

1977
ANNIE HALL ....Charles H. Joffe★★
THE GOODBYE GIRL ....Ray Stark
JULIA ....Richard Roth
STAR WARS ....Gary Kurtz
THE TURNING POINT .....Herbert Ross & Arthur Laurents

1978
COMING HOME ....Jerome Hellman
THE DEER HUNTER ...Barry Spikings, Michael Deeley,
        Michael Cimino & John Peverall★★
HEAVEN CAN WAIT ....Warren Beatty
MIDNIGHT EXPRESS ......Alan Marshall & David Puttnam
AN UNMARRIED WOMAN .....Paul Mazursky & Tony Ray

1979
ALL THAT JAZZ ....Robert Alan Aurthur
APOCALYPSE NOW..........................Francis Coppola
BREAKING AWAY ....Peter Yates
KRAMER VS. KRAMER ....Stanley R. Jaffe★★
NORMA RAE ....Tamara Asseyev & Alex Rose

1980
COAL MINER'S DAUGHTER ....Bernard Schwartz
THE ELEPHANT MAN ....Jonathan Sanger
ORDINARY PEOPLE ....Ronald L. Schwary★★
RAGING BULL ....Irwin Winkler & Robert Chartoff
TESS ....Claude Berri & Timothy Burrill

1981
ATLANTIC CITY ....Denis Heroux & John Kemeny
CHARIOTS OF FIRE ....David Puttnam★★
ON GOLDEN POND ....Bruce Gilbert
RAIDERS OF THE LOST ARK .... Frank Marshall
REDS .... Warren Beatty

1982
E.T. THE EXTRA-TERRESTRIAL .....Steven Spielberg
        & Kathleen Kennedy
GANDHI ....Richard Attenborough★★
MISSING ....Edward Lewis & Mildred Lewis
TOOTSIE ....Sydney Pollack & Dick Richards
THE VERDICT ....Richard D. Zanuck & David Brown

1983
THE BIG CHILL ....Michael Shamberg
THE DRESSER ....Peter Yates
THE RIGHT STUFF .....Irwin Winkler & Robert Chartoff
TENDER MERCIES ....Philip S. Hobel
TERMS OF ENDEARMENT ....James L. Brooks★★

1984
AMADEUS...Saul Zaentz★★
THE KILLING FIELDS ....David Puttnam
A PASSAGE
        TO INDIA ....John Brabourne & Richard Goodwin
PLACES IN THE HEART ....Arlene Donovan
A SOLDIER'S STORY ....Norman Jewison, Ronald L.
        Schwary & Patrick Palmer

1985
THE COLOR PURPLE ....Steven Spielberg, Kathleen
        Kennedy, Frank Marshall & Quincy Jones
KISS OF THE SPIDER WOMAN ....David Weisman
OUT OF AFRICA ....Sydney Pollack★★
PRIZZI'S HONOR ....John Foreman
WITNESS ....Edward S. Feldman

1986
CHILDREN OF A
        LESSER GOD ......Burt Sugarman & Patrick Palmer
HANNAH AND HER SISTERS ....Robert Greenhut
THE MISSION ....Fernando Ghia & David Puttnam
PLATOON ....Arnold Kopelson★★
A ROOM WITH A VIEW ....Ismail Merchant

1987
BROADCAST NEWS ....James L. Brooks
FATAL
        ATTRACTION .....Stanley R. Jaffe & Sherry Lansing
HOPE AND GLORY ....John Boorman
THE LAST EMPEROR ....Jeremy Thomas★★
MOONSTRUCK ....Norman Jewison

1988
THE ACCIDENTAL
        TOURIST ....Lawrence Kasdan, Charles Okun &
        Michael Grillo
DANGEROUS
        LIAISONS ....Norma Heyman & Hank Moonjean
MISSISSIPPI
        BURNING ....Frederick Zollo & Robert F. Colesberry
RAIN MAN ....Mark Johnson★★
WORKING GIRL ....Douglas Wick

1989
BORN ON THE FOURTH
        OF JULY ....Oliver Stone & A. Kitman Ho
DEAD POETS
        SOCIETY ....Steven Haft, Tony Thomas &
        Paul Junger Witt
DRIVING MISS
        DAISY ....Lili Fini Zanuck & Richard D. Zanuck★★
FIELD OF
        DREAMS ....Charles Gordon & Lawrence Gordon
MY LEFT FOOT ....Noel Pearson & Arthur Lappin

1990
AWAKENINGS ....Lawrence Lasker & Walter F. Parkes
DANCES WITH
        WOLVES ....Kevin Costner & Jim Wilson★★
GHOST...Lisa Weinstein
THE GODFATHER PART III ....Francis Ford Coppola
GOODFELLAS ....Irwin Winkler

★ ★ ★ ★

A

ELLIOT ABBOTT
Business: Parkway Productions, 10202 W. Washington Blvd., Culver City, CA, 310/280-4474; Fax: 310/280-1474

HOME OF THE BRAVE (FD) Cinecom, 1986, EP
AWAKENINGS ★ Columbia, 1990, EP w/Penny Marshall & Arne L. Schmidt

STEVE ABBOTT
Business: Prominent Features Ltd., 68A Delancey St., London NW1 7RY, 071/284-0242; Fax: 071/284-1004

A FISH CALLED WANDA MGM/UA, 1988, EP w/John Cleese
AMERICAN FRIENDS MCEG Virgin Vision, 1991, w/Patrick Cassavetti
BLAME IT ON THE BELLBOY Buena Vista, 1992, EP

NICK ABDO
Agent: David Shapira & Associates - Sherman Oaks, 818/906-9845
Contact: Directors Guild of America - Los Angeles, 213/289-2000

YOUNG DOCTORS IN LOVE 20th Century Fox, 1982, AP w/Jeffrey Ganz
THE FLAMINGO KID 20th Century Fox, 1984, AP
NOTHING IN COMMON TriStar, 1986, AP
OVERBOARD MGM, 1987, AP
BEACHES Buena Vista, 1988, CP

ALAN ABEL
(credit w/Jeanne Abel)

IS THERE SEX AFTER DEATH Abel-Child, 1971
THE FAKING OF THE PRESIDENT Spencer, 1976

JEANNE ABEL
(credit w/Alan Abel)

IS THERE SEX AFTER DEATH Abel-Child, 1971
THE FAKING OF THE PRESIDENT Spencer, 1976

ROBERT ABEL
(credit w/Pierre Adidge)
Contact: Directors Guild of America - Los Angeles, 213/289-2000

JOE COCKER/MAD DOGS AND ENGLISHMEN (FD) MGM, 1971, w/Harry Marks
ELVIS ON TOUR (FD) MGM, 1972

MARC ABRAHAM
Business: Beacon Pictures, 1041 North Formosa Ave., Hollywood, CA 90046, 213/850-2651; Fax: 213/850-2613

A MIDNIGHT CLEAR Interstar, 1991, EP w/Armyan Bernstein & Tom Rosenberg

JIM ABRAHAMS
Agent: United Talent - Beverly Hills, 310/273-6700
Business: Abrahams Boy, Inc., c/o Howard & Cohen, 11835 W. Olympic, Suite 1160, Los Angeles, CA 90064

AIRPLANE! Paramount, 1980, EP w/David Zucker & Jerry Zucker
THE NAKED GUN: FROM THE FILES OF POLICE SQUAD! Paramount, 1988, EP w/David Zucker & Jerry Zucker
CRY-BABY Universal, 1990, EP w/Brian Grazer
THE NAKED GUN 2 1/2: THE SMELL OF FEAR Paramount, 1991, EP w/Jerry Zucker & Gil Netter

MORT ABRAHAMS
GOODBYE, MR. CHIPS MGM, 1969, AP
THE CHAIRMAN 20th Century Fox, 1969
BENEATH THE PLANET OF THE APES 20th Century Fox, 1970, AP
TO FIND A MAN *THE BOY NEXT DOOR/SEX AND THE TEENAGER* Columbia, 1972, EP
LUTHER American Film Theatre, 1974, EP
THE MAN IN THE GLASS BOOTH American Film Theatre, 1975, EP
THE GREEK TYCOON Universal, 1978, EP w/Peter Howarth & Les Landau
THE HOLCROFT COVENANT Universal, 1985, EP
SEVEN HOURS TO JUDGMENT Trans World Entertainment, 1988

JACK ABRAMOFF
RED SCORPION Shapiro Glickenhaus, 1989

ROBERT ABRAMOFF
RED SCORPION Shapiro Glickenhaus, 1989, EP w/Paul Erickson & Daniel Sklar

GERALD W. ABRAMS
Business: Hearst Entertainment, 1640 S. Sepulveda Blvd., 4th Floor, Los Angeles, CA 90025, 310/478-1700; Fax: 310/478-2202

HEARTS OF FIRE Lorimar, 1988, EP w/Doug Harris

JEFFREY ABRAMS
REGARDING HENRY Paramount, 1991, CP

PETER ABRAMS
Business: Tapestry Films, c/o Writers Building, Suite 12, 1041 North Formosa Ave., West Hollywood, CA 90046-6798, 213/850-3591; Fax: 213/850-3571

THE KILLING TIME New World, 1987, w/Robert L. Levy

RICHARD GILBERT ABRAMSON
(credit w/William E. McEuen)

BANJOMAN Blue Pacific, 1975, w/Robert French & Michael Varhol
PEE-WEE'S BIG ADVENTURE Warner Bros., 1985, w/Robert Shapiro*
BIG TOP PEE-WEE Paramount, 1988, EP
THE BIG PICTURE Columbia, 1989, EP

BERLE ADAMS
BRASS TARGET United Artists, 1978, EP

FILM
PRODUCERS,
STUDIOS,
AGENTS AND
CASTING
DIRECTORS
GUIDE

CATLIN ADAMS
Agent: Triad Artists, Inc. - Los Angeles, 310/556-2727
Contact: Directors Guild of America - Los Angeles,
213/289-2000

STICKY FINGERS   Spectrafilm, 1988, w/Melanie Mayron

LLOYD N. ADAMS, JR.
THE BILLION DOLLAR HOBO   International Picture
Show, 1977, EP w/Darrell McGowan
THEY WENT THAT-A-WAY AND THAT-A-WAY
International Picture Show, 1978, EP

RICHARD MORRIS-ADAMS
(see Richard MORRIS-Adams)

TONY ADAMS
Business: Blake Edwards Entertainment, 9336
W. Washington Blvd., Culver City, CA 90230,
310/202-3375; Fax: 310/202-3412

THE RETURN OF THE PINK PANTHER   United Artists,
1975, AP
THE PINK PANTHER STRIKES AGAIN   United Artists,
1976, AP
REVENGE OF THE PINK PANTHER   United Artists,
1978, EP
10   Orion/Warner Bros., 1979, w/Blake Edwards
S.O.B.   Lorimar/Paramount, 1981, w/Blake Edwards
VICTOR/VICTORIA   MGM/UA, 1982, w/Blake Edwards
TRAIL OF THE PINK PANTHER   MGM/UA, 1982,
w/Blake Edwards
CURSE OF THE PINK PANTHER   MGM/UA, 1983,
w/Blake Edwards
THE MAN WHO LOVED WOMEN   Columbia, 1983,
w/Blake Edwards
MICKI & MAUDE   Columbia, 1984
A FINE MESS   Columbia, 1986
THAT'S LIFE!   Columbia, 1986
BLIND DATE   TriStar, 1987
SUNSET   TriStar, 1988
SKIN DEEP   20th Century Fox, 1989
SWITCH   Warner Bros., 1991

AL ADAMSON
HAMMER   United Artists, 1972

KEITH ADDIS
Business: Addis-Wechsler & Associates, 955 S.
Carrillo Dr., 3rd Floor, Los Angeles, CA 90048,
310/954-9000; Fax: 310/954-0990

BREATHLESS   Orion, 1983, EP
THE BRIDE   Columbia, 1985, EP

GARY ADELSON
Business: Adelson-Baumgarten Productions, 1041 North
Formosa Ace., Suite 202, West Hollywood, CA 90046,
213/850-2660; Fax: 213/850-2661

THE LAST STARFIGHTER   Universal, 1984,
w/Edward O. DeNault
THE BOY WHO COULD FLY   Lorimar, 1986
IN THE MOOD   Lorimar, 1987, w/Karen Mack
TAP   TriStar, 1989, w/Richard Vane
HARD TO KILL   Warner Bros., 1990, w/Joel Simon &
Bill Todman, Jr.
HOOK   TriStar, 1991, CP w/Craig Baumgarten

MERV ADELSON
(credit w/Lee Rich)

TWILIGHT'S LAST GLEAMING   Allied Artists, 1977
THE CHOIRBOYS   Universal, 1977
WHO IS KILLING THE GREAT CHEFS OF EUROPE?
Warner Bros., 1978, EP
THE BIG RED ONE   United Artists, 1980, EP

MICHELE ADER
Contact: Directors Guild of America - Los Angeles,
213/289-2000

TURNER & HOOCH   Buena Vista, 1989, CP

MISHAAL KAMAL ADHAM
THE NEW ADVENTURES OF PIPPI LONGSTOCKING
Columbia, 1988, EP

PIERRE ADIDGE
(credit w/Robert Abel)

JOE COCKER/MAD DOGS AND ENGLISHMEN (FD)
MGM, 1971, w/Harry Marks
ELVIS ON TOUR (FD)   MGM, 1972

ALLEN ADLER
MAKING LOVE   20th Century Fox, 1982,
w/Daniel Melnick

GILBERT ADLER
BASIC TRAINING   Moviestore, 1985, w/Otto Salamon
CERTAIN FURY   New World, 1985

LOU ADLER
Business Manager: Dick Deblois, Ernst & Whinney, 1875
Century Park East, Los Angeles, CA 90067,
310/553-2800
Contact: Directors Guild of America - Los Angeles,
213/289-2000

BREWSTER MCCLOUD   MGM, 1970
THE ROCKY HORROR PICTURE SHOW   20th Century
Fox, 1975, EP
UP IN SMOKE   Paramount, 1978, w/Lou Lombardo
SHOCK TREATMENT   20th Century Fox, 1981,
EP w/Michael White

ELEONORE ADLON
(credit w/Percy Adlon)
Contact: German Film & TV Academy, Pommernallee 1,
1 Berlin 19, 0311/302-6096

BAGDAD CAFE   Island Pictures, 1988
ROSALIE GOES SHOPPING   Four Seasons, 1990

PERCY ADLON
(credit w/Eleonore Adlon)
Agent: Robinson, Weintraub, Gross & Associates -
Los Angeles, 213/653-5802
Contact: German Film & TV Academy, Pommernallee 1,
1 Berlin 19, 0311/302-6096

BAGDAD CAFE   Island Pictures, 1988
ROSALIE GOES SHOPPING   Four Seasons, 1990

STAFFAN AHRENBERG
Business: Electric Pictures, 8771 Sunset Blvd., Suite 202,
    Los Angeles, CA 90069, 310/657-6363;
    Fax: 310/657-7888

WAXWORK   Vestron, 1988

JOSEPH L. AKERMAN
ERNEST SAVES CHRISTMAS   Buena Vista, 1988,
    EP w/Martin Erlichman

MOUSTAPHA AKKAD
Business: Trancas International Films, Inc., 9229 Sunset
    Blvd., Suite 415, Los Angeles, CA 90069, 310/657-7670;
    Fax: 310/271-4156

MOHAMMAD, MESSENGER OF GOD   Tarik, 1977
LION OF THE DESERT   UFD, 1981
APPOINTMENT WITH DEATH   Galaxy, 1985, EP
HALLOWEEN 4: THE RETURN OF MICHAEL MYERS
    Galaxy, 1988, EP
HALLOWEEN 5: THE REVENGE OF MICHAEL MYERS
    Galaxy, 1989, EP

NORMAN ALADJEM
FIREWALKER   Cannon, 1986,
    EP w/Jeffrey M. Rosenbaum

RICHARD L. ALBERT
THE FORBIDDEN DANCE   Columbia, 1990,
    w/Marc S. Fischer
SPACE AVENGER   Manley, 1990, EP w/Timothy McGinn
    & David Smith
OUT OF SIGHT, OUT OF MIND   Spectrum
    Entertainment, 1990

ROBERT ALDEN
STREETWALKIN'   Concorde, 1985
SATISFACTION   20th Century Fox, 1988,
    EP w/Armyan Bernstein

WILLIAM ALDRICH
HUSTLE   Paramount, 1975, AP
WHO IS KILLING THE GREAT CHEFS OF EUROPE?
    Warner Bros., 1978
...ALL THE MARBLES   MGM/UA, 1981
THE SHELTERING SKY   Warner Bros., 1990, EP

JEAN-PIERRE ALESSANDRI
TO KILL A PRIEST   Columbia, 1990, EP

JANE ALEXANDER
Agent: Joan Hyler, William Morris Agency - Beverly Hills,
    310/274-7451

SQUARE DANCE   *HOME IS WHERE THE HEART IS*
    Island Pictures, 1987, EP w/Charles Haid

LES ALEXANDER
Business: Alexander/Enright & Associates, 201 Wilshire
    Blvd., Santa Monica, CA 90401, 310/458-3003;
    Fax: 310/393-8111

NEXT OF KIN   Warner Bros., 1989, w/Don Enright

RICHARD ALFIERI
Business: Entertainment Professionals, 1015 Gayley,
    Suite 1149, Los Angeles, CA 90024, 310/473-5711;
    Fax: 310/575-0822

RESCUE ME   Cannon, 1991

MALIK B. ALI
Business: MPI Home Video, 15825 Rob Roy Dr., Oak Forest,
    IL 60452, 312/687-7881

HENRY: PORTRAIT OF A SERIAL KILLER   Greycat Films,
    1990, EP w/Waleed B. Ali

WALEED B. ALI
Business: MPI Home Video, 15825 Rob Roy Dr., Oak Forest,
    IL 60452, 312/687-7881

HENRY: PORTRAIT OF A SERIAL KILLER   Greycat Films,
    1990, EP w/Malik B. Ali

ANTHONY HAVELOCK-ALLAN
(see Anthony HAVELOCK-Allan)

DEDE ALLEN
Agent: UTA - Beverly Hills, 310/273-6700

REDS ★   Paramount, 1981, EP w/Simon Relph

JAY PRESSON ALLEN
Agent: ICM - New York, 212/556-5600
Contact: Writers Guild of America - New York, 212/245-6180

IT'S MY TURN   Columbia, 1980, EP
JUST TELL ME WHAT YOU WANT   Warner Bros., 1980,
    w/Sidney Lumet
PRINCE OF THE CITY   Orion, 1981, EP
DEATHTRAP   Warner Bros., 1982, EP

LEWIS ALLEN
Business: Lewis Allen Productions, 1501 Broadway,
    Suite 1614, New York, NY 10036, 212/768-4610

FARENHEIT 451   Universal, 1967
FORTUNE AND MEN'S EYES   MGM, 1971,
    w/Lester Persky
NEVER CRY WOLF   Buena Vista, 1983, w/Jack Couffer &
    Joseph Strick
1918   Cinecom, 1985, EP w/Peter Newman
ON VALENTINE'S DAY   Angelika, 1986, EP w/Lindsay
    Law, Ross E. Milloy & Peter Newman
SWIMMING TO CAMBODIA   Cinecom, 1987, EP w/Ira
    Deutchman, Amir J. Malin & Peter Newman
O. C. AND STIGGS   MGM/UA, 1987, EP
END OF THE LINE   Orion Classics, 1987,
    w/Peter Newman
MISS FIRECRACKER   Corsair, 1989, EP w/Ross E. Milloy
LORD OF THE FLIES   Castle Rock/Columbia, 1990,
    EP w/Peter Newman

DAN ALLINGHAM
Contact: Directors Guild of America - Los Angeles,
    213/289-2000

THE CHICKEN CHRONICLES   Avco Embassy, 1977, AP
REUBEN, REUBEN   20th Century Fox International
    Classics, 1983, AP
A BREED APART   Orion, 1984, AP

AI

**FILM
PRODUCERS,
STUDIOS,
AGENTS AND
CASTING
DIRECTORS
GUIDE**

F
I
L
M

P
R
O
D
U
C
E
R
S

INTO THE NIGHT   Universal, 1985, EP
COMMUNION   New Line, 1989, w/Philippe Mora &
   Whitley Strieber

B R I A N   A L L M A N
Business: Evenstar Pictures, 8233 Manchester Ave.,
   Suite 5, Playa del Rey, CA 90293, 310/306-0368

APARTMENT ZERO   Skouras Pictures, 1989, CP

W I L L I A M   A L L Y N
Business: Allyn Films, 152 N. Mansfield Av., Los Angeles,
   CA 90036 213/937-8162; Fax: 213/937-8164

RICH & FAMOUS   MGM/UA, 1981
COUSINS   Paramount, 1989

M E L A N I E   J .   A L S C H U L E R
PRETTY SMART   New World, 1987, CP

H O W A R D   A L S T O N
Business: Marstar Productions, 20th Century Fox,
   10201 W. Pico Blvd., Los Angeles, CA 90035,
   310/203-3943; Fax: 310/203-2576
Contact: Directors Guild of America - Los Angeles,
   213/289-2000

CODE NAME: EMERALD   MGM/UA, 1985,
   CP w/Jonathan Sanger
MASK   Universal, 1985, CP

R O B E R T   A L T M A N
Business: Sand Castle 5 Productions, 502 Park Ave.,
   Suite 156, New York, NY 10022, 212/826-6641
Agent: ICM - Los Angeles, 310/550-4000
Contact: Writers Guild of America - Los Angeles,
   310/550-1000

THE DELINQUENTS   United Artists, 1957
THE JAMES DEAN STORY   Warner Bros., 1957,
   w/George W. George
NIGHTMARE IN CHICAGO   Universal, 1964
MCCABE & MRS. MILLER   Warner Bros., 1971, EP
CALIFORNIA SPLIT   Columbia, 1974,
   w/Joseph Walsh
NASHVILLE ★   Paramount, 1975
BUFFALO BILL & THE INDIANS or SITTING BULL'S
   HISTORY LESSON   United Artists, 1976
THE LATE SHOW   Warner Bros., 1977
WELCOME TO L.A.   United Artists, 1977
3 WOMEN   20th Century Fox, 1977
A WEDDING   20th Century Fox, 1978
REMEMBER MY NAME   Columbia, 1978
QUINTET   20th Century Fox, 1979
A PERFECT COUPLE   20th Century Fox, 1979
RICH KIDS   United Artists, 1979, EP
HEALTH   20th Century Fox, 1980
STREAMERS   United Artists Classics, 1983,
   w/Nick J. Mileti
SECRET HONOR   Cinecom, 1985
O. C. AND STIGGS   MGM/UA, 1987,
   w/Peter Newman

C A R L O S   A L V A R E Z
WALKER   Universal, 1987, LP

J E N N I F E R   A L W A R D
Business: Hearst Entertainment, 1640 S. Sepulveda Blvd.,
   4th Floor, Los Angeles, CA 90025, 310/478-1700;
   Fax: 310/478-2202

HEARTS OF FIRE   Lorimar, 1988, w/Richard Marquand &
   Jennifer Miller

R O D   A M A T E A U
Agent: Martin Baum, CAA - Los Angeles, 310/288-4545
Contact: Directors Guild of America - Los Angeles,
   213/289-2000

WHERE DOES IT HURT?   Cinerama, 1972,
   w/Bill Schwartz
THE GARBAGE PAIL KIDS MOVIE   Atlantic, 1987

C H R I S T O P H E R   A M E S
Agent: UTA - Beverly Hills, 310/273-6700
Business: North Beach Productions, P.O. Box 9119,
   Calabasas, CA 91372 818/591-2222

CLASS ACTION   20th Century Fox, 1991,
   CP w/Carolyn Shelby

Y O R A M   B E N - A M I
(see Yoram BEN-Ami)

A L A N   A M I E L
COMMANDO SQUAD   Trans World, 1987

M A R K   A M I N
Business: Trimark Pictures, 2901 Ocean Park Blvd.,
   Suite 123, Santa Monica, CA 90405, 310/399-8877;
   Fax: 310/399-4238

THE SLEEPING CAR   Vidmark, 1990, EP
BLACK MAGIC WOMAN   Trimark, 1991,
   EP w/Joan Baribeault
WHORE   Trimark, 1991, EP
THE SERVANTS OF TWILIGHT   Trimark, 1991,
   EP w/Andrew Lane, Joel Levine, Wayne Crawford
INTO THE SUN   Trimark, 1991, EP

G I D E O N   A M I R
Business: Action Plus Pictures, 999 North Doheny Drive,
   Suite 411, Los Angeles, CA 90069, 310/271-8596;
   Fax: 310/271-8695

SURVIVAL GAME   Trans World, 1987

T A R A K   B E N   A M M A R
(see Tarak BEN Ammar)

R O B E R T   A M R A M
THE LATE GREAT PLANET EARTH (FD)   Pacific
   International, 1979, w/Alan Belkin

A S H O K   A M R I T R A J
NIGHT EYES   Amritraj-Baldwin Entertainment, 1990
SCHWEITZER   Concorde, 1990
POPCORN   Studio Three, 1991, w/Gary Goch &
   Torben Johnke

D O M I N I C   A N C I A N O
Business: Fugitive Features, Unit 1, 14 Williams Road, London
   NW1 3EN, England, 071/383-4373; Fax: 071/383-5681

THE KRAYS   Miramax, 1990, w/Ray Burdis

Ar

FILM
PRODUCERS,
STUDIOS,
AGENTS AND
CASTING
DIRECTORS
GUIDE

ANDY ANDERSON
Agent: Joel Millner, Triad Artists, Inc. - Los Angeles,
310/556-2727

POSITIVE I.D.   Universal, 1987

BILL ANDERSON
THIRD MAN ON THE MOUNTAIN   Buena Vista, 1959
SWISS FAMILY ROBINSON   Buena Vista, 1960
THE SIGN OF ZORRO   Buena Vista, 1960
MOON PILOT   Buena Vista, 1962, CP
SAVAGE SAM   Buena Vista, 1963, CP
A TIGER WALKS   Buena Vista, 1964, CP
THE MOON-SPINNERS   Buena Vista, 1964, CP
THE FIGHTING PRINCE OF DONEGAL   Buena Vista,
   1966, CP
THE ADVENTURES OF BULLWHIP GRIFFIN   Buena
   Vista, 1967, CP
THE HAPPIEST MILLIONAIRE   Buena Vista, 1967, CP
THE ONE & ONLY GENUINE ORIGINAL FAMILY BAND
   Buena Vista, 1968
SMITH!   Buena Vista, 1969
THE COMPUTER WORE TENNIS SHOES
   Buena Vista, 1970
THE BAREFOOT EXECUTIVE   Buena Vista, 1971
THE $1,000,000 DUCK   Buena Vista, 1971
THE BISCUIT EATER   Buena Vista, 1972
CHARLEY AND THE ANGEL   Buena Vista, 1973
SUPERDAD   Buena Vista, 1974
THE STRONGEST MAN IN THE WORLD   Buena
   Vista, 1975
THE APPLE DUMPLING GANG   Buena Vista, 1975
DR. SYN, ALIAS THE SCARECROW   Buena Vista,
   1975, CP
TREASURE OF MATECUMBE   Buena Vista, 1976
THE SHAGGY D.A.   Buena Vista, 1976

KURT ANDERSON
PARTY LINE   SVS Films, 1988, w/Thomas S. Byrnes &
   William Webb

LINDSAY ANDERSON
O LUCKY MAN!   Warner Bros., 1973,
   w/Lindsay Anderson

ROBERT J. ANDERSON
AARON LOVES ANGELA   Columbia, 1975

PETER ANDREWS
THE BLOOD ON SATAN'S CLAW   Cannon, 1971,
   w/Malcolm Heyworth

RENATE ANGIOLINI
SHANGHAI JOE   United International, 1976,
   w/Roberto Bessi

KEN ANNAKIN
Contact: Directors Guild of America - Los Angeles,
   213/289-2000

THOSE DARING YOUNG MEN IN THEIR JAUNTY
   JALOPIES   Paramount, 1969
THE NEW ADVENTURES OF PIPPI LONGSTOCKING
   Columbia, 1988, CP

DEE ANTHONY
SGT. PEPPER'S LONELY HEARTS CLUB BAND
   Universal, 1978, EP

TONY ANTHONY
COMETOGETHER   Allied Artists, 1971, w/Saul Swimmer
BLINDMAN   20th Century Fox, 1972, w/Saul Swimmer
THE SILENT STRANGER   MGM, 1975
WILD ORCHID   Triumph, 1990, w/Mark Damon
HONEYMOON ACADEMY   Triumph, 1990

LOU ANTONIO
Agent: InterTalent Agency, Inc. - Los Angeles, 310/858-6200
Contact: Directors Guild of America - Los Angeles,
   213/289-2000

MICKI & MAUDE   Columbia, 1984,
   EP w/Jonathan D. Krane

MICHAEL APTED
Business: Osiris Films, 300 South Lorimar, Bldg 137,
   Burbank, CA 91505, 818/954-7696; Fax: 213/656-3449
Agent: CAA - Beverly Hills, 310/288-4545

THE RIVER RAT   Paramount, 1984, EP

SHIMON ARAMA
TRIUMPH OF THE SPIRIT   Triumph, 1989,
   w/Arnold Kopelson

RUTA K. ARAS
RAW NERVE   Pyramid, 1991

PAUL ARATOW
SHEENA   Columbia, 1984

BEN ARBEID
HOFFMAN   Levitt-Pickman, 1971
THE HIRELING   Columbia, 1973
ENIGMA   Embassy, 1983, w/Andre Pergament &
   Peter Shaw

MANUEL ARCE
CROSSOVER DREAMS   Miramax, 1985

ALAN ARKIN
Agent: ICM - Los Angeles, 310/550-4000
Contact: Directors Guild of America - New York,
   212/581-0370

THE IN-LAWS   Warner Bros., 1979, EP

LOUIS S. ARKOFF
Business: AIP/Marathon, Producers Bldg., Room 215, 10202
   W. Washington Blvd., Culver City, CA 90232,
   310/280-8243; Fax: 310/280-1390

A SMALL TOWN IN TEXAS   AIP, 1976, EP
CALIFORNIA DREAMING   AIP, 1979, EP
UP THE CREEK   Orion, 1984, EP w/Samuel Z. Arkoff

SAMUEL Z. ARKOFF
Business: Arkoff International Pictures, Lakeside Plaza,
   3801 Barham, Suite 178, Los Angeles, CA 90068,
   213/882-1161; Fax: 213/882-1039

THE PIT & THE PENDULUM   AIP, 1961,
   EP w/James H. Nicholson
TALES OF TERROR   AIP, 1962, EP w/James H. Nicholson
THE RAVEN   AIP, 1963, EP w/James H. Nicholson
X - THE MAN WITH X-RAY EYES   AIP, 1963,
   EP w/James H. Nicholson

Ar

FILM
PRODUCERS,
STUDIOS,
AGENTS AND
CASTING
DIRECTORS
GUIDE

F
I
L
M

P
R
O
D
U
C
E
R
S

BEACH PARTY   AIP, 1963
BIKINI BEACH   AIP, 1964, w/James H. Nicholson
MUSCLE BEACH PARTY   AIP, 1964, EP
BEACH BLANKET BINGO   AIP, 1965,
   w/James H. Nicholson
FIREBALL 500   AIP, 1966, w/James H. Nicholson
WILD IN THE STREETS   AIP, 1968,
   w/James H. Nicholson
THE DUNWICH HORROR   AIP, 1970,
   w/James H. Nicholson
BLOODY MAMA   AIP, 1970, EP w/James H. Nicholson
UP IN THE CELLAR   AIP, 1970, w/James H. Nicholson
WUTHERING HEIGHTS   AIP, 1971,
   w/James H. Nicholson
MURDERS IN THE RUE MORGUE   AIP, 1971,
   EP w/James H. Nicholson
WHO SLEW AUNTIE ROO?   AIP, 1971,
   w/James H. Nicholson
BUNNY O'HARE   AIP, 1971, EP w/James H. Nicholson
DR. PHIBES RISES AGAIN   AIP, 1972,
   EP w/James H. Nicholson
BLACULA   AIP, 1972, EP w/James H. Nicholson
DILLINGER   AIP, 1973, w/Lawrence Gordon
LITTLE CIGARS   AIP, 1973, EP
MADHOUSE   AIP, 1974, EP w/James H. Nicholson
SUGAR HILL   AIP, 1974, EP
HENNESSY   AIP, 1975, EP
COOLEY HIGH   AIP, 1975, EP
RETURN TO MACON COUNTY   AIP, 1975, EP
FOOD OF THE GODS   AIP, 1976
A MATTER OF TIME   AIP, 1976, EP w/Giulio Sbarigia
ONE SUMMER LOVE   AIP, 1976, EP
FUTUREWORLD   AIP, 1976, EP
THE FOOD OF THE GODS   AIP, 1976, EP
DRAGONFLY   AIP, 1976, EP
THE GREAT SCOUT & CATHOUSE THURSDAY   AIP,
   1976, EP
THE ISLAND OF DR. MOREAU   AIP, 1977,
   EP w/Sandy Howard
EMPIRE OF THE ANTS   AIP, 1977, EP
OUR WINNING SEASON   AIP, 1978, EP
FORCE 10 FROM NAVARONE   AIP, 1978
CALIFORNIA DREAMING   AIP, 1979, EP
C.H.O.M.P.S.   AIP, 1979, EP
THE AMITYVILLE HORROR   AIP, 1979, EP
HOW TO BEAT THE HIGH COST OF LIVING   AIP,
   1980, EP
DRESSED TO KILL   Filmways, 1980, EP
UNDERGROUND ACES   Filmways, 1981, EP
UP THE CREEK   Orion, 1984, EP w/Louis S. Arkoff

ALICE ARLEN
Agent: ICM - New York, 212/556-5600
Contact: Writers Guild of America - New York, 212/245-6180

COOKIE   Warner Bros., 1989, EP w/Nora Ephron &
   Susan Seidelman
A SHOCK TO THE SYSTEM   Corsair, 1990, AP

RICHARD ARLOOK
AFTER MIDNIGHT   MGM/UA, 1989, w/Peter Greene,
   Jim Wheat & Ken Wheat

GEORGE ARMITAGE
Business: Pentamerica Pictures, 11111 Santa Monica Blvd.,
   Suite 1100, Los Angeles, CA 90025, 310/473-5199;
   Fax: 310/477-5879
Agent: The Artists Agency - Los Angeles, 310/277-7779

PRIVATE DUTY NURSES   New World, 1972

MARK ARMSTRONG
HELLRAISER   New World, 1987, EP w/David Saunders &
   Christopher Webster

ROBIN B. ARMSTRONG
ONE CUP OF COFFEE   Miramax, 1991,
   w/Eric Tynan Young

SU ARMSTRONG
THE PUNISHER   New World, 1990, CP

DANNY ARNOLD
Contact: Writers Guild of America - Los Angeles,
   310/550-1000

THE WAR BETWEEN MEN AND WOMEN   National
   General, 1972

J. GORDON ARNOLD
THE RETURN OF THE SOLDIER   European Classics,
   1985, EP w/John Quested & Edward Simons

PETER ARNOW
TORN APART   Castle Hill, 1990, EP

AMI ARTZI
Business: 21st Century Film Corporation, 7000 W. 3rd St.,
   Los Angeles, CA 90048, 213/658-3000;
   Fax: 213/658-3002

MAID IN SWEDEN   Cannon, 1971
LUPO   Cannon, 1971, w/Yoram Globus
SUGAR COOKIES   General Film, 1973
PURGATORY   New Star Entertainment, 1989
THE FORBIDDEN DANCE   Columbia, 1990,
   EP w/Menahem Golan
NIGHT OF THE LIVING DEAD   Columbia, 1990,
   EP w/Menahem Golan & George Romero

WILLIAM ASHER
Agent: UTA - Beverly Hills, 310/273-6700
Contact: Directors Guild of America - Los Angeles,
   213/289-2000

MOVERS & SHAKERS   MGM/UA, 1985, w/Charles Grodin

TAMARA ASSEYEV
Contact: New World Entertainment, 1440 S. Sepulveda Blvd.,
   Los Angeles, CA 90025, 310/444-8116;
   Fax: 310/444-8101

THE WILD RACERS   AIP, 1968, AP
PADDY   Allied Artists, 1970
THE AROUSERS   *SWEET KILL*   New World, 1970
DRIVE-IN   Columbia, 1976, w/Alex Rose
I WANNA HOLD YOUR HAND   Universal, 1978,
   w/Alex Rose
BIG WEDNESDAY   Warner Bros., 1978, EP w/Alex Rose
NORMA RAE ★   20th Century Fox, 1979, w/Alex Rose

OVIDIO G. ASSONITIS
BEYOND THE DOOR   FVI, 1975
TENTACLES   AIP, 1977, EP
THE VISITOR   International Picture Show, 1979
PIRANHA II: THE SPAWNING   Saturn International,
   1983, EP
CHOKE CANYON   United Films, 1986

IRON WARRIOR   Trans World, 1987
   (under the pseudonym "Sam Sill")
THE CURSE   Trans World, 1987
SONNY BOY   Triumph, 1990

JARVIS ASTAIRE
Business: Viewsport Ltd., Broughton House, 6-8 Sackville
   Street, London W1 England, 071/287-4601

AGATHA   Warner Bros., 1979, w/Gavrik Losey

NAIM ATTALLAH
Business: Namara Films, Ltd., 45 Poland St., London
   W1V 4AV England, 071/439-6422; Fax: 071/439-6489

BRIMSTONE AND TREACLE   United Artists Classics,
   1982, EP

SIR RICHARD ATTENBOROUGH
Business: Lambeth Productions, Twickenham Studios, St.
   Margaret's, Twickenham TW1 2AW England,
   081/892-4477; Fax: 081/891-0168
Agent: Marty Baum, CAA - Beverly Hills, 310/288-4545

THE L-SHAPED ROOM   Columbia, 1963,
   w/Sir John Woolf
GANDHI ★★   Columbia, 1982
CRY FREEDOM   Universal, 1987

JAMES T. AUBREY
FUTUREWORLD   AIP, 1976, w/Richard T. Heffron &
   Paul N. Lazarus III

GABRIEL AUER
SALAAM BOMBAY!   Cinecom, 1988, EP w/Michael
   Nozik, Cherie Rodgers & Anil Tejani

JEFFREY AUERBACH
Business: Blake Edwards Entertainment, 9336 W.
   Washington Blvd., Culver City, CA 90232,
   310/202-3502; Fax: 310/202-3224

JUDGMENT IN BERLIN   New Line, 1988,
   EP w/William R. Greenblatt & Martin Sheen

BOB AUGUR
THE TROUBLE WITH DICK   Fever Dream, 1989,
   w/Gary Walkow

JOE AUGUSTYN
NIGHT OF THE DEMONS   International Film
   Marketing, 1988
NIGHT ANGEL   Fries Entertainment, 1990,
   w/Gerald Geoffray

CARLOS AURED
ALIEN PREDATOR   Trans World, 1987, w/Deran Sarafian

BUD AUSTIN
MIKEY & NICKY   Paramount, 1976, EP
JOHNNY DANGEROUSLY   20th Century Fox,
   EP w/Harry Colomby

FRANKIE AVALON
BACK TO THE BEACH   Paramount, 1987,
   EP w/Annette Funicello

CLARENCE AVANT
SAVE THE CHILDREN (FD)   Paramount, 1973, EP

HOWARD AVEDIS
Business: Hickmar, 4000 Warner Blvd., Producers 4,
   Burbank, CA 91522, 818/954-5104
Attorney: Jerome E. Weinstein, Weinstein & Hart,
   433 N. Camden Dr., Suite 600, Beverly Hills, CA 90210,
   310/274-7157

THE STEPMOTHER   Crown International, 1973
THE TEACHER   Crown International, 1974
DR. MINX   Dimension, 1975
THE SPECIALIST   Crown International, 1975
SCORCHY   AIP, 1976

FRANK AVIANCA
CLAY PIGEON   MGM, 1971, EP w/Ronald L. Buck
THE HUMAN FACTOR   Bryanston, 1975

JOHN G. AVILDSEN
Agent: UTA - Beverly Hills, 310/273-6700
Contact: Directors Guild of America - Los Angeles,
   213/289-2000

OUT OF IT   United Artists, 1970, AP
SLOW DANCING IN THE BIG CITY   United Artists, 1978,
   w/Michael Levee
LEAN ON ME   Warner Bros., 1989, EP

JON AVNET
Business: Avnet-Kerner Company, 3815 Hughes Av., Culver
   City, CA 90232, 310/838-2500; Fax: 310/204-4208

COAST TO COAST   Paramount, 1980, w/Steve Tisch
RISKY BUSINESS   Geffen/Warner Bros., 1983,
   w/Steve Tisch
DEAL OF THE CENTURY   Warner Bros., 1983,
   EP w/Paul Brickman & Steve Tisch
LESS THAN ZERO   20th Century Fox, 1987,
   w/Jordan Kerner
MEN DON'T LEAVE   Geffen/Warner Bros., 1990
FUNNY ABOUT LOVE   Paramount, 1990, w/Jordan Kerner
FRIED GREEN TOMATOES   Universal, 1991,
   w/Jordan Kerner

IRVING AXELRAD
THE COLOR OF MONEY   Buena Vista, 1986,
   w/Barbara DeFina

DAVID R. AXELROD
WINNERS TAKE ALL   Apollo, 1987, EP

DAN AYKROYD
Attorney: Alan Hergott - Los Angeles, 213/859-6800
Agent: CAA - Beverly Hills, 310/288-4545

ONE MORE SATURDAY NIGHT   Columbia, 1986, EP

GERALD AYRES
Agent: Broder-Kurland-Webb-Uffner Agency - Los Angeles,
   213/656-9262

CISCO PIKE   Columbia, 1972
THE LAST DETAIL   Columbia, 1973
FOXES   United Artists, 1980, w/David Puttnam

Ay

FILM
PRODUCERS,
STUDIOS,
AGENTS and
CASTING
DIRECTORS
GUIDE

F
I
L
M

P
R
O
D
U
C
E
R
S

Az

FILM
PRODUCERS,
STUDIOS,
AGENTS AND
CASTING
DIRECTORS
GUIDE

F
I
L
M

P
R
O
D
U
C
E
R
S

IRVING AZOFF
Business: Azoff Entertainment, 345 N. Maple Dr., Suite 205,
Beverly Hills, CA 90210, 310/288-5595;
Fax: 310/288-5532

URBAN COWBOY   Paramount, 1980, w/Robert Evans
FAST TIMES AT RIDGEMONT HIGH   Universal, 1982,
w/Art Linson

B

BETH B
SALVATION!   Circle Releasing, 1987,
w/Michael Shamberg

DANIEL F. BACANER
Business: Fremont II, 8489 W. 3rd St., Los Angeles, CA
90048, 213/852-0934

BLOOD SIMPLE   Circle Releasing Corporation, 1985, EP
SCARED STIFF   International Film Marketing, 1987

STEVEN BACH
MR. BILLION   20th Century Fox, 1977, w/Ken Friedman
BUTCH & SUNDANCE: THE EARLY DAYS   20th Century
Fox, 1979, w/Gabriel Katzka

LAWRENCE P. BACHMANN
WHOSE LIFE IS IT ANYWAY?   MGM, 1981

DORO BACHRACH
Business: 250 W. 57th St., Suite 1905, New York, NY
10019, 212/582-5689

DIRTY DANCING   Vestron, 1987, AP
LOVE HURTS   Vestron, 1990, w/Bud Yorkin

JOHN D. BACKE
Business: Tomorrow Entertainment, 327 East 50th St.,
New York, NY 10022, 212/355-7737

BRENDA STARR   New World, 1987, EP
A KILLING AFFAIR   Hemdale, 1988, EP
w/Myron A. Hyman

PETER BACSO
LILY IN LOVE   New Line, 1985, EP w/Robert Halmi Jr.

WILLIAM BADALATO
Agent: Triad Artists, Inc., - Los Angeles, 310/556-2727
Contact: Directors Guild of America - Los Angeles,
213/289-2000

LET'S SCARE JESSICA TO DEATH   Paramount,
1971, CP
BANG THE DRUM SLOWLY   Paramount, 1973, AP
TOP GUN   Paramount, 1986, EP
WEEDS   DEG, 1987
LAGUNA HEAT (CTF)   HBO Pictures/Jay Weston
Productions, 1987

1969   Atlantic, 1988, w/Daniel Grodnik
DEAD SOLID PERFECT (CTF)   HBO Pictures/David Merrick
Productions, 1988
FIRE BIRDS   Buena Vista, 1990
HOT SHOTS!   20th Century-Fox, 1991

SUE BADEN-POWELL
CHATTAHOOCHEE   Hemdale, 1990, CP

JOHN BADHAM
Business: Badham-Cohen Group, 100 Universal City Plaza,
Bldg. 82, Universal City, CA 91608, 818/777-3477;
Fax: 818/777-8226
Agent: Triad Artists, Inc. - Los Angeles, 310/556-2727

STAKEOUT   Buena Vista, 1987, EP
DISORGANIZED CRIME   Buena Vista, 1989,
EP w/Rob Cohen

MAX BAER
Contact: Directors Guild of America - Los Angeles,
213/289-2000

MACON COUNTY LINE   AIP, 1974
THE WILD MCCULLOCHS   AIP, 1975
ODE TO BILLY JOE   Warner Bros., 1976, w/Roger Camras

NORMAN BAER
THE DESERTER   Paramount, 1971, w/Ralph Serpe

THOMAS BAER
Business: Baer Entertainment Group, c/o Orion Pictures,
1888 Century Park East, Los Angeles, CA 90067,
310/282-2776; Fax: 310/785-1800

LOST ANGELS   Orion, 1989, w/Howard Rosenman

JERRY A. BAERWITZ
Contact: Directors Guild of America - Los Angeles,
213/289-2000

FRIGHT NIGHT   Columbia, 1985, AP
STEWARDESS SCHOOL   Columbia, 1987,
CP w/Michael Kane
LISTEN TO ME   WEG/Columbia, 1989, CP
COUPE DE VILLE   Universal, 1990, AP

TED BAFALOUKOS
Agent: Triad Artists - Los Angeles, 310/556-2727

MARTIANS GO HOME   Taurus, 1990,
CP w/Anthony Santa Crose

PATRICK BAILEY
Contact: Directors Guild of America - Los Angeles,
213/289-2000

SPACECAMP   20th Century Fox, 1986, w/Walter Coblenz

ROY BAIRD
WOMEN IN LOVE   United Artists, 1969, AP
THE DEVILS   Warner Bros., 1971, AP
THE MUSIC LOVERS   United Artists, 1971, EP
HENRY VIII AND HIS SIX WIVES   Anglo EMI, 1973
THAT'LL BE THE DAY   EMI, 1974, EP
THE LAST DAYS OF MAN ON EARTH   *THE FINAL
PROGRAMME*   New World, 1974, EP w/Michael
Moorcock & David Puttnam

MAHLER   Mayfair, 1975
LISZTOMANIA   Warner Bros., 1975, w/David Puttnam
STARDUST   Columbia, 1975, EP
QUADROPHENIA   World Northal, 1979, w/Bill Curbishley
McVICAR   Crown International, 1982, w/Bill Curbishley &
   Roger Daltrey

TERENCE BAKER
THE HIRELING   Columbia, 1973, EP

RALPH BAKSHI
Business Manager: Howard Bernstein, Kaufman &
   Bernstein, 1900 Avenue of the Stars, Suite 2270,
   Los Angeles, CA 90067, 310/277-1900
Business: Ralph Bakshi Productions, 8125 Lankershim
   Blvd., North Hollywood, CA 91605

WIZARDS (AF)   20th Century Fox, 1977
AMERICAN POP (AF)   Paramount, 1981,
   w/Martin Ransohoff
HEY GOOD LOOKIN' (AF)   Warner Bros., 1982
FIRE AND ICE (AF)   20th Century Fox, 1983,
   w/Frank Frazetta

DECLAN BALDWIN
NIGHT OF THE LIVING DEAD   Columbia, 1990, LP

HOWARD L. BALDWIN
Business: 9832 Charleville Rd., Beverly Hills, CA 90212,
   310/551-1214; Fax: 310/551-1217

BILLY GALVIN   Vestron, 1986, EP w/Stuart Benjamin,
   Lindsay Law & William Minot
FROM THE HIP   DEG, 1987, EP w/William Minot &
   Brian Russell
SPELLBINDER   MGM/UA, 1988, EP w/Richard Cohen
NIGHT EYES   Amritraj-Baldwin Entertainment, 1990, EP
POPCORN   Studio Three, 1991, EP w/Karl
   Hendrickson & Howard Hurst

KATE BALES
MANNEQUIN TWO: ON THE MOVE   20th Century Fox,
   1991, AP

HAIG BALIAN
THE GIRL WITH THE RED HAIR   United Artists Classics,
   1983, w/Chris Brouwer

DAVID BALL
CREEPSHOW 2   New World, 1987

JACK BALLARD
MAHOGANY   Paramount, 1975, w/Rob Cohen

MARK BALSAM
MATEWAN   Cinecom, 1987, EP w/Amir J. Malin &
   Jerry Silva

MICHAEL BALSON
BAT 21   TriStar, 1988, w/David Fisher & Gary A. Neill

ALBERT BAND
Business: Full Moon Entertainment, 6930 Sunset Blvd, Los
   Angeles, CA 90028, 213/957-0091; Fax: 213/957-0092

LITTLE CIGARS   AIP, 1973
DRACULA'S DOG   Crown International, 1978,
   w/Frank Ray Perilli

SHE CAME TO THE VALLEY   R&V Pictures, 1979,
   w/Frank Ray Perilli
TERRORVISION   Empire, 1986
TROLL   Empire, 1986
GHOST WARRIOR   Empire, 1986, EP w/Efrem Harkham,
   Uri Harkham & Arthur H. Maslansky
THE PIT AND THE PENDULUM   1991

CHARLES BAND
Business: Full Moon Entertainment, 6930 Sunset Blvd, Los
   Angeles, CA 90028, 213/957-0091; Fax: 213/957-0092

LAST FOXTROT IN BURBANK   Federated Films, 1973
MANSION OF THE DOOMED   Group I, 1976
END OF THE WORLD   Irwin Yablans, 1977
CINDERELLA   Group I, 1977
CRASH   Group I, 1977
LASERBLAST   Irwin Yablans, 1978
FAIRY TALES   Fairy Tales, 1979
TOURIST TRAP   Compass International, 1979, EP
PARASITE   Embassy, 1982
FUTURE COP   Empire, 1985
THE DUNGEONMASTER   Empire, 1985
FROM BEYOND   Empire, 1986, EP
ZONE TROOPERS   Empire, 1986, EP
TERRORVISION   Empire, 1986, EP
ELIMINATORS   Empire, 1986
GHOST WARRIOR   Empire, 1986
ENEMY TERRITORY   Empire, 1987, EP
DOLLS   Empire, 1987, EP
PRISON   Empire, 1988, EP
DEADLY WEAPON   Empire, 1988, EP
GHOST TOWN   Trans World, 1988, EP
BUY & CELL   Empire, 1989, EP
SHADOWZONE   JGM Enterprises, 1990, EP
TRANCERS II   1991
THE PIT AND THE PENDULUM   1991, EP

MIRRA BANK
ENORMOUS CHANGES AT THE LAST MINUTE   TC Films
   International, 1985

STEPHEN K. BANNON
THE INDIAN RUNNER   1991, EP w/Thom Mount &
   Mark Bisgeier

TOM BARAD
Business: Paramount Pictures, 5555 Melrose Ave.,
   Hollywood, CA 90035, 213/956-5801

CRAZY PEOPLE   Paramount, 1990

GARY BARBER
(credit w/David Nicksay & James G. Robinson)
Business: Morgan Creek Productions, 1875 Century Park
   East, Suite 200, Los Angeles, CA 90067, 310/284-8884;
   Fax: 310/282-8794

MIDNIGHT CROSSING   Vestron, 1988, EP w/Gregory
   Cascante, Dan Ireland & Wanda S. Rayle*
COMMUNION   New Line, 1989, EP w/Paul Redshaw*
YOUNG GUNS II   20th Century Fox, 1990, EP w/John
   Fusco & Joe Roth
PACIFIC HEIGHTS   20th Century Fox, 1990,
   EP w/Joe Roth
ROBIN HOOD: PRINCE OF THIEVES   Warner Bros.,
   1991, EP
FREEJACK   Warner Bros., 1991, EP

Ba - FILM PRODUCERS, STUDIOS, AGENTS and CASTING DIRECTORS GUIDE - FILM PRODUCERS

Ba

FILM
PRODUCERS,
STUDIOS,
AGENTS AND
CASTING
DIRECTORS
GUIDE

F
I
L
M

P
R
O
D
U
C
E
R
S

Ba

FILM
PRODUCERS,
STUDIOS,
AGENTS AND
CASTING
DIRECTORS
GUIDE

F
I
L
M

P
R
O
D
U
C
E
R
S

JOSEPH BARBERA
(credit w/William Hanna)
Business: Hanna-Barbera Productions, Inc., 3400
    Cahuenga Blvd. West, Los Angeles, CA 90068,
    213/851-5000; Fax: 213/969-1201

CHARLOTTE'S WEB (AF)   Paramount, 1974
MOTHER, JUGS & SPEED   20th Century Fox, 1976, EP*
C.H.O.M.P.S.   AIP, 1979*
JETSONS: THE MOVIE (AF)   Universal, 1990

VICTOR BARDAK
THE GUMSHOE KID   Skouras, 1990, EP

BEN BARENHOLTZ
Business: Circle Releasing, 239 1/2 East 32nd St.,
    New York, NY 10016, 212/686-0822

MILLER'S CROSSING   20th Century Fox, 1990, EP
BARTON FINK   20th Century Fox, 1991, EP w/Ted
    Pedas & Jim Pedas & Bill Durkin

JOAN BARIBEAULT
BLACK MAGIC WOMAN   Trimark, 1991, EP w/Mark Amin

KEITH BARISH
Business: Keith Barish Productions, P.O. Box 93969,
    Los Angeles, CA 90093, 213/471-0945;
    Fax: 213/476-3576

ENDLESS LOVE   Universal, 1981, EP
SOPHIE'S CHOICE   Universal, 1982, w/Alan J. Pakula
MISUNDERSTOOD   MGM/UA, 1984,
    EP w/Craig Baumgarten
9 1/2 WEEKS   MGM/UA, 1986, EP w/Frank
    Konigsberg & F. Richard Northcott
BIG TROUBLE IN LITTLE CHINA   20th Century Fox,
    1986, EP w/Paul Monash
LIGHT OF DAY   TriStar, 1987, w/Rob Cohen
THE MONSTER SQUAD   TriStar, 1987, EP w/Rob
    Cohen & Peter Hyams
THE RUNNING MAN   TriStar, 1987, EP w/Rob Cohen
IRONWEED   TriStar, 1987, w/Marcia Nasatir
THE SERPENT & THE RAINBOW   Universal, 1988,
    EP w/Rob Cohen
HER ALIBI   Warner Bros., 1989
FIRE BIRDS   Buena Vista, 1990, EP w/Arnold Kopelson

MOSHE BARKAT
(co-producers: Moshe Diamant & Sunil R. Shah)

PRAY FOR DEATH   American Distribution Group,
    1986, EP
RAGE OF HONOR   Trans World, 1987, EP

CLIVE BARKER
Agent: CAA - Beverly Hills, 310/288-4545

HELLBOUND: HELLRAISER II   New World, 1988,
    EP w/Christopher Webster

LYNN BARKER
VICIOUS   SVS Films, 1988, LP

HOWARD G. BARNES
BAXTER   National General, 1973,
    EP w/John L. Hargreaves

JOHN BARNETT
STRANGE BEHAVIOR   World Northal, 1981,
    w/Antony I. Ginnane
WILD HORSES   Satori, 1984

SAUL BARNETT
RICHARD PRYOR LIVE IN CONCERT (FD)   Special Event
    Entertainment, 1979, EP
SAMMY STOPS THE WORLD   Special Event
    Entertainment, 1979, EP w/Hillard Elkins

ALAN BARNETTE
OFF LIMITS   20th Century Fox, 1988

EARL BARRET
Business Manager: Jamner, Pariser & Meschures -
    Los Angeles, 213/652-0222
Contact: Writers Guild of America - Los Angeles, 310/550-1000

SEE NO EVIL, HEAR NO EVIL   TriStar, 1989, EP w/Burtt
    Harris & Arne Sultan

BRUNO BARRETO
Business: Producoes Cinematograficas L.C. Barreto Ltd.,
    Rua Visconde De Caravelas, 28-Botafogos, Rio de Janeiro,
    Brazil, 021/286-7186

WHERE THE RIVER RUNS BLACK   MGM/UA, 1986,
    LP w/Flavio R. Tambellini

ERIC BARRETT
I'M GONNA GIT YOU SUCKA   MGM/UA, 1989,
    CP w/Tamara Rawitt

GEORGE BARRIE
WHIFFS   20th Century Fox, 1975
HEDDA   Brut, 1975, EP
I WILL, WILL...FOR NOW   20th Century Fox, 1976
HUGO THE HIPPO (AF)   20th Century Fox, 1976, EP
THIEVES   Paramount, 1977
NASTY HABITS   Brut, 1977, EP
FINGERS   Brut, 1978
THE CLASS OF MISS MacMICHAEL   Brut, 1979, EP

LISA BARSAMIAN
FRIDAY THE 13TH PART 2   Paramount, 1981,
    EP w/Tom Gruenberg
FRIDAY THE 13TH PART 3   Paramount, 1982, EP
OFF THE WALL   Jensen Farley Pictures, 1983, EP
MEATBALLS PART II   TriStar, 1984, EP

PETER BART
Business: Variety, 475 Park Ave. South, New York, NY
    10016, 212/779-1100

FUN WITH DICK & JANE   Columbia, 1977,
    w/Max Palevsky
ISLANDS IN THE STREAM   Paramount, 1977,
    w/Max Palevsky
REVENGE OF THE NERDS   20th Century Fox, 1984,
    EP w/David Obst
YOUNGBLOOD   MGM/UA, 1986, w/Patrick C. Wells
REVENGE OF THE NERDS II   20th Century Fox, 1987,
    w/Robert W. Cort & Ted Field

HALL BARTLETT
Contact: Writers Guild of America - Los Angeles, 310/550-1000

CHANGES   Cinerama, 1969

THE WILD PACK   AIP, 1972
JONATHAN LIVINGSTON SEAGULL   Paramount, 1973
THE CHILDREN OF SANCHEZ   Lone-Star, 1978

GEOF BARTZ
STRIPPER (FD)   20th Century Fox, 1986, w/Melvyn J.
   Estrin & Jerome Gary

ROBERT BARUC
Business: Academy Entertainment, 1 Pine Haven
   Shore Rd., Shelburne, VT 05482, 800/972-0001

PRAYER OF THE ROLLERBOYS   Academy
   Entertainment, 1991, EP w/Tetsu Fujimara,
   Martin F. Gold & Richard Lorber

HAL BARWOOD
Contact: Directors Guild of America - Los Angeles,
   213/289-2000
Agent: ICM - Los Angeles, 310/550-4000

CORVETTE SUMMER   MGM/UA, 1978
DRAGONSLAYER   Paramount, 1981

JOHN F. BASSETT
PAPERBACK HERO   Runson, 1975, w/James Margellos

KENT BATEMAN
Contact: Directors Guild of America - Los Angeles,
   213/289-2000

LAND OF NO RETURN   International Picture Show, 1978
TEEN WOLF TOO   Atlantic, 1987

FRED BAUER
THE BUDDY HOLLY STORY   Columbia, 1978

CAROL BAUM
Business: Sandollar Productions, 8730 Sunset Blvd.,
   Penthouse, Los Angeles, CA 90069, 310/659-5933;
   Fax: 310/659-0433

DEAD RINGERS   20th Century Fox, 1988,
   EP w/Sylvio Tabet
JACKNIFE   Cineplex Odeon, 1989, w/Robert Schaffel
GROSS ANATOMY   Buena Vista, 1989,
   EP w/Sandy Gallin
FATHER OF THE BRIDE   Buena Vista, 1991, w/Nancy
   Meyers & Howard Rosenman

FRED BAUM
UP THE CREEK   Orion, 1984, CP

MARTIN BAUM
Business: CAA - Los Angeles, 310/288-4545

BRING ME THE HEAD OF ALFREDO GARCIA   United
   Artists, 1974
THE WILBY CONSPIRACY   United Artists, 1975
THE KILLER ELITE   United Artists, 1975, w/Arthur Lewis

CRAIG BAUMGARTEN
Business: Adelson-Baumgarten Productions, 1041 N.
   Formosa Ave., Formosa Bldg. Suite 202, West Hollywood,
   CA 90046, 213/850-2660; Fax: 213/850-2661

MISUNDERSTOOD   MGM/UA, 1984, EP w/Keith Barish
HOOK   TriStar, 1991, CP w/Gary Adelson

ROBERT BAYLIS
CHILD UNDER A LEAF   Cinema National, 1975,
   w/Murray Shostak
AGENCY   Jensen Farley, 1981, AP
DEATH HUNT   20th Century Fox, 1981, AP
SILENCE OF THE NORTH   Universal, 1982, CP
LOVE SONGS   Spectrafilm, 1986, w/Elie Chouraqui
MARIA CHAPDELAINE   Moviestore, 1986,
   w/Murray Shostak

JIM BEACH
Business: Fugitive Features, Unit 1, 14 William Rd., London
   NW1 3EN England, 071/383-4373; Fax: 071/383-5681

THE KRAYS   Miramax, 1990, EP w/Michele Kimche

PETER BEALE
Business: Showscan Film Corporation, 3939 Landmark St.,
   Culver City, CA 90230, 310/558-0150
Contact: Directors Guild of America - Los Angeles,
   213/289-2000

FIVE DAYS ONE SUMMER   Warner Bros., 1982, EP

RAY BEATTIE
YOUNG EINSTEIN   Warner Bros., 1989, EP w/Graham Burke

WARREN BEATTY
Agent: CAA - Beverly Hills, 310/288-4545
Business Manager: Traubner & Flynn, 2029 Century Park
   East, Los Angeles, CA 90067

BONNIE & CLYDE ★   Warner Bros., 1967
SHAMPOO   Columbia, 1975
HEAVEN CAN WAIT ★   Paramount, 1978
REDS ★   Paramount, 1981
ISHTAR   Columbia, 1987
DICK TRACY   Buena Vista, 1990
BUGSY   Tristar, 1991, w/Mark Johnson & Barry Levinson

JOSEPH BEAUBIEN
ATLANTIC CITY ★   Paramount, 1981,
   EP w/Gabriel Boustani

WILLIAM BEAUDINE, JR.
Contact: Directors Guild of America - Los Angeles,
   213/289-2000

COUNTRY   Buena Vista, 1984, LP

GABRIELLE BEAUMONT
CRUCIBLE OF HORROR   Cannon, 1971

STANLEY BECK
STRAIGHT TIME   Warner Bros., 1978, w/Tim Zinnemann
DEATH VALLEY   Universal, 1982, CP w/Richard Rothstein
MAN, WOMAN & CHILD   Paramount, 1983, EP

RICHARD BECKER
Business: Producers Representation Organization, 11849 W.
   Olympic Blvd., Suite 200, Los Angeles, CA 90064,
   310/478-5159; Fax: 310/479-0617

BAD INFLUENCE   Triumph, 1990, EP w/Morrie Eisenman
LOVE STINKS   Live Entertainment, 1991,
   EP w/Richard Gladstein

Be

FILM
PRODUCERS,
STUDIOS,
AGENTS AND
CASTING
DIRECTORS
GUIDE

F
I
L
M

P
R
O
D
U
C
E
R
S

Be

FILM
PRODUCERS,
STUDIOS,
AGENTS AND
CASTING
DIRECTORS
GUIDE

F
I
L
M

P
R
O
D
U
C
E
R
S

BARRY BECKERMAN
Contact: Writers Guild of America - Los Angeles,
310/550-1000

RED DAWN   MGM/UA, 1984, w/Buzz Feitshans

SIDNEY BECKERMAN
LAST SUMMER   Allied Artists, 1969, w/Alfred W. Crown
MARLOWE   MGM, 1969, w/Gabriel Katzka
KELLY'S HEROES   MGM, 1970, w/Gabriel Katzka
JOE KIDD   Universal, 1972
MARATHON MAN   Paramount, 1976, w/Robert Evans
THE RIVER NIGER   Cine Artists, 1976, w/Isaac L. Jones
SIDNEY SHELDON'S BLOODLINE   Paramount, 1979,
   w/David V. Picker
SERIAL   Paramount, 1980
BLOOD BEACH   Jerry Gross Organization, 1981, EP
A STRANGER IS WATCHING   MGM/UA, 1982
THE ADVENTURES OF BUCKAROO BANZAI ACROSS
   THE EIGHTH DIMENSION   20th Century Fox,
   1984, EP
RED DAWN   MGM/UA, 1984, EP
INSIDE OUT   Hemdale, 1986
THE SICILIAN   20th Century Fox, 1987, EP

CHRIS BECKMAN
HOLLYWOOD BOULEVARD II   Concorde, 1991,
   w/Tom Merchant

RON BECKMAN
Business: Apollo Pictures, 6071 Bristol Parkway,
   Culver City, CA 90230, 310/568-8282

THE CHALLENGE   Embassy, 1982, w/Robert L. Rosen
CAN'T BUY ME LOVE   Buena Vista, 1987,
   EP w/Jere Henshaw

DAVID BEGELMAN
Business: Gladden Entertainment, 10100 Santa Monica
   Blvd., Suite 600, Los Angeles, CA 90067,
   310/282-7500; Fax: 310/282-8262

WHOLLY MOSES!   Columbia, 1980

JEFF BEGUN
SWITCHBLADE SISTERS   Centaur, 1975,
   EP w/Frank Moreno
STREET GIRLS   New World, 1975, w/Paul Ponpian
JACKSON COUNTY JAIL   New World, 1976
HARDBODIES   Columbia, 1984, w/Ken Dalton
PRETTY SMART   New World, 1987, w/Ken Solomon

DON BEHRNS
Contact: Directors Guild of America - Los Angeles,
   213/289-2000

FRIDAY THE 13TH, PART VI: JASON LIVES
   Paramount, 1986

HARRY BELAFONTE
Agent: Triad Artists, Inc. - Los Angeles, 310/556-2727

BEAT STREET   Orion, 1984, w/David V. Picker

WILLIAM BELASCO
THEY ONLY KILL THEIR MASTERS   MGM, 1972
THE CAREY TREATMENT   MGM, 1972
THE SUPER COPS   MGM, 1974
THE LAST HARD MEN   20th Century Fox, 1976, EP

GRAHAM BELIN
UNION CITY   Kinesis, 1980

ALAN BELKIN
Business: Alan Belkin Productions, Inc., 720 N. Seward St.,
   Hollywood, CA 90038, 213/465-9815
Contact: Directors Guild of America - Los Angeles,
   213/289-2000

A DIFFERENT STORY   Avco Embassy, 1978
THE LATE GREAT PLANET EARTH (FD)   Pacific
   International, 1979, w/Robert Amram
A FORCE OF ONE   American Cinema, 1979
THE OCTAGON   American Cinema, 1980,
   EP w/Michael C. Leone
CHARLIE CHAN & THE CURSE OF THE DRAGON QUEEN
   American Cinema, 1981, EP w/Michael C. Leone
THAT WAS THEN...THIS IS NOW   Paramount, 1985,
   EP w/Brandon K. Phillips
GETTING EVEN   American Distribution Group, 1986, EP

DAVE BELL
Contact: 3211 Cahuenga West, Los Angeles, CA 90068,
   213/851-7801; Fax: 213/851-9349

THE LONG WALK HOME   Miramax, 1990,
   w/Howard W. Koch Jr.

RICHARD BELL
GREASED LIGHTNING   Warner Bros., 1977,
   EP w/J. Lloyd Grant

TOM BELLAGIO
CHAMPIONS FOREVER (FD)   Ion, 1989,
   EP w/Hollister Whitworth

DAVINA BELLING
(credit w/Clive Parsons)
Business: Film & General Productions, Ltd., 10 Pembridge
   Place, London W2 4XB, 071/221-1141; Fax: 071/792-1167
Contact: 1362 N. Wetherly Drive, Los Angeles, CA 90069,
   310/274-4773; Fax: 310/274-7947

INSERTS   United Artists, 1976
SCUM   Berwick Street Films, 1979
THAT SUMMER   Columbia, 1979
BREAKING GLASS   Paramount, 1980
BRITTANIA HOSPITAL   United Artists Classics, 1982
GREGORY'S GIRL   Samuel Goldwyn Company, 1982
COMFORT AND JOY   Universal, 1984

DONALD BELLISARIO
Business: Belisarius Productions, 100 Universal City Plaza,
   Universal City, CA 91608, 818/777-3381;
   Fax: 818/777-0475
Agent: Broder/Kurland/Webb/Uffner - Los Angeles,
   213/274-8921

LAST RITES   MGM/UA, 1988, w/Patrick McCormick

HERCULES BELLVILLE
Business: The Recorded Picture Company Ltd., 8-12
   Broadwick Street, London W1V 1FH England,
   071/439-0607; Fax: 071/434-1192

STRANGERS KISS   Orion Classics, 1984, CP

Be

FILM
PRODUCERS,
STUDIOS,
AGENTS AND
CASTING
DIRECTORS
GUIDE

HENRI BELOLO
CAN'T STOP THE MUSIC   AFD, 1980, w/Allan Carr &
   Jacques Morali

JERRY BELSON
Agent: CAA - Beverly Hills, 310/288-4545
Contact: Directors Guild of America - Los Angeles,
   213/289-2000

HOW SWEET IT IS!   National General, 1968,
   w/Garry Marshall
THE GRASSHOPPER   National General, 1979,
   w/Garry Marshall
STUDENT BODIES   Paramount, 1981,
   EP w/Harvey Miller
FOR KEEPS   TriStar, 1988, w/Walter Coblenz

LESLIE BELZBERG
INTO THE NIGHT   Universal, 1985, AP
SPIES LIKE US   Warner Bros., 1985, AP
COMING TO AMERICA   Paramount, 1988,
   EP w/Mark Lipsky
OSCAR   Buena Vista, 1991

YORAM BEN-AMI
Business: Triumph Pictures, Inc., 6111 Shirley Ave.,
   Tarzana, CA 91356, 818/708-1384

LONE WOLF MCQUADE   Orion, 1982
SHEENA   Columbia, 1984, EP
STONE COLD   Columbia, 1991

TARAK BEN AMMAR
LA TRAVIATA   Universal Classics, 1983
MISUNDERSTOOD   MGM/UA, 1984
PIRATES   Cannon, 1986

MICHAEL BENDER
BEETLEJUICE   Warner Bros., 1988, w/Richard
   Hashimoto & Larry Wilson

BILL BENENSON
Business: Bill Benenson Productions, 321 Hampton Dr.,
   Suite 209, Venice, CA 90291, 310/399-7793

BOULEVARD NIGHTS   Warner Bros., 1979
THE LIGHTSHIP   Castle Hill, 1986, w/Moritz Borman
MR. JOHNSON   Avenue Pictures, 1991, EP

STUART BENJAMIN
Business: New Visions Entertainment Corporation,
   5750 Wilshire Blvd., 6th Floor, Los Angeles, CA 90036,
   213/965-2500; Fax: 213/965-2599

BILLY GALVIN   Vestron, 1986, EP w/Howard L. Baldwin,
   Lindsay Law & William Minot
LA BAMBA   Columbia, 1987, EP
EVERYBODY'S ALL-AMERICAN   Warner Bros.,
   1988, EP
ROOFTOPS   New Visions, 1989, EP w/Taylor Hackford
THE LONG WALK HOME   Miramax, 1990,
   EP w/Taylor Hackford
QUEENS LOGIC   Seven Arts, 1991,
   EP w/Taylor Hackford
MORTAL THOUGHTS   Columbia, 1991,
   EP w/Taylor Hackford

HARRY BENN
THE BOY FRIEND   MGM, 1971, AP
SAVAGE MESSIAH   MGM, 1972, AP
TOMMY   Columbia, 1975, AP
CALLAN   Cinema National, 1975, AP
INSERTS   United Artists, 1976, AP
VALENTINO   United Artists, 1977, AP
THE RAZOR'S EDGE   Columbia, 1984,
   w/Robert P. Marcucci
YOUNG SHERLOCK HOLMES   Paramount, 1985, AP
GOOD MORNING, VIETNAM   Buena Vista, 1987,
   CP w/Ben Moses

BILL BENNETT
BACKLASH   Samuel Goldwyn Company, 1987

HARVE BENNETT
Attorney: Ziffren, Brittenham & Branca - Los Angeles,
   213/552-3388
Contact: Writers Guild of America - Los Angeles,
   310/550-1000

STAR TREK II: THE WRATH OF KHAN   Paramount,
   1982, EP
STAR TREK III: THE SEARCH FOR SPOCK
   Paramount, 1984
STAR TREK IV: THE VOYAGE HOME   Paramount, 1986
STAR TREK V: THE FINAL FRONTIER   Paramount, 1989

JOHN B. BENNETT
WATERMELON MAN   Columbia, 1970
A MAN, A WOMAN, AND A BANK   Avco Embassy, 1979,
   w/Peter Samuelson
TULIPS   Avco Embassy, 1981, EP w/Harold Greenberg

STEPHANIE BENNETT
Business: Delilah Pictures, c/o The Mount Company, 3723
   W. Olive Ave., Burbank, CA 91505, 818/846-1500

THE COMPLEAT BEATLES (FD)   TeleCulture, 1984,
   w/Patrick Montgomery
CHUCK BERRY: HAIL! HAIL! ROCK 'N' ROLL! (FD)
   Universal, 1987, w/Chuck Berry

GRAHAM BENSON
Business: Telso International, 84-85 Buckingham Gate,
   London, SW1E 6PD, 071/976-7188; Fax: 071/976-7113

QUEEN OF HEARTS   Cinecom, 1989, EP

JAY BENSON
THE STEPFATHER   New Century/Vista, 1987

LEON BENSON
CHOSEN SURVIVORS   Columbia, 1974, CP

ROBBY BENSON
Attorney: Lloyd Braun, Silverberg Katz, 11766 Wilshire Blvd.,
   7th Floor, Los Angeles, CA 90025, 310/445-5801
Contact: Directors Guild of America - Los Angeles,
   213/289-2000

MODERN LOVE   Triumph, 1990

MARK BENTLEY
RESTLESS NATIVES   Orion Classics, 1986, EP
CROOKED HEARTS   MGM, 1991, AP w/Lianne Halfon

KATE BENTON
SPELLBINDER   MGM/UA, 1988, CP w/Steve Berman, Todd Black & Mickey Borofsky

ROBERT BENTON
Business: 110 W. 57th St., 5th Floor, New York, NY 10019, 212/247-5652
Agent: ICM - New York, 212/556-5600

THE HOUSE ON CARROLL STREET   Orion, 1988, EP w/Arlene Donovan

OBIE BENZ
HEAVY PETTING (FD)   Skouras Pictures, 1989

ERIC BERCOVICI
Agent: CAA - Beverly Hills, 310/288-4545
Contact: Writers Guild of America - Los Angeles, 310/550-1000

OUT OF SEASON   Athenaeum, 1975, w/Reuben Bercovitch

REUBEN BERCOVITCH
Contact: Writers Guild of America - Los Angeles, 310/550-1000

OUT OF SEASON   Athenaeum, 1975, w/Eric Bercovici

BENJAMIN BERG
LATINO   Cinecom, 1986

DICK BERG
Business: Stonehenge Productions c/o Viacom, 10 Universal Plaza, 32nd Floor, Universal City, CA 91608, 818/505-7566
Contact: Writers Guild of America - Los Angeles, 310/550-1000

SHOOT   Avco Embassy, 1976, EP
SPECIAL DELIVERY   AIP, 1976
FRESH HORSES   WEG/Columbia, 1988

ANDREW BERGMAN
Business: Lobell-Bergman Productions, 9336 W. Washington Blvd., Culver City, CA 90230, 310/202-3362; Fax: 310/202-3272
Agent: ICM - New York, 212/556-5600

CHANCES ARE   TriStar, 1989, EP w/Neil Machlis
WHITE FANG   Buena Vista, 1991, EP w/Michael Lobell

JULIE BERGMAN
Contact: Spring Creek Productions, 4000 Warner Blvd., Producers Bldg. 7, Room #8, Burbank, CA 91522, 818/954-1210; Fax: 818/954-2737

MAJOR LEAGUE   Paramount, 1989, CP
KING RALPH   Universal, 1991, CP w/John Comfort

MEL BERGMAN
DEATH GAME   Levitt-Pickman, 1977, EP w/William Duffy
SURVIVAL RUN   Film Ventures International, 1980, EP w/Ruben Broido
REMO WILLIAMS: THE ADVENTURE BEGINS...
Orion, 1985, EP w/Dick Clark

ELEANOR BERGSTEIN
Agent: CAA - Beverly Hills, 310/288-4545
Contact: Writers Guild of America - New York, 212/245-6180

DIRTY DANCING   Vestron, 1987, CP

DORI BERINSTEIN
ENID IS SLEEPING   Vestron, 1990, EP w/Mitchell Cannold & Adam Platnick

ROGER BERLIND
BEYOND THERAPY   New World, 1987, EP

GERALD BERMAN
THE GUEST   RM Productions, 1984

LESTER BERMAN
Contact: Direcotrs Guild of America - New York, 212/581-0370

THE GREAT BANK HOAX   *SHENANIGANS*   Warner Bros., 1979, AP
SOMETHING SHORT OF PARADISE   AIP, 1979, w/James C. Gutman

STEVEN E. BERMAN
Business: Patrick C. Wells Associates, Inc., 2415 Vado Drive, Los Angeles, CA 90046, 213/650-8544

SPELLBINDER   MGM/UA, 1988, CP w/Kate Benton, Todd Black & Mickey Borofsky

JUDD BERNARD
Agent: CAA - Beverly Hills, 310/288-4545

DOUBLE TROUBLE   MGM, 1967, w/Irwin Winkler
POINT BLANK   MGM, 1967, w/Robert Chartoff
BLUE   Paramount, 1968, w/Irwin Winkler
THE MAN WHO HAD POWER OVER WOMEN   Avco Embassy, 1971
THE DESTRUCTORS   AIP, 1974
INSIDE OUT   Warner Bros., 1976
THE CLASS OF MISS MacMICHAEL   Brut, 1979
ENTER THE NINJA   Cannon, 1981, w/Yoram Globus

SAM BERNARD
Agent: The Gage Group - Los Angeles, 310/859-8777

RAD   TriStar, 1986, CP

YANNICK BERNARD
BABAR: THE MOVIE   New Line, 1989, EP w/Pierre Bertrand-Jaume & Stephane Sperry

BARRY BERNARDI
Contact: Steve White Productions, 7920 Sunset Blvd., 4th Floor, Los Angeles, CA 90046, 213/962-1923; Fax: 213/871-2963

ESCAPE FROM NEW YORK   Avco Embassy, 1981, AP
CHRISTINE   Columbia, 1983, AP
STARMAN   Columbia, 1984, CP
WANTED DEAD OR ALIVE   New World, 1986, CP
POLTERGEIST III   MGM/UA, 1988

MAURICE BERNART
THE KING'S WHORE   J&M, 1990, w/Wieland Schulz-Keil & Paolo Zaccaria

Be

FILM
PRODUCERS,
STUDIOS,
AGENTS AND
CASTING
DIRECTORS
GUIDE

GUSTAVE BERNE
ASYLUM   Cinerama, 1972, EP
THEATRE OF BLOOD   United Artists, 1973,
   EP w/Sam Jaffe
CRAZE   Warner Bros., 1974, EP
PHANTOM OF THE PARADISE   20th Century Fox,
   1974, EP
THE STEPFORD WIVES   Columbia, 1975, EP
CANNONBALL   New World, 1976, EP w/Run Run Shaw
THE STRANGER AND THE GUNFIGHTER   Columbia,
   1976, w/Run Run Shaw

FRED BERNER
Business: Berner/Schlamme Productions, 1619 Broadway,
   9th Floor, New York, NY 10019, 212/603-0609
Contact: Directors Guild of America - New York,
   212/581-0370

MISS FIRECRACKER   Corsair, 1989

HARVEY BERNHARD
Business: Bernhard-Robson Entertainment, 100 Universal
   City Plaza, Bldg. 507, Suite 3B, Universal City, CA
   91608, 818/777-3012; Fax: 818/777-0428

THE MACK   Cinerama, 1973
THOMASINE AND BUSHROD   Columbia, 1974,
   w/Max Julien
THE OMEN   20th Century Fox, 1976
DAMIEN - OMEN II   20th Century Fox, 1978
THE FINAL CONFLICT   20th Century Fox, 1981
THE BEAST WITHIN   MGM/UA, 1982,
   w/Gabriel Katzka
LADYHAWKE   Warner Bros., 1985, EP
THE GOONIES   Warner Bros., 1985,
   w/Richard Donner
THE LOST BOYS   Warner Bros., 1987

STEVEN BERNHARDT
Contact: Directors Guild of America - Los Angeles,
   213/289-2000

GET TO KNOW YOUR RABBIT   Warner Bros., 1972,
   w/Paul Gaer
THE FUNHOUSE   Universal, 1981, w/Derek Power
TEMPEST   Columbia, 1982, CP w/Pato Guzman

ALAIN BERNHEIM
Contact: Alma Productions, 9219 Cordell Drive,
   Los Angeles, CA 90069, 310/550-7603

BUDDY BUDDY   MGM, 1981, EP
YES, GIORGIO   MGM, 1982, EP w/Herbert H. Breslin
RACING WITH THE MOON   Paramount, 1984,
   w/John Kohn

HARMON BERNS
NATIONAL LAMPOON'S CLASS REUNION   20th Century
   Fox, 1982, w/Peter V. Herald

WILLIAM A. BERNS
THE GAMBLERS   UMC, 1970

HARRY BERNSEN
Business: Tartarus Productions, 15260 Ventura Blvd.,
   Suite 1160, Sherman Oaks, CA 91403, 818/377-2222;
   Fax: 818/784-0104

SOMETHING BIG   National General, 1971, AP

FOOLS' PARADE   Columbia, 1971, AP
THREE THE HARD WAY   Allied Artists, 1974
TAKE A HARD RIDE   20th Century Fox, 1975

ARMYAN BERNSTEIN
Business: Beacon Pictures, 1041 Formosa Ave., Hollywood,
   CA 90046, 213/850-2651; Fax: 213/850-2613
Agent: CAA - Beverly Hills, 310/288-4545

ONE FROM THE HEART   Columbia, 1982, CP
SATISFACTION   20th Century Fox, 1988,
   EP w/Robert Alden
A MIDNIGHT CLEAR   Interstar, 1991, EP w/Marc Abraham
   & Tom Rosenberg

JACK B. BERNSTEIN
Business: MGM Pictures, 10000 W. Washington Blvd.,
   Culver City, CA 90232, 310/280-6000; Fax: 310/836-1680
Agent: The Gersh Agency - Beverly Hills, 310/274-6611

THE FURY   20th Century Fox, 1978, AP
BUTCH AND SUNDANCE: THE EARLY DAYS   20th
   Century Fox, 1979, AP
NORTH DALLAS FORTY   Paramount, 1979, EP
UNFAITHFULLY YOURS   20th Century Fox, 1984, AP

JAY BERNSTEIN
Business: Jay Bernstein Productions, P.O. Box 1148,
   Beverly Hills, CA 90213, 818/905-3223

SUNBURN   Paramount, 1979, EP w/John Quested
NOTHING PERSONAL   AIP, 1980, EP w/Alan Hamel &
   Norman Hirschfield

JONATHAN BERNSTEIN
Business: FNM, Inc., 11833 Mississippi Ave., Los Angeles,
   CA 90025, 310/447-7300
Contact: Directors Guild of America - Los Angeles,
   213/289-2000

THE CHOSEN   20th Century Fox International
   Classics, 1982
TESTAMENT   Paramount, 1983, w/Lynne Littman
ONE MORE SATURDAY NIGHT   Columbia, 1986,
   w/Robert Kosberg & Tova Laiter

RAY BERNSTEIN
THE RETURN OF SUPERFLY   Triton, 1990, CP w/Hank
   Blumenthal, Robert Freibrun & Tom Gruenberg

WALTER BERNSTEIN
Agent: ICM - New York, 212/556-5600
Contact: Writers Guild of America - New York, 212/245-6180

THE MOLLY MAGUIRES   Paramount, 1970, CP

ERIC BERNT
MONSTER HIGH   Lightyear, 1990

VON BERNUTH
THE GIANT OF THUNDER MOUNTAIN   Castle Hill, 1991,
   LP w/Joan Weidman

CHUCK BERRY
Agent: William Morris Agency - Beverly Hills, 310/274-7451

CHUCK BERRY: HAIL! HAIL! ROCK 'N' ROLL! (FD)
   Universal, 1987, w/Stephanie Bennett

Be

FILM
PRODUCERS,
STUDIOS,
AGENTS AND
CASTING
DIRECTORS
GUIDE

F
I
L
M

P
R
O
D
U
C
E
R
S

JOHN BERRY
A CAPTIVE IN THE LAND   1991, w/Malcolm Stuart

TOM BERRY
TWIN SISTERS   IMAGE, 1991

GIOVANNI BERTOLUCCI
THE CONFORMIST   Paramount, 1971, EP
THE SPIDER'S STRATAGEM   New Yorker, 1973
TERESA THE THIEF   World Northal, 1979
THE INNOCENT   Analysis, 1979
LUNA   20th Century Fox, 1979

PIERRE BERTRAND-JAUME
BABAR: THE MOVIE (AF)   New Line, 1989,
    EP w/Yannick Bernard & Stephane Sperry

JOSEPH BERUH
THE WILD PARTY   AIP, 1975, EP w/Edgar Lansbury

ROBERTO BESSI
Business: Trans World, 3330 Cahuenga Blvd. West,
    Suite 500, Los Angeles, CA 90068, 213/969-2800

SHANGHAI JOE   United International, 1976,
    w/Renate Angiolini
WARRIORS OF THE LOST WORLD   Vista, 1985,
    w/Frank E. Hildebrand
FROM BEYOND   Empire, 1986, LP

DAN BESSIE
EXECUTIVE ACTION   National General, 1973,
    CP w/Gary Horowitz

JUST BETZER
Business: Just Betzer Films, Inc., c/o Raleigh Studios,
    5300 Melrose Ave., Suite 250B, Los Angeles, CA 90038,
    213/960-4026; Fax: 213/960-4021

BABETTE'S FEAST   Orion Classics, 1987, EP
THE MISFIT BRIGADE   *WHEELS OF TERROR*
    Trans World, 1987, w/Benni Korzen
THE GIRL IN A SWING   Millimeter Films, 1989

CURTIS BEUSMAN
TRUST ME   Cinecom, 1989, EP

TIM BEVAN
Business: Working Title Films, 1 Water Lane, Kentish
    Town Lane, London NW1 8NZ, 071/911-6100;
    Fax: 071/911-6150
Contact: 1416 N. La Brea Ave., Hollywood, CA 90028,
    213/856-2779; Fax: 213/856-2615

MY BEAUTIFUL LAUNDRETTE   Orion Classics, 1986,
    w/Sarah Radclyffe
PERSONAL SERVICES   Vestron, 1987
SAMMY & ROSIE GET LAID   Cinecom, 1987,
    w/Sarah Radclyffe
A WORLD APART   Atlantic, 1988,
    EP w/Graham Bradstreet
PAPERHOUSE   Vestron, 1989, w/Sarah Radclyffe
FOR QUEEN & COUNTRY   Atlantic, 1989
DARK OBSESSION   Circle Releasing, 1990
THE TALL GUY   Miramax, 1990, EP
CHICAGO JOE AND THE SHOWGIRL   New Line, 1990
FOOLS OF FORTUNE   New Line, 1990,
    EP w/Graham Bradstreet

DROP DEAD FRED   NEW LINE, 1991, EP
    w/Carlos Davis & Anthony Fingleton
HEAR MY SONG   Miramax, 1992

VICTOR BHALLA
NIGHT EYES   Amritraj-Baldwin Entertainment, 1990, LP

JERRY BICK
THE LONG GOODBYE   United Artists, 1973
THIEVES LIKE US   United Artists, 1974
RUSSIAN ROULETTE   Avco Embassy, 1975
FAREWELL, MY LOVELY   Avco Embassy, 1975,
    EP w/Elliott Kastner
SWING SHIFT   Warner Bros., 1984
AGAINST ALL ODDS   Columbia, 1984, EP

RICK BIEBER
Business: Stonebridge Productions, Columbia Pictures,
    10401 Venice Blvd., Suite 200, Los Angeles, CA 90034,
    310/280-6800; Fax: 310/280-1473

FLATLINERS   Columbia, 1990, w/Michael Douglas

WALTER BIEN
TOM SAWYER   United Artists, 1973, EP

LYNN BIGELOW
Business: Kouf-Bigelow Productions, Walt Disney Pictures,
    500 S. Buena Vista St., Burbank, CA 91521,
    818/560-5103; Fax: 213/560-1930

DISORGANIZED CRIME   Buena Vista, 1989

DAN BIGGS
Business: Millennium Pictures, Inc., 2580 N.W. Upshur,
    Portland, OR, 97210, 503/227-7041

SHADOW PLAY   New World, 1986, w/Susan Shadburne &
Will Vinton

JOE BILELLA
TOO MUCH SUN   New Line, 1990,
    CP w/John V. Stuckmeyer

TONY BILL
Business: Tony Bill Productions, 73 Market St., Venice, CA
    90291, 310/396-5937; Fax: 310/450-4988
Agent: ICM - Los Angeles, 310/550-4000

DEADHEAD MILES   Paramount, 1971,
    w/Vernon Zimmerman
STEELYARD BLUES   Warner Bros., 1973, w/Julia &
    Michael Phillips
THE STING ★★   Universal, 1973, w/Julia &
    Michael Phillips
HEARTS OF THE WEST   United Artists, 1975
HARRY & WALTER GO TO NEW YORK   Columbia,
    1976, EP
GOING IN STYLE   Warner Bros., 1979, w/Fred T. Gallo
BOULEVARD NIGHTS   Warner Bros., 1979, EP
THE LITTLE DRAGONS   Aurora, 1980,
    EP w/Robert S. Bremson
FIVE CORNERS   Cineplex Odeon, 1988, w/Forrest Murray

SALVATORE BILLITTERI
COFFY   AIP, 1973, EP

FILM
PRODUCERS,
STUDIOS,
AGENTS AND
CASTING
DIRECTORS
GUIDE

F
I
L
M

P
R
O
D
U
C
E
R
S

MIKE BINDER
Contact: Writers Guild of America - Los Angeles,
310/550-1000

COUPE DE VILLE   Universal, 1990, CP

MACK BING
Agent: Gray/Goodman, Inc. - Beverly Hills, 310/276-7070
Contact: Directors Guild of America - Los Angeles,
213/289-2000

HARD COUNTRY   AFD, 1981, w/David Greene
LICENSE TO DRIVE   20th Century Fox, 1988, AP

THOMAS BIRD
DEAR AMERICA (FD)   Corsair, 1988, w/Bill Couturié

MARVIN BIRDT
THE CAR   Universal, 1977, w/Elliot Silverstein

ROGER BIRNBAUM
Business: 20th Century Fox Film Corporation, 10201 W.
Pico Blvd., Los Angeles, CA 90035, 310/277-2111

THE SURE THING   Embassy, 1985
WHO'S THAT GIRL   Warner Bros., 1987, EP w/Peter
Guber & Jon Peters

MARK BISGEIER
THE INDIAN RUNNER   1991, EP w/Thom Mount &
Stephon K. Bannon

JOSEPH E. BISHOP
THE DIRT GANG   AIP, 1972, w/Art Jacobs

TONY BISHOP
FRIDAY THE 13TH PART 3   Paramount, 1982, CP
MEATBALLS PART II   TriStar, 1984, w/Stephen Poe

WES BISHOP
THE THING WITH TWO HEADS   AIP, 1972
POLICEWOMEN   Crown International, 1974
RACE WITH THE DEVIL   20th Century Fox, 1975
THE BLACK GESTAPO   Bryanston, 1975

MICHAEL BITTINS
DAS BOOT   Columbia, 1982, CP

CAROL BLACK
Business: The Black/Marlens Company, 17351 Sunset
Blvd., Suite 504, Pacific Palisades, CA 90272,
310/573-1717; Fax: 310/573-1704
Agent: UTA - Beverly Hills, 310/273-6700

SOUL MAN   New World, 1986, CP w/Neal Marlens

JOHN D.F. BLACK
Agent: Triad Artists, Inc. - Los Angeles, 310/556-2727
Contact: Writers Guild of America - Los Angeles,
310/550-1000

TROUBLE MAN   20th Century Fox, 1972, EP

NOEL BLACK
Agent: The Chasin Agency - Beverly Hills, 310/278-7505
Contact: Directors Guild of America - Los Angeles,
213/289-2000

MISCHIEF   20th Century Fox, 1985, EP

SARAH RYAN BLACK
BREAKING IN   Samuel Goldwyn Company, 1989,
EP w/Andrew Meyer

SHANE BLACK
Agent: InterTalent - Beverly Hills, 310858-6200

THE LAST BOY SCOUT   Warner Bros., 1991,
EP w/Barry Josephson

TODD BLACK
(credit w/Mickey Borofsky)
Business: Wizan/Black Films, 11999 San Vicente Blvd.,
Suite 450, Los Angeles, CA 90049, 310/472-6133;
Fax: 310/471-9074

SPELLBINDER   MGM/UA, 1988, CP w/Kate Benton &
Steve Berman
SPLIT DECISIONS   New Century/Vista, 1988, CP
THE GUARDIAN   Universal, 1990, CP w/Dan Greenburg
SHORT TIME   20th Century Fox, 1990*
STOP OR MY MOTHER WILL SHOOT   Universal, 1991,
EP w/Joe Wizan

BARRY BLACKMORE
Business: Futuregood Ltd., 16 Talbot Road, London W2 5OH
England, 071/229-6650

DANNY BOY   Triumph/Columbia, 1984

CHRIS BLACKWELL
Business: Island Pictures, 9000 Sunset Blvd., Suite 700,
Los Angeles, CA 90069, 310/276-4500
Contact: The Howard Brandy Company, Inc. - Los Angeles,
213/657-8320

GOOD TO GO   Island Pictures, 1986, EP w/Jeremy Thomas
BIG TIME (FD)   Island Pictures, 1988, EP

GREGORY S. BLACKWELL
TAKE THIS JOB AND SHOVE IT   Embassy, 1981
UNDER THE BOARDWALK   New World, 1989,
w/Steven H. Chanin

BILL BLAKE
RHINESTONE   20th Century Fox, 1984,
CP w/Richard M. Spitalny

GRACE BLAKE
STAR 80   The Ladd Company/Warner Bros., 1983, AP
SCHOOL DAZE   Columbia, 1988, EP
THE SILENCE OF THE LAMBS   Orion, 1991, AP

DANIEL H. BLATT
Business: Daniel H. Blatt Productions, 300 S. Lorimar Plaza,
Bldg. 140, Burbank, CA 91505, 818/954-2227;
Fax: 818/954-7678

I NEVER PROMISED YOU A ROSE GARDEN   New World,
1977, w/Terence F. Deane & Michael Hausman
THE AMERICAN SUCCESS COMPANY   *SUCCESS*
Columbia, 1979, w/Edgar J. Scherick
THE HOWLING   Avco Embassy, 1980,
EP w/Steven A. Lane
INDEPENDENCE DAY   Warner Bros., 1983,
w/Robert Singer
CUJO   Warner Bros., 1983, w/Robert Singer
LET'S GET HARRY   TriStar, 1986, w/Robert Singer
THE BOOST   Herndale, 1988

WILLIAM PETER BLATTY
Agent: William Morris Agency - Beverly Hills, 310/274-7451
Contact: Writers Guild of America - Los Angeles, 310/550-1000

THE EXORCIST ★   Warner Bros., 1973
THE NINTH CONFIGURATION *TWINKLE, TWINKLE, "KILLER" KANE*   Warner Bros., 1979

STEVE BLAUNER
DRIVE, HE SAID   Columbia, 1971, w/Jack Nicholson
THE KING OF MARVIN GARDENS   Columbia, 1972, EP

ANDRE BLAY
Business: Palisades Pictures, 1875 Century Park East, 3rd Floor, Los Angeles, CA 90067, 310/785-3100

PRINCE OF DARKNESS   Universal, 1987, EP w/Shep Gordon
THEY LIVE   Universal, 1988, EP w/Shep Gordon
BRAIN DAMAGE   Palisades Entertainment, 1988, EP w/Al Eicher
THE BLOB   TriStar, 1988, EP
A CHORUS OF DISAPPROVAL   South Gate Entertainment, 1989, EP w/Elliott Kastner

WILLIAM WARREN BLAYLOCK
GRANDVIEW, U.S.A.   Warner Bros., 1984, w/Peter W. Rea

CHARLES B. BLOCH
THE FOG   Avco Embassy, 1980, EP

IVAN BLOCH
THE STONE BOY   20th Century Fox, 1984, w/Joe Roth

DAVID BLOCKER
Business: Raincity Inc., 550 N. Larchmont Blvd., Suite 202, Los Angeles, CA 90004, 213/461-0195
Contact: Directors Guild of America - Los Angeles, 213/289-2000

CHOOSE ME   Island Alive, 1984, w/Carolyn Pfeiffer
TROUBLE IN MIND   Alive Films, 1985, w/Carolyn Pfeiffer
MADE IN HEAVEN   Lorimar, 1987, w/Bruce A. Evans & Raynold Gideon
THE MODERNS   Alive Films, 1988, w/Carolyn Pfeiffer
LOVE AT LARGE   Orion, 1990

ALAN C. BLOMQUIST
Contact: Directors Guild of America - Los Angeles, 213/289-2000

EVERYBODY'S ALL-AMERICAN   Warner Bros., 1988, CP
GUILTY BY SUSPICION   Warner Bros., 1991, CP

JEFFREY BLOOM
Agent: William Morris Agency - Beverly Hills, 310/274-7451
Contact: Writers Guild of America - Los Angeles, 310/550-1000

DOGPOUND SHUFFLE   Paramount, 1977

JIM BLOOM
Business: Blue Iris, Inc., 850 Keeler Ave., Berkeley, CA 94708, 415/526-1996
Contact: Directors Guild of America - Los Angeles, 213/289-2000

CLOSE ENCOUNTERS OF THE THIRD KIND?
THE EMPIRE STRIKES BACK   20th Century Fox, 1980, AP w/Robert Watts
RETURN OF THE JEDI   20th Century Fox, 1983, CP w/Robert Watts
WARNING SIGN   20th Century Fox, 1985
FIRES WITHIN   Pathe, 1990, EP

JOHN BLOOMGARDEN
DEAD OF WINTER   MGM/UA, 1987, w/Marc Shmuger

PHILIPPE BLOT
THE ARROGANT   Cannon, 1987

DENIS BLOUIN
IRONWEED   TriStar, 1987, EP w/Rob Cohen & Joseph H. Kanter

BOB BLUES
WEDNESDAY'S CHILD   *FAMILY LIFE*   Cinema 5, 1972, EP

DEBORAH BLUM
(credit w/Tony Ganz)
Business: Blum-Ganz Productions, 8265 Sunset Blvd., Suite 202, Los Angeles, CA 90046, 213/654-1411; Fax: 213/654-0863

GUNG HO   Paramount, 1986
VIBES   Columbia, 1988
CLEAN AND SOBER   Warner Bros., 1988

HARRY N. BLUM
Business: The Blum Group, 494 Tuallitan Road, Los Angeles, CA 90049, 310/476-2229

DIAMONDS   Avco Embassy, 1975, EP
DRIVE-IN   Columbia, 1976, AP w/Robert S. Bremson
AT THE EARTH'S CORE   AIP, 1976, EP
OBSESSION   Columbia, 1976, w/George Litto
SKATEBOARD   Universal, 1978, w/Richard A. Wolf
THE MAGICIAN OF LUBLIN   Cannon, 1979, EP

LEN BLUM
Agent: CAA - Beverly Hills, 310/288-4545

FEDS   Warner Bros., 1988, w/Ilona Herzberg

HANK BLUMENTHAL
THE RETURN OF SUPERFLY   Triton, 1990, CP w/Ray Bernstein, Robert Freibrun & Tom Gruenberg

RICK BLUMENTHAL
Business: Skybird Films, 4425 Ventura Canyon Ave., Suite 5, Sherman Oaks, CA 91423, 818/788-3770

TRUCKIN' BUDDY MCCOY   Bedford Entertainment, 1984, w/Richard DeMarco
KANDYLAND   New World, 1988
GRIM PRAIRIE TALES   East/West Film Partners, 1990, EP w/Larry Haber
BLOODMATCH   21st Century, 1991, w/Corinne Olivo

Bo

FILM
PRODUCERS,
STUDIOS,
AGENTS and
CASTING
DIRECTORS
GUIDE

F
I
L
M

P
R
O
D
U
C
E
R
S

ROBERT F. BLUMOFE
Contact: 1100 Alta Loma Drive, Los Angeles, CA 90069, 213/657-7000

YOURS, MINE, AND OURS   United Artists, 1968
PIECES OF DREAMS   United Artists, 1970
BOUND FOR GLORY ★   United Artists, 1976,
   w/Harold Leventhal

DON BLUTH
(credit w/Gary Goldman & John Pomeroy)
Business: Sullivan/Bluth Studios, 2501 W. Burbank Blvd., Suite 201, Burbank, CA 91505, 818/840-9446; Fax: 818/840-0487

THE SECRET OF N.I.M.H. (AF)   MGM/UA, 1982
AN AMERICAN TAIL (AF)   Universal, 1986
THE LAND BEFORE TIME (AF)   Universal, 1988
ALL DOGS GO TO HEAVEN (AF)   Universal, 1989

BRUCE BODNER
Business: Cornelius Productions, 4000 Warner Blvd., Burbank, CA 91522, 818/954-2782; Fax: 818/954-4326

FUNNY FARM   Warner Bros., 1988, EP w/Patrick Kelley
FLETCH LIVES   Universal, 1989, EP w/Robert Larson
MEMOIRS OF AN INVISIBLE MAN   Warner Bros., 1991,
   w/Dan Kolsrud

ALLAN F. BODOH
DOGS   R.C. Riddell, 1977, w/Bruce Cohn
ACAPULCO GOLD   R.C. Riddell, 1978, w/Bruce Cohn
GOOD GUYS WEAR BLACK   American Cinema, 1978
GO TELL THE SPARTANS   Avco Embassy, 1978,
   w/Mitchell Cannold
THE GREAT SMOKEY ROADBLOCK   *THE LAST OF THE COWBOYS*   Dimension, 1978
DIRT   American Cinema, 1979, w/John Patrick Graham

LUDI BOEKEN
VINCENT AND THEO   Hemdale, 1990

PAUL BOGART
Agent: CAA - Beverly Hills, 310/288-4545
Contact: Directors Guild of America - Los Angeles, 213/289-2000

CLASS OF '44   Warner Bros., 1973

YUREK BOGAYEVICZ
Agent: CAA - Beverly Hills, 310/288-4545

ANNA   Vestron, 1987, w/Zanne Devine

PETER BOGDANOVICH
Business: 2040 Avenue of the Stars, Suite 400, Los Angeles, CA 90067, 310/203-8055
Agent: CAA - Beverly Hills, 310/288-4545

TARGETS   Paramount, 1968
WHAT'S UP, DOC?   Warner Bros., 1972
PAPER MOON   Paramount, 1973
DAISY MILLER   Paramount, 1974
AT LONG LAST LOVE   20th Century Fox, 1975
ILLEGALLY YOURS   DEG, 1988
TEXASVILLE   Columbia, 1990, w/Barry Spikings
NOISES OFF   Buena Vista, 1991,
   EP w/Kathleen Kennedy

ANNE BOHLEN
BLOOD IN THE FACE (FD)   First Run Features, 1991,
   w/Kevin Rafferty & James Ridgeway

JACK BOHRER
Agent: Gerald K. Smith Agency - Los Angeles, 213/849-5388
Contact: Directors Guild of America - Los Angeles, 213/289-2000

UNHOLY ROLLERS   AIP, 1972, w/John Prizer

ANDRE BOISSIER
BROTHERS IN ARMS   Ablo, 1988, EP w/Jan Erik Lunde

NICOLE BOISVERT
BLACKOUT   New World, 1978, w/John Dunning & Eddy Matalon

EDGAR BOLD
STEEL DAWN   Vestron, 1987, AP
OPTIONS   Vestron, 1989, CP w/Conrad Hool
SCHWEITZER   Concorde, 1990, EP

CRAIG BOLOTIN
Agent: CAA - Beverly Hills, 310/288-4545
Contact: Writers Guild of America - Los Angeles, 310/550-1000

BLACK RAIN   Paramount, 1989, EP w/Julie Kirkham

JAMES BOND III
DEF BY TEMPTATION   Troma, 1990

LOIS BONFIGLIO
Business: Isis Productions c/o Orion Pictures, 1888 Century Park East, 6th Floor, Los Angeles, CA 90067, 310/282-2952; Fax: 310/282-8607

THE MORNING AFTER   20th Century Fox, 1986,
   AP w/Wolfgang Glattes
OLD GRINGO   Columbia, 1989

BOB BOOKER
Contact: 11811 W. Olympic Blvd., Los Angeles, CA 90064, 310/478-7878; Fax: 310/479-6257

THE PHYNX   Warner Bros., 1970, w/George Foster

JOHN BOORMAN
Business: 9696 Culver Blvd., Suite 203, Culver City, CA 90232, 310/558-8110
Agent: ICM - Los Angeles, 310/550-4000

DELIVERANCE ★   Warner Bros., 1972
ZARDOZ   20th Century Fox, 1974
EXORCIST II: THE HERETIC   Warner Bros., 1977,
   w/Richard Lederer
EXCALIBUR   Orion, 1981
DANNY BOY   Triumph/Columbia, 1984, EP
THE EMERALD FOREST   Embassy, 1985
HOPE AND GLORY ★   Columbia, 1987
WHERE THE HEART IS   Buena Vista, 1990

JON BOORSTIN
Agent: Camden Artists, Ltd. - Los Angeles, 213/556-2022

ALL THE PRESIDENT'S MEN   Warner Bros., 1976, AP
DREAM LOVER   MGM/UA, 1986, w/Alan J. Pakula

Bo

**FILM
PRODUCERS,
STUDIOS,
AGENTS AND
CASTING
DIRECTORS**
GUIDE

F
I
L
M

P
R
O
D
U
C
E
R
S

MARGARET BOOTH
THE CHEAP DETECTIVE   Columbia, 1978, AP
CHAPTER TWO   Columbia, 1979, AP
THE SLUGGER'S WIFE   Columbia, 1985, EP

CARL BORACK
THE BIG FIX   Universal, 1978, w/Richard Dreyfuss

PHIL BORACK
Business: April Fools Productions, Inc., 636 Northland Blvd.,
   Cincinnati, OH 45250, 513/851-5700

HARPER VALLEY P.T.A.   April Fools, 1978, EP
CHATTANOOGA CHOO CHOO   April Fools, 1984, EP

JOSE LUIS BORAU
Business: El Iman S.A., Alberto Aleocer 42, Madrid 16,
   Spain, 01/250-5534

ON THE LINE   Miramax, 1987, w/Steven Kovacs

DONALD P. BORCHERS
ANGEL   New World, 1984, w/Roy Watts
CHILDREN OF THE CORN   New World, 1984,
   w/Terrence Kirby
TUFF TURF   New World, 1985
VAMP   New World, 1986
TWO MOON JUNCTION   Lorimar, 1988
FAR FROM HOME   Vestron, 1989

BILL BORDEN
Contact: First Street Films c/o A&M Films, 1416 N. La Brea
   Ave., Hollywood, CA 90028, 213/856-2795;
   Fax: 213/856-2740

AGAINST ALL ODDS   Columbia, 1984, AP
WHITE NIGHTS   Columbia, 1985, AP
LA BAMBA   Columbia, 1987, w/Taylor Hackford
A MIDNIGHT CLEAR   Interstar, 1991, Dale Pollock

LIZZIE BORDEN
BORN IN FLAMES   First Run Features, 1983
WORKING GIRLS   Miramax, 1987, w/Andi Gladstone

MORITZ BORMAN
Business: Picture Fund, Inc., 1350 Abbot Kinney Blvd.,
   Suite 203, Venice, CA 90291, 310/296-4374;
   Fax: 310/392-3102

UNDER THE VOLCANO   Universal, 1984,
   w/Wieland Schulz-Keil
THE LIGHTSHIP   Castle Hill, 1986, w/Bill Benenson
HOMER AND EDDIE   Skouras, 1990, w/James Cady

MICKEY BOROFSKY
(credit w/Todd Black)
Business: Wizan/Black Films, 11999 San Vicente Blvd.,
   Suite 450, Los Angeles, CA 90049, 310/472-6133;
   Fax: 310/471-9074

PRIME CUT   National General, 1972, AP*
JUNIOR BONNER   Cinerama, 1972, AP*
99 & 44/100 PERCENT DEAD   20th Century Fox,
   1974, AP*
SPELLBINDER   MGM/UA, 1988, CP w/Kate Benton &
   Steve Berman
SPLIT DECISIONS   New Century/Vista, 1988, CP

THE GUARDIAN   Universal, 1990, CP w/Todd Black &
   Dan Greenburg
SHORT TIME   20th Century Fox, 1990, EP w/Joe Wizan*

PHILLIP BORSOS
Business: 1800 Century Park East, Suite 300, Los Angeles,
   CA 90067, 310/203-0777
Agent: UTA - Beverly Hills, 310/273-6700

THE GREY FOX   United Artists Classics, 1983,
   CP w/Barry Healey
ONE MAGIC CHRISTMAS   Buena Vista, 1985, EP

SIMON BOSANQUET
Business: Aritsan Films, Twickenham Film Studios, The
   Barons, St. Margaret's, Twickenham, Middlesex TW1 2AW
   England, 081/892-4477; Fax: 081/892-3899

NUNS ON THE RUN   20th Century Fox, 1990, CP

FREDERIC BOURBOULON
WAITING FOR THE MOON   Skouras Pictures, 1987, LP

GABRIEL BOUSTANI
ATLANTIC CITY ★   Paramount, 1981,
   EP w/Joseph Beaubien
DEATHWATCH   Quartet, 1982, w/Janine Rubeiz

TOM BOUTROSS
Contact: Directors Guild of America - Los Angeles,
   213/289-2000

THE HOUSE ON SKULL MOUNTAIN   20th Century Fox,
   1974, CP
APPOINTMENT WITH DEATH   Galaxy, 1985

JOHN R. BOWEY
Business: Howard International, 6565 Sunset Blvd., Suite
   400, Hollywood, CA 90028, 213/463-2226

PRETTYKILL   Spectrafilm, 1987, w/Martin Walters
TIME OF THE BEAST   Liberty Films, 1989, EP

KENNETH BOWSER
Agent: Lucy Kroll Agency - New York, 212/877-0627

IN A SHALLOW GRAVE   Skouras Pictures, 1988,
   w/Barry Jossen

BETTY E. BOX
SOME GIRLS DO   United Artists, 1971
IT'S NOT THE SIZE THAT COUNTS   Joseph Brenner
   Associates, 1974

JOHN BOX
THE LOOKING GLASS WAR   Columbia, 1970

DON BOYD
Business: Anglo-International Films, 21a Kingly Court,
   London W1R 5LE England, 071/734-5747;
   Fax: 071/734-5784

HONKY TONK FREEWAY   Universal/AFD, 1981,
   w/Howard W. Koch Jr.
SCRUBBERS   Orion Classics, 1984
ARIA   Miramax, 1988
WAR REQUIEM   Anglo International, 1988

FILM
PRODUCERS,
STUDIOS,
AGENTS AND
CASTING
DIRECTORS
GUIDE

JOE BOYD
Business: Rykodisc, P.O. Box 2401, London W2 5SF,
071/727-7480; Fax: 071/229-4190

JIMI HENDRIX (FD)   Warner Bros., 1973, w/John Head &
Gary Weis
SCANDAL   Miramax, 1989, EP w/Nik Powell, Bob
Weinstein & Harvey Weinstein

ROBERT BOYETT
Business: Miller-Boyett Productions, 10202 W. Washington
Blvd., Culver City, CA 90232, 310/558-6555

THE BEST LITTLE WHOREHOUSE IN TEXAS   Universal,
1982, w/Edward K. Milkis & Thomas L. Miller

BARBARA BOYLE
Business: Sovereign Pictures, Inc., 11845 W. Olympic
Blvd., Suite 1055, Los Angeles, CA 90064,
310/312-1001; Fax: 310/478-7707

CAMPUS MAN   Paramount, 1987, EP w/Marc E. Platt
EIGHT MEN OUT   Orion, 1988, EP w/Jerry Offsay

KERRY BOYLE
Business: Palace Pictures, 8170 Beverly Blvd., Suite 203,
Los Angeles, CA 90048, 213/655-1114;
Fax: 213/655-1195

A RAGE IN HARLEM   Miramax, 1991, w/Stephen Woolley

MARC BOYMAN
THE INCUBUS   FIlm Ventures International, 1982,
w/John M. Eckert
THE FLY   20th Century Fox, 1986, CP w Kip Ohman
DEAD RINGERS   20th Century Fox, 1988,
w/David Cronenberg

RON BOZMAN
Contact: Directors Guild of America - New York,
212/581-0370

SOMETHING WILD   Orion, 1986, AP
MARRIED TO THE MOB   Orion, 1988, AP
MIAMI BLUES   Orion, 1990, CP w/Kenneth Utt
WAITING FOR THE LIGHT   Triumph, 1990,
w/Caldecot Chubb
THE SILENCE OF THE LAMBS   Orion, 1991,
w/Edward Saxon & Kenneth Utt

LORD JOHN BRABOURNE
(credit w/Richard Goodwin)
Business: Mersham Productions, Ltd., 41 Montpelier
Walk, London SW7 1JH, England, 071/589-8829;
Fax: 071/584-0024

ROMEO & JULIET ★   Paramount, 1968,
w/Anthony Havelock-Allan*
THE DANCE OF DEATH   Paramount, 1968*
PETER RABBIT AND TALES OF BEATRIX POTTER
MGM, 1971, EP*
MURDER ON THE ORIENT EXPRESS   Paramount, 1974
DEATH ON THE NILE   Paramount, 1978
STORIES FROM A FLYING TRUNK   EMI, 1979
THE MIRROR CRACK'D   AFD, 1980
EVIL UNDER THE SUN   AFD/Universal, 1982
A PASSAGE TO INDIA ★   Columbia, 1984
LITTLE DORRIT   Cannon, 1988

JACOB BRACKMAN
Agent: ICM - New York, 212/556-5600
Contact: Writers Guild of America - New York, 212/245-6180

DAYS OF HEAVEN   Paramount, 1978, EP
TIMES SQUARE   AFD, 1980, w/Robert Stigwood

PAUL BRADLEY
THE BALLAD OF THE SAD CAFE   Angelika, 1991, EP

GRAHAM BRADSTREET
(credit w/Tim Bevan)
Contact: Working Title Films, 1416 N. La Brea Ave.,
Hollywood, CA 90028, 213/856-2779; Fax: 213/856-2615;
1 Water Lane, Kentish Town Lane, London NW1 8NZ
England, 071/911-6100; Fax: 071/911-6150

A WORLD APART   Atlantic, 1988, EP
FOOLS OF FORTUNE   New Line, 1990, EP
HEAR MY SONG   Miramax, 1992

DAVID H. BRADY
THE GREY FOX   United Artists Classics, 1983, EP

ARNE BRANDHILD
AWOL   BFB, 1973, w/Herb Freed

SAUL BRANDMAN
THE JESUS TRIP   EMCO, 1971, EP

JERROLD BRANDT, JR.
Agent: The Gersh Agency - Beverly Hills, 310/274-6611
Contact: Directors Guild of America - Los Angeles,
213/289-2000

THE BELL JAR   Avco Embassy, 1979,
w/Michael Todd, Jr.

HOWARD BRANDY
Business: The Howard Brandy Company, Inc., 755 N. La
Cienega Blvd., Los Angeles, CA 90069, 213/657-8320;
75 Rockfeller Plaza, Suite 1706, New York, NY 10019

THE TAKE   Columbia, 1974

RICHARD BRANSON
Business: The Virgin Group, 328 Kensal Rd., London W10
5XJ England, 081/968-6688; Fax: 081/968-6533

ELECTRIC DREAMS   MGM/UA, 1984, EP

STEVEN J. BRATTER
INSTANT KARMA   MGM, 1990, EP w/Craig Sheffer

ZEV BRAUN
Business: Zev Braun Pictures, 1440 S. Sepulveda Blvd., Los
Angeles, CA 90025, 310/444-8457; Fax: 310/444-8137

THE PEDESTRIAN   Cinerama, 1974, CP
THE LITTLE GIRL WHO LIVES DOWN THE LANE
AIP, 1977
THE SENSUOUS NURSE   Mid-Broadway, 1979
ANGELA   Embassy, 1984, EP
WHERE ARE THE CHILDREN   Columbia, 1986

ARTUR BRAUNER
CALL OF THE WILD   Constantin, 1975
THE ROSE GARDEN   Cannon, 1989

ANDREW BRAUNSBERG

WONDERWALL   Cinecenta, 1969
MACBETH   Columbia, 1971
WHAT?   Avco Embassy, 1973, EP
ANDY WARHOL'S DRACULA   Bryanston, 1974, w/Carlo
   Ponti & Jean Pierre Rassam
ANDY WARHOL'S FRANKENSTEIN   Bryanston, 1974,
   w/Carlo Ponti & Jean Pierre Rassam
THE TENANT   Paramount, 1976
BEING THERE   United Artists, 1979
THE HOUND OF THE BASKERVILLES   Atlantic, 1979,
   EP w/Michael White
THE POSTMAN ALWAYS RINGS TWICE   Paramount,
   1981, EP
LOOKIN' TO GET OUT   Paramount, 1982, EP
ALPHABET CITY   Atlantic, 1984
CRUSOE   Island Pictures, 1989
DRIVING ME CRAZY   First Run Features, 1990

GEORGE BRAUNSTEIN
(credit w/Ron Hamady)

TRAIN RIDE TO HOLLYWOOD   Taylor-Laughlin,
   1975, EP
FADE TO BLACK   American Cinema, 1980
SURF II   International Films, 1984
AND GOD CREATED WOMAN   Vestron, 1988
OUT COLD   Hemdale, 1989
DON'T TELL HER IT'S ME   Hemdale, 1990

WILLIAM BRAUNSTEIN
Business: Bima Entertainment, Ltd., 2049 Century Park
   East, Suite 4050, Los Angeles, CA 90067, 310/203-8488

SLIPSTREAM   Entertainment Films, 1989, EP w/Nigel
   Green & Arthur Maslansky

PHILIP M. BREEN
Business: Rolling Hills Productions, 204 South Beverly Dr.,
   Suite 166, Beverly Hills, CA 90212, 310/275-0872

SWORD OF THE VALIANT   Cannon, 1984,
   EP w/Michael J. Kagan
THE NATURAL   TriStar, 1984, EP w/Roger Towne

MARTIN BREGMAN
Business: Martin Bregman Productions, 100 Universal City
   Plaza, Universal City, CA 91608, 818/777-4950;
   Fax: 818/777-4971; 642 Lexington Ave., Suite 1400,
   New York, NY, 10022, 212/421-6161
Agent: UTA - Beverly Hills, 310/273-6700

SERPICO   Paramount, 1973
DOG DAY AFTERNOON ★   Warner Bros., 1975,
   w/Martin Elfand
THE NEXT MAN   Allied Artists, 1976
THE SEDUCTION OF JOE TYNAN   Universal, 1979
SIMON   Orion, 1980
THE FOUR SEASONS   Universal, 1981
VENOM   Paramount, 1982
SCARFACE   Universal, 1983
SWEET LIBERTY   Universal, 1986
REAL MEN   MGM/UA, 1987
A NEW LIFE   Paramount, 1988
LISTEN TO ME   WEG/Columbia, 1989, EP
SEA OF LOVE   Universal, 1989, w/Louis A. Stroller
BETSY'S WEDDING   Buena Vista, 1990,
   w/Louis A. Stroller

MARIO BREGUI
Business: Produzioni Atlas Consorziate SRL, Viale Rigina
   Margherita 279, 00198 Roma, Italy, 06-4403797

THE CHOIRBOYS   Universal, 1977, EP w/Pietro Bregui &
   Mark Damon

PIETRO BREGUI
Business: Produzioni Atlas Consorziate SRL, Viale Rigina
   Margherita 279, 00198 Roma, Italy, 06-4403797

THE CHOIRBOYS   Universal, 1977, EP w/Mario Bregui &
   Mark Damon

ROBERT S. BREMSON
DRIVE-IN   Columbia, 1976, AP w/Harry N. Blum
OBSESSION   Columbia, 1976, EP
FIVE DAYS FROM HOME   Universal, 1979, EP
SHE CAME TO THE VALLEY   R&V Pictures, 1979, EP
THE LITTLE DRAGONS   Aurora, 1980, EP w/Tony Bill

HERBERT H. BRESLIN
YES, GIORGIO   MGM, 1982, EP w/Alain Bernheim

KEVIN BRESLIN
UHF   Orion, 1989, CP w/Deren Getz

MARTIN BREST
Business: City Lights Films, 2110 Main St., Suite 200, Santa
   Monica, CA 90405, 310/314-3500; Fax: 310/314-3525
Agent: CAA - Beverly Hills, 310/288-4545

HOT TOMORROWS   AFI, 1978
MIDNIGHT RUN   Universal, 1988

JASON BRETT
Business: Jason Brett Productions, c/o New World
   Entertainment, 1440 S. Sepulveda Blvd., Los Angeles, CA
   90025, 310/444-8623; Fax: 310/444-8101
Agent: UTA - Beverly Hills, 310/273-6700

ABOUT LAST NIGHT...   TriStar, 1986, w/Stuart Oken

JONATHAN BRETT
SHE-DEVIL   Orion, 1989, w/Susan Seidelman

ALAN BREWER
PLAYING FOR KEEPS   Universal, 1986, w/Bob Weinstein
   & Harvey Weinstein

COLIN M. BREWER
ESCAPE TO ATHENA   AFD, 1979, AP
THE KEEP   Paramount, 1983, EP

LARRY BREZNER
Business: Morra, Brezner & Steinberg, Inc., c/o 20th Century
   Fox, 10201 Pico Blvd., Bldg. 58, Los Angeles, 90035,
   310/203-1090; Fax: 310/203-2883

THROW MOMMA FROM THE TRAIN   Orion, 1987
GOOD MORNING, VIETNAM   Buena Vista, 1987,
   w/Mark Johnson
THE 'BURBS   Universal, 1989, w/Michael Finnell
COUPE DE VILLE   Universal, 1990, w/Paul Schiff

RICHARD BRICK
Business: Silo Cinema, Inc., 70 Grand St., New York, NY
10013, 212/925-8877
Contact: Directors Guild of America - New York,
212/581-0370

HANGIN' WITH THE HOMEBOYS   New Line, 1991

MARSHALL BRICKMAN
Agent: ICM - Los Angeles, 310/550-4000
Contact: WGA - New York,
212/245-6180

THE MANHATTAN PROJECT   20th Century Fox, 1986,
w/Jennifer Ogden

PAUL BRICKMAN
Agent: CAA - Beverly Hills, 310/288-4545
Contact: Directors Guild of America - Los Angeles,
213/289-2000

CITIZENS BAND *HANDLE WITH CARE*   Paramount,
1977, AP
DEAL OF THE CENTURY   Warner Bros., 1983,
EP w/Jon Avnet & Steve Tisch
MEN DON'T LEAVE   Geffen/Warner Bros., 1990, EP

HOWARD M. BRICKNER
SIDEWALK STORIES   Island Pictures, 1989,
EP w/Vicki Lebenbaum

LESLIE BRICUSSE
Contact: Writers Guild of America - Los Angeles,
310/550-1000

SCROOGE   National General, 1970, EP

JAMES BRIDGES
Agent: CAA - Beverly Hills, 310/288-4545
Contact: Directors Guild of America - Los Angeles,
213/289-2000

PERFECT   Columbia, 1985

RICHARD F. BRIDGES
THE GREAT BANK HOAX *SHENANIGANS*   Warner
Bros., 1979, EP w/Laurence Klausner & T. Carlyle Scales

DANIEL BRIGGS
SEXTETTE   Crown International, 1979, w/Robert Sullivan

JACK BRIGGS
EAT & RUN   New World, 1987

RICHARD S. BRIGHT
TRIBUTE   20th Century Fox, 1980, EP w/David Foster &
Lawrence Turman

BILL BRIGODE
ENID IS SLEEPING   Vestron, 1990, CP

JOHN BRILEY
Agent: ICM - Los Angeles, 310/550-4000
Contact: Writers Guild of America - Los Angeles,
310/550-1000

POPE JOAN   Columbia, 1972, AP
CRY FREEDOM   Universal, 1987, CP w/Norman Spencer

BERNIE BRILLSTEIN
Business: The Brillstein Company, 9200 Sunset Blvd.,
Suite 428, Los Angeles, CA 90069, 310/275-6135;
Fax: 310/275-6180

THE BLUES BROTHERS   Universal, 1980, EP
MAD MAGAZINE PRESENTS UP THE ACADEMY   Warner
Bros., 1980, EP
CONTINENTAL DIVIDE   Universal, 1981,
EP w/Steven Spielberg
NEIGHBORS   Columbia, 1981, EP w/Irving Paul Lazar
DOCTOR DETROIT   Universal, 1983, EP
GHOSTBUSTERS   Columbia, 1984, EP
SUMMER RENTAL   Paramount, 1985, EP
SPIES LIKE US   Warner Bros., 1985, EP
DRAGNET   Universal, 1987, EP
GHOSTBUSTERS II   Columbia, 1989, EP w/Michael C.
Gross & Joe Medjuck

BO BRINKMAN
ICE HOUSE   Upfront Films, 1989

JOEL BRISKIN
BEN   Cinerama, 1972, AP
WALKING TALL   Cinerama, 1973, AP
FRAMED   Paramount, 1975, w/Mort Briskin

MORT BRISKIN
Contact: Writers Guild of America - Los Angeles,
310/550-1000

WILLARD   Cinerama, 1971
BEN   Cinerama, 1972
YOU'LL LIKE MY MOTHER   Universal, 1972
WALKING TALL   Cinerama, 1973
FRAMED   Paramount, 1975, w/Joel Briskin

TOM BROADBRIDGE
Business: Broadstar Entertainment, 6464 Sunset Blvd., Suite
1130 Penthouse, Hollywood, CA 90028, 213/962-4950,
Fax: 213/962-8922; P.O. Box 256, Pennant Hills, NSW,
2120, Australia, 02/634-7855

VICIOUS   SVS Films, 1988, EP
NIGHT VISITOR   MGM/UA, 1989, EP w/Shelley E. Reid

ALBERT R. BROCCOLI
Business: Warfield Productions, 10000 W. Washington Blvd.,
Culver City, CA 90232, 310/280-6565

RED BERET *PARATROOPER*   1954, w/Irving Allen &
Anthony Bushell
THE BLACK KNIGHT   Columbia, 1954, w/Irving Allen &
Phil C. Samuel
HELL BELOW ZERO   Columbia, 1954, w/Irving Allen &
George W. Willoughby
PRIZE OF GOLD   Columbia, 1955, w/Irving Allen
ODONGO   Columbia, 1956, EP w/Irving Allen
THE COCKLESHELL HEROES   Columbia, 1956,
w/Irving Allen
SAFARI   Columbia, 1956, EP w/Irving Allen
ZARAK   Columbia, 1957, w/Irving Allen
FIRE DOWN BELOW   Columbia, 1957, w/Irving Allen
PICKUP ALLEY   Columbia, 1957, w/Irving Allen
HIGH FLIGHT   Columbia, 1958, w/Irving Allen
THE MAN INSIDE   Columbia, 1958, w/Irving Allen
HOW TO MURDER A RICH UNCLE   Columbia, 1958,
EP w/Irving Allen
NO TIME TO DIE *TANK FORCE*   Columbia, 1958,
w/Irving Allen

Br

FILM
PRODUCERS,
STUDIOS,
AGENTS AND
CASTING
DIRECTORS
GUIDE

F
I
L
M

P
R
O
D
U
C
E
R
S

Br

FILM
PRODUCERS,
STUDIOS,
AGENTS AND
CASTING
DIRECTORS
GUIDE

F
I
L
M

P
R
O
D
U
C
E
R
S

26

THE BANDIT OF ZHOBE   Columbia, 1959, w/Irving Allen
KILLERS OF KILIMANJARO   Columbia, 1960,
   EP w/Irving Allen
JAZZ BOAT   Columbia, 1960, w/Irving Allen
THE TRIALS OF OSCAR WILDE   Kingsley International,
   1960, EP w/Irving Allen
PLAY IT COOLER   Columbia, 1961, EP w/Irving Allen
DR. NO   United Artists, 1962, w/Harry Saltzman
CALL ME BWANA   United Artists, 1963, w/Harry Saltzman
FROM RUSSIA WITH LOVE   United Artists, 1963,
   w/Harry Saltzman
GOLDFINGER   United Artists, 1964, w/Harry Saltzman
YOU ONLY LIVE TWICE   United Artists, 1967,
   w/Harry Saltzman
CHITTY CHITTY BANG BANG   United Artists, 1968
ON HER MAJESTY'S SECRET SERVICE   United Artists,
   1969, w/Harry Saltzman
DIAMONDS ARE FOREVER   United Artists, 1971,
   w/Harry Saltzman
LIVE AND LET DIE   United Artists, 1973,
   w/Harry Saltzman
THE MAN WITH THE GOLDEN GUN   United Artists,
   1974, w/Harry Saltzman
THE SPY WHO LOVED ME   United Artists, 1977
MOONRAKER   United Artists, 1979
FOR YOUR EYES ONLY   United Artists, 1981
OCTOPUSSY   MGM/UA, 1983
A VIEW TO A KILL   MGM/UA, 1985, w/Michael G. Wilson
THE LIVING DAYLIGHTS   MGM/UA, 1987,
   w/Michael G. Wilson
LICENCE TO KILL   MGM/UA, 1989, w/Michael G. Wilson

THOMAS H. BRODEK
Business: ABC Productions, 2020 Avenue of the Stars,
   Los Angeles, CA 90067, 310/557-7777
Contact: Directors Guild of America - Los Angeles,
   213/289-2000

TRANSYLVANIA 6-5000   New World, 1985,
   w/Mace Neufeld
THE AVIATOR   MGM/UA, 1985, w/Mace Neufeld
THE BOSS' WIFE   TriStar, 1986
THE PRINCIPAL   TriStar, 1987

JOHN C. BRODERICK
Agent: Gray/Goodman, Inc. - Beverly Hills, 310/276-7070
Contact: Directors Guild of America - Los Angeles,
   213/289-2000

DIRTY O'NEIL   AIP, 1974

STEVE BRODIE
Contact: Directors Guild of America - Los Angeles,
   213/289-2000

BOBBIE JO AND THE OUTLAW   AIP, 1976,
   CP w/Lynn Ross

HERBERT BRODKIN
THE PEOPLE NEXT DOOR   Avco Embassy, 1970

JACK BRODSKY
Business: JBRO Productions, c/o 20th Century Fox Film
   Corporation, 10201 W. Pico Blvd., Los Angeles, CA
   90035, 310/203-2629
Mail: P.O. Box 900, Beverly Hills, CA 90213

LITTLE MURDERS   20th Century Fox, 1971
EVERYTHING YOU ALWAYS WANTED TO KNOW ABOUT
   SEX* (*BUT WERE AFRAID TO ASK)   United Artists,
   1972, EP

SUMMER WISHES, WINTER DREAMS   Columbia, 1973
ROMANCING THE STONE   20th Century Fox, 1984,
   CP w/Joel Douglas
THE JEWEL OF THE NILE   20th Century Fox, 1985,
   CP w/Joel Douglas
DANCERS   Cannon, 1987, EP w/Nora Kaye
KING RALPH   Universal, 1991

DENNIS BRODY
3:15 THE MOMENT OF TRUTH   Dakota Entertainment,
   1986, w/Robert Kenner

MERRILL S. BRODY
AWOL   BFB, 1973, EP

RUBEN BROIDO
SURVIVAL RUN   Film Ventures International, 1980,
   EP w/Mel Bergman

CARY BROKAW
Business: Avenue Entertainment, 12100 Wilshire Blvd.,
   Suite 1650, Los Angeles, CA 90025, 310/442-2200;
   Fax: 310/207-1753

TROUBLE IN MIND   Alive Films, 1985, EP
NOBODY'S FOOL   Island Pictures, 1986, EP
DOWN BY LAW   Island Pictures, 1986,
   EP w/Otto Grokenberger
SLAMDANCE   Island Pictures, 1987, EP
PASCALI'S ISLAND   Avenue Pictures, 1988, EP
STRAIGHT TO HELL   Island Pictures, 1988,
   EP w/Scott Millaney
SIGNS OF LIFE   Avenue Pictures, 1989,
   EP w/Lindsay Law
COLD FEET   Avenue Pictures, 1989, EP
DRUGSTORE COWBOY   Avenue Pictures, 1989, EP
AFTER DARK, MY SWEET   Avenue Pictures, 1990, EP
THE OBJECT OF BEAUTY   Avenue Pictures, 1991, EP
THE PLAYER   AVENUE, 1991, EP

EDGAR BRONFMAN, JR.
Business: Joseph E. Seagram & Sons, Inc., 375 Park
   Avenue, New York, NY 10152, 212/572-7000

THE BLOCKHOUSE   Cannon, 1974, w/Lord Anthony
   Rufus Isaacs
THE BORDER   Universal, 1982

JAMES L. BROOKS
Business: Gracie Films, 20th Century Fox, 10201 W. Pico
   Blvd., Los Angeles, CA 90035, 310/280-4222;
   Fax: 310/203-3770
Agent: ICM - Los Angeles, 310/550-4000

STARTING OVER   Paramount, 1979, w/Alan J. Pakula
TERMS OF ENDEARMENT ★★   Paramount, 1983
BROADCAST NEWS ★   20th Century Fox, 1987
BIG   20th Century Fox, 1988, w/Robert Greenhut
SAY ANYTHING   20th Century Fox, 1989, EP
WAR OF THE ROSES   20th Century Fox, 1989,
   w/Arnon Milchan

JOSEPH BROOKS
Business: Chancery Lane Films, Inc., 41-A E. 74th St., New
   York, NY 10021, 212/759-8720
Contact: Directors Guild of America - New York,
   212/581-0370

YOU LIGHT UP MY LIFE   Columbia, 1977
IF EVER I SEE YOU AGAIN   Columbia, 1978

MEL BROOKS
Business: Brooksfilms, Ltd., P.O. Box 900, Beverly Hills,
   CA 90213, 310/203-1375
Contact: Directors Guild of America - Los Angeles,
   213/289-2000

HIGH ANXIETY   20th Century Fox, 1977
THE HISTORY OF THE WORLD - PART I   20th Century
   Fox, 1981
TO BE OR NOT TO BE   20th Century Fox, 1983
THE DOCTOR AND THE DEVILS   20th Century Fox,
   1985, EP
84 CHARING CROSS ROAD   Columbia, 1987, EP
SPACEBALLS   MGM/UA, 1987
LIFE STINKS   MGM, 1991
THE VAGRANT   MGM, 1991, EP

RICHARD BROOKS
Agent: Irving Paul Lazar - Beverly Hills, 310/275-6153
Contact: Directors Guild of America - Los Angeles,
   213/289-2000

LORD JIM   Columbia, 1964
THE PROFESSIONALS   Columbia, 1966
IN COLD BLOOD   Columbia, 1967
THE HAPPY ENDING   United Artists, 1969
   BITE THE BULLET   Columbia, 1975

MITCHELL BROWER
MCCABE & MRS. MILLER   Warner Bros., 1971,
   w/David Foster
THE GETAWAY   National General, 1972,
   w/David Foster

CHRIS BROUWER
THE GIRL WITH THE RED HAIR   United Artists Classics,
   1983, w/Haig Balian

ANDREW BROWN
Business: Euston Films, 365 Euston Road, London
   NW1 3AR England, 071/387-0911; Fax: 071/388-2122

PRICK UP YOUR EARS   Samuel Goldwyn
   Company, 1987
DEALERS   Skouras Pictures, 1989,
   EP w/John Hambley

BRUCE W. BROWN
WELCOME TO 18   American Distribution Group,
   1986, EP

BRYAN BROWN
F/X 2 — THE DEADLY ART OF ILLUSION   Orion, 1991,
   EP w/Lee R. Mayes

CHRIS BROWN
Business: Portman Entertainment, Pinewood Studios,
   Iver Heath, Bucks SL0 0NH England, 0753/630-366;
   Fax: 0753/630-332

THE COMPANY OF WOLVES   Cannon, 1985,
   w/Stephen Woolley
ABSOLUTE BEGINNERS   Orion, 1986,
   w/Stephen Woolley
MONA LISA   Island Pictures, 1986, CP w/Ray Cooper
SIESTA   Lorimar, 1987, CP

DAVID BROWN
(credit w/Richard D. Zanuck)
Business: The Manhattan Project, 1270 Avenue of the
   Americas, Suite 609, New York, NY 10020,
   212/632-3461; Fax: 212/632-3459

SSSSSSS   Universal, 1973, EP
WILLIE DYNAMITE   Universal, 1974
THE SUGARLAND EXPRESS   Universal, 1974
THE GIRL FROM PETROVKA   Universal, 1974
THE BLACK WINDMILL   Universal, 1974
THE EIGER SANCTION   Universal, 1975, EP
JAWS ★   Universal, 1975
MACARTHUR   Universal, 1977, EP
JAWS II   Universal, 1978
THE ISLAND   Universal, 1980
NEIGHBORS   Columbia, 1981
THE VERDICT ★   20th Century Fox, 1982
COCOON   20th Century Fox, 1985, w/Lili Fini Zanuck
TARGET   Warner Bros., 1985
COCOON: THE RETURN   20th Century Fox, 1988,
   w/Lili Fini Zanuck
DRIVING MISS DAISY   Warner Bros., 1989,
   EP w/Jake Eberts*
THE PLAYER   Avenue, 1991, w/Michael Tolkin &
   Nick Wechsler

G. MAC BROWN
Contact: Directors Guild of America - New York,
   212/581-0370
Agent: Sandra Marsh Management - Beverly Hills,
   310/285-0303

HELLO AGAIN   Buena Vista, 1987, CP w/Thomas Folino,
   Susan Isaacs & Martin Mickelson
SHE-DEVIL   Orion, 1989, CP
ONCE AROUND   Universal, 1991, EP

GEORGE H. BROWN
OPEN SEASON   Columbia, 1974, EP

HOWARD BROWN
CHEECH & CHONG'S NEXT MOVIE   Universal, 1980
CHEECH & CHONG'S NICE DREAMS   Columbia, 1981
THINGS ARE TOUGH ALL OVER   Columbia, 1982
FAR OUT MAN   New Line, 1990, CP

PETER BROWN
THE FIRST NUDIE MUSICAL   Paramount, 1976,
   EP w/Stuart W. Phelps
SPARKLE   Warner Bros., 1976, EP w/Beryl Vertue

ROBERT LATHAM BROWN
Contact: Directors Guild of America - Los Angeles,
   213/289-2000

TOM   Four Star International, 1973, EP w/Mardi Rustam
THE BAD BUNCH   Dimension, 1976,
   EP w/Mardi Rustam
WARNING SIGN   20th Century Fox, 1985, AP
HOWARD THE DUCK   Universal, 1986, CP
CHILD'S PLAY 2   Universal, 1990, EP
CHILD'S PLAY 3   Universal, 1991, w/David Kirschner &
   Laura Moskowitz

SIR WILLIAM PIGGOTT-BROWN
(see Sir William PIGGOTT-Brown)

Br

FILM
PRODUCERS,
STUDIOS,
AGENTS AND
CASTING
DIRECTORS
GUIDE

F
I
L
M

P
R
O
D
U
C
E
R
S

Br

FILM
PRODUCERS,
STUDIOS,
AGENTS AND
CASTING
DIRECTORS
GUIDE

F
I
L
M

P
R
O
D
U
C
E
R
S

JEROME BROWNSTEIN
Contact: True Fiction Pictures, 12 W. 27th Street,
10th Floor, New York, NY 10001, 212/684-4284;
Fax: 212/686-6109

THE UNBELIEVABLE TRUTH   Miramax, 1990, EP

JAMES BRUBAKER
Business: Sidewalk Productions, 1253 7th Street,
Suite 100, Santa Monica, CA 90401, 310/576-6094;
Fax: 310/576-6098
Contact: Directors Guild of America - Los Angeles,
213/289-2000

TRUE CONFESSIONS   United Artists, 1981, AP
THE RIGHT STUFF ★   The Ladd Company/Warner
Bros., 1983, EP
RHINESTONE   20th Century Fox, 1984, AP
ROCKY IV   MGM/UA, 1985, EP w/Arthur Chobanian
BEER   Orion, 1986, EP
COBRA   Warner Bros., 1986, EP
OVER THE TOP   Cannon, 1987, EP
PATTY HEARST   Atlantic, 1988, LP
PROBLEM CHILD   Universal, 1990, EP

BONNIE BRUCKHEIMER-MARTELL
Business: All-Girl Productions, Walt Disney Pictures,
500 S. Buena Vista St., Burbank, CA 91521,
818/560-6547; Fax: 818/560-1930

BEACHES   Buena Vista, 1988, w/Bette Midler &
Margaret Jennings South
FOR THE BOYS   Buena Vista, 1991, w/Bette Midler &
Margaret Jennings South

JERRY BRUCKHEIMER
Business: Simpson-Bruckheimer Productions, Hollywood
Pictures, 500 S. Buena Vista St., Burbank, CA 91521,
818/560-7711

THE CULPEPPER CATTLE COMPANY   20th Century
Fox, 1972, AP
FAREWELL, MY LOVELY   Avco Embassy, 1975,
w/George Pappas
RAFFERTY & THE GOLD DUST TWINS   Warner Bros.,
1975, AP
MARCH OR DIE   Columbia, 1977, w/Dick Richards
AMERICAN GIGOLO   Paramount, 1980
DEFIANCE   AIP, 1980, w/William S. Gilmore
THIEF   United Artists, 1981, w/Ronnie Caan
CAT PEOPLE   Universal, 1982, EP
YOUNG DOCTORS IN LOVE   20th Century Fox, 1982
FLASHDANCE   Paramount, 1983, w/Don Simpson
BEVERLY HILLS COP   Paramount, 1984,
w/Don Simpson
THIEF OF HEARTS   Paramount, 1984, w/Don Simpson
TOP GUN   Paramount, 1986, w/Don Simpson
BEVERLY HILLS COP II   Paramount, 1987,
w/Don Simpson
DAYS OF THUNDER   Paramount, 1990, w/Don Simpson

PIETER JAN BRUGGE
Contact: Directors Guild of America - Los Angeles,
213/289-2000

MY DEMON LOVER   New Line, 1987, LP
GLORY   TriStar, 1989, CP

STANLEY F. BUCHTHAL
Business: Buckeye Entertainment, 919 3rd. Ave., 18th Floor,
New York, NY 10022, 212/888-9399

HAIRSPRAY   New Line, 1988, CP w/John Waters

JULES BUCK
THE RULING CLASS   Avco Embassy, 1972,
w/Jack Hawkins
MAN FRIDAY   Avco Embassy, 1975, EP w/Gerald Green
THE GREAT SCOUT & CATHOUSE THURSDAY   AIP,
1976, w/David Korda

RONALD L. BUCK
Agent: William Morris Agency - Beverly Hills, 310/274-7451
Contact: Writers Guild of America - Los Angeles,
310/550-1000

CLAY PIGEON   MGM, 1971, EP w/Frank Avianca
BREAKOUT   Columbia, 1975, EP
HARRY & SON   Orion, 1984, w/Paul Newman

ANTHONY BUCKLEY
CADDIE   Australian Films, 1979
THE NIGHT OF THE PROWLER   International
Harmony, 1979
BLISS   New World, 1986

ZEV BUFMAN
THE NAKED APE   Universal, 1973

JEFF BUHAI
(credit w/David Obst & Steve Zacharias)
Agent: UTA - Beverly Hills, 310/273-6700
Contact: Writers Guild of America - Los Angeles,
310/550-1000

THE WHOOPEE BOYS   Paramount, 1986, EP
JOHNNY BE GOOD   Orion, 1988, EP

ANDREW BULLIANS
(credit w/Jean Bullians)

3:15 THE MOMENT OF TRUTH   Dakota Entertainment,
1986, EP w/Sandy Climan & Charles C. Thieriot
THE BIKINI SHOP   *THE MALIBU BIKINI SHOP*
International Film Marketing, 1987, EP w/Sandy
Climan & Charles C. Thieriot
BORN TO RACE   MGM/UA, 1988

JEAN BULLIANS
(credit w/Andrew Bullians)

3:15 THE MOMENT OF TRUTH   Dakota Entertainment,
1986, EP w/Sandy Climan & Charles C. Thieriot
THE BIKINI SHOP   *THE MALIBU BIKINI SHOP*
International Film Marketing, 1987, EP w/Sandy
Climan & Charles C. Thieriot
BORN TO RACE   MGM/UA, 1988

MARK BUNTZMAN
Business: Artists Alliance Productions, Inc., 7979 Willow
Glen Rd., Los Angeles, CA 90046, 310/650-6042
Contact: Writers Guild of America - Los Angeles,
310/550-1000

THE ASTROLOGER   Interstar, 1979
EXTERMINATOR 2   Cannon, 1984

By

FILM
PRODUCERS,
STUDIOS,
AGENTS AND
CASTING
DIRECTORS
GUIDE

F
I
L
M

P
R
O
D
U
C
E
R
S

RAY BURDIS
THE KRAYS   Miramax, 1990, w/Dominic Anciano

MARK BURG
Business: Island Pictures, 8920 Sunset Blvd., 2nd Floor,
   Los Angeles, CA 90069, 310/276-4500;
   Fax: 310/271-7840

CAN'T BUY ME LOVE   Buena Vista, 1987, CP
BULL DURHAM   Orion, 1988, w/Thom Mount
TOY SOLDIERS   TriStar, 1991, EP w/Chris Zarpas

BOB BURGE
KEATON'S COP   Cannon, 1990

GRAHAM BURKE
YOUNG EINSTEIN   Warner Bros., 1989,
   EP w/Ray Beattie

STEVEN E. BURMAN
THE CELLAR   Moviestore, 1990, w/Patrick C. Wells &
   John Woodward

ALLAN BURNS
Agent: APA - Los Angeles, 310/273-0744
Contact: Turnaround Productions c/o Raleigh Studios,
   5358 Melrose, Suite 406W, Los Angeles, CA 90038,
   213/960-4068; Fax: 213/960-4069

JUST BETWEEN FRIENDS   Orion, 1986,
   w/Edward Teets

MICHAEL BURNS
THRESHOLD   20th Century Fox International Classics,
   1983, w/Jon Slan

WILLIAM BURR
STEPFATHER II   Millimeter, 1989, w/Darin Scott

PETER BURRELL
Contact: Directors Guild of America - Los Angeles,
   213/289-2000

SMOKEY & THE BANDIT II   Universal, 1980, AP
ZOOT SUIT   Universal, 1982
DEATH OF AN ANGEL   20th Century Fox, 1986
STACKING   Spectrafilm, 1987, CP w/Patrick Markey
JACK THE BEAR   20th Century Fox, 1991, AP

TIMOTHY BURRILL
Business: Burrill Productions, 19 Cranbury Road, London
   SW6 2NS England, 071-736-8673; Fax: 071/731-3921

PRIVILEGE   Universal, 1967, AP
MACBETH   Columbia, 1971, AP
THREE SISTERS   American Film Theatre, 1974,
   AP w/James C. Katz
THAT LUCKY TOUCH   Allied Artists, 1975, AP
ALPHA BETA   Cine III, 1976
TESS ★   Columbia, 1980, CP
THE PIRATES OF PENZANCE   Universal, 1983, CP
ANOTHER TIME, ANOTHER PLACE   Samuel Goldwyn
   Company, 1984, EP
SUPERGIRL   Warner Bros., 1984
THE FOURTH PROTOCOL   Lorimar, 1987
TO KILL A PRIEST   Columbia, 1990, SP

GEOFF BURROWES
Contact: Australian Film Commission, 9229 Sunset Blvd.,
   Los Angeles, CA 90069, 310/275-7074

THE MAN FROM SNOWY RIVER   20th Century Fox, 1983
RETURN TO SNOWY RIVER   Buena Vista, 1988
BACKSTAGE   Hoyts, 1988

CHRIS BURT
Business: Elmgate Fils Ltd., 46 Grange Road, London
   W4 4DD England, 0932/562-611; Fax: 0932/569-918

REVOLUTION   Warner Bros., 1985, EP

TIM BURTON
Business: Tlm Burton Productions, c/o Warner Bros., 4000
   Warner Blvd., Bungalow #1, Room 209, Burbank, CA
   91522, 818/954-3810; Fax: 818/954-3842
Agent: William Morris Agency - Beverly Hills, 310/274-7451

EDWARD SCISSORHANDS   20th Century Fox, 1990,
   w/Denise DiNovi

HENRY BUSHKIN
SPONTANEOUS COMBUSTION   Taurus, 1990,
   EP w/Arthur Sarkissian

SCOTT BUSHNELL
Business: Sand Castle 5 Productions, 502 Park Ave., Suite
   156, New York, NY 10022, 212/826-6641

NASHVILLE ★   Paramount, 1975, AP
BUFFALO BILL & THE INDIANS or SITTING BULL'S
   HISTORY LESSON   United Artists, 1976, AP
THE LATE SHOW   Warner Bros., 1977, AP
3 WOMEN   20th Century Fox, 1977, AP
A WEDDING   20th Century Fox, 1978, AP
A PERFECT COUPLE   20th Century Fox, 1979, AP
RICH KIDS   United Artists, 1979, EP
HEALTH   20th Century Fox, 1980, AP
POPEYE   Paramount/Buena Vista, 1980, AP
COME BACK TO THE 5 & DIME, JIMMY DEAN, JIMMY
   DEAN   Cinecom, 1982
STREAMERS   United Artists Classics, 1983, AP
SECRET HONOR   Cinecom, 1985, EP
FOOL FOR LOVE   Cannon, 1986, AP
BEYOND THERAPY   New World, 1987, AP
O.C. AND STIGGS   MGM/UA, 1987, AP

GEORGE BUTLER
Agent: William Morris Agency - Beverly Hills, 310/274-7451

PUMPING IRON (FD)   Cinema 5, 1977, w/Jerome Gary

MICHAEL BUTLER
HAIR   United Artists, 1979, w/Lester Persky

FRITZ BUTTENSTEDT
SINGING THE BLUES IN RED   Angelika, 1988, CP

DANN BYCK
Business: 2427 Cazaux Pl., Los Angeles, CA 90068,
   213/856-9025; Fax: 213/856-0436

'NIGHT, MOTHER   Universal, 1986,
   EP w/David Lancaster

By

FILM
PRODUCERS,
STUDIOS,
AGENTS AND
CASTING
DIRECTORS
GUIDE

F
I
L
M

P
R
O
D
U
C
E
R
S

MARK BYERS
STRIPPED TO KILL   Concorde, 1987, w/Matt Leipzig & Andy Ruben

BILL BYRNE
FROM HOLLYWOOD TO DEADWOOD   Island Pictures, 1989, EP

THOMAS S. BYRNES
Business: Byrnes Entertainment Co., 9595 Wilshire Blvd., Suite 606, Beverly Hills, CA 90212, 310/278-6000; Fax: 310/278-3961

PARTY LINE   SVS Films, 1988, w/Kurt Anderson & William Webb
TO SLEEP WITH ANGER   Samuel Goldwyn Company, 1990, w/Caldecot Chubb & Darin Scott

C

RONNIE CAAN
THIEF   United Artists, 1981, w/Jerry Bruckheimer

DANIEL B. CADY
SWEET JESUS, PREACHER MAN   MGM, 1973

FITCH CADY
RUN   Buena Vista, 1991, CP

JAMES CADY
Contact: Directors Guild of America - Los Angeles, 213/289-2000

HOMER AND EDDIE   Skouras, 1990, w/Moritz Borman

RICHARD CAFFEY
BUCK ROGERS IN THE 25TH CENTURY   Universal, 1979

BARRY CAHN
THE HILLS HAVE EYES II   Castle Hill, 1985, w/Peter Locke

CHRISTOPHER CAIN
Agent: CAA - Beverly Hills, 310/288-4545
Contact: Directors Guild of America - Los Angeles, 213/289-2000

YOUNG GUNS   20th Century Fox, 1988, w/Joe Roth

MICHAEL CAINE
Agent: ICM - Los Angeles, 310/550-4000

THE FOURTH PROTOCOL   Lorimar, 1987, EP w/Frederick Forsyth & Wafic Said

MITCHELL CALDER
Business: Ion Pictures, 3122 Santa Monica Blvd., Santa Monica, CA 90404, 310/453-4466

THE CLOSER   Ion, 1991, EP w/Tony Conforti, Roy Medawar & George Pappas

WILLIAM A. CALIHAN
THE MAGNIFICENT SEVEN RIDE!   United Artists, 1972

COLIN CALLENDER
Business: HBO, 1100 Avenue of the Americas, New York, NY 10036, 212/512-1000; Fax: 212/512-5517

THE BELLY OF AN ARCHITECT   Hemdale, 1990, w/Walter Donohue

JOHN CALLEY
Contact: Firefly Farm, P.O. Box 446, Washington Depot, CT 06795

THE CINCINNATI KID   MGM, 1965, AP
ICE STATION ZEBRA   MGM, 1968, w/Martin Ransohoff
CASTLE KEEP   Columbia, 1969, w/Martin Ransohoff
CATCH 22   Paramount, 1970, w/Martin Ransohoff
FAT MAN AND LITTLE BOY   Paramount, 1989, EP
POSTCARDS FROM THE EDGE   Columbia, 1990, w/Mike Nichols

DAVID CALLOWAY
WILD THING   Atlantic, 1987, w/Nicolas Clermont

JAMES CAMERON
Contact: Lightstorm Entertainment, 3100 Darmon Way, Burbank, CA 91505, 818/562-1301; Fax: 818/562-1814

TERMINATOR 2: JUDGMENT DAY   TriStar, 1991

BEVERLY J. CAMHE
THE BELIEVERS   Orion, 1987, w/Michael Childers & John Schlesinger
THE PACKAGE   Orion, 1989, w/Tobie Haggerty

ALIDA CAMP
Business: Concorde Films, 11600 San Vicente Blvd., Los Angeles, CA 90049, 310/820-6733

BODY CHEMISTRY   Concorde, 1990
THE HAUNTING OF MORELLA   Concorde, 1990, AP w/Rodman Flender
TRANSYLVANIA TWIST   Concorde, 1990

CAROLYN CAMP
Business: Mulberry Square Productions, One Glen Lakes, 8140 Walnut Hill Lane, Suite 301, Dallas, TX 75231, 214/369-2430
Contact: Directors Guild of America - Los Angeles, 213/289-2000

BENJI THE HUNTED   Buena Vista, 1987, SP

JOE CAMP
Business: Mulberry Square Productions, One Glen Lakes, 8140 Walnut Hill Lane, Suite 301, Dallas, TX 75231, 214/369-2430

BENJI   Mulberry Square, 1974
HAWMPS   Mulberry Square, 1976
FOR THE LOVE OF BENJI   Mulberry Square, 1977, EP
THE DOUBLE McGUFFIN   Mulberry Square, 1979

BRUCE CAMPBELL
Business: Renaissance MotionPictures, Inc., 28 East 10th St., New York, NY 10003, 212/477-0432

THE EVIL DEAD   New Line, 1983, EP w/Samuel M. Raimi
EASY WHEELS   Fries Entertainment, 1989, EP w/Robert Tapert

ROGER CAMRAS
MACON COUNTY LINE   AIP, 1974, EP
THE WILD MCCULLOCHS   AIP, 1975, EP
ODE TO BILLY JOE   Warner Bros., 1976, w/Max Baer
HOMETOWN U.S.A.   Film Ventures International, 1979,
   w/Jesse Vint

JOHN CANDY
Agent: APA - Los Angeles, 310/273-0744

WHO'S HARRY CRUMB?   TriStar, 1989, EP

JAMES CANNADY
THE WHITE GIRL   Tony Brown Prods., 1990

SHERYL CANNADY
THE WHITE GIRL   Tony Brown Prods., 1990, EP

MITCHELL CANNOLD
(credit w/Steven Reuther)
Business: Lilly Anna Productions, 500 S. Buena Vista St.,
   Animation 1G-13, Burbank, CA 91521, 818/560-1800;
   Fax: 818/563-3650

GO TELL THE SPARTANS   Avco Embassy, 1978,
   w/Allan F. Bodoh*
CHINA GIRL   Vestron, 1987, EP
DIRTY DANCING   Vestron, 1987, EP
AND GOD CREATED WOMAN   Vestron, 1988,
   EP w/Ruth Vitale
CALL ME   Vestron, 1988, EP w/Ruth Vitale
BIG MAN ON CAMPUS   Vestron, 1989, EP
PARENTS   Vestron, 1989, EP
LITTLE MONSTERS   MGM/UA, 1989,
   EP w/Dori B. Wasserman*
ENID IS SLEEPING   Vestron, 1990, EP w/Dori
   Berinstein & Adam Platnick
CATCHFIRE   1991, EP

LARRY CANO
SILKWOOD   20th Century Fox, 1983, EP w/Buzz Hirsch

MILENA CANONERO
NAKED TANGO   Scotia International, 1990,
   CP w/Michael Maiello

STANLEY S. CANTER
HORNETS' NEST   United Artists, 1970
W.W. AND THE DIXIE DANCEKINGS   20th Century
   Fox, 1975
ST. IVES   Warner Bros., 1976, w/Pancho Kohner
GREYSTOKE: THE LEGEND OF TARZAN, LORD OF
   THE APES   Warner Bros., 1984, w/Hugh Hudson

ELIZABETH CANTILLON
HOW I GOT INTO COLLEGE   20th Century Fox, 1989, CP

MARIE CANTIN
Contact: Directors Guild of America - Los Angeles,
   213/289-2000

HEART CONDITION   New Line, 1990,
   CP w/Bernie Goldmann

NEIL CANTON
BLOOD BEACH   Jerry Gross Organization, 1981, AP
THE ADVENTURES OF BUCKAROO BANZAI ACROSS
   THE EIGHTH DIMENSION   20th Century Fox, 1984,
   w/W. D. Richter

BACK TO THE FUTURE   Universal, 1985, w/Bob Gale
THE WITCHES OF EASTWICK   Warner Bros., 1987,
   w/Peter Guber & Jon Peters
CADDYSHACK II   Warner Bros., 1988, w/Peter Guber &
   Jon Peters
BACK TO THE FUTURE II   Universal, 1989, w/Bob Gale
BACK TO THE FUTURE III   Universal, 1990, w/Bob Gale

LEON CAPETANOS
Agent: William Morris Agency - Los Angeles, 310/274-7451

DIRTY O'NEIL   AIP, 1974, EP

SIDNEY L. CAPLAN
NECROMANCY   Cinerama, 1972, EP w/Robert J. Stone

LEE CAPLIN
(credit w/Greg H. Sims)
Business: Caplin Productions, 8274 Grand View,
   Los Angeles, CA 90046, 310/650-1882

TO DIE FOR   Skouras Pictures, 1989, EP
SON OF DARKNESS: TO DIE FOR II   Trimark, 1991, EP

DEBORAH CAPOGROSSO
Business: American Road Productions, 3000 Olympic Blvd.,
   Suite 2428, Santa Monica, CA 90404, 310/315-4735;
   Fax: 310/315-4800
Agent: Gray/Goodman, Inc. - Beverly Hills, 310/276-7070

THE HOT SPOT   Orion, 1990, CP

SYD CAPPE
(credit w/Nicolas Stiliadis)
Business: SC Entertainment, 1326 Londonderry View, Los
   Angeles, CA 90069, 310/854-0337; Fax: 310/854-0737

FRIENDS, LOVERS & LUNATICS   Fries Entertainment,
   1989, EP
PUMP UP THE VOLUME   New Line, 1990,
   EP w/Sara Risher

FRANK CAPRA, JR.
Business: Bonjo Productions, Ltd., One Transglobal Square,
   P.O. Box 7005, Long Beach, CA 90807, 310/426-3622
Agent: The Gersh Agency - Beverly Hills, 310/274-6611

MAROONED   Columbia, 1969, AP
ESCAPE FROM THE PLANET OF THE APES   20th
   Century Fox, 1971, AP
CONQUEST OF THE PLANET OF THE APES   20th
   Century Fox, 1972, AP
PLAY IT AGAIN, SAM   Paramount, 1972, AP
BATTLE FOR THE PLANET OF THE APES   20th Century
   Fox, 1973, AP
TOM SAWYER   United Artists, 1973, AP
BILLY JACK GOES TO WASHINGTON
   Taylor-Laughlin, 1978
BORN AGAIN   Avco Embassy, 1978
THE BLACK MARBLE   Avco Embassy, 1980
AN EYE FOR AN EYE   Avco Embassy, 1981
THE SEDUCTION   Avco Embassy, 1982, EP w/Chuck
   Russell & Joseph Wolf
VICE SQUAD   Avco Embassy, 1982, EP w/Sandy Howard
   & Bob Rehme
FIRESTARTER   Universal, 1984
MARIE   MGM/UA, 1985

Ca

FILM
PRODUCERS,
STUDIOS,
AGENTS AND
CASTING
DIRECTORS
GUIDE

F
I
L
M

P
R
O
D
U
C
E
R
S

FILM
PRODUCERS,
STUDIOS,
AGENTS AND
CASTING
DIRECTORS
GUIDE

JIM CARABATSOS
Agent: Martin Shapiro, Shapiro-Lichtman, Inc., -
Los Angeles, 310/859-8877

NO MERCY   TriStar, 1986, CP
HAMBURGER HILL   Paramount, 1987, w/Marcia Nasatir

JOSEPH M. CARACCIOLO
Contact: Directors Guild of America - Los Angeles,
213/289-2000

A CHORUS LINE   Columbia, 1985, AP
BRIGHTON BEACH MEMOIRS   Universal, 1986, AP
THE GLASS MENAGERIE   Cineplex Odeon, 1987, AP
THE SECRET OF MY SUCCESS   Universal, 1987, LP
BILOXI BLUES   Universal, 1988, EP w/Marykay Powell
THE DREAM TEAM   Universal, 1989, EP
PARENTHOOD   Universal, 1989, EP
SECOND SIGHT   Warner Bros., 1989, EP
MY BLUE HEAVEN   Warner Bros., 1990, CP
TUNE IN TOMORROW...   Cinecom, 1990, EP
TRUE COLORS   Paramount, 1991, EP
MY GIRL   Columbia, 1991, EP w/David Friendly

JOANN CARELLI
THE DEER HUNTER   Universal, 1978, AP
HEAVEN'S GATE   United Artists, 1980
THE SICILIAN   20th Century Fox, 1987, w/Michael Cimino

TOPPER CAREW
Contact: Directors Guild of America - Los Angeles,
213/289-2000

D.C. CAB   Universal, 1983

ED CARLIN
BLOOD AND LACE   AIP, 1971, w/Gil Lasky
MAMA'S DIRTY GIRLS   Premiere, 1974, w/Gil Lasky
THE SWINGING BARMAIDS   Premiere, 1975
THE NIGHT GOD SCREAMED   Cinemation, 1975,
w/Gil Lasky
THE STUDENT BODY   Surrogate, 1976
THE EVIL   New World, 1978
BATTLE BEYOND THE STARS   New World, 1980

MARK CARLINER
Business: Mark Carliner Productions, 11700 Laurelwood
Dr., Studio City, CA 91604, 818/763-4783

HEAVEN HELP US   TriStar, 1985, w/Dan Wigutow
CROSSROADS   Columbia, 1986

LEWIS JOHN CARLINO
Agent: CAA - Beverly Hills, 310/288-4545
Contact: Writers Guild of America - Los Angeles,
310/550-1000

THE MECHANIC   United Artists, 1972, w/Robert
Chartoff & Irwin Winkler

PHYLLIS CARLYLE
Business: Carlyle Productions, 639 N. Larchmont Dr.,
Suite 207, Los Angeles, CA 90004, 213/469-3086;
Fax: 213/469-9558

THE ACCIDENTAL TOURIST ★   Warner Bros., 1988,
EP w/John Malkovich

DON CARMODY
Agent: Gray/Goodman, Inc. - Beverly Hills, 310/276-7070

TULIPS   Avco Embassy, 1981
PORKY'S   20th Century Fox, 1982, w/Bob Clark
PORKY'S II: THE NEXT DAY   20th Century Fox, 1983,
w/Bob Clark
SPACEHUNTER: ADVENTURES IN THE FORBIDDEN
ZONE   Columbia, 1983, w/John Dunning & Andre Link
MEATBALLS III   Moviestore, 1986, w/John Dunning
THE BIG TOWN   Columbia, 1987, CP
SWITCHING CHANNELS   TriStar, 1988, EP
PHYSICAL EVIDENCE   Columbia, 1988
WELCOME HOME   Columbia, 1989, EP
WHISPERS   ITC, 1990, w/John Dunning
PRIMARY MOTIVE   Hemdale, 1991,
EP w/Richard K. Rosenberg

JULIO CARO
Business: Siren Pictures, 10 East 22nd St., New York, NY
10010, 212/254-9770

SIESTA   Lorimar, 1987, EP w/Zalman King & Nik Powell
STATIC   MCEG, 1988, EP

DON CARPENTER
PAYDAY   Cinerama, 1973, CP

JOHN CARPENTER
Agent: ICM - Los Angeles, 310/550-4000

DARK STAR   Jack H. Harris, 1974
HALLOWEEN II   Universal, 1981, w/Debra Hill
HALLOWEEN III: SEASON OF THE WITCH   Universal,
1982, w/Debra Hill
THE PHILADELPHIA EXPERIMENT   New World,
1984, EP

ALLAN CARR
Business: Allan Carr Enterprises, P.O. Box 691670, Los
Angeles, CA 90069, 213/278-2490; Fax: 310/274-2278

THE FIRST TIME   United Artists, 1969, w/Roger Smith
C.C. & COMPANY   Avco Embassy, 1970, w/Roger Smith
GREASE   Paramount, 1978, w/Robert Stigwood
CAN'T STOP THE MUSIC   AFD, 1980, w/Henri Belolo &
Jacques Morali
GREASE 2   Paramount, 1982, w/Robert Stigwood
WHERE THE BOYS ARE '84   TriStar, 1984
CLOAK & DAGGER   Universal, 1984

RON CARR
BURNING SECRET   Vestron, 1988, SP

TERRY CARR
Agent: Gray/Goodman, Inc. - Beverly Hills, 310/276-7070
Contact: Directors Guild of America - Los Angeles,
213/289-2000

THE BAD NEWS BEARS GO TO JAPAN   Paramount,
1977, AP
AN ALMOST PERFECT AFFAIR   Paramount, 1979
COAST TO COAST   Paramount, 1980, EP
YES, GIORGIO   MGM, 1982, AP

PAUL CARRAN
WIRED   Taurus, 1989, EP w/P. Michael Smith

Ca

FILM
PRODUCERS,
STUDIOS,
AGENTS AND
CASTING
DIRECTORS
GUIDE

MICHAEL CARRERAS
Contact: British Academy of Film & Television Arts,
195 Piccadilly, London W1 England, 071/734-0022

MOON ZERO TWO   Warner Bros., 1970
CREATURES THE WORLD FORGOT   Columbia, 1971
CRESCENDO   Warner Bros., 1972
FEAR IN THE NIGHT   International Co-Productions,
1974, EP
STRAIGHT ON TILL MORNING   International
Co-Productions, 1974, EP
THE LADY VANISHES   Rank, 1979, EP w/Arlene
Sellers & Alex Winitsky

GORDON CARROLL
Business: Brandywine Films, 1211 N. Wetherly Dr.,
Los Angeles, CA 90069

HOW TO MURDER YOUR WIFE   United Artists, 1965, EP
LUV   Columbia, 1967, EP
COOL HAND LUKE   Warner Bros., 1967
THE APRIL FOOLS   National General, 1969
PAT GARRETT & BILLY THE KID   MGM, 1973
ALIEN   20th Century Fox, 1979, w/David Giler &
Walter Hill
BLUE THUNDER   Columbia, 1983
THE BEST OF TIMES   Universal, 1986
ALIENS   20th Century Fox, 1986, EP w/David Giler &
Walter Hill
RED HEAT   TriStar, 1988, w/Walter Hill

J. LARRY CARROLL
TOURIST TRAP   Compass International, 1979

WILLARD CARROLL
Business: Hyperion Entertainment, 837 Traction Ave.,
Suite 402, Los Angeles, CA 90013, 213/625-2921;
Fax: 213/687-4955

NUTCRACKER   Atlantic, 1986, w/Donald Kushner,
Peter Locke & Thomas L. Wilhite

RODNEY CARR-SMITH
LOLLY-MADONNA XXX   *THE LOLLY-MADONNA WAR*
MGM, 1973

RICHARD CARTER
KOTCH   Cinerama, 1971

WILLIAM P. CARTLIDGE
Fax: 071/328-5052

PAUL AND MICHELLE   Paramount, 1974, AP
MOONRAKER   United Artists, 1979, AP
EDUCATING RITA   Columbia, 1983, CP
NOT QUITE PARADISE   New World, 1986, CP
CONSUMING PASSIONS   Samuel Goldwyn
Company, 1988
DEALERS   Skouras Pictures, 1989

FRED CARUSO
Business: Warner Bros., 4000 Warner Blvd., Producers
Bldg. 5, Suite 114, Burbank, CA 91522, 818/954-3382
Agent: UTA - Beverly Hills, 310/273-6700

WHO IS HARRY KELLERMAN AND WHY IS HE SAYING
THOSE TERRIBLE THINGS ABOUT ME?   National
General, 1971, AP
LAW AND DISORDER   Columbia, 1974, AP

THE HAPPY HOOKER   Cannon, 1975
NETWORK ★   United Artists, 1976, AP
THE WANDERERS   Orion, 1979, AP
WINTER KILLS   Avco Embassy, 1979
DRESSED TO KILL   Filmways, 1980, AP
BLOW OUT   Filmways, 1981, EP
BLUE VELVET   DEG, 1986
THE PRESIDIO   Paramount, 1988, CP
CASUALTIES OF WAR   Columbia, 1989, CP
WE'RE NO ANGELS   Paramount, 1989, CP
THE BONFIRE OF THE VANITIES   Warner Bros.,
1990, CP

GREGORY CASCANTE
Business: August Entertainment, 838 N. Fairfax Ave.,
Los Angeles, CA 90046, 213/658-8888;
Fax: 213/658-7654

MIDNIGHT CROSSING   Vestron, 1988, EP w/Gary Barber,
Dan Ireland & Wanda S. Rayle
WAXWORK   Vestron, 1988, EP w/Dan Ireland, William J.
Quigley & Mario Sotela

PATRICIA CASEY
THE MAN WHO HAD POWER OVER WOMEN   Avco
Embassy, 1971, AP
AND NOW FOR SOMETHING COMPLETELY DIFFERENT
Columbia, 1972

EUGENE C. CASHMAN
RETURN OF THE LIVING DEAD PART II   Lorimar,
1988, EP

PATRICK CASSAVETTI
Business: Greenpoint Films, 5a Noel Street, London
W1V 3RB England, 071/437-6492; Fax: 071/437-0644

BRAZIL   Universal, 1985, CP
MONA LISA   Island Pictures, 1986, w/Stephen Woolley
PARIS BY NIGHT   Cineplex Odeon, 1990
AMERICAN FRIENDS   MCEG Virgin Vision, 1991,
w/Steve Abbott

T. J. CASTRONOVO
DOUBLE REVENGE   Smart Egg Releasing, 1988,
w/John S. Curran

GILBERT CATES
Business: Cates Productions, 10920 Wilshire Blvd.,
Suite 600, Los Angeles, CA 90024, 310/208-2134
Agent: William Morris Agency - Beverly Hills, 310/274-7451

I NEVER SANG FOR MY FATHER   Columbia, 1970
DRAGONFLY   *ONE SUMMER LOVE*   AIP, 1976, CP
THE LAST MARRIED COUPLE IN AMERICA   Universal,
1980, EP w/Joseph Cates

JOSEPH CATES
Business: Cates Films, 57 E. 74th St., New York, NY
10021, 212/517-7100
Contact: Directors Guild of America - Los Angeles,
213/289-2000

THE LAST MARRIED COUPLE IN AMERICA   Universal,
1980, EP w/Gilbert Cates

CEVIN CATHELL
DELUSION   Cineville, 1991, CP w/Cevin Cathell

Ca

FILM
PRODUCERS,
STUDIOS,
AGENTS AND
CASTING
DIRECTORS
GUIDE

F
I
L
M

P
R
O
D
U
C
E
R
S

ROBERT CAVALLO
(credit w/Steven Fargnoli & Joseph Ruffalo)
Business: Roven-Cavallo Entertainment, Raleigh Studios, 650 Bronson Ave., Suite 218 West, Los Angeles, CA 90038, 213/960-4921

PURPLE RAIN   Warner Bros., 1984
UNDER THE CHERRY MOON   Warner Bros., 1986
SIGN O' THE TIMES   Cineplex Odeon, 1987

SUSAN CAVAN
Contact: Accent Entertainment Group, 8282 Sunset Blvd., Suite C, Los Angeles, CA 90046, 213/654-0231; Fax: 213/654-1372

THE BAY BOY   Orion, 1985, EP w/Frank Jacobs

MARIO CECCHI GORI
(credit w/Vittorio Cecchi Gori)
MAN TROUBLE   1991
FOLKS!   1991

VITTORIO CECCHI GORI
(credit w/Mario Cecchi Gori)
MAN TROUBLE   1991
FOLKS!   1991

ALAIN CHAMMAS
THE BUDDY SYSTEM   20th Century Fox, 1984

GILL CHAMPION
FUN AND GAMES   Audubon, 1973, w/Martin Richards

GREGG CHAMPION
Agent: ICM - Los Angeles, 310/550-4000
Contact: Directors Guild of America - Los Angeles, 213/289-2000

BLUE THUNDER   Columbia, 1983, AP
AMERICAN FLYERS   Warner Bros., 1985, AP
SHORT CIRCUIT   TriStar, 1986, SP
STAKEOUT   Buena Vista, 1987, SP

JOHN CHAMPION
MUSTANG COUNTRY   Universal, 1976

DAVID CHAN
Business: Golden Harvest Films, Inc., 9884 Santa Monica Blvd., Beverly Hills, CA 90212, 310/203-0722; Fax: 310/556-3214

THE PROTECTOR   Golden Harvest, 1985
TEENAGE MUTANT NINJA TURTLES   New Line Cinema, 1990, w/Kim Dawson & Simon Fields
TEENAGE MUTANT NINJA TURTLES II: THE SECRET OF THE OOZE   New Line, 1991, w/Kim Dawson & Thomas K. Gray

JOHN K. CHAN
Business: C.I.M. Productions, 665 Bush St., San Francisco, CA 94108, 415/433-2342

EAT A BOWL OF TEA   Columbia, 1989, EP w/Lindsay Law
LIFE IS CHEAP...BUT TOILET PAPER IS EXPENSIVE   Silverlight, 1990, EP w/Wayne Wang

WARREN CHANEY
ALOHA SUMMER   Spectrafilm, 1988, EP

STEVEN H. CHANIN
UNDER THE BOARDWALK   New World, 1989, w/Gregory S. Blackwell

SIMON CHANNING-WILLIAMS
Business: Imagine Productions Ltd., 9 Greek Street, London W1V 5LE England, 071/734-7372; Fax: 071/287-5228

HIGH HOPES   Skouras Pictures, 1989, w/Victor Glynn
WHEN THE WHALES CAME   20th Century Fox, 1989

DOUG CHAPIN
Business: Krost/Chapin Productions, 4000 Warner Blvd., Burbank, CA 91522, 818/954-6526

WHEN A STRANGER CALLS   Columbia, 1979, w/Steve Feke
PANDEMONIUM   MGM/UA, 1982
AMERICAN DREAMER   Warner Bros., 1984
AMERICAN ANTHEM   Columbia, 1986, w/Robert Schaffel

SAUL CHAPLIN
Business: 8969 Sunset Blvd., Los Angeles, CA 90069, 310/271-2904

THE SOUND OF MUSIC   20th Century Fox, 1965, AP
STAR!   20th Century Fox, 1968
MAN OF LA MANCHA   United Artists, 1972, AP
THAT'S ENTERTAINMENT, PART 2   MGM/UA, 1976, w/Daniel Melnick

CHRISTIAN CHARRET
WAIT UNTIL SPRING, BANDINI   Orion, 1990, EP w/Cyril de Rouvre, Amadeo Pagani & Giorgio Silvago

ROBERT CHARTOFF
(credit w/Irwin Winkler)
Business: Robert Chartoff Productions, 1250 6th St., Suite 201, Santa Monica, CA 90401, 310/472-8775

POINT BLANK   MGM, 1967, w/Judd Bernard*
THE SPLIT   MGM, 1968
THEY SHOOT HORSES, DON'T THEY?   Cinerama Releasing Corporation, 1969, w/Sydney Pollack
LEO THE LAST   United Artists, 1970
THE STRAWBERRY STATEMENT   MGM, 1970
BELIEVE IN ME   MGM, 1971
THE GANG THAT COULDN'T SHOOT STRAIGHT   MGM, 1971
THE MECHANIC   United Artists, 1972, w/Lewis John Carlino
THE NEW CENTURIONS   Columbia, 1972
THUMB TRIPPING   Avco Embassy, 1972
UP THE SANDBOX   National General, 1972
BUSTING   United Artists, 1974
S*P*Y*S   20th Century Fox, 1974
BREAKOUT   Columbia, 1975
THE GAMBLER   Paramount, 1974
PEEPER   20th Century Fox, 1976
NICKELODEON   Columbia, 1976
ROCKY ★★   United Artists, 1976
NEW YORK, NEW YORK   United Artists, 1977
VALENTINO   United Artists, 1977
COMES A HORSEMAN   United Artists, 1978, EP
UNCLE JOE SHANNON   United Artists, 1978
ROCKY II   United Artists, 1979
RAGING BULL ★   United Artists, 1980
TRUE CONFESSIONS   United Artists, 1981
ROCKY III   MGM/UA, 1982
THE RIGHT STUFF ★   The Ladd Company/ Warner Bros., 1983

ROCKY IV   MGM/UA, 1985
BEER   Orion, 1986*
ROCKY V   MGM/UA, 1990

STANLEY CHASE
Contact: 1937 S. Beverly Glen, Suite 20, Los Angeles, CA
    90025, 310/475-4236; Fax: 310/474-5720

COLOSSUS: THE FORBIN PROJECT   Universal, 1970
HIGH-BALLIN'   AIP, 1978, EP w/William Hayward
MACK THE KNIFE   21st Century, 1989

DAVID CHASMAN
BRIGHTON BEACH MEMOIRS   Universal, 1986, EP
THE SECRET OF MY SUCCESS   Universal, 1987, EP

JULIA CHASMAN
Business: Universal Pictures, 445 Park Ave., New York,
    NY 10022, 212/759-7500

SHAG: THE MOVIE   Hemdale, 1989, w/Stephen Woolley

AMIN Q. CHAUDHRI
Business: Continental Film Group, Ltd., 321 W. 44th St.,
    Suite 405, New York, NY 10036, 212/265-2530;
    Fax: 212/245-6275; Park St., Sharon, PA 16146,
    412/981-3456; Fax: 412/981-2668

TIGER WARSAW   Sony Pictures, 1988
AN UNREMARKABLE LIFE   SVS Films, 1989

JOHN CHAVEZ
MEET THE HOLLOWHEADS   Moviestore, 1989,
    w/Joseph Grace

STEPHEN G. CHEIKES
THE HEAVENLY KID   Orion, 1985, EP w/Gabe Sumner

JOEL CHERNOFF
Contact: 310/273-1302

LOOSE SHOES   *COMING ATTRACTIONS*
    National-American, 1979

JEFFREY CHERNOV
Business: Walt Disney Pictures, 500 S. Buena Vista St.,
    Burbank, CA 91521, 818/840-1000
Contact: Directors Guild of America - Los Angeles,
    213/289-2000

CUTTER'S WAY   United Artists Classics, 1981, AP
EDDIE MURPHY RAW   Paramount, 1987, CP
SLEEPING WITH THE ENEMY   20th Century Fox,
    1991, EP

CHRIS CHESSER
Business: 4212 Costello Ave., Sherman Oaks, CA 91423,
    818/789-0851

MAJOR LEAGUE   Paramount, 1989, w/Irby Smith
WAR PARTY   Hemdale, 1989, EP w/Franc Roddam

GIRAUD CHESTER
Business: Mark Goodson Productions, 375 Park Ave., New
    York, NY 10152, 212/751-0600; Fax: 212/319-0013; 5750
    Wilshire Blvd., Los Angeles, CA 90036, 213/965-6500

COME BACK TO THE 5 & DIME, JIMMY DEAN, JIMMY
    DEAN   Cinecom, 1982, EP

RANDOLPH CHEVELDAVE
FRIDAY THE 13TH PART VIII - JASON TAKES
    MANHATTAN   Paramount, 1989

DEVEN CHIERIGHINO
THE WIZARD OF SPEED AND TIME   Shapiro- Glickenhaus
    Entertainment, 1989, w/Richard Kaye

MICHAEL CHILDERS
Contact: Directors Guild of America - Los Angeles,
    213/289-2000

THE BELIEVERS   Orion, 1987, w/Beverly J. Camhe &
    John Schlesinger

MICHAEL CHINICH
Business: Hughes Entertainment, 100 Universal Plaza,
    Universal City, CA 91608, 818/777-6363

THE BINGO LONG TRAVELING ALL-STARS AND MOTOR
    KINGS   Universal, 1976, AP
WHICH WAY IS UP?   Universal, 1977, AP
PRETTY IN PINK   Paramount, 1986, EP w/John Hughes
FERRIS BUELLER'S DAY OFF   Paramount, 1986, EP
SOME KIND OF WONDERFUL   Paramount, 1987,
    EP w/Ronald Colby
PLANES, TRAINS AND AUTOMOBILES   Paramount, 1987,
    EP w/Neil Machlis

DAVID CHISOLM
Agent: CAA - Beverly Hills, 310/288-4545

THE WIZARD   Universal, 1989, w/Ken Topolsky

ARTHUR CHOBANIAN
PARADISE ALLEY   Universal, 1978, AP
ROCKY II   United Artists, 1979, AP
ROCKY III   MGM/UA, 1982
ROCKY IV   MGM/UA, 1985, EP w/James D. Brubaker

ELIE CHOURAQUI
Contact: French Film Office, 745 Fifth Ave., New York, NY
    10151, 212/832-8860

LOVE SONGS   Spectrafilm, 1986, w/Robert Baylis

MARIE-CHRISTINE CHOURAQUI
Contact: French Film Office, 745 Fifth Ave., New York, NY
    10151, 212/832-8860

LOVE SONGS   Spectrafilm, 1986, EP w/Murray Shostak

RAYMOND CHOW
Business: Golden Harvest Films, Inc., 9884 Santa Monica
    Blvd., Beverly Hills, CA 90212, 310/203-0722;
    Fax: 310/556-3214

DEEP THRUST   AIP, 1973
FISTS OF FURY   National General, 1973
LADY KUNG FU   National General, 1973
ENTER THE DRAGON   Warner Bros., 1973, AP
RETURN OF THE DRAGON   Bryanston, 1974,
    EP w/Bruce Lee
THE CHINESE PROFESSIONALS   National General, 1974
THE DRAGON FLIES   20th Century Fox, 1975,
    w/John Fraser
THE AMSTERDAM KILL   Columbia, 1978, EP
THE BOYS IN COMPANY C   Columbia, 1978, EP

Ch

FILM
PRODUCERS,
STUDIOS,
AGENTS and
CASTING
DIRECTORS
GUIDE

F
I
L
M

P
R
O
D
U
C
E
R
S

GAME OF DEATH   Columbia, 1979
THE CANNONBALL RUN   20th Century Fox, 1981, EP
DEATH HUNT   20th Century Fox, 1981,
   EP w/Albert S. Ruddy
MEGAFORCE   20th Century Fox, 1982, EP
BETTER LATE THAN NEVER   Warner Bros., 1983, EP
HIGH ROAD TO CHINA   Warner Bros., 1983, EP
LASSITER   Warner Bros., 1984, EP w/Andre Morgan
THE PROTECTOR   Golden Harvest, 1985, EP
TEENAGE MUTANT NINJA TURTLES   New Line
   Cinema, 1990, EP
A SHOW OF FORCE   Paramount, 1990, EP
TEENAGE MUTANT NINJA TURTLES II: THE SECRET
   OF THE OOZE   New Line, 1991, EP

BO CHRISTENSEN
BABETTE'S FEAST   Orion Classics, 1987

BRIAN CHRISTIAN
RETRIBUTION   Taurus Entertainment, 1988,
   EP w/Scott Lavin

ROBERT CHRISTIANSEN
(credit w/Rick Rosenberg)
Business: Chris-Rose Productions, 4000 Warner Blvd.,
   Producers 2, Suite 1104-A, Burbank, CA 91522,
   818/954-1748; Fax: 818/954-4822

ADAM AT SIX A.M.   National General, 1970
HIDE IN PLAIN SIGHT   MGM/UA, 1980

CALDECOT CHUBB
Business: Edward R. Pressman Film Corporation, 445 N.
   Bedford Dr., Penthouse, Beverly Hills, CA 90210,
   310/271-8383; Fax: 310/271-9497

GOOD MORNING BABYLON   Vestron, 1987,
   AP w/Lloyd Fonvielle
CHERRY 2000   Orion, 1988, w/Edward R. Pressman
TO SLEEP WITH ANGER   Samuel Goldwyn Company,
   1990, w/Thomas S. Byrnes & Darin Scott
WAITING FOR THE LIGHT   Triumph, 1990,
   w/Ron Bozman

DAVID CHUDNOW
Business: Rosamond Productions, 7461 Beverly Blvd.,
   Los Angeles, CA 90036

THE DOBERMAN GANG   1972
THE DARING DOBERMANS   Dimension, 1973
THE AMAZING DOBERMANS   Golden, 1977

MICHAEL CIMINO
Attorney: Barry Hirsch, Armstrong & Hirsch, 1888 Century
   Park East, Los Angeles, CA 90067, 310/553-0305
Business Manager: Alan Cohen & Co. - New York,
   212/755-0750

THE DEER HUNTER ★★   Universal, 1978, w/Michael
   Deeley, John Peverall & Barry Spikings
THE SICILIAN   20th Century Fox, 1987, w/Joann Carelli

TONY CINCIRIPINI
THE LAWLESS LAND   Concorde, 1988, w/Larry Leahy

LUIGI CINGOLANI
Business: Smart Egg Pictures, 8733 Sunset Blvd.,
   Suite 200, Los Angeles, CA 90069, 310/659-1801;
   Fax: 310/659-1739

OMEGA SYNDROME   New World, 1987
DOUBLE REVENGE   Smart Egg Releasing, 1988,
   EP w/George Zecevic
CAMERON'S CLOSET   SVS Films, 1989
SPACED INVADERS   Buena Vista, 1990

CARLA CIPRIANI
SALON KITTY   *MADAME KITTY*   AIP, 1976, EP

ANNETTE CIRILLO
THE RETURN OF SWAMP THING   Miramax, 1989, CP
MONSTER HIGH   Lightyear, 1990, EP w/Tom Kuhn

NICHOLAS CLAINOS
THE DOORS   TriStar, 1991, EP w/Brian Grazer &
   Mario Kassar

AL CLARK
(credit w/Robert Devereux)

1984   Atlantic, 1985, CP
ABSOLUTE BEGINNERS   Orion, 1986,
   EP w/Nik Powell
GOTHIC   Vestron, 1987, EP
ARIA   Miramax, 1988, CP w/Mike Watts

BOB CLARK
Business Manager: Harold D. Cohen - Los Angeles,
   310/550-0570
Contact: Directors Guild of America - Los Angeles,
   213/289-2000

CHILDREN SHOULDN'T PLAY WITH DEAD THINGS
   Europix International, 1974, w/Gary Goch
DEAD OF NIGHT   Europix International, 1974
BREAKING POINT   20th Century Fox, 1976,
   w/Claude Héroux
MURDER BY DECREE   Avco Embassy, 1979,
   w/Rene Dupont
PORKY'S   20th Century Fox, 1982, w/Don Carmody
PORKY'S II: THE NEXT DAY   20th Century Fox, 1983,
   w/Don Carmody
A CHRISTMAS STORY   MGM/UA, 1983,
   w/Rene Dupont
FROM THE HIP   DEG, 1987, w/Rene Dupont

DICK CLARK
Business: Dick Clark Productions, Inc., 3003 W. Olive Ave.,
   Burbank, CA 91510, 818/954-8609; Fax: 818/841-3003

THE DARK   Film Ventures International, 1979,
   w/Edward L. Montoro
REMO WILLIAMS: THE ADVENTURE BEGINS...   Orion,
   1985, EP w/Mel Bergman
CATCHFIRE   1991, w/Dan Paulson

GAIL CLARK
BLACK OAK CONSPIRACY   New World, 1977, EP

GREYDON CLARK
PSYCHIC KILLER   Avco Embassy, 1975, AP
JOYSTICKS   Jensen-Farley, 1983

LOUISE CLARK
A WINTER TAN   Circle Releasing, 1989

NIGEL STAFFORD-CLARK
(see Nigel STAFFORD-Clark)

TOM CLARK
BLACK OAK CONSPIRACY   New World, 1977,
   w/Jesse Vint

FRANK CLARKE
LETTER TO BREZHNEV   Circle Releasing, 1985, EP

JAMES CLAVELL
Agent: CAA - Beverly Hills, 310/288-4545
Contact: Writers Guild of America - Los Angeles,
   310/550-1000

FIVE GATES TO HELL   20th Century Fox, 1959
WALK LIKE A DRAGON   Paramount, 1960
TO SIR WITH LOVE   Columbia, 1967
THE SWEET AND THE BITTER   Monarch, 1968
WHERE'S JACK?   Paramount, 1969
THE LAST VALLEY   Cinerama, 1971

TIM CLAWSON
Contact: Propaganda Films, 940 N. Mansfield Ave., Los
   Angeles, CA 90038, 310/462-6400; Fax: 310/463-7874

DICE RULES   Seven Arts, 1991, CP

DOUG CLAYBOURNE
Business: Claybourne Productions, 848 Fuller Ave.,
   Los Angeles, CA 90046, 213/930-1112
Contact: Directors Guild of America - Los Angeles,
   213/289-2000

THE ESCAPE ARTIST   Orion, 1982, w/Buck Houghton
RUMBLE FISH   Universal, 1983, w/Fred Roos
THE BLACK STALLION RETURNS   MGM/UA, 1983,
   w/Fred Roos & Tom Sternberg
LIGHT OF DAY   TriStar, 1987, EP
THE SERPENT & THE RAINBOW   Universal, 1988,
   w/David Ladd
ERNEST SAVES CHRISTMAS   Buena Vista, 1988,
   w/Stacy Williams
THE WAR OF THE ROSES   20th Century Fox, 1989,
   EP w/Polly Platt
HEARTS OF DARKNESS: A FILMMAKER'S
   APOCALYPSE   Avenue, 1991, EP w/Fred Roos

JOHN CLEESE
Business: Prominent Features Ltd., 68A Delancey St.,
   London NW1 7RY, England, 071/284-0242
   Fax: 071/284-1004

A FISH CALLED WANDA   MGM/UA, 1988,
   EP w/Steve Abbott

TERENCE CLEGG
Business: Convergence Productions, 177 Oxford Gardens,
   London W10 6NE England, 081/960-7426;
   Fax: 081/968-5138

CAL   Warner Bros., 1984, EP
OUT OF AFRICA ★★   Universal, 1985, CP
CRY FREEDOM   Universal, 1987, EP
GORILLAS IN THE MIST   Universal, 1988, w/Arnold Glimcher

RENE CLEITMAN
THE BAY BOY   Orion, 1985, CP

BRIAN H. CLEMENS
(credit w/Albert Fennell)
Agent: Paul Kohner Agency - Los Angeles,
   310/550-1060

AND SOON THE DARKNESS   Levitt-Pickman, 1971
DR. JEKYLL AND SISTER HYDE   AIP, 1972
CAPTAIN KRONOS: VAMPIRE HUNTER
   Paramount, 1974

DICK CLEMENT
Agent: Broder-Kurland-Webb-Uffner Agency - Los Angeles,
   213/656-9262
Contact: Directors Guild of America - Los Angeles,
   213/289-2000

VICE VERSA   Columbia, 1988, w/Ian La Frenais

NICOLAS CLERMONT
Business: Filmline International Inc., 109 ouest rue St. Paul,
   Montreal, H2Y 2A1, 514/288-5888; Fax: 514/288-8083

WILD THING   Atlantic, 1987, w/David Calloway
BETHUNE: THE MAKING OF A HERO   Filmline
   International, 1990, w/Pieter Kroonenburg

GRAEME CLIFFORD
Agent: ICM - Los Angeles, 310/550-4000
Contact: Directors Guild of America - Los Angeles,
   213/289-2000

BURKE & WILLS   Hemdale, 1987, w/John Sexton

SANDY CLIMAN
(credit w/Charles C. Thieriot)

ALMOST YOU   20th Century Fox, 1984,
   EP w/Stephen J. Levin
3:15 THE MOMENT OF TRUTH   Dakota Entertainment,
   1986, EP w/Andrew Bullians & Jean Bullians
THE BIKINI SHOP   *THE MALIBU BIKINI SHOP*
   International Film Marketing, 1987, EP w/Andrew
   Bullians & Jean Bullians

ALAN CLORE
THREE SISTERS   American Film Theatre, 1974

LEON CLORE
Contact: Terence Baker Ltd., 17 Grove Hill Road,
   Camberwell, London SE5 8DF England, 071/926-0122;
   Fax: 071/737-5971

MORGAN; A SUITABLE CASE FOR TREATMENT
   Cinema 5, 1966
ALL NEAT IN BLACK STOCKINGS   National
   General, 1969
THE FRENCH LIEUTENANT'S WOMAN   United
   Artists, 1981

ROBERT CLOUSE
Agent: ICM - Los Angeles, 310/550-4000
Contact: Directors Guild of America - Los Angeles,
   213/289-2000

DREAMS OF GLASS   Universal, 1970

CI

FILM
PRODUCERS,
STUDIOS,
AGENTS AND
CASTING
DIRECTORS
GUIDE

F
I
L
M

P
R
O
D
U
C
E
R
S

Co

FILM
PRODUCERS,
STUDIOS,
AGENTS AND
CASTING
DIRECTORS
GUIDE

F
I
L
M

P
R
O
D
U
C
E
R
S

ANNE V. COATES
THE MEDUSA TOUCH   Warner Bros., 1978,
   w/Jack Gold

WALTER COBLENZ
Business: Bellisle Productions, 2348 Apollo Dr.,
   Los Angeles, CA 90046, 213/469-0896
Contact: Directors Guild of America - Los Angeles,
   213/289-2000

THE CANDIDATE   Warner Bros., 1972
ALL THE PRESIDENT'S MEN ★   Warner Bros., 1976
THE ONION FIELD   Avco Embassy, 1979
THE LEGEND OF THE LONE RANGER
   AFD/Universal, 1981
STRANGE INVADERS   Orion, 1983
SPACECAMP   20th Century Fox, 1986, w/Patrick Bailey
FOR KEEPS   TriStar, 1988, w/Jerry Belson
SISTER SISTER   New World, 1988
18 AGAIN   New World, 1988
THE BABE   Universal, 1991, EP w/William Finnegan

MICHAEL CODRON
CLOCKWISE   Universal, 1986

EDWARD COE
Business: Entertainment Productions, Inc., 2210 Wilshire
   Blvd., Suite 744, Santa Monica, CA 90403,
   310/456-3143; Fax: 310/828-0427

GHOST FEVER   Miramax, 1987, w/Ron Rich

ETHAN COEN
Agent: UTA - Beverly Hills, 310/273-6700

BLOOD SIMPLE   Circle Releasing Corporation, 1985
RAISING ARIZONA   20th Century Fox, 1987
MILLER'S CROSSING   20th Century Fox, 1990
BARTON FINK   20th Century Fox, 1991

ADRIANNA A. J. COHEN
MINDWALK   Mindwalk Productions, 1990

EDWARD H. COHEN
THE BUDDY HOLLY STORY   Columbia, 1978,
   EP w/Fred T. Kuehnert

HAROLD D. COHEN
I WALK THE LINE   Columbia, 1970

HERB COHEN
200 MOTELS   United Artists, 1971, w/Jerry Good

HERMAN COHEN
Business: Herman Cohen Productions, 650 N. Bronson
   Ave., Hollywood, CA 90004, 213/466-3388

CRAZE   Warner Bros., 1974

JANELLE COHEN
HELL UP IN HARLEM   AIP, 1973, CP
BLACK CAESAR   AIP, 1973, AP
IT'S ALIVE   Warner Bros., 1974, CP

JONATHAN COHEN
MARIGOLDS IN AUGUST   RM Productions, 1984,
   w/Mark Forstater

LARRY COHEN
Attorney: Skip Brittenham, Ziffren, Brittenham & Branca,
   2049 Century Park East, Los Angeles, CA 90067,
   310/552-3388
Agent: Robert Littman, The Robert Littman Company -
   Los Angeles, 310/278-1572

BONE   Jack H. Harris, 1972
HELL UP IN HARLEM   AIP, 1973
BLACK CAESAR   AIP, 1973
IT'S ALIVE   Warner Bros., 1974
GOD TOLD ME TO   New World, 1976
DEMON   New World, 1977
IT LIVES AGAIN   Warner Bros., 1978
THE PRIVATE FILES OF J. EDGAR HOOVER   AIP, 1978
Q   UFD, 1982
THE STUFF   New World, 1985, EP
FULL MOON HIGH   Orion, 1986
IT'S ALIVE III: ISLAND OF THE ALIVE   Warner Bros.,
   1987, EP
WICKED STEPMOTHER   MGM/UA, 1989, EP
MANIAC COP 2 Movie House Sales, 1990

LAWRENCE J. COHEN
Agent: CAA - Beverly Hills, 310/288-4545

THE BIG BUS   Paramount, 1976, w/Fred Freeman

MARTIN B. COHEN
Business: Martin B. Cohen Productions, Inc., 9962 Durant
   Dr., Beverly Hills, CA 90212, 310/552-2958
Agent: Diamond Artists, Ltd. - Los Angeles, 310/278-8146

REBEL ROUSERS   Four Star Excelsior, 1970
HUMANOIDS FROM THE DEEP   New World, 1980,
   w/Hunt Lowry

NAT COHEN
CLOCKWISE   Universal, 1986, EP w/Verity Lambert

NORMAN I. COHEN
Business: Co-Star Entertainment c/o P.O. Box 806, 241 Little
   Deer Rd., Woodstock, NY 12498, 518/474-4812;
   Fax: 518/474-8733

I COULD NEVER HAVE SEX WITH ANY MAN WHO HAS
   SO LITTLE REGARD FOR MY HUSBAND   Cinema 5,
   1973, EP
CONFESSIONS OF A WINDOW CLEANER   Columbia,
   1974, EP w/Michael Klinger
DEATH PLAY   New Line, 1976
THE KILLER INSIDE ME   Warner Bros., 1976, EP
TRACKS   Castle Hill, 1976, w/Ted Shapiro &
   Howard Zucker
THE GIG   Castle Hill, 1985
THE LUCKIEST MAN IN THE WORLD   Castle Hill, 1989

RICHARD COHEN
SPELLBINDER   MGM/UA, 1988, EP w/Howard Baldwin

ROB COHEN
Business: Badham-Cohen Group, 100 Universal City Plaza,
   Bldg. 82, Universal City, CA 91608, 818/777-3477;
   Fax: 818/777-8226
Agent: UTA - Beverly Hills, 310/273-6700

MAHOGANY   Paramount, 1975, w/Jack Ballard
THE BINGO LONG TRAVELING ALL-STARS & MOTOR
   KINGS   Universal, 1976

SCOTT JOPLIN   Universal, 1977, EP
THE WIZ   Universal, 1978
THANK GOD IT'S FRIDAY   Columbia, 1978
ALMOST SUMMER   Universal, 1978
THE RAZOR'S EDGE   Columbia, 1984, EP
THE LEGEND OF BILLIE JEAN   TriStar, 1985
LIGHT OF DAY   TriStar, 1987, w/Keith Barish
THE MONSTER SQUAD   TriStar, 1987, EP w/Keith
   Barish & Peter Hyams
THE RUNNING MAN   TriStar, 1987, EP w/Keith Barish
THE WITCHES OF EASTWICK   Warner Bros., 1987,
   EP w/Don Devlin
IRONWEED   TriStar, 1987, EP w/Denis Blouin &
   Joseph H. Kanter
THE SERPENT & THE RAINBOW   Universal, 1988,
   EP w/Keith Barish
DISORGANIZED CRIME   Buena Vista, 1989,
   EP w/John Badham
BIRD ON A WIRE   Universal, 1990
THE HARD WAY   Universal, 1991, w/William Sackheim

RONALD I. COHEN
Business: Ronald I. Cohen Productions Inc., 1155 Blvd.
   René-Lévesque, Suite 4103, Montreal, Quebec H3B 3V6,
   Canada, 514/397-1511

RUNNING   Universal, 1979, w/Robert Cooper
MIDDLE AGE CRAZY   20th Century Fox, 1980,
   w/Robert Cooper
TICKET TO HEAVEN   United Artists Classics, 1981, EP
CROSS COUNTRY   New World, 1983, EP
HARRY TRACY   Quartet/Films, Inc., 1983

RUDY COHEN
Contact: Karen Films, 755 N. La Cienega Blvd.,
   Suite 201, Los Angeles, CA 90069, 310/289-0270;
   Fax: 310/289-0169

THE RETURN OF SUPERFLY   Triton, 1990,
   EP w/Jon Goldwater

BRUCE COHN
(credit w/Allan F. Bodoh)

DOGS   R.C. Riddell, 1977
ACAPULCO GOLD   R.C. Riddell, 1978

RONALD COLBY
Contact: Directors Guild of America - Los Angeles,
   213/289-2000

THE RAIN PEOPLE   Warner Bros., 1969, w/Bart Patton
HAMMETT   Orion, 1982, w/Don Guest & Fred Roos
SOME KIND OF WONDERFUL   Paramount, 1987,
   EP w/Michael Chinich
SHE'S HAVING A BABY   Paramount, 1988, EP
LISA   MGM/UA, 1990, AP

STEPHEN J. COLE
APARTMENT ZERO   Skouras Pictures, 1989, EP

STAN COLEMAN
Contact: One Bean Productions c/o 20th Century Fox TV,
   10201 W. Pico Blvd., Los Angeles, CA 90035,
   310/203-1086

BORN IN EAST L.A.   Universal, 1987, EP

THOMAS COLEMAN
(credit w/Michael Rosenblatt)

THE DAY THE MUSIC DIED (FD)   Atlantic, 1977, EP
VALLEY GIRL   Atlantic, 1983, EP
ROADHOUSE 66   Atlantic, 1984, EP
TEEN WOLF   Atlantic, 1985, EP
THE MEN'S CLUB   Atlantic, 1986, EP w/John Harada
EXTREMITIES   Atlantic, 1986, EP
NUTCRACKER   Atlantic, 1986, EP
SUMMER HEAT   Atlantic, 1987, EP
STEEL JUSTICE   Atlantic, 1987, EP
WILD THING   Atlantic, 1987, EP
THE GARBAGE PAIL KIDS MOVIE   Atlantic, 1987, EP
TEEN WOLF TOO   Atlantic, 1987, EP
COP   Atlantic, 1988, EP
PATTY HEARST   Atlantic, 1988, EP
1969   Atlantic, 1988, EP*

ROBERT F. COLESBERRY
Contact: David Alexander, Peyser & Alexander 500 Fifth
   Avenue, Suite 2800, New York, NY, 212/7646455
Contact: Directors Guild of America - New York,
   212/581-0370

TATTOO   20th Century Fox, 1981, AP
BABY, IT'S YOU   Paramount, 1983, AP
THE KING OF COMEDY   20th Century Fox, 1983, AP
FALLING IN LOVE   Paramount, 1984, AP
THE NATURAL   TriStar, 1984, AP
AFTER HOURS   Geffen/Warner Bros., 1985, w/Griffin
   Dunne & Amy Robinson
HOUSEKEEPING   Columbia, 1987
THE HOUSE ON CARROLL STREET   Orion, 1988,
   w/Peter Yates
MISSISSIPPI BURNING ★   Orion, 1988, w/Frederick Zollo
COME SEE THE PARADISE   20th Century Fox, 1990

PAUL COLICHMAN
(credit w/Miles A. Copeland III)
Business: I.R.S. World Media, 3939 Lankershim Blvd.,
   Universal City, CA 91604, 818/505-0555;
   Fax: 818/505-1318

THE DECLINE OF WESTERN CIVILIZATION PART II:
   THE METAL YEARS (FD)   New Line, 1988, EP
A SINFUL LIFE   New Line, 1989, EP
CIRCUITRY MAN   Skouras, 1990, EP
GENUINE RISK   I.R.S., 1990, EP
BLOOD AND CONCRETE   I.R.S., 1991, EP w/Harold Welb
GUILTY AS CHARGED   I.R.S., 1991, EP

RICHARD COLL
MISS FIRECRACKER   Corsair, 1989, CP

RICHARD A. COLLA
OLLY OLLY OXEN FREE   Sanrio, 1978

ELLEN COLLETT
Contact: Collett/Dozoretz Productions, 500 S. Buena Vista
   St., Animation 2G-4, Burbank, CA 91521, 818/560-4637;
   Fax: 818/567-2966

DECEIVED   Buena Vista, 1991, w/Wendy Dozoretz &
   Michael Finnell

DAVID COLLINS
EAT THE PEACH   Skouras Pictures, 1987, EP

Co

FILM
PRODUCERS,
STUDIOS,
AGENTS AND
CASTING
DIRECTORS
GUIDE

F
I
L
M

P
R
O
D
U
C
E
R
S

PETER COLLINSON
STRAIGHT ON TILL MORNING   International
Co-Productions, 1974

PETER COLLISTER
KGB: THE SECRET WAR   Cinema Group, 1986, EP

HARRY COLOMBY
Agent: Coxson & Carleton - Los Angeles, 213/924-2028

MR. MOM   20th Century Fox, 1983, CP
JOHNNY DANGEROUSLY   20th Century Fox,
    EP w/Bud Austin
THE SQUEEZE   TriStar, 1987, EP w/David
    Shamroy Hamburger
TOUCH AND GO   TriStar, 1987, EP

JOHN COMFORT
KING RALPH   Universal, 1991, CP w/Julie Bergman

FRANCO COMMITTERI
MACARONI   Paramount, 1985, w/Aurelio &
    Luigi De Laurentiis

ROD CONFESOR
DRIVING FORCE   J&M Entertainment, 1990,
    w/Howard Grigsby

TONY CONFORTI
Business: Ion Pictures, 3122 Santa Monica Blvd.,
    Santa Monica, CA 90404, 310/453-4466

THE CLOSER   Ion, 1991, EP w/Mitchell Calder, Roy
    Medawar & George Pappas

SEAN CONNERY
Agent: CAA - Beverly Hills, 310/288-4545

THE LAST DAYS OF EDEN   Buena Vista, 1991, EP

JON CONNOLLY
Agent: CAA - Beverly Hills, 310/288-4545
Contact: Writers Guild of America - Los Angeles,
    310/550-1000

THE DREAM TEAM   Universal, 1989, CP w/David Loucka

JACK CONRAD
THE HOWLING   Avco Embassy, 1980, w/Michael Finnell

DAVID CONROY
Business: Arena Fils, Twickenham Film Studios,
    The Barons, St. Margaret's, Twickenham, Middlesex
    TW1 2AW, 081/892-4477; Fax: 081/891-0168

VINCENT AND THEO   Hemdale, 1990, EP

D. CONSTANTINE CONTE
CONAN THE BARBARIAN   Universal, 1982,
    EP w/Edward R. Pressman
FIGHTING BACK   Paramount, 1982
48 HOURS   Paramount, 1982, EP
HARD TO HOLD   Universal, 1984
NO MERCY   TriStar, 1986
THE PRESIDIO   Paramount, 1988
ANOTHER 48 HOURS   Paramount, 1990, CP

GARY CONWAY
Contact: Screen Actors Guild - Los Angeles, 213/465-4600

THE FARMER   Columbia, 1977

JAMES L. CONWAY
(credit w/Charles E. Sellier, Jr.)

THE MYSTERIOUS MONSTERS (FD)   Sunn Classic,
    1976, AP*
THE BERMUDA TRIANGLE (FD)   Sunn Classic, 1979
THE LEGEND OF SLEEPY HOLLOW   Sunn Classic, 1979
IN SEARCH OF HISTORIC JESUS (FD)   Sunn
    Classic, 1979

JOAN GANZ COONEY
Business: Children's Television Workshop, One Lincoln
    Plaza, 4th Floor, New York, NY 10023, 212/595-3456

SESAME STREET PRESENTS: FOLLOW THAT BIRD
    Warner Bros., 1985, EP

RAY COONEY
WHOSE LIFE IS IT ANYWAY?   MGM, 1981,
    EP w/Martin C. Schute

HARRY COOPER
HEARTBREAKERS   Orion, 1985, EP w/Joseph Franck &
Lee Muhl

MARC COOPER
Contact: Writers Guild of America - Los Angeles,
    310/550-1000

SHARK   Excelsior, 1970, w/Skip Steloff

NESSA COOPER
LAST RESORT   Concorde, 1986, EP

RAY COOPER
MONA LISA   Island Pictures, 1986, CP w/Chris Brown
THE ADVENTURES OF BARON MUNCHAUSEN
    Columbia, 1989, CP
HOW TO GET AHEAD IN ADVERTISING   Warner Bros.,
    1989, CP

ROBERT COOPER
Business: Robert Cooper Productions Inc., 11340 W.
    Olympic Blvd., Suite 100, Los Angeles, CA 90064,
    310/477-5118

RUNNING   Universal, 1979, w/Ronald I. Cohen
MIDDLE AGE CRAZY   20th Century Fox, 1980,
    w/Ronald I. Cohen
TRULY, MADLY, DEEPLY   Samuel Goldwyn
    Company, 1991

MILES A. COPELAND III
(credit w/Paul Colichman)
Business: I.R.S. World Media, 3939 Lankershim Blvd.,
    Universal City, CA 91604, 818/505-0555;
    Fax: 818/505-1318

LUCKY STIFF   New Line, 1988, EP w/Laurie Perlman,
    Derek Power & Pat Proft*
THE DECLINE OF WESTERN CIVILIZATION PART II: THE
    METAL YEARS (FD)   New Line, 1988, EP

Co

FILM
PRODUCERS,
STUDIOS,
AGENTS AND
CASTING
DIRECTORS
GUIDE

F
I
L
M

P
R
O
D
U
C
E
R
S

A SINFUL LIFE   New Line, 1989, EP
CIRCUITRY MAN   Skouras, 1990, EP
GENUINE RISK   I.R.S., 1990, EP
BLOOD AND CONCRETE   I.R.S., 1991,
    EP w/Harold Welb
GUILTY AS CHARGED   I.R.S., 1991, EP

FRANCIS FORD COPPOLA
Business: Zoetrope Studios, Sentinel Bldg., 916 Kearny
    St., San Francisco, CA 94133, 415/788-7500;
    Fax: 415/989-7910
Agent: ICM - Los Angeles, 310/550-4000

TONIGHT FOR SURE   Premier Pictures, 1962
THE TERROR   AIP, 1963, AP
THX 1138   Warner Bros., 1971, EP
AMERICAN GRAFFITI ★   Universal, 1973
THE CONVERSATION ★   Paramount, 1974
THE GODFATHER - PART II ★★   Paramount, 1974
APOCALYPSE NOW ★   United Artists, 1979
THE BLACK STALLION   United Artists, 1979, EP
HAMMETT   Orion, 1982, EP
THE ESCAPE ARTIST   Orion, 1982, EP w/Fred Roos
PARSIFAL   Triumph/Columbia, 1983
THE BLACK STALLION RETURNS   MGM/UA, 1983, EP
RUMBLE FISH   Universal, 1983, EP
MISHIMA: A LIFE IN FOUR CHAPTERS   Warner Bros.,
    1985, EP w/George Lucas
GARDENS OF STONE   TriStar, 1987, w/Michael I. Levy
TOUGH GUYS DON'T DANCE   Cannon, 1987,
    EP w/Tom Luddy
LION HEART   Orion, 1987, EP w/Jack Schwartzman
THE GODFATHER PART III ★   Paramount, 1990

PENNY CORKE
GOTHIC   Vestron, 1987
SALOME'S LAST DANCE   Vestron, 1988

CIS CORMAN
Business: Barwood Films, 75 Rockefeller Plaza, 18th
    Floor, New York, NY 10019, 212/484-7300

NUTS   Warner Bros., 1987, EP w/Teri Schwartz

GENE CORMAN
Business: 21st Century Film Corporation, 8200 Wilshire
    Blvd., Beverly Hills, CA 90211, 213/658-3000

YOU CAN'T WIN 'EM ALL   Columbia, 1970
VON RICHTHOFEN & BROWN   United Artists, 1971
PRIVATE PARTS   MGM, 1972
COOL BREEZE   MGM, 1972
HIT MAN   MGM, 1972
I ESCAPED FROM DEVIL'S ISLAND   United Artists,
    1973, w/Roger Corman
THE SLAMS   MGM, 1973
VIGILANTE FORCE   United Artists, 1976
F.I.S.T.   United Artists, 1978, EP
TARGET: HARRY   ABC Pictures International, 1979, EP
THE BIG RED ONE   United Artists, 1980
IF YOU COULD SEE WHAT I HEAR   Jensen Farley
    Pictures, 1982, EP w/Dale Falconer
A MAN CALLED SARGE   Cannon, 1990

JULIE CORMAN
Business: Concorde Films, 11600 San Vicente Blvd., Los
    Angeles, CA 90049, 310/820-6733; Fax: 310/207-6816

BOXCAR BERTHA   AIP, 1972, AP
THE STUDENT TEACHERS   New World, 1973

THE YOUNG NURSES   New World, 1973
NIGHT CALL NURSES   New World, 1974
CANDY STRIPE NURSES   New World, 1974
CRAZY MAMA   New World, 1975
SUMMER SCHOOL TEACHERS   New World, 1975
MOVING VIOLATION   20th Century Fox, 1976
THE LADY IN RED   New World, 1979
SATURDAY THE 14TH   New World, 1981
THE DIRT BIKE KID   Concorde, 1985
CHOPPING MALL   Concorde, 1986
LAST RESORT   Concorde, 1986
DA   FilmDallas, 1988
NIGHTFALL   Concorde, 1989
NOWHERE TO RUN   *TEMPTATION BLUES*
    Concorde, 1989
SATURDAY THE 14TH STRIKES BACK   Concorde, 1989
PATHFINDER   Concorde, 1989
BRAIN DEAD   Concorde, 1990
A CRY IN THE WILD   Concorde, 1990
CORPORATE AFFAIRS   Concorde, 1990

ROGER CORMAN
Business: Concorde Films, 11600 San Vicente Blvd., Los
    Angeles, CA 90049, 310/820-6733; Fax: 310/207-6816

HIGHWAY DRAGNET   Allied Artists, 1954, AP
CRY BABY KILLER   AIP, 1954
THE MONSTER FROM THE OCEAN FLOOR   AIP, 1954
THE FAST AND THE FURIOUS   American
    International, 1954
STAKEOUT ON DOPE STREET   American
    International, 1958
HIGH SCHOOL BIG SHOT   AIP, 1958
T-BIRD GANG   AIP, 1958
THE WILD RIDE   AIP, 1960
THE BATTLE OF BLOOD ISLAND   American
    International, 1960
LITTLE SHOP OF HORRORS   Filmgroup, 1960
BATTLE BEYOND THE SUN   American International, 1962
THE MAGIC VOYAGE OF SINBAD   American
    International, 1962
DEMENTIA 13   AIP, 1963
PIT STOP   AIP, 1963
MOVING VIOLATION   AIP, 1963
BEACH BALL   AIP, 1965
QUEEN OF BLOOD   AIP, 1965
TARGETS   AIP, 1967, EP
DEVIL'S ANGELS   AIP, 1967
THE WILD RACERS   AIP, 1967
BLOODY MAMA   AIP, 1970
THE DUNWICH HORROR   AIP, 1970, EP
GAS-S-S-S!   AIP, 1970
THE STUDENT NURSES   AIP, 1970, EP
BOXCAR BERTHA   AIP, 1972
THE DIRT GANG   AIP, 1972, EP
UNHOLY ROLLERS   AIP, 1972, EP
I ESCAPED FROM DEVIL'S ISLAND   United Artists, 1973,
    w/Gene Corman
BIG BAD MAMA   New World, 1974
BORN TO KILL   *COCKFIGHTER*   New World, 1974
DEATH RACE 2000   New World, 1975
CAPONE   20th Century Fox, 1975
MOVING VIOLATION   20th Century Fox, 1976, EP
JACKSON COUNTY JAIL   New World, 1976, EP
FIGHTING MAD   20th Century Fox, 1976
EAT MY DUST   New World, 1976
I NEVER PROMISED YOU A ROSE GARDEN   New World,
    1977, EP w/Edgar J. Scherick
THUNDER & LIGHTNING   20th Century Fox, 1977
GRAND THEFT AUTO   New World, 1977, EP
PIRANHA   New World, 1978, EP w/Jeff Schechtman

Co

FILM
PRODUCERS,
STUDIOS,
AGENTS and
CASTING
DIRECTORS
GUIDE

F
I
L
M

P
R
O
D
U
C
E
R
S

DEATHSPORT   New World, 1978
AVALANCHE   New World, 1978
SAINT JACK   New World, 1979
TARGET: HARRY   ABC Pictures International, 1979
FAST CHARLIE...THE MOONBEAM RIDER   Universal,
   1979, w/Saul Krugman
ROCK 'N' ROLL HIGH SCHOOL   New World, 1979, EP
BATTLE BEYOND THE STARS   New World, 1980, EP
SMOKEY BITES THE DUST   New World, 1981
GALAXY OF TERROR   New World, 1981
FORBIDDEN WORLD   New World, 1982
LOVE LETTERS   New World, 1983
COCAINE WARS   Concorde, 1985, w/Alex Sessa
STREETWALKIN'   Concorde, 1985, EP
MUNCHIES   Concorde, 1987
BIG BAD MAMA II   Concorde, 1987
STRIPPED TO KILL   Concorde, 1987, EP
SWEET REVENGE   Concorde, 1987, EP
HOUR OF THE ASSASSIN   Concorde, 1987, EP
DADDY'S BOYS   Concorde, 1988
THE DRIFTER   Concorde, 1988, EP
WATCHERS   TriStar, 1988, EP
CRIME ZONE   Concorde, 1988, EP
THE LAWLESS LAND   Concorde, 1988,
   EP w/Juan Forch
THE TERROR WITHIN   Concorde, 1989
LORDS OF THE DEEP   Concorde, 1989
STRIPPED TO KILL 2   Concorde, 1989, EP
TRANSYLVANIA TWIST   Concorde, 1989, EP
BLOODFIST   Concorde, 1989
STREETS   Concorde, 1990, EP
FRANKENSTEIN UNBOUND   20th Century Fox, 1990,
   w/Kabi Jaeger & Thom Mount
THE HAUNTING OF MORELLA   Concorde, 1990
ANDY AND THE AIRWAVE RANGERS   Concorde,
   1990, EP
OVEREXPOSED   Concorde, 1990
BACK TO BACK   Concorde, 1990, EP
WATCHERS II   Concorde, 1990
HOLLYWOOD BOULEVARD II   Concorde, 1991, EP

JOHN CORNELL
Business: Paramount Pictures, 5555 Melrose Ave.,
   Los Angeles, CA 90038, 213/956-5796

"CROCODILE" DUNDEE   Paramount, 1986
CROCODILE DUNDEE II   Paramount, 1988,
   w/Jane Scott
ALMOST AN ANGEL   Paramount, 1990

STUART CORNFELD
Business: Baltimore Pictures, Culver Studios, 9336 W.
   Washington Blvd., Culver City, CA 90230,
   310/202-3334; Fax: 310/202-3206

FATSO   20th Century Fox, 1980
THE ELEPHANT MAN ★   Paramount, 1980, EP
THE HISTORY OF THE WORLD - PART I   20th Century
   Fox, 1981, AP
GIRLS JUST WANT TO HAVE FUN   New World,
   1985, EP
NATIONAL LAMPOON'S EUROPEAN VACATION
   Warner Bros., 1985, CP
THE FLY   20th Century Fox, 1986
MOVING   Warner Bros., 1988
THE FLY II   20th Century Fox, 1989, EP
HIDER IN THE HOUSE   Vestron, 1989,
   CP w/Lem Dobbs

ROBERT W. CORT
(credit w/Ted Field)
Business: Interscope Communications, 10900 Wilshire Blvd.,
   Suite 1400, Los Angeles, CA 90024, 310/208-8525;
   Fax: 310/208-1764

TURK 182   20th Century Fox, 1985,
   EP w/Peter Samuelson*
REVENGE OF THE NERDS II   20th Century Fox, 1987,
   w/Peter Bart
OUTRAGEOUS FORTUNE   Buena Vista, 1987
THREE MEN AND A BABY   Buena Vista, 1987
CRITICAL CONDITION   Paramount, 1987
COLLISION COURSE   DEG, 1988
THE SEVENTH SIGN   TriStar, 1988
COCKTAIL   Buena Vista, 1988
BILL & TED'S EXCELLENT ADVENTURE   Orion, 1989,
   EP w/Stephen Deutsch
RENEGADES   Universal, 1989, EP w/James G. Robinson
   & Joe Roth
AN INNOCENT MAN   Buena Vista, 1989
BLIND FURY   TriStar, 1990, EP w/David Madden*
THE FIRST POWER   Orion, 1990, w/Melinda Jason
BIRD ON A WIRE   Universal, 1990, EP
ARACHNOPHOBIA   Buena Vista, 1990, EP w/Frank
   Marshall & Steven Spielberg
THREE MEN AND A LITTLE LADY   Buena Vista, 1990
EVE OF DESTRUCTION   Orion, 1991, EP w/Rick
   Finkelstein, Graham Henderson & Melinda Jason*
CLASS ACTION   20th Century Fox, 1991, w/Scott Kroopf
BILL & TED'S BOGUS JOURNEY   Orion, 1991,
   EP w/Rick Finkelstein
PARADISE   Buena Vista, 1991, EP
WELCOME TO BUZZSAW   Universal, 1992,
   w/Michael Hertzberg
THE HAND THAT ROCKS THE CRADLE   Buena Vista,
   1992, EP w/Rick Jaffa
THE CUTTING EDGE   MGM, 1992, w/Karen Murphy &
   Dean O'Brien

ROBERT CORTES
(credit w/Edward Lewis)

CRACKERS   Universal, 1984
THE RIVER   Universal, 1984

FRANCESCO CORTI
THE URANIUM CONSPIRACY   Noah Films, 1978,
   w/Yoram Globus

SHERRILL C. CORWIN
VIVA KNIEVEL!   Warner Bros., 1977, EP

BILL COSBY
Business: SAH Enterprises, Inc., 205 Hill St., Santa Monica,
   CA 90405, 310/457-8023
Agent: William Morris Agency - Beverly Hills, 310/274-7451

MAN & BOY   Levitt-Pickman, 1972, EP
LEONARD PART 6   Columbia, 1987

DAC COSCARELLI
Business: Stairway International, 15445 Ventura Blvd.,
   Suite 10, Sherman Oaks, CA 91413, 818/784-8822

JIM - THE WORLD'S GREATEST   Universal, 1976,
   EP w/S.T. Coscarelli
PHANTASM II   Universal, 1988, EP
SURVIVAL QUEST   MGM/UA, 1990, EP

Cr

FILM
PRODUCERS,
STUDIOS,
AGENTS AND
CASTING
DIRECTORS
GUIDE

F
I
L
M

P
R
O
D
U
C
E
R
S

DON COSCARELLI
Business: Stairway International, 15445 Ventura Blvd.,
   Suite 10, Sherman Oaks, CA 91413, 818/784-8822

KENNY AND COMPANY   20th Century Fox, 1976
JIM - THE WORLD'S GREATEST   Universal, 1976
PHANTASM   Avco Embassy, 1979

S. T. COSCARELLI
Business: Stairway International, 15445 Ventura Blvd.,
   Suite 10, Sherman Oaks, CA 91413, 818/784-8822

JIM - THE WORLD'S GREATEST   Universal, 1976,
   EP w/Dac Coscarelli

KEVIN COSTNER
Business: Tig Productions, 4000 Warner Blvd., Burbank,
   CA 91522, 818/954-4500; Fax: 818/954-4882
Agent: CAA - Beverly Hills, 310/288-4545

REVENGE   Columbia, 1990, EP
DANCES WITH WOLVES ★★   Orion, 1990, w/Jim Wilson

MARIO COTONE
EVERYBODY'S FINE   Miramax, 1990, EP
THE COMFORT OF STRANGERS   Skouras, 1990, EP

GRAHAM COTTLE
Contact: Directors Guild of America - Los Angeles,
   213/289-2000

TRIPLE ECHO   Altura, 1973
UNDER THE CHERRY MOON   Warner Bros., 1986, AP
MIRACLE MILE   Hemdale, 1989, CP
TEENAGE MUTANT NINJA TURTLES   New Line,
   1990, CP

PIERRE COTTRELL
MY NIGHT AT MAUD'S   Pathe, 1970,
   w/Barbet Schroeder

JACK COUFFER
Agent: ICM - Los Angeles, 310/550-4000
Contact: Directors Guild of America - Los Angeles,
   213/289-2000

NEVER CRY WOLF   Buena Vista, 1983, w/Lewis Allen &
   Joseph Strick

JEROME COURTLAND
Agent: Sanford-Skouras-Gross - Los Angeles,
   310/208-2100
Contact: Directors Guild of America - Los Angeles,
   213/289-2000

ESCAPE TO WITCH MOUNTAIN   Buena Vista, 1975
RIDE A WILD PONY   Buena Vista, 1975
PETE'S DRAGON   Buena Vista, 1977, w/Ron Miller
RETURN FROM WITCH MOUNTAIN   Buena Vista,
   1978, w/Ron Miller
THE DEVIL AND MAX DEVLIN   Buena Vista, 1981
AMY   Buena Vista, 1981

JAMES A. COURTNEY
MOONTRAP   Shapiro-Glickenhaus Entertainment, 1989,
   EP w/Brian C. Manoogian & Alan M. Solomon

BILL COUTURIÉ
Agent: CAA - Beverly Hills, 310/288-4545

TWICE UPON A TIME (AF)   Warner Bros., 1983
DEAR AMERICA (FD)   Corsair, 1988, w/Thomas Bird

PAUL COWAN
ANOTHER TIME, ANOTHER PLACE   Samuel Goldwyn
   Company, 1984, AP
DANCE WITH A STRANGER   Samuel Goldwyn Company,
   1985, AP
RIDERS OF THE STORM   *THE AMERICAN WAY*
   Miramax, 1987, w/Laurie Keller
WE THINK THE WORLD OF YOU   Cinecom,
   1989, CP
THE KRAYS   Miramax, 1990, AP

ROB COWAN
SHORT TIME   20th Century Fox, 1990, CP

BRIAN COX
Business: Distant Horizon, 52 Crescent Ave., St. George,
   Staten Island, NY 10301, 718/816-6732;
   5-6 Portman Mews South, London W1H 9AU,
   071/493-1625; Fax: 071/493-3429

TERMINAL BLISS   Distant Horizon, 1990

PENNEY FINKELMAN COX
Contact: Directors Guild of America - Los Angeles,
   213/289-2000

TERMS OF ENDEARMENT   Paramount, 1983,
   CP w/Martin Jurow
BROADCAST NEWS   20th Century Fox, 1987, CP
HONEY, I SHRUNK THE KIDS   Buena Vista, 1989
WELCOME HOME, ROXY CARMICHAEL
   Paramount, 1990

RONNY COX
RAW COURAGE   *COURAGE*   New World, 1984,
   w/Robert L. Rosen

MALCOLM CRADDOCK
Business: Picture Palace Productions, 65-71 Beak Street,
   London W1R 3LF England, 071/439-9882;
   Fax: 071/734-8574

PING PONG   Samuel Goldwyn Company, 1987,
   w/Michael Guest

CARL CRAIG
HOLLYWOOD SHUFFLE   Samuel Goldwyn Company,
   1987, EP
I'M GONNA GIT YOU SUCKA   MGM/UA, 1989,
   w/Peter McCarthy

STUART CRAIG
CAL   Warner Bros., 1984, w/David Puttnam

JOE CRAMER
THE TRIAL OF BILLY JACK   Taylor-Laughlin, 1974

JENNY CRAVEN
ORDEAL BY INNOCENCE   Cannon, 1985

FILM
PRODUCERS,
STUDIOS,
AGENTS AND
CASTING
DIRECTORS
GUIDE

WES CRAVEN

Business: Wes Craven Films, 10000 W. Washington Blvd.,
Suite 3016, Culver City, CA 90232, 310/280-6033;
Fax: 310/558-5964
Agent: ICM - Los Angeles, 310/550-4000

TOGETHER (FD)   Hallmark, 1971, AP
A NIGHTMARE ON ELM STREET 3: DREAM WARRIORS
New Line, 1987, EP w/Stephen Diener
SHOCKER   Universal, 1989, EP w/Shep Gordon

ROBERT L. CRAWFORD

Business: Pan Arts Productions, 4000 Warner Blvd.,
Burbank, CA 91522, 818/954-3631

THE STING   Universal, 1973, AP
THE GREAT WALDO PEPPER   Universal, 1975, AP
SLAP SHOT   Universal, 1977, AP
A LITTLE ROMANCE   Orion/Warner Bros., 1979,
w/Yves Rousset-Rouard
THE WORLD ACCORDING TO GARP   Warner Bros.,
1982, w/George Roy Hill
THE LITTLE DRUMMER GIRL   Warner Bros., 1984
DEADLY FRIEND   Warner Bros., 1986, CP
FUNNY FARM   Warner Bros., 1988

WAYNE CRAWFORD
(credit w/Andrew Lane)

Business: Gibraltar Entertainment, 14101 Valleyheart Dr.,
Suite 205, Sherman Oaks, CA 91423, 818/501-2076;
Fax: 818/501-5138
Agent: The Richland-Wunsch-Hohman Agency -
Los Angeles, 310/278-1955

GOD'S BLOODY ACRE   Omni, 1975
CHEERING SECTION   Dimension, 1977
TOMCATS   Dimension, 1977
BARRACUDA   Republic, 1979, w/Harry Kerwin
VALLEY GIRL   Atlantic, 1983
NIGHT OF THE COMET   Atlantic, 1984
JAKE SPEED   New World, 1986, w/William Fay
MORTAL PASSIONS   MGM/UA, 1990, EP w/Joel Levine
THE SERVANTS OF TWILIGHT   Trimark, 1991,
EP w/Joel Levine & Mark Amin

JAMES CRESSON
(credit w/Robert Fryer)

Agent: William Morris Agency - Beverly Hills, 310/274-7451

TRAVELS WITH MY AUNT   MGM, 1972, w/George Cukor
THE ABDICATION   Warner Bros., 1974
MAME   Warner Bros., 1974

FRANCO CRISTALDI

Business: Cristaldi Film, Via Mangili, 5, 00100 Rome, Italy,
321-5010; Fax: 322-1036

IN THE NAME OF THE FATHER   Vides, 1971
THE RED TENT   Paramount, 1971
LADY CAROLINE LAMB   United Artists, 1973, EP
THE MATTEI AFFAIR   Paramount, 1973
RE: LUCKY LUCIANO   Avco Embassy, 1974
AMARCORD   New World, 1974
WIFEMISTRESS   Quartet Films, 1979
THE NAME OF THE ROSE   20th Century Fox, 1986, CP
w/Alexandre Mnouchkine
CINEMA PARADISO   Miramax, 1990

KEITH CRITCHLOW

THE CALIFORNIA REICH (FD)   Intercontinental, 1976,
w/Walter F. Parkes

GERARD CROCE

ONCE IN PARIS   Leigh-McLaughlin, 1978,
CP w/Manny Fuchs

AL C. CROFT

THE CRAZIES   *CODE NAME TRIXIE*   Cambist, 1973

DAVID CRONENBERG

Business: 217 Avenue Rd., Toronto, Ontario M5R 2J3,
Canada, 416/961-3432
Agent: CAA - Beverly Hills, 310/288-4545

DEAD RINGERS   20th Century Fox, 1988, w/Marc Boyman

ANTHONY SANTA CROSE
(see Anthony SANTA Crose)

BILLY CROSS

WEEDS   DEG, 1987, EP w/Mel Pearl

PAUL F. CROUCH

CHINA CRY   Penland, 1990

EMILIA CROW

AND GOD CREATED WOMAN   Vestron, 1988,
CP w/Robert Crow

ROBERT CROW

AND GOD CREATED WOMAN   Vestron, 1988,
CP w/Emilia Crow

CAMERON CROWE

Agent: William Morris Agency - Beverly Hills, 310/274-7451
Contact: Writers Guild of America - Los Angeles,
310/550-1000

THE WILD LIFE   Universal, 1984, w/Art Linson
SINGLES   Warner Bros., 1991, w/Richard Hashimoto

MART CROWLEY

Agent: ICM - Los Angeles, 310/550-4000
Contact: Writers Guild of America - Los Angeles,
310/550-1000

THE BOYS IN THE BAND   National General, 1970

PATRICK CROWLEY

Contact: Directors Guild of America - Los Angeles,
213/289-2000

TRUE BELIEVER   Columbia, 1989, CP
ROBOCOP 2   Orion, 1990, EP
ROBOCOP 3   Orion, 1991

ALFRED W. CROWN

LAST SUMMER   Allied Artists, 1969, w/Sidney Beckerman
TAKING OFF   Universal, 1971

JIM CRUICKSHANK

Contact: Orr & Cruickshank Productions, 500 S. Buena Vista
St., Animation 2G-11, Burbank, CA 91521, 818/560-6423;
Fax: 818/566-7310

MR. DESTINY   Buena Vista, 1990, w/James Orr
FATHER OF THE BRIDE   Buena Vista 1991, EP w/Sandy
Gallin & James Orr

Cu

FILM
PRODUCERS,
STUDIOS,
AGENTS and
CASTING
DIRECTORS
GUIDE

F
I
L
M

P
R
O
D
U
C
E
R
S

OWEN CRUMP
Contact: Directors Guild of America - Los Angeles,
213/289-2000

DARLING LILI   Paramount, 1970, EP

BILLY CRYSTAL
Agent: ICM - Los Angeles, 310/550-4000

MEMORIES OF ME   MGM/UA, 1988, w/Michael
   Hertzberg & Alan King
CITY SLICKERS   Columbia, 1991, EP

JAMES V. CULLEN
THE DEVIL'S RAIN   Bryanston, 1975,
   w/Michael S. Glick

GREGORY M. CUMMINS
PATTI ROCKS   FilmDallas, 1988, w/Gwen Field

GENE CUNNINGHAM
FORBIDDEN ZONE   Samuel Goldwyn Company,
   1980, EP

JERE CUNNINGHAM
Agent: CAA - Beverly Hills, 310/288-4545
Contact: Writers Guild of America - Los Angeles,
   310/550-1000

THE LAST OF THE FINEST   Orion, 1990, EP

SEAN S. CUNNINGHAM
Agent: ICM - Los Angeles, 310/550-4000
Contact: Directors Guild of America - Los Angeles,
   213/289-2000

TOGETHER (FD)   Hallmark, 1971, w/Roger Murphy
LAST HOUSE ON THE LEFT   Hallmark Releasing
   Corporation, 1972
HERE COME THE TIGERS   AIP, 1978,
   w/Stephen Miner
FRIDAY THE 13TH   Paramount, 1980
SPRING BREAK   Columbia, 1983
THE NEW KIDS   Columbia, 1985, w/Andrew Fogelson
HOUSE   New World, 1986
HOUSE II: THE SECOND STORY   New World, 1987
THE HORROR SHOW   MGM/UA, 1989
DEEPSTAR SIX   TriStar, 1989, w/Patrick Markey

CAROLE CURB
Business: Curb-Musifilm, 3907 W. Alameda Ave.,
   Burbank, CA 91505, 818/843-2872

TWENTY-ONE   Triton, 1991, EP w/Mike Curb &
   Lester Korn
NO SECRETS   I.R.S., 1991, EP w/David Jackson

MIKE CURB
Business: Curb-Musifilm, 3907 W. Alameda Ave.,
   Burbank, CA 91505, 818/843-2872

CYCLE SAVAGES   Trans American, 1970,
   EP w/Casey Kasem
BODY SLAM   DEG, 1987, w/Shel Lytton
TWENTY-ONE   Triton, 1991, EP w/Carole Curb &
   Lester Korn

BILL CURBISHLEY
Contact: Castle-Target - England, 081/877-3331;
   Los Angeles, 213/576-7043

THE KIDS ARE ALRIGHT (FD)   New World, 1979,
   w/Tony Klinger
QUADROPHENIA   World Northal, 1979, w/Roy Baird
McVICAR   Crown International, 1982, w/Roy Baird &
   Roger Daltrey

JOHN S. CURRAN
Contact: Smart Egg Pictures, 8733 Sunset Blvd., Suite 200,
   Los Angeles, CA 90069, 310/659-1801;
   Fax: 310/659-1739

DOUBLE REVENGE   Smart Egg Releasing, 1988,
   w/T.J. Castronovo
CAMERON'S CLOSET   SVS Films, 1989, LP
SPACED INVADERS   Buena Vista, 1990, LP

BRUCE COHN CURTIS
LONG AGO, TOMORROW   *THE RAGING MOON*
   Cinema 5, 1971
JOYRIDE   AIP, 1977
CHATTERBOX   AIP, 1977
ROLLER BOOGIE   United Artists, 1979
HELL NIGHT   Aquarius, 1981, w/Irwin Yablans
THE SEDUCTION   Avco Embassy, 1982, w/Irwin Yablans
DREAMSCAPE   20th Century Fox, 1984
FEAR CITY   Zupnik-Curtis Enterprises, 1985

DAN CURTIS
Business: Dan Curtis Productions Inc., 10000 W. Washington
   Blvd., Suite 3014, Culver City, CA 90232, 310/280-6567;
   Fax: 310/836-1680
Business Manager: Michael Rutman, Breslauer, Jacobson &
   Rutman, 10880 Wilshire Blvd., Los Angeles, CA 90024,
   310/553-1707

HOUSE OF DARK SHADOWS   MGM, 1970
NIGHT OF DARK SHADOWS   MGM, 1971
BURNT OFFERINGS   United Artists, 1976

DOUGLAS CURTIS
THE HAZING   Miraleste, 1978, w/Bruce Shelly
THE PHILADELPHIA EXPERIMENT   New World, 1984,
   w/Joel B. Michaels
BLACK MOON RISING   New World, 1986,
   w/Joel B. Michaels
NICE GIRLS DON'T EXPLODE   New World, 1987,
   w/John Wells
THE SLEEPING CAR   Vidmark, 1990

PATRICK CURTIS
HANNIE CAULDER   Paramount, 1972

TOM CURTIS
DREAMSCAPE   20th Century Fox, 1984,
   EP w/Stanley R. Zupnik

JOHN H. CUSHINGHAM
THE EXTRAORDINARY SEAMAN   MGM, 1968, CP
QUACKSER FORTUNE HAS A COUSIN IN THE BRONX
   UMC, 1970, w/Mel Howard
WELCOME TO ARROW BEACH   Warner Bros., 1974,
   w/Steven North

Cu

FILM
PRODUCERS,
STUDIOS,
AGENTS AND
CASTING
DIRECTORS
GUIDE

F
I
L
M

P
R
O
D
U
C
E
R
S

JOSEPH CUSUMANO
THE COTTON CLUB   Orion, 1984,
   LP w/Barrie M. Osborne

JOHN CUTTS
THE LAST AMERICAN HERO   *HARD DRIVER*   20th
   Century Fox, 1973, w/William Roberts
GOIN' COCONUTS   Osmond, 1978

CATHERINE CYRAN
SLUMBER PARTY MASSACRE 3   Concorde, 1990
KISS ME A KILLER   Califilm, 1991
ULTRAVIOLET   Concorde, 1991

JIM CZARNECKI
WITHOUT YOU I'M NOTHING   MCEG, 1990, LP

D

BOUDJEMAA DAHMANE
THE LAST BUTTERFLY   1991, EP w/Jacques Methe,
   Patrick Dromgoole

ROBERT DALEY
Business: 1900 Avenue of the Stars, Suite 2270,
   Los Angeles, CA 90067, 310/277-1900
Contact: Directors Guild of America - Los Angeles,
   213/289-2000

DIRTY HARRY   Warner Bros., 1971, EP
PLAY MISTY FOR ME   Universal, 1971
JOE KIDD   Universal, 1972, EP
HIGH PLAINS DRIFTER   Universal, 1973
BREEZY   Universal, 1973
MAGNUM FORCE   Warner Bros., 1973
THUNDERBOLT & LIGHTFOOT   United Artists, 1974
THE EIGER SANCTION   Universal, 1975
THE OUTLAW JOSEY WALES   Warner Bros., 1976
THE ENFORCER   Warner Bros., 1976
THE GAUNTLET   Warner Bros., 1977
EVERY WHICH WAY BUT LOOSE   Warner
   Bros., 1978
ESCAPE FROM ALCATRAZ   Paramount, 1979, EP
BRONCO BILLY   Warner Bros., 1980, EP
ANY WHICH WAY YOU CAN   Warner Bros.,
   1980, EP
STICK   Universal, 1985, EP w/William Gordean
REAL GENIUS   TriStar, 1985, EP

KEN DALTON
HARDBODIES   Columbia, 1984, w/Jeff Begun

RICHARD DALTON
JESUS   Warner Bros., 1979, CP
MARTIN'S DAY   MGM/UA, 1985, w/Roy Krost

ROBIN DALTON
MADAME SOUSATZKA   Cineplex Odeon, 1988

ROGER DALTREY
Agent: The Lantz Office - New York, 212/586-0200
Contact: Castle-Target - England, 081/877-3331;
   Los Angeles, 213/576-7043

QUADROPHENIA   World Northal, 1979, EP w/John
   Entwistle, Keith Moon & Pete Townshend
McVICAR   Crown International, 1982, w/Roy Baird &
   Bill Curbishley

JOHN DALY
(credit w/Derek Gibson)
Business: Hemdale Film Corporation, 7966 Beverly Blvd.,
   Los Angeles, CA 90048, 213/966-3700; Fax: 213/651-3107;
   21 Albion Street, London W2 2AS England, 071/724-1010;
   Fax: 071/724-9168

VALLEY OF BLOOD   Mica, 1973*
THE PASSAGE   United Artists, 1979,
   EP w/Derek Dawson*
SUNBURN   Paramount, 1979, w/Gerald Green*
CARBON COPY   Avco Embassy, 1981, EP*
CATTLE ANNIE & LITTLE BRITCHES   Universal,
   1981, EP
STRANGE BEHAVIOR   World Northal, 1981, EP w/William
   Fayman & David Hemmings
GOING APE!   Paramount, 1981, EP*
HIGH RISK   American Cinema, 1981, EP*
YELLOWBEARD   Orion, 1983, EP*
DEADLY FORCE   Embassy, 1983, EP*
A BREED APART   Orion, 1984
THE TERMINATOR   Orion, 1984, EP
RETURN OF THE LIVING DEAD   Orion, 1985, EP
THE FALCON & THE SNOWMAN   Orion, 1985, EP*
AT CLOSE RANGE   Orion, 1986, EP
SALVADOR   Hemdale, 1986, EP
HOOSIERS   Orion, 1986, EP
PLATOON ★★   Orion, 1986, EP
RIVER'S EDGE   Island Pictures, 1987, EP
BEST SELLER   Orion, 1987, EP
BUSTER   Hemdale, 1988, EP
THE BOOST   Hemdale, 1988, EP
MADE IN U.S.A.   TriStar, 1988, EP
LOVE AT STAKE   TriStar, 1988, EP
SHAG: THE MOVIE   Hemdale, 1989, EP w/Nik Powell
MIRACLE MILE   Hemdale, 1989
CRIMINAL LAW   Hemdale, 1989, EP
WAR PARTY   Hemdale, 1989, w/Bernard Williams
VAMPIRE'S KISS   Hemdale, 1989, EP
OUT COLD   Hemdale, 1989, EP
STAYING TOGETHER   Hemdale, 1989, EP
DON'T TELL HER IT'S ME   Hemdale, 1990, EP
HIDDEN AGENDA   Hemdale, 1990, EP

MARK DAMON
Business: Vision International, 3330 W. Cahuenga Blvd.,
   Suite 500, Los Angeles, CA 90068, 213/969-2900;
   Fax: 213/851-7212

THE ARENA   New World, 1974
THE CHOIRBOYS   Universal, 1977, EP w/Mario Bregui &
   Pietro Bregui
DAS BOOT   Columbia, 1982, EP w/John Hyde &
   Edward R. Pressman
THE NEVERENDING STORY   Warner Bros., 1984,
   EP w/John Hyde
FLIGHT OF THE NAVIGATOR   Buena Vista, 1986,
   EP w/Malcolm R. Harding, John Hyde & Jonathan Sanger
THE CLAN OF THE CAVE BEAR   Warner Bros., 1986, EP
   w/Peter Guber, John Hyde, Sidney Kimmel & Jon Peters

SHORT CIRCUIT   TriStar, 1986, EP w/John Hyde
THE LOST BOYS   Warner Bros., 1987, EP w/Richard
   Donner & John Hyde
BAT 21   TriStar, 1988, CP w/David Saunders
HIGH SPIRITS   TriStar, 1988, EP w/Moshe Diamant &
   Eduard Sarlui
MAC & ME   Orion, 1988, EP w/William B. Kerr
WILD ORCHID   Triumph Releasing, 1990,
   w/Tony Anthony
I COME IN PEACE   Triumph, 1990,
   EP w/David Saunders

GEORGES DANCIGERS
(credit w/Alexandre Mnouchkine)

THAT MAN FROM RIO   Lopert, 1964
LOVE IS A FUNNY THING   United Artists, 1970
STAVISKY   Cinemation, 1974, EP
TOUCH AND GO   Libra, 1975
A PAIN IN THE A...   Corwin-Mahler, 1975
ANOTHER MAN, ANOTHER CHANCE
   United Artists, 1977
DEAR DETECTIVE   *DEAR INSPECTOR*
   Cinema 5, 1978
JUPITER'S THIGH   Quartet, 1981
LA BALANCE   Spectrafilm, 1983

JAY DANIEL
Agent: William Morris Agency - Beverly Hills, 310/274-7451
Contact: Directors Guild of America - Los Angeles,
   213/289-2000

CLEAN AND SOBER   Warner Bros., 1987, CP

JEFF DANNENBAUM
(credit w/Kathleen Dowdey)
Business: Five Point Films, Inc., 915 Highland View N.E.,
   Suite B, Atlanta, GA 30306, 404/875-6076

BLUE HEAVEN   Vestron/Shapiro Entertainment,
   1985, EP

HELMUT DANTINE
BRING ME THE HEAD OF ALFREDO GARCIA   United
   Artists, 1974, EP
THE WILBY CONSPIRACY   United Artists, 1975, EP
THE KILLER ELITE   United Artists, 1975, EP

PHILIP D'ANTONI
Contact: D'Antoni Productions Group, c/o Viacom,
   1515 Broadway, 40th Floor, New York, NY 10036,
   212/258-7190; Fax: 212/258-7130

BULLITT   Warner Bros., 1968
THE FRENCH CONNECTION ★★   20th Century
   Fox, 1971
THE SEVEN-UPS   20th Century Fox, 1973

JOHN DARK
HALF A SIXPENCE   Paramount, 1967, EP
THERE'S A GIRL IN MY SOUP   Columbia, 1970, EP
THE BEAST MUST DIE   Cinerama, 1974. AP
I, MONSTER   Cannon, 1974, AP
THE LAND THAT TIME FORGOT   AIP, 1975
AT THE EARTH'S CORE   AIP, 1976
WARLORDS OF ATLANTIS   Columbia, 1978
MADHOUSE   AIP, 1974, AP
SLAYGROUND   Universal, 1984, w/Gower Frost
SHIRLEY VALENTINE   Paramount, 1989, EP

STEPHEN DART
THE HANOI HILTON   Cannon, 1987, EP

JULIE DASH
DAUGHTERS OF THE DUST   American Playhouse
   Theatrical Films, 1991

DAVID DASHEV
Agent: The Gersh Agency - Beverly Hills, 310/274-6611

THE FISH THAT SAVED PITTSBURGH   United Artists,
   1979, w/Gary Stromberg

ANATOLE DAUMAN
WINGS OF DESIRE   Orion Classics, 1988,
   w/Wim Wenders

PASCALE DAUMAN
THE COOK, THE THIEF, HIS WIFE & HER LOVER
   Miramax, 1990, CP w/Daniel Toscan duPlantier &
   Denis Wigman

BRUCE DAVEY
Contact: Icon Productions, 4000 Warner Blvd., Burbank, CA
   91522, 818/954-2960; Fax: 818/954-4212

HAMLET   Warner Bros., 1990, EP

PIERRE DAVID
Business: The Image Organization, 9000 Sunset Blvd.,
   Suite 915, Los Angeles, CA 90069, 310/278-8751,
   Fax: 213/278-3967; 1207 St. Andre St., Montreal, Quebec
   H2L 3S8, 514/844-4555, Fax: 514/844-1471

THE BROOD   New World, 1979, EP w/Victor Solnicki
HOG WILD   Avco Embassy, 1980, EP w/Victor Solnicki &
   Stephen Miller
SCANNERS   Avco Embassy, 1981, EP w/Victor Solnicki
DIRTY TRICKS   Avco Embassy, 1981, EP w/Arnold
   Kopelson & Victor Solnicki
GAS   Paramount, 1981, EP w/Victor Solnicki
VISITING HOURS   20th Century Fox, 1982,
   EP w/Victor Solnicki
VIDEODROME   Universal, 1983, EP w/Victor Solnicki
THE FUNNY FARM   New World, 1983, EP
GOING BERSERK   Universal, 1983, EP
OF UNKNOWN ORIGIN   Warner Bros., 1983, EP
COVERGIRL   New World, 1984, EP w/Victor Solnicki
QUIET COOL   New Line, 1986, EP w/Arthur Sarkissian &
   Larry Thompson
HOT PURSUIT   Paramount, 1987, w/Theodore R. Parvin
MY DEMON LOVER   New Line, 1987,
   EP w/Larry Thompson
INTERNAL AFFAIRS   Paramount, 1990, EP w/René Malo
   & David Streit
THE PERFECT WEAPON   Paramount, 1991,
   w/Mark DiSalle
TWIN SISTERS   Image, 1991, EP w/Andre Koob
MARTIAL LAW UNDERCOVER   Image, 1991,
   EP w/Robert W. Mann

SAUL DAVID
Contact: Writers Guild of America - Los Angeles,
   310/550-1000

VON RYAN'S EXPRESS   20th Century Fox, 1965
OUR MAN FLINT   20th Century Fox, 1966
FANTASTIC VOYAGE   20th Century Fox, 1966
IN LIKE FLINT   20th Century Fox, 1967

Da

**FILM
PRODUCERS,
STUDIOS,
AGENTS AND
CASTING
DIRECTORS
GUIDE**

F
I
L
M

P
R
O
D
U
C
E
R
S

Da

FILM
PRODUCERS,
STUDIOS,
AGENTS AND
CASTING
DIRECTORS
GUIDE

F
I
L
M

P
R
O
D
U
C
E
R
S

SKULLDUGGERY   Universal, 1970
LOGAN'S RUN   MGM/UA, 1976
RAVAGERS   Columbia, 1979, EP

GORDON DAVIDSON
Business: Mark Taper Forum, 135 N. Grand Ave.,
    Los Angeles, CA 90012, 213/972-7353
Agent: William Morris Agency - Beverly Hills,
    310/274-7451

ZOOT SUIT   Universal, 1982, EP

JAY DAVIDSON
HEADHUNTER   Academy Entertainment, 1989

MARTIN DAVIDSON
Agent: Harris & Goldberg - Los Angeles, 310/553-5200
Contact: Directors Guild of America - Los Angeles,
    213/289-2000

HEART OF DIXIE   Orion, 1989, EP

WILLIAM DAVIDSON
THE SHAPE OF THINGS TO COME   Film
    Ventures, 1979

ANDREW DAVIS
Attorney: Peter Dekom, Bloom & Dekom, 9255 Sunset
    Blvd., Los Angeles, CA 90069, 310/278-8622
Agent: The Agency - Los Angeles, 310/551-3000

STONY ISLAND   World Northal, 1980,
    w/Tamar Simon Hoffs
ABOVE THE LAW   Warner Bros., 1988,
    w/Steven Seagal
THE PACKAGE   Orion, 1989, CP w/Dennis Haggerty

ANDREW Z. DAVIS
Contact: Walt Disney Studios, 5000 S. Buena Vista St.,
    Burbank, CA 91521, 818/972-3562

LOST ANGELS   Orion, 1989, LP

CARLOS DAVIS
DROP DEAD FRED   New Line, 1991, EP w/Tim
    Bevan & Anthony Fingleton

JOHN A. DAVIS
Business: Davis Entertainment, 2121 Avenue of the Stars,
    Suite 2900, Los Angeles, CA 90067, 310/556-3550;
    Fax: 310/556-3760

PREDATOR   20th Century Fox, 1987, w/Lawrence
    Gordon & Joel Silver
THREE O'CLOCK HIGH   Universal, 1987,
    CP w/Neil Israel
TAFFIN   MGM/UA, 1988, AP
LICENSE TO DRIVE   20th Century Fox, 1988, EP
LITTLE MONSTERS   United Artists, 1989, w/Andrew
    Licht & Jeffrey Mueller
THE LAST OF THE FINEST   Orion, 1990
ENID IS SLEEPING   Vestron, 1990, w/Howard Malin
STORYVILLE   20th Century Fox, 1991,
    EP w/John Flock

PETER S. DAVIS
(credit w/William N. Panzer)
Business: Davis-Panzer Productions, 1754 N. Serrano,
    Suite 401, Hollywood, CA 90027, 213/463-2343;
    Fax: 213/465-0948

DEATH COLLECTOR   Epoh, 1976, EP*
STUNTS   New Line, 1977, EP w/Robert Shaye*
FAMILY ENFORCER   First American, 1978, EP*
STEEL   World Northal, 1980
ST. HELENS   Parnell, 1981, AP
THE OSTERMAN WEEKEND   20th Century Fox, 1983
O'HARA'S WIFE   Enfield, 1984
HIGHLANDER   20th Century Fox, 1986
FREEWAY   New World, 1988

RANDALL DAVIS
JULIA HAS TWO LOVERS   South Gate Entertainment,
    1991, EP w/C.H. Lehenhof

RICHARD DAVIS
PHAR LAP   20th Century Fox, 1984, EP
CADENCE   New Line, 1991

W. TERRY DAVIS
H.O.T.S.   Derio, 1979, w/Don Schain

JON DAVISON
Business: Davison/Doel, 10202 W. Washington Blvd., Culver
    City, CA 90232, 310/280-7888; Fax: 310/280-1574

BIG BAD MAMA   New World, 1974, AP
HOLLYWOOD BOULEVARD   New World, 1977
GRAND THEFT AUTO   New World, 1977
PIRANHA   New World, 1978
AIRPLANE!   Paramount, 1980
WHITE DOG   *TRAINED TO KILL*   Paramount, 1982
TWILIGHT ZONE - THE MOVIE   Warner Bros.,
    1983, AP
TOP SECRET!   Paramount, 1984, w/Hunt Lowry
ROBOCOP   Orion, 1987, EP
ROBOCOP 2   Orion, 1990

DEREK DAWSON
THE PASSAGE   United Artists, 1979, EP w/John Daly

KIM DAWSON
(credit w/David Chan)

TEENAGE MUTANT NINJA TURTLES   New Line Cinema,
    1990, w/Simon Fields
TEENAGE MUTANT NINJA TURTLES II: THE SECRET OF
    THE OOZE   New Line, 1991, w/Thomas K. Gray

RAYMOND DAY
KNIGHTS & EMERALDS   Warner Bros., 1986,
    w/Susan Richards
SINGING THE BLUES IN RED   Angelika, 1988

JONATHAN DAYTON
THE DECLINE OF WESTERN CIVILIZATION PART II: THE
    METAL YEARS (FD)   New Line, 1988, w/Valerie Faris

JOEL DEAN
SUMMER LOVERS   Filmways, 1982, EP

De

FILM
PRODUCERS,
STUDIOS,
AGENTS AND
CASTING
DIRECTORS
GUIDE

F
I
L
M

P
R
O
D
U
C
E
R
S

TERENCE F. DEANE

HOMER   National General, 1970, w/Steven North
I NEVER PROMISED YOU A ROSE GARDEN   New
   World, 1977, w/Michael Hausman & Daniel H. Blatt

WILLIAM DEAR

Agent: CAA - Beverly Hills, 310/288-4545
Contact: Directors Guild of America - Los Angeles,
   213/289-2000

THE NORTHVILLE CEMETERY MASSACRE   Cannon,
   1976, w/Thomas L. Dyke
HARRY AND THE HENDERSONS   Universal, 1987,
   w/Richard Vane

GERALD B. DEARING

CANDY MOUNTAIN   International Film Exchange,
   1988, EP

GEORGES DeBEAUREGARD

LA COLLECTIONNEUSE   Pathe, 1971,
   w/Barbet Schroeder
THE NUN   Altura, 1971

ALEX DeBENEDETTI

FIGHTING BACK   Paramount, 1982, CP w/David Lowe
PUMPKINHEAD   United Artists, 1988, EP

ALLEN DeBEVOISE

BREAKIN'   Cannon, 1984, w/David Zito

DAVID DeCOTEAU

TRANCERS II   1991, LP w/John Schouweiler

LISA DEDMOND

HENRY: PORTRAIT OF A SERIAL KILLER   Greycat
   Films, 1990, w/John McNaughton

MICHAEL DEELEY

Business: Consolidated Entertainment, 9000 Sunset Blvd.,
   Suite 415, Los Angeles, CA 90069, 310-275-5719

THE KNACK - AND HOW TO GET IT   United Artists,
   1965, AP
WHERE'S JACK?   Paramount, 1969, EP
MURPHY'S WAR   Paramount, 1971
CONDUCT UNBECOMING   Allied Artists, 1975,
   w/Barry Spikings
THE MAN WHO FELL TO EARTH   Cinema 5, 1976,
   w/Barry Spikings
CONVOY   United Artists, 1978, EP w/Barry Spikings
THE DEER HUNTER ★★   Universal, 1978, w/Michael
   Cimino, John Peverall & Barry Spikings
BLADE RUNNER   The Ladd Company/Warner
   Bros., 1982

WALT DeFARIA

COME TO YOUR SENSES   National General, 1971
THE MOUSE AND HIS CHILD (AF)   Sanrio, 1978

FRANK DeFELITTA

Agent: The Artists Agency - Los Angeles, 310/277-7779
Contact: Writers Guild of America - Los Angeles,
   310/550-1000

AUDREY ROSE   United Artists, 1977, w/Joe Wizan

BARBARA DeFINA

Business: Scorsese Productions, 1619 Broadway, New York,
   NY 10019, 212/603-0617
Agent: CAA - Beverly Hills, 310/288-4545

SPRING BREAK   Columbia, 1983, AP
THE NEW KIDS   Columbia, 1985, AP
THE COLOR OF MONEY   Buena Vista, 1986,
   w/Irving Axelrad
THE LAST TEMPTATION OF CHRIST   Universal, 1988
NEW YORK STORIES   "Life Lessons"   Buena Vista, 1989
GOOD FELLAS ★   Warner Bros., 1990, EP
THE GRIFTERS   Miramax, 1990, EP
CAPE FEAR   Universal, 1991

THIERRY DeGANAY

SOMEONE TO WATCH OVER ME   Columbia, 1987,
   w/Harold Schneider

DIMITRI DeGRUNWALD

THAT LUCKY TOUCH   Allied Artists, 1975

CARTER DeHAVEN

Attorney: Eric Weissmann, Weissmann, Wolff, 9655 Wilshire
   Blvd., Beverly Hills, CA 90212, 310/858-7888
Contact: Directors Guild of America - Los Angeles,
   213/289-2000

A WALK WITH LOVE AND DEATH   20th Century Fox, 1969
THE KREMLIN LETTER   20th Century Fox, 1970,
   w/Sam Wiesenthal
THE LAST RUN   MGM, 1971
ULZANA'S RAID   Universal, 1972
THE OUTFIT   MGM, 1973
OPERATION DAYBREAK   Warner Bros., 1975
SENIORS   Cinema Shares International, 1978,
   w/Stanley Shapiro
CARBON COPY   Avco Embassy, 1981, w/Stanley Shapiro
YELLOWBEARD   Orion, 1983
SCANDALOUS   Orion, 1984, EP
SPECIAL EFFECTS   New Line, 1984, EP
PERFECT STRANGERS   New Line, 1984
MAXIE   Orion, 1985
HOOSIERS   Orion, 1986, w/Angelo Pizzo
BEST SELLER   Orion, 1987
THE EXORCIST III   20th Century Fox, 1990

DONNA DEITCH

Business: Desert Heart Productions, 685 Venice Blvd.,
   Venice, CA 90291, 310/827-1515; Fax: 310/827-8717
Agent: Robinson, Weintraub, Gross - Los Angeles,
   213/653-5802

DESERT HEARTS   Samuel Goldwyn Company, 1986

RICHARD DeKOKER

JUGGERNAUT   United Artists, 1974

AURELIO DeLAURENTIIS
(credit w/Luigi De Laurentiis)
Business: De Laurentiis Ricordi Video, Via Berchet 2, 20121
   Milano, Italy, 02-8881

MACARONI   Paramount, 1985, w/Franco Committeri
LEVIATHAN   MGM/UA, 1989

FILM
PRODUCERS,
STUDIOS,
AGENTS AND
CASTING
DIRECTORS
GUIDE

F
I
L
M

P
R
O
D
U
C
E
R
S

DINO DeLAURENTIIS
Business: De Laurentiis Communications, 8670 Wilshire
Blvd., 3rd Floor, Beverly Hills, CA 90211, 310/289-6100

THE BIBLE   20th Century Fox, 1966
BARBARELLA   Paramount, 1968
WATERLOO   Paramount, 1971
A MAN CALLED SLEDGE   Columbia, 1971
THE VALACHI PAPERS   Columbia, 1972
MANDINGO   Paramount, 1975
THE SHOOTIST   Paramount, 1976, EP
DRUM   United Artists, 1976, EP
LIPSTICK   Paramount, 1976, EP
KING KONG   Paramount, 1976
THE SERPENT'S EGG   Paramount, 1977
HURRICANE   Paramount, 1979
FLASH GORDON   Universal, 1980
RAGTIME   Paramount, 1981
YEAR OF THE DRAGON   MGM/UA, 1985
THE DESPERATE HOURS   MGM/UA, 1990
RETURNING NAPOLEON   Universal, 1991

LUIGI DeLAURENTIIS
(credit w/Aurelio De Laurentiis)
Business: De Laurentiis Ricordi Video, Via Berchet 2,
20121 Milano, Italy, 02-8881

MACARONI   Paramount, 1985, w/Franco Committeri
LEVIATHAN   MGM/UA, 1989

RAFFAELLA DeLAURENTIIS
Business: Rafaella Productions, Universal Pictures, 100
Universal City Plaza, Bungalow 121-C, Universal City,
CA 91608, 818/777-2655; Fax: 818/777-7158

BEYOND THE REEF   Universal, 1981
CONAN THE BARBARIAN   Universal, 1982,
w/Buzz Feitshans
DUNE   Universal, 1984
CONAN THE DESTROYER   Universal, 1984
JAMES CLAVELL'S TAI-PAN   DEG, 1986
PRANCER   Orion, 1989
BACKDRAFT   Universal, 1991, EP w/Brian Grazer

ROBERT DeLAURENTIS
Agent: BBMW - Los Angeles, 310/247-5500

A LITTLE SEX   Universal, 1982, w/Bruce Paltrow

MARCUS DeLEON
BORDER RADIO   Coyote Films, 1987

WANDA DELL
Business: Dell Films, 1905 Powers Ferry Rd., Suite 260,
Atlanta, GA 30067, 404/955-6924

THEY WENT THAT-A-WAY AND THAT-A-WAY
International Picture Show, 1978, AP
THE PRIZE FIGHTER   New World, 1979, CP
THE PRIVATE EYES   New World, 1981,
w/Lang Elliott
MARVIN AND TIGE   *LIKE FATHER AND SON*   Fox
International Classics, 1985

MEL DELLAR
THE DESPERATE HOURS   MGM/UA, 1990, LP

RICHARD DeMARCO
Contact: 609/779-9111

TRUCKIN' BUDDY MCCOY   Bedford Entertainment, 1984,
w/Rick Blumenthal

LISA DEMBERG
Contact: NBC Entertainment, 3000 W. Alameda Blvd.,
Burbank, CA 91523, 818/840-4444

CATCHFIRE   1991, CP

BOB DEMCHUK
Business: Scene East Productions, Ltd., 153 Mercer St.,
New York, NY 10012, 212/226-6525
Contact: Directors Guild of America - New York,
212/581-0370

WHATEVER IT TAKES   Aquarius Films, 1986

FRANCOIS DeMENIL
GIZMO (FD)   New Line, 1977, EP

PAUL DeMEO
Agent: Robinson, Weintraub, Gross - Los Angeles,
213/653-5802

ZONE TROOPERS   Empire, 1986
THE WRONG GUYS   New World, 1988, CP

JONATHAN DEMME
Business: Clinica Estetico Ltd., 1600 Broadway, Suite 503,
New York, NY 10019, 212/262-2777
Agent: CAA - Beverly Hills, 310/288-4545

ANGELS HARD AS THEY COME   New World, 1971
SOMETHING WILD   Orion, 1986, w/Kenneth Utt
MIAMI BLUES   Orion, 1990, w/Gary Goetzman

EDWARD O. DeNAULT
Contact: Directors Guild of America - Los Angeles,
213/289-2000

THE LAST STARFIGHTER   Universal, 1984,
w/Gary Adelson

GIULIANI DeNEGRI
GOOD MORNING BABYLON   Vestron, 1987

ROBERT DeNIRO
Business: Tribeca Productions, 375 Greenwich St.,
New York, NY 10013, 212/941-4040
Agent: CAA - Beverly Hills, 310/288-4545

WE'RE NO ANGELS   Paramount, 1989, EP

ALLAN DENNIS
Contact: Directors Guild of America - New York,
212/581-0370

AFTER MIDNIGHT   MGM/UA, 1989, EP w/Barry J. Hirsch

JON S. DENNY
NOBODY'S FOOL   Island Pictures, 1986, w/James C. Katz
THE OBJECT OF BEAUTY   Avenue, 1991

De

FILM
PRODUCERS,
STUDIOS,
AGENTS AND
CASTING
DIRECTORS
GUIDE

F
I
L
M

P
R
O
D
U
C
E
R
S

PEN DENSHAM
(credit w/John Watson)
Business: Trilogy Entertainment Group, c/o Sony Studios,
10202 West Washington Blvd., Culver City, CA 90232,
310/204-3133; Fax: 310/204-1160
Agent: William Morris Agency - Beverly Hills,
310/274-7451

THE ZOO GANG   New World, 1985
THE KISS   TriStar, 1988
BACKDRAFT   Universal, 1991, w/Richard B. Lewis
ROBIN HOOD: PRINCE OF THIEVES   Warner Bros.,
1991, w/Richard B. Lewis

BRIAN DePALMA
Agent: UTA - Beverly Hills, 310/273-6700
Contact: Directors Guild of America - New York,
212/581-0370

DIONYSUS IN '69   Sigma III, 1970, w/Robert Fiore &
Bruce Joel Rubin
BODY DOUBLE   Columbia, 1984
THE BONFIRE OF THE VANITIES   Warner Bros., 1990

CYNTHIA DePAULA
ENEMY TERRITORY   Empire, 1987, w/Tim Kincaid
NECROPOLIS   Empire, 1987, w/Tim Kincaid
SHE'S BACK   Vestron, 1989

BO DEREK
Agent: CAA - Beverly Hills, 310/288-4545

TARZAN, THE APE MAN   MGM/UA, 1981
BOLERO   Cannon, 1984
GHOSTS CAN'T DO IT   Triumph, 1990

JULIAN DERODE
THE DAY OF THE JACKAL   Universal, 1973,
CP w/David Deutsch
JULIA ★   20th Century Fox, 1977, EP

CYRIL DeROUVRE
WAIT UNTIL SPRING, BANDINI   Orion, 1990,
EP w/Christian Charret, Amadeo Pagani &
Giorgio Silvago

ELON DERSHOWITZ
Business: Edward R. Pressman Film Corporation, 4000
Warner Blvd., Prod. 5, Room 114, Burbank, CA 91522,
818/954-3315

REVERSAL OF FORTUNE   Warner Bros., 1990,
CP w/Nicholas Kazan

NAVIN DESAI
Business: Continental Film Group, Ltd., 321 W. 44th St.,
Suite 405, New York, NY 10036, 212/265-2530;
Fax: 212/245-6275; Park St., Sharon, PA 16146,
412/981-3456; Fax: 412/981-2668

TIGER WARSAW   Sony Pictures, 1988, EP w/Gay
Mayer & Watson Warriner

DAVID DeSILVA
FAME   MGM/UA, 1980, w/Alan Marshall

IRA DEUTCHMAN
Business: Fine Line Features, c/o NYC New Line office

SWIMMING TO CAMBODIA   Cinecom, 1987, EP w/Lewis
Allen, Amir J. Malin & Peter Newman
MATEWAN   Cinecom, 1987, AP
SCENES FROM THE CLASS STRUGGLE IN BEVERLY
HILLS   Cinecom, 1989, EP w/Amir J. Malin
STRAIGHT OUT OF BROOKLYN   Samuel Goldwyn
Company, 1991, EP w/Lindsay Law

DAVID DEUTSCH
Agent: Petes, Fraser & Dunlop, 5th Floor, The Chambers,
Chelsea Harbour, Lots Road, London SW10 0XF England,
071/376-7676; Fax: 071/352-7356

A DAY IN THE DEATH OF JOE EGG   Columbia, 1972
THE DAY OF THE JACKAL   Universal, 1973,
CP w/Julien Derode

STEPHEN DEUTSCH
Business: De Laurentiis Communications, 8670 Wilshire
Blvd., 3rd Floor, Beverly Hills, CA 90211, 310/289-6100;
Fax: 310/855-0562

SOMEWHERE IN TIME   Universal, 1980
ALL THE RIGHT MOVES   20th Century Fox, 1983
RUSSKIES   New Century/Vista, 1987, EP w/Mort Engelberg
BILL & TED'S EXCELLENT ADVENTURE   Orion, 1989,
EP w/Robert W. Cort & Ted Field
SHE'S OUT OF CONTROL   WEG/Columbia, 1989

ROBERT DEVEREUX
(credit w/Al Clark)
Contact: Virgin Communications, 338 Ladbroke Grove,
London W10, 081/960-2255; Fax: 081/960-4890

1984   Atlantic, 1985, CP
ABSOLUTE BEGINNERS   Orion, 1986, EP w/Nik Powell
GOTHIC   Vestron, 1987, EP
ARIA   Miramax, 1988, CP w/Mike Watts

ZANNE DEVINE
Business: 100 Universal City Plaza, Universal City, CA
91608, 818/777-1000

ANNA   Vestron, 1987, w/Yurek Bogayevicz
PRISONERS OF INERTIA   North Winds Entertainment, 1989

MATT DEVLEN
Business: Boomerang Pictures - Los Angeles, 213/312-5850

OZONE   Muther Pictures, 1989
UNDERGROUND   Vista Street Entertainment, 1990
BODY PARTS   Raedon Entertainment, 1990,
w/Holly MacConkey
INVISIBLE MANIAC   Republic Pictures, 1990, w/Tony Markes
SOULMATES   Overseas Film Group, 1991
LOVE IS LIKE THAT   Boomerang Pictures, 1991,
w/Johnathan Reiss
MAD AT THE MOON   Boomerang Pictures, 1991,
w/Cassian Elwes, Michael Kastenbaum & Seth Kastenbaum

DON DEVLIN
PETULIA   Warner Bros./7 Arts, 1968, EP
LOVING   Columbia, 1970
THE FORTUNE   Columbia, 1975, w/Mike Nichols
HARRY & WALTER GO TO NEW YORK   Columbia, 1976,
w/Harry Gittes

MY BODYGUARD   20th Century Fox, 1980
THE WITCHES OF EASTWICK   Warner Bros., 1987,
EP w/Rob Cohen

GARY DeVORE
Agent: ICM - Los Angeles, 310/550-4000

TRAXX   DEG, 1988

LARRY DeWAAY
Business: Paramount Pictures, 5555 Melrose Ave.,
Los Angeles, CA 90038, 213/956-4824
Contact: Directors Guild of America - Los Angeles,
213/289-2000

YENTL   MGM/UA, 1983, EP
THE DOGS OF WAR   United Artists, 1981
ELECTRIC DREAMS   MGM/UA, 1984,
w/Rusty Lemorande
HAMBURGER HILL   Paramount, 1987, CP
NEXT OF KIN   Warner Bros., 1989, EP
THE HUNT FOR RED OCTOBER   Paramount, 1990,
EP w/Jerry Sherlock
BACKDRAFT   Universal, 1991, CP

CHRISTOPHER C. DEWEY
(credit w/Dennis Friedland)

JOE   Cannon, 1970, EP
MAID IN SWEDEN   Cannon, 1971, EP
LUPO   Cannon, 1971, EP
JUMP   Cannon, 1971*
WHO KILLED MARY WHAT'S 'ERNAME?   Cannon,
1971, EP*

MATTHIAS DEYLE
OUT OF ORDER   Sandstar Releasing, 1985,
w/Thomas Schuehly

MOSHE DIAMANT
Business: Epic Productions, Inc., 3330 W. Cahuenga Blvd.,
Suite 500, Los Angeles, CA 90068, 213/969-2800;
Fax: 213/969-8211

PRAY FOR DEATH   American Distribution Group, 1986,
EP w/Moshe Barkat & Sunil R. Shah
CATCH THE HEAT   Trans World, 1987,
EP w/Stirling Silliphant
THE CURSE   Trans World, 1987, EP
RAGE OF HONOR   Trans World, 1987, EP w/Moshe
Barkat & Sunil R. Shah
SURVIVAL GAME   Trans World, 1987, EP
KANSAS   Trans Word Entertainment, 1988, CP
HIGH SPIRITS   TriStar, 1988, EP w/Mark Damon &
Eduard Sarlui
FULL MOON IN BLUE WATER   Trans World
Entertainment, 1988, EP w/Eduard Sarlui
THE FURTHER ADVENTURES OF TENNESSEE BUCK
Trans World, 1988
NIGHT GAME   Trans World, 1989, EP w/Eduard Sarlui
TEEN WITCH   Trans World, 1989, EP w/Eduard Sarlui
MEN AT WORK   Triumph, 1990, EP w/Irwin Yablans

RON DIAMOND
SORORITY HOUSE MASSACRE   Concorde, 1987
THE DARK BACKWARD   RCA/Columbia, 1991, CP

CHARLES BEACH DICKERSON
ANGELS DIE HARD   New World, 1970

STEPHEN DIENER
Business: New Line, 116 N. Robertson Blvd., Suite 808,
Los Angeles, CA 90048, 310/854-5811

A NIGHTMARE ON ELM STREET 2: FREDDY'S
REVENGE   New Line, 1985, EP w/Stanley Dudelson
THE HIDDEN   New Line, 1987, EP w/Dennis Harris,
Jeffrey Klein & Lee Muhl
A NIGHTMARE ON ELM STREET 3: DREAM WARRIORS
New Line, 1987, EP w/Wes Craven
NIGHTMARE ON ELM STREET 4: THE DREAM MASTER
New Line, 1988, EP w/Sara Risher

JIM DiGANGI
THE STEAGLE   Avco Embassy, 1971

DOUGLAS DILGE
STRANGERS KISS   Orion Classics, 1984
GOOD TO GO   Island Pictures, 1986, w/Sean Ferrer

ROBERT DILLON
Agent: CAA - Beverly Hills, 310/288-4545
Contact: Writers Guild of America - Los Angeles,
310/550-1000

MUSCLE BEACH PARTY   AIP, 1964,
w/James H. Nicholson

DENISE DiNOVI
Business: Tim Burton Productions, c/o Warner Bros., 4000
Warner Blvd., Bungalow 1, Suite 209, Burbank, CA 91522,
818/954-3810; Fax: 818/954-3842

GOING BERSERK   Universal, 1983, AP
FRATERNITY VACATION   New World, 1985, EP
HEATHERS   New World, 1989
MEET THE APPLEGATES   Triton, 1991
EDWARD SCISSORHANDS   20th Century Fox, 1990,
w/Tim Burton

MARK DiSALLE
KICKBOXER   Cannon, 1989
DEATH WARRANT   MGM/UA, 1990
THE PERFECT WEAPON   Paramount, 1991,
w/Pierre David

DAVID DISICK
CRY UNCLE   Cambist, 1971
OKAY BILL   Four Star Excelsior, 1971

ROY EDWARD DISNEY
Business: The Walt Disney Company, 500 S. Buena Vista
St., Burbank, CA 91521, 818/560-1000
Contact: Directors Guild of America - Los Angeles,
213/289-2000

CHEETAH   Buena Vista, 1989, EP

IVAN DIXON
Contact: Directors Guild of America - Los Angeles,
213/289-2000

THE SPOOK WHO SAT BY THE DOOR   United Artists,
1973, w/Sam Greenlee

LESLIE DIXON
Agent: ICM - Los Angeles, 310/550-4000

LOVERBOY   TriStar, 1989, EP w/Tom Ropelewski
MADHOUSE   Orion, 1990

Do

FILM
PRODUCERS,
STUDIOS,
AGENTS and
CASTING
DIRECTORS
GUIDE

F
I
L
M

P
R
O
D
U
C
E
R
S

DALE DJERASSI
'68   New World, 1988, w/Steven Kovacs & Isabel Maxwell

BOSKO DJORDJEVIC
MARIA'S LOVERS   Cannon, 1984, w/Lawrence Mortorff

LEM DOBBS
Agent: UTA - Beverly Hills, 310/273-6700
Contact: Writers Guild of America - Los Angeles,
   310/550-1000

HIDER IN THE HOUSE   Vestron, 1989,
   CP w/Stuart Cornfeld

NEAL DOBROFSKY
(credit w/Dennis Hackin)

WANDA NEVADA   United Artists, 1979
BRONCO BILLY   Warner Bros., 1980

E. L. DOCTOROW
Agent: ICM - New York, 212/556-5600

DANIEL   Paramount, 1983, EP w/Sidney Lumet

RONALD DOMONT
CINDERELLA   Group I, 1977, EP w/Lenny Shabes

TOM DONAHUE
MEDICINE BALL CARAVAN (FD)   Warner Bros., 1971,
   w/Francois Reichenbach

TOM DONALD
HIGH HOPES   Skouras Pictures, 1989, EP

ROGER DONALDSON
Agent: CAA - Beverly Hills, 310/288-4545
Contact: Directors Guild of America - Los Angeles,
   213/289-2000

SMASH PALACE   ARC, 1981
CADILLAC MAN   Orion, 1990, w/Charles Roven

ANDREW DONALLY
CROMWELL   Columbia, 1970, AP
NICHOLAS AND ALEXANDRA   Columbia, 1971, AP
THE INTERNECINE PROJECT   Allied Artists, 1974, CP
THE DEATH WHEELERS   Scotia International, 1974
CONDUCT UNBECOMING   Allied Artists, 1975, CP

STANLEY DONEN
Agent: ICM - Los Angeles, 310/550-4000
Contact: Directors Guild of America - Los Angeles,
   213/289-2000

CHARADE   Universal, 1963
ARABESQUE   Universal, 1966
BEDAZZLED   20th Century Fox, 1967
TWO FOR THE ROAD   20th Century Fox, 1967
THE LITTLE PRINCE   Paramount, 1974
MOVIE MOVIE   Warner Bros., 1978
SATURN 3   AFD, 1980
BLAME IT ON RIO   20th Century Fox, 1984

WALTER DONIGER
Contact: Bettino Productions, 6245 S. June St., Los
   Angeles, CA 90005, 213/937-2101; Fax: 213/937-2103

STONE COLD   Columbia, 1991, EP W/Gary Wichard

LAUREN SHULER-DONNER
(see Lauren SHULER-Donner)

RICHARD DONNER
Business: Richard Donner Productions, Warner Bros., 4000
   Warner Blvd., Burbank, CA 91522, 818/954-4437
Business Manager: Gerald Breslauer, Breslauer, Jacobson &
   Rutman - Los Angeles, 213/879-0167
Agent: CAA - Beverly Hills, 310/288-4545

THE FINAL CONFLICT   20th Century Fox, 1981, EP
THE GOONIES   Warner Bros., 1985, w/Harvey Bernhard
LADYHAWKE   Warner Bros., 1985,
   w/Lauren Shuler-Donner
LETHAL WEAPON   Warner Bros., 1987, w/Joel Silver
THE LOST BOYS   Warner Bros., 1987, EP w/Mark Damon
   & John Hyde
SCROOGED   Paramount, 1988, w/Art Linson
LETHAL WEAPON 2   Warner Bros., 1989, w/Joel Silver

WALTER DONOHUE
THE BELLY OF AN ARCHITECT   Hemdale, 1990,
   w/Colin Callender

ARLENE DONOVAN
Business: 110 W. 57th St., 5th Floor, New York, NY 10019,
   212/247-5652

STILL OF THE NIGHT   MGM/UA, 1982
PLACES IN THE HEART ★   TriStar, 1984
NADINE   TriStar, 1987
THE HOUSE ON CARROLL STREET   Orion, 1988,
   EP w/Robert Benton

MARTIN DONOVAN
APARTMENT ZERO   Skouras Pictures, 1989,
   w/David Koepp

ANITA DOOHAN
EMBRYO   Cine Artists, 1976, w/Arnold Orgolini

LINDSAY DORAN
Contact: Mirage Enterprises, 100 Universal City Plaza,
   Universal City, CA 91608, 818/777-2000;
   Fax: 818/777-5416

LEAVING NORMAL   Universal, 1991

ENZO DORIA
TENTACLES   AIP, 1977

ROBIN DOUET
WINTER FLIGHT   Cinecom, 1986, w/Susan Richards
MR. LOVE   Warner Bros., 1986, w/Susan Richards
SHANGHAI SURPRISE   MGM, 1986, CP
DEFENSE OF THE REALM   Hemdale, 1987,
   w/Lynda Myles
WONDERLAND   Vestron, 1988, CP

MARION DOUGHERTY
Business: Warner Bros., 4000 Warner Blvd., Burbank, CA
   91522, 818/954-3021

SMILE   United Artists, 1975, EP w/David V. Picker

FILM
PRODUCERS,
STUDIOS,
AGENTS AND
CASTING
DIRECTORS
GUIDE

ANNE DOUGLAS
Business: The Bryna Company, 141 El Camino Dr., Beverly
Hills, CA 90212, 310/274-5294; Fax: 310/274-2537

SCALAWAG   Paramount, 1973

JOEL DOUGLAS
Business: Studios La Victorine, 16 Avenue Edouard
Grinda, 06200 Nice, France. 011/33/9321-2552;
Fax: 011/33/9322-1281

ROMANCING THE STONE   20th Century Fox, 1984,
CP w/Jack Brodsky
TORCHLIGHT   UCO Films, 1985
THE JEWEL OF THE NILE   20th Century Fox, 1985,
CP w/Jack Brodsky
COURAGE MOUNTAIN   Triumph, 1990, EP

KIRK DOUGLAS
Business: The Bryna Company, 141 El Camino Dr.,
Beverly Hills, CA 90212, 310/274-5294;
Fax: 310/274-2537
Agent: CAA - Beverly Hills, 310/288-4545

THE INDIAN FIGHTER   United Artists, 1955
THE VIKINGS   United Artists, 1958
SPARTACUS   Universal, 1960, EP
LONELY ARE THE BRAVE   Universal, 1962
THE LIST OF ADRIAN MESSENGER   Universal, 1963
SEVEN DAYS IN MAY   Paramount, 1964
THE BROTHERHOOD   Paramount, 1968
SUMMERTREE   Columbia, 1971
THE LIGHT AT THE EDGE OF THE WORLD
National General, 1971
POSSE   Paramount, 1975

MICHAEL DOUGLAS
Business: Stonebridge Productions, Columbia Pictures,
10401 Venice Blvd., Suite 200, Los Angeles, CA 90034,
310/280-6800; Fax: 310/280-1473
Agent: CAA - Beverly Hills, 310/288-4545

ONE FLEW OVER THE CUCKOO'S NEST ★★   United
Artists, 1975, w/Saul Zaentz
THE CHINA SYNDROME   Columbia, 1979
RUNNING   Universal, 1979
ROMANCING THE STONE   20th Century Fox, 1984
STARMAN   Columbia, 1984, EP
THE JEWEL OF THE NILE   20th Century Fox, 1985
FLATLINERS   Columbia, 1990, w/Rick Bieber

PETER VINCENT DOUGLAS
Business: UniversalPictures, Bldg. 473, 2nd Flr., Universal
City, CA 91408, 818/777-3138
Agent: CAA - Beverly Hills, 310/288-4545

THE FINAL COUNTDOWN   United Artists, 1980
SOMETHING WICKED THIS WAY COMES   Buena
Vista, 1983
FLETCH   Universal, 1985, w/Alan Greisman
A TIGER'S TALE   Atlantic, 1988
FLETCH LIVES   Universal, 1989, w/Alan Greisman

NED DOWD
(credit w/Randy Ostrow)
Contact: Dean Avedon & Co., Inc., 11022 Santa Monica
Blvd., Los Angeles, CA 90025, 310/444-9776

THINGS CHANGE   Columbia, 1988, AP*

LET IT RIDE   Paramount, 1989, CP
STATE OF GRACE   Orion, 1990, w/Ron Rotholz

KATHLEEN DOWDEY
(credit w/Jeff Dannenbaum)
Business: Five Point Films, Inc., 915 Highland View N.E.,
Suite B, Atlanta, GA 30306, 404/875-6076

A CELTIC TRILOGY (FD)   First Run Features, 1979
BLUE HEAVEN   Vestron/Shapiro Entertainment, 1985, CP

WENDY DOZORETZ
Contact: Collett-Dozoretz Productions, 500 S. Buena Vista
St., Animation Bldg. 2-F4, Burbank, CA 91521,
818/560-4637; Fax: 818/567-2966

DECEIVED   Buena Vista, 1991, w/Ellen Collett &
Michael Finnell

GARTH DRABINSKY
(credit w/Joel B. Michaels)
Business: Alive Entertainment Corporation of Canada, 1300
Young, 2nd Floor, Toronto, M4T 1X2, 416/324-5800

THE SILENT PARTNER   EMC Films/Aurora, 1979, EP
THE CHANGELING   AFD, 1980
TRIBUTE   20th Century Fox, 1980
THE AMATEUR   20th Century Fox, 1981
LOSIN' IT   Embassy, 1983, EP

BERT DRAGIN
SUBURBIA *THE WILD SIDE*   New Horizons, 1984

STAN DRAGOTI
Agent: CAA - Beverly Hills, 310/288-4545

DIRTY LITTLE BILLY   Columbia, 1972, w/Jack L. Warner

VICTOR DRAI
Business: Victor Drai Productions, 4117 Radford Ave., Studio
City, CA 91604, 818/505-6626; Fax: 818/505-6628

THE WOMAN IN RED   Orion, 1984
THE MAN WITH ONE RED SHOE   20th Century Fox, 1985
THE BRIDE   Columbia, 1985
WEEKEND AT BERNIE'S   20th Century Fox, 1989

DOUG DRAIZIN
Business: Elsboy Entertainment, 7920 Sunset Blvd.,
Suite 350, Los Angeles, CA 90046, 213/851-5700;
Fax: 213/851-5157

MOVING VIOLATIONS   20th Century Fox, 1985,
EP w/Pat Proft

PAUL DRANE
THE MAN WHO SAW TOMORROW (FD)   Warner Bros.,
1981, w/Robert Guenette & Lee Kramer

LORIN DREYFUSS
SKATETOWN U.S.A.   Columbia, 1979, w/William A. Levey

RICHARD DREYFUSS
Business: Dreyfuss/James Productions, c/o Walt Disney
Pictures, 500 S. Buena Vista St., Burbank, CA 91505,
818/560-7100; Fax: 818/567-1263

THE BIG FIX   Universal, 1978, w/Carl Borack
ONCE AROUND   Universal, 1991, CP w/Judith James

Du

FILM
PRODUCERS,
STUDIOS,
AGENTS AND
CASTING
DIRECTORS
GUIDE

F
I
L
M

P
R
O
D
U
C
E
R
S

SARA DRIVER
STRANGER THAN PARADISE   Samuel Goldwyn
Company, 1984

PATRICK DROMGOOLE
THE LAST BUTTERFLY   1991, EP w/Boudjemaa
Dahmane & Jacques Methe

MICHAEL DRYHURST
Agent: BBMW - Los Angeles, 310/247-5500

THE TERMINAL MAN   Warner Bros., 1974, AP
EXCALIBUR   Orion, 1981, AP
NEVER SAY NEVER AGAIN   Warner Bros., 1983, AP
THE EMERALD FOREST   Embassy, 1985, CP
HOPE AND GLORY ★   Columbia, 1987, CP
HUDSON HAWK   TriStar, 1991, CP

RANI DUBE
GANDHI ★★   Columbia, 1982, CP

DONNA DUBROW
THE LAST DAYS OF EDEN   Buena Vista, 1991,
w/Tom Schulman & Andy Vajna

STANLEY DUDELSON
Business: Artist Entertainment Group, Inc., 5455 Wilshire
Blvd., Suite 1715, Los Angeles, CA 90036,
213/933-7496

A NIGHTMARE ON ELM STREET   New Line, 1984,
EP w/Joseph Wolf
A NIGHTMARE ON ELM STREET 2: FREDDY'S
REVENGE   New Line, 1985, EP w/Stephen Diener

MAURICE DUKE
KEATON'S COP   Cannon, 1990, EP

PATRICIA DUFF
LIMIT UP   MCEG, 1990, CP

WILLIAM DUFFY
DEATH GAME   Levitt-Pickman, 1977, EP w/Mel Bergman

RON DUMAS
THE ABOMINABLE DR. PHIBES   AIP, 1971,
w/Louis M. Heyward

WILLIAM J. DUNN
STEPHEN KING'S GRAVEYARD SHIFT   Paramount,
1990, w/Ralph S. Singleton

DOMINICK DUNNE
THE BOYS IN THE BAND   National General, 1970,
EP w/Robert Jiras
THE PANIC IN NEEDLE PARK   20th Century Fox, 1971
PLAY IT AS IT LAYS   Universal, 1972, CP
ASH WEDNESDAY   Paramount, 1973

GRIFFIN DUNNE
(credit w/Amy Robinson)
Business: Double Play Productions, 445 Park Ave.,
8th Floor, New York, NY 10022, 212/605-2722

CHILLY SCENES OF WINTER   *HEAD OVER HEELS*
United Artists, 1979, w/Mark Metcalf
BABY IT'S YOU   Paramount, 1983

AFTER HOURS   Geffen/Warner Bros., 1985,
w/Robert F. Colesberry
RUNNING ON EMPTY   Warner Bros., 1988
WHITE PALACE   Universal, 1990, w/Mark Rosenberg
ONCE AROUND   Universal, 1991

JOHN DUNNING
(credit w/Andre Link)
Business: Cinepix Inc., 8275 Mayrand St., Montreal, H4P
2C8, 514/342-2340; Fax: 514/342-1922

THEY CAME FROM WITHIN   Trans-America, 1976,
w/Alfred Pariser
THE HOUSE BY THE LAKE   AIP, 1977, EP
RABID   New World, 1977*
BLACKOUT   New World, 1978, w/Nicole Boisvert &
Eddy Matalon*
MEATBALLS   Paramount, 1979, EP
MY BLOODY VALENTINE   Paramount, 1981,
w/Stephen Miller
HAPPY BIRTHDAY TO ME   Columbia, 1981
SPACEHUNTER: ADVENTURES IN THE FORBIDDEN
ZONE   Columbia, 1983, w/Don Carmody
MEATBALLS III   Moviestore, 1986, w/Don Carmody*
SNAKE EATER   Moviestore, 1990*
WHISPERS   ITC, 1990, w/Don Carmody*

DANIEL TOSCAN duPLANTIER
Business: Unifrance Film International, 4 Villa Bosquet, Paris
75007, 47.53.95.80; Fax: 47.05.96.55

THE COOK, THE THIEF, HIS WIFE & HER LOVER
Miramax, 1990, CP w/Pascale Dauman & Denis Wigman

RENE DUPONT
THE LAST GRENADE   Cinerama, 1970, AP
SHAFT IN AFRICA   MGM, 1973, AP
MURDER BY DECREE   Avco Embassy, 1979, w/Bob Clark
SILVER DREAM RACER   Almi Cinema 5, 1980
A CHRISTMAS STORY   MGM/UA, 1983, w/Bob Clark
TURK 182   20th Century Fox, 1985, w/Ted Field
FROM THE HIP   DEG, 1987, w/Bob Clark
COLLISION COURSE   DEG, 1988, EP
LOOSE CANNONS   TriStar, 1990, EP

ALLAN L. DURAND
BELIZAIRE THE CAJUN   Skouras Pictures, 1986,
w/Glen Pitre

RUDY DURAND
Business: Koala Productions, Ltd., 361 N. Canon Dr.,
Beverly Hills, CA 90212, 310/476-1949
Contact: Directors Guild of America - Los Angeles,
213/289-2000

TILT   Warner Bros., 1979

BILL DURKIN
BARTON FINK   20th Century Fox, 1991, EP w/Ted Pedas
& Ben Barenholtz

DENNIS DURNEY
MOLLY AND LAWLESS JOHN   Producers Distributing
Corp., 1972

MICHEL DUVAL
SALVATION!   Circle Releasing, 1987, EP w/Irving Ong &
Ned Richardson

Du

**FILM
PRODUCERS,
STUDIOS,
AGENTS** AND
**CASTING
DIRECTORS
GUIDE**

F
I
L
M

P
R
O
D
U
C
E
R
S

ROBERT DUVALL
Agent: ICM - Los Angeles, 310/550-4000

TENDER MERCIES ★   Universal, 1983,
    CP w/Horton Foote

DALE DYE
FIRE BIRDS   Buena Vista, 1990, CP w/John K. Swensson

JAMES DYER
Contact: Directors Guild of America - Los Angeles,
    213/289-2000

WILD ORCHID   Triumph Releasing, 1990,
    EP w/David Saunders

ROBERT DYKE
MOONTRAP   Shapiro Glickenhaus Entertainment, 1989

THOMAS L. DYKE
THE NORTHVILLE CEMETERY MASSACRE   Cannon,
    1976, w/William Dear

JOHN DYKSTRA
BATTLESTAR GALACTI CA   Universal, 1979

BRIAN EASTMAN
Business: Carnival, 12 Raddington Road, London W10 5TG
    England, 081/968-1818; Fax: 081/968-0155

WHOOPS APOCALYPSE   MGM, 1986
THE MISADVENTURES OF MR. WILT   Samuel Goldwyn
    Company, 1990
THE OTHER WOMAN   Columbia, 1991

GRAHAM EASTON
Business: Film Finances, Ltd., 9000 Sunset Blvd., Los
    Angeles, CA 90069, 310/275-7323; 1/11 Hay Hill,
    Berkeley Square, London, W1X 7LF, 071/629-6557;
    Fax: 071/491-7530

STRIKE IT RICH   Miramax, 1989, w/Christine Oestricher

CLINT EASTWOOD
Business: Malpaso Productions, 4000 Warner Blvd.,
    Burbank, CA 91522, 818/954-3367
Agent: William Morris Agency - Beverly Hills, 310/274-7451

FIREFOX   Warner Bros., 1982
HONKY TONK MAN   Warner Bros., 1982
SUDDEN IMPACT   Warner Bros., 1983
TIGHTROPE   Warner Bros., 1984, w/Fritz Manes
PALE RIDER   Warner Bros., 1985
HEARTBREAK RIDGE   Warner Bros., 1986
BIRD   Warner Bros., 1988
THELONIOUS MONK: STRAIGHT, NO CHASER (FD)
    Warner Bros., 1988, EP
WHITE HUNTER, BLACK HEART   Warner Bros., 1990

JAKE EBERTS
Contact: Kate Vale Productions - London, 071/2299173

THE NAME OF THE ROSE   20th Century Fox, 1986,
    EP w/Thomas Schuehly
HOPE & GLORY   Columbia, 1987,
    EP w/Edgar F. Gross
THE ADVENTURES OF BARON MUNCHAUSEN
    Columbia, 1989, EP
DRIVING MISS DAISY ★   Warner Bros., 1989,
    EP w/David Brown
ME AND HIM   Columbia, 1989, AP
TEXASVILLE   Columbia, 1990, EP w/Bill Peiffer
DANCES WITH WOLVES ★★   Orion, 1990, EP
CITY OF JOY   TriStar, 1991, w/Roland Joffe

MASAHIRO EBISAWA
CLASS OF NUKE 'EM HIGH PART II: SUBHUMANOID
    MELTDOWN   Troma, 1991, EP w/Tetsu Fujimura &
    Sammy O. Masada

JOHN M. ECKERT
Business: John M. Eckert Productions Ltd., 385 Carlton St.,
    Toronto, M5A 2M3, 416/960-4961

RUNNING   Universal, 1979, CP
THE INCUBUS   FIlm Ventures International, 1982,
    w/Marc Boyman
HOME IS WHERE THE HART IS   Atlantic, 1987
MILLENNIUM   20th Century Fox, 1989, SP

MICHAEL EDGLEY
THE MAN FROM SNOWY RIVER   20th Century Fox, 1983,
    EP w/Simon Wincer

BOBBIE EDRICK
Business: Artists Circle Entertainment, 8955 Norma Place,
    Los Angeles, CA 90069, 213/275-6330

DADDY'S DYIN'...WHO'S GOT THE WILL?   MGM/UA,
    1990, EP w/Michael Kuhn, Del Shores & Nigel Sinclair

BLAKE EDWARDS
Business: Blake Edwards Entertainment, 9336 W.
    Washington Blvd., Culver City, CA 90230,
    310/202-3502; Fax: 310/202-3224
Agent: Triad Artists, Inc. - Los Angeles,
    310/556-2727

DARLING LILI   Paramount, 1970
WILD ROVERS   MGM, 1971, w/Ken Wales
THE RETURN OF THE PINK PANTHER   United
    Artists, 1975
THE PINK PANTHER STRIKES AGAIN   United
    Artists, 1976
REVENGE OF THE PINK PANTHER   United
    Artists, 1978
10   Orion/Warner Bros., 1979, w/Tony Adams
S.O.B.   Lorimar/Paramount, 1981, w/Tony Adams
VICTOR/VICTORIA   MGM/UA, 1982, w/Tony Adams
TRAIL OF THE PINK PANTHER   MGM/UA, 1982,
    w/Tony Adams
CURSE OF THE PINK PANTHER   MGM/UA, 1983,
    w/Tony Adams
THE MAN WHO LOVED WOMEN   Columbia, 1983,
    w/Tony Adams

GEORGE EDWARDS
Business: Desert Wind Productions, Raleigh Studios, 5300 Melrose Ave., Los Angeles, CA 90038, 213/464-3082
Agent: Artists Group, Inc. - Los Angeles, 310/552-1100

WHAT'S THE MATTER WITH HELEN?   United Artists, 1971
FUZZ   United Artists, 1972, EP
FROGS   AIP, 1972, w/Peter Thomas
OUTSIDE IN   Robbins International, 1972
THE KILLING KIND   Media Trend, 1974
RUBY   Dimension, 1977
HARPER VALLEY P.T.A.   April Fools, 1978
CHATTANOOGA CHOO CHOO   April Fools, 1984, w/Jill Griffith
TRUST ME   Cinecom, 1989
INSTANT KARMA   MGM, 1990, w/Dale Rosenbloom & Bruce A. Taylor

ROBERT GORDON EDWARDS
LUDWIG   MGM, 1973, EP
THE NIGHT PORTER   Avco Embassy, 1974

R. BEN EFRAIM
THE JERUSALEM FILE   MGM, 1972
MITCHELL   Allied Artists, 1975
STRIKING BACK   Film Ventures International, 1981, EP
PRIVATE LESSONS   Jensen Farley, 1981
PRIVATE SCHOOL   Universal, 1983, w/Don Enright
NASTY HERO   Private Movie Co., 1990
THE SHRIMP ON THE BARBIE   Unity Pictures, 1990

MEL EFROS
Contact: Directors Guild of America - Los Angeles, 213/289-2000

STAR TREK V: THE FINAL FRONTIER   Paramount, 1989, CP

AL EICHER
BRAIN DAMAGE   Palisades Entertainment, 1988, EP w/Andre Blay

BERND EICHINGER
Contact: 9200 Sunset Blvd., Suite 730, Los Angeles, CA 90069, 310/247-0300; Fax: 310/247-0305
Business: Constantin Film, GMBH & Co, Verleih KG, Kaiserstraße 39, D-8000 München 40, West Germany, 38-60-90

THE WILD DUCK   New Yorker, 1977
THE CONSEQUENCE   Libra, 1979
CHRISTIANE F.   New World, 1982, w/Hans Weth
THE NEVERENDING STORY   Warner Bros., 1984, w/Dieter Geissler
THE NAME OF THE ROSE   20th Century Fox, 1986
ME AND HIM   Columbia, 1989
LAST EXIT TO BROOKLYN   Cinecom, 1990

MARY EILTS
Contact: Directors Guild of America - Los Angeles, 213/289-2000

WATCHERS   Universal, 1988, CP
NARROW MARGIN   TriStar, 1990, AP

D. E. EISENBERG
DREAM A LITTLE DREAM   Vestron, 1989, w/Marc Rocco

MORRIE EISENMAN
Business: Producers Representation Organization, 11849 W. Olympic Blvd., Suite 200, Los Angeles, CA 90064, 310/478-5159; Fax: 310/479-0617

BAD INFLUENCE   Triumph, 1990, EP w/Richard Becker
LOVE STINKS   Live Entertainment, 1991, w/Wayne Rice

RAFAEL EISENMAN
I, MADMAN   Trans World, 1989
TEEN WITCH   Trans World, 1989, w/Alana H. Lambros
I COME IN PEACE   Triumph, 1990, CP w/Jon Turtle

ZAN EISLEY
COOL BLUE   Cinema Corporation of America, 1990, CP

ED ELBERT
THE MIGHTY QUINN   MGM/UA, 1989, w/Marion Hunt & Sandy Lieberson
HOTEL OKLAHOMA   1991, w/Terry Kahn & Gregory Vanger

KEVIN ELDERS
IRON EAGLE   TriStar, 1986, EP

MARTIN ELFAND
KANSAS CITY BOMBER   MGM, 1972
DOG DAY AFTERNOON ★   Warner Bros., 1975, w/Martin Bregman
IT'S MY TURN   Columbia, 1980
AN OFFICER & A GENTLEMAN   Paramount, 1982
KING DAVID   Paramount, 1985
CLARA'S HEART   Warner Bros., 1988
HER ALIBI   Warner Bros., 1989, EP

RICHARD ELFMAN
Business: Richard Elfman Productions, 723 Ocean Front Walk, Venice, CA 90291, 310/399-9118

FORBIDDEN ZONE   Samuel Goldwyn Company, 1980

HILLARD ELKINS
Contact: Elkins Entertainment, 8306 Wilshire Blvd., Suite 438, Beverly Hills, CA 90211, 310/285-0700; Fax: 310/273-4999

OH! CALCUTTA!   Cinemation, 1972
A DOLL'S HOUSE   Paramount, 1973
SAMMY STOPS THE WORLD   Special Event Entertainment, 1979, EP w/Saul Barnett

ERIC ELLENBOGEN
Contact: Broadway Video, 5555 Melrose Ave., Dressing Room #305, Los Angeles, CA 90038, 213/956-5729; Fax: 213/956-8605

HONEYMOON ACADEMY   Triumph, 1990, EP w/Paul Maslansky

LANG ELLIOTT
Business: Performance Pictures, 17030 Ventura Blvd., Penthouse, Encino, CA 91316, 818/501-1821; Fax: 818/501-5370
Contact: Directors Guild of America - Los Angeles, 213/289-2000

THE FARMER   Columbia, 1977, AP

F I L M   P R O D U C E R S

EI

**FILM
PRODUCERS,
STUDIOS,
AGENTS AND
CASTING
DIRECTORS
GUIDE**

F
I
L
M

P
R
O
D
U
C
E
R
S

THE BILLION DOLLAR HOBO   International Picture
   Show, 1977
THEY WENT THAT-A-WAY AND THAT-A-WAY
   International Picture Show, 1978
THE PRIZE FIGHTER   New World, 1979
THE PRIVATE EYES   New World, 1981, w/Wanda Dell
THE LONGSHOT   Orion, 1986
CAGE   New Century/Vista, 1989

MIKE ELLIOTT
Business: Concorde Films, 11600 San Vicente Blvd.,
   Los Angeles, CA 90049, 310/820-6733

KISS ME A KILLER   Califilm, 1991, EP
THE UNBORN   Califilm, 1991, EP
DEAD SPACE   Califilm, 1991
HEAT OF PASSION   Concorde, 1991
FINAL EMBRACE   Concorde, 1991

PAUL ELLSWORTH
THE HOUSE THAT DRIPPED BLOOD   Cinerama, 1971,
   EP w/Gordon Wescourt

CASSIAN ELWES
Business: Smoking Gun Pictures, 1445 S. Beverly Dr.,
   Penthouse, Beverly Hills, CA 90212, 310/278-7186;
   Fax: 310/278-7239; Winkast Programming Ltd.,
   Pinewood Studios, Iver Heath, Bucks., SL0 0NH,
   0753/651-700; Fax: 0753/652-525

OXFORD BLUES   MGM/UA, 1984, w/Elliott Kastner
NOMADS   Atlantic, 1986, w/George Pappas
WHITE OF THE EYE   Palisades Entertainment, 1987,
   w/Brad Wyman
ZOMBIE HIGH   Cinema Group, 1987, EP
NEVER ON TUESDAY   Palisades Entertainment,
   1987, EP
COLD FEET   Avenue Entertainment, 1989
COOL BLUE   Cinema Corporation of America, 1990, EP
WARM SUMMER RAIN   Trans World, 1990,
   w/Lionel Wigram
MEN AT WORK   Triumph, 1990
THE DARK BACKWARD   RCA/Columbia, 1991,
   w/Brad Wyman
LIQUID DREAMS   1991, EP w/Ted Fox
MAD AT THE MOON   Boomerang Pictures, 1991, w/Matt
   Devlen, Michael Kastenbaum & Seth Kastenbaum

JAY EMMETT
GARDENS OF STONE   TriStar, 1987, EP w/Fred Roos,
   David Valdes & Stan Weston

ROBERT J. ENDERS
HOW DO I LOVE THEE   Cinerama, 1970,
   w/Everett Freeman
ZIGZAG   MGM, 1970, w/Everett Freeman
OUT OF SEASON   Athenaeum, 1975, EP
HEDDA   Brut, 1975
THE MAIDS   American Film Theatre, 1975
NASTY HABITS   Brut, 1977
STEVIE   First Artists, 1978

MICHAEL S. ENDLER
BACK TO SCHOOL   Orion, 1986, EP w/Estelle Endler &
   Harold Ramis

MORT ENGELBERG
Business: The Vista Organization, 8439 Sunset Blvd., Suite
   200, Los Angeles, CA 90069, 213/656-9130

SMOKEY & THE BANDIT   Universal, 1977
HOT STUFF   Columbia, 1979
THE VILLAIN   Columbia, 1979
THE HUNTER   Paramount, 1980
NOBODY'S PERFEKT   Columbia, 1981
SMOKEY & THE BANDIT PART 3   Universal, 1983
THE HEAVENLY KID   Orion, 1985
THE BIG EASY   Columbia, 1987, EP
MAID TO ORDER   New Century/Vista, 1987, w/Herb Jaffe
RUSSKIES   New Century/Vista, 1987, w/Stephen Deutsch
THREE FOR THE ROAD   New Century/Vista, 1987,
   w/Herb Jaffe
FRIGHT NIGHT PART 2   New Century/Vista, 1988,
   w/Herb Jaffe
PASS THE AMMO   New Century/Vista, 1988, w/Herb Jaffe
DUDES   New Century/Vista, 1988, EP
RENTED LIPS   CineWorld Enterprises, 1988, w/Martin Mull
TRADING HEARTS   New Century/Vista, 1988, EP w/Herb Jaffe

ROBERT ENGELMAN
Contact: Directors Guild of America - Los Angeles,
   213/289-2000

LEATHERFACE: THE TEXAS CHAINSAW MASSACRE III
   New Line, 1990

IRA ENGLANDER
RUNNING BRAVE   Buena Vista, 1983

GEORGE ENGLUND
Agent: CAA - Beverly Hills, 310/288-4545
Contact: Directors Guild of America - Los Angeles, 213/289-2000

DARK OF THE SUN *THE MERCENARIES*   MGM, 1968
THE SHOES OF THE FISHERMAN   MGM, 1968
ZACHARIAH   Cinerama, 1971

DAN ENRIGHT
Business: Barry & Enright Productions, 201 Wilshire Blvd.,
   2nd Floor, Santa Monica, CA 90401, 310/556-1000;
   Fax: 310/393-8111
Agent: David Shapira & Associates - Sherman Oaks,
   818/906-0322

PRIVATE LESSONS   Jensen Farley, 1981,
   EP w/Jack Barry
MAKING MR. RIGHT   Orion, 1987, EP w/Susan Seidelman

DON ENRIGHT
Business: Alexander/Enright & Asso., 201 Wilshire Blvd., Santa
   Monica, CA 90401, 310/458-3003; Fax: 310/393-8111
Agent: ICM - Los Angeles, 310/550-4000

PRIVATE SCHOOL   Universal, 1983, w/R. Ben Efraim
NEXT OF KIN   Warner Bros., 1989, w/Les Alexander

JOHN ENTWISTLE
QUADROPHENIA   World Northal, 1979, EP w/Roger
   Daltrey, Keith Moon & Pete Townshend

ANDROS EPAMINONDAS
GIVE MY REGARDS TO BROAD STREET   20th Century
   Fox, 1984
STEALING HEAVEN   Scotti Bros., 1989,
   w/Simon MacCorkindale

Ev

FILM
PRODUCERS,
STUDIOS,
AGENTS AND
CASTING
DIRECTORS
GUIDE

NORA EPHRON
Agent: ICM - New York, 212/556-5600

COOKIE   Warner Bros., 1989, EP w/Alice Arlen &
Susan Seidelman
MY BLUE HEAVEN   Warner Bros., 1990, EP w/Goldie
Hawn & Andrew Stone

JULIUS J. EPSTEIN
Agent: ICM - Los Angeles, 310/550-4000

PETE 'N' TILLIE   Universal, 1972
REUBEN, REUBEN   20th Century Fox International
Classics, 1983, CP

MITCH EPSTEIN
SALAAM BOMBAY!   Cinecom, 1988, CP

NORMAN EPSTEIN
REAL LIFE   Paramount, 1979, EP w/Jonathan Kovler

DORON ERAN
TORN APART   Castle Hill, 1990, CP

C. O. ERICKSON
Business: Paramount Pictures, 5555 Melrose Ave., Los
Angeles, CA 90038, 213/956-5729
Agent: The Gersh Agency - Beverly Hills, 310/274-6611
Contact: Directors Guild of America - Los Angeles,
213/289-2000

BUONA SERA, MRS. CAMPBELL   United Artists,
1968, EP
THERE WAS A CROOKED MAN   Warner Bros., 1970, EP
CHINATOWN   Paramount, 1974, AP
MAGIC   20th Century Fox, 1978, EP
URBAN COWBOY   Paramount, 1980, EP
POPEYE   Paramount/Buena Vista, 1980, EP
ZORRO, THE GAY BLADE   20th Century Fox, 1981,
w/George Hamilton
FAST TIMES AT RIDGEMONT HIGH   Universal,
1982, EP
THE LONELY GUY   Universal, 1984,
EP w/William E. McEuen
CLOAK & DAGGER   Universal, 1984, EP
THE WILD LIFE   Universal, 1984, EP
SECRET ADMIRER   Orion, 1985, EP
PROJECT X   20th Century Fox, 1987, EP
IRONWEED   TriStar, 1987, CP w/Gene Kirkwood
MOBSTERS   Universal, 1991, EP

PAUL ERICKSON
RED SCORPION   Shapiro Glickenhaus, 1989,
EP w/Robert Abramoff & Daniel Sklar

MARTIN ERLICHMAN
UP THE SANDBOX   National General, 1972, AP
FOR PETE'S SAKE   Columbia, 1974, w/Stanley Shapiro
COMA   United Artists, 1978
BREATHLESS   Orion, 1983
ERNEST GOES TO CAMP   Buena Vista, 1987,
EP w/Elmo Williams
ERNEST SAVES CHRISTMAS   Buena Vista, 1988,
EP w/Joseph L. Akerman
ERNEST GOES TO JAIL   Buena Vista, 1990, EP

MIKE ERWIN
Business: Blueline Prods., 9107 Wilshire Blvd., #427, Beverly
Hills, CA 90210, 310/271-2572; Fax: 310/271-9316

DEADLINE   Studio Three, 1991, w/J. Max Krishima
MOM AND DAD SAVE THE WORLD   Warner Bros., 1991,
w/Michael Phillips

JOHN ESKOW
Agent: ICM - Los Angeles, 310/550-4000

AIR AMERICA   TriStar, 1990, CP w/Allen Shapiro

MOCTESUMA ESPARZA
Contact: Esparza-Katz Prods., 3330 Cahuenga West, Ste 500,
Los Angeles, CA 90068, 213/969-2896; Fax: 213/851-5797

ONLY ONCE IN A LIFETIME   Movietime Films, 1979
THE BALLAD OF GREGORIO CORTEZ   Embassy, 1983,
w/Michael Hausman
RADIOACTIVE DREAMS   DEG, 1986, w/Tom Karnowski
THE TELEPHONE   New World, 1988, w/Robert Katz
THE MILAGRO BEANFIELD WAR   Universal, 1988,
w/Robert Redford

KAREN ESSEX
THE IN CROWD   Orion, 1988, CP w/Jeffrey Hornaday

MELVYN J. ESTRIN
STRIPPER (FD)   20th Century Fox, 1986, w/Geof Bartz &
Jerome Gary

JOE ESZTERHAS
(credit w/Hal W. Polaire)
Agent: ICM - Los Angeles, 310/550-4000
Contact: Writers Guild of America - Los Angeles, 310/550-1000

BETRAYED   MGM/UA, 1988, EP
MUSIC BOX   TriStar, 1989, EP

BRUCE A. EVANS
(credit w/Raynold Gideon)
Business: Evans-Gideon Productions, Universal Studios,
100 Universal City Plaza, Universal City, CA 91608,
818/777-3121; Fax: 818/777-8857
Agent: CAA - Beverly Hills, 310/288-4545

STARMAN   Columbia, 1984, AP
STAND BY ME   Columbia, 1986, w/Andrew Scheinman
MADE IN HEAVEN   Lorimar, 1987, w/David Blocker

CHARLES EVANS
TOOTSIE ★   Columbia, 1982, EP
MONKEY SHINES   Orion, 1988

KENNETH EVANS
PRIME CUT   National General, 1972, EP

MICHAEL STANLEY-EVANS
(see Michael STANLEY-Evans)

ROBERT EVANS
Business: Robert Evans Productions, c/o Paramount Studios,
5555 Melrose Ave., Los Angeles, CA 90038,
213/956-8800; Fax: 213/956-0070

CHINATOWN ★   Paramount, 1974
MARATHON MAN   Paramount, 1976, w/Sidney Beckerman

Ev

FILM
PRODUCERS,
STUDIOS,
AGENTS and
CASTING
DIRECTORS
GUIDE

F
I
L
M

P
R
O
D
U
C
E
R
S

BLACK SUNDAY   Paramount, 1977
PLAYERS   Paramount, 1979
URBAN COWBOY   Paramount, 1980, w/Irving Azoff
POPEYE   Paramount/Buena Vista, 1980
THE COTTON CLUB   Orion, 1984
THE TWO JAKES   Paramount, 1990, w/Harold Schneider

STEPHEN EVANS
HENRY V   Samuel Goldwyn Company, 1989, EP

TED EVANSON
WHAT COMES AROUND   W.O. Associates, 1986

WILLIAM EWART
GENUINE RISK   I.R.S., 1990, w/Guy J. Louthan &
   Larry J. Rattner
DELUSION   Cineville, 1991, CP w/Cevin Cathell

F

DALE FALCONER
IF YOU COULD SEE WHAT I HEAR   Jensen Farley
   Pictures, 1982, EP w/Gene Corman

JAMAA FANAKA
WELCOME HOME, BROTHER CHARLES   Crown
   International, 1975
EMMA MAE   Pro-International, 1977
PENITENTIARY   Jerry Gross, 1979

HAMPTON FANCHER
Agent: UTA - Beverly Hills, 310/273-6700
Contact: Writers Guild of America - Los Angeles,
   310/550-1000

BLADE RUNNER   The Ladd Company/Warner Bros.,
   1982, EP w/Brian Kelly

WILLIAM FARALLA
Contact: Directors Guild of America - Los Angeles,
   213/289-2000

THE BALLAD OF CABLE HOGUE   Warner Bros.,
   1970, CP

STEVEN FARGNOLI
(credit w/Robert Cavallo & Joseph Ruffalo)
Business: Steven Fargnoli & Associates, 35 Harwood Road,
   London SW6 4QP, 071/371-5633; Fax: 071/371-5515

PURPLE RAIN   Warner Bros., 1984
UNDER THE CHERRY MOON   Warner Bros., 1986
SIGN O' THE TIMES   Cineplex Odeon, 1987

VALERIE FARIS
THE DECLINE OF WESTERN CIVILIZATION PART II:
   THE METAL YEARS (FD)   New Line Cinema, 1988,
   w/Jonathan Dayton

DAN FARRELL
WHERE THE RIVER RUNS BLACK   MGM, 1986, CP

JOSEPH FARRELL
Business: The National Research Group, Inc., 7046
   Hollywood Blvd., Los Angeles, CA 90028, 213/856-4400

MANNEQUIN   20th Century Fox, 1987,
   EP w/Edward Rugoff

MIKE FARRELL
Business: Farrell-Minoff Productions, 14755 Ventura Blvd.,
   Suite 203, Sherman Oaks, CA 91403, 818/789-5766;
   Fax: 818/789-7459
Contact: Directors Guild of America - Los Angeles,
   213/289-2000

DOMINICK & EUGENE   Orion, 1988, w/Marvin Minoff

JACK FARREN
FUZZ   United Artists, 1972

ALVIN L. FAST
THE INCREDIBLE TWO-HEADED TRANSPLANT   AIP,
   1971, AP
TOM   Four Star International, 1973
THE BAD BUNCH   Dimension, 1976
BLACK SHAMPOO   Dimension, 1976
EATEN ALIVE   Virgo International, 1977, CP
SATAN'S CHEERLEADERS   World Amusement, 1977

WILLIAM FAY
JAKE SPEED   New World, 1986, w/Wayne Crawford &
   Andrew Lane

DODI FAYED
Business: Allied Stars, 55 Park Lane, London W1Y 3DH,
   071/493-1050; Fax: 071/499-5889; 10202 W. Washington
   Blvd., Culver City, CA 90232-3195, 310/280-7700

BREAKING GLASS   Paramount, 1980, EP
CHARIOTS OF FIRE ★★   The Ladd Company/Warner
   Bros., 1981, EP
F/X   Orion, 1986, w/Jack Wiener
F/X 2 — THE DEADLY ART OF ILLUSION   Orion, 1991,
   EP w/Jack Wiener

WILLIAM FAYMAN
STRANGE BEHAVIOR   World Northal, 1981, EP w/John
   Daly & David Hemmings
HARLEQUIN   New Image, 1983, EP

MAURIZIO LODI-FE
(see Maurizio LODI-Fe)

IRVING FEIN
JUST YOU AND ME, KID   Columbia, 1979,
   w/Jerome M. Zeitman
OH, GOD! YOU DEVIL   Warner Bros., 1984, EP
18 AGAIN   New World, 1988, EP w/Michael Jaffe

BUZZ FEITSHANS
Business: Carolco Pictures, 8800 Sunset Blvd., Los Angeles,
   CA 90069, 310/850-8800; Fax: 310/657-1629

DILLINGER   AIP, 1973
ACT OF VENGEANCE   AIP, 1974
FOXY BROWN   AIP, 1974

BIG WEDNESDAY   Warner Bros., 1978
HARDCORE   Columbia, 1979
1941   Columbia/Universal, 1979
CONAN THE BARBARIAN   Universal, 1982,
    w/Raffaella De Laurentiis
FIRST BLOOD   Orion, 1982
UNCOMMON VALOR   Paramount, 1983, w/John Milius
RED DAWN   MGM/UA, 1984, w/Barry Beckerman
RAMBO: FIRST BLOOD PART II   TriStar, 1985
EXTREME PREJUDICE   TriStar, 1987
RAMBO III   Carolco, 1988
TOTAL RECALL   TriStar, 1990, w/Ronald Shusett

STEPHEN J. FEKE
Business: Parnassus Productions, 10000 W. Washington
    Blvd., Suite 3007, Culver City, CA 90232,
    310/280-6538; Fax: 310/558-5896
Agent: Camden Artists, Ltd. - Los Angeles, 213/556-2022

WHEN A STRANGER CALLS   Columbia, 1979,
    w/Doug Chapin

DENNIS J. FELDMAN
Agent: ICM - Los Angeles, 310/550-4000
Contact: Writers Guild of America - Los Angeles,
    310/550-1000

THE GOLDEN CHILD   Paramount, 1986, CP

EDWARD S. FELDMAN
Business: The Edward S. Feldman Company, c/o Icon
    Productions, 4000 Warner Blvd., Burbank, CA
    91522-0001, 818/954-6000

WHAT'S THE MATTER WITH HELEN?   United Artists,
    1971, EP
FUZZ   United Artists, 1972, EP
SAVE THE TIGER   Paramount, 1973, EP
THE OTHER SIDE OF THE MOUNTAIN
    Universal, 1975
TWO-MINUTE WARNING   Universal, 1976
THE OTHER SIDE OF THE MOUNTAIN - PART 2
    Universal, 1978
THE LAST MARRIED COUPLE IN AMERICA   Universal,
    1980, w/John Herman Shaner
SIX PACK   20th Century Fox, 1982, EP w/Ted Witzer
THE SENDER   Paramount, 1982
HOT DOG   MGM/UA, 1984
WITNESS ★   Paramount, 1985
EXPLORERS   Paramount, 1985, w/David Bombyk
THE HITCHER   TriStar, 1986, EP w/Charles R. Meeker
HAMBURGER: THE MOTION PICTURE   FM
    Entertainment, 1986, w/Charles R. Meeker
THE GOLDEN CHILD   Paramount, 1986,
    w/Robert D. Wachs
NEAR DARK   DEG, 1987, EP w/Charles R. Meeker
WIRED   Taurus, 1989, w/Charles R. Meeker
GREEN CARD   Buena Vista, 1990, EP

PHIL FELDMAN
YOU'RE A BIG BOY NOW   7 Arts, 1966
THE WILD BUNCH   Warner Bros./7 Arts, 1969
THE BALLAD OF CABLE HOGUE   Warner Bros.,
    1970, EP
FOR PETE'S SAKE   Columbia, 1974, EP
POSSE   Paramount, 1975, EP
THE TOY   Columbia, 1982
BLUE THUNDER   Columbia, 1983,
    EP w/Andrew Fogelson
STEWARDESS SCHOOL   Columbia, 1987

ERIC FELLNER
Business: Initial Film & Television., 211 East 17th St., Ste 1,
    New York, NY 10003, 212/254-7026; Fax: 212/398-9877;
    74 Black Lion Lane, London W6 9BE England,
    081/745-4500; Fax: 081/741-9416

SID & NANCY   Samuel Goldwyn Company, 1986
STRAIGHT TO HELL   Island Pictures, 1987
PASCALI'S ISLAND   Avenue Entertainment, 1988
THE RACHEL PAPERS   United Artists, 1989,
    EP w/James T. Roe III
HIDDEN AGENDA   Hemdale, 1990
A KISS BEFORE DYING   Universal, 1991, EP

JON FELTHEIMER
Business: New World Television, 1440 S. Sepulveda Blvd.,
    Los Angeles, CA 90025, 310/444-8350;
    Fax: 310/444-8407

BODY ROCK   New World, 1984, EP w/Phil Ramone &
    Charles J. Weber

ANDREW J. FENADY
Business: Fenady Associates, Inc., 249 N. Larchmont Blvd.,
    Suite 6, Los Angeles, CA 90004, 213/466-6375;
    Fax: 213/466-6376
Agent: ICM - Los Angeles, 310/550-4000

CHISUM   Warner Bros., 1970
TERROR IN THE WAX MUSEUM   Cinerama, 1973
ARNOLD   Cinerama, 1973
THE MAN WITH BOGART'S FACE   *SAM MARLOW,
    PRIVATE EYE*   20th Century Fox, 1980

ALBERT FENNELL
(credit w/Brian H. Clemens)

AND SOON THE DARKNESS   Levitt-Pickman, 1971
DR. JEKYLL AND SISTER HYDE   AIP, 1972
THE LEGEND OF HELL HOUSE   20th Century Fox, 1973,
    w/Norman T. Herman
CAPTAIN KRONOS: VAMPIRE HUNTER
    Paramount, 1974

ROBERT FENTRESS
DEAD & BURIED   Avco Embassy, 1981,
    w/Ronald Shusett

MEL FERRER
THE NIGHT VISITOR   UMC, 1971
"W"   Cinerama, 1974

SEAN FERRER
STRANGERS KISS   Orion Classics, 1984, AP
GOOD TO GO   Island Pictures, 1986, w/Douglas Dilge

BETH FERRIS
HEARTLAND   Levitt-Pickman, 1979,
    w/Michael Hausman

CHRISTIAN FERRY
KING KONG   Paramount, 1976,
    EP w/Federico DeLaurentiis
SHEENA   Columbia, 1984, AP
RED SONJA   MGM/UA, 1985

Fe

FILM
PRODUCERS,
STUDIOS,
AGENTS and
CASTING
DIRECTORS
GUIDE

F
I
L
M

P
R
O
D
U
C
E
R
S

Fe

FILM
PRODUCERS,
STUDIOS,
AGENTS AND
CASTING
DIRECTORS
GUIDE

F
I
L
M

P
R
O
D
U
C
E
R
S

PETER FETTERMAN
Business: Peter Fetterman Productions, 818 21st St.,
    Suite B, Santa Monica, CA 90403, 310/453-6463;
    Siege Productions Ltd., 17 Adam's Row, London W1,
    071/493-4441

NEITHER THE SEA NOR THE SAND   International
    Amusement Corp., 1974, w/Jack Smith
THE HAUNTING OF JULIA   Discovery, 1981,
    w/Alfred Pariser
YES, GIORGIO   MGM/UA, 1982

CY FEUER
CABARET   Allied Artists, 1972
PIAF - THE EARLY YEARS   20th Century Fox
    International Classics, 1982
A CHORUS LINE   Columbia, 1985, w/Ernest Martin

JOSEPH FEURY
Business: Joseph Feury Productions, 120 Riverside Dr.,
    Suite 5-E, New York, NY 10024, 212/877-7700;
    Fax: 212/595-2864
Contact: Directors Guild of America - Los Angeles,
    213/289-2000

THE PLEASURE GAME   Eve, 1970
THE JESUS TRIP   EMCO, 1971
STAYING TOGETHER   Hemdale, 1989

JOHN FIEDLER
(credit w/Mark Tarlov)

THE BEAST   Columbia, 1988
TUNE IN TOMORROW...   Cinecom, 1990
MORTAL THOUGHTS   Columbia, 1991

DAVID M. FIELD
Business: Paramount Pictures, 5555 Melrose Ave.,
    Los Angeles, CA 90038, 213/956-4706
Agent: William Morris Agency - Beverly Hills, 310/274-7451

AMAZING GRACE AND CHUCK   TriStar, 1987

GWEN FIELD
Contact: Paul Sandberg, c/o Sinclair-Tennenbaum,
    335 N. Maple Dr., Suite 352, Beverly Hills, CA 90210,
    310/285-6222

PATTI ROCKS   FilmDallas, 1988,
    w/Gregory M. Cummins
MORTAL PASSIONS   MGM/UA, 1990

SALLY FIELD
Business: Fogwood Films, 825 South Barrington,
    Suite 204, Los Angeles, CA 90049, 310/820-3443;
    Fax: 310/820-2227

DYING YOUNG   20th Century Fox, 1991,
    w/Kevin McCormick

TED FIELD
(credit w/Robert W. Cort)
Business: Interscope Communications, 10900 Wilshire Blvd.,
    Suite 1400, Los Angeles, CA 90024, 310/208-8525

REVENGE OF THE NERDS   20th Century Fox, 1984,
    w/Peter Samuelson*
TURK 182   20th Century Fox, 1985, w/Rene Dupont*

REVENGE OF THE NERDS II   20th Century Fox, 1987,
    w/Peter Bart
OUTRAGEOUS FORTUNE   Buena Vista, 1987
CRITICAL CONDITION   Paramount, 1987
THREE MEN & A BABY   Buena Vista, 1987
THE SEVENTH SIGN   TriStar, 1988
COLLISION COURSE   DEG, 1988
COCKTAIL   Buena Vista, 1988
BILL & TED'S EXCELLENT ADVENTURE   Orion, 1989,
    EP w/Stephen Deutsch
RENEGADES   Universal, 1989, EP w/James G. Robinson
    & Joe Roth
AN INNOCENT MAN   Buena Vista, 1989
THE FIRST POWER   Orion, 1990, w/Melinda Jason
BIRD ON A WIRE   Universal, 1990, EP
ARACHNOPHOBIA   Buena Vista, 1990, EP w/Frank
    Marshall & Steven Spielberg
THREE MEN AND A LITTLE LADY   Buena Vista, 1990
CLASS ACTION   20th Century Fox, 1991, w/Scott Kroopf
BILL & TED'S BOGUS JOURNEY   Orion, 1991,
    EP w/Rick Finkelstein
PARADISE   Buena Vista, 1991, EP
WELCOME TO BUZZSAW   Universal, 1992,
    w/Michael Hertzberg
THE HAND THAT ROCKS THE CRADLE   Buena Vista,
    1992, EP w/Rick Jaffa

ADAM FIELDS
VISION QUEST   Warner Bros., 1985, EP w/Stan Weston
THE WHOOPEE BOYS   Paramount, 1986,
    w/Peter MacGregor-Scott
JOHNNY BE GOOD   Orion, 1988
GREAT BALLS OF FIRE   Orion, 1989
JOURNEY TO THE CENTER OF THE EARTH   Cannon,
    1989, EP w/Avi Lerner & Tom Udell

FREDDIE FIELDS
Business: Freddie Fields Productions, 152 N. La Peer Dr.,
    Los Angeles, CA 90048, 310/276-6555;
    Fax: 310/276-6794

LIPSTICK   Paramount, 1976
CITIZENS BAND   *HANDLE WITH CARE*
    Paramount, 1977
LOOKING FOR MR. GOODBAR   Paramount, 1977
AMERICAN GIGOLO   Paramount, 1980, EP
WHOLLY MOSES!   Columbia, 1980
VICTORY   Paramount, 1981
FEVER PITCH   MGM/UA, 1985
POLTERGEIST II: THE OTHER SIDE   MGM/UA,
    1986, EP
AMERICAN ANTHEM   Columbia, 1986, EP
CRIMES OF THE HEART   DEG, 1986
MILLENNIUM   20th Century Fox, 1989, EP w/John
    Foreman, P. Gael Mourant & Louis M. Silverstein
GLORY   TriStar, 1989

SHEP FIELDS
CITIZENS BAND   *HANDLE WITH CARE*   Paramount,
    1977, EP

SIMON FIELDS
Business: Limelight Productions, 6806 Lexington Ave., Los
    Angeles, CA 90038, 213/464-5808; Fax: 213/464-3109

SIGN O' THE TIMES   Cineplex Odeon, 1987, CP
TEENAGE MUTANT NINJA TURTLES   New Line, 1990,
    w/David Chan & Kim Dawson

Fi

FILM
PRODUCERS,
STUDIOS,
AGENTS AND
CASTING
DIRECTORS
GUIDE

STEVEN FIERBERG
Business: 668 Washington St., Suite 3A, New York, NY
10014, 212/929-4199

FORTY-DEUCE   Island Alive, 1982, AP
MIXED BLOOD   Sara/Cinevista, 1985,
   w/Antoine Gannage

RONALD K. FIERSTEIN
TORCH SONG TRILOGY   New Line, 1988, EP

CHRISTOPHER FIGG
Business: Blue Dolphin Films, 15-17 Old Compton Street,
   London W1V 6JR England, 071/439-9511;
   Fax: 071/287-0370

HELLRAISER   New World, 1987
HELLBOUND: HELLRAISER II   New World, 1988
NIGHTBREED   20th Century Fox, 1990

PETER FILARDI
Agent: ICM - Los Angeles, 310/550-4000

FLATLINERS   Columbia, 1990, EP w/Michael Rachmil &
   Scott Rudin

HARRY FINE
(credit w/Michael Style)

VAMPIRE LOVERS   AIP, 1970
LUST FOR A VAMPIRE   American Continental, 1971
TWINS OF EVIL   Universal, 1972

ANTHONY FINGLETON
DROP DEAD FRED   New Line, 1991, EP w/Tim Bevan &
   Carlos Davis

MARTIN FINK
Business: Complete Film Corp., 3000 Oympic Blvd.,
   Santa Monica, CA 90404, 310/315-4767

SKULLDUGGERY   Universal, 1970, AP
PAYDAY   Cinerama, 1973

PENNEY FINKELMAN COX
(see Penney Finkelman COX)

RICK FINKELSTEIN
Contact: 310/285-6204

EVE OF DESTRUCTION   Orion, 1991, EP w/Robert W.
   Cort, Graham Henderson & Melinda Jason
BILL & TED'S BOGUS JOURNEY   Orion, 1991,
   EP w/Robert W. Cort & Ted Field

WILLIAM FINNEGAN
Business: Finnegan-Pinchuk Company, 4225 Coldwater
   Canyon, Studio City, CA 91604, 818/985-0430;
   Fax: 818/985-3853

SUPPORT YOUR LOCAL GUNFIGHTER   United
   Artists, 1971
NIGHT OF THE CREEPS   TriStar, 1986, EP
NORTH SHORE   Universal, 1987
THE FABULOUS BAKER BOYS   20th Century Fox,
   1989, CP
WHITE PALACE   Universal, 1990, CP
THE BABE   Universal, 1991, EP w/Walter Coblenz

MICHAEL FINNELL
Business: Renfield Productions, 100 Universal Plaza,
   Bungalow 424, Universal City, CA 91608, 818/777-8330

ROCK 'N' ROLL HIGH SCHOOL   New World, 1979
THE HOWLING   Avco Embassy, 1980, w/Jack Conrad
TWILIGHT ZONE - THE MOVIE   Warner Bros.,
   1983, AP
GREMLINS   Warner Bros., 1984
EXPLORERS   Paramount, 1985, EP
INNERSPACE   Warner Bros., 1987
THE 'BURBS   Universal, 1988, w/Larry Brezner
GREMLINS 2: THE NEW BATCH   Warner Bros., 1990
NEWSIES   BUENA VISTA, 1991
DECEIVED   Buena Vista, 1991, w/Ellen Collett &
   Wendy Dozoretz

ROBERT FIORE
DIONYSUS IN '69   Sigma III, 1970, w/Brian DePalma &
   Bruce Joel Rubin

TOM FIORELLO
FORT APACHE, THE BRONX   20th Century Fox, 1981,
   w/Martin Richards

DIANE FIRESTONE
Business: Zeta Entertainment, 814 North Highland Avenue,
   Hollywood, CA 90038, 213/466-8066; Fax: 213/466-0322

LIQUID DREAMS   1991, w/Zane W. Levitt

MARC S. FISCHER
Business: Marble Films, 16133 Ventura Blvd., Suite 600,
   Encino, CA 91436, 818/884-8911; Fax: 818/995-7432

THE FORBIDDEN DANCE   Columbia, 1990,
   w/Richard L. Albert

MARTIN J. FISCHER
BLOOD SALVAGE   Paragon Arts International, 1990,
   w/Ken Sanders

RICHARD FISCHOFF
Business: TriStar Pictures, 10202 West Washington Blvd.,
   Culver City, CA 90232-3195, 310/280-7700

KRAMER VS. KRAMER ★★   Columbia, 1979, AP
DESERT BLOOM   Columbia, 1986, EP

DANNY FISHER
TORN APART   Castle Hill, 1990, w/Jerry Menkin

DAVID FISHER
BAT 21   TriStar, 1988, w/Michael Balson &
   Gary A. Neill

MARY ANN FISHER
ANDROID   Island Alive, 1984
HOUR OF THE ASSASSIN   Concorde, 1987, CP

ROBERT FISHER
Contact: Directors Guild of America - New York,
   212/581-0370

ROCKET GIBRALTAR   Columbia, 1988, EP w/Geoffrey
   Mayo & Michael Ulick

Fi

FILM
PRODUCERS,
STUDIOS,
AGENTS AND
CASTING
DIRECTORS
GUIDE

F
I
L
M

P
R
O
D
U
C
E
R
S

ARNOLD FISHMAN
(credit w/Paul Lichtman)

OUT OF CONTROL   New World, 1985, EP
TRANSYLVANIA 6-5000   New World, 1985, EP

JOAN FISHMAN
THE PRINCE OF PENNSYLVANIA   New Line, 1988

MELVIN FISHMAN
STEPPENWOLF   D/R Films, 1974, w/Richard Herland

KATHY FITZGERALD
WISE BLOOD   New Line, 1980, w/Michael Fitzgerald

MICHAEL FITZGERALD
WISE BLOOD   New Line, 1980, w/Kathy Fitzgerald
UNDER THE VOLCANO   Universal, 1984, EP
THE PENITENT   Cineworld, 1988
MR. JOHNSON   Avenue Pictures, 1991

RODMAN FLENDER
Business: Concorde Films, 11600 San Vicente Blvd.,
   Los Angeles, CA 90049, 310/820-6733

LORDS OF THE DEEP   Concorde, 1989, AP
STRIPPED TO KILL 2   Concorde, 1989, AP
THE TERROR WITHIN   Concorde, 1989,
   CP w/Reid Shane
STREETS   Concorde, 1990, AP
THE HAUNTING OF MORELLA   Concorde, 1990,
   AP w/Alida Camp
BODY CHEMISTRY   Concorde, 1990, EP
FULL FATHOM FIVE   Concorde, 1990, EP
WATCHERS II   Concorde, 1990, CP
THE RAIN KILLER   Concorde, 1990
NAKED OBSESSION   Concorde, 1991, EP
THE UNBORN   Califilm, 1991

JOHN FLOCK
Business: Village Roadshow, 2121 Avenue of the Stars,
   22nd Floor, Los Angeles, CA 90067, 310/282-8926;
   Fax: 310/282-8992

STORYVILLE   20th Century Fox, 1991, EP w/John Davis

ANGEL FLORES-MARINI
Business: Accent Entertainment, 8439 Sunset Blvd.,
   Suite 302, Los Angeles, CA 90069, 213/654-0231

WALKER   Universal, 1987, w/Lorenzo O'Brien
THE BLUE IGUANA   Paramount, 1988,
   CP w/Othon Roffiel

ANDREW FOGELSON
WRONG IS RIGHT   Columbia, 1982, EP
BLUE THUNDER   Columbia, 1983, EP w/Phil Feldman
THE NEW KIDS   Columbia, 1985, w/Sean S. Cunningham
JUST ONE OF THE GUYS   Columbia, 1985

LAWRENCE D. FOLDES
Business: Star Cinema Production Group, Inc., 6253
   Hollywood Blvd., Suite 927, Los Angeles, CA 90028,
   213/462-2000
Attorney: Ronald G. Gabler, 9606 Santa Monica Blvd.,
   Beverly Hills, CA 90210, 310/205-8908

MALIBU HIGH   Crown International, 1979

THOMAS FOLINO
HELLO AGAIN   Buena Vista, 1987, CP w/G. Mac Brown,
   Susan Isaacs & Martin Mickelson

GEORGE FOLSEY, JR.
Business: Q Sound, 9401 Wilshire Blvd., Suite 1201,
   Beverly Hills, CA 90212, 310/278-2829
Contact: Directors Guild of America - Los Angeles,
   213/289-2000

GLASS HOUSES   Columbia, 1972
SCHLOCK *BANANA MONSTER*   Jack H. Harris
   Enterprises, 1973, EP
THE BLUES BROTHERS   Universal, 1980, AP
AN AMERICAN WEREWOLF IN LONDON   Universal, 1981
TWILIGHT ZONE - THE MOVIE   Warner Bros., 1983, AP
TRADING PLACES   Paramount, 1983, EP
INTO THE NIGHT   Universal, 1985, w/Ron Koslow
SPIES LIKE US   Warner Bros., 1985, w/Brian Grazer
CLUE   Paramount, 1985, EP w/Peter Guber, John Landis
   & Jon Peters
THREE AMIGOS   Orion, 1986, w/Lorne Michaels
AMAZON WOMEN ON THE MOON   Universal, 1987,
   EP w/John Landis
COMING TO AMERICA   Paramount, 1988,
   w/Robert D. Wachs

JANE FONDA
Business: Fonda Films, P.O. Box 1198, Santa Monica, CA
   90406, 310/458-4545

F.T.A.   AIP, 1972, w/Francine Parker & Donald Sutherland

PETER FONDA
Business Manager: Lawrence J. Stern, Nanas, Stern, Biers &
   Company, 9434 Wilshire Blvd., Beverly Hills, CA 90212,
   310/273-2501
Contact: Directors Guild of America - Los Angeles,
   213/289-2000

EASY RIDER   Columbia, 1969

NAOMI FONER
Agent: CAA - Beverly Hills, 310/288-4545
Contact: Writers Guild of America - Los Angeles,
   310/550-1000

RUNNING ON EMPTY   Warner Bros., 1988,
   EP w/Burtt Harris

LLOYD FONVIELLE
Agent: ICM - Los Angeles, 310/550-4000
Contact: Writers Guild of America - Los Angeles,
   310/550-1000

THE BRIDE   Columbia, 1985, AP
GOOD MORNING BABYLON   Vestron, 1987,
   AP w/Caldecot Chubb
CHERRY 2000   Orion, 1988, EP

HORTON FOOTE
Agent: Lucy Kroll Agency - New York, 212/877-0627
Contact: Writers Guild of America - New York,
   212/245-6180

TENDER MERCIES ★   Universal, 1983,
   CP w/Robert Duvall
THE TRIP TO BOUNTIFUL   Island Pictures, 1985,
   w/Sterling Van Wagenen

Fo

FILM
PRODUCERS,
STUDIOS,
AGENTS AND
CASTING
DIRECTORS
GUIDE

F
I
L
M

P
R
O
D
U
C
E
R
S

LILLIAN V. FOOTE
1918   Cinecom, 1985, w/Ross E. Milloy
ON VALENTINE'S DAY   Angelika, 1986,
   w/Calvin Skaggs

BRYAN FORBES
Agent: The Artists Agency - Los Angeles, 310/277-7779

INTERNATIONAL VELVET   United Artists, 1978

DAVID FORBES
THE BIG SCORE   Almi, 1983, EP w/Harry Hurwitz

JUAN FORCH
THE LAWLESS LAND   Concorde, 1988,
   EP w/Roger Corman

JOHN FOREMAN
BUTCH CASSIDY AND THE SUNDANCE KID ★   20th
   Century Fox, 1969
WINNING   Universal, 1969
WUSA   Paramount, 1970, w/Paul Newman
PUZZLE OF A DOWNFALL CHILD   Universal, 1970
SOMETIMES A GREAT NOTION   Universal, 1971
THEY MIGHT BE GIANTS   Universal, 1971,
   w/Paul Newman
THE LIFE & TIMES OF JUDGE ROY BEAN   National
   General, 1972
POCKET MONEY   National General, 1972
THE EFFECT OF GAMMA RAYS ON MAN-IN-THE-
   MOON MARIGOLDS   20th Century Fox, 1972, EP
THE MACKINTOSH MAN   Warner Bros., 1973
THE MAN WHO WOULD BE KING   Allied Artists/
   Columbia, 1975
BOBBY DEERFIELD   Columbia, 1977, EP
THE GREAT TRAIN ROBBERY   United Artists, 1979
THE ICE PIRATES   MGM/UA, 1984
EUREKA   MGM/UA, 1984, EP
PRIZZI'S HONOR ★   20th Century Fox, 1985
MILLENNIUM   20th Century Fox, 1989,
   EP w/Freddie Fields, P. Gael Mourant &
   Louis M. Silverstein
MANNEQUIN TWO: ON THE MOVE   20th Century Fox,
   1991, EP

MARK FORSTATER
Business: Mark Forstater Productions, Ltd.,
   8A Trebeck St., London, W1Y 7RL, 071/408-0733;
   Fax: 071/499-8772

MONTY PYTHON AND THE HOLY GRAIL
   Cinema 5, 1975
XTRO   New Line, 1983
KILLING HEAT   Satori, 1984
NOT FOR PUBLICATION   Samuel Goldwyn Company,
   1984, EP
MARIGOLDS IN AUGUST   RM Productions, 1984,
   w/Jonathan Cohen
PAINT IT BLACK   Vestron, 1989, w/Anne Kimmel

BILL FORSYTH
Agent: CAA - Beverly Hills, 310/288-4545
Contact: Directors Guild of America - Los Angeles,
   213/289-2000

THAT SINKING FEELING   Samuel Goldwyn
   Company, 1984

FREDERICK FORSYTH
Agent: Perry Knowlton, Curtis Brown, Inc., 10 Astor Place,
   New York, NY 10003, 212/473-5400

THE FOURTH PROTOCOL   Lorimar, 1987, EP w/Michael
   Caine & Wafic Said

DAVID FOSTER
(credit w/Lawrence Turman)
Business: The Turman-Foster Company, 1041 N. Formosa,
   Formosa Bldg., West Hollywood, CA 90046,
   213/850-3161; Fax: 213/850-3181

MCCABE & MRS. MILLER   Warner Bros., 1971,
   w/Mitchell Brower*
THE GETAWAY   National General, 1972,
   w/Mitchell Brower*
THE NICKEL RIDE   20th Century Fox, 1974, EP
THE DROWNING POOL   Warner Bros., 1975
FIRST LOVE   Paramount, 1977
HEROES   Universal, 1977
THE LEGACY   Columbia, 1978*
TRIBUTE   20th Century Fox, 1980, EP w/Richard S. Bright
CAVEMAN   United Artists, 1981
THE THING   Universal, 1982
SECOND THOUGHTS   Universal, 1983
MASS APPEAL   Universal, 1984
THE MEAN SEASON   Orion, 1985
SHORT CIRCUIT   TriStar, 1986
RUNNING SCARED   MGM, 1986
FULL MOON IN BLUE WATER   Trans World
   Entertainment, 1988, w/John Turman
SHORT CIRCUIT II   TriStar, 1988, w/Gary Foster
GLEAMING THE CUBE   20th Century Fox, 1989

GARY FOSTER
Business: TriStar Pictures, 1990 S. Bundy, Penthouse Suite
   836, Los Angeles, CA 90025, 310/442-3509;
   Fax: 310/207-4973

SHORT CIRCUIT   TriStar, 1986, AP
SHORT CIRCUIT II   TriStar, 1988, w/David Foster &
   Lawrence Turman
LOVERBOY   TriStar, 1989, w/Willie Hunt
SIDEOUT   TriStar, 1990

GEORGE FOSTER
THE PHYNX   Warner Bros., 1970, w/Bob Booker

PATRICIA FOULKROD
Business: 213/664-1408

BETTER WATCH OUT   Carolco
WARM SUMMER RAIN   Trans World Entertainment, 1990
COOL BLUE   Cinema Corporation of America, 1990, LP
DISTURBED   Live Entertainment/Odyssey, 1990, CP

PEGGY FOWLER
CAMPUS MAN   Paramount, 1987, w/Jon Landau

ROBERT FOX
Business: World Film Services Ltd.,Pinewood Studios, Iver
   Heath, Bucks., SL0 0NH, England, 0753/656501;
   Fax: 0753/656475

ANOTHER COUNTRY   Orion Classics, 1984,
   EP w/Julian Seymour

TED FOX
LIQUID DREAMS   1991, EP w/Cassian Elwes

TOM FOX
RETURN OF THE LIVING DEAD   Orion, 1985
BLUE MONKEY   Spectrafilm, 1987, EP
RETURN OF THE LIVING DEAD PART II   Lorimar, 1988

JOSEPH FRANCK
HEARTBREAKERS   Orion, 1985, EP w/Harry Cooper &
Lee Muhl

LARRY J. FRANCO
Agent: The Gersh Agency - Beverly Hills, 310/274-6611
Contact: Directors Guild of America - Los Angeles,
   213/289-2000

CUTTER'S WAY   United Artists Classics, 1981,
   AP w/Jeffrey Chernov
ESCAPE FROM NEW YORK   Avco Embassy, 1981,
   w/Debra Hill
THE THING   Universal, 1982, AP
CHRISTINE   Columbia, 1983, CP
STARMAN   Columbia, 1984
BIG TROUBLE IN LITTLE CHINA   20th Century Fox, 1986
PRINCE OF DARKNESS   Universal, 1987
THEY LIVE   Universal, 1988
TANGO & CASH   Warner Bros., 1989, CP
THE ROCKETEER   Buena Vista, 1991, EP

HARRIET FRANK, JR.
Contact: Writers Guild of America - Los Angeles,
   310/550-1000

CONRACK   20th Century Fox, 1974, w/Martin Ritt

ILANA FRANK
PROM NIGHT III; THE LAST KISS   Norstar, 1990,
   EP w/Dan Johnson

JERRY FRANKEL
FAST BREAK   Columbia, 1979, EP

BRIAN FRANKISH
Business: Universal Studios, 100 Universal City Plaza,
   Universal City, CA 91608, 818/777-5177
Contact: Directors Guild of America - Los Angeles,
   213/289-2000

VICE SQUAD   Avco Embassy, 1982
STRANGE BREW   MGM/UA, 1983, AP
THE BOY WHO COULD FLY   Lorimar, 1986, AP
IN THE MOOD   Lorimar, 1987, AP
FIELD OF DREAMS   Universal, 1989, EP
FLIGHT OF THE INTRUDER   Paramount, 1991,
   EP w/Ralph Winter

JEFF FRANKLIN
Business: Jeff Franklin Productions, 10202 W. Washington
   Blvd., Gable Bldg. 103, Culver City, CA 90232,
   310/280-5428; Fax: 310/280-1431
Agent: BBMW - Los Angeles, 310/247-5500

JUST ONE OF THE GUYS   Columbia, 1985, EP
SUMMER SCHOOL   Paramount, 1987, AP
THE IN CROWD   Orion, 1988, EP w/John F. Roach

RICHARD FRANKLIN
Agent: The Daniel Ostroff Agency - Los Angeles,
   310/278-1955
Contact: Directors Guild of America - Los Angeles,
   213/289-2000

PATRICK   Monarch-Vanguard, 1979,
   w/Antony I. Ginnane
THE BLUE LAGOON   Columbia, 1980, CP
ROAD GAMES   Avco Embassy, 1981
LINK   Cannon, 1986

M. J. FRANKOVICH
Business: Frankovich Productions, 9200 Sunset Blvd.,
   Suite 801, Los Angeles, CA 90069, 310/278-0920

BOB & CAROL & TED & ALICE   Columbia, 1969, EP
THERE'S A GIRL IN MY SOUP   Columbia, 1970,
   w/John Boulting
THE LOOKING GLASS WAR   Columbia, 1970, EP
DOCTORS' WIVES   Columbia, 1971
THE LOVE MACHINE   Columbia, 1971
$ DOLLARS   Columbia, 1971
STAND UP AND BE COUNTED   Columbia, 1972
BUTTERFLIES ARE FREE   Columbia, 1972
40 CARATS   Columbia, 1973
REPORT TO THE COMMISSIONER   United Artists, 1975
THE SHOOTIST   Paramount, 1976, w/William Self
FROM NOON TILL THREE   United Artists, 1976,
   w/William Self

JOHN FRASER
THE DRAGON FLIES   20th Century Fox, 1975,
   w/Raymond Chow

FRANK FRAZETTA
FIRE & ICE (AF)   20th Century Fox, 1983,
   w/Ralph Bakshi

RONALD E. FRAZIER
THE WRONG GUYS   New World, 1988,
   w/Charles Gordon

GRAY FREDERICKSON
MAKING IT   20th Century Fox, 1971, AP
THE GODFATHER ★★   Paramount, 1972, AP
HIT!   Paramount, 1973, EP
THE GODFATHER - PART II ★★   Paramount, 1974,
   CP w/Fred Roos
APOCALYPSE NOW ★   United Artists, 1979, CP w/Fred
   Roos & Tom Sternberg
ONE FROM THE HEART   Columbia, 1982,
   w/Fred Roos
THE OUTSIDERS   Warner Bros., 1983, w/Fred Roos
UHF   Orion, 1989, EP
THE GODFATHER PART III ★   Paramount, 1990,
   EP w/Nicholas Gage*
THE GODFATHER PART III ★   Paramount, 1990,
   CP w/Charles Mulvehill & Fred Roos

WINNIE FREDRIKSZ
LIFE IS CHEAP...BUT TOILET PAPER IS EXPENSIVE
   Silverlight, 1990

HERB FREED
AWOL   BFB, 1973, w/Arne Brandhild
HAUNTS   Intercontinental, 1977, w/Burt Weissbourd

JACK E. FREEDMAN
Business: Jack Freedman Productions, 14225 Ventura
   Blvd., Suite 200, Sherman Oaks, CA 91423,
   818/789-9306; Fax: 818/789-2632

TOY SOLDIERS   TriStar, 1991, w/Patricia Herskovic &
   Wayne S. Williams

JOEL L. FREEDMAN
BRAINSTORM   MGM/UA, 1983, EP

FRED FREEMAN
Agent: CAA - Beverly Hills, 310/288-4545
Contact: Writers Guild of America - Los Angeles,
   310/550-1000

THE BIG BUS   Paramount, 1976, w/Lawrence J. Cohen

JOEL FREEMAN
Agent: Triad Artists, Inc. - Los Angeles, 310/556-2727
Contact: Directors Guild of America - Los Angeles,
   213/289-2000

CAMELOT   Warner Bros., 1967, AP
FINIAN'S RAINBOW   Warner Bros., 1968, AP
THE HEART IS A LONELY HUNTER   Warner Bros.,
   1968, EP
SHAFT   MGM, 1971
TROUBLE MAN   20th Century Fox, 1972
THE KILLER ELITE   United Artists, 1975, AP
LOVE AT FIRST BITE   AIP, 1979
THE OCTAGON   American Cinema, 1980
THE KINDRED   FM Entertainment, 1987, EP
SOAPDISH   Paramount, 1991, CP w/Victoria White

PAUL FREEMAN
HALLOWEEN 4: THE RETURN OF MICHAEL MYERS
   Galaxy, 1988

ROBERT FREIBRUN
THE RETURN OF SUPERFLY   Triton, 1990, CP w/Ray
   Bernstein, Hank Blumenthal & Tom Gruenberg

ROBERT FRENCH
BANJOMAN   Blue Pacific, 1975, w/Richard Gilbert
   Abramson & Michael Varhol

ROBIN FRENCH
BLUE COLLAR   Universal, 1978, EP

EUGENE FRENKE
THE LAST SUNSET   Universal, 1961, w/Edward Lewis

WILLIAM FRIEDKIN
SORCERER   Paramount/Universal, 1977

DENNIS FRIEDLAND
(credit w/Christopher C. Dewey)

JOE   Cannon, 1970, EP
CRUCIBLE OF HORROR   Cannon, 1971, EP*
MAID IN SWEDEN   Cannon, 1971, EP
LUPO   Cannon, 1971, EP
THE HAPPY HOOKER   Cannon, 1975,
   EP w/Marlene Hess*

KEN FRIEDMAN
Agent: UTA - Beverly Hills, 310/273-6700
Contact: Writers Guild of America - Los Angeles,
   310/550-1000

MR. BILLION   20th Century Fox, 1977, w/Steven Bach

STEPHEN J. FRIEDMAN
Business: Kings Road Entertainment, 1901 Avenue of the
   Stars, Suite 605, Los Angeles, CA 90067, 310/552-0057;
   Fax: 310/277-4468

THE LAST PICTURE SHOW ★   Columbia, 1971
LOVIN' MOLLY   Columbia, 1974
SLAP SHOT   Universal, 1977, w/Robert J. Wunsch
BLOODBROTHERS   Warner Bros., 1978
FAST BREAK   Columbia, 1979
HERO AT LARGE   MGM/UA, 1980
LITTLE DARLINGS   Paramount, 1980
EYE OF THE NEEDLE   United Artists, 1981
THE INCUBUS   Film Ventures International, 1982, EP
ALL OF ME   Universal, 1984
ENEMY MINE   20th Century Fox, 1985
CREATOR   Universal, 1985
MORGAN STEWART'S COMING HOME   New Century/
   Vista, 1987
TOUCH AND GO   TriStar, 1987
THE BIG EASY   Columbia, 1987

TULLY FRIEDMAN
THE PROMISE   Universal, 1979, EP

DAVID FRIENDLY
Contact: Imagine Films, 1925 Century Park East,
   23rd Floor, Los Angeles, CA 90067, 310/277-1665;
   Fax: 310/785-0107

MY GIRL   Columbia, 1991, EP w/Joseph M. Caracciolo

AVA OSTERN FRIES
Business: Fries Entertainment, 6922 Hollywood Blvd.,
   12th Floor, Hollywood, CA 90028, 213/466-2266;
   Fax: 213/466-5603

TROOP BEVERLY HILLS   WEG/Columbia, 1989

CHARLES FRIES
Business: Fries Entertainment, 6922 Hollywood Blvd.,
   12th Floor, Hollywood, CA 90028, 213/466-2266;
   Fax: 213/466-5603

TALES FROM THE CRYPT   Cinerama, 1972, EP
THE VAULT OF HORROR   Cinerama, 1973, EP
LET THE GOOD TIMES ROLL (FD)   Columbia,
   1973, EP
CATCH MY SOUL   Cinerama, 1974, EP
CHOSEN SURVIVORS   Columbia, 1974
CAT PEOPLE   Universal, 1982
THRASHIN'   Fries Entertainment, 1986,
   EP w/Mike Rosenfeld
OUT OF BOUNDS   Columbia, 1986, w/Mike Rosenfeld
TROOP BEVERLY HILLS   WEG/Columbia, 1989, EP
UNDER SURVEILLANCE   Fries Entertainment, 1991, EP

THOMAS FRIES
FLOWERS IN THE ATTIC   New World, 1987, w/Sy Levin
UNDER SURVEILLANCE   Fries Entertainment, 1991

Fr

FILM
PRODUCERS,
STUDIOS,
AGENTS AND
CASTING
DIRECTORS
GUIDE

F
I
L
M

P
R
O
D
U
C
E
R
S

Fr

FILM
PRODUCERS,
STUDIOS,
AGENTS AND
CASTING
DIRECTORS
GUIDE

F
I
L
M

P
R
O
D
U
C
E
R
S

GIL FRIESEN
Contact: 770 Bonhill Road, Los Angeles, CA 90049,
310/471-0514

THE BREAKFAST CLUB   Universal, 1985,
EP w/Andrew Meyer
BETTER OFF DEAD   Warner Bros., 1985,
EP w/Andrew Meyer
BRING ON THE NIGHT (FD)   Samuel Goldwyn
Company, 1985, EP w/Andrew Meyer
ONE CRAZY SUMMER   Warner Bros., 1986,
EP w/Andrew Meyer
THE BEAST   Columbia, 1988, EP w/Dale Pollock
THE MIGHTY QUINN   MGM/UA, 1989,
EP w/Dale Pollock
WORTH WINNING   20th Century Fox, 1989,
w/Dale Pollock
BLAZE   Buena Vista, 1989, w/Dale Pollock
CROOKED HEARTS   MGM, 1991, w/Rick Stevenson &
Dale Pollock

LEON FROMKESS
RAGE   Warner Bros., 1972, w/J. Ronald Getty

GOWER FROST
Business; Jennie & Co., 3 Duck Lane, London W1V 1FL
England, 071/437-0600; Fax: 071/439-2377; 120
Wooster Street, New York, NY 10012, 212/941-9880

SLAYGROUND   Universal, 1984, w/John Dark

WILLIAM FRYE
AIRPORT 1975   Universal, 1974
AIRPORT '77   Universal, 1977
THE CONCORDE - AIRPORT '79   Universal, 1979
RAISE THE TITANIC   AFD, 1980

ROBERT FRYER
MYRA BRECKINRIDGE   20th Century Fox, 1970
TRAVELS WITH MY AUNT   MGM, 1972, w/James
Cresson & George Cukor
THE ABDICATION   Warner Bros., 1974,
w/James Cresson
MAME   Warner Bros., 1974, w/James Cresson
VOYAGE OF THE DAMNED   Avco Embassy, 1976
THE BOYS FROM BRAZIL   20th Century Fox,
1978, EP

FRED FUCHS
(credit w/Fred Roos)
Business: Zoetrope Studios, Sentinel Bldg., 916
Kearny St., San Francisco, CA 94133,
415/789-7500; Fax: 415/989-7910

TUCKER: THE MAN AND HIS DREAM
Paramount, 1988
NEW YORK STORIES   "Life Without Zoe"   Buena
Vista, 1989
THE GODFATHER PART III ★   Paramount, 1990,
EP w/Nicholas Gage*

LEO L. FUCHS
THE FRENCH WAY   *LOVE AT THE TOP*
Peppercorn-Wormser, 1975
CATHERINE & CO.   Warner Bros., 1976
SUNDAY LOVERS   United Artists, 1981
JUST THE WAY YOU ARE   MGM/UA, 1984
MALONE   Orion, 1987

MANNY FUCHS
ONCE IN PARIS   Leigh-McLaughlin, 1978,
CP w/Gerard Croce

TETSU FUJIMARA
PRAYER OF THE ROLLERBOYS   Academy Entertainment,
1991, EP w/Robert Baruc, Martin F. Gold &
Richard Lorber
CLASS OF NUKE 'EM HIGH PART II: SUBHUMANOID
MELTDOWN   Troma, 1991, EP w/Masahiro Ebisawa &
Sammy O. Masada

ANNETTE FUNICELLO
BACK TO THE BEACH   Paramount, 1987,
EP w/Frankie Avalon

ALLEN FUNT
WHAT DO YOU SAY TO A NAKED LADY? (FD)   United
Artists, 1970
MONEY TALKS (FD)   United Artists, 1972

SIDNEY J. FURIE
Business: Furie Productions, 9169 Sunset Blvd.,
Los Angeles, CA 90069
Agent: ICM - Los Angeles, 310/550-4000

PURPLE HEARTS   Warner Bros., 1984

JOHN FUSCO
Agent: William Morris Agency - Beverly Hills,
310/274-7451
Contact: Writers Guild of America - Los Angeles,
310/550-1000

YOUNG GUNS   20th Century Fox, 1988,
EP w/James G. Robinson
YOUNG GUNS II   20th Century Fox, 1990,
EP w/Gary Barber, David Nicksay, James G.
Robinson & Joe Roth
THE BABE   Universal, 1991

G

RICHARD GABOURIE
BUYING TIME   MGM/UA, 1989

PAUL GAER
GET TO KNOW YOUR RABBIT   Warner Bros., 1972,
   w/Steven Bernhardt

NICHOLAS GAGE
Contact: Writers Guild of America - New York,
   212/245-6180

ELENI   Warner Bros., 1985, w/Mark Pick & Nick Vanoff
THE GODFATHER PART III ★   Paramount, 1990,
   EP w/Fred Fuchs*

LEONARD GAINES
GOING IN STYLE   Warner Bros., 1979, EP

DEIRDRE GAINER
Contact: Northwinds Entertainment, 1223 Wilshire Blvd.,
   Suite 565, Santa Monica, CA 90403; 310/558-4504

ANNA   Vestron, 1987, EP w/Julianne Gilliam

BOB GALE
Agent: CAA - Beverly Hills, 310/288-4545
Contact: Writers Guild of America - Los Angeles,
   310/550-1000

I WANNA HOLD YOUR HAND   Universal, 1977, AP
USED CARS   Columbia, 1980
BACK TO THE FUTURE   Universal, 1985, w/Neil Canton
BACK TO THE FUTURE II   Universal, 1989,
   w/Neil Canton
BACK TO THE FUTURE III   Universal, 1990,
   w/Neil Canton

RANDOLPH GALE
GUILTY AS CHARGED   I.R.S., 1991

MITCHELL GALIN
Business: Laurel Entertainment, Inc., 928 Broadway,
   12th Floor, New York, NY 10010, 212/674-3800;
   Fax: 212/777-6426

PET SEMATARY   Paramount, 1989, CP
TALES FROM THE DARKSIDE: THE MOVIE
   Paramount, 1990, w/Richard P. Rubinstein

SANDY GALLIN
Business: Sandollar Productions, 8730 Sunset Blvd.,
   W. Penthouse, Los Angeles, CA 90069, 310/659-5933;
   Fax: 310/659-0433

JACKNIFE   Cineplex Odeon, 1989, EP
GROSS ANATOMY   Buena Vista, 1989,
   EP w/Carol Baum
FATHER OF THE BRIDE   Buena Vista, 1991, EP w/Jim
   Cruickshank & James Orr

FRED T. GALLO
Business: Whitestone Productions, Warner Bros., 4000
   Warner Blvd., Burbank, CA 91522, 818/954-1881
Contact: Directors Guild of America - Los Angeles,
   213/289-2000

LOVE AND DEATH   United Artists, 1975, AP
ANNIE HALL   United Artists, 1977, AP
GOING IN STYLE   Warner Bros., 1979,
   w/Tony Bill
BODY HEAT   Warner Bros., 1981

TIMOTHY GAMBLE
CADENCE   New Line, 1991, EP w/Frank Giustra &
   Peter E. Strauss

MICHEL GAMES
SCHWEITZER   Concorde, 1990, LP

ANTOINE GANNAGE
MIXED BLOOD   Sara Films/Cinevista, 1985,
   w/Steven Fierberg

BEN GANNON
TRAVELLING NORTH   Cineplex Odeon, 1988

JEFFREY GANZ
Contact: Writers Guild of America - Los Angeles,
   310/550-1000

YOUNG DOCTORS IN LOVE   20th Century Fox, 1982,
   AP w/Nick Abdo
BAD MEDICINE   20th Century Fox, 1985, CP

TONY GANZ
Business: Blum-Ganz Productions, 8265 Sunset Blvd.,
   Suite 202, Los Angeles, CA 90046, 213/654-1411;
   Fax: 213/654-0863
Contact: Directors Guild of America - Los Angeles,
   213/289-2000

GUNG HO   Paramount, 1986, w/Deborah Blum
NO MAN'S LAND   Orion, 1987, EP w/Ron Howard
CLEAN & SOBER   Warner Bros., 1988,
   w/Deborah Blum
VIBES   Columbia, 1988, w/Deborah Blum

ARTHUR GARDNER
(credit w/Jules Levy)
Business: Levy-Gardner-Laven Productions, 9595 Wilshire
   Blvd., Suite 610, Beverly Hills, CA 90212, 310/278-9820;
   Fax: 310/278-2632

THE McKENZIE BREAK   United Artists, 1970
UNDERGROUND   United Artists, 1970
THE HUNTING PARTY   United Artists, 1971, EP
THE HONKERS   United Artists, 1972
KANSAS CITY BOMBER   MGM, 1972, EP
WHITE LIGHTNING   United Artists, 1973
McQ   Warner Bros., 1974
BRANNIGAN   United Artists, 1975
GATOR   United Artists, 1976

ERIC GARDNER
ELVIRA, MISTRESS OF THE DARK   New World, 1988,
   w/Mark Pierson

Ga

FILM
PRODUCERS,
STUDIOS,
AGENTS AND
CASTING
DIRECTORS
GUIDE

F
I
L
M

P
R
O
D
U
C
E
R
S

Ga

**FILM
PRODUCERS,
STUDIOS,
AGENTS AND
CASTING
DIRECTORS
GUIDE**

F
I
L
M

P
R
O
D
U
C
E
R
S

HERB GARDNER
Agent: The Lantz Office - New York, 212/586-0200
Contact: Writers Guild of America - New York,
212/245-6180

WHO IS HARRY KELLERMAN AND WHY IS HE SAYING
THOSE TERRIBLE THINGS ABOUT ME?   National
General, 1971, w/Ulu Grosbard

ROBERT GARLAND
Agent: CAA - Beverly Hills, 310/288-4545
Contact: Writers Guild of America - Los Angeles,
310/550-1000

NO WAY OUT   Orion, 1987, w/Laura Ziskin

TONY GARNETT
Business: Island World Prods., 12-14 Argyll Street, London
W1V 1AB England, 071/734-3536; Fax: 071/734-3585
Attorney: Barry Hirsch - Los Angeles, 213/553-0305

KES   United Artists, 1970
THE BODY   Anglo-EMI, 1971
WEDNESDAY'S CHILD   *FAMILY LIFE*   Cinema 5, 1972
DEEP IN THE HEART   *HANDGUN*   Warner Bros., 1984
SESAME STREET PRESENTS FOLLOW THAT BIRD
Warner Bros., 1985
EARTH GIRLS ARE EASY   Vestron, 1989
FAT MAN AND LITTLE BOY   Paramount, 1989

HELEN GARVY
HARD TRAVELING   New World, 1986

JEROME GARY
Agent: The Agency - Los Angeles, 310/551-3000
Contact: Directors Guild of America - New York,
212/581-0370

PUMPING IRON (FD)   Cinema 5, 1977, w/George Butler
STRIPPER (FD)   20th Century Fox, 1986, w/Geof
Bartz & Melvyn J. Estrin

ANDREW GATY
Contact: Norman Rudman, Esq., Slaff, Mosk & Rudman,
9200 Sunset Blvd., Suite 825, Los Angeles, CA 90069,
310/275-5351

HEART OF MIDNIGHT   Samuel Goldwyn
Company, 1988

BILL GAVIN
Business: Gavin Film Ltd., 120 Wardour St., London,
W1V 3LA, 071/439-6655; Fax: 071/439-0472

THE HOT SPOT   Orion, 1990, EP w/Derek Power &
Steve Ujlaki

MICHELE RAY-GAVRAS
(see Michele RAY-Gavras)

ADRIAN GAYE
THE OPTIMISTS   Paramount, 1973, w/Victor Lyndon

E.K. GAYLORD II
MY HEROES HAVE ALWAYS BEEN COWBOYS
Samuel Goldwyn Company, 1991, w/Martin Poll

SARA GEATER
BUSINESS AS USUAL   Cannon, 1988

DAVID GEFFEN
Business: The Geffen Company, 9130 Sunset Blvd., Los
Angeles, CA 90069, 310/278-9010; Fax: 310/273-1692

PERSONAL BEST   Warner Bros., 1982, EP
LITTLE SHOP OF HORRORS   Geffen/Warner Bros., 1986

ELLIOTT GEISINGER
Contact: Directors Guild of America - New York,
212/581-0370

THE AMITYVILLE HORROR   AIP, 1979, w/Ronald Saland
CHILD'S PLAY   MGM/UA, 1988, EP w/Barrie M. Osborne

DIETER GEISSLER
THE NEVERENDING STORY   Warner Bros., 1984,
w/Bernd Eichinger
THE NEVERENDING STORY II: THE NEXT CHAPTER
Warner Bros., 1991

LARRY GELBART
Business Manager: Barry Pollack - Los Angeles,
310/550-4525
Contact: Writers Guild of America - Los Angeles,
310/550-1000

BLAME IT ON RIO   20th Century Fox, 1984, EP

HERB GELBSPAN
FOUR CLOWNS (FD)   20th Century Fox, 1970, AP
THE WORLD OF HANS CHRISTIAN ANDERSEN (AF)
United Artists, 1971, EP w/Bill Yellin

RICHARD GELFAND
Contact: New Regency Films, 4000 Warner Blvd., Burbank,
CA 91522, 818/954-3044; Fax: 818/954-3295

CALL ME   Vestron, 1988, LP w/Mary Kane

SAMUEL W. GELFMAN
CAGED HEAT   New World, 1974, EP
BORN TO KILL   *COCKFIGHTER*   New World, 1974, AP
CANNONBALL   New World, 1976
THE INCREDIBLE MELTING MAN   AIP, 1977

BRUCE GELLER
CORKY   MGM, 1972
HARRY IN YOUR POCKET   United Artists, 1973

ANDREW GELLIS
GRANDVIEW, U.S.A.   Warner Bros., 1984,
EP w/Jonathan T. Taplin

HENRY GELLIS
SHADOW OF THE HAWK   Columbia, 1976, EP

GERALD (JEFF) GEOFFRAY
Business: Paragon Arts International, 6777 Hollywood Blvd.,
Suite 520, Hollywood, CA 90028, 213/465-5355;
Fax: 213/465-9029

WITCHBOARD   Cinema Group, 1987
NIGHT ANGEL   Fries Entertainment, 1990,
w/Joe Augustyn

GEORGE W. GEORGE
THE JAMES DEAN STORY   Warner Bros., 1957,
   w/Robert Altman
TWISTED NERVE   National General, 1969,
   w/Frank Granat
NIGHT WATCH   Avco Embassy, 1973, w/Martin
   Poll & Barnard Straus
RICH KIDS   United Artists, 1979, w/Michael Hausman
MY DINNER WITH ANDRE   New Yorker, 1981,
   w/Beverly Karp

LOU GEORGE
Business: Arista Films, Inc., 16027 Ventura Blvd., Encino,
   CA 91436, 818/907-7660; Fax: 818/905-6872

SURF II   International Films, 1984, EP w/Frank D. Tolin

LOUCAS GEORGE
DICE RULES   Seven Arts, 1991, LP

NELSON GEORGE
DEF BY TEMPTATION   Troma, 1990, EP w/Kevin
   Harewood & Charles Huggins

SUSAN GEORGE
Business: Amy International Prods., 2a Park Avenue,
   Wraysbury, Middlesex TW19 5ET England,
   0784/483-131; Fax: 0784/483-812
Agent: APA - Los Angeles, 310/273-0744

STEALING HEAVEN   Scotti Bros., 1989, EP

BILL GERBER
Business: Warner Bros., 4000 Warner Blvd., Burbank, CA
   91522, 818/954-2777

CRIMES OF THE HEART   DEG, 1986,
   CP w/Arlyne Rothberg

RICHARD GERE
Contact: Gere Productions, 10202 W. Washington Blvd.,
   Metro #282, Culver City, CA 90232, 310/280-8410;
   Fax: 310/280-1598

FINAL ANALYSIS   Warner Bros., 1991,
   EP w/Maggie Wilde

PATRICIA GERRETSEN
NIGHT FRIEND   Cineplex Odeon, 1988

WILLIAM C. GERRITY
Agent: Gray/Goodman, Inc. - Beverly Hills, 310/276-7070
Contact: Directors Guild of America - New York,
   212/581-0370

SOPHIE'S CHOICE   Universal, 1982, AP
DREAM LOVER   MGM/UA, 1986, EP

JERRY GERSHWIN
Business: Winkast II Film Productions, 9507 Santa Monica
   Blvd., Suite 224, Beverly Hills, CA 90210, 310/285-9533

HARPER   Warner Bros., 1966, w/Elliott Kastner
A SEVERED HEAD   Columbia, 1971, EP w/Elliott Kastner
YOUR THREE MINUTES ARE UP   Cinerama, 1973,
   w/Mark C. Levy
BREAKHEART PASS   United Artists, 1976
NOMADS   Atlantic, 1986, EP

BERNARD GERSTEN
Business: Lincoln Center Theater, 150 W. 65th St., New
   York, NY 10023, 212/362-7600

ONE FROM THE HEART   Columbia, 1982, EP

J. RONALD GETTY
RAGE   Warner Bros., 1972, w/Leon Fromkess
THE MUTATIONS   Columbia, 1974, EP

DEREN GETZ
UHF   Orion, 1989, CP w/Kevin Breslin

AZIZ GHAZAL
ZOMBIE HIGH   Cinema Group, 1987, w/Marc Toberoff

FERNANDO GHIA
THE RED TENT   Paramount, 1971, AP
LADY CAROLINE LAMB   United Artists, 1973
THE MISSION ★   Warner Bros., 1986, w/David Puttnam

STACEY GIACHINO
THE POWER   Film Ventures International, 1984, AP
THE KINDRED   FM Entertainment, 1987, CP

DEREK GIBSON
(credit w/John Daly)
Business: Hemdale Film Corporation, 7966 Beverly Blvd.,
   Los Angeles, CA 90048, 213/966-3700;
   Fax: 213/651-3107; 21 Albion Street, London W2 2AS
   England, 071/724-1010; Fax: 071/724-9168

JAGUAR LIVES!   AIP, 1979
DEATH SHIP   Avco Embassy, 1980, w/Harold Greenberg*
A BREED APART   Orion, 1984
THE TERMINATOR   Orion, 1984, EP
TRIUMPHS OF A MAN CALLED HORSE   Jensen
   Farley, 1984*
RETURN OF THE LIVING DEAD   Orion, 1985, EP
AT CLOSE RANGE   Orion, 1986, EP
SALVADOR   Hemdale, 1986, EP
HOOSIERS   Orion, 1986, EP
PLATOON ★★   Orion, 1986, EP
RIVER'S EDGE   Island Pictures, 1987, EP
BEST SELLER   Orion, 1987, EP
BUSTER   Hemdale, 1988, EP
THE BOOST   Hemdale, 1988, EP
MADE IN U.S.A.   TriStar, 1988, EP
LOVE AT STAKE   TriStar, 1988, EP
SHAG: THE MOVIE   Hemdale, 1989, EP w/Nik Powell
MIRACLE MILE   Hemdale, 1989
CRIMINAL LAW   Hemdale, 1989, EP
WAR PARTY   Hemdale, 1989, w/Bernard Williams
VAMPIRE'S KISS   Hemdale, 1989, EP
OUT COLD   Hemdale, 1989, EP
STAYING TOGETHER   Hemdale, 1989, EP
DON'T TELL HER IT'S ME   Hemdale, 1990, EP
HIDDEN AGENDA   Hemdale, 1990, EP

RAYNOLD GIDEON
(credit w/Bruce A. Evans)
Business: Evans-Gideon Productions, Universal Studios,
   100 Universal City Plaza, Universal City, CA 91608,
   818/777-3121; Fax: 818/777-8857
Agent: CAA - Beverly Hills, 310/288-4545

STARMAN   Columbia, 1984, AP
STAND BY ME   Columbia, 1986, w/Andrew Scheinman

Gi

FILM
PRODUCERS,
STUDIOS,
AGENTS AND
CASTING
DIRECTORS
GUIDE

F
I
L
M

P
R
O
D
U
C
E
R
S

Gi

FILM
PRODUCERS,
STUDIOS,
AGENTS AND
CASTING
DIRECTORS
GUIDE

F I L M

P R O D U C E R S

MADE IN HEAVEN   Lorimar, 1987, w/David Blocker
HERO WANTED   Universal, 1991

DAVID GIL
JOE   Cannon, 1970
GUESS WHAT WE LEARNED IN SCHOOL TODAY?
   Cannon, 1970
JOURNEY THROUGH ROSEBUD   GSF, 1972

BRAD GILBERT
Contact: Monument Pictures, 8271 Melrose Ave.,
   Suite 105, Los Angeles, CA 90046, 213/852-1275;
   Fax: 213/852-1279

LITTLE NOISES   Monument Pictures, 1991,
   w/Michael Spielberg

BRUCE GILBERT
Business: American Filmworks, c/o 20th Century-Fox,
   P.O. Box 900, Beverly Hills, CA 90213, 310/203-1707;
   Fax: 310/557-2760

THE CHINA SYNDROME   Columbia, 1979, EP
NINE TO FIVE   20th Century Fox, 1980
ROLLOVER   Orion, 1981
ON GOLDEN POND ★   Universal/AFD, 1981
THE MORNING AFTER   20th Century Fox, 1986
JACK THE BEAR   20th Century Fox, 1991
MAN TROUBLE   1991, w/Carole Eastman

LEWIS GILBERT
Business: c/o Baker Rooke, Clement House, 99 Aldwych,
   London WC2 BJY, England
Contact: Directors Guild of America - Los Angeles,
   213/289-2000

ALFIE ★   Paramount, 1966
THE ADVENTURERS   Paramount, 1970
FRIENDS   Paramount, 1971
PAUL AND MICHELLE   Paramount, 1974
EDUCATING RITA   Columbia, 1983
NOT QUITE PARADISE   New World, 1986
SHIRLEY VALENTINE   Paramount, 1989

DAVID GILER
Business: The Phoenix Company, c/o Nelson Films,
   335 N. Maple Dr., Suite 350, Beverly Hills, CA 90210,
   310/285-6424
Agent: ICM - Los Angeles, 310/550-4000

ALIEN   20th Century Fox, 1979, w/Gordon Carroll &
   Walter Hill
SOUTHERN COMFORT   20th Century Fox, 1981
RUSTLER'S RHAPSODY   Paramount, 1985
ALIENS   20th Century Fox, 1986, EP w/Gordon Carroll &
   Walter Hill
THE MONEY PIT   Universal, 1986,
   EP w/Steven Spielberg
LET IT RIDE   Paramount, 1989

JULIANNE GILLIAM
ANNA   Vestron, 1987, EP w/Deirdre Gainor

TERRY GILLIAM
Business: 51 South Hill Park, London NW3, England
Agent: CAA - Beverly Hills, 310/288-4545

TIME BANDITS   Avco Embassy, 1981

LESLIE GILLIAT
THE VIRGIN SOLDIERS   Columbia, 1970, w/Ned Sherrin
THE BUTTERCUP CHAIN   Columbia, 1971, EP

GARY GILLINGHAM
HAMBONE AND HILLIE   New World, 1984,
   w/Sandy Howard

WILLIAM S. GILMORE
Contact: Directors Guild of America - Los Angeles,
   213/289-2000

SOLDIER BLUE   Avco Embassy, 1970, AP
SWASHBUCKLER   Universal, 1976, AP
THE LAST REMAKE OF BEAU GESTE   Universal, 1977
DEFIANCE   AIP, 1980, w/Jerry Bruckheimer
DEADLY BLESSING   United Artists, 1981
TOUGH ENOUGH   20th Century Fox, 1983
AGAINST ALL ODDS   Columbia, 1984, w/Taylor Hackford
WHITE NIGHTS   Columbia, 1985, w/Taylor Hackford
LITTLE SHOP OF HORRORS   Geffen/Warner Bros.,
   1986, LP
MIDNIGHT RUN   Universal, 1988, EP
RETURN OF THE LIVING DEAD PART II   Lorimar,
   1988, CP

FRANK D. GILROY
Agent: William Morris Agency - New York, 212/586-5100

DESPERATE CHARACTERS   ITC, 1971
ONCE IN PARIS   Leigh-McLaughlin, 1978

ROGER GIMBEL
Business: The Gimbel Production Group, 8439 Sunset Blvd.,
   Suite 201, Los Angeles, CA 90069, 213/656-9756;
   Fax: 213/656-1592

GRAVY TRAIN   Columbia, 1974, EP

ANTONY I. GINNANE
Business: International Film Management Ltd., Level 4, 64
   Stead St., South Melbourne, 3205 Australia, 03/699-6133

FANTASM   Filmways Australasian, 1977
PATRICK   Monarch-Vanguard, 1979, w/Richard Franklin
THIRST   Greater Union Film Distribution, 1979
STRANGE BEHAVIOR   World Northal, 1981,
   w/John Barnett
HARLEQUIN   New Image, 1983
HIGH TIDE   TriStar, 1987, EP w/Joseph Skrzynski
THE EVERLASTING SECRET FAMILY   International Film
   Exchange, 1990, EP
DRIVING FORCE   J&M Entertainment, 1990,
   EP w/Marilyn Ong

DONALD GINSBERG
FORTUNE & MEN'S EYES   MGM, 1971, CP

VINCENT GIORDANO
TOUGHER THAN LEATHER   New Line, 1988

HARRY GITTES
Business: Columbia Pictures, 10202 W. Washington Blvd.,
   Producers Bldg., Room 121, Culver City, CA 90232,
   310/280-4333

DRIVE, HE SAID   Columbia, 1971, CP
HARRY & WALTER GO TO NEW YORK   Columbia, 1976,
   w/Don Devlin

GI

FILM
PRODUCERS,
STUDIOS,
AGENTS AND
CASTING
DIRECTORS
GUIDE

GOIN' SOUTH   Paramount, 1978, w/Harold Schneider
TIMERIDER: THE ADVENTURE OF LYLE SWANN
   Jensen Farley, 1983
LITTLE NIKITA   Columbia, 1988
BREAKING IN   Samuel Goldwyn Company, 1989

FRANK GIUSTRA
BUSTER   TriStar, 1988, EP w/Peter E. Strauss
BEST OF THE BEST   Taurus, 1989, EP w/Michael
   Holzman & Jeff Ringler
CADENCE   New Line, 1991, EP w/Timothy Gamble &
   Peter E. Strauss

RICHARD GLADSTEIN
LOVE STINKS   Live Entertainment, 1991,
   EP w/Morrie Eisenman

ANDI GLADSTONE
WORKING GIRLS   Miramax, 1987, w/Lizzie Borden

ALLAN GLASER
LUST IN THE DUST   New World, 1985, w/Tab Hunter

PENELOPE GLASS
MR. JOHNSON   Avenue Pictures, 1991, CP

WOLFGANG GLATTES
Contact: Directors Guild of America - Los Angeles,
   213/289-2000

ALL THAT JAZZ   20th Century Fox, 1979,
   AP w/Kenneth Utt
STILL OF THE NIGHT   MGM/UA, 1982,
   AP w/Kenneth Utt
STAR 80   The Ladd Company/Warner Bros., 1983,
   w/Kenneth Utt
THE MORNING AFTER   20th Century Fox, 1986,
   AP w/Lois Bonfiglio
POWER   20th Century Fox, 1986, AP w/Kenneth Utt
WHITE WATER SUMMER   Columbia, 1987, EP
NADINE   TriStar, 1987, EP
SING   TriStar, 1989, EP
THE HANDMAID'S TALE   Cinecom, 1990, EP

SIDNEY GLAZIER
QUACKSER FORTUNE HAS A COUSIN IN THE BRONX
   UMC, 1970, EP
THE TWELVE CHAIRS   UMC, 1970, w/Michael Hertzberg
THE GAMBLERS   UMC, 1970, EP
GLEN AND RANDA   UMC, 1971, EP

GARRARD GLENN
THE BATTLE OF LOVE'S RETURN   Standard, 1971, EP
SEIZURE   Cinerama, 1974, w/Jeffrey Kapelman

EARL A. GLICK
THE GROUNDSTAR CONSPIRACY   Universal, 1972, EP
STARSHIP INVASIONS   Warner Bros., 1977, EP
CHILDREN OF THE CORN   New World, 1984,
   EP w/Charles J. Weber

MICHAEL S. GLICK
Contact: Directors Guild of America - Los Angeles,
   213/289-2000

THE DEVIL'S RAIN   Bryanston, 1975, w/James V. Cullen
BUSTIN' LOOSE   Universal, 1981, w/Richard Pryor
LOCK UP   TriStar, 1989, EP
ROCKY V   MGM/UA, 1990, EP

NORMAN GLICK
STARSHIP INVASIONS   Warner Bros., 1977, w/Ken Gord
   & Ed Hunt

JAMES GLICKENHAUS
Business: Shapiro-Glickenhaus Entertainment, 1619
   Broadway, New York, NY 10019, 212/265-1150; 12001
   Ventura Pl., Studio City, CA 91604, 818/766-8500;
   Fax: 818/766-7873
Agent: William Morris Agency - Beverly Hills, 310/274-7451

BASKET CASE 2   Shapiro-Glickenhaus Entertainment,
   1990, EP
FRANKENHOOKER   Shapiro-Glickenhaus Entertainment,
   1990, EP

JOEL GLICKMAN
BROTHER JOHN   Columbia, 1971
THE TRIAL OF THE CATONSVILLE NINE   Cinema 5,
   1972, EP
BUCK AND THE PREACHER   Columbia, 1972

CARY GLIEBERMAN
PEACEMAKER   Fries Entertainment, 1990, CP
BACKSTREET DREAMS   Vidmark, 1990, LP

ARNOLD GLIMCHER
Agent: CAA - Beverly Hills, 310/288-4545

LEGAL EAGLES   Universal, 1986, AP w/Sheldon Kahn
GORILLAS IN THE MIST   Universal, 1988,
   w/Terence Clegg
THE GOOD MOTHER   Buena Vista, 1988
THE MAMBO KINGS   Warner Bros., 1991,
   w/Arnon Milchan

TERRY GLINWOOD
Business: Glinwood Films Ltd., Swan House, 52 Poland St.,
   London W1V 3DF, 071/437-1181; Fax: 071/494-0634

THINK DIRTY   Quartet, 1978, AP
THE NATIONAL HEALTH   Columbia, 1979, w/Ned Sherrin
MERRY CHRISTMAS, MR. LAWRENCE   Universal, 1983,
   EP w/Masato Hara, Geoffrey Nethercott & Eiko Oshima
ERIK THE VIKING   Orion, 1989, EP
EVERYBODY WINS   Orion, 1990, EP w/Linda Yellen
A RAGE IN HARLEM   Miramax, 1991, EP w/William
   Horberg, Nik Powell, Bob Weinstein & Harvey Weinstein

YORAM GLOBUS
(credit w/Menahem Golan)
Business: Cannon Productions, 5757 Wilshire Blvd., Suite
   721, Los Angeles, CA 90036, 213/965-0901

LUPO   Cannon, 1971, w/Ami Artzi*
I LOVE YOU ROSA   Leisure Media, 1973, EP*
THE HOUSE ON CHELOUCHE STREET   Productions
   Unlimited, 1974, EP*
DAUGHTERS! DAUGHTERS!   Steinmann-Baxter,
   1975, EP*
DIAMONDS   Avco Embassy, 1975, CP*
LEPKE   Warner Bros., 1975, EP*
THE FOUR DEUCES   Avco Embassy, 1976*
KID VENGEANCE   Irwin Yablans, 1977, EP*
OPERATION THUNDERBOLT   Cinema Shares
   International, 1978
GOD'S GUN   Irwin Yablans, 1978
THE URANIUM CONSPIRACY   Noah Films, 1978,
   w/Francesco Corti*

GI

**FILM
PRODUCERS,
STUDIOS,
AGENTS AND
CASTING
DIRECTORS
GUIDE**

**F
I
L
M

P
R
O
D
U
C
E
R
S**

IT'S A FUNNY FUNNY WORLD   Noah Films, 1978
THE MAGICIAN OF LUBLIN   Cannon, 1979
THE APPLE   Cannon, 1980
THE HAPPY HOOKER GOES HOLLYWOOD
   Cannon, 1980
SCHIZOID   Cannon, 1980
THE GODSEND   Cannon, 1980
ENTER THE NINJA   Cannon, 1981, w/Judd Bernard*
BODY AND SOUL   Cannon, 1981
HOSPITAL MASSACRE   Cannon, 1982
DEATH WISH II   Filmways, 1982
THAT CHAMPIONSHIP SEASON   Cannon, 1982
THE WICKED LADY   Cannon, 1983
REVENGE OF THE NINJA   Cannon, 1983
THE LAST AMERICAN VIRGIN   Cannon, 1983
HERCULES   Cannon, 1983
10 TO MIDNIGHT   Cannon, 1983, EP
LOVE STREAMS   Cannon, 1984
GRACE QUIGLEY   *THE ULTIMATE SOLUTION OF
   GRACE QUIGLEY*   Cannon, 1984
DEJA VU   Cannon, 1984
SAHARA   Cannon, 1984
THE NAKED FACE   Cannon, 1984
BOLERO   Cannon, 1984
MISSING IN ACTION
BREAKIN'   MGM/UA/Cannon, 1984, EP
BREAKIN' 2: ELECTRIC BOOGALOO   TriStar, 1984
HOUSE OF THE LONG SHADOWS   Cannon, 1984
EXTERMINATOR 2   Cannon, 1984
NINJA III: THE DOMINATION   Cannon, 1984
SWORD OF THE VALIANT   Cannon, 1984
MISSING IN ACTION 2: THE BEGINNING   Cannon, 1985
INVASION U.S.A.   Cannon, 1985
DEATH WISH 3   Cannon, 1985
ORDEAL BY INNOCENCE   Cannon, 1985, EP
KING SOLOMON'S MINES   Cannon, 1985
FOOL FOR LOVE   Cannon, 1985
RUNAWAY TRAIN   Cannon, 1985
HOT RESORT   Cannon, 1985
RAPPIN'   Cannon, 1985
LIFEFORCE   TriStar, 1985
AMERICAN NINJA   Cannon, 1985
HOT CHILI   Cannon, 1985
THE SEVEN MAGNIFICENT GLADIATORS
   Cannon, 1985
THE ASSISI UNDERGROUND   Cannon, 1985
MARIA'S LOVERS   Cannon, 1985, EP
THE AMBASSADOR   Cannon, 1985
THE DELTA FORCE   Cannon, 1986
THE NAKED CAGE   Cannon, 1986, EP
AMERICA 3000   Cannon, 1986
DETECTIVE SCHOOL DROPOUTS   *DUMB DICKS*
   Cannon, 1986
INVADERS FROM MARS   Cannon, 1986
THE TEXAS CHAINSAW MASSACRE PART 2
   Cannon, 1986
AVENGING FORCE   Cannon, 1986
MURPHY'S LAW   Cannon, 1986, EP
COBRA   Warner Bros., 1986
P.O.W. THE ESCAPE   Cannon, 1986
OTELLO   Cannon, 1986
52 PICK-UP   Cannon, 1986
FIREWALKER   Cannon, 1986
DANGEROUSLY CLOSE   Cannon, 1986, EP
ALLAN QUATERMAIN AND THE LOST CITY OF GOLD
   Cannon, 1987
NUMBER ONE WITH A BULLET   Cannon, 1987
ASSASSINATION   Cannon, 1987, EP
DOWN TWISTED   Cannon, 1987
RUMPLESTILTSKIN   Cannon, 1987

BEAUTY AND THE BEAST   Cannon, 1987
AMERICAN NINJA 2   Cannon, 1987
HELL SQUAD   Cannon, 1987, EP
TOO MUCH   Cannon, 1987
DUET FOR ONE   Cannon, 1987
MASTERS OF THE UNIVERSE   Cannon, 1987
STREET SMART   Cannon, 1987
OVER THE TOP   Cannon, 1987
SUPERMAN IV: THE QUEST FOR PEACE   Warner
   Bros., 1987
THE HANOI HILTON   Cannon, 1987
BARFLY   Cannon, 1987, EP
DANCERS   Cannon, 1987
UNDER COVER   Cannon, 1987
DUTCH TREAT   Cannon, 1987
SURRENDER   Warner Bros., 1987, EP
TOUGH GUYS DON'T DANCE   Cannon, 1987
DEATH WISH 4: THE CRACKDOWN   Cannon, 1987, EP
SHY PEOPLE   Cannon, 1987
HANNA'S WAR   Cannon, 1988
BRADDOCK: MISSING IN ACTION III   Cannon, 1988
MESSENGER OF DEATH   Cannon, 1988, EP
HERO AND THE TERROR   Cannon, 1988, EP
A CRY IN THE DARK   Warner Bros., 1988, EP
THE KITCHEN TOTO   Cannon, 1988
POWAQQATSI   Cannon, 1988
SALSA   Cannon, 1988
APPOINTMENT WITH DEATH   Cannon, 1988
KING LEAR   Cannon, 1988
ALIEN FROM L.A.   Cannon, 1988
BUSINESS AS USUAL   Cannon, 1988, EP
HAUNTED SUMMER   Cannon, 1989
PUSS IN BOOTS   Cannon, 1989
KINJITE (FORBIDDEN SUBJECTS)   Cannon, 1989, EP
THE ROSE GARDEN   Cannon, 1989,
   EP w/Christopher Pearce*
CYBORG   Cannon, 1989
MANIFESTO   Cannon, 1989
DOIN' TIME ON PLANET EARTH   Cannon, 1990
A MAN CALLED SARGE   Cannon, 1990,
   EP w/Christopher Pearce*
DELTA FORCE 2   Cannon, 1990, w/Christopher Pearce*
ROCKULA   Cannon, 1990, EP w/Christopher Pearce*

DANNY GLOVER
Agent: Triad Artists, Inc. - Los Angeles, 310/556-2727
Contact: Carrie Productions, 4000 Warner Blvd., 16th Floor,
   Burbank, CA 91522, 818/972-1747; Fax: 818/972-9021

TO SLEEP WITH ANGER   Samuel Goldwyn Company,
   1990, EP w/Edward R. Pressman & Harris E. Tulchin

RICHARD GLOVER
NO HOLDS BARRED   New Line, 1989, EP w/Hulk Hogan
   & Vince McMahon

VICTOR GLYNN
Business: Portman Entertainment, Pinewood Studios,
   Iver Heath, Bucks., SL0 0NH, 0753/630-366;
   Fax: 0753/630-332

HIGH HOPES   Skouras Pictures, 1989, w/Simon
   Channing-Williams

GARY GOCH
CHILDREN SHOULDN'T PLAY WITH DEAD THINGS
   Europix International, 1974, w/Bob Clark
POPCORN   Studio Three, 1991, w/Ashok Amritraj &
   Torben Johnke

JANET GODDARD
Business: Pankino Productions Ltd., 134 Royal College
  Street, London NW1 0TA England, 071/267-0972;
  Fax: 071/267-7678

LETTER TO BREZHNEV   Circle Releasing, 1986

MELISSA GODDARD
Contact: New Line Cinema, 116 N. Robertson, Suite 401,
  Los Angeles, CA 90048, 818/891-6325

POISON IVY   New Line, 1991, EP w/Peter Morgan

GARY GOETZMAN
Business: Clinica Estetico Ltd., 1600 Broadway, Suite 503,
  New York, NY 10019, 212/262-2777

STOP MAKING SENSE (FD)   Cinecom, 1984
MODERN GIRLS   Atlantic, 1986
MIAMI BLUES   Orion, 1990, w/Jonathan Demme
THE SILENCE OF THE LAMBS   Orion, 1991, EP

ALEX GOHAR
THE OBJECT OF BEAUTY   Avenue, 1991, CP

ALEX E. GOITEIN
CHERRY HILL HIGH   Cannon, 1977
CHEERLEADERS' BEACH PARTY   Cannon, 1978,
  w/Dennis Murphy

MENAHEM GOLAN
(credit w/Yoram Globus)
Business: 21st Century Film Corporation, 7000 W. 3rd St.,
  Los Angeles, CA 90048, 213/658-3000;
  Fax: 213/658-3002

ESCAPE TO THE SUN   Cinevision, 1972*
999 - ALIZA THE POLICEMAN   Baruch-Mayfair, 1972*
I LOVE YOU ROSA   Leisure Media, 1973*
KAZABLAN   MGM/UA, 1974*
THE HOUSE ON CHELOUCHE STREET   Productions
  Unlimited, 1974*
TOPELE   Risto, 1975*
DAUGHTERS! DAUGHTERS!   Steinmann-Baxter, 1975*
DIAMONDS   Avco Embassy, 1975*
LEPKE   Warner Bros., 1975*
THE FOUR DEUCES   Avco Embassy, 1976, EP*
THE PASSOVER PLOT   Atlas, 1977, EP*
KID VENGEANCE   Irwin Yablans, 1977*
OPERATION THUNDERBOLT   Cinema Shares
  International, 1978
GOD'S GUN   Irwin Yablans, 1978
IT'S A FUNNY FUNNY WORLD   Noah Films, 1978
THE MAGICIAN OF LUBLIN   Cannon, 1979
THE APPLE   Cannon, 1980
THE HAPPY HOOKER GOES HOLLYWOOD
  Cannon, 1980
SCHIZOID   Cannon, 1980
THE GODSEND   Cannon, 1980
BODY AND SOUL   Cannon, 1981
HOSPITAL MASSACRE   Cannon, 1982
DEATH WISH II   Filmways, 1982
THAT CHAMPIONSHIP SEASON   Cannon, 1982
THE WICKED LADY   Cannon, 1983
10 TO MIDNIGHT   Cannon, 1983, EP
REVENGE OF THE NINJA   Cannon, 1983
THE LAST AMERICAN VIRGIN   Cannon, 1983
HERCULES   Cannon, 1983
LOVE STREAMS   Cannon, 1984

GRACE QUIGLEY   *THE ULTIMATE SOLUTION OF
  GRACE QUIGLEY*   Cannon, 1984
DEJA VU   Cannon, 1984
SAHARA   Cannon, 1984
THE NAKED FACE   Cannon, 1984
BOLERO   Cannon, 1984
MISSING IN ACTION
BREAKIN'   MGM/UA/Cannon, 1984, EP
BREAKIN' 2: ELECTRIC BOOGALOO   TriStar, 1984
HOUSE OF THE LONG SHADOWS   Cannon, 1984
EXTERMINATOR 2   Cannon, 1984
NINJA III: THE DOMINATION   Cannon, 1984
SWORD OF THE VALIANT   Cannon, 1984
MISSING IN ACTION 2: THE BEGINNING   Cannon, 1985
INVASION U.S.A.   Cannon, 1985
DEATH WISH 3   Cannon, 1985
ORDEAL BY INNOCENCE   Cannon, 1985, EP
KING SOLOMON'S MINES   Cannon, 1985
FOOL FOR LOVE   Cannon, 1985
RUNAWAY TRAIN   Cannon, 1985
HOT RESORT   Cannon, 1985
RAPPIN'   Cannon, 1985
LIFEFORCE   TriStar, 1985
AMERICAN NINJA   Cannon, 1985
HOT CHILI   Cannon, 1985
THE SEVEN MAGNIFICENT GLADIATORS   Cannon, 1985
THE ASSISI UNDERGROUND   Cannon, 1985
MARIA'S LOVERS   Cannon, 1985, EP
THE AMBASSADOR   Cannon, 1985
THE DELTA FORCE   Cannon, 1986
THE NAKED CAGE   Cannon, 1986, EP
AMERICA 3000   Cannon, 1986
DETECTIVE SCHOOL DROPOUTS   *DUMB DICKS*
  Cannon, 1986
INVADERS FROM MARS   Cannon, 1986
THE TEXAS CHAINSAW MASSACRE PART 2
  Cannon, 1986
AVENGING FORCE   Cannon, 1986
MURPHY'S LAW   Cannon, 1986, EP
COBRA   Warner Bros., 1986
P.O.W. THE ESCAPE   Cannon, 1986
OTELLO   Cannon, 1986
52 PICK-UP   Cannon, 1986
FIREWALKER   Cannon, 1986
DANGEROUSLY CLOSE   Cannon, 1986, EP
ALLAN QUATERMAIN AND THE LOST CITY OF GOLD
  Cannon, 1987
NUMBER ONE WITH A BULLET   Cannon, 1987
ASSASSINATION   Cannon, 1987, EP
DOWN TWISTED   Cannon, 1987
BEAUTY AND THE BEAST   Cannon, 1987
RUMPLESTILTSKIN   Cannon, 1987
AMERICAN NINJA 2   Cannon, 1987
HELL SQUAD   Cannon, 1987, EP
TOO MUCH   Cannon, 1987
DUET FOR ONE   Cannon, 1987
MASTERS OF THE UNIVERSE   Cannon, 1987
STREET SMART   Cannon, 1987
OVER THE TOP   Cannon, 1987
SUPERMAN IV: THE QUEST FOR PEACE   Warner
  Bros., 1987
THE HANOI HILTON   Cannon, 1987
BARFLY   Cannon, 1987, EP
DANCERS   Cannon, 1987
UNDER COVER   Cannon, 1987
DUTCH TREAT   Cannon, 1987
SURRENDER   Warner Bros., 1987, EP
TOUGH GUYS DON'T DANCE   Cannon, 1987
DEATH WISH 4: THE CRACKDOWN   Cannon, 1987, EP
SHY PEOPLE   Cannon, 1987
HANNA'S WAR   Cannon, 1988

Go

FILM
PRODUCERS,
STUDIOS,
AGENTS AND
CASTING
DIRECTORS
GUIDE

F
I
L
M

P
R
O
D
U
C
E
R
S

Go

FILM
PRODUCERS,
STUDIOS,
AGENTS AND
CASTING
DIRECTORS
GUIDE

F
I
L
M

P
R
O
D
U
C
E
R
S

BRADDOCK: MISSING IN ACTION III
Cannon, 1988
MESSENGER OF DEATH   Cannon, 1988, EP
HERO AND THE TERROR   Cannon, 1988, EP
A CRY IN THE DARK   Warner Bros., 1988, EP
THE KITCHEN TOTO   Cannon, 1988
POWAQQATSI   Cannon, 1988
SALSA   Cannon, 1988
APPOINTMENT WITH DEATH   Cannon, 1988
KING LEAR   Cannon, 1988
ALIEN FROM L.A.   Cannon, 1988
BUSINESS AS USUAL   Cannon, 1988, EP
HAUNTED SUMMER   Cannon, 1989
PUSS IN BOOTS   Cannon, 1989
KINJITE (FORBIDDEN SUBJECTS)   Cannon,
1989, EP
THE ROSE GARDEN   Cannon, 1989, EP
CYBORG   Cannon, 1989
MANIFESTO   Cannon, 1989
DOIN' TIME ON PLANET EARTH   Cannon, 1990
MACK THE KNIFE   21st Century, EP*
THE PHANTOM OF THE OPERA   21st Century,
1989, EP*
THE FORBIDDEN DANCE   Columbia, 1990,
EP w/Ami Artzi*
NIGHT OF THE LIVING DEAD   Columbia, 1990,
EP w/Ami Artzi & George Romero

FREDERIC GOLCHAN
Business: Frederic Golchan Productions, 9255 Doheny
Road, Suite 1106, Los Angeles, CA 90069,
310/858-4939; Fax: 310/858-7698

QUICK CHANGE   Warner Bros., 1990, EP

ERIC L. GOLD
Contact: Ivory Way Productions, c/o KTTV, 5746 Sunset
Blvd., Hollywood, CA 90028, 213/856-1190;
Fax: 213/462-7382

I'M GONNA GIT YOU SUCKA   MGM/UA, 1989,
EP w/Raymond Katz

JACK GOLD
Agent: InterTalent - Los Angeles, 310/858-6200

THE MEDUSA TOUCH   Warner Bros., 1978,
w/Anne V. Coates

MARTIN F. GOLD
PRAYER OF THE ROLLERBOYS   Academy
Entertainment, 1991, EP w/Robert Baruc, Tetsu
Fujimara & Richard Lorber

PETER S. GOLD
A CAPTIVE IN THE LAND   1991, EP

DAN GOLDBERG
Agent: CAA - Beverly Hills, 310/288-4545
Contact: Ivan Reitman Productions, 100 Universal Plaza,
Suite 415B, Universal City, CA 91608, 818/777-8080;
Fax: 818/777-0689

CANNIBAL GIRLS   AIP, 1973
RABID   New World, 1977, AP
MEATBALLS   Paramount, 1979
STRIPES   Columbia, 1981, w/Ivan Reitman

DANNY GOLDBERG
Business: Gold Mountain Entertainment, 3575 Cahuenga
Blvd. West, Suite 470, Los Angeles, CA 90068,
213/850-5660

NO NUKES (FD)   Warner Bros., 1980,
w/Julian Schlossberg

GARY DAVID GOLDBERG
Business: UBU Productions, 5555 Melrose Ave., Los
Angeles, CA 90038, 213/956-5058; Fax: 213/956-1678
Agent: The Jim Preminger Agency - Los Angeles,
310/475-9491

DAD   Universal, 1989, w/Joseph Stern

LEONARD J. GOLDBERG
Business: Mandy Films, 500 S. Buena Vista St., Animation
2D-12, Burbank, CA 91521, 818/560-6440;
Fax: 818/954-8411

CALIFORNIA SPLIT   Columbia, 1974,
EP w/Aaron Spelling
BABY BLUE MARINE   Columbia, 1976,
w/Aaron Spelling
THE BAD NEWS BEARS IN BREAKING TRAINING
Paramount, 1977
WINTER KILLS   Avco Embassy, 1979,
EP w/Robert Sterling
ALL NIGHT LONG   Universal, 1981, w/Jerry Weintraub
WARGAMES   MGM/UA, 1983, EP
SPACECAMP   20th Century Fox, 1986, EP
SLEEPING WITH THE ENEMY   20th Century
Fox, 1991

TIKKI GOLDBERG
Business: Melinda Jason Productions, c/o Walt Disney
Pictures, 500 S. Buena Vista, Tower - 28th Floor, Burbank,
CA 91521, 818/567-5760; Fax: 818/563-1263

LIMIT UP   MCEG, 1990, LP

WARREN GOLDBERG
CITY LIMITS   Atlantic, 1985, EP

DAVID GOLDEN
LOVE STORY ★   Paramount, 1970, EP
SHAFT   MGM, 1971, AP
SHAFT'S BIG SCORE!   MGM, 1972, AP
THE EDUCATION OF SONNY CARSON   Paramount,
1974, AP

PHILLIP GOLDFARB
Business: Steven Bochco Productions, 20th Century Fox,
10201 W. Pico Blvd., Los Angeles, CA 90035,
310/203-2400; Fax: 310/203-3236
Contact: Directors Guild of America - Los Angeles,
213/289-2000

TAXI DRIVER   Columbia, 1976, AP
ALL THE RIGHT MOVES   20th Century Fox,
1983, CP

PHILLIP B. GOLDFINE
SKI PATROL   Triumph Releasing, 1990,
w/Donald L. West

GARY GOLDMAN
(credit w/Don Bluth & John Pomeroy)
Business: Sullivan/Bluth Studios, 2501 W. Burbank, Suite 201, Burbank, CA 91505, 818/840-9446; Fax: 818/840-0487

THE SECRET OF N.I.M.H. (AF)   MGM/UA, 1982
AN AMERICAN TAIL (AF)   Universal, 1986
THE LAND BEFORE TIME (AF)   Universal, 1988
ALL DOGS GO TO HEAVEN (AF)   Universal, 1989

LES GOLDMAN
THE PHANTOM TOLLBOOTH (AF)   MGM, 1970, CP w/Abe Levitow

RONALD K. GOLDMAN
Business: Euro-American Films, 4818 Yuma St., N.W., Washington, DC 20016, 202/363-8800

SWEET JESUS, PREACHER MAN   MGM, 1973, EP
THE BLACK GESTAPO   Bryanston, 1975, EP

BERNIE GOLDMANN
Business: The Steve Tisch Co., 3815 Hughes Ave., Culver City, CA 90232, 310/838-2500; Fax: 310/204-2713

HEART CONDITION   New Line, 1990, CP w/Marie Cantin
BAD INFLUENCE   Triumph, 1990, CP

ALLAN GOLDSTEIN
Agent: Devra Lieb, Triad Artists, Inc., 10100 Santa Monica Blvd., 16th Floor, Los Angeles, CA 90067, 310/556-2727
Contact: Directors Guild of America - Los Angeles, 213/289-2000

ROOFTOPS   New Visions, 1989, CP w/Sue Jett & Tony Mark

GARY W. GOLDSTEIN
Business: The Goldstein Co., 864 S. Robertson Blvd., Ste. 304, Los Angeles, CA 90035, 310/659-9511; Fax: 310/659-8779

CANNIBAL WOMEN IN THE AVOCADO JUNGLE OF DEATH   Paramount, 1989
PRETTY WOMAN   Buena Vista, 1990, CP
PIZZA MAN   Meglomania, 1991
VICTIM OF LOVE   Academy, 1991

JUDY GOLDSTEIN
Business: Appledown, 9687 Olympic Blvd., Beverly Hills, CA 90212, 310/552-1833

REMO WILLIAMS: THE ADVENTURE BEGINS...   Orion, 1985, CP

MILTON GOLDSTEIN
Business: HKM Films, 1641 N. Ivar Ave., Hollywood, CA 90028, 213/465-9191

PORKY'S REVENGE   20th Century Fox, 1985, EP w/Melvin Simon
CAPTIVE HEARTS   MGM/UA, 1987, EP

ROBERT A. GOLDSTON
A SEPARATE PEACE   Paramount, 1972, w/Otto Plaschkes
THE BELL JAR   Avco Embassy, 1979, EP
RUNAWAY TRAIN   Cannon, 1985, EP w/Henry T. Weinstein & Robert Whitmore

DUKE GOLDSTONE
THE HARRAD SUMMER   Cinerama, 1974, EP

JOHN GOLDSTONE
THE THREE SISTERS   American Film Theatre, 1974
THE LAST DAYS OF MAN ON EARTH *THE FINAL PROGRAMME*   New World, 1974, w/Sandy Lieberson
MONTY PYTHON & THE HOLY GRAIL   Cinema 5, 1975, EP
THE ROCKY HORROR PICTURE SHOW   20th Century Fox, 1975, AP
JABBERWOCKY   Cinema 5, 1977, EP
THE HOUND OF THE BASKERVILLES   Atlantic Entertainment, 1979
MONTY PYTHON'S LIFE OF BRIAN   Orion/Warner Bros., 1979
SHOCK TREATMENT   20th Century Fox, 1981
MONTY PYTHON'S THE MEANING OF LIFE   Universal, 1983
ERIK THE VIKING   Orion, 1989

RICHARD GOLDSTONE
THE BABY MAKER   National General, 1970

JON GOLDWATER
THE RETURN OF SUPERFLY   Triton, 1990, EP w/Rudy Cohen

JOHN GOLDWYN
Business: Paramount Pictures, 5555 Melrose Ave., Hollywood, CA 90038, 213/956-5000

POLICE ACADEMY 2: THEIR FIRST ASSIGNMENT   Warner Bros., 1985, EP

SAMUEL GOLDWYN, JR.
Business: The Samuel Goldwyn Company, 10203 Santa Monica Blvd., Suite 500, Los Angeles, CA 90067, 310/552-2255; Fax: 310/284-8493

COTTON COMES TO HARLEM   United Artists, 1970
COME BACK CHARLESTON BLUE   Warner Bros., 1972
THE GOLDEN SEAL   Samuel Goldwyn Company, 1983
ONCE BITTEN   Samuel Goldwyn Company, 1985, EP
MYSTIC PIZZA   Samuel Goldwyn Company, 1988, EP
STELLA   Samuel Goldwyn Company/Buena Vista, 1990

STEVEN GOLIN
(credit w/Sigurjon Sighvatsson)
Business: Propaganda Films, 940 N. Mansfield Ave., Los Angeles, CA 90038, 213/462-6400; Fax: 213/463-7874

PRIVATE INVESTIGATIONS   MGM, 1987
THE BLUE IGUANA   Paramount, 1988
FEAR, ANXIETY, AND DEPRESSION   Samuel Goldwyn Company, 1989, w/Stanley Wlodkowski
KILL ME AGAIN   MGM/UA, 1989, w/David W. Warfield
DADDY'S DYIN'...WHO'S GOT THE WILL?   MGM/UA, 1990, w/Monty Montgomery
WILD AT HEART   Samuel Goldwyn Company, 1990, w/Monty Montgomery
A ROW OF CROWS   1991, EP

SY GOMBERG
THREE WARRIORS   Fantasy Films, 1977, w/Saul Zaentz

STEVE GOMER
Contact: Directors Guild of America - New York,
212/581-0370

SWEET LORRAINE   Angelika Films, 1987

JEAN GONTIER
Business: FilmAccord Corp., 3619 Motor Ave., Los Angeles,
CA 90034, 310/204-6270; Fax: 310/204-6295

GREEN CARD   Buena Vista, 1990,
CP w/Duncan Henderson

JACK GOOD
CATCH MY SOUL   Cinerama, 1974,
w/Richard Rosenbloom

JERRY GOOD
200 MOTELS   United Artists, 1971, w/Herb Cohen
CHEAP (AF)   New World, 1974
DIRTY DUCK (AF)   New World, 1977

GEORGE GOODMAN
Contact: Directors Guild of America - Los Angeles,
213/289-2000

THE HAPPINESS CAGE   Cinerama, 1972
COUSINS   Paramount, 1989, EP

JOHNNY GOODMAN
Agent: London Management, 235-241 Regent Street,
London W1A 7AG England, 071/493-1610;
Fax: 071/408-0065

BELLMAN AND TRUE   Island Pictures, 1987,
EP w/John Hambley, George Harrison & Denis O'Brien

R. W. GOODWIN
INSIDE MOVES   AFD, 1980, w/Mark M. Tanz

RICHARD GOODWIN
(credit w/Lord John Brabourne)
Business: Sands Films, 119 Rotherhithe Street, London
SE16 4NF England, 071/231-2209; Fax: 071/231-2119

THE DANCE OF DEATH   Paramount, 1968, AP*
PETER RABBIT AND TALES OF BEATRIX POTTER
MGM, 1971*
MURDER ON THE ORIENT EXPRESS   Paramount, 1974
DEATH ON THE NILE   Paramount, 1978
STORIES FROM A FLYING TRUNK   EMI, 1979
THE MIRROR CRACK'D   AFD, 1980
EVIL UNDER THE SUN   Universal/AFD, 1982
BIDDY   Sands Films Ltd., 1983*
A PASSAGE TO INDIA ★   Columbia, 1984
LITTLE DORRIT   Cannon, 1988

ROBERT H. GOODMAN
DOOR TO DOOR   Castle Hill Productions, 1984, EP

KEN GORD
Contact: Accent Entertainment, 8282 Sunset Blvd.,
Suite C, Los Angeles, CA 90046, 213/654-0231;
Fax: 213/654-1372

STARSHIP INVASIONS   Warner Bros., 1977, w/Norman
Glick & Ed Hunt
CRIMINAL LAW   Hemdale, 1989, CP

WILLIAM GORDEAN
STICK   Universal, 1985, EP w/Robert Daley

BERT I. GORDON
Business: Bert I. Gordon Films, 9640 Arby Dr., Beverly Hills,
CA 90210
Agent: Contemporary Artists Agency - Beverly Hills,
213/278-8250

NECROMANCY   Cinerama, 1972
THE MAD BOMBER   *THE POLICE CONNECTION*
Cinemation, 1973
FOOD OF THE GODS   AIP, 1976
EMPIRE OF THE ANTS   AIP, 1977
SATAN'S PRINCESS   Sun Heat Pictures, 1990

CHARLES GORDON
(credit w/Lawrence Gordon)
Business: Daybreak Productions, c/o 20th Century Fox,
10201 W. Pico Blvd., Bldg. 58, Los Angeles, CA 90035,
310/203-3046; Fax: 310/203-3400

NIGHT OF THE CREEPS   TriStar, 1986*
DIE HARD   20th Century Fox, 1988, EP*
THE WRONG GUYS   New World, 1988,
w/Ronald E. Frazier*
K-9   Universal, 1989
FIELD OF DREAMS ★   Universal, 1989
LEVIATHAN   MGM/UA, 1989, EP
LOCK UP   TriStar, 1989
DIE HARD 2   20th Century Fox, 1990, w/Joel Silver
THE ROCKETEER   Buena Vista, 1991, w/Lloyd Levin

JON GORDON
Business: 213/472-3439

RACE TO GLORY   New Century/Vista, 1989,
w/Daniel A. Sherkow
ALL'S FAIR   Moviestore Entertainment, 1989

LAWRENCE GORDON
Business: Largo Entertainment, c/o 20th Century Fox, 10201
W. Pico Blvd., Los Angeles, CA 90035, 310/203-3600;
Fax: 310/203-4133

DILLINGER   AIP, 1973, EP w/Samuel Z. Arkoff
IT'S NOT THE SIZE THAT COUNTS   Joseph Brenner
Associates, 1974, EP
HARD TIMES   Columbia, 1975
ROLLING THUNDER   AIP, 1977, EP
THE DRIVER   20th Century Fox, 1978
THE END   United Artists, 1978
HOOPER   Warner Bros., 1978, EP
THE WARRIORS   Paramount, 1979
XANADU   Universal, 1980
PATERNITY   Paramount, 1981, w/Hank Moonjean
JEKYLL & HYDE...TOGETHER AGAIN   Paramount, 1982
48 HOURS   Paramount, 1982, w/Joel Silver
STREETS OF FIRE   Universal, 1984, w/Joel Silver
BREWSTER'S MILLIONS   Universal, 1985, w/Joel Silver
JUMPIN' JACK FLASH   20th Century Fox, 1986,
w/Joel Silver
PREDATOR   20th Century Fox, 1987, w/John Davis &
Joel Silver
THE COUCH TRIP   Orion, 1988
DIE HARD   20th Century Fox, 1988, w/Joel Silver
FIELD OF DREAMS ★   Universal, 1989, w/Charles Gordon
FAMILY BUSINESS   TriStar, 1989
DIE HARD 2   20th Century Fox, 1990, w/Charles Gordon &
Joel Silver

ANOTHER 48 HOURS Paramount, 1990,
  w/Robert D. Wachs
THE ROCKETEER Buena Vista, 1991, w/Lloyd Levin

MARK R. GORDON
(credit w/Chris Meledandri)

BROTHERS IN ARMS Ablo, 1988
OPPORTUNITY KNOCKS Universal, 1990

SHEP GORDON
Business: Alive Films, 8912 Burton Way, Beverly Hills, CA
  90211, 310/247-7800; Fax: 310/247-7823

PRINCE OF DARKNESS Universal, 1987,
  EP w/Andre Blay
THE WHALES OF AUGUST Alive Films, 1987, EP
FAR NORTH Alive Films, 1988, EP
THEY LIVE Universal, 1988, w/Andre Blay
A TIME OF DESTINY Columbia, 1988,
  EP w/Carolyn Pfeiffer
THE MODERNS Alive Films, 1988, EP
SHOCKER Universal, 1989, EP w/Wes Craven

BERRY GORDY
Business: Gordy/de Passe Productions, 6255 Sunset Blvd.,
  Suite 1800, Los Angeles, CA 90028, 213/461-9954
Contact: Directors Guild of America - Los Angeles,
  213/289-2000

LADY SINGS THE BLUES Paramount, 1972, EP
THE BINGO LONG TRAVELING ALL-STARS & MOTOR
  KINGS Universal, 1976, EP
THE LAST DRAGON TriStar, 1985, EP

MARJOE GORTNER
WHEN YOU COMIN' BACK, RED RYDER?
  Columbia, 1979

TARQUIN GOTCH
DUTCH 20th Century Fox, 1991, EP
ONLY THE LONELY 20th Century Fox, 1991, EP

HOWARD GOTTFRIED
THE HOSPITAL United Artists, 1971
NETWORK ★ MGM/UA, 1976
ALTERED STATES Warner Bros., 1980
BODY DOUBLE Columbia, 1984, EP
THE MEN'S CLUB Atlantic, 1986
TORCH SONG TRILOGY New Line, 1988

JOE GOTTFRIED
HARD TO HOLD Universal, 1984, EP

CARL GOTTLIEB
Agent: Larry Grossman & Associates - Beverly Hills,
  310/550-8127

CELEBRATION AT BIG SUR (FD) 20th Century
  Fox, 1971

LINDA GOTTLIEB
Business: Taurusfilm, 56 W. 66th St., New York, NY
  10023, 212/456-3607; Fax: 212/456-2755

LIMBO Universal, 1972
DIRTY DANCING Vestron, 1987

MORTON GOTTLIEB
SLEUTH 20th Century Fox, 1972
SAME TIME, NEXT YEAR Universal, 1978,
  w/Walter Mirisch
ROMANTIC COMEDY MGM/UA, 1983, w/Walter Mirisch

SAM GOWAN
A FLASH OF GREEN Spectrafilm, 1985, EP

JOSEPH GRACE
Business: Linden Productions, 10850 Wilshire Blvd.,
  Suite 250, Los Angeles, CA 90024, 310/474-2234;
  Fax: 310/474-8773

MEET THE HOLLOWHEADS Moviestore, 1989,
  w/John Chavez

LORD LEW GRADE
Business: The Grade Company, 7 Queen Street, London,
  W1X 7PH, 071/409-1925; Fax: 071/408-2042

THE MEDUSA TOUCH Warner Bros., 1978, EP w/Elliott
  Kastner & Arnon Milchan
FROM THE LIFE OF THE MARIONETTES Universal/ AFD,
  1980, EP w/Martin Starger

ROGER GRAEF
MONTY PYTHON MEETS BEYOND THE FRINGE
  New Line, 1978

JOHN PATRICK GRAHAM
DIRT American Cinema, 1979, w/Allan F. Bodoh

J. EDMUND GRAINGER
A MATTER OF TIME AIP, 1976, w/Jack H. Skirball

MICHAEL GRAIS
(credit w/Mark Victor)
Agent: CAA - Beverly Hills, 310/288-4545
Contact: Writers Guild of America - Los Angeles,
  310/550-1000

POLTERGEIST II: THE OTHER SIDE MGM, 1986
GREAT BALLS OF FIRE Orion, 1989, EP
MARKED FOR DEATH 20th Century Fox, 1990,
  w/Steven Seagal

FRANK GRANAT
TWISTED NERVE National General, 1969,
  w/George W. George

ROBERT GRAND
DEFENDING YOUR LIFE Geffen/Warner Bros., 1991, CP

DEREK GRANGER
Business: Centre Entertainment PLC, 118 Cleveland Street,
  London W1P 5DN England, 071/387-4045;
  Fax: 071/388-0408

A HANDFUL OF DUST New Line, 1988

J. LLOYD GRANT
CLAUDINE 20th Century Fox, 1974
GREASED LIGHTNING Warner Bros., 1977,
  EP w/Richard Bell

Gr

FILM
PRODUCERS,
STUDIOS,
AGENTS AND
CASTING
DIRECTORS
GUIDE

F
I
L
M

P
R
O
D
U
C
E
R
S

BOB GRAY
LOOK WHO'S TALKING TriStar, 1989, LP
LOOK WHO'S TALKING TOO TriStar, 1990, CP

THOMAS K. GRAY
Business: Golden Harvest Films, Inc., 9884 Santa Monica
Blvd., Beverly Hills, CA 90212, 310/203-0722;
Fax: 310/556-3214

TEENAGE MUTANT NINJA TURTLES II: THE SECRET
OF THE OOZE New Line, 1991, w/David Chan &
Kim Dawson

BRIAN GRAZER
Business: Imagine Entertainment, 1925 Century Park East,
23rd Floor, Los Angeles, CA 90067, 310/277-1665;
Fax: 310/785-0107

NIGHT SHIFT The Ladd Company/Warner Bros., 1982
SPLASH Buena Vista, 1984
REAL GENIUS TriStar, 1985
SPIES LIKE US Warner Bros., 1985,
w/George Folsey, Jr.
ARMED & DANGEROUS Columbia, 1986,
w/James Keach
LIKE FATHER, LIKE SON TriStar, 1987, w/David Valdes
PARENTHOOD Universal, 1989
CRY BABY Universal, 1990, EP w/Jim Abrahams
KINDERGARTEN COP Universal, 1990, w/Ivan Reitman
CLOSET LAND Universal, 1991, EP w/Ron Howard
THE DOORS TriStar, 1991, EP w/Nicholas Clainos &
Mario Kassar
BACKDRAFT Universal, 1991,
EP w/Raffaella DeLaurentiis
MY GIRL Columbia, 1991
AN IRISH STORY Universal, 1992, w/Ron Howard

WENDY GREAN
SPEED ZONE Orion, 1989, LP
EDDIE & THE CRUISERS II: EDDIE LIVES Scotti Bros.,
1989, LP

WILLIAM GREAVES
Business: William Greaves Productions, 80 8th Ave.,
New York, NY 10011, 212/206-1213
Contact: Directors Guild of America - New York,
212/581-0370

ALI THE MAN; ALI THE FIGHTER (FD) CinAmerica,
1975, w/Shintaro Katsu
BUSTIN' LOOSE Universal, 1981, EP

MIKE GRECO
ALOHA SUMMER Spectrafilm, 1988

DOUGLAS GREEN
Contact: Directors Guild of America - Los Angeles,
213/289-2000

GHOST STORY Universal, 1981, CP
HEARTBEEPS Universal, 1981, EP

GERALD GREEN
Business: Omniquest - Los Angeles, 213/854-5947

MAN FRIDAY Avco Embassy, 1975, EP w/Jules Buck
OTHER SIDE OF PARADISE *FOXTROT* New
World, 1977

TINTORERA United Film, 1978
SUNBURN Paramount, 1979, w/John Daly &
Derek Gibson
HIGH RISK American Cinema, 1981, w/Joe Raffill
SALVADOR Hemdale, 1986, w/Oliver Stone

HILTON A. GREEN
Contact: Directors Guild of America - Los Angeles,
213/289-2000

PSYCHO II Universal, 1983
SIXTEEN CANDLES Universal, 1984
PSYCHO III Universal, 1986

NIGEL GREEN
Business: Entertainment Film Productions Ltd., 27 Soho
Square, London, W1V 5FL, 071/439-1606;
Fax: 071/734-2483

SLIPSTREAM Entertainment Films, 1989, EP w/William
Braunstein & Arthur Maslansky

SARAH GREEN
Business: 1 Christopher St., New York, NY 10014,
212/243-1716

THOUSAND PIECES OF GOLD Greycat, 1991, CP
CITY OF HOPE Samuel Goldwyn Company, 1991,
w/Maggie Renzi

WALON GREEN
Agent: William Morris Agency - Beverly Hills, 310/274-7451
Contact: Writers Guild of America - Los Angeles,
310/550-1000

THE HELLSTROM CHRONICLE Cinema 5, 1971

BRIAN GREENBAUM
POISON Zeitgeist, 1991, EP w/James Schamus

HAROLD GREENBERG
Business: Astral Film Enterprises, Inc., 2100 rue
Ste-Catherine ouest, bureau 900, Montreal, H3H 2T3,
514/939-5000; Fax: 514/939-1515; 720 King St. West,
Toronto M5V 2T3, 416/364-3894; Fax: 416/364-3894

THE NEPTUNE FACTOR 20th Century Fox, 1973,
EP w/David M. Perlmutter
BREAKING POINT 20th Century Fox, 1976,
EP w/Alfred Pariser
THE LITTLE GIRL WHO LIVES DOWN THE LANE AIP,
1977, EP w/Alfred Pariser
IN PRAISE OF OLDER WOMEN Avco Embassy, 1979,
w/Stephen J. Roth
CITY ON FIRE Avco Embassy, 1979,
EP w/Sandy Howard
TULIPS Avco Embassy, 1981, EP w/John B. Bennett
PORKY'S 20th Century Fox, 1982, EP w/Melvin Simon
PORKY'S II: THE NEXT DAY 20th Century Fox, 1983,
EP w/Alan Landsburg & Melvin Simon
MARIA CHAPDELAINE Moviestore, 1986, EP
HANG TOUGH Moviestore Entertainment, 1990

ROBERT E. GREENBERG
BLACK GIRL Cinerama, 1972, EP
THE BEAST MUST DIE Cinerama, 1974. EP
THE LAND THAT TIME FORGOT AIP, 1975, EP

WILLIAM R. GREENBLATT
(credit w/Martin Sheen)
Business: Symphony Pictures, 5711 W. Slauson Blvd., Suite 226, Culver City, CA 90230, 310/649-3668; Fax: 310/649-4272

DA   FilmDallas, 1988, EP w/Sam Grogg
JUDGMENT IN BERLIN   New Line, 1988, EP w/Jeffery Auerbach

DAN GREENBURG
Agent: Susan Smith & Associates - Beverly Hills, 310/658-7170
Contact: Writers Guild of America - Los Angeles, 310/550-1000

THE GUARDIAN   Universal, 1990, CP w/Mickey Borofsky & Todd Black

MICHAEL GREENBURG
ALLAN QUATERMAIN & THE LOST CITY OF GOLD   Cannon, 1987, LP

CHRIS GREENBURY
THE WORLD'S GREATEST LOVER   20th Century Fox, 1977, CP w/Terence Marsh

CAROL LYNN GREENE
BURNING SECRET   Vestron, 1988, w/Norma Heyman & Eberhard Junkersdorf

DAVID GREENE
Agent: CAA - Beverly Hills, 310/288-4545
Contact: Directors Guild of America - Los Angeles, 213/289-2000

I START COUNTING   United Artists, 1970
HARD COUNTRY   AFD, 1981, w/Mack Bing

JUSTIS GREENE
ERNEST SAVES CHRISTMAS   Buena Vista, 1988, CP w/Coke Sams

PETER GREENE
AFTER MIDNIGHT   MGM/UA, 1989, w/Richard Arlook, Jim Wheat & Ken Wheat

ROBERT GREENHUT
Contact: Directors Guild of America - New York, 212/581-0370

HUCKLEBERRY FINN   United Artists, 1974, AP
LENNY ★   United Artists, 1974, AP
DOG DAY AFTERNOON   Warner Bros., 1975, AP
THE FRONT   Columbia, 1976, AP
ANNIE HALL ★★   United Artists, 1977, EP
INTERIORS   United Artists, 1978, EP
HAIR   United Artists, 1979, AP
MANHATTAN   United Artists, 1979, EP
STARDUST MEMORIES   United Artists, 1980
ARTHUR   Orion/Warner Bros., 1981
A MIDSUMMER NIGHT'S SEX COMEDY   Orion/Warner Bros., 1982
THE KING OF COMEDY   20th Century Fox, 1983
ZELIG   Orion/Warner Bros., 1983
BROADWAY DANNY ROSE   Orion, 1984
THE PURPLE ROSE OF CAIRO   Orion, 1985
HANNAH & HER SISTERS ★   Orion, 1986

HEARTBURN   Paramount, 1986, w/Mike Nichols
RADIO DAYS   Orion, 1987
SEPTEMBER   Orion, 1987
ANOTHER WOMAN   Orion, 1988
BIG   20th Century Fox, 1988, w/James L. Brooks
WORKING GIRL ★   20th Century Fox, 1988, EP w/Laurence Mark
NEW YORK STORIES   Buena Vista, 1989
CRIMES & MISDEMEANORS   Orion, 1989
POSTCARDS FROM THE EDGE   Columbia, 1990, EP w/Neil Machlis
QUICK CHANGE   Warner Bros., 1990, w/Bill Murray
ALICE   Orion, 1990
REGARDING HENRY   Paramount, 1991, EP

SAM GREENLEE
THE SPOOK WHO SAT BY THE DOOR   United Artists, 1973, w/Ivan Dixon

ROBERT GREENWALD
Business: Robert Greenwald Productions, 10510 Culver Blvd., Culver City, CA 90232, 310/204-0404; Fax: 310/204-0174
Contact: Directors Guild of America - Los Angeles, 213/289-2000

SWEET HEARTS DANCE   TriStar, 1988, EP w/Gabrielle Mandelik & Lauren Weissman

STEPHEN R. GREENWALD
AMITYVILLE II: THE POSSESSION   Orion, 1982, w/Ira N. Smith

DAVID GREENWALT
Agent: ICM - Los Angeles, 310/550-4000
Contact: Directors Guild of America - Los Angeles, 213/289-2000

MIRACLES   Orion, 1986, EP

EILEEN GREGORY
DEEP BLUES   1991, w/John Stewart

RICHARD GREGSON
Business: UBA, Pinewood Studios, Iver Heath, Bucks SL0 0NH England, 0753/651-700; Fax: 0753/656-844

DOWNHILL RACER   Paramount, 1969

ALAN GREISMAN
Business: Rastar, 335 N. Maple, Beverly Hills, CA 90210, 310/247-0130; Fax: 310/247-9120

HEART BEAT   Orion/Warner Bros., 1980, w/Michael Shamberg
MODERN PROBLEMS   20th Century Fox, 1981, w/Michael Shamberg
WINDY CITY   Warner Bros., 1984
FLETCH   Universal, 1985, w/Peter Vincent Douglas
CLUB PARADISE   Warner Bros., 1986, EP
'NIGHT, MOTHER   Universal, 1986, w/Aaron Spelling
CROSS MY HEART   Universal, 1987, EP w/Aaron Spelling
THREE O'CLOCK HIGH   Universal, 1987, EP w/Aaron Spelling
SURRENDER   Warner Bros., 1987, w/Aaron Spelling
SATISFACTION   20th Century Fox, 1988, w/Aaron Spelling
FLETCH LIVES   Universal, 1989, w/Peter Vincent Douglas
LOOSE CANNONS   TriStar, 1990, w/Aaron Spelling
SOAPDISH   Paramount, 1991, w/Aaron Spelling

Gr

FILM
PRODUCERS,
STUDIOS,
AGENTS AND
CASTING
DIRECTORS
GUIDE

F
I
L
M

P
R
O
D
U
C
E
R
S

BRAD GREY
Business: The Brillstein Company, 9200 Sunset Blvd.,
Suite 428, Los Angeles, CA 90069, 310/275-6135;
Fax: 310/275-6180

OPPORTUNITY KNOCKS   Universal, 1990, EP

CHRIS GRIFFIN
Business: The Old Post House, Wilmcote, Stratford-Upon-
Avon CV37 9UX, 0789/292-142

EXPERIENCE PREFERRED...BUT NOT ESSENTIAL
Samuel Goldwyn Company, 1983
KIPPERBANG   P'TANG YANG, KIPPERBANG   UA
Classics, 1984
SECRETS   Samuel Goldwyn Company, 1984
SHARMA & BEYOND   Cinecom, 1986
FOREVER YOUNG   Cinecom, 1986
THOSE GLORY, GLORY DAYS   Cinecom, 1986
ARTHUR'S HALLOWED GROUND   Cinecom, 1986

JILL GRIFFITH
Contact: Directors Guild of America - Los Angeles,
213/289-2000

CHATTANOOGA CHOO CHOO   April Fools, 1984,
w/George Edwards
84 CHARLIE MOPIC   New Century/Vista, 1989, CP
ROSALIE GOES SHOPPING   Four Seasons, 1990, LP

HOWARD GRIGSBY
DRIVING FORCE   J&M Entertainment, 1990,
w/Rod Confesor

EDD GRILES
Contact: Directors Guild of America - New York,
212/581-0370

POUND PUPPIES & THE LEGEND OF BIG PAW (AF)
TriStar, 1988, w/Ray Volpe

JANET GRILLO
Business: New Line, 575 Eighth Ave., 15th Floor,
New York, NY 10018, 212/239-8880

HANGIN' WITH THE HOMEBOYS   New Line, 1991, EP

MICHAEL GRILLO
(credit w/Charles Okun)
Business: 650 N. Bronson Ave., Rm 306, Hollywood, CA 90004
Contact: Directors Guild of America - Los Angeles,
213/289-2000

SILVERADO   Columbia, 1985, EP
CROSS MY HEART   Universal, 1987, CP
THE ACCIDENTAL TOURIST ★   Warner Bros., 1988,
w/Lawrence Kasdan
I LOVE YOU TO DEATH   TriStar, 1990, EP
DEFENDING YOUR LIFE   Geffen/Warner Bros., 1991*
GRAND CANYON   20th Century Fox, 1991,
w/Lawrence Kasdan

NICK GRILLO
Contact: Neufeld/Rehme Productions, Paramount,
Dressing #112, 5555 Melrose Ave., Los Angeles, CA
90038, 213/956-4816; Fax: 213/956-2571

YOUNGBLOOD   AIP, 1978, w/Alan Riche
STONE COLD   Columbia, 1991, CP w/Andrew D.T. Pfeffer

ALBERTO GRIMALDI
Business: P.E.A. Films, 9320 Wilshire Blvd., Ste 207, Beverly
Hills, CA 90212, 310/858-6725; Fax: 310/858-7040

FOR A FEW DOLLARS MORE   United Artists, 1967
THE GOOD, THE BAD & THE UGLY   United Artists, 1968
A QUIET PLACE IN THE COUNTRY   United Artists, 1968
SPIRITS OF THE DEAD   AIP, 1969
FELLINI SATYRICON   United Artists, 1970
BURN!   United Artists, 1970
THE MERCENARY   United Artists, 1970
SABATA   United Artists, 1970
ADIOS SABATA   United Artists, 1971
THE DECAMERON   United Artists, 1971
MAN OF LA MANCHA   United Artists, 1972, EP
LAST TANGO IN PARIS   United Artists, 1973
A MAN FROM THE EAST   United Artists, 1974
THE CANTERBURY TALES   United Artists, 1974
THE ARABIAN NIGHTS   United Artists, 1974
ILLUSTRIOUS CORPSES   United Artists, 1976
SALO: THE LAST 120 DAYS OF SODOM   Zebra, 1977, EP
1900   Paramount, 1977
FELLINI'S CASANOVA   Universal, 1977
LOVERS AND LIARS   Levitt-Pickman, 1979
HURRICANE ROSY   United Artists, 1979
GINGER AND FRED   MGM/UA, 1986

CHARLES GRODIN
Agent: UTA - Beverly Hills, 310/273-6700
Contact: Writers Guild of America - Los Angeles,
310/550-1000

MOVERS & SHAKERS   MGM/UA, 1985, w/William Asher

DANIEL GRODNIK
Business: Paragon Entertainment Corp., 2211 Corinth Ave.,
Suite 305, Los Angeles, CA 90064, 310/478-7272;
Fax: 310/479-2314

STARHOPS   First American, 1978, EP w/Jack Rose &
Robert Sharpe
OUT OF CONTROL   New World, 1985, w/Fred Weintraub
1969   Atlantic, 1988, w/Bill Badalato
BLIND FURY   TriStar, 1990, w/Tim Matheson

FERDE GROFE, JR.
THE PROUD AND THE DAMNED   Prestige, 1972

SAM GROGG
Business: Magic Pictures, 6842 Valjean, Van Nuys, CA
91406, 818/989-5757; Fax: 818/781-6671

THE TRIP TO BOUNTIFUL   Island Pictures, 1985,
EP w/George Yaneff
PATTI ROCKS   FilmDallas, 1987, EP
DA   FilmDallas, 1988, EP w/William R. Greenblatt &
Martin Sheen

OTTO GROKENBERGER
STRANGER THAN PARADISE   Samuel Goldwyn
Company, 1984, EP
DOWN BY LAW   Island Pictures, 1986, EP w/Cary Brokaw

ULU GROSBARD
Agent: ICM - New York, 212/556-5600

WHO IS HARRY KELLERMAN AND WHY IS HE SAYING
THOSE TERRIBLE THINGS ABOUT ME?   National
General, 1971, w/Herb Gardner

EDGAR F. GROSS

Business: 9696 Culver Blvd., Suite 203, Culver City, CA
90232, 310/558-8110

THE EMERALD FOREST   Embassy, 1985, EP
HOPE & GLORY   Columbia, 1987, EP w/Jake Eberts
WHERE THE HEART IS   Buena Vista, 1990, EP

MICHAEL C. GROSS

(credit w/Joe Medjuck)
Business: Ivan Reitman Productions, 100 Universal Plaza,
Suite 415B, Universal City, CA 91608, 818/777-8080;
Fax: 818/777-0689

HEAVY METAL (AF)   Columbia, 1981,
AP w/Lawrence Nesis*
GHOSTBUSTERS   Columbia, 1984, AP
LEGAL EAGLES   Universal, 1986, EP
BIG SHOTS   20th Century Fox, 1987
TWINS   Universal, 1988, EP
GHOSTBUSTERS II   Columbia, 1989,
EP w/Bernie Brillstein
KINDERGARTEN COP   Universal, 1990, EP
BEETHOVEN   UNIVERSAL, 1991
STOP OR MY MOTHER WILL SHOOT   Universal, 1991,
w/Ivan Reitman

JACK GROSSBERG

Contact: Directors Guild of America - Los Angeles,
213/289-2000

PRETTY POISON   20th Century Fox, 1968, AP
THE PRODUCERS   Avco Embassy, 1968, AP
DON'T DRINK THE WATER   Avco Embassy, 1969, AP
TAKE THE MONEY AND RUN   Cinerama Releasing
Corporation, 1969, AP
BANANAS   United Artists, 1971
THE HOSPITAL   United Artists, 1971, AP
EVERYTHING YOU ALWAYS WANTED TO KNOW
ABOUT SEX* (*BUT WERE AFRAID TO ASK)
United Artists, 1972, AP
SLEEPER   United Artists, 1973
LEADBELLY   Paramount, 1976, AP
THE BETSY   Allied Artists, 1978, AP
FAST BREAK   Columbia, 1979, AP
A STRANGER IS WATCHING   MGM/UA, 1982, AP
STRANGE BREW   MGM/UA, 1983, EP
THE EXPERTS   Paramount, 1989,
EP w/Jonathan D. Krane
LITTLE MONSTERS   MGM/UA, 1989, SP

HOWARD K. GROSSMAN

Business: NorthernLights Entertainment, Ltd., Weston
Woods, Weston, CT 06883-1199, 203/226-5231

APPRENTICE TO MURDER   New World, 1988

TOM GRUENBERG

Business: Blossom Pictures, Inc., 1414 Ave. of the
Americas, 18th Floor, New York, NY 10019,
212/486-8880

FRIDAY THE 13TH PART 2   Paramount, 1981,
EP w/Lisa Barsamian
THE RETURN OF SUPERFLY   Triton, 1990, CP w/Ray
Bernstein, Hank Blumenthal & Robert Freibrun
PRIMARY MOTIVE   Hemdale, 1991,
EP w/Richard K. Rosenberg

PETER GRUNWALD

MONKEY SHINES   Orion, 1988, EP w/Gerald S. Paonessa

MICHAEL GRUSKOFF

Business: The Gruskoff-Levy Company, 8737 Clifton Way,
Beverly Hills, CA 90211, 310/550-7302
Contact: The Howard Brandy Company, Inc., 755 N. La
Cienega Blvd., Los Angeles, CA 90069, 310/657-8320;
75 Rockfeller Plaza, Suite 1706, New York, NY 10019

THE LAST MOVIE   Universal, 1971, EP
SILENT RUNNING   Universal, 1972
YOUNG FRANKENSTEIN   20th Century Fox, 1974
LUCKY LADY   20th Century Fox, 1975
RAFFERTY & THE GOLD DUST TWINS   Warner Bros.,
1975, w/Art Linson
QUEST FOR FIRE   20th Century Fox, 1982, EP
MY FAVORITE YEAR   MGM/UA, 1982
UNTIL SEPTEMBER   MGM/UA, 1984
LOVE AT STAKE   TriStar, 1988
PINK CADILLAC   Warner Bros., 1989, EP
PRELUDE TO A KISS   20th Century Fox, 1992,
w/Michael I. Levy

RICHARD GUAY

Business: Forward Films, 2445 Herring Ave., Bronx,
NY 10469
Agent: Susan H. Bodine, Esq., 477 Madison Av., 15th Floor,
New York, NY 10022 212/758-7474

TRUE LOVE   United Artists, 1989, w/Shelley Houis

PETER GUBER

(credit w/Jon Peters)
Business: Sony Pictures Entertainment, 10202 W.
Washington Blvd., Culver City, CA 90232, 310/280-7200

THE DEEP   Columbia, 1977*
MIDNIGHT EXPRESS   Columbia, 1978, EP*
AN AMERICAN WEREWOLF IN LONDON   Universal,
1981, EP
SIX WEEKS   Universal, 1982, EP
MISSING ★   Universal, 1983, EP
FLASHDANCE   Paramount, 1983, EP
D.C. CAB   Universal, 1983, EP
HEAD OFFICE   TriStar, 1985, EP
VISION QUEST   Warner Bros., 1985
THE LEGEND OF BILLIE JEAN   TriStar, 1985, EP
CLUE   Paramount, 1985, EP w/George Folsey Jr. &
John Landis
THE COLOR PURPLE ★   Warner Bros., 1985, EP
THE CLAN OF THE CAVE BEAR   Warner Bros., 1986,
EP w/Mark Damon, John Hyde & Sidney Kimmel
YOUNGBLOOD   MGM/UA, 1986, EP
THE WITCHES OF EASTWICK   Warner Bros., 1987,
w/Neil Canton
INNERSPACE   Warner Bros., 1987, EP w/Kathleen
Kennedy, Frank Marshall & Steven Spielberg
WHO'S THAT GIRL   Warner Bros., 1987,
EP w/Roger Birnbaum
GORILLAS IN THE MIST   Universal, 1988, EP
CADDYSHACK II   Warner Bros., 1988, w/Neil Canton
RAIN MAN ★★   MGM/UA, 1988, EP
BATMAN   Warner Bros., 1989
TANGO & CASH   Warner Bros., 1989
MISSING LINK   Universal, 1989, EP
THE BONFIRE OF THE VANITIES   Warner Bros.,
1990, EP

Gu

FILM
PRODUCERS,
STUDIOS,
AGENTS AND
CASTING
DIRECTORS
GUIDE

F
I
L
M

P
R
O
D
U
C
E
R
S

Gu

FILM
PRODUCERS,
STUDIOS,
AGENTS AND
CASTING
DIRECTORS
GUIDE

F
I
L
M

P
R
O
D
U
C
E
R
S

ROBERT GUENETTE
Business: 1551 S. Robertson Blvd., Suite 200, Los Angeles, CA 90035, 310/785-9312; Fax: 310/277-2369
Contact: Directors Guild of America - Los Angeles, 213/289-2000
Contact: Writers Guild of America - Los Angeles, 310/550-1000

THE MYSTERIOUS MONSTERS (FD)   Sunn Classic, 1976, CP
THE MAN WHO SAW TOMORROW (FD)   Warner Bros., 1981, w/Paul Drane & Lee Kramer

JAMES WILLIAM GUERCIO
Business: Caribou Ranch, Nederland, CO 80466, 303/258-3215
Agent: Jeff Berg, ICM - Los Angeles, 310/550-4000

ELECTRA GLIDE IN BLUE   United Artists, 1973
SECOND HAND HEARTS   *THE HAMSTER OF HAPPINESS*   Lorimar/Paramount, 1981

J. P. GUERIN
THE KILLING TIME   New World, 1987, EP

DON GUEST
Business: American Road Productions, 3000 Olympic Blvd., Suite 2428, Santa Monica, CA 90404, 310/315-4735; Fax: 310/315-4800
Agent: Gray/Goodman, Inc. - Beverly Hills, 310/276-7070
Contact: Directors Guild of America - Los Angeles, 213/289-2000

THE WHITE DAWN   Paramount, 1974, AP
BLUE COLLAR   Universal, 1978
THE OSTERMAN WEEKEND   20th Century Fox, 1983, AP
HAMMETT   Orion, 1982, w/Ronald Colby & Fred Roos
PARIS, TEXAS   20th Century Fox, 1984
AT CLOSE RANGE   Orion, 1986, w/Elliott Lewitt
SHADOW OF CHINA   New Line, 1991, w/Elliott Lewitt

MICHAEL GUEST
PING PONG   Samuel Goldwyn Company, 1987, w/Malcolm Craddock

ROBERT GURALNICK
Business: Warner Bros., 4000 Warner Blvd., Burbank, CA 91522, 818/954-2966

MUSTANG: THE HOUSE THAT JOE BUILT (FD)   RG Productions, 1978
THE PUNISHER   New World, 1990, EP

CARL GUREVICH
FOREPLAY   Cinema National, 1975, EP

PAUL R. GURIAN
Business: Gurian Productions, c/o TriStar Pictures, 3400 Riverside Dr., Bungalow 3, Room 10, Burbank, CA 91505, 818/954-5721

CUTTER'S WAY   United Artists Classics, 1981
PEGGY SUE GOT MARRIED   TriStar, 1986
THE SEVENTH SIGN   TriStar, 1988, EP
THE ARROWTOOTH WALTZ   Warner Bros., 1991, EP

J.R. GUTERMAN
DICE RULES   Seven Arts, 1991, EP w/Jana Sue Memel

JAMES C. GUTMAN
SOMETHING SHORT OF PARADISE   AIP, 1979, w/Lester Berman

GENE GUTOWSKI
ROMANCE OF A HORSETHIEF   Allied Artists, 1971

H

LARRY HABER
GRIM PRAIRIE TALES   East/West Film Partners, 1990, EP w/Rick Blumenthal

TAYLOR HACKFORD
Agent: CAA - Beverly Hills, 310/288-4545

AGAINST ALL ODDS   Columbia, 1984, w/William S. Gilmore
WHITE NIGHTS   Columbia, 1985, w/William S. Gilmore
LA BAMBA   Columbia, 1987, w/Bill Borden
EVERYBODY'S ALL-AMERICAN   Warner Bros., 1988, w/Laura Ziskin & Ian Sander
ROOFTOPS   New Visions, 1989, EP w/Stuart Benjamin
THE LONG WALK HOME   Miramax, 1990, EP w/Stuart Benjamin
QUEENS LOGIC   Seven Arts, 1991, EP w/Stuart Benjamin
MORTAL THOUGHTS   Columbia, 1991, EP w/Stuart Benjamin

DENNIS HACKIN
(credit w/Neal Dobrofsky)

WANDA NEVADA   United Artists, 1979
BRONCO BILLY   Warner Bros., 1980

RONNIE HADAR
Business: Ronnie Hadar Productions, 1551 N. La Brea Ave., Hollywood, CA 90028, 213/850-6110

THE TOMB   Trans World, 1986, w/Fred Olen Ray
CARTEL   Shapiro Glickenhaus, 1990

MARILYN G. HAFT
IN A SHALLOW GRAVE   Skouras Pictures, 1988, EP w/Lindsay Law

STEVEN M. HAFT
Business: Haft Nasatir Productions, 136 East 57th St., 12th Floor, New York, NY 10022, 212/754-3016 or 20th Century Fox, P.O. Box 900, Los Angeles, CA 90035, 310/203-2974; Fax: 310/788-9753

BEYOND THERAPY   New World, 1987
MR. NORTH   Samuel Goldwyn Company, 1988, w/Skip Steloff
DEAD POETS SOCIETY ★   Buena Vista, 1989, w/Tony Thomas & Paul Junger Witt

Ha

FILM
PRODUCERS,
STUDIOS,
AGENTS AND
CASTING
DIRECTORS
GUIDE

DENNIS HAGGERTY
THE PACKAGE   Orion, 1989, CP w/Andrew Davis

TOBIE HAGGERTY
THE PACKAGE   Orion, 1989, w/Beverly J. Camhe

RICHARD HAHN
Business: East/West Film Partners, 279 S. Beverly Dr.,
   Suite 934, Beverly Hills, CA 90212, 310/858-3091;
   Fax: 310/858-0703

KANDYLAND   New World, 1988, CP w/Leo Leichter
GRIM PRAIRIE TALES   East/West Film Partners, 1990

CHARLES HAID
Agent: Writers & Artists Agency, 11726 San Vicente Blvd.,
   Suite 300, Los Angeles, CA 90049, 310/820-2240

SQUARE DANCE   *HOME IS WHERE THE HEART IS*
Island Pictures, 1987, EP w/Jane Alexander

DON HAIG
Business: Film Arts Ltd., 424 Adelaide St. East, Toronto,
   M5A 1N4, 416/368-9925

I'VE HEARD THE MERMAIDS SINGING   Miramax,
   1987, EP
NIGHT FRIEND   Cineplex Odeon, 1988, EP
COMIC BOOK CONFIDENTIAL (FD)   Cinecom, 1989,
   w/Martin Harbury & Ron Mann

RICHARD HAINES
SPACE AVENGER   Manley, 1990, CP

JOE HALE
THE BLACK CAULDRON (AF)   Buena Vista, 1985

JACK HALEY, JR.
Business: Jack Haley Jr. Productions, 8255 Beverly Blvd.,
   Los Angeles, CA 90048, 213/655-1106
Contact: Directors Guild of America - Los Angeles,
   213/289-2000

THAT'S ENTERTAINMENT! (FD)   MGM/UA, 1974
BETTER LATE THAN NEVER   Warner Bros., 1983,
   w/David Niven Jr.
THAT'S DANCING! (FD)   MGM, 1985, w/David Niven Jr.

PETER HALEY
Business: Norstar Entertainment, Inc., 86 Bloor Street W.,
   5th Floor, Toronto, Ontario M5S 1M5, Canada,
   416/961-6278

BULLIES   Universal, 1986, EP
HELLO MARY LOU: PROM NIGHT II   Samuel Goldwyn
   Company, 1987, EP

LIANNE HALFON
Contact: A&M Films, 1416 N. La Brea Ave., Hollywood, CA
   90028, 213/469-2411; Fax: 213/856-2740

CROOKED HEARTS   MGM, 1991, AP w/Mark Bentley

KATHY HALLBERG
THE SEVENTH SIGN   TriStar, 1988, CP

TODD HALLOWELL
AN IRISH STORY   Universal, 1991, EP

ROBERT HALMI, JR.
Business: RHI, 720 5th Ave., 9th Floor, New York, NY
   10019, 212/977-9001
Contact: Directors Guild of America - Los Angeles,
   213/289-2000

BRADY'S ESCAPE   Satori, 1984, AP
LILY IN LOVE   New Line, 1985, EP w/Peter Bacso

ROBERT HALMI, SR.
Business: RHI, 156 W. 56th Street, Suite 1901, New York,
   NY 10019, 212/977-9001; Fax: 212/977-9049

VISIT TO A CHIEF'S SON   United Artists, 1974
HUGO THE HIPPO (AF)   20th Century Fox, 1976
BRADY'S ESCAPE   Satori, 1984
THE ONE AND ONLY   Paramount, 1978, EP
LILY IN LOVE   New Line, 1985
CHEETAH   Buena Vista, 1989
MR. & MRS. BRIDGE   Miramax, 1990, EP

RON HAMADY
(credit w/George Braunstein)

TRAIN RIDE TO HOLLYWOOD   Taylor-Laughlin,
   1975, EP
FADE TO BLACK   American Cinema, 1980
SURF II   International Films, 1984
AND GOD CREATED WOMAN   Vestron, 1988
OUT COLD   Hemdale, 1989
DON'T TELL HER IT'S ME   Hemdale, 1990

JOHN HAMBLEY
Business: Euston Films, 365 Euston Road, London NW1
   3AR England, 071/387-0911; Fax: 071/388-2122

BELLMAN AND TRUE   Island Pictures, 1987, EP w/Johnny
   Goodman, George Harrison & Denis O'Brien
DEALERS   Skouras Pictures, 1989, EP w/Andrew Brown

DAVID SHAMROY HAMBURGER
Contact: Directors Guild of America - Los Angeles,
   213/289-2000

THE CANNONBALL RUN   20th Century Fox, 1981, AP
MEGAFORCE   20th Century Fox, 1982, AP
THE SQUEEZE   TriStar, 1987, EP w/Harry Colomby
THE INDIAN RUNNER   1991, LP

ALAN HAMEL
NOTHING PERSONAL   AIP, 1980, EP w/Jay Bernstein &
   Norman Hirschfield

MICHAEL HAMILBURG
Business: The Mitchell J. Hamilburg Agency - Beverly Hills,
   310/657-1501

THE YAKUZA   Warner Bros., 1975, CP

GEORGE HAMILTON
Agent: APA - Los Angeles, 310/273-0744

EVEL KNIEVEL   Fanfare, 1971, w/Joe Solomon
LOVE AT FIRST BITE   AIP, 1979, EP w/Robert Kaufman
ZORRO, THE GAY BLADE   20th Century Fox, 1981,
   w/C. O. Erickson

Ha

FILM
PRODUCERS,
STUDIOS,
AGENTS AND
CASTING
DIRECTORS
GUIDE

F
I
L
M

P
R
O
D
U
C
E
R
S

MICHAEL HAMLYN
Business: Midnight Films, 4th Floor, Ramillies House,
   1/2 Ramillies St., London W1V 1DF, 071/494-0926;
   Fax: 071/494-2676

U2: RATTLE & HUM (FD)   Paramount, 1988

ANDRAS HAMORI
Business: Accent Entertainment, 8282 Sunset Blvd.,
   Suite C, Los Angeles, CA 90046, 213/654-0231;
   Fax: 213/654-1372

HEAVENLY BODIES   MGM/UA, 1985, AP
SEPARATE VACATIONS   RSK Entertainment, 1986, AP
THE GATE   New Century/Vista, 1987, CP
NOWHERE TO HIDE   New Century/Vista, 1987
IRON EAGLE II   TriStar, 1988, EP
FOOD OF THE GODS II   Concorde, 1989,
   EP w/Robert Misiorowski

CHRISTOPHER HAMPTON
Agent: William Morris Agency - Beverly Hills, 310/274-7451

DANGEROUS LIAISONS ★   Warner Bros., 1988, CP

TIM HAMPTON
MONTY PYTHON'S LIFE OF BRIAN   Orion/Warner Bros.,
   1979, AP
LEGEND   Universal, 1986, CP
FRANTIC   Warner Bros., 1988, w/Thom Mount
A DRY WHITE SEASON   MGM, 1989, EP
THE NEVERENDING STORY II: THE NEXT CHAPTER
   Warner Bros., 1991, EP

CHARLES HANAWALT
THE HARD RIDE   AIP, 1971

BARRY HANKERSON
PIPE DREAMS   Avco Embassy, 1976, EP

WILLIAM HANNA
(credit w/Joseph Barbera)
Business: Hanna-Barbera Productions, Inc., 3400
   Cahuenga Blvd. West, Los Angeles, CA 90068,
   213/851-5000; Fax: 213/969-1201

CHARLOTTE'S WEB (AF)   Paramount, 1974
JETSONS: THE MOVIE (AF)   Universal, 1990

CHARLES HANNAH
VICIOUS   SVS Films, 1988, w/David Hannah

DAVID HANNAH
VICIOUS   SVS Films, 1988, w/Charles Hannah

GARY HANNAM
THE NAVIGATOR: AN ODYSSEY ACROSS TIME
   Circle Releasing, 1989, CP

LISA M. HANSEN
Business: CineTel Films, Inc., 3800 W. Alameda Ave.,
   Suite 825, Burbank, CA 91505, 818/955-9551;
   Fax: 818/955-9616

ARMED RESPONSE   CineTel, 1986, EP
BULLETPROOF   CineTel, 1987, EP
COLD STEEL   CineTel, 1987

976-EVIL   New Line, 1989
HIT LIST   New Line, 1989, EP
RELENTLESS   New Line, 1989, EP w/Paul Hertzberg
MASTERS OF MENACE   New Line, 1990, w/Tino Insana
FAR OUT MAN   New Line, 1990
TOO MUCH SUN   New Line, 1990
HORROSCOPE   New Line, 1991, EP
PAST MIDNIGHT   New Line, 1991
SERIOUS MONEY   New Line, 1991

BARRY HANSON
THE LONG GOOD FRIDAY   Embassy, 1982
MORONS FROM OUTER SPACE   Universal, 1985

JOHN HANSON
Business: New Front Films, 125 W. Richmond Ave.,
   Point Richmond, CA 94801, 415/231-0225
Agent: Scott Harris, Harris & Goldberg - Los Angeles,
   310/553-5200

NORTHERN LIGHTS   Cine Manifest, 1979, w/Rob Nilsson
WILDROSE   Troma, 1985, CP

MASATO HARA
MERRY CHRISTMAS, MR. LAWRENCE   Universal, 1983,
   EP w/Terry Glinwood, Geoffrey Nethercott & Eiko Oshima
RAN   Orion Classics, 1985, w/Serge Silberman

JOHN HARADA
THE MEN'S CLUB   Atlantic, 1986, EP w/Thomas Coleman
   & Michael Rosenblatt

SASHA HARARI
THE DOORS   TriStar, 1991, w/Bill Graham & A. Kitman Ho

MARTIN HARBURY
COMIC BOOK CONFIDENTIAL (FD)   Cinecom, 1989,
   w/Don Haig & Ron Mann

MALCOLM R. HARDING
Contact: Directors Guild of America - Los Angeles,
   213/289-2000

HARRY AND SON   Orion, 1984, AP
FLIGHT OF THE NAVIGATOR   Buena Vista, 1986,
   EP w/Mark Damon, John Hyde & Jonathan Sanger
FAR NORTH   Alive Films, 1988, w/Carolyn Pfeiffer
WEEKEND AT BERNIE'S   20th Century Fox, 1989,
   EP w/Robert Klane
SHORT TIME   20th Century Fox, 1990, SP
MANNEQUIN TWO: ON THE MOVE   20th Century Fox,
   1991, CP

STEWART HARDING
HAPPY BIRTHDAY TO ME   Columbia, 1981, LP
FALLING OVER BACKWARDS   Astral Films, 1990,
   w/Mort Ransen

KARL HARDMAN
NIGHT OF THE LIVING DEAD   Continental, 1968,
   w/Russell W. Streiner

JOHN HARDY
sex, lies, & videotape   Miramax, 1989, w/Robert Newmyer
TWENTY-ONE   Triton, 1991, w/Morgan Mason
NO SECRETS   I.R.S., 1991, w/Morgan Mason &
   Shauna Shapiro

Ha

FILM
PRODUCERS,
STUDIOS,
AGENTS AND
CASTING
DIRECTORS
GUIDE

JOHN HARDY

Business: Enterprise Pictures, Ltd., 113 Wardour St.,
London, W1V 3TD, 071/734-3372; Fax: 071/734-7626

QUEEN OF HEARTS   Cinecom, 1989

SHARON HAREL
(credit w/Jacob Kotzky)
Business: Capitol Films, Ltd., 24 Upper Brook St., London
W1Y 1PD, 071/872-0154; Fax: 071/495-0640

EVERY TIME WE SAY GOODBYE   TriStar, 1986
IRON EAGLE II   TriStar, 1988, w/John Kemeny

KEVIN HAREWOOD

DEF BY TEMPTATION   Troma, 1990, EP w/Nelson
George & Charles Huggins

JOHN L. HARGREAVES

BAXTER   National General, 1973,
EP w/Howard G. Barnes
DON QUIXOTE   Continental, 1973

EFREM HARKHAM
(credit w/Uri Harkham)

GORKY PARK   Orion, 1983, AP
GHOST WARRIOR   Empire, 1986, EP w/Albert Band &
Arthur H. Maslansky

URI HARKHAM
(credit w/Efrem Harkham)
Business: Karen Films, 755 N. La Cienega Blvd.,
Suite 201, Los Angeles, CA 90069, 310/289-0270

GORKY PARK   Orion, 1983, AP
GHOST WARRIOR   Empire, 1986, EP w/Albert Band &
Arthur H. Maslansky

JAN HARLAN

BARRY LYNDON   Warner Bros., 1975, EP
FULL METAL JACKET   Warner Bros., 1987, EP

J. BOYCE HARMAN, JR.

Contact: Directors Guild of America - New York,
212/581-0370

SHAKEDOWN   Universal, 1988

KENNETH HARPER

THE VIRGIN AND THE GYPSY   Chevron, 1970
THE WIZ   Universal, 1978, EP

BURTT HARRIS

LITTLE MURDERS   20th Century Fox, 1971, AP
THE NEXT MAN   Allied Artists, 1976, CP
THE WIZ   Universal, 1978, AP
CRUISING   United Artists, 1980, AP
JUST TELL ME WHAT YOU WANT   Warner Bros.,
1980, EP
PRINCE OF THE CITY   Orion/Warner Bros., 1981
DEATHTRAP   Warner Bros., 1982
THE VERDICT ★   20th Century Fox, 1982, EP
DANIEL   Paramount, 1983
GARBO TALKS   MGM/UA, 1984, w/Elliott Kastner
D.A.R.Y.L.   Paramount, 1985, CP w/Gabrielle Kelly
THE GLASS MENAGERIE   Cineplex Odeon, 1987
RUNNING ON EMPTY   Warner Bros., 1988, EP w/Naomi Foner

SEE NO EVIL, HEAR NO EVIL   TriStar, 1989,
EP w/Earl Barret & Arne Sultan
FAMILY BUSINESS   TriStar, 1989, EP w/Jennifer Ogden
Q&A   TriStar, 1990, w/Arnon Milchan

DENNIS HARRIS

SILENT SCREAM   American Cinema, 1979,
EP w/Joan Harris
THE HIDDEN   New Line, 1987, EP w/Stephen Diener,
Jeffrey Klein & Lee Muhl

DOUG HARRIS

HEARTS OF FIRE   Lorimar, 1988,
EP w/Gerald W. Abrams

GRAHAM HARRIS

THE BEAST IN THE CELLAR   Cannon, 1971

JACK H. HARRIS

DARK STAR   Jack H. Harris, 1974, EP
EYES OF LAURA MARS   Columbia, 1978, EP
THE BLOB   TriStar, 1988, w/Elliott Kastner

JAMES B. HARRIS

Business: James B. Harris Productions, 248 1/2 Lasky Dr.,
Beverly Hills, CA 90212, 310/273-4270
Attorney: Louis C. Blau, Loeb & Loeb, 10100 Santa Monica
Blvd., Los Angeles, CA 90067, 310/552-7700
Agent: ICM - Los Angeles, 310/550-4000

THE KILLING   United Artists, 1956
PATHS OF GLORY   United Artists, 1957
LOLITA   MGM, 1962
THE BEDFORD INCIDENT   Columbia, 1965
SOME CALL IT LOVING   Cine Globe, 1973
TELEFON   MGM/UA, 1977
FAST-WALKING   Pickman, 1982
COP   Atlantic, 1988, w/James Woods

JOAN HARRIS

SILENT SCREAM   American Cinema, 1979,
EP w/Dennis Harris

LEWIS HARRIS

SHORT EYES   Paramount, 1977

RICHARD HARRIS

ECHOES OF A SUMMER   Cine Artists, 1976,
EP w/Sandy Howard

ROBERT HARRIS

Business: Davnor Productions, Ltd., 300 Phillips Park Rd.,
Mamaroneck, NY 10543, 914/381-2994

SPACE AVENGER   Manley, 1990, w/Ray Sundlin
THE GRIFTERS   Miramax, 1990, w/James Painten &
Martin Scorsese

GEORGE HARRISON
(credit w/Denis O'Brien)
Business: HandMade Films, Ltd., 26 Cadogan Square,
London SW1X 0JP, England, 071/581-1265,
071/581-8345; Fax: 071/584-7338

THE CONCERT FOR BANGLADESH (FD)   20th Century
Fox, 1972, w/Allen Klein*
LITTLE MALCOLM AND HIS STRUGGLE AGAINST THE
EUNUCHS   Multicetera Investments, 1974, EP*

Ha

FILM
PRODUCERS,
STUDIOS,
AGENTS AND
CASTING
DIRECTORS
GUIDE

F
I
L
M

P
R
O
D
U
C
E
R
S

MONTY PYTHON'S LIFE OF BRIAN   Orion/Warner Bros.,
   1979, EP
TIME BANDITS   Avco Embassy, 1981, EP
THE MISSIONARY   Columbia, 1982, EP
PRIVATES ON PARADE   Orion Classics, 1984, EP
SCRUBBERS   Orion Classics, 1984, EP
BULLSHOT   Island Alive, 1985, EP
A PRIVATE FUNCTION   Island Alive, 1985, EP
MONA LISA   Island Pictures, 1986, EP
SHANGHAI SURPRISE   MGM, 1986, EP
WATER   Atlantic, 1986, EP
WITHNAIL & I   Cineplex Odeon, 1987, EP
THE LONELY PASSION OF JUDITH HEARNE   Island
   Pictures, 1987, EP
BELLMAN & TRUE   Island Pictures, 1987,
   EP w/Johnny Goodman & John Hambley
FIVE CORNERS   Cineplex Odeon, 1988, EP
TRACK 29   Island Pictures, 1988, EP
POWWOW HIGHWAY   Warner Bros., 1989, EP
CHECKING OUT   Warner Bros., 1989, EP
HOW TO GET AHEAD IN ADVERTISING   Warner Bros.,
   1989, EP
NUNS ON THE RUN   20th Century Fox, 1990, EP
THE RAGGEDY RAWNEY   Four Seasons Entertainment,
   1990, EP

CHRIS HARROP
LEOPARD IN THE SNOW   New World, 1979,
   w/John Quested

RAY HARRYHAUSEN
(credit w/Charles H. Schneer)

THE GOLDEN VOYAGE OF SINBAD   Columbia, 1974
SINBAD AND THE EYE OF THE TIGER   Columbia, 1977
CLASH OF THE TITANS   MGM/UA, 1981

JIM V. HART
Agent: CAA - Beverly Hills, 310/288-4545

HOOK   TriStar, 1991, EP

KENNETH HARTFORD
HELL SQUAD   Cannon, 1987

HAL HARTLEY
Contact: True Fiction Pictures, 12 W. 27th St., 10th Floor,
   New York, NY 10001, 212/684-4284; Fax: 212/686-6109

THE UNBELIEVABLE TRUTH   Miramax, 1990,
   w/Bruce Weiss

NEIL HARTLEY
Business: Woodfall Ltd., Hill House, 1 Little New St.,
   London EC4A 3TR, England or 1478 N. Kings Rd.,
   Los Angeles, CA 90069

HAMLET   Columbia, 1969
A DELICATE BALANCE   American Film Theatre, 1973, EP
JOSEPH ANDREWS   Paramount, 1977
THE BORDER   Universal, 1982, EP
THE HOTEL NEW HAMPSHIRE   Orion, 1984

TED HARTLEY
Contact: RKO/Pavilion Productions, 1801 Avenue of the
   Stars, Suite 498, Los Angeles, CA 90067, 310/277-0707;
   Fax: 310/284-8574

FALSE IDENTITY   RKO, 1990, EP w/Gerald Offsay &
   Daniel Sarnoff

JOE R. HARTSFIELD
THE HOUSE ON SKULL MOUNTAIN   20th Century Fox,
   1974, EP

RAY HARTWICK
Contact: Directors Guild of America - Los Angeles,
   213/289-2000

SO FINE   Warner Bros., 1981, AP
PRINCE OF THE CITY   Orion/Warner Bros., 1981, AP
OUT OF BOUNDS   Columbia, 1986,
   EP w/John Tarnoff
THE UNTOUCHABLES   Paramount, 1987, AP
VIBES   Columbia, 1988, CP
SCROOGED   Paramount, 1988, CP
OPPORTUNITY KNOCKS   Universal, 1990, CP

WOLF C. HARTWIG
OFFICE GIRLS   International Producers, 1974
CAMPUS SWINGERS   Hemisphere, 1974
WOMEN FOR SALE   Independent International, 1975
THE MAKING OF A LADY   Sunset International, 1976
CROSS OF IRON   Avco Embassy, 1977

RUPERT HARVEY
Business: Sho Films, 2300 Duane St., Suite 9, Los Angeles,
   CA 90039, 213/665-9088; Fax: 213/665-7087

ANDROID   Island Alive, 1984, EP w/Barry Opper
CITY LIMITS   Atlantic, 1985, w/Barry Opper
CRITTERS   New Line, 1986
SLAMDANCE   Island Pictures, 1987, w/Barry Opper
THE BLOB   TriStar, 1988, LP
A NIGHTMARE ON ELM STREET, PART 5: THE DREAM
   CHILD   New Line, 1989, w/Robert Shaye
PUMP UP THE VOLUME   New Line, 1990,
   w/Sandy Stern

RICHARD HASHIMOTO
Contact: Directors Guild of America - Los Angeles,
   213/289-2000

TOUGH GUYS   Buena Vista, 1986,
   CP w/Jana Sue Memel
BEETLEJUICE   Warner Bros., 1988, w/Michael Bender &
   Larry Wilson
EDWARD SCISSORHANDS   20th Century Fox, 1990, EP
SINGLES   Warner Bros., 1991, w/Cameron Crowe

DANIEL HASSID
DELUSION   Cineville, 1991

SALAH M. HASSANEIN
Business: 516/921-3802

KNIGHTRIDERS   UFD, 1981, EP
CREEPSHOW   Warner Bros., 1982, EP
DAY OF THE DEAD   UFD, 1985, EP
COMPROMISING POSITIONS   Paramount, 1985, EP
HELLO AGAIN   Buena Vista, 1987, EP

BOB HATHCOCK
DUCK TALES: THE MOVIE - TREASURE OF THE LOST
   LAMP (AF)   Buena Vista, 1990

GARY HAUNAN
WILD HORSES   Satori, 1984, EP

MICHAEL HAUSMAN

Business: Cinehaus, 245 W. 55th St., Suite 1011, New York, NY 10019, 212/245-9060
Contact: Directors Guild of America - New York, 212/581-0370

TAKING OFF   Universal, 1971, AP
THE HEARTBREAK KID   20th Century Fox, 1972, AP
MIKEY AND NICKY   Paramount, 1976
I NEVER PROMISED YOU A ROSE GARDEN   New World, 1977, w/Daniel H. Blatt & Terence F. Deane
ALAMBRISTA!   Bobwin/Film Haus, 1979, w/Irwin Young
HEARTLAND   Levitt-Pickman, 1979, w/Beth Ferris
RICH KIDS   United Artists, 1979, w/George W. George
ONE-TRICK PONY   Warner Bros., 1980, CP
RAGTIME   Paramount, 1981, EP w/Bernard Williams
SILKWOOD   20th Century Fox, 1983, w/Mike Nichols
THE BALLAD OF GREGORIO CORTEZ   Embassy, 1983, w/Moctesuma Esparza
PLACES IN THE HEART ★   TriStar, 1984, EP
AMADEUS ★★   Orion, 1984, EP w/Bertil Ohlsson
NO MERCY   TriStar, 1986, EP
DESERT BLOOM   Columbia, 1986
THE FLIGHT OF THE SPRUCE GOOSE   Film Haus, 1986
HOUSE OF GAMES   Orion, 1987
THINGS CHANGE   Columbia, 1988
VALMONT   Orion, 1989, w/Paul Rannam
STATE OF GRACE   Orion, 1990, EP
HOMICIDE   Triumph, 1991, w/Edward R. Pressman

ANTHONY HAVELOCK-ALLAN

ROMEO & JULIET ★   Paramount, 1968, w/Lord John Brabourne
RYAN'S DAUGHTER   MGM, 1970

GOLDIE HAWN

Business: Hawn/Sylbert Productions, Hollywood Pictures, 500 S. Buena Vista St., Animation 1D-6, Burbank, CA 91521, 818/560-6120; Fax: 818/566-4141

PRIVATE BENJAMIN   Warner Bros., 1980, EP
PROTOCOL   Warner Bros., 1984, EP
MY BLUE HEAVEN   Warner Bros., 1990, EP w/Nora Ephron & Andrew Stone

DENNIS HAYASHI

LIVING ON TOKYO TIME   Skouras Pictures, 1987, w/Lynn O'Donnell

MATHEW HAYDEN

MIDNIGHT CROSSING   Vestron, 1988

JEFFREY HAYES

Contact: Directors Guild of America - New York, 212/581-0370

ON THE EDGE   Skouras Pictures, 1986, w/Rob Nilsson

TERRY HAYES

(credit w/Doug Mitchell)
Business: Kennedy Miller Productions, 30 Orwell St., Kings Cross, Sydney, Australia

MAD MAX BEYOND THUNDERDOME   Warner Bros., 1985, CP
DEAD CALM   Warner Bros., 1989, w/George Miller

WILLIAM HAYWARD

EASY RIDER   Columbia, 1969, AP
THE HIRED HAND   Universal, 1971
IDAHO TRANSFER   Cinemation, 1975
HIGH-BALLIN'   AIP, 1978, EP w/Stanley Chase
WANDA NEVADA   United Artists, 1979, EP
BLUE CITY   Paramount, 1986, w/Walter Hill

PHILLIP HAZELTON

EYE OF THE CAT   Universal, 1969, w/Bernard Schwartz
JENNIFER ON MY MIND   United Artists, 1971, AP
HAMMER   United Artists, 1972, EP w/Bernard Schwartz
THE ZEBRA KILLER   General Film, 1974, EP
BUCKTOWN   AIP, 1975, AP

JOHN HEAD

Business: Broadway Video, 1619 Broadway, 9th Floor, New York, NY 10019, 212/265-7621

JIMI HENDRIX (FD)   Warner Bros., 1973, w/Joe Boyd & Gary Weis
NOTHING LASTS FOREVER   MGM/UA, 1984, CP

BARRY HEALEY

THE GREY FOX   United Artists Classics, 1983, CP w/Phillip Borsos

HILARY HEATH

Business: Portman Entertainment, Pinewood Studios, Iver Heath, Bucks SL0 0NH England, 0753/630-366; Fax: 0753/630-332

CRIMINAL LAW   Hemdale, 1989, w/Robert MacLean

RICHARD T. HEFFRON

Agent: CAA - Beverly Hills, 310/288-4545
Contact: Directors Guild of America - Los Angeles, 213/289-2000

FUTUREWORLD   AIP, 1976, w/James T. Aubrey & Paul N. Lazarus III

HUGH M. HEFNER

Business: Playboy, 919 N. Michigan Ave., Chicago, IL 60611

MACBETH   Columbia, 1971, EP w/Victor Lownes
THE NAKED APE   Universal, 1973, EP
THE CRAZY WORLD OF JULIUS VROODER   20th Century Fox, 1974, EP
SAINT JACK   New World, 1979, EP w/Edward L. Rissien

ALBERT P. HEINER

THE GREAT AMERICAN COWBOY (FD)   Sun International, 1974, EP

W. LAWRENCE HEISEY

LEOPARD IN THE SNOW   New World, 1979, EP

PAUL HELLER

(credit w/Fred Weintraub)
Business: Paul Heller Productions, 1666 N. Beverly Dr., Beverly Hills, CA 90210, 310/275-4477; Fax: 310/275-1406
Contact: Directors Guild of America - Los Angeles, 213/289-2000

DAVID & LISA   Continental, 1962*
THE EAVESDROPPER   Royal Films International, 1966*

FILM
PRODUCERS,
STUDIOS,
AGENTS AND
CASTING
DIRECTORS
GUIDE

SECRET CEREMONY   Universal, 1969, EP*
ENTER THE DRAGON   Warner Bros., 1973
THE NEW YORK EXPERIENCE (FD)   Trans-Lux, 1973*
BLACK BELT JONES   Warner Bros., 1974
TRUCK TURNER   AIP, 1974
GOLDEN NEEDLES   AIP, 1974
THE ULTIMATE WARRIOR   Warner Bros., 1976
DIRTY KNIGHTS' WORK   Gamma III, 1976
IT'S SHOWTIME (FD)   United Artists, 1976
HOT POTATO   Warner Bros., 1976
OUTLAW BLUES   Warner Bros., 1977, EP
THE PACK   Warner Bros., 1978
CHECKERED FLAG OR CRASH   Universal, 1978
THE PROMISE   Universal, 1979
FIRST MONDAY IN OCTOBER   Paramount, 1981,
    w/Martha Scott*
WITHNAIL & I   Cineplex Odeon, 1987,
    w/Lawrence Kirstein*
MY LEFT FOOT ★   Miramax, 1989,
    EP w/Steve Morrison*

ROSILYN HELLER
Business: Productions, 2237 Nichols Canyon Rd., Los
    Angeles, CA 90046, 213/876-2820

ICE CASTLES   Columbia, 1978, EP
WHO'S THAT GIRL   Warner Bros., 1987,
    w/Bernard Williams

JEROME HELLMAN
Business: Jerome Hellman Productions, 68 Malibu Colony
    Dr., Malibu, CA 90265, 310/456-3361
Contact: Directors Guild of America - Los Angeles,
    213/289-2000

THE WORLD OF HENRY ORIENT   United Artists, 1964
A FINE MADNESS   Warner Bros., 1966
MIDNIGHT COWBOY ★★   United Artists, 1969
THE DAY OF THE LOCUST   Paramount, 1975
COMING HOME ★   United Artists, 1978
PROMISES IN THE DARK   Orion/Warner Bros., 1979
THE MOSQUITO COAST   Warner Bros., 1986

GEOFFREY HELMAN
Business: 9D Logan Place, London W8 6QN England,
    071/373-6288

FRIENDS   Paramount, 1971, AP
THE PASSAGE   United Artists, 1979, AP
THE FRENCH LIEUTENANT'S WOMAN   United
    Artists, 1981, AP
KRULL   Columbia, 1983, AP
THE DOCTOR AND THE DEVILS   20th Century Fox,
    1985, AP
84 CHARING CROSS ROAD   Columbia, 1987

RICHARD HELMAN
SWEET MOVIE   Biograph, 1975, w/Vincent Malle

PAUL A. HELMICK
THE CULPEPPER CATTLE COMPANY   20th Century
    Fox, 1972

LYNE HELMS
20TH CENTURY OZ   Inter-Planetary, 1977,
    w/Chris Lofven

DAVID HELPERN
DEAD HEAT   New World, 1988, w/Michael Meltzer

DAVID HEMMINGS
Business: A-L Productions, 3500 W. Olive, Suite 650,
    Burbank, CA 91505, 818/953-4114

STRANGE BEHAVIOR   World Northal, 1981, EP w/John
    Daly & William Fayman

DUNCAN HENDERSON
TAKING CARE OF BUSINESS   Buena Vista, 1990, CP
GREEN CARD   Buena Vista, 1990, CP w/Jean Gontier
DYING YOUNG   20th Century Fox, 1991, CP

GRAHAM HENDERSON
Contact: Directors Guild of America - Los Angeles,
    213/289-2000

BODY SLAM   DEG, 1987, CP
EVE OF DESTRUCTION   Orion, 1991, EP w/Robert W.
    Cort, Rick Finkelstein & Melinda Jason

KARL HENDRICKSON
POPCORN   Studio Three, 1991, EP w/Howard Baldwin &
    Howard Hurst

DORIAN HENDRIX
MONDO NEW YORK   4th & Broadway, 1988, EP

LUTZ HENGST
KING, QUEEN, KNAVE   Avco Embassy, 1972,
    w/David L. Wolper
DESPAIR   New Line, 1979, EP w/Edward R. Pressman

CHRISTOPH HENKEL
DELUSION   Cineville, 1991, EP w/Seth M. Willenson

KIM HENKEL
Contact: Writers Guild of America - Los Angeles,
    310/550-1000

THE TEXAS CHAINSAW MASSACRE   Bryanston,
    1974, AP
LAST NIGHT AT THE ALAMO   Cinecom, 1984,
    w/Eagle Pennell

MIKE HENRY
(credit w/Gordon C. Layne)

THE ZEBRA KILLER   General Film, 1974
ABBY   AIP, 1974, w/William Girdler

JERE HENSHAW
Business: Cannon Productions, 8200 Wilshire Blvd.,
    Beverly Hills, CA 90212, 213/966-5600;
    Fax: 213/653-5485

CAN'T BUY ME LOVE   Buena Vista, 1988,
    EP w/Ron Beckman
HAPPY TOGETHER   Borde Releasing, 1990
RESCUE ME   Cannon, 1991, w/David A. Smitas

PAUL G. HENSLER
GOTCHA!   Universal, 1985

PERRY HENZELL
THE HARDER THEY COME   New World, 1973

He

FILM
PRODUCERS,
STUDIOS,
AGENTS AND
CASTING
DIRECTORS
GUIDE

F
I
L
M

P
R
O
D
U
C
E
R
S

PETER V. HERALD
Agent: The Gersh Agency - Beverly Hills, 310/274-6611
Contact: Directors Guild of America - Los Angeles,
   213/289-2000

MIRACLE OF THE WHITE STALLIONS   Buena Vista,
   1963, AP
EMIL & THE DETECTIVES   Buena Vista, 1964, AP
THE GREAT WALTZ   MGM, 1972, AP
FOUL PLAY   Paramount, 1978, AP
NIGHTWING   Columbia, 1979, AP
NATIONAL LAMPOON'S CLASS REUNION   20th Century
   Fox, 1982, CP w/Harmon Berns
DOCTOR DETROIT   Universal, 1983, AP
D.C. CAB   Universal, 1983, AP
OUTRAGEOUS FORTUNE   Buena Vista, 1987,
   CP w/Scott Kroopf & Martin Mickelson

LEN HERBERMAN
MURDER BY DECREE   Avco Embassy, 1979, EP

DAVID HERBERT
OLD EXPLORERS   Taurus, 1991, w/Tom Jenz &
   William Pohlad

JAMES HERBERT
DREAMER   20th Century Fox, 1979, AP
DIE HARD 2   20th Century Fox, 1990, LP

JOHN HERKLOTZ
THE GIANT OF THUNDER MOUNTAIN   Castle Hill,
   1991, EP w/Richard Kiel

RICHARD HERLAND
STEPPENWOLF   D/R Films, 1974, w/Melvin Fishman
SKY BANDITS   Galaxy, 1986

NORMAN T. HERMAN
Contact: Directors Guild of America - Los Angeles,
   213/289-2000

ANGEL UNCHAINED   AIP, 1970, CP
UP IN THE CELLAR   AIP, 1970, CP
BLOODY MAMA   AIP, 1970, CP
BUNNY O'HARE   AIP, 1971, w/Gerd Oswald
FROGS   AIP, 1972, EP
THE LEGEND OF HELL HOUSE   20th Century Fox,
   1973, w/Albert Fennell
DIRTY MARY CRAZY LARRY   20th Century Fox, 1974
ROLLING THUNDER   AIP, 1977
IN GOD WE TRUST   Universal, 1980, EP

CLAUDE HÉROUX
JACQUES BREL IS ALIVE AND WELL AND LIVING IN
   PARIS   American Film Theatre, 1975, EP
BREAKING POINT   20th Century Fox, 1976, w/Bob Clark
IN PRAISE OF OLDER WOMEN   Avco Embassy, 1979,
   w/Robert Lantos
THE BROOD   New World, 1979
CITY ON FIRE   Avco Embassy, 1979
HOG WILD   Avco Embassy, 1980
SCANNERS   Avco Embassy, 1981
DIRTY TRICKS   Avco Embassy, 1981
GAS   Paramount, 1981
VISITING HOURS   20th Century Fox, 1982
VIDEODROME   Universal, 1983
GOING BERSERK   Universal, 1983
THE FUNNY FARM   New World, 1983

OF UNKNOWN ORIGIN   Warner Bros., 1983
COVERGIRL   New World, 1984
ANGELA   Embassy, 1984, w/Julian Melzack

DENIS HÉROUX
Business: Alliance Entertainment Corporation, 8439 Sunset
   Blvd., Suite 404, Los Angeles, CA 90069, 213/654-9488;
   Fax: 213/654-9786; 920 Yonge Street, Suite 400, Toronto,
   Ontario, M4W 3C7, Canada, 416/967-1174;
   Fax: 416/960-0971

THE LITTLE GIRL WHO LIVES DOWN THE LANE   AIP,
   1977, CP w/Eugene Lepicier & Leland Nolan
VIOLETTE   Gaumont/New Yorker, 1978,
   EP w/Eugene Lepicier
ATLANTIC CITY ★   Paramount, 1981
QUEST FOR FIRE   20th Century Fox, 1982,
   w/John Kemeny
THE BAY BOY   Orion, 1985, w/John Kemeny
EDDIE & THE CRUISERS II: EDDIE LIVES   Scotti Bros.,
   1989, EP w/Victor Loewy, James L. Stewart &
   William Stuart

GERRY HERROD
BOARDWALK   ARC, 1979, EP

PATRICIA HERSKOVIC
Business: Jack Freedman Productions, 14225 Ventura Blvd.,
   Suite 200, Sherman Oaks, CA 91423, 818/789-9306;
   Fax: 818/789-2632

TOY SOLDIERS   TriStar, 1991, w/Jack E. Freedman &
   Wayne S. Williams

MICHAEL HERTZBERG
Contact: Directors Guild of America - Los Angeles,
   213/289-2000

THE TWELVE CHAIRS   UMC, 1970, w/Sidney Glazier
BLAZING SADDLES   Warner Bros., 1974
SILENT MOVIE   20th Century Fox, 1976
JOHNNY DANGEROUSLY   20th Century Fox, 1984
MEMORIES OF ME   MGM/UA, 1988, w/Billy Crystal &
   Alan King
TURNER & HOOCH   Buena Vista, 1989,
   EP w/Daniel Petrie Jr.
WELCOME TO BUZZSAW   Universal, 1991, w/Robert W.
   Cort & Ted Field

PAUL HERTZBERG
Business: CineTel Films, Inc., 3800 W. Alameda Ave.,
   Suite 825, Burbank, CA 91505, 818/955-9551;
   Fax: 818/955-9616

ARMED RESPONSE   CineTel, 1986
THE TOMB   Trans World, 1986, EP w/Richard Kaye
BULLETPROOF   CineTel, 1987
CYCLONE   CineTel, 1987
COLD STEEL   CineTel, 1987, EP
976-EVIL   New Line, 1989, EP
HIT LIST   New Line, 1989
RELENTLESS   New Line, 1989, EP w/Lisa M. Hansen
FAR OUT MAN   New Line, 1990, EP
TOO MUCH SUN   New Line, 1990, EP w/Seymour
   Morgenstern & Al Schwartz
HORROSCOPE   New Line, 1991
PAST MIDNIGHT   New Line, 1991, EP
SERIOUS MONEY   New Line, 1991, EP

He

FILM
PRODUCERS,
STUDIOS,
AGENTS AND
CASTING
DIRECTORS
GUIDE

F
I
L
M

P
R
O
D
U
C
E
R
S

MICHAEL HERZ
Business: Troma, Inc., 733 Ninth Ave., New York, NY
10019, 212/757-4555; Fax: 212/399-9885

CLASS OF NUKE 'EM HIGH PART II: SUBHUMANOID
MELTDOWN   Troma, 1991, w/Lloyd Kaufman

ILONA HERZBERG
FEDS   Warner Bros., 1988, w/Len Blum
CASUAL SEX?   Universal, 1980, w/Sheldon Kahn
IRON MAZE   Trans-Tokyo, 1991, w/Hidenori Ueki

WERNER HERZOG
Contact: German Film & TV Academy, Pommemallee 1,
1 Berlin 19, Germany, 0311/302-6096

AGUIRRE, THE WRATH OF GOD   New Yorker, 1977
HEART OF GLASS   New Yorker, 1977
STROSZEK   New Yorker, 1977

MARLENE HESS
THE HAPPY HOOKER   Cannon, 1975,
EP w/Dennis Friedland

OLIVER HESS
INTO THE SUN   Trimark, 1991, w/Kevin Kallberg

GORDON HESSLER
Agent: Triad Artists, Inc. - Los Angeles, 310/556-2727

CRY OF THE BANSHEE   AIP, 1970

JOHN HEYMAN
Business: World Film Services Ltd., Pinewood Studios,
Iver Heath, Bucks., SL0 0NH, 0753/656-501;
Fax: 0753/656-475

PRIVILEGE   Universal, 1967
SECRET CEREMONY   Universal, 1968
LOLA   TWINKY   AIP, 1971, EP
THE GO-BETWEEN   Columbia, 1971, w/Norman Priggen
THE HERO   Avco Embassy, 1972, w/Wolf Mankowitz
BLACK GUNN   Columbia, 1972, w/Norman Priggen
HITLER: THE LAST TEN DAYS   Paramount, 1973
JESUS   Warner Bros., 1979
DANIEL   Paramount, 1983, EP
D.A.R.Y.L.   Paramount, 1985

NORMA HEYMAN
BEYOND THE LIMIT   Paramount, 1983
BURNING SECRET   Vestron, 1988, w/Carol Lynn
Greene & Eberhard Junkersdorf
BUSTER   Hemdale, 1988
DANGEROUS LIAISONS ★   Warner Bros., 1988,
w/Hank Moonjean

LOUIS M. HEYWARD
SCREAM AND SCREAM AGAIN   AIP, 1969, EP
THE CRIMSON CULT   AIP, 1970
CRY OF THE BANSHEE   AIP, 1970, EP
WHO SLEW AUNTIE ROO?   AIP, 1971, EP
THE ABOMINABLE DR. PHIBES   AIP, 1971,
w/Ron Dumas
WUTHERING HEIGHTS   AIP, 1971, EP
MURDERS IN THE RUE MORGUE   AIP, 1971
DR. PHIBES RISES AGAIN   AIP, 1972

MALCOLM HEYWORTH
THE BLOOD ON SATAN'S CLAW   Cannon, 1971,
w/Peter Andrews

SALLY HIBBIN
Business: Parallax Pictures, 7 Denmark Street, London
WC2H 8LS England, 071/836-1478; Fax: 071/497-8062

RIFF RAFF   Fine Line, 1992

JEAN HIGGINS
Contact: Directors Guild of America - Los Angeles,
213/289-2000

GETTING EVEN   American Distribution Group,
1986, LP
REPOSSESSED   New Line, 1990, CP

PADDY HIGSON
Business: Antonine Films Ltd., 4/5 Queen Margaret Road,
Glasgow G20 5DP Scotland, 041/945-5552

COMFORT AND JOY   Universal, 1984, AP
THE GIRL IN THE PICTURE   Samuel Goldwyn
Company, 1986

FRANK E. HILDEBRAND
VICE SQUAD   Avco Embassy, 1982, AP
WARRIORS OF THE LOST WORLD   Vista, 1985,
w/Roberto Bessi
ONCE BITTEN   Samuel Goldwyn Company, 1985,
w/Dimitri Villard & Robby Wald

DEBRA HILL
Business: Debra Hill Productions, c/o Walt Disney Studios,
500 S. Buena Vista St., Burbank, CA 91521,
818/560-1951; Fax: 818/567-7395

HALLOWEEN   Compass International, 1978
THE FOG   Avco Embassy, 1980
HALLOWEEN II   Universal, 1981, w/John Carpenter
ESCAPE FROM NEW YORK   Avco Embassy, 1981,
w/Larry Franco
HALLOWEEN III: SEASON OF THE WITCH   Universal,
1982, w/John Carpenter
THE DEAD ZONE   Paramount, 1983
CLUE   Paramount, 1985
HEAD OFFICE   TriStar, 1985
ADVENTURES IN BABYSITTING   Buena Vista, 1987,
w/Lynda Obst
HEARTBREAK HOTEL   Buena Vista, 1988,
w/Lynda Obst
BIG TOP PEE-WEE   Paramount, 1988, w/Paul Reubens
GROSS ANATOMY   Buena Vista, 1989,
w/Howard Rosenman
THE FISHER KING   TriStar, 1991

GEORGE ROY HILL
Business Manager: Edwins, Brown, McGladrey,
Hendrickson & Pulle, 1133 Ave. of the Americas, New
York, NY 10019, 212/382-0024
Business: Pan Arts Productions, 4000 Warner Blvd.,
Burbank, CA 91522, 818/954-3631

THE GREAT WALDO PEPPER   Universal, 1975
THE WORLD ACCORDING TO GARP   Warner Bros.,
1982, w/Robert L. Crawford

WALTER HILL
Business: Warner Hollywood Studios, 1041 N. Formosa,
   Los Angeles, CA 90046, 213/850-2901
Agent: ICM - Los Angeles, 310/550-4000

ALIEN   20th Century Fox, 1979, w/Gordon Carroll &
   David Giler
BLUE CITY   Paramount, 1986, w/William Hayward
ALIENS   20th Century Fox, 1986, EP w/Gordon Carroll &
   David Giler
RED HEAT   TriStar, 1988, w/Gordon Carroll

ARTHUR HILLER
Business: 100 Universal Plaza, Universal City, CA 91608,
   818/777-7377
Agent: The Gersh Agency - Beverly Hills, 310/274-6611

MAN OF LA MANCHA   United Artists, 1972
THE CRAZY WORLD OF JULIUS VROODER   20th
   Century Fox, 1974, w/Edward L. Rissien
THE IN-LAWS   Warner Bros., 1979, w/William Sackheim
THE LONELY GUY   Universal, 1984

KUNJIRO HIRATA
MYSTERY TRAIN   Orion Classics, 1989,
   EP w/Hideaki Suda

BARRY J. HIRSCH
AFTER MIDNIGHT   MGM/UA, 1989, EP w/Allan Dennis

BUZZ HIRSCH
SILKWOOD   20th Century Fox, 1983, EP w/Larry Cano

CHARLES HIRSCH
Personal Manager: Carol Akiyama - Sherman Oaks,
   818/906-3639
Contact: Writers Guild of America - Los Angeles,
   310/550-1000

GREETINGS   Sigma III, 1968
HI, MOM!   Sigma III, 1970

NORMAN HIRSCHFIELD
NOTHING PERSONAL   AIP, 1980, EP w/Jay Bernstein &
   Alan Hamel

CHARLES HIRSCHHORN
Business: Hollywood Pictures, 500 S. Buena Vista St.,
   Burbank, CA 91521, 818/560-2795; Fax: 818/841-9463

BULL DURHAM   Orion, 1988, AP
DIRTY ROTTEN SCOUNDRELS   Orion, 1988,
   EP w/Dale Launer

HERBERT HIRSCHMAN
HALLS OF ANGER   United Artists, 1970
THEY CALL ME MISTER TIBBS   United Artists, 1970

MICHAEL HIRSH
Business: Nelvana Ltd., 32 Atlantic Ave., Toronto,
   M6K 1X8, 416/588-5571; Fax: 416/588-5588;
   9000 Sunset Blvd., Suite 911, Los Angeles, CA 90069,
   310/278-8466; Fax: 310/278-4872

THE CARE BEARS MOVIE (AF)   Samuel Goldwyn
   Company, 1985, w/Patrick Loubert & Clive A. Smith
ROCK & RULE (AF)   MGM/UA, 1985, w/Patrick Loubert

CARE BEARS MOVIE II: A NEW GENERATION (AF)
   Columbia, 1986, w/Patrick Loubert & Clive A. Smith
THE CARE BEARS ADVENTURE IN WONDERLAND (AF)
   Cineplex Odeon, 1987, w/Patrick Loubert & Clive A. Smith
BURGLAR   Warner Bros., 1987, w/Kevin McCormick
BABAR: THE MOVIE (AF)   New Line, 1989

RUPERT HITZIG
Business: 73 Market St., Venice, CA 90201, 310/396-5937
Contact: Directors Guild of America - Los Angeles,
   213/289-2000

ELECTRA GLIDE IN BLUE   United Artists, 1973, EP
HAPPY BIRTHDAY, GEMINI   United Artists, 1980
CATTLE ANNIE & LITTLE BRITCHES   Universal, 1981,
   w/Alan King
WOLFEN   Orion, 1981
JAWS 3-D   Universal, 1983
THE LAST DRAGON   TriStar, 1985
THE SQUEEZE   TriStar, 1987, w/Michael Tannen

A. KITMAN HO
Business: Ixtlan, Inc., 321 Hampton, Suite 105, Venice, CA
   90291, 310/399-2550
Contact: Directors Guild of America - Los Angeles,
   213/289-2000

THE LOVELESS   Atlantic, 1984, w/Grafton Nunes
PLATOON ★★   Orion, 1986, CP
WALL STREET   20th Century Fox, 1987, CP
TALK RADIO   Universal, 1988, w/Edward R. Pressman
BORN ON THE FOURTH OF JULY ★   Universal, 1989,
   w/Oliver Stone
THE DOORS   TriStar, 1991, w/Bill Graham & Sasha Harari
JFK   WARNER BROS., 1991

PHILIP HOBBS
FULL METAL JACKET   Warner Bros., 1987, CP

PHILIP S. HOBEL
Business: 1697 Broadway, Suite 802, New York, NY 10019,
   212/246-5522; Fax: 212/246-5525

TENDER MERCIES ★   Universal, 1983

MIKE HODGES
Contact: "Websley," Durweston, Blanford Farm, Doreset,
   England, 02/585-3188
Agent: Terence Baker, Hatton & Baker, 18 Jermyn St.,
   London W1, England, 071/439-2971

THE TERMINAL MAN   Warner Bros., 1974

MARK HOFFMAN
RICH GIRL   Studio Three, 1991, EP w/Steven H. Parker

PETER HOFFMAN
VALENTINO RETURNS   Skouras Pictures, 1989,
   w/David Wisnievitz

TAMAR SIMON HOFFS
Agent: The Gersh Agency - Beverly Hills, 310/274-6611
Contact: Directors Guild of America - Los Angeles,
   213/289-2000

STONY ISLAND   World Northal, 1980, w/Andrew Davis
STAND ALONE   New World, 1985, AP
THE ALLNIGHTER   Universal, 1987

Ho

FILM
PRODUCERS,
STUDIOS,
AGENTS AND
CASTING
DIRECTORS
GUIDE

F
I
L
M

P
R
O
D
U
C
E
R
S

Ho

FILM
PRODUCERS,
STUDIOS,
AGENTS AND
CASTING
DIRECTORS GUIDE

F
I
L
M

P
R
O
D
U
C
E
R
S

HULK HOGAN
Business: World Wrestling Federation, P.O. Box 3857,
   Stamford, CT 06905

NO HOLDS BARRED   New Line, 1989, EP w/Richard
   Glover & Vince McMahon

PAUL HOGAN
Business: Paramount Pictures, 5555 Melrose Ave.,
   Hollywood, CA 90067, 213/956-5796

CROCODILE DUNDEE II   Paramount, 1988, EP
ALMOST AN ANGEL   Paramount, 1990, EP

ARNOLD J. HOLLAND
Business: Lightyear Entertainment, 350 5th Ave.,
   Suite 5101, New York, NY 10118,

THE LEMON SISTERS   Miramax, 1990, EP w/Tom
   Kuhn & Charles Mitchell

JULIAN HOLLOWAY
LOOPHOLE   Almi Pictures, 1986, w/David Korda

HENRY HOLMES
THE TEXAS CHAINSAW MASSACRE PART 2   Cannon,
   1986, EP w/James Jorgensen

MILTON HOLMES
A MATTER OF WHO   MGM, 1962,
   w/Walter Shenson

PRESTON L. HOLMES
NEW JACK CITY   Warner Bros., 1991, CP

RAND HOLSTON
Business: CAA - Beverly Hills, 310/288-4545

FM   Universal, 1978, CP

EVANDER HOLYFIELD
BLOOD SALVAGE   Paragon Arts International,
   1990, EP

MICHAEL HOLZMAN
Business: SVS, Inc., 1700 Broadway, New York, NY
   10019, 212/757-4990; Fax: 212/956-3792

BEST OF THE BEST   Taurus, 1989, EP w/Frank
   Giustra & Jeff Ringler

RAY HOMER
Contact: Directors Guild of America - New York,
   212/581-0370

AMERICAN GOTHIC   Vidmark Entertainment, 1988,
   EP w/Michael Manley & George Walker

CONRAD HOOL
Business: Silver Lion Films, 715 Broadway, Suite 320,
   Santa Monica, CA 90401, 310/393-9177

STEEL DAWN   Vestron, 1987, w/Lance Hool
OPTIONS   Vestron, 1989, CP w/Edgar Bold
DAMNED RIVER   MGM/UA, 1989, CP

LANCE HOOL
Business: Silver Lion Films, 715 Broadway, Suite 210,
   Santa Monica, CA 90401, 310/393-9177
Agent: William Morris Agency - Beverly Hills, 310/274-7451

10 TO MIDNIGHT   Cannon, 1983, w/Pancho Kohner
MISSING IN ACTION   Cannon, 1984, EP
STEEL DAWN   Vestron, 1987, w/Conrad Hool
OPTIONS   Vestron, 1989
DAMNED RIVER   MGM/UA, 1989

TOBE HOOPER
Business Manager: Joel Behr - Los Angeles, 213/551-2320
Contact: Directors Guild of America - Los Angeles,
   213/289-2000

THE TEXAS CHAINSAW MASSACRE   Bryanston, 1974
THE TEXAS CHAINSAW MASSACRE PART 2   Cannon,
   1986, CP

KAREN LEIGH HOPKINS
Agent: InterTalent Agency, Inc. - Los Angeles, 310/858-6200

WELCOME HOME, ROXY CARMICHAEL   Paramount,
   1990, EP

ROY HORAN
NO RETREAT, NO SURRENDER II   Shapiro
   Glickenhaus, 1989

WILLIAM HORBERG
Business: Paramount Pictures, 5555 Melrose Ave.,
   Hollywood, CA 90038, 213/956-5162

MIAMI BLUES   Orion, 1990, AP
A RAGE IN HARLEM   Miramax, 1991, EP w/Terry
   Glinwood, Nik Powell, Bob Weinstein & Harvey Weinstein

JEFFREY HORNADAY
Contact: Directors Guild of America - Los Angeles,
   213/289-2000

THE IN CROWD   Orion, 1988, CP w/Karen Essex

DEREK HORNE
ALICE'S ADVENTURES IN WONDERLAND   American
   National, 1972
CALLAN   Cinema National, 1975

RICHARD HORNER
RAGGEDY ANN AND ANDY (AF)   20th Century Fox, 1977

MARTIN HORNSTEIN
Contact: Directors Guild of America - Los Angeles,
   213/289-2000

SILENT RUNNING   Universal, 1972, AP
TRUCK TURNER   AIP, 1974, AP
ONE ON ONE   Warner Bros., 1977
I, THE JURY   20th Century Fox, 1982, AP
BAD BOYS   Universal, 1983, AP
THE WOMEN'S CLUB   Lightning, 1987, CP
PERMANENT RECORD   Paramount, 1988, EP

TED HOROVITZ
ANDY AND THE AIRWAVE RANGERS   Concorde, 1988

GARY HOROWITZ
Contact: Directors Guild of America - Los Angeles,
213/289-2000

EXECUTIVE ACTION   National General, 1973,
CP w/Dan Bessie

LEWIS M. HORWITZ
PRISONERS   American Films Ltd., 1975, w/W. John Seig

BUCK HOUGHTON
THE ESCAPE ARTIST   Orion, 1982, w/Doug Claybourne

SHELLEY HOUIS
TRUE LOVE   MGM/UA, 1989, w/Richard Guay

MEL HOWARD
Contact: Directors Guild of America - Los Angeles,
213/289-2000

QUACKSER FORTUNE HAS A COUSIN IN THE BRONX
UMC, 1970, w/John H. Cushingham
RENTED LIPS   Cineworld, 1988, LP

RON HOWARD
Business: Imagine Entertainment, 1925 Century Park East,
23rd Floor, Los Angeles, CA 90067, 310/277-1665;
Fax: 310/785-0107
Agent: CAA - Beverly Hills, 310/288-4545

LEO AND LOREE   United Artists, 1980, EP
GUNG HO   Paramount, 1986, EP
NO MAN'S LAND   Orion, 1987, EP w/Tony Ganz
CLEAN AND SOBER   Warner Bros., 1988, EP
VIBES   Columbia, 1988, EP
CLOSET LAND   Universal, 1991, EP w/Brian Grazer
AN IRISH STORY   Universal, 1991, w/Brian Grazer

SANDY HOWARD
Business: World Entertainment & Business Network, Inc.,
7060 Hollywood Blvd., Suite 1204, Los Angeles, CA
90028, 213/467-4151

A MAN CALLED HORSE   National General, 1970
THE NEPTUNE FACTOR   20th Century Fox, 1973
TOGETHER BROTHERS   20th Century Fox, 1974, EP
THE DEVIL'S RAIN   Bryanston, 1975, EP
EMBRYO   Cine Artists, 1976, EP
SKY RIDERS   20th Century Fox, 1976, EP
ECHOES OF A SUMMER   Cine Artists, 1976,
EP w/Richard Harris
RETURN OF A MAN CALLED HORSE   United Artists,
1976, EP
THE ISLAND OF DR. MOREAU   AIP, 1977,
EP w/Samuel Z. Arkoff
CITY ON FIRE   Avco Embassy, 1979,
EP w/Harold Greenberg
METEOR   AIP, 1979, EP w/Gabriel Katzka
JAGUAR LIVES!   AIP, 1979, EP
CIRCLE OF IRON   Avco Embassy, 1979,
w/Paul Maslansky
DEATH SHIP   Avco Embassy, 1980, EP
VICE SQUAD   Avco Embassy, 1982, EP w/Frank
Capra Jr. & Bob Rehme
DEADLY FORCE   Embassy, 1983
TRIUMPHS OF A MAN CALLED HORSE   Jensen Farley,
1984, EP
HAMBONE & HILLIE   New World, 1984,
w/Gary Gillingham

THE BOYS NEXT DOOR   New World, 1985,
w/Keith Rubinstein
AVENGING ANGEL   New World, 1985, w/Keith Rubinstein
KGB: THE SECRET WAR   Cinema Group, 1986,
w/Keith Rubinstein
HOLLYWOOD VICE SQUAD   Cinema Group, 1986,
w/Arnold Orgolini
PRETTYKILL   Spectrafilm, 1987, EP

JENNIFER HOWARTH
Agent: ICM - Duncan Heath, 071/439-1471

DISTANT VOICES, STILL LIVES   Avenue Pictures, 1989
BLAME IT ON THE BELLBOY   Buena Vista, 1991

PETER HOWARTH
THE GREEK TYCOON   Universal, 1978, EP w/Mort
Abrahams & Les Landau

WARRINGTON HUDLIN
Agent: Triad Artists, Inc. - Los Angeles, 310/556-2727
Contact: Tribeca Film Center, 375 Greenwich St., New York,
NY 10013, 212/941-4004

HOUSE PARTY   New Line, 1990

HUGH HUDSON
Business: Hudson Film, Ltd., 11 Queen's Gate Place Mews,
London SW7 5BG, England, 071/581-3133
Agent: CAA - Beverly Hills, 310/288-4545

GREYSTOKE: THE LEGEND OF TARZAN, LORD OF
THE APES   Warner Bros., 1984, w/Stanley S. Canter

CHARLES HUGGINS
DEF BY TEMPTATION   Troma, 1990, EP w/Nelson
George & Kevin Harewood

JOHN HUGHES
Business: Hughes Entertainment, 254 Market St., Lake
Forest, IL 60045, 708/615-0030
Agent: CAA - Beverly Hills, 310/288-4545

PRETTY IN PINK   Paramount, 1986, EP w/Michael Chinich
FERRIS BUELLER'S DAY OFF   Paramount, 1986,
w/Tom Jacobson
SOME KIND OF WONDERFUL   Paramount, 1987
PLANES, TRAINS & AUTOMOBILES   Paramount, 1987
SHE'S HAVING A BABY   Paramount, 1988
THE GREAT OUTDOORS   Universal, 1988,
EP w/Tom Jacobson
UNCLE BUCK   Universal, 1989, w/Tom Jacobson
NATIONAL LAMPOON'S CHRISTMAS VACATION   Warner
Bros., 1989, w/Tom Jacobson
HOME ALONE   20th Century Fox, 1990
CAREER OPPORTUNITIES   Universal, 1991,
w/Hunt Lowry
DUTCH   20th Century Fox, 1991, w/Richard Vane
ONLY THE LONELY   20th Century Fox, 1991,
w/Hunt Lowry

LENORA HUME
Business: Disney TV, 500 S. Buena Vista St., Burbank, CA
91521, 818/560-1000

CARE BEARS MOVIE II: A NEW GENERATION (AF)
Columbia, 1986, SP
THE CARE BEARS ADVENTURE IN WONDERLAND (AF)
Cineplex Odeon, 1987, SP

FILM
PRODUCERS,
STUDIOS,
AGENTS AND
CASTING
DIRECTORS
GUIDE

F
I
L
M

P
R
O
D
U
C
E
R
S

Hu

FILM
PRODUCERS,
STUDIOS,
AGENTS AND
CASTING
DIRECTORS GUIDE

F
I
L
M

P
R
O
D
U
C
E
R
S

ED HUNT
STARSHIP INVASIONS   Warner Bros., 1977, w/Norman
   Glick & Ken Gord
PLAGUE   Group I, 1979, w/Barry Pearson

JESSICA SALEH HUNT
Business: Angelika Films, 1974 Broadway, New York, NY
   10023, 212/769-1400

BAIL JUMPER   Angelika Films, 1990, EP

MARION HUNT
SHE DANCES ALONE   Continental, 1982, EP
THE MIGHTY QUINN   MGM/UA, 1989, w/Ed Elbert &
   Sandy Lieberson

WILLIE HUNT
LOVERBOY   TriStar, 1989, w/Gary Foster

JOHN HUNTER
JOHN AND THE MISSUS   Cinema Group, 1987

TAB HUNTER
Agent: The Craig Agency - Los Angeles, 213/655-0236

LUST IN THE DUST   New World, 1985, w/Allan Glaser

GALE ANNE HURD
Business: Pacific Western Productions, 1401 Ocean Ave.,
   Suite 200, Santa Monica, CA 90401, 310/451-9818;
   Fax: 310/451-8801

SMOKEY BITES THE DUST   New World, 1981, CP
THE TERMINATOR   Orion, 1984
ALIENS   20th Century Fox, 1986
ALIEN NATION   20th Century Fox, 1988,
   w/Richard Kobritz
BAD DREAMS   20th Century Fox, 1988
THE ABYSS   20th Century Fox, 1989
DOWNTOWN   20th Century Fox, 1990, EP
TREMORS   Universal, 1990, EP
TERMINATOR 2: JUDGMENT DAY   TriStar, 1991,
   EP w/Mario Kassar

HOWARD HURST
POPCORN   Studio Three, 1991, EP w/Howard Baldwin &
   Karl Hendrickson

SOPHIE HURST
POPCORN   Studio Three, 1991, CP

HARRY HURWITZ
Business: RSM Productions, Inc., 450 N. Rossmore Ave.,
   Los Angeles, CA 90004, 213/466-5225; 42 West End
   Ave., New York, NY 10024, 212/496-1357
Agent: Shapiro-Lichtman, Inc. - Los Angeles, 310/859-8877

THE PROJECTIONIST   Maron Films Limited, 1971
THE COMEBACK TRAIL   Dynamite Entertainment/
   Rearguard Productions, 1971
RICHARD   Billings Associates, 1972, w/Lorees Yerby
CHAPLINESQUE, MY LIFE & HARD TIMES (FD)
   Xanadu, 1972
THE ROSEBUD BEACH HOTEL   THE BIG LOBBY   Almi,
   1984, w/Irving Schwartz
THAT'S ADEQUATE   That's Adequate Company, 1986,
   w/Irving Schwartz
THE BIG SCORE   Almi, 1983, EP w/David Forbes

DALE HUTCHINSON
Contact: Directors Guild of America - Los Angeles,
   213/289-2000

ELVIS: THAT'S THE WAY IT IS (FD)   MGM, 1970

WILLARD HUYCK
Agent: CAA - Beverly Hills, 310/288-4545
Contact: Directors Guild of America - Los Angeles,
   213/289-2000

MESSIAH OF EVIL   DEAD PEOPLE   International
   Cinefilm, 1975, w/Gloria Katz

PETER HYAMS
Business: Peter Hyams, Inc., Paramount Pictures, 5555
   Melrose Ave., Los Angeles, CA 90038, 213/956-5977;
   Fax: 213/956-8590
Agent: CAA - Beverly Hills, 310/288-4545

T.R. BASKIN   Paramount, 1971
2010   MGM/UA, 1984
RUNNING SCARED   MGM, 1986, EP
THE MONSTER SQUAD   TriStar, 1987, EP w/Keith Barish
   & Rob Cohen

JOHN HYDE
Business: Patriot Entertainment, 4000 Warner Blvd.,
   Producers Bldg. 1, Suite 103, Burbank, CA 91522,
   818/954-1679
Contact: The Howard Brandy Company, Inc. - Los Angeles,
   213/657-8320

RAVAGERS   Columbia, 1979
DAS BOOT   Columbia, 1982, EP w/Mark Damon &
   Edward R. Pressman
FIRE & ICE (AF)   20th Century Fox, 1983,
   EP w/Richard R. St. Johns
THE NEVERENDING STORY   Warner Bros., 1984,
   EP w/Mark Damon
FLIGHT OF THE NAVIGATOR   Buena Vista, 1986,
   EP w/Mark Damon, Malcolm R. Harding & Jonathan Sanger
THE CLAN OF THE CAVE BEAR   Warner Bros.,
   1986, EP w/Mark Damon, Peter Guber, Sidney
   Kimmel & Jon Peters
SHORT CIRCUIT   TriStar, 1986, EP w/Mark Damon
THE LOST BOYS   Warner Bros., 1987, EP w/Mark Damon
   & Richard Donner
UHF   Orion, 1989, w/Gene Kirkwood

MYRON A. HYMAN
BRENDA STARR   New World, 1987
A KILLING AFFAIR   Hemdale, 1988, EP w/John D. Backe

I

EDGAR IEVINS
Business: Ievins/Henenlotter, 443 W. 43rd St., Suite 1,
  New York, NY 10036, 212/265-2166

BASKET CASE   Analysis Releasing, 1982
BRAIN DAMAGE   Palisades Entertainment, 1988
BASKET CASE 2   Shapiro-Glickenhaus
  Entertainment, 1990
FRANKENHOOKER   Shapiro-Glickenhaus
  Entertainment, 1990

BRIDGET IKIN
AN ANGEL AT MY TABLE   Fine Line, 1991

WILLIAM J. IMMERMAN
Business: Cannon Productions, 5757 Wilshire Blvd.,
  Suite 721, Los Angeles, CA 90036, 213/965-0901

SOUTHERN COMFORT   20th Century Fox, 1981, EP
TAKE THIS JOB AND SHOVE IT   Embassy, 1981,
  EP w/J. David Marks

ROBERTO INFASCELLI
BLINDMAN   20th Century Fox, 1972, EP

MICHAEL INGBER
SOMETHING SHORT OF PARADISE   AIP, 1979,
  EP w/Herbert Swartz

TINO INSANA
Contact: Writers Guild of America - Los Angeles,
  310/550-1000

MASTERS OF MENACE   New Line, 1990,
  w/Lisa M. Hansen

BEVERLY IRBY
IN THE SPIRIT   Castle Hill, 1990, w/Julian Schlossberg

DAN IRELAND
(credit w/William J. Quigley)
Business: M.L. International Pictures, 6413 Colgate Ave., Los
  Angeles, CA 90048, 213/954-0932; Fax: 213/954-0933

MIDNIGHT CROSSING   Vestron, 1988, EP w/Gary
  Barber, Gregory Cascante & Wanda S. Rayle*
WAXWORK   Vestron, 1988, EP w/Gregory Cascante &
  Mario Sotela
THE LAIR OF THE WHITE WORM   Vestron, 1988, EP
PAPERHOUSE   Vestron, 1989, EP w/M. J. Peckos*
THE RAINBOW   Vestron, 1989, EP
TWISTER   Vestron, 1990, EP
WHORE   Trimark, 1991, w/Ronaldo Vasconcellos

MATTHEW IRMAS
UNDER THE BOARDWALK   New World, 1989, CP

SAM IRVIN
THE FIRST TIME   New Line, 1982

RICH IRVINE
(credit w/James L. Stewart)

WHY WOULD I LIE?   MGM/UA, 1980, EP
HEART LIKE A WHEEL   20th Century Fox, 1983, EP
MAXIE   Orion, 1985, EP

RICHARD IRVING
NEWMAN'S LAW   Universal, 1974
SIDECAR RACERS   Universal, 1975

FRANK ISAAC
Contact: Shapiro-Glickenhaus, 12001 Ventura Place, Suite 404,
  Studio City, CA 91604, 818/766-8500; Fax: 818/766-7873

WIZARDS OF THE LOST KINGDOM   Concorde, 1985,
  w/Alex Sessa
BARBARIAN QUEEN   Concorde, 1985, w/Alex Sessa

LORD ANTHONY RUFUS ISAACS
(see Lord Anthony RUFUS Isaacs)

SUSAN ISAACS
Agent: William Morris Agency - New York, 212/586-5100

HELLO AGAIN   Buena Vista, 1987, CP w/G. Mac Brown,
  Thomas Folino & Martin Mickelson

SATORU ISEKI
SHADOW OF CHINA   New Line, 1991, EP

CAROLE ISENBERG
Contact: Big Light Films, 201 Wilshire Blvd., 3rd Floor,
  Santa Monica, CA 90401, 310/395-0670

THIS IS MY LIFE   20th Century Fox, 1991,
  EP w/Patricia Meyer

GERALD I. ISENBERG
Business: Hearst Entertainment, 1640 S. Sepulveda Blvd.,
  4th Floor, Los Angeles, CA 90025, 310/478-2700;
  Fax: 310/478-2202

LET THE GOOD TIMES ROLL (FD)   Columbia, 1973
THE CLAN OF THE CAVE BEAR   Warner Bros., 1986

MARJORIE ISRAEL
WHY ME?   Triumph, 1990

NANCY ISRAEL
Contact: Directors Guild of America - Los Angeles,
  213/289-2000

THE ALLNIGHTER   Universal, 1987, CP
THE FIVE HEARTBEATS   20th Century Fox, 1991, CP

NEIL ISRAEL
Agent: ICM - Los Angeles, 310/550-4000

TUNNELVISION   World Wide, 1976, EP
THREE O'CLOCK HIGH   Universal, 1987,
  CP w/John Davis

ROBERT ISRAEL
BACHELOR PARTY   20th Century Fox, 1984, w/Ron Moler
MOVING VIOLATIONS   20th Century Fox, 1985, CP

Is

FILM
PRODUCERS,
STUDIOS,
AGENTS AND
CASTING
DIRECTORS
GUIDE

F
I
L
M

P
R
O
D
U
C
E
R
S

FILM
PRODUCERS,
STUDIOS,
AGENTS AND
CASTING
DIRECTORS
GUIDE

F
I
L
M

P
R
O
D
U
C
E
R
S

J

DEL JACK
(credit w/J. Mark Travis)

RICHARD PRYOR LIVE IN CONCERT (FD)   Special
  Event Entertainment, 1979
SAMMY STOPS THE WORLD   Special Event
  Entertainment, 1979

JAMES JACKS
Business: Universal Pictures, 100 Universal City Plaza,
  Universal City, CA 91608, 818/777-1000

RAISING ARIZONA   20th Century Fox, 1987, EP

DAVID JACKSON
NO SECRETS   I.R.S., 1991, EP w/Carole Curb

GEORGE A. JACKSON
Contact: Jackson McHenry, 4000 Warner Blvd., Burbank,
  CA 91522, 818/954-3221

KRUSH GROOVE   Warner Bros., 1985,
  EP w/Robert O. Kaplan
DISORDERLIES   Warner Bros., 1987, w/Michael Jaffe &
  Michael Schultz
NEW JACK CITY   Warner Bros., 1991, w/Doug McHenry

ART JACOBS
THE DIRT GANG   AIP, 1972, w/Joseph E. Bishop

FRANK JACOBS
THE BAY BOY   Orion, 1985, EP w/Susan Cavan

NEWTON P. JACOBS
VAN NUYS BLVD.   Crown International, 1979, EP

JOHN M. JACOBSEN
SHIPWRECKED   Buena Vista, 1991

TOM JACOBSON
Business: 20th Century Fox, 10201 W. Pico Blvd.,
  Los Angeles, CA 90035, 310/277-2211
Contact: Directors Guild of America - Los Angeles,
  213/289-2000

FLASHDANCE   Paramount, 1983, AP w/Lynda Obst
TOP SECRET!   Paramount, 1984, AP
EXPLORERS   Paramount, 1985, AP
THIEF OF HEARTS   Paramount, 1985, AP
FERRIS BUELLER'S DAY OFF   Paramount, 1986,
  w/John Hughes
BURGLAR   Warner Bros., 1987, EP
THE GREAT OUTDOORS   Universal, 1988,
  EP w/John Hughes
UNCLE BUCK   Universal, 1989, w/John Hughes
NATIONAL LAMPOON'S CHRISTMAS VACATION
  Warner Bros., 1989, w/John Hughes

JOSEPH JACOBY
HURRY UP, OR I'LL BE 30   Avco Embassy, 1973
THE GREAT BANK HOAX   *SHENANIGANS*   Warner
  Bros., 1979, w/Ralph Rosenblum

KOBI JAEGER
Business: Santa Ana Productions

KAMA SUTRA   Trans America, 1971, w/Richard R. Rimmel
SALTY   Saltwater, 1975
FRANKENSTEIN UNBOUND   20th Century Fox, 1990,
  w/Roger Corman & Thom Mount

RICK JAFFA
THE HAND THAT ROCKS THE CRADLE   Buena Vista,
  1992, EP w/Robert W. Cort & Ted Field

HERB JAFFE
THE WIND & THE LION   MGM/UA, 1975
DEMON SEED   MGM/UA, 1977
WHO'LL STOP THE RAIN   United Artists, 1978,
  w/Gabriel Katzka
TIME AFTER TIME   Orion/Warner Bros., 1979
THOSE LIPS, THOSE EYES   United Artists, 1980, EP
MOTEL HELL   United Artists, 1980, EP
JINXED   MGM/UA, 1982
THE LORDS OF DISCIPLINE   Paramount, 1983,
  w/Gabriel Katzka
LITTLE TREASURE   TriStar, 1985
FRIGHT NIGHT   Columbia, 1985
MAID TO ORDER   New Century/Vista, 1987,
  w/Mort Engelberg
THREE FOR THE ROAD   New Century/Vista, 1987,
  w/Mort Engelberg
NIGHTFLYERS   New Century/Vista, 1987, EP
TRADING HEARTS   New Century/Vista, 1988,
  EP w/Mort Engelberg
FRIGHT NIGHT PART 2   New Century/Vista, 1988,
  w/Mort Engelberg
DUDES   New Century/Vista, 1988, w/Miguel Tejada-Flores
PASS THE AMMO   New Century/Vista, 1988,
  w/Mort Engelberg

HOWARD B. JAFFE
A REFLECTION OF FEAR   Columbia, 1973
MAN ON A SWING   Paramount, 1974
TAPS   20th Century Fox, 1981, w/Stanley R. Jaffe

MICHAEL JAFFE
Business: Spectacor Films, 7920 Sunset Blvd., 4th Floor, Los
  Angeles, CA 90046, 213/871-2777; Fax: 213/871-2963

BETTER OFF DEAD   Warner Bros., 1985
BAD MEDICINE   20th Century Fox, 1985, EP w/Sam
  Manners & Myles Osterneck
ONE CRAZY SUMMER   Warner Bros., 1986
DISORDERLIES   Warner Bros., 1987, w/George A.
  Jackson & Michael Schultz
18 AGAIN   New World, 1988, EP w/Irving Fein

ROBERT JAFFE
Business: Columbia Pictures, 10202 W. Washington Blvd.,
  Culver City, CA 90232, 310/280-8017
Agent: Camden Artists, Ltd. - Los Angeles, 213/556-2022

MOTEL HELL   United Artists, 1980, w/Steven Charles Jaffe
NIGHTFLYERS   New Century/Vista, 1987

Je

FILM
PRODUCERS,
STUDIOS,
AGENTS AND
CASTING
DIRECTORS
GUIDE

F
I
L
M

P
R
O
D
U
C
E
R
S

STANLEY R. JAFFE

Business: Paramount Pictures, 5555 Melrose Ave., Los
Angeles, CA 90038, 213/956-5000

GOODBYE, COLUMBUS   Paramount, 1969
I START COUNTING   United Artists, 1969
BAD COMPANY   Paramount, 1972
MAN ON A SWING   Paramount, 1974, EP
THE BAD NEWS BEARS   Paramount, 1976
KRAMER VS. KRAMER ★★   Columbia, 1979
TAPS   20th Century Fox, 1981, w/Howard B. Jaffe
WITHOUT A TRACE   20th Century Fox, 1983
RACING WITH THE MOON   Paramount, 1984,
EP w/Sherry Lansing
FIRSTBORN   Paramount, 1984, EP w/Sherry Lansing
FATAL ATTRACTION ★   Paramount, 1987,
w/Sherry Lansing
THE ACCUSED   Paramount, 1988, w/Sherry Lansing
BLACK RAIN   Paramount, 1989, w/Sherry Lansing

STEVEN-CHARLES JAFFE

Business: Pari Passu Productions, Paramount Pictures,
5555 Melrose Ave., Los Angeles, CA 90038,
213/956-5841; Fax: 213/956-4827
Business Manager: Laurence Rose, Esq., Gang, Tyre,
Ramer & Brown, 6400 Sunset Blvd., Los Angeles,
CA 90028
Agent: Camden Artists, Ltd. - Los Angeles, 213/556-2022

DEMON SEED   MGM, 1977, AP
TIME AFTER TIME   Orion/Warner Bros., 1979, AP
MOTEL HELL   United Artists, 1980, w/Robert Jaffe
THOSE LIPS, THOSE EYES   United Artists, 1980,
w/Michael Pressman
NEAR DARK   DEG, 1987
PLAIN CLOTHES   Paramount, 1988, EP
THE FLY II   20th Century Fox, 1989
GHOST ★   Paramount, 1990, EP w/Howard W. Koch
STAR TREK VI: THE UNDISCOVERED COUNTRY
Paramount, 1991, w/Ralph Winter

JUDITH JAMES

Business: Dreyfuss/James Productions, c/o Walt Disney
Pictures, 500 S. Buena Vista St., Burbank, CA 91521,
818/560-7100; Fax: 818/563-1263

ONCE AROUND   Universal, 1991, CP w/Richard Dreyfuss

PETER JAMES

DEAD OF NIGHT   Europix International, 1974,
EP w/John Trent

TOMMASO JANDELLI

Business: Gold Screen Films, 28 Draycott Place, Flat 6,
London SW3 2SB, 071/584-9466; Fax: 071/5899680
Attorney: Nigel Bennet, Simkins Partnership, 51 Whitfield
St., London W1 P5R, England, 071/631-1050

WE THINK THE WORLD OF YOU   Cinecom, 1989

PETAR JANKOVIC

HEY BABU RIBA   Orion Classics, 1987,
EP w/George Zecevic

JOSEPH JANNI

A KIND OF LOVING   Continental, 1962
BILLY LIAR   Continental, 1963
DARLING ★   Embassy, 1965
FAR FROM THE MADDING CROWD   MGM, 1967

POOR COW   National General, 1967
IN SEARCH OF GREGORY   Universal, 1970,
w/Daniel Senatore
SUNDAY BLOODY SUNDAY   United Artists, 1971
DEAF SMITH AND JOHNNY EARS   MGM, 1973,
w/Luciano Perugia
MADE   International Co-Productions, 1975
YANKS   Universal, 1979, w/Lester Persky

MELINDA JASON

Business: Melinda Jason Company, c/o Walt Disney
Pictures, 500 S. Buena Vista, Tower - 28th Floor, Burbank,
CA 91521, 818/567-5760; Fax: 818/563-1263

THE FIRST POWER   Orion, 1990, EP w/Robert W. Cort &
Ted Field
EVE OF DESTRUCTION   Orion, 1991, EP w/Robert W.
Cort, Rick Finkelstein & Graham Henderson

HELMUT JEDELE

DEEP END   Paramount, 1971
TWILIGHT'S LAST GLEAMING   Allied Artists, 1977, EP

GRAHAME JENNINGS

HOWLING II...YOUR SISTER IS A WEREWOLF   Thorn
EMI, 1986, EP

MARGARET JENNINGS SOUTH

(see Margaret Jennings SOUTH)

ANDERS P. JENSEN

ANGEL TOWN   Taurus, 1990, EP w/Sundip R. Shah &
Sunil R. Shah

RAYLAN D. JENSEN

THE MYSTERIOUS MONSTERS (FD)   Sunn Classic,
1976, EP
IN SEARCH OF NOAH'S ARK (FD)   Sunn Classic,
1976, EP
THE ADVENTURES OF FRONTIER FREMONT   Sunn
Classic, 1976, EP
THE LINCOLN CONSPIRACY (FD)   Sunn Classic, 1977,
w/Charles E. Sellier, Jr.

TOM JENZ

OLD EXPLORERS   Taurus, 1991, w/David Herbert &
William Pohlad

SUE JETT

(credit w/Tony Mark)
Agent: CAA - Beverly Hills, 310/288-4545

BILLY GALVIN   Vestron, 1986
ZELLY AND ME   Columbia, 1988
ROOFTOPS   New Visions, 1989, CP w/Allan Goldstein

NORMAN JEWISON

Business: Yorktown Productions Ltd., 9336 W. Washington
Blvd., Culver City, CA 90232, 310/202-3434;
Fax: 310/202-3339
Agent: William Morris Agency - Beverly Hills, 310/274-7451

THE RUSSIANS ARE COMING, THE RUSSIANS ARE
COMING ★   United Artists, 1966
GAILY, GAILY   United Artists, 1969
THE LANDLORD   United Artists, 1970
FIDDLER ON THE ROOF ★   United Artists, 1971

JESUS CHRIST SUPERSTAR   Universal, 1973,
   w/Robert Stigwood
BILLY TWO HATS   United Artists, 1974, w/Patrick Palmer
ROLLERBALL   United Artists, 1975
F.I.S.T.   United Artists, 1978
...AND JUSTICE FOR ALL   Columbia, 1979,
   w/Patrick Palmer
THE DOGS OF WAR   United Artists, 1981,
   EP w/Patrick Palmer
BEST FRIENDS   Warner Bros., 1982, w/Patrick Palmer
ICEMAN   Universal, 1984, w/Patrick Palmer
A SOLDIER'S STORY ★   Columbia, 1984, w/Patrick
   Palmer & Ronald L. Schwary
AGNES OF GOD   Columbia, 1985, w/Patrick Palmer
MOONSTRUCK ★   MGM, 1987, w/Patrick Palmer
THE JANUARY MAN   MGM/UA, 1989, w/Ezra Swerdlow
IN COUNTRY   Warner Bros., 1989, w/Richard Roth

ROBERT JIRAS
THE BOYS IN THE BAND   National General, 1970,
   EP w/Dominick Dunne

CHARLES H. JOFFE
(credit w/Jack Rollins)
Business: Rollins-Joffe Productions, 130 W. 57th Street,
   New York, NY 10019, 212/582-9062; 300 S. Lorimar
   Plaza, Rm. 1016, Burbank, CA 91505, 818/954-7036;
   Fax: 818/954-7874

TAKE THE MONEY AND RUN   Cinerama, 1969*
DON'T DRINK THE WATER   Avco Embassy, 1969*
BANANAS   United Artists, 1971, EP*
PLAY IT AGAIN, SAM   Paramount, 1972, EP*
EVERYTHING YOU ALWAYS WANTED TO KNOW
   ABOUT SEX* (*BUT WERE AFRAID TO ASK)
   United Artists, 1972*
SLEEPER   United Artists, 1973, EP
LOVE AND DEATH   United Artists, 1975*
THE FRONT   Columbia, 1976, EP*
ANNIE HALL ★★   United Artists, 1977*
INTERIORS   United Artists, 1978*
MANHATTAN   United Artists, 1979*
STARDUST MEMORIES   United Artists, 1980, EP
ARTHUR   Orion/Warner Bros., 1981, EP*
A MIDSUMMER NIGHT'S SEX COMEDY   Orion/Warner
   Bros., 1982*
ZELIG   Orion/Warner Bros., 1983, EP
BROADWAY DANNY ROSE   Orion, 1984, EP*
THE HOUSE OF GOD   United Artists, 1984,
   w/Harold Schneider*
THE PURPLE ROSE OF CAIRO   Orion, 1985, EP*
HANNAH AND HER SISTERS ★   Orion, 1986, EP
RADIO DAYS   Orion, 1987, EP
SEPTEMBER   Orion, 1987, EP
ANOTHER WOMAN   Orion, 1988, EP
NEW YORK STORIES   Buena Vista, 1989, EP
CRIMES & MISDEMEANORS   Orion, 1989, EP
ALICE   Orion, 1990, EP

ROLAND JOFFE
Contact: Lightmotive, Inc., 662 N. Robertson Blvd., Los
   Angeles, CA 90069, 310/659-6200; Fax: 310/659-6688

CITY OF JOY   TriStar, 1991, w/Jake Eberts

TORBEN JOHNKE
POPCORN   Studio Three, 1991, w/Ashok Amritraj &
   Gary Goch

BRUCE JOHNSON
Contact: Hanna-Barbera Productions, 3400 Cahuenga West,
   Hollywood, CA 90068, 213/851-5000; Fax: 213/969-1201

JETSONS: THE MOVIE (AF)   Universal, 1990, SP

DAN JOHNSON
PROM NIGHT III; THE LAST KISS   Norstar, 1990,
   EP w/Ilana Frank

KRISTINE JOHNSON
THROW MOMMA FROM THE TRAIN   Orion, 1987, CP

MARK JOHNSON
Business: Baltimore Pictures, 10201 W. Pico Blvd., Suite 12,
   Los Angeles, CA 90035, 310/203-2525;
   Fax: 310/203-3806
Agent: CAA - Beverly Hills, 310/288-4545

DINER   MGM/UA, 1982, EP
THE NATURAL   TriStar, 1984
YOUNG SHERLOCK HOLMES   Paramount, 1985
TIN MEN   Buena Vista, 1987
GOOD MORNING, VIETNAM   Buena Vista, 1987,
   w/Larry Brezner
RAIN MAN ★★   MGM/UA, 1988
AVALON   TriStar, 1990, w/Barry Levinson
BUGSY   TriStar, 1991, w/Warren Beatty & Barry Levinson

RICHARD JOHNSON
TURTLE DIARY   Samuel Goldwyn Company, 1985
CASTAWAY   Cannon, 1987, EP w/Peter Shaw
THE LONELY PASSION OF JUDITH HEARNE   Island
   Pictures, 1987, w/Peter Nelson
AMBITION   Miramax, 1991, CP

DAVID B. JOHNSTON
TAKE DOWN   Buena Vista, 1979, EP

ANTHONY JONES
BLUE CITY   Paramount, 1986, EP w/Robert Kenner

CHUCK JONES
THE PHANTOM TOLLBOOTH (AF)   MGM, 1970
THE BUGS BUNNY/ROAD RUNNER MOVIE (AF)   Warner
   Bros., 1979

DENNIS JONES
Agent: Gray/Goodman, Inc. - Beverly Hills, 310/276-7070
Contact: Directors Guild of America - Los Angeles,
   213/289-2000

MRS. SOFFEL   MGM/UA, 1984, AP
SHORT CIRCUIT   TriStar, 1986, CP
PACIFIC HEIGHTS   20th Century Fox, 1990, CP

ISAAC L. JONES
THE RIVER NIGER   Cine Artists, 1976,
   w/Sidney Beckerman

L. Q. JONES
Agent: Contemporary Artists - Beverly Hills, 310/278-8250

THE BROTHERHOOD OF SATAN   Columbia, 1971,
   w/Alvy Moore

Ju

FILM
PRODUCERS,
STUDIOS,
AGENTS AND
CASTING
DIRECTORS
GUIDE

F
I
L
M

P
R
O
D
U
C
E
R
S

LORETHA C. JONES
SCHOOL DAZE   Columbia, 1988, CP w/Monty Ross
THE FIVE HEARTBEATS   20th Century Fox, 1991

QUINCY JONES
Business: Qwest Records, 7250 Beverly Blvd., Suite 207,
   Los Angeles, CA 90036, 213/874-2009;
   Fax: 213/874-3364
Agent: Triad Artists, Inc. - Los Angeles, 310/556-2727

THE COLOR PURPLE ★   Warner Bros., 1985,
   w/Kathleen Kennedy, Frank Marshall & Steven Spielberg

STEVEN JONES
DAUGHTERS OF THE DUST   American Playhouse
   Theatrical Films, 1991, LP

JACK JORDAN
GEORGIA, GEORGIA   Cinerama, 1972
GANJA & HESS *BLOOD COUPLE*   Kelly-Jordan,
   1973, EP
HONEYBABY, HONEYBABY   Kelly-Jordan, 1974

RICHARD JORDAN
A FLASH OF GREEN   Spectrafilm, 1985

JAMES JORGENSEN
THE TEXAS CHAINSAW MASSACRE PART 2   Cannon,
   1986, EP w/Henry Holmes

KIM JORGENSEN
THE KENTUCKY FRIED MOVIE   UFD, 1977, EP
OUT OF AFRICA ★★   Universal, 1985, EP

DAVID JOSEPH
FLIGHT OF THE NAVIGATOR   Buena Vista, 1986, CP

PAUL A. JOSEPH
THE EVIL   New World, 1978, EP w/Malcolm Levinthal

ROBERT L. JOSEPH
ECHOES OF A SUMMER   Cine Artists, 1976

BARRY JOSEPHSON
Contact: Silver Pictures, 4000 Warner Blvd., Bldg. 90,
   Burbank, CA 91522, 818/954-4490; Fax: 818/954-3237

THE LAST BOY SCOUT   Warner Bros., 1991,
   EP w/Shane Black
RICOCHET   Warner Bros., 1991, EP

BARRY JOSSEN
IN A SHALLOW GRAVE   Skouras Pictures, 1988,
   w/Kenneth Bowser

WALTER JOSTEN
Business: Paragon Arts International, 6777 Hollywood
   Blvd., Suite 520, Hollywood, CA 90028, 213/465-5355;
   Fax: 213/465-9029

WITCHBOARD   Cinema Group, 1987, EP
NIGHT OF THE DEMONS   International Film Marketing,
   1988, EP
NIGHT ANGEL   Fries Entertainment, 1990, EP

RON JOY
TILT   Warner Bros., 1979, EP

TOM JOYNER
Contact: Directors Guild of America - Los Angeles,
   213/289-2000

WORTH WINNING   20th Century Fox, 1989, EP
VITAL SIGNS   20th Century Fox, 1990, AP

JAY JULIEN
KING OF NEW YORK   Seven Arts, 1990,
   EP w/Vittoria Squillante

MAX JULIEN
CLEOPATRA JONES   Warner Bros., 1973, CP
THOMASINE AND BUSHROD   Columbia, 1974,
   w/Harvey Bernhard

EBERHARD JUNKERSDORF
THE LOST HONOR OF KATHARINA BLUM   New World,
   1975, EP
COUP DE GRACE   Cinema 5, 1978
THE SECOND AWAKENING OF CHRISTA KLAGES   New
   Line, 1979, EP
SISTERS, OR THE BALANCE OF HAPPINESS
   Cinema 5, 1982
MARIANNE & JULIANE   New Yorker, 1982
CIRCLE OF DECEIT   United Artists Classics, 1982
SHEER MADNESS   R5/S8, 1985
ROSA LUXEMBURG   New Yorker Films, 1987
BURNING SECRET   Vestron, 1988, w/Carol Lynn
   Greene & Norma Heyman

MARTIN JUROW
Business: 3505 Rankin St., Dallas, TX 75205

THE HANGING TREE   Warner Bros., 1959,
   w/Richard Shepherd
THE FUGITIVE KIND   United Artists, 1960,
   w/Richard Shepherd
BREAKFAST AT TIFFANY'S   Paramount, 1961,
   w/Richard Shepherd
SOLDIER IN THE RAIN   Allied Artists, 1963
THE PINK PANTHER   United Artists, 1964
THE GREAT RACE   Warner Bros., 1965
WALTZ ACROSS TEXAS   Atlantic, 1983
TERMS OF ENDEARMENT   Paramount, 1983,
   CP w/Penny Finkelman Cox
SYLVESTER   Columbia, 1985

MILTON JUSTICE
STAYING TOGETHER   Hemdale, 1989, CP

GEORGE JUSTIN
Contact: Directors Guild of America - Los Angeles,
   213/289-2000

THE OWL & THE PUSSYCAT   Columbia, 1970, AP
THE ANDERSON TAPES   Columbia, 1971, AP
THE DEEP   Columbia, 1977, AP
NO SMALL AFFAIR   Columbia, 1984, EP

Ka

FILM
PRODUCERS,
STUDIOS,
AGENTS AND
CASTING
DIRECTORS
GUIDE

F
I
L
M

P
R
O
D
U
C
E
R
S

K

MICHAEL J. KAGAN
Agent: Sandra Marsh Management - Beverly Hills,
310285-0303

DEJA VU   Cannon, 1984, AP
SWORD OF THE VALIANT   Cannon, 1984,
   EP w/Philip M. Breen
ORDEAL BY INNOCENCE   Cannon, 1985, AP
LIFEFORCE   TriStar, 1985, AP
DEATH WISH 3   Cannon, 1985, AP
THREE KINDS OF HEAT   Cannon, 1987
DUET FOR ONE   Cannon, 1987, AP
SUPERMAN IV: THE QUEST FOR PEACE   Warner
   Bros., 1987, EP
AIR AMERICA   TriStar, 1990, LP
ROBIN HOOD: PRINCE OF THIEVES   Warner Bros.,
   1991, CP

MARCEL KAHN
POWAQQATSI (FD)   Cannon, 1988,
   LP w/Tom Luddy

SHELDON KAHN
Business: Ivan Reitman Productions, 100 Universal Plaza
   415B, Universal City, CA 91608, 818/777-8080;
   Fax: 818/777-0689

LEGAL EAGLES   Universal, 1986,
   AP w/Arnold Glimcher
CASUAL SEX?   Universal, 1988, w/Ilona Herzberg
GHOSTBUSTERS II   Columbia, 1989,
   AP w/Gordon Webb
KINDERGARTEN COP   Universal, 1990,
   AP w/Gordon Webb
BEETHOVEN   Universal, 1991, AP

TERRY KAHN
HOTEL OKLAHOMA   1991, w/Ed Elbert &
   Gregory Vanger

CONNIE KAISERMAN
Business: Merchant Ivory Productions, 250 West 57th St.,
   Suite 1913-A, New York, NY 10023, 212/582-8049

HEAT AND DUST   Universal Classics, 1983, AP
THE BOSTONIANS   Almi, 1984, AP
MY LITTLE GIRL   Hemdale, 1987

KEVIN KALLBERG
INTO THE SUN   Trimark, 1991, w/Oliver Hess

MISHAAL KAMAL ADHAM
(see Mishaal Kamal ADHAM)

ROBERT KAMEN
THE PUNISHER   New World, 1990

ANDRZEJ KAMROWSKI
Contact: East-West Film Partners, 279 S. Beverly Dr.,
   Suite 934, Beverly Hills, CA 90212, 310/858-3091;
   Fax: 310/858-0703

GRIM PRAIRIE TALES   East/West Film Partners,
   1990, CP

DENNIS D. KANE
MISSING LINK   Universal, 1989

MARY KANE
Contact: Directors Guild of America - New York,
   212/581-0370

CALL ME   Vestron, 1988, LP w/Richard Gelfand
KING OF NEW YORK   Seven Arts, 1990
MR. & MRS. BRIDGE   Miramax, 1990, AP

MICHAEL KANE
Contact: Directors Guild of America - Los Angeles,
   213/289-2000

STEWARDESS SCHOOL   Columbia, 1987,
   CP w/Jerry A. Baerwitz

JAY KANTER
(credit w/Alan Ladd, Jr.)
Business: MGM-Pathe Communications, 10000 W.
   Washington Blvd., Culver City, CA 90232, 310/280-6000

VILLAIN   MGM, 1971
X, Y, & ZEE   Columbia, 1971
FEAR IS THE KEY   Paramount, 1973

JOSEPH H. KANTER
IRONWEED   TriStar, 1987, EP w/Denis Blouin &
   Rob Cohen
THE BIG BANG (FD)   Triton, 1990

JEFFREY KAPELMAN
SEIZURE   Cinerama, 1974, w/Garrard Glenn

J. STEIN KAPLAN
ASSAULT ON PRECINCT 13   Turtle Releasing, 1976
THE FINAL TERROR   Aquarius, 1984, CP

MIKE KAPLAN
THE WHALES OF AUGUST   Alive Films, 1987,
   w/Carolyn Pfeiffer

PAUL A. KAPLAN
PARTING GLANCES   Cinecom, 1986, EP

ROBERT O. KAPLAN
MR. SYCAMORE   Film Venture, 1975, EP
KRUSH GROOVE   Warner Bros., 1985, EP
   w/George A. Jackson

DAVID R. KAPPES
TALES FROM THE DARKSIDE: THE MOVIE   Paramount,
   1990, CP

TOM KARNOWSKI
RADIOACTIVE DREAMS   DEG, 1986,
   w/Moctesuma Esparza
DOWN TWISTED   Cannon, 1987, AP

CYBORG   Cannon, 1989, LP
KICKBOXER 2: THE ROAD BACK   Entertainment Film
   Distributors, 1991

CONSTANTINE P. KAROS
THE TROUBLE WITH SPIES   DEG, 1987, EP

BEVERLY KARP
MY DINNER WITH ANDRE   New Yorker, 1981,
   w/George W. George

ANDREW S. KARSCH
Business: 10000 W. Washington Blvd., Suite 3024,
   Culver City, CA 90232, 310/280-6522

THE RACHEL PAPERS   MGM/UA, 1989

ERIC KARSON
Business: Imperial Entertainment Corp., 4640 Lankershim
   Blvd., 4th Floor, North Hollywood, CA 91602,
   818/762-0005; Fax: 818/762-0006
Agent: Shapiro-Lichtman Talent Agency - Los Angeles,
   310/859-8877
Contact: Directors Guild of America - Los Angeles,
   213/289-2000

ANGEL TOWN   Taurus, 1990, w/Ash R. Shah

KEES KASANDER
THE COOK, THE THIEF, HIS WIFE & HER LOVER
   Miramax, 1990

LAWRENCE KASANOFF
Business: Lightstorm Entertainment, 3100 Damon Way,
   Burbank, CA 91505, 818/562-1301; Fax: 818/562-1814

BLOOD DINER   Vestron, 1987, EP w/Ellen Steloff
THE BEAT   Vestron, 1988, EP w/Ruth Vitale
YOU CAN'T HURRY LOVE   Vestron, 1988,
   w/Jonathan D. Krane & Ellen Steloff
DREAM A LITTLE DREAM   Vestron, 1989,
   EP w/Ellen Steloff
FAR FROM HOME   Vestron, 1989, EP w/Ellen Steloff
SHE'S BACK   Vestron, 1989, EP w/Richard Kestinge
BLUE STEEL   MGM/UA, 1990, EP
CLASS OF 1999   Taurus, 1990, EP w/Ellen Steloff

LAWRENCE KASDAN
Agent: UTA - Beverly Hills, 310/273-6700
Contact: 20th Century-Fox, 10201 W. Pico, Bldg. 78, Los
   Angeles, CA 90035, 310/203-1890; Fax: 310/203-3839

THE BIG CHILL ★   Columbia, 1983,
   EP w/Marcia Nasatir
SILVERADO   Columbia, 1985
CROSS MY HEART   Universal, 1987
THE ACCIDENTAL TOURIST ★   Warner Bros., 1988,
   w/Michael Grillo & Charles Okun
IMMEDIATE FAMILY   Columbia, 1989, EP
GRAND CANYON   20th Century Fox, 1991, w/Michael
   Grillo & Charles Okun

CASEY KASEM
Agent: ICM - Los Angeles, 310/550-4000

CYCLE SAVAGES   Trans American, 1970,
   EP w/Mike Curb

DARYL KASS
Contact: Directors Guild of America - Los Angeles,
   213/289-2000

DARKMAN   Universal, 1990, LP

RONALD S. KASS
MELODY   Levitt-Pickman, 1971, EP
THE OPTIMISTS   Paramount, 1973, EP
THE STUD   Trans-American, 1979

MARIO KASSAR
(credit w/Andrew Vajna)
Business: Carolco Pictures, 8800 Sunset Blvd., Los Angeles,
   CA 90069, 310/850-8800; Fax: 310/657-1629

THE AMATEUR   20th Century Fox, 1981, EP
FIRST BLOOD   Orion, 1982
SUPERSTITION   Almi Pictures, 1985
RAMBO: FIRST BLOOD PART II   TriStar, 1985, EP
EXTREME PREJUDICE   TriStar, 1987, EP
ANGEL HEART   TriStar, 1987, EP
RAMBO III   TriStar, 1988
RED HEAT   TriStar, 1988, EP
DEEPSTAR SIX   TriStar, 1989, EP
JOHNNY HANDSOME   TriStar, 1989, EP
MOUNTAINS OF THE MOON   TriStar, 1990, EP
NARROW MARGIN   TriStar, 1990, EP
TOTAL RECALL   TriStar, 1990, EP
AIR AMERICA   TriStar, 1990, EP
JACOB'S LADDER   TriStar, 1990, EP
L.A. STORY   TriStar, 1991, EP w/Steve Martin*
THE DOORS   TriStar, 1991, EP w/Nicholas Clainos &
   Brian Grazer*
TERMINATOR 2: JUDGMENT DAY   TriStar, 1991,
   EP w/Gale Ann Hurd*
BASIC INSTINCT   TriStar, 1992, EP*

MICHAEL KASTENBAUM
Contact: 213/476-0374

MAD AT THE MOON   Boomerang Pictures, 1991, w/Matt
   Devlen, Cassian Elwes & Seth Kastenbaum

SETH KASTENBAUM
MAD AT THE MOON   Boomerang Pictures, 1991, w/Matt
   Devlen, Cassian Elwes & Michael Kastenbaum

ELLIOTT KASTNER
Business: Cinema Seven Productions, 154 West 57th St.,
   Suite 112, New York, NY 10019, 212/315-1060;
   Fax: 212/315-1085; Winkast Programming Ltd.,
   Pinewood Studios, Iver Heath, Bucks SL0 0NH,
   0753/651-700; Fax: 0753/652-525

HARPER   Warner Bros., 1966, w/Jerry Gershwin
WHERE EAGLES DARE   MGM, 1968
A SEVERED HEAD   Columbia, 1971, EP w/Jerry Gershwin
WHEN EIGHT BELLS TOLL   Cinerama, 1971
VILLAIN   MGM, 1971, EP
X, Y, & ZEE   Columbia, 1971, EP
FEAR IS THE KEY   EMI, 1972, EP
COUNT YOUR BULLETS   Brut, 1972
THE LONG GOODBYE   United Artists, 1973, EP
JEREMY   United Artists, 1973, EP
COPS & ROBBERS   United Artists, 1973
FACE TO THE WIND   Warner Bros., 1974, EP
11 HARROW HOUSE   20th Century Fox, 1974
92 IN THE SHADE   United Artists, 1975, EP

Ka

FILM
PRODUCERS,
STUDIOS,
AGENTS AND
CASTING
DIRECTORS
GUIDE

F
I
L
M

P
R
O
D
U
C
E
R
S

Ka

**FILM
PRODUCERS,
STUDIOS,
AGENTS** AND
**CASTING
DIRECTORS
GUIDE**

F
I
L
M

P
R
O
D
U
C
E
R
S

RANCHO DELUXE   United Artists, 1975
FAREWELL, MY LOVELY   Avco Embassy, 1975,
   EP w/Jerry Bick
BREAKHEART PASS   United Artists, 1976, EP
RUSSIAN ROULETTE   Avco Embassy, 1975, EP
THE MISSOURI BREAKS   United Artists, 1976,
   w/Robert M. Sherman
SWASHBUCKLER   Universal, 1976, EP
EQUUS   United Artists, 1977, w/Lester Persky
BLACK JOY   Hemdale, 1977, w/Arnon Milchan
THE BIG SLEEP   United Artists, 1978,
   w/Michael Winner
A LITTLE NIGHT MUSIC   New World, 1978
THE MEDUSA TOUCH   Warner Bros., 1978, EP w/Lew
   Grade & Arnon Milchan
YESTERDAY'S HERO   EMI, 1979, EP
GOLDENGIRL   Avco Embassy, 1979, EP
THE FIRST DEADLY SIN   Filmways, 1980,
   EP w/Frank Sinatra
ffolkes   Universal, 1980
DEATH VALLEY   Universal, 1982
MAN, WOMAN & CHILD   Paramount, 1983,
   w/Elmo Williams
GARBO TALKS   MGM/UA, 1984, w/Burtt Harris
OXFORD BLUES   MGM/UA, 1984, w/Cassian Elwes
ANGEL HEART   TriStar, 1987, w/Alan Marshall
ABSOLUTION   Trans World, 1988, w/Danny O'Donovan
JACK'S BACK   Palisades Entertainment, 1988
THE BLOB   TriStar, 1988, w/Jack H. Harris
A CHORUS OF DISAPPROVAL   South Gate
   Entertainment, 1989, EP w/Andre Blay
HOMEBOY   Homeboy Productions, 1990,
   w/Alan Marshall

SHINTARO KATSU
ALI THE MAN; ALI THE FIGHTER (FD)   CinAmerica,
   1975, w/William Greaves

GLORIA KATZ
Agent: CAA - Beverly Hills, 310/288-4545
Contact: Writers Guild of America - Los Angeles,
   310/550-1000

MESSIAH OF EVIL   *DEAD PEOPLE*   International
   Cinefilm, 1975, w/Willard Huyck
FRENCH POSTCARDS   Paramount, 1979
BEST DEFENSE   Paramount, 1984
HOWARD THE DUCK   Universal, 1986

JAMES C. KATZ
THREE SISTERS   American Film Theatre, 1974,
   AP w/Timothy Burrill
NOBODY'S FOOL   Island Pictures, 1986,
   w/Jon S. Denny
SCENES FROM THE CLASS STRUGGLE IN BEVERLY
   HILLS   Cinecom, 1989

MARTY KATZ
Business: Walt Disney Pictures, 500 S. Buena Vista St.,
   Burbank, CA 91521, 818/560-5151
Contact: Directors Guild of America - Los Angeles,
   213/289-2000

HEART LIKE A WHEEL   20th Century Fox, 1983, SP
LOST IN AMERI CA   Warner Bros., 1985

PETER KATZ
DON'T LOOK NOW   Paramount, 1974

RAYMOND KATZ
Business: Katz/Rush Entertainment, Suite 115, 9255 Sunset
   Blvd., Suite 115, Los Angeles, CA 90069, 310/273-4211;
   Fax: 310/273-7062

I'M GONNA GIT YOU SUCKA   MGM/UA, 1989,
   EP w/Eric L. Gold

ROBERT KATZ
Contact: Esparza-Katz Productions, 3330 Cahuenga West,
   Suite 500, Los Angeles, CA 90068, 213/969-2896;
   Fax: 213/851-5797

THE TELEPHONE   New World, 1988,
   w/Moctesuma Esparza

JOSEPH KAUFMAN
ASSAULT ON PRECINCT 13   Turtle Releasing, 1976, EP

LLOYD KAUFMAN
Business: Troma, Inc., 733 Ninth Ave., New York, NY
   10019, 212/757-4555; Fax: 212/399-9885

THE BATTLE OF LOVE'S RETURN   Standard, 1971,
   w/Frank Vitale
SUGAR COOKIES   General Film, 1973, EP
CLASS OF NUKE 'EM HIGH PART II: SUBHUMANOID
   MELTDOWN   Troma, 1991, w/Michael Herz

PETER KAUFMAN
HENRY & JUNE   Universal, 1990

ROBERT KAUFMAN
Contact: Writers Guild of America - Los Angeles,
   310/550-1000

I LOVE MY WIFE   Universal, 1970, AP
LOVE AT FIRST BITE   AIP, 1979,
   EP w/George Hamilton
HOW TO BEAT THE HIGH COST OF LIVING   AIP, 1980,
   w/Jerome M. Zeitman
THE CHECK IS IN THE MAIL   Ascot Entertainment, 1986,
   w/Robert Krause
SHE'S OUT OF CONTROL   WEG/Columbia, 1989, EP

DEREK KAVANAGH
DANCES WITH WOLVES ★★   Orion, 1990

TAKESHI KAWATA
SOLAR CRISIS   NHK, 1990, EP w/Takehito Sadamura

RICHARD KAYE
THE TOMB   Trans World, 1986, EP w/Paul Hertzberg
THE WIZARD OF SPEED AND TIME   Shapiro-Glickenhaus
   Entertainment, 1989, w/Deven Chierighino

ELIA KAZAN
Business: 174 East 95th St., New York, NY 10128
Contact: Directors Guild of America - Los Angeles,
   213/289-2000
Contact: Writers Guild of America - New York,
   212/245-6180

AMERICA, AMERICA ★   Warner Bros., 1963
THE ARRANGEMENT   Warner Bros./7 Arts, 1969

Ke

FILM
PRODUCERS,
STUDIOS,
AGENTS AND
CASTING
DIRECTORS
GUIDE

F
I
L
M

P
R
O
D
U
C
E
R
S

NICHOLAS KAZAN
Agent: Sanford-Skouras-Gross - Los Angeles, 310/208-2100

REVERSAL OF FORTUNE   Warner Bros., 1990,
CP w/Elon Dershowitz

HOWARD KAZANJIAN
Business: Tricor Entertainment, 3855 Lankershim Blvd.,
North Hollywood, CA 91614, 818/766-3157 or
213/956-4506
Contact: Directors Guild of America - Los Angeles,
213/289-2000

ROLLERCOASTER   Universal, 1977, EP
MORE AMERICAN GRAFFITI   Universal, 1979
RAIDERS OF THE LOST ARK ★   Parmount, 1981,
EP w/George Lucas
RETURN OF THE JEDI   20th Century Fox, 1983
THE ROOKIE   Warner Bros., 1990, w/Steven Siebert &
David Valdes

JAMES KEACH
Contact: Writers Guild of America - Los Angeles,
310/550-1000

THE LONG RIDERS   United Artists, 1980,
EP w/Stacy Keach
ARMED & DANGEROUS   Columbia, 1986,
w/Brian Grazer
THE EXPERTS   Paramount, 1989

STACY KEACH
Agent: William Morris Agency - Beverly Hills, 310/274-7451
Contact: Directors Guild of America - Los Angeles,
213/289-2000

THE LONG RIDERS   United Artists, 1980,
EP w/James Keach

JOHN KEARNEY
GROUND ZERO   Avenue, 1988, EP w/Kent Lovell &
Dennis Wright

DIANE KEATON
Agent: William Morris Agency - Beverly Hills, 310/274-7451

THE LEMON SISTERS   Miramax, 1990, w/Joe Kelly

NIETZCHKA KEENE
THE JUNIPER TREE   Keene/Moyroud, 1991

PAT KEHOE
Contact: Directors Guild of America - Los Angeles,
213/289-2000

FANDANGO   Warner Bros., 1985,
AP w/Barrie M. Osborne
TUFF TURF   New World, 1985, CP

JOHN KELLEHER
Business: Strongbow, 2 Upper Mount Street, Dublin 2,
Ireland, 785-622

EAT THE PEACH   Skouras Pictures, 1987
WAR REQUIEM   Anglo International, 1988, EP

HARRY KELLER
CLASS OF '44   Warner Bros., 1973, EP

LAURIE KELLER
RIDERS OF THE STORM   *THE AMERICAN WAY*
Miramax, 1987, w/Paul Cowan

PATRICK KELLEY
Business: Pan Arts Productions, 4000 Warner Blvd.,
Burbank, CA 91522, 818/954-3631

A LITTLE ROMANCE   Orion/Warner Bros., 1979, EP
DEADLY FRIEND   Warner Bros., 1986, EP
THE WORLD ACCORDING TO GARP
THE LITTLE DRUMMER GIRL   Warner Bros., 1984, EP
FUNNY FARM   Warner Bros., 1988, EP w/Bruce Bodner

BRIAN KELLY
BLADE RUNNER   The Ladd Company/Warner Bros., 1982,
EP w/Hampton Fancher

GABRIELLE KELLY
D.A.R.Y.L.   Paramount, 1985, CP w/Burtt Harris

GENE KELLY
Agent: ICM - Los Angeles, 310/550-4000

THAT'S DANCING! (FD)   MGM, 1985, EP

JOE KELLY
HEAVEN (FD)   Island Pictures, 1987
THE LEMON SISTERS   Miramax, 1990, w/Diane Keaton

JOHN B. KELLY
STARHOPS   First American, 1978, w/Robert D. Krintzman

QUENTIN KELLY
GEORGIA, GEORGIA   Cinerama, 1972, EP
GANJA & HESS   *BLOOD COUPLE*   Kelly-Jordan, 1973, EP
HONEYBABY, HONEYBABY   Kelly-Jordan, 1974, EP

JOHN KEMENY
Business: Alliance Entertainment Corporation, 8439 Sunset
Blvd., Suite 404, Los Angeles, CA 90069, 213/654-9488;
920 Yonge Street, Suite 400, Toronto, Ontario, M4W 3C7,
Canada, 416/967-1174

THE APPRENTICESHIP OF DUDDY KRAVITZ
Paramount, 1974
WHITE LINE FEVER   Columbia, 1975
SHADOW OF THE HAWK   Columbia, 1976
ICE CASTLES   Columbia, 1978
QUEST FOR FIRE   20th Century Fox, 1982,
w/Denis Héroux
THE BAY BOY   Orion, 1985, w/Denis Héroux
THE BOY IN BLUE   20th Century Fox, 1986
THE WRAITH   New Century, 1986
THE GATE   New Century/Vista, 1987
NOWHERE TO HIDE   New Century/Vista, 1987, EP
IRON EAGLE II   TriStar, 1988, w/Sharon Harel &
Jacob Kotzky

BURT KENNEDY
Business: 13138 Magnolia Blvd., Sherman Oaks, CA 91403,
818/986-8759
Agent: Sanford-Skouras-Gross - Los Angeles, 310/208-2100

DIRTY DINGUS MAGEE   MGM, 1970
SUPPORT YOUR LOCAL GUNFIGHTER   United Artists,
1971, EP
THE TROUBLE WITH SPIES   DEG, 1987

Ke

FILM
PRODUCERS,
STUDIOS,
AGENTS AND
CASTING
DIRECTORS
GUIDE

F
I
L
M

P
R
O
D
U
C
E
R
S

KATHLEEN KENNEDY

Business: Amblin Entertainment, Universal Studios,
100 Universal Plaza, Bungalow 477, Universal City,
CA 91608, 818/777-4600

POLTERGEIST   MGM/UA, 1982, AP
E.T. THE EXTRA-TERRESTRIAL ★   Universal, 1982,
w/Steven Spielberg
TWILIGHT ZONE - THE MOVIE   Warner Bros.,
1983, AP
GREMLINS   Warner Bros., 1984, EP w/Frank Marshall &
Steven Spielberg
INDIANA JONES & THE TEMPLE OF DOOM
Paramount, 1984, AP
FANDANGO   Warner Bros., 1985, EP w/Frank Marshall
THE GOONIES   Warner Bros., 1985, EP w/Frank
Marshall & Steven Spielberg
BACK TO THE FUTURE   Universal, 1985, EP w/Frank
Marshall & Steven Spielberg
YOUNG SHERLOCK HOLMES   Paramount, 1985,
EP w/Frank Marshall & Steven Spielberg
THE COLOR PURPLE ★   Warner Bros., 1985,
w/Quincy Jones, Frank Marshall & Steven Spielberg
THE MONEY PIT   Universal, 1986, w/Art Levinson &
Frank Marshall
AN AMERICAN TAIL (AF)   Universal, 1986, EP w/David
Kirschner, Frank Marshall & Steven Spielberg
INNERSPACE   Warner Bros., 1987, EP w/Peter Guber,
Frank Marshall, Jon Peters & Steven Spielberg
BATTERIES NOT INCLUDED   Universal, 1987,
EP w/Frank Marshall & Steven Spielberg
EMPIRE OF THE SUN   Warner Bros., 1987, w/Frank
Marshall & Steven Spielberg
WHO FRAMED ROGER RABBIT   Buena Vista, 1988,
EP w/Steven Spielberg
THE LAND BEFORE TIME (AF)   Universal, 1988,
EP w/George Lucas, Frank Marshall & Steven Spielberg
INDIANA JONES & THE LAST CRUSADE   Paramount,
1989, EP w/George Lucas & Frank Marshall
DAD   Universal, 1989, EP w/Frank Marshall &
Steven Spielberg
BACK TO THE FUTURE PART II   Universal, 1989,
EP w/Frank Marshall & Steven Spielberg
ALWAYS   Universal, 1989, w/Frank Marshall &
Steven Spielberg
BACK TO THE FUTURE PART III   Universal, 1990,
EP w/Frank Marshall & Steven Spielberg
GREMLINS 2: THE NEW BATCH   Warner Bros., 1990,
EP w/Frank Marshall & Steven Spielberg
JOE VERSUS THE VOLCANO   Warner Bros., 1990,
EP w/Frank Marshall & Steven Spielberg
ARACHNOPHOBIA   Buena Vista, 1990,
w/Richard Vane
CAPE FEAR   Universal, 1991, EP w/Frank Marshall &
Steven Spielberg
HOOK   TriStar, 1991, w/Frank Marshall &
Gerald R. Molen
NOISES OFF   Buena Vista, 1991,
EP w/Peter Bogdanovich

ROBERT KENNER

BLUE CITY   Paramount, 1986, EP w/Anthony Jones

CHRIS KENNY

THE BRIDE   Columbia, 1985, CP
EMPIRE OF THE SUN   Warner Bros., 1987, AP
BATMAN   Warner Bros., 1989, CP

JORDAN KERNER
(credit w/Jon Avnet)

Business: Avnet-Kerner Company, 3815 Hughes Av., Culver
City, CA 90232, 310/838-2500; Fax: 310/204-4208

LESS THAN ZERO   20th Century Fox, 1987
FUNNY ABOUT LOVE   Paramount, 1990
FRIED GREEN TOMATOES   Universal, 1991,
w/Jon Avnet

SARAH KERNOCHAN

MARJOE (FD)   Cinema 5, 1972, w/Howard Smith

WILLIAM B. KERR

Contact: Directors Guild of America - Los Angeles,
213/289-2000

MAC & ME   Orion, 1988, EP w/Mark Damon

IRVIN KERSHNER

Business: 9229 Sunset Blvd., Suite 818, Los Angeles,
CA 90069
Agent: CAA - Beverly Hills, 310/288-4545

WILDFIRE   Cinema Group, 1988,
EP w/Stanley R. Zupnik

HARRY KERWIN

BARRACUDA   Republic, 1979, w/Wayne Crawford &
Andrew Lane

JUDY KESSLER

GORILLAS IN THE MIST   Universal, 1988,
CP w/Robert Nixon

STEPHEN F. KESTEN

Contact: Directors Guild of America - New York,
212/581-0370

END OF THE ROAD   Allied Artists, 1970,
w/Terry Southern
THE TAKING OF PELHAM 1-2-3   United Artists,
1974, AP
FOUR FRIENDS   Filmways, 1981, AP
A LITTLE SEX   Universal, 1982, AP
CONAN THE DESTROYER   Universal, 1984, EP
MILLION DOLLAR MYSTERY   DEG, 1987

RICHARD KESTINGE

SHE'S BACK   Vestron, 1989, EP w/Lawrence Kasanoff

CALLIE KHOURI

THELMA & LOUISE   MGM-Pathe, 1991,
CP w/Dean O'Brien

RIC KIDNEY

Business: Yorktown Productions Ltd., 9336 W. Washington
Blvd., Bldg. H, Culver City, CA 90232, 310/202-3434;
Fax: 310/202-3339

AFTER DARK, MY SWEET   Avenue Pictures, 1990,
w/Robert Redlin

RICHARD KIEL

THE GIANT OF THUNDER MOUNTAIN   Castle Hill, 1991,
EP w/John Herklotz

FATHER ELLWOOD E. KIESER

Business: Paulist Productions, P.O. Box 1057, 17575 Pacific Coast Highway, Pacific Palisades, CA 90272, 310/454-0688; Fax: 310/459-6549
Contact: The Howard Brandy Company, Inc. - Los Angeles, 213/657-8320

ROMERO Four Seasons Entertainment, 1989

JON KILIK

Business: 40 Acres & A Mule Filmworks, 124 Dekalb Ave., Brooklyn, NY 11217, 718/624-3703; Fax: 718/961-2008
Contact: 230 Central Park West, New York, NY 10024

THE BEAT Vestron, 1988, w/Julia Phillips & Nick Wechsler
DO THE RIGHT THING Universal, 1989, LP
MO' BETTER BLUES Universal, 1990, LP
JUNGLE FEVER Universal, 1991, LP
FATHERS AND SONS RCA/Columbia, 1992
MALCOLM X Warner Bros., 1992

MICHELE KIMCHE

THE KRAYS Miramax, 1990, EP w/Jim Beach

ANNE KIMMEL

Business: Kimmel-Lucas Productions, 932 N. La Brea Ave., Hollywood, CA 90038, 213/874-0436

EATING RAOUL 20th Century Fox International Classics, 1982
NOT FOR PUBLICATION Samuel Goldwyn Company, 1984
PAINT IT BLACK Vestron, 1989, w/Mark Forstater

SIDNEY KIMMEL

THE CLAN OF THE CAVE BEAR Warner Bros., 1986, EP w/Mark Damon, Peter Guber, John Hyde & Jon Peters

KATSUMI KIMURA

IRON MAZE Trans-Tokyo, 1991, EP w/Edward R. Pressman, Oliver Stone & Hidenori Taga

TIM KINCAID

(credit w/Cynthia DePaula)

ENEMY TERRITORY Empire, 1987
NECROPOLIS Empire, 1987

ALAN KING

Business: Odyssey Film Partners, Ltd., 6500 Wilshire Blvd., Suite 400, Los Angeles, CA 90048, 213/655-9335

HAPPY BIRTHDAY GEMINI United Artists, 1980, EP
CATTLE ANNIE & LITTLE BRITCHES Universal, 1981, w/Rupert Hitzig
WOLFEN Orion/Warner Bros., 1981, EP
MEMORIES OF ME MGM/UA, 1988, w/Billy Crystal & Michael Hertzberg

KANDICE KING

MIDNIGHT HEAT NEW LINE, 1991, w/Lance King

LANCE KING

MIDNIGHT HEAT NEW LINE, 1991, w/Kandice King

ZALMAN KING

Agent: Arnold Rifkin, Triad Artists, Inc. - Los Angeles, 310/556-2727
Contact: Directors Guild of America - Los Angeles, 213/289-2000

ROADIE United Artists, 1980, EP
ENDANGERED SPECIES MGM/UA, 1982
9 1/2 WEEKS MGM/UA, 1986, w/Lord Anthony Rufus Isaacs
SIESTA Lorimar, 1987, EP w/Julio Caro & Nik Powell

TERRENCE KIRBY

CHILDREN OF THE CORN New World, 1984, w/Donald P. Borchers

J. MAX KIRISHIMA

Business: Blueline Productions, 9107 Wilshire Blvd., Suite 427, Beverly Hills, CA 90210 310/271-2572; Fax: 310/271-9316

DEADLINE Studio Three, 1991, w/Mike Erwin

JULIE KIRKHAM

BLACK RAIN Paramount, 1989, EP w/Craig Bolotin

GENE KIRKWOOD

Business: Cinecorp, 4000 Warner Blvd., Producers Bldg. 1, Suite 103, Burbank, CA 91522, 818/954-1677
Contact: The Howard Brandy Company, Inc. - Los Angeles, 213/657-8320

ROCKY ★★ United Artists, 1976, EP
NEW YORK, NEW YORK United Artists, 1977, AP
COMES A HORSEMAN United Artists, 1978, w/Dan Paulson
UNCLE JOE SHANNON United Artists, 1978, EP
THE IDOLMAKER United Artists, 1980, w/Howard W. Koch Jr.
THE KEEP Paramount, 1983, w/Howard W. Koch Jr.
GORKY PARK Orion, 1983, w/Howard W. Koch Jr.
A NIGHT IN HEAVEN 20th Century Fox, 1983, w/Howard W. Koch Jr.
THE POPE OF GREENWICH VILLAGE MGM/UA, 1984, w/Howard W. Koch Jr.
IRONWEED TriStar, 1987, CP w/C. O. Erickson
UHF Orion, 1989, w/John Hyde

DAVID KIRSCHNER

Business: Hanna-Barbera Productions, Inc., 3400 Cahuenga Blvd. West, Los Angeles, CA 90068, 213/851-5000; Fax: 213/969-1201
Contact: Writers Guild of America - Los Angeles, 310/550-1000

AN AMERICAN TAIL (AF) Universal, 1986, EP w/Kathleen Kennedy, Frank Marshall & Steven Spielberg
CHILD'S PLAY MGM/UA, 1988
CHILD'S PLAY 2 Universal, 1990
CHILD'S PLAY 3 Universal, 1991, w/Robert Latham Brown & Laura Moskowitz

LAWRENCE KIRSTEIN

WITHNAIL & I Cineplex Odeon, 1987, w/Paul Heller

FILM
PRODUCERS,
STUDIOS,
AGENTS AND
CASTING
DIRECTORS
GUIDE

EPHRAIM KISHON
THE POLICEMAN   Cinema 5, 1972, w/Itzik Kol

MARK KITCHELL
BERKELEY IN THE SIXTIES (FD)   P.O.V. Theatrical
Films, 1990

ROBERT KLANE
Agent: ICM - Los Angeles, 310/550-4000
Contact: Writers Guild of America - Los Angeles,
310/550-1000

WALK LIKE A MAN   MGM/UA, 1987, EP
WEEKEND AT BERNIE'S   20th Century Fox, 1989,
EP w/Malcolm R. Harding

RIC KLASS
ELLIOT FAUMAN, PH.D.   Taurus, 1990

LAURENCE KLAUSNER
THE GREAT BANK HOAX   *SHENANIGANS*   Warner
Bros., 1979, EP w/Richard F. Bridges &
T. Carlyle Scales

ALLEN KLEIN
Business: Abkco Records, Inc., 1700 Broadway, New York,
NY 212/399-0300

MRS. BROWN, YOU'VE GOT A LOVELY DAUGHTER
MGM, 1968
THE CONCERT FOR BANGLADESH (FD)   20th Century
Fox, 1972, w/George Harrison
THE GREEK TYCOON   Universal, 1978, w/Ely Landau

HAL KLEIN
ANGEL UNCHAINED   AIP, 1970, EP

JEFFREY KLEIN
Business: Jaguar Distribution Corp., 3415 S. Sepulveda
Blvd., Los Angeles, CA 90034, 310/391-6666

THE HIDDEN   New Line, 1987, EP w/Stephen Diener,
Dennis Harris & Lee Muhl

MEL KLEIN
A NIGHT IN THE LIFE OF JIMMY REARDON
20th Century Fox, 1988, EP w/Noel Marshall

PAUL KLEIN
BASIC TRAINING   Moviestore, 1985,
EP w/Lawrence Vanger

ALAN KLEINBERG
DOWN BY LAW   Island Pictures, 1986

RANDAL KLEISER
Business: Randal Kleiser Productions, 3050 Runyon
Canyon Rd., Los Angeles, CA 90046, 213/851-5224
Agent: ICM - Los Angeles, 310/550-4000

THE BLUE LAGOON   Columbia, 1980
NORTH SHORE   Universal, 1987, EP
GETTING IT RIGHT   MCEG, 1989,
w/Jonathan D. Krane

MICHAEL KLINGER
GET CARTER   MGM, 1971
PULP   United Artists, 1972
CONFESSIONS OF A WINDOW CLEANER   Columbia,
1974, EP w/Norman Cohen
GOLD   Allied Artists, 1974
SOMETHING TO HIDE   Atlantic, 1976
SHOUT AT THE DEVIL   AIP, 1976

TONY KLINGER
THE KIDS ARE ALRIGHT (FD)   New World, 1979,
w/Bill Curbishley

DONALD C. KLUNE
Agent: Gray/Goodman, Inc. - Beverly Hills, 310/276-7070
Contact: Directors Guild of America - Los Angeles,
213/289-2000

MADHOUSE   Orion, 1990, CP
TOY SOLDIERS   TriStar, 1991, CP

CHRISTOPHER W. KNIGHT
Business: Knight-Tyson Productions, 127 Broadway,
Suite 220, Santa Monica, CA 90401, 310/395-7100;
Fax: 310/395-7099

HOT DOG...THE MOVIE   MGM/UA, 1984, EP
WINNERS TAKE ALL   Apollo, 1987, w/Tom Tatum
THE DREAM TEAM   Universal, 1989

RICHARD KOBRITZ
Contact: Directors Guild of America - Los Angeles,
213/289-2000

CONRACK   20th Century Fox, 1974, AP
CHRISTINE   Columbia, 1983
ALIEN NATION   20th Century Fox, 1988,
w/Gale Anne Hurd

HOWARD W. KOCH
Business: Aries Films, Inc., Paramount Pictures, 5555
Melrose Ave., Los Angeles, CA 90038, 213/956-5996;
Fax: 213/956-8466
Contact: Directors Guild of America - Los Angeles,
213/289-2000

COME BLOW YOUR HORN   Paramount, 1963, EP
THE MANCHURIAN CANDIDATE   United Artists,
1962, EP
THE PRESIDENT'S ANALYST   Paramount, 1967, EP
THE ODD COUPLE   Paramount, 1968
ON A CLEAR DAY YOU CAN SEE FOREVER
Paramount, 1970
PLAZA SUITE   Paramount, 1971
STAR SPANGLED GIRL   Paramount, 1971
LAST OF THE RED HOT LOVERS   Paramount, 1972
BADGE 373   Paramount, 1973
JACQUELINE SUSANN'S ONCE IS NOT ENOUGH
Paramount, 1975
AIRPLANE!   Paramount, 1980, EP
DRAGONSLAYER   Paramount, 1981, EP
SOME KIND OF HERO   Paramount, 1982
AIRPLANE II: THE SEQUEL   Paramount, 1983
GHOST ★   Paramount, 1990,
EP w/Steven-Charles Jaffe

FILM
PRODUCERS,
STUDIOS,
AGENTS AND
CASTING
DIRECTORS
GUIDE

HOWARD W. KOCH, JR.

Business: The Koch Company, Paramount Pictures, 5555 Melrose Ave., Los Angeles, CA 90038, 213/956-8219

THE DROWNING POOL   Warner Bros., 1975, AP
THE OTHER SIDE OF MIDNIGHT   20th Century Fox, 1977, EP
THE IDOLMAKER   United Artists, 1980, w/Gene Kirkwood
HEAVEN CAN WAIT   Paramount, 1978,
   EP w/Charles H. Maguire
THE FRISCO KID   Warner Bros., 1979, EP
HONKY TONK FREEWAY   Universal/AFD, 1981,
   w/Don Boyd
THE KEEP   Paramount, 1983, w/Gene Kirkwood
GORKY PARK   Orion, 1983, w/Gene Kirkwood
A NIGHT IN HEAVEN   20th Century Fox, 1983,
   w/Gene Kirkwood
THE POPE OF GREENWICH VILLAGE   MGM/UA, 1984,
   w/Gene Kirkwood
ROOFTOPS   New Visions, 1989
THE LONG WALK HOME   Miramax, 1990, w/Dave Bell
NECESSARY ROUGHNESS   Paramount, 1991, EP
WAYNE'S WORLD   Paramount, 1992

KAREN KOCH

THE RAPTURE   Fine Line, 1991, w/Nick Wechsler & Nancy Tenenbaum

DAVID KOEPP

Agent: UTA - Beverly Hills, 310/273-6700
Contact: Writers Guild of America - Los Angeles, 310/550-1000

APARTMENT ZERO   Skouras Pictures, 1989,
   w/Martin Donovan

JOHN KOHN

Contact: Writers Guild of America - Los Angeles, 310/550-1000

FIGURES IN A LANDSCAPE   National General, 1971
THE STRANGE VENGEANCE OF ROSALIE
   20th Century Fox, 1972
THEATRE OF BLOOD   United Artists, 1973,
   w/Stanley Mann
RACING WITH THE MOON   Paramount, 1984,
   w/Alain Bernheim
SHANGHAI SURPRISE   MGM/UA, 1986

PANCHO KOHNER

Business: Capricorn Productions, Inc., 1527 Tigertail Rd., Los Angeles, CA 90049
Agent: Paul Kohner, Inc. - Los Angeles, CA 90069, 310/550-1060

THE BRIDGE IN THE JUNGLE   United Artists, 1971
MR. SYCAMORE   Film Venture, 1975
ST. IVES   Warner Bros., 1976, w/Stanley S. Canter
THE WHITE BUFFALO   United Artists, 1977
LOVE AND BULLETS   AFD, 1979
WHY WOULD I LIE?   MGM/UA, 1980
10 TO MIDNIGHT   Cannon, 1983, w/Lance Hool
THE EVIL THAT MEN DO   TriStar, 1984
MURPHY'S LAW   Cannon, 1986
ASSASSINATION   Cannon, 1987
DEATH WISH 4: THE CRACKDOWN   Cannon, 1987
MESSENGER OF DEATH   Cannon, 1988
KINJITE (FORBIDDEN SUBJECTS)   Cannon, 1989

SHUNDO KOJI

THE YAKUZA   Warner Bros., 1975, EP

ITZIK KOL

THE POLICEMAN   Cinema 5, 1972, w/Ephraim Kishon
THE AMBASSADOR   Cannon, 1985, AP
BEAUTY AND THE BEAST   Cannon, 1987, EP
RUMPLESTILTSKIN   Cannon, 1987, EP

CEDOMIR KOLAR

THE ARROWTOOTH WALTZ   Warner Bros., 1991,
   w/Claude Ossard

EVZEN W. KOLAR

STREET SMART   Cannon, 1987, AP
MASTERS OF THE UNIVERSE   Cannon, 1987, AP
BAT 21   TriStar, 1988, LP

DAN KOLSRUD

Contact: Directors Guild of America - Los Angeles, 213/289-2000

IMPULSE   Warner Bros., 1990, EP
MEMOIRS OF AN INVISIBLE MAN   Warner Bros., 1991,
   w/Bruce Bodner

DANIEL P. KONDOS
(credit w/George Kondos)

STAND ALONE   New World, 1985, EP

GEORGE KONDOS
(credit w/Daniel P. Kondos)

STAND ALONE   New World, 1985, EP

JACKIE KONG

Attorney: Bob Brenner, Esq., 213/553-2525

NIGHT PATROL   New World, 1984, CP
BLOOD DINER   Vestron, 1987, CP

FRANK KONIGSBERG

Business: The Konigsberg-Sanitsky Company, 1930 Century Park West, Suite 400, Los Angeles, CA 90067, 310/277-6850; Fax: 310/277-7965

JOY OF SEX   Paramount, 1984
9 1/2 WEEKS   MGM/UA, 1986, EP w/Keith Barish & F. Richard Northcott

LAWRENCE KONNER

Business: Konner-Rosenthal Productions, Paramount Pictures, 5555 Melrose Ave., Los Angeles, LA 90038, 213/956-5909
Agent: CAA - Beverly Hills, 310/288-4545

THE LEGEND OF BILLIE JEAN   TriStar, 1985,
   CP w/Mark Rosenthal
THE IN CROWD   Orion, 1988, w/Keith Rubinstein

HIDETAKA KONNO

BRIDE OF RE-ANIMATOR   50th St. Films, 1991,
   EP w/Keith Walley & Paul White

FILM
PRODUCERS,
STUDIOS,
AGENTS AND
CASTING
DIRECTORS
GUIDE

F
I
L
M

P
R
O
D
U
C
E
R
S

JOSI W. KONSKI
Business: Laguna Productions, Inc., 6854 NW 77 Court, Miami, FL 33166, 305/594-5674
Contact: Directors Guild of America - Los Angeles, 213/289-2000

TRADING HEARTS   New Century/Vista, 1988

JEFFREY KONVITZ
Agent: Shapiro-Lichtman, Inc. - Los Angeles, 310/859-8877
Contact: Writers Guild of America - Los Angeles, 310/550-1000

THE SENTINEL   Universal, 1977, w/Michael Winner

ANDRE KOOB
TWIN SISTERS   Image, 1991, EP w/Pierre David

DAVID KOONTZ
MOMMIE DEAREST   Paramount, 1981, EP w/Terence O'Neill

ARNOLD KOPELSON
Business: 6100 Wilshire Blvd., Suite 1500, Los Angeles, CA 90048, 213/932-0500; Fax: 213/932-0238

LOST AND FOUND   Columbia, 1979, EP
THE LEGACY   Universal, 1979, EP
FOOLIN' AROUND   Columbia, 1980
NIGHT OF THE JUGGLER   Columbia, 1980, EP
DIRTY TRICKS   Avco Embassy, 1981, EP w/Pierre David & Victor Solnicki
PLATOON ★★   Orion, 1986
TRIUMPH OF THE SPIRIT   Triumph, 1989, w/Shimon Arama
FIRE BIRDS   Buena Vista, 1990, EP w/Keith Barish
WARLOCK   Trimark, 1991, EP
OUT FOR JUSTICE   Warner Bros., 1991, w/Steven Seagal

BARBARA KOPPLE
Business: Cabin Creek Films, 58 E. 11th St., New York, NY 10003, 212/533-7157

HARLAN COUNTY, U.S.A. (FD)   Cabin Creek, 1977

DAVID KORDA
Business: Capella Films, 9242 Beverly Blvd., Suite 280, Beverly Hills, CA 90210, 310/247-4700

THE RULING CLASS   Avco Embassy, 1972, AP
MAN FRIDAY   Avco Embassy, 1975
THE GREAT SCOUT & CATHOUSE THURSDAY   AIP, 1976, w/Jules Buck
SUNBURN   Paramount, 1979, AP
CATTLE ANNIE & LITTLE BRITCHES   Universal, 1981, AP
HALF MOON STREET   20th Century Fox, 1986, EP w/Edward R. Pressman
LOOPHOLE   Almi Pictures, 1986, w/Julian Holloway
HAMBURGER HILL   Paramount, 1987, EP w/Jerry Offsay
SHATTERED   MGM-Pathe, 1991, CP
THE NUTTY NUT   1992, EP

LESTER KORN
TWENTY-ONE   Triton, 1991, EP w/Carole Curb & Mike Curb

HARRY KORSHAK
CALLIOPE   Moonstone, 1971
HIT!   Paramount, 1973
SHEILA LEVINE IS DEAD AND LIVING IN NEW YORK   Paramount, 1975
GABLE AND LOMBARD   Universal, 1976

BENNI KORZEN
I COULD NEVER HAVE SEX WITH ANY MAN WHO HAS SO LITTLE REGARD FOR MY HUSBAND   Cinema 5, 1973, AP
FOREPLAY   Cinema National, 1975, w/David G. Witter
RENT CONTROL   Group 5 Films, 1984
THE MISFIT BRIGADE   *WHEELS OF TERROR*   Trans World, 1987, w/Just Betzer
THE GIRL IN A SWING   Millimeter Films, 1989, CP

ROBERT KOSBERG
Business: 10202 W. Washington Blvd., Culver City, CA 90232, 310/280-4774; Fax: 310/280-1514

COMMANDO   20th Century Fox, 1985, AP
ONE MORE SATURDAY NIGHT   Columbia, 1986, w/Jonathan Bernstein & Tova Laiter

RON KOSLOW
Agent: CAA - Beverly Hills, 310/288-4545
Contact: Writers Guild of America - Los Angeles, 310/550-1000

FIRSTBORN   Paramount, 1984, CP
INTO THE NIGHT   Universal, 1985, w/George Folsey Jr.

MICHEL KOSSAK
Business: Ion Pictures, 3122 Santa Monica Blvd., Santa Monica, CA 90404, 310/453-4466

THE CLOSER   Ion, 1991, SP w/F. Daniel Somrack

DOROTHY KOSTER PAUL
(see Dorothy Koster PAUL)

LARRY KOSTROFF
Contact: Directors Guild of America - Los Angeles, 213/289-2000

WHEN A STRANGER CALLS   Columbia, 1979, AP
THE GUMSHOE KID   Skouras, 1990, CP

TED KOTCHEFF
Agent: CAA - Beverly Hills, 310/288-4545
Contact: Directors Guild of America - Los Angeles, 213/289-2000

SPLIT IMAGE   Orion, 1982

CAROL KOTTENBROOK
SHADOWZONE   JGM Enterprises, 1990
RICH GIRL   Studio Three, 1991, AP w/Richard Mann
A ROW OF CROWS   1991

JACOB KOTZKY
(credit w/Sharon Harel)
Business: Capitol Films, Ltd., 24 Upper Brook St., London W1Y 1PD, 071/872-0017

EVERY TIME WE SAY GOODBYE   TriStar, 1986
IRON EAGLE II   TriStar, 1988, w/John Kemeny

JIM KOUF
Business: Kouf-Bigelow Productions, Walt Disney Pictures,
   Animation 1A11, 500 S. Buena Vista St., Burbank, CA
   91521, 818/560-5103; Fax: 213/560-1930
Agent: ICM - Los Angeles, 310/550-4000

CLASS   Orion, 1983, AP
SECRET ADMIRER   Orion, 1985, CP
STAKEOUT   Buena Vista, 1987, w/Cathleen Summers

STEVEN KOVACS
THE LADY IN RED   New World, 1979, CP
ON THE LINE   Miramax, 1987, w/Jose Luis Borau
'68   New World, 1988, w/Dale Djerassi & Isabel Maxwell

JONATHAN KOVLER
REAL LIFE   Paramount, 1979, EP w/Norman Epstein

WOLODYMYR KOWAL
THE INCREDIBLE TWO-HEADED TRANSPLANT   AIP,
   1971, CP

BERNARD L. KOWALSKI
MACHO CALLAHAN   Avco Embassy, 1970,
   w/Martin C. Schute

GENE KRAFT
Business: Gene Kraft Productions, 7556 Woodrow Wilson
   Dr., Los Angeles, CA 90046, 213/851-5322
Contact: Directors Guild of America - Los Angeles,
   213/289-2000

THE BIG TOWN   Columbia, 1987, EP

ROBERT KRAFT
HUDSON HAWK   TriStar, 1991, EP

LARRY KRAMER
WOMEN IN LOVE   United Artists, 1970

LEE KRAMER
XANADU   Universal, 1980, EP
THE MAN WHO SAW TOMORROW (FD)   Warner Bros.,
   1981, w/Paul Drane & Robert Guenette

STANLEY KRAMER
Business: Stanley Kramer Productions, 12386 Ridge Circle,
   Los Angeles, CA 90049, 213/472-0065
Agent: Paul Kohner, Inc. - Los Angeles, 310/550-1060

CHAMPION   United Artists, 1949
HOME OF THE BRAVE   United Artists, 1949
THE MEN   Columbia, 1950
CYRANO DE BERGERAC   United Artists, 1950
DEATH OF A SALESMAN   Columbia, 1951
HIGH NOON ★   United Artists, 1952
MY SIX CONVICTS   Universal, 1952
THE SNIPER   Columbia, 1952
THE HAPPY TIME   Columbia, 1952
EIGHT IRON MEN   Columbia, 1952
THE FOUR POSTER   Columbia, 1953
THE 5000 FINGERS OF DR. T   Columbia, 1953
THE JUGGLER   Columbia, 1953
THE WILD ONE   Columbia, 1954
THE CAINE MUTINY ★   Columbia, 1954
NOT AS A STRANGER   United Artists, 1955
THE PRIDE AND THE PASSION   United Artists, 1957
THE DEFIANT ONES ★   United Artists, 1958

ON THE BEACH   United Artists, 1959
INHERIT THE WIND   United Artists, 1960
JUDGMENT AT NUREMBERG ★   United Artists, 1961
A CHILD IS WAITING   United Artists, 1962
IT'S A MAD, MAD, MAD, MAD WORLD   United
   Artists, 1963
SHIP OF FOOLS ★   Columbia, 1965
GUESS WHO'S COMING TO DINNER ★   Columbia, 1967
THE SECRET OF SANTA VITTORIA   United Artists, 1969
R.P.M.   Columbia, 1970
BLESS THE BEASTS AND CHILDREN   Columbia, 1971
OKLAHOMA CRUDE   Columbia, 1973
THE DOMINO PRINCIPLE   Avco Embassy, 1977
THE RUNNER STUMBLES   20th Century Fox, 1979

JONATHAN D. KRANE
Contact: TriStar Pictures, 7944 Woodrow Wilson,
   Los Angeles, CA 90046, 213/650-0942;
   Fax: 213/654-8944

TRAIL OF THE PINK PANTHER   MGM/UA, 1982, EP
CURSE OF THE PINK PANTHER   MGM/UA, 1983, EP
THE MAN WHO LOVED WOMEN   Columbia, 1983, EP
MICKI AND MAUDE   Columbia, 1984, EP w/Lou Antonio
A FINE MESS   Columbia, 1986, EP
THAT'S LIFE!   Columbia, 1986, EP
BLIND DATE   TriStar, 1987, EP w/Gary Hendler &
   David Permut
SLIPPING INTO DARKNESS   MCEG, 1988
THE CHOCOLATE WAR   MCEG, 1988
YOU CAN'T HURRY LOVE   MCEG, 1988, w/Lawrence
   Kasanoff & Ellen Steloff
C.H.U.D. II   Vestron, 1988
GETTING IT RIGHT   MCEG, 1989, w/Randal Kleiser
THE EXPERTS   Paramount, 1989, EP w/Jack Grossberg
LOOK WHO'S TALKING   TriStar, 1989
WITHOUT YOU I'M NOTHING   MCEG, 1990
LIMIT UP   MCEG, 1990
LOOK WHO'S TALKING TOO   TriStar, 1990

STEVE KRANTZ
Business: Steve Krantz Productions, 8439 Sunset Blvd.,
   Suite 200, Los Angeles, CA 90069, 213/848-1384;
   Fax: 213/656-1647

FRITZ THE CAT (AF)   Cinemation, 1972
HEAVY TRAFFIC (AF)   AIP, 1973
THE NINE LIVES OF FRITZ THE CAT (AF)   AIP, 1974
COOLEY HIGH   AIP, 1975
RUBY   Dimension, 1977, EP
WHICH WAY IS UP?   Universal, 1977
JENNIFER   AIP, 1978
SWAP MEET   Dimension Pictures, 1979

DONALD KRANZE
Contact: Directors Guild of America - Los Angeles,
   213/289-2000

SUMMER OF '42   Warner Bros., 1971, AP
THE OTHER   20th Century Fox, 1972, AP
THE PURSUIT OF D. B. COOPER   Universal, 1981,
   EP w/William Tennant
NIGHT SHIFT   The Ladd Company/Warner Bros.,
   1982, EP

ROBERT KRAUSE
THE CHECK IS IN THE MAIL   Ascot Entertainment, 1986,
   w/Robert Kaufman

Kr

FILM
PRODUCERS,
STUDIOS,
AGENTS and
CASTING
DIRECTORS
GUIDE

F
I
L
M

P
R
O
D
U
C
E
R
S

FILM
PRODUCERS,
STUDIOS,
AGENTS AND
CASTING
DIRECTORS
GUIDE

DAVID KREBS
BEATLEMANIA American Cinema, 1981, w/Edie
Landau, Ely Landau & Steven Leber

HOWARD B. KREITSEK
Contact: Writers Guild of America - Los Angeles,
310/550-1000

THE ILLUSTRATED MAN Warner Bros., 1969,
w/Ted Mann
RABBIT, RUN Warner Bros., 1970

BRAD KREVOY
(credit w/Steven Stabler)
Business: Motion Picture Corporation of America, 1401
Ocean Ave., 3rd Floor, Santa Monica, CA 90401,
310/319-9500; Fax: 310/319-9501

SWEET REVENGE Concorde, 1987
DANGEROUS LOVE Concorde, 1988
PURPLE PEOPLE EATER Concorde, 1988
MEMORIAL VALLEY MASSACRE Nelson
Entertainment, 1989
MINISTRY OF VENGEANCE Motion Picture Corp. of
America, 1989
THINK BIG Concorde, 1990
BACK TO BACK Concorde, 1990
HANGFIRE Motion Picture Corp. of America, 1991

ROBERT D. KRINTZMAN
STARHOPS First American, 1978, w/John B. Kelly

NINO KRISMAN
THE VALACHI PAPERS Columbia, 1972, EP

JONATHAN KRIVINE
THE SISTER-IN-LAW Crown International, 1975,
w/Joseph Ruben

MARTY KROFFT
(credit w/Sid Krofft)
Business: Sid and Marty Krofft Picture Corporation,
1040 N. Las Palmas Ave., Hollywood, CA 90038,
213/467-3125; Fax: 213/850-2484

PUFNSTUF Universal, 1970, EP
HARRY TRACY Quartet/Films, 1983,
EP w/Albert J. Tenser

SID KROFFT
(credit w/Marty Krofft)
Business: Sid and Marty Krofft Picture Corporation,
1040 N. Las Palmas Ave., Hollywood, CA 90038,
213/467-3125; Fax: 213/850-2484

PUFNSTUF Universal, 1970, EP
HARRY TRACY Quartet/Films, 1983,
EP w/Albert J. Tenser

LEONARD KROLL
Contact: MGM-Pathe, 10000 W. Washington Blvd.,
Culver City, CA 90232, 310/280-6000

POLICE ACADEMY 2: THEIR FIRST ASSIGNMENT
Warner Bros., 1985, CP
WALK LIKE A MAN MGM/UA, 1987
FATAL BEAUTY MGM, 1987

PIETER KROONENBURG
Business: Filmline International Inc., 109 ouest rue St. Paul,
Montreal, H2Y 2A1, 514/288-5888; Fax: 514/288-8083

BETHUNE: THE MAKING OF A HERO Filmline
International, 1990, w/Nicolas Clermont

SCOTT KROOPF
Business: Interscope Communications, 10900 Wilshire Blvd.,
Suite 1400, Los Angeles, CA 90024, 310/208-8525;
Fax: 310/208-1764

OUTRAGEOUS FORTUNE Buena Vista, 1987,
CP w/Peter V. Herald & Martin Mickelson
NO MAN'S LAND Orion, 1987, AP
BILL & TED'S EXCELLENT ADVENTURE Orion, 1989,
w/Michael S. Murphey & Joel Soisson
AN INNOCENT MAN Buena Vista, 1989, EP
CLASS ACTION 20th Century Fox, 1991, w/Robert W.
Cort & Ted Field
BILL & TED'S BOGUS JOURNEY Orion, 1991
PARADISE Buena Vista, 1991, EP w/Patrick Palmer

BARRY KROST
Business: Krost/Chapin Productions, 4000 Warner Blvd.,
Burbank, CA 91522, 818/954-6526

WHEN A STRANGER CALLS Columbia, 1979,
EP w/Melvin Simon
PANDEMONIUM MGM/UA, 1982, EP
AMERICAN DREAMER Warner Bros., 1984, EP
UFORIA Universal, 1985, EP w/Melvin Simon

ROY KROST
MARTIN'S DAY MGM/UA, 1985, w/Richard Dalton
TOO OUTRAGEOUS! Spectrafilm, 1987

SAUL KRUGMAN
THE ALL-AMERICAN BOY Warner Bros., 1973,
w/Joseph T. Naar
FAST CHARLIE...THE MOONBEAM RIDER Universal,
1979, w/Roger Corman

LAWRENCE KUBIK
Business: The Kubik Company - Los Angeles,
213/859-9777
Contact: Writers Guild of America - Los Angeles,
310/550-1000

ZACHARIAH Cinerama, 1970, CP
DEATH BEFORE DISHONOR New World, 1987

STANLEY KUBRICK
Attorney: Louis C. Blau, Loeb & Loeb, 10100 Santa Monica
Blvd., Los Angeles, CA 90067, 310/552-7774
Contact: Directors Guild of America - Los Angeles,
213/656-1220

DR. STRANGELOVE OR: HOW I LEARNED TO
STOP WORRYING & LOVE THE BOMB ★
Columbia, 1964
2001: A SPACE ODYSSEY MGM, 1968
A CLOCKWORK ORANGE ★ Warner Bros., 1971
BARRY LYNDON ★ Warner Bros., 1975
THE SHINING Warner Bros., 1980
FULL METAL JACKET Warner Bros., 1987

ANDREW J. KUEHN

Business: Kaleidoscope Films Ltd., 844 N. Seward St., Hollywood, CA 90038, 213/465-1151
Contact: Directors Guild of America - Los Angeles, 213/289-2000

TERROR IN THE AISLES   Universal, 1984, w/Stephen J. Netburn
D.O.A.   Buena Vista, 1988, CP w/Cathleen Summers

FRED T. KUEHNERT

Contact: Houston International Film Festival

THE BUDDY HOLLY STORY   Columbia, 1978, EP w/Edward H. Cohen

MICHAEL KUHN

(credit w/Nigel Sinclair)
Business: Propaganda Films, 940 N. Mansfield Ave., Los Angeles, CA 90038, 213/462-6400

THE BLUE IGUANA   Paramount, 1988
FEAR, ANXIETY, AND DEPRESSION   Samuel Goldwyn Company, 1989, EP
KILL ME AGAIN   MGM/UA, 1989, EP
DADDY'S DYIN'...WHO'S GOT THE WILL?   MGM/UA, 1990, EP w/Bobbie Edrick & Del Shores

TOM KUHN

(credit w/Charles Mitchell)
Business: Lightyear Entertainment, 350 5th Ave., Suite 5101, New York, NY 10118,

HEAVEN (FD)   Island Pictures, 1987, EP w/Arlyne Rothberg
ARIA   Miramax, 1988, EP
THE RETURN OF SWAMP THING   Miramax, 1989, EP
THE LEMON SISTERS   Miramax, 1990, EP w/Arnold J. Holland
MONSTER HIGH   Lightyear, 1990, EP w/Annette Cirillo*

DARRYL J. KUNTZ

(credit w/Frank J. Kuntz)

DAKOTA   Miramax, 1988

FRANK J. KUNTZ

(credit w/Darryl J. Kuntz)

DAKOTA   Miramax, 1988

GARY KURFIRST

Business: 1775 Broadway, 7th Floor, New York, NY 10019, 212/957-0900

STOP MAKING SENSE (FD)   Cinecom, 1984, EP
TRUE STORIES   Warner Bros., 1986
SIESTA   Lorimar, 1987

JOHN A. KURI

Business: Sheffield Entertainment Corporation, 16133 Ventura Blvd., Suite 700, Encino, CA 91436, 818/501-8471
Contact: Directors Guild of America - Los Angeles, 213/289-2000

CAPTIVE HEARTS   MGM/UA, 1987

HISAO KUROSAWA

RHAPSODY IN AUGUST   1991

PAUL KURTA

Contact: Directors Guild of America - New York, 212/581-0370

Q   UFD, 1982, AP
PERFECT STRANGERS   New Line, 1984
SPECIAL EFFECTS   New Line, 1984
THE STUFF   New World, 1985
KEY EXCHANGE   20th Century Fox, 1985
RETURN TO SALEM'S LOT   Warner Bros., 1987
MILES FROM HOME   Cinecom, 1988, w/Frederick Zollo
HEART OF DIXIE   Orion, 1989, CP

GARY KURTZ

Business: Pinewood Studios, Iver Heath, Bucks., SL0 0NH, England, 0753/651-700; Fax: 0753/656-564

TWO-LANE BLACKTOP   Universal, 1971, AP
AMERICAN GRAFFITI ★   Universal, 1973, CP
STAR WARS ★   20th Century Fox, 1977
THE EMPIRE STRIKES BACK   20th Century Fox, 1980
THE DARK CRYSTAL   Universal/AFD, 1982, w/Jim Henson
RETURN TO OZ   Buena Vista, 1985, EP
SLIPSTREAM   Entertainment Films, 1989

KIM KURUMADA

Contact: Directors Guild of America - Los Angeles, 213/289-2000

MIKE'S MURDER   Warner Bros., 1984, EP
PERFECT   Columbia, 1985, EP
MOVING   Warner Bros., 1988, AP
CLASS ACTION   20th Century Fox, 1991, AP
LIFE STINKS   MGM, 1991, AP

DONALD KUSHNER

(credit w/Peter Locke)
Business: The Kushner-Locke Company, 11601 Wilshire Blvd., 21st Floor, Los Angeles, CA 90025, 310/445-1111; Fax: 310/445-1191

TRON   Buena Vista, 1982*
NUTCRACKER   Atlantic, 1986, w/Willard Carroll & Thomas L. Wilhite
POUND PUPPIES & THE LEGEND OF BIG PAW (AF)   TriStar, 1988

KAZ KUZUI

Business: Kuzui Enterprises, 220 Fifth Ave., New York, NY 10001, 212/683-9198 or Jingumae-Otowa Heights 201, 5-503 Jingumae, Shibuya-ku, Tokyo

TOKYO POP   Spectrafilm, 1988, w/Joel Tuber

La

FILM
PRODUCERS,
STUDIOS,
AGENTS AND
CASTING
DIRECTORS
GUIDE

F
I
L
M

P
R
O
D
U
C
E
R
S

L

RICHARD LaBRIE
BLOOD AND CONCRETE   I.R.S., 1991

ALAN LADD, JR.
Business: MGM-Pathe Communications, 10000 W.
   Washington Blvd., Culver City, CA 90232,
   310/280-6000

THE WALKING STICK   MGM, 1969
A SEVERED HEAD   Columbia, 1971
VILLAIN   MGM, 1971, w/Jay Kanter
X, Y, & ZEE   Columbia, 1971, w/Jay Kanter
THE DEVIL'S WIDOW   *TAM LIN*   AIP, 1972,
   w/Stanley Mann
FEAR IS THE KEY   Paramount, 1973, w/Jay Kanter
VICE VERSA   Columbia, 1988, EP

DAVID LADD
Business: MGM-Pathe Communications, 8670 Wilshire
   Blvd., Beverly Hills, CA 90211, 310/967-2225

THE SERPENT AND THE RAINBOW   Universal, 1988,
   w/Doug Claybourne

IAN LaFRENAIS
Agent: Broder-Kurland-Webb-Uffner Agency - Los Angeles,
   213/656-9262
Contact: Writers Guild of America - Los Angeles,
   310/550-1000

BULLSHOT   Island Alive, 1985
WATER   Atlantic, 1986
VICE VERSA   Columbia, 1988, w/Dick Clement

TOVA LAITER
Business: Imagine Entertainment, 1925 Century Park East,
   23rd Floor, Los Angeles, CA 90067, 310/277-1665; Fax:
   310/785-0107

ONE MORE SATURDAY NIGHT   Columbia, 1986,
   w/Jonathan Bernstein & Robert Kosberg
FIRE WITH FIRE   Paramount, 1986, EP

ARNIE LAKEYN
Business: Xenon Entertainment, 211 Arizona Ave.,
   Suite 25, Santa Monica, CA 90401, 310/451-5510;
   Fax: 310/395-4058

TWISTED JUSTICE   Seymour Borde & Associates, 1990,
   EP w/Gerald Milton & S. Leigh Savidge

CHARLES M. LaLOGGIA
Business: LaLoggia Productions - Los Angeles,
   213/462-3055

FEAR NO EVIL   Avco Embassy, 1981, w/Frank LaLoggia
THE LADY IN WHITE   New Century/Vista, 1988,
   EP w/Cliff Payne

FRANK LaLOGGIA
Business: LaLoggia Productions - Los Angeles,
   213/462-3055

FEAR NO EVIL   Avco Embassy, 1981,
   w/Charles M. LaLoggia
THE LADY IN WHITE   New Century/Vista, 1988,
   w/Andrew G. La Marca

ANDREW G. LaMARCA
THE LADY IN WHITE   New Century/Vista, 1988,
   w/Frank LaLoggia
ROBOCOP 3   Orion, 1991, AP

JOHN LAMB
DELINQUENT SCHOOLGIRLS   *CARNAL MADNESS*
   Rainbow, 1975, EP

JERROLD W. LAMBERT
SPONTANEOUS COMBUSTION   Taurus, 1990, CP

VERITY LAMBERT
Business: Cinema Verity, Ltd., The Mill House, Millers Way,
   1A Shepherds Bush Rd., London, W6 7NA, 081/749-8485;
   Fax: 081/743-5062
Agent: ICM - Los Angeles, 310/550-4000

DREAMCHILD   Universal, 1985, EP w/Dennis Potter
MORONS FROM OUTER SPACE   Universal, 1985, EP
CLOCKWISE   Universal, 1986, EP w/Nat Cohen
LINK   Cannon, 1986, EP
A CRY IN THE DARK   Warner Bros., 1988

ALANA H. LAMBROS
TEEN WITCH   Trans World, 1989, w/Rafael Eisenman

LEONARD LAMENSDORF
CORNBREAD, EARL AND ME   AIP, 1975, EP

HUGO LAMONICA
THE STRANGER   Columbia, 1987

CAROL LAMPMAN
STEPFATHER II   Millimeter Films, 1989, EP

DAVID LANCASTER
Business: 3356 Bennett Dr., Los Angeles, CA 90068,
   213/874-1415

'NIGHT, MOTHER   Universal, 1986, EP w/Dann Byck

JOANNA LANCASTER
(credit w/Richard Wagner)

LITTLE TREASURE   TriStar, 1985, EP
RUTHLESS PEOPLE   Buena Vista, 1986,
   EP w/Walter Yetnikoff

EDIE LANDAU
(credit w/Ely Landau)
Business: Edie & Ely Landau, Inc., 8863 Alcott St., Suite 1,
   Los Angeles, CA 90035, 310/274-9993

HOPSCOTCH   Avco Embassy, 1980
BEATLEMANIA   American Cinema, 1981, w/David Krebs &
   Steven Leber

THE CHOSEN   20th Century Fox International
   Classics, 1982
THE HOLCROFT COVENANT   Universal, 1985

ELY LANDAU
Business: Edie & Ely Landau, Inc., 8863 Alcott St., Suite 1,
   Los Angeles, CA 90035, 310/274-9993

LONG DAY'S JOURNEY INTO NIGHT   Embassy,
   1962, EP
THE PAWNBROKER   Allied Artists, 1965,
   w/Herbert R. Steinman
THE MADWOMAN OF CHAILLOT   Warner Bros., 1969
KING: A FILMED RECORD...MONTGOMERY TO
   MEMPHIS (FD)   Commonwealth, 1970
A DELICATE BALANCE   American Film Theatre, 1973
THE ICEMAN COMETH   American Film Theatre, 1973
THE HOMECOMING   American Film Theatre, 1973
BUTLEY   American Film Theatre, 1974
LUTHER   American Film Theatre, 1974
RHINOCEROS   American Film Theatre, 1974
LOST IN THE STARS   American Film Theatre, 1974
THE THREE SISTERS   American Film Theatre, 1974, EP
IN CELEBRATION   American Film Theatre, 1975
GALILEO   American Film Theatre, 1975
THE MAN IN THE GLASS BOOTH   American Film
   Theatre, 1975
THE GREEK TYCOON   Universal, 1978, w/Allen Klein
HOPSCOTCH   Avco Embassy, 1980, w/Edie Landau
BEATLEMANIA   American Cinema, 1981, w/David Krebs,
   Edie Landau & Steven Leber
THE CHOSEN   20th Century Fox International Classics,
   1982, w/Edie Landau
THE HOLCROFT COVENANT   Universal, 1985,
   w/Edie Landau

JON LANDAU
Contact: Directors Guild of America - Los Angeles,
   213/289-2000

CAMPUS MAN   Paramount, 1987, w/Peggy Fowler

SUSAN B. LANDAU
Contact: Orr & Cruickshank Productions, c/o Walt Disney
   Studios, 500 S. Buena Vista St., Animation 2G11,
   Burbank, CA 91521, 818/560-6423; Fax: 818/566-7310

MR. DESTINY   Buena Vista, 1990, cp

HAL LANDERS
(credit w/Bobby Roberts)

THE GYPSY MOTHS   MGM, 1969
MONTE WALSH   National General, 1970
THE HOT ROCK   20th Century Fox, 1972
THE BANK SHOT   United Artists, 1974
DEATH WISH   Paramount, 1974
DAMNATION ALLEY   20th Century Fox, 1977, EP
JOYRIDE   AIP, 1977, EP
DEATH WISH II   Filmways, 1982, EP

MICHAEL S. LANDES
(credit w/Albert Schwartz)
Business: The Almi Group, 1900 Broadway, New York, NY
   10023, 212/769-6400; Fax: 212/769-9295

THE BIG SCORE   Almi, 1983
I AM THE CHEESE   Almi, 1983, EP w/Jack Schwartzman
THE BOSTONIANS   Almi, 1984, EP

JOHN LANDIS
Agent: CAA - Beverly Hills, 310/288-4545
Contact: Directors Guild of America - Los Angeles,
   213/289-2000

TWILIGHT ZONE - THE MOVIE   Warner Bros., 1983,
   w/Steven Spielberg
CLUE   Paramount, 1985, EP w/George Folsey Jr., Peter
   Guber & Jon Peters
AMAZON WOMEN ON THE MOON   Universal, 1987,
   EP w/George Folsey Jr.

ALAN LANDSBURG
Business: The Landsburg Company, 11811 W. Olympic
   Blvd., Los Angeles, CA 90064, 310/478-7878;
   Fax: 310/477-7166
Contact: Directors Guild of America - Los Angeles,
   213/289-2000

THE OUTER SPACE CONNECTION (FD)   Sunn
   Classic, 1975
JAWS 3-D   Universal, 1983, EP w/Howard Lipstone
PORKY'S II: THE NEXT DAY   20th Century Fox, 1983,
   EP w/Harold Greenberg & Melvin Simon

ANDREW LANE
(credit w/Wayne Crawford)
Business: Gibraltar Entertainment, 14101 Valleyheart Dr.,
   Suite 205, Sherman Oaks, CA 91423, 818/501-2076;
   Fax: 818/501-5138
Agent: The Richland-Wunsch-Hohman Agency -
   Los Angeles, 310/278-1955

GOD'S BLOODY ACRE   Omni, 1975
CHEERING SECTION   Dimension, 1977
TOMCATS   Dimension, 1977
BARRACUDA   Republic, 1979, w/Harry Kerwin
VALLEY GIRL   Atlantic, 1983
NIGHT OF THE COMET   Atlantic, 1984
JAKE SPEED   New World, 1986, w/William Fay
MORTAL PASSIONS   MGM/UA, 1990, EP w/Joel Levine
PEACEMAKER   Fries Entertainment, 1990
THE SERVANTS OF TWILIGHT   Trimark, 1991,
   EP w/Mark Amin, Joel Levine

CHARLES LANE
SIDEWALK STORIES   Island Pictures, 1989

LEONARD C. LANE
POPE JOAN   Columbia, 1972, EP

STEVEN LANE
THE HOWLING   Avco Embassy, 1980,
   EP w/Daniel H. Blatt
HOWLING II...YOUR SISTER IS A WEREWOLF   Thorn
   EMI, 1986
HOWLING III: THE MARSUPIALS   Square Pictures, 1987,
   EP w/Robert Pringle & Edward Simons
HOWLING IV...THE ORIGINAL NIGHTMARE   Allied
   Entertainment, 1988, EP w/Avi Lerner, Robert Pringle &
   Edward Simons

JENNINGS LANG
SLAUGHTERHOUSE-FIVE   Universal, 1972, EP
PETE 'N' TILLIE   Universal, 1972, EP
HIGH PLAINS DRIFTER   Universal, 1973, EP
THE GREAT NORTHFIELD, MINNESOTA RAID
   Universal, 1972
CHARLEY VARRICK   Universal, 1973, EP

La

FILM
PRODUCERS,
STUDIOS,
AGENTS AND
CASTING
DIRECTORS
GUIDE

FILM PRODUCERS

La

**FILM
PRODUCERS,
STUDIOS,
AGENTS** AND
**CASTING
DIRECTORS
GUIDE**

**F
I
L
M

P
R
O
D
U
C
E
R
S**

BREEZY   Universal, 1973, EP
EARTHQUAKE   Universal, 1974, EP
AIRPORT '75   Universal, 1974, EP
THE FRONT PAGE   Universal, 1974, EP
SWASHBUCKLER   Universal, 1976
ROLLERCOASTER   Universal, 1977
AIRPORT '77   Universal, 1977, EP
NUNZIO   Universal, 1978
HOUSE CALLS   Universal, 1978, EP
THE CONCORDE - AIRPORT '79   Universal, 1979
LITTLE MISS MARKER   Universal, 1980
THE STING II   Universal, 1983
STICK   Universal, 1985

DAVID LANGE
KLUTE   Warner Bros., 1971, CP
I AM THE CHEESE   Almi, 1983

JESSICA LANGE
Business: Prairie Films, Orion Pictures, 1888 Century
   Park East, Los Angeles, CA 90067, 310/282-2975;
   Fax: 310/201-0798
Agent: CAA - Beverly Hills, 310/288-4545

COUNTRY   Buena Vista, 1984,
   w/William D. Wittliff

STEVE LANNING
SLIPSTREAM   Entertainment Films, 1989, CP

EDGAR LANSBURY
Contact: 450 W. 42nd Street, Suite 2C, New York, NY
   10036, 212/564-2770

GODSPELL   Columbia, 1973
THE WILD PARTY   AIP, 1975, EP w/Joseph Beruh

SHERRY LANSING
(credit w/Stanley R. Jaffe)
Business: Sherry Lansing Productions, 5555 Melrose
   Avenue, Lucille Ball Bldg., Los Angeles, CA 90038,
   213/956-4575; Fax: 213/956-8510

RACING WITH THE MOON   Paramount, 1984, EP
FIRSTBORN   Paramount, 1984, EP
FATAL ATTRACTION ★   Paramount, 1987
THE ACCUSED   Paramount, 1988
BLACK RAIN   Paramount, 1989

ROBERT LANTOS
(credit w/Stephen J. Roth)
Business: Alliance Entertainment Corporation, 8439
   Sunset Blvd., Suite 404, Los Angeles, CA 90069,
   213/654-9488; Fax: 213/654-9786; 920 Yonge Street,
   Suite 400, Toronto, Ontario, M4W 3C7, Canada,
   416/967-1174; Fax: 416/960-0971

IN PRAISE OF OLDER WOMEN   Avco Embassy, 1979,
   w/Claude Héroux*
SUZANNE   RSL/Ambassador, 1980*
AGENCY   Jensen Farley, 1981
PARADISE   Embassy, 1982
HEAVENLY BODIES   MGM/UA, 1985
JOSHUA THEN & NOW   20th Century Fox, 1985
SEPARATE VACATIONS   RSK Entertainment, 1986
BEDROOM EYES   Aquarius Releasing, 1986

ROGER LaPAGE
Contact: Directors Guild of America - Los Angeles,
   213/289-2000

HAMBONE & HILLIE   New World, 1984, CP

ARTHUR LAPPIN
MY LEFT FOOT ★   Miramax, 1989, LP
THE FIELD   Avenue Pictures, 1990, LP

GLEN A. LARSON
Business: Glen Larson Productions, 12300 Wilshire Blvd.,
   Suite 300, Los Angeles, CA 90025, 310/447-8484;
   Fax: 310/447-8486

BATTLESTAR GALACTI CA   Universal, 1979, EP
BUCK ROGERS IN THE 25TH CENTURY   Universal,
   1979, EP

JACK LARSON
MIKE'S MURDER   Warner Bros., 1984, AP
PERFECT   Columbia, 1985, CP

ROBERT LARSON
Contact: Directors Guild of America - Los Angeles,
   213/289-2000

PLAY MISTY FOR ME   Universal, 1971, AP
FM   Universal, 1978, CP
COAL MINER'S DAUGHTER   Universal, 1980, EP
CONTINENTAL DIVIDE   Universal, 1981
GORKY PARK   Orion, 1983, EP
THE RIVER RAT   Paramount, 1984
CRITICAL CONDITION   Paramount, 1987, EP
FLETCH LIVES   Universal, 1989, EP w/Bruce Bodner

LAWRENCE LASKER
(credit w/Walter F. Parkes)
Business: Lasker-Parkes, 10202 W. Washington Blvd.,
   Producers Bldg., Suite 142, Culver City, CA 90232,
   310/280-4267
Agent: InterTalent Agency, Inc. - Los Angeles, 310/858-6200

PROJECT X   20th Century Fox, 1987
TRUE BELIEVER   Columbia, 1989
AWAKENINGS ★   Columbia, 1990

GENE LASKO
Contact: Directors Guild of America - New York,
   212/581-0370

LITTLE BIG MAN   National General, 1970, AP
WHEN THE LEGENDS DIE   20th Century Fox, 1972, CP
NIGHT MOVES   Warner Bros., 1975, AP
FOUR FRIENDS   Filmways, 1981, w/Arthur Penn

BYRON H. LASKY
LOOSE SHOES   COMING ATTRACTIONS
   National-American, 1979, EP w/Lee D. Weisel

GIL LASKY
(credit w/Ed Carlin)

BLOOD AND LACE   AIP, 1971
MAMA'S DIRTY GIRLS   Premiere, 1974
THE NIGHT GOD SCREAMED   Cinemation, 1975

MICHAEL S. LAUGHLIN
Contact: 212/249-0431

THE WHISPERERS   United Artists, 1967,
   w/Ronald Shedlo
DUSTY AND SWEETS McGEE   Warner Bros., 1971
TWO-LANE BLACKTOP   Universal, 1971
THE CHRISTIAN LICORICE STORE   National General,
   1971, w/Floyd Mutrux
CHANDLER   MGM, 1972

DALE LAUNER
Business: Anarchy Productions, 20th Century Fox,
   10201 W. Pico Blvd., Bldg. 1, Suite 146, Los Angeles,
   CA 90035, 310/203-2081; Fax: 310/203-2081
Contact: Writers Guild of America - Los Angeles,
   310/550-1000

DIRTY ROTTEN SCOUNDRELS   Orion, 1988,
   EP w/Charles Hirschhorn

ROBERT G. LAUREL
THE ROSARY MURDERS   New Line, 1987

ARTHUR LAURENTS
Contact: Writers Guild of America - Los Angeles,
   310/550-1000

THE TURNING POINT ★   20th Century Fox, 1977,
   w/Herbert Ross

JOHN LAURICELLA
SOME OF MY BEST FRIENDS ARE...   AIP, 1971,
   w/Martin Richards

SCOTT LAVIN
RETRIBUTION   Taurus Entertainment, 1988,
   EP w/Brian Christian

LINDSAY LAW
Business: American Playhouse, 1776 Broadway, 9th Floor,
   New York, NY 10019, 212/757-4300; Fax: 212/333-7552

SMOOTH TALK   Spectrafilm, 1985, EP
BILLY GALVIN   Vestron, 1986, EP w/Howard L.
   Baldwin, Stuart Benjamin & William Minot
NATIVE SON   Cinecom, 1986, EP
ON VALENTINE'S DAY   Angelika, 1986, EP w/Lewis
   Allen, Ross E. Milloy, & Peter Newman
STACKING   Spectrafilm, 1987, EP
WAITING FOR THE MOON   Skouras Pictures, 1987, EP
IN A SHALLOW GRAVE   Skouras Pictures, 1988,
   EP w/Marilyn G. Haft
STAND & DELIVER   Warner Bros., 1988, EP
THE WIZARD OF LONELINESS   Skouras Pictures,
   1988, EP
THE THIN BLUE LINE (FD)   Miramax, 1988, EP
THE WASH   Skouras Pictures, 1988, EP
RACHEL RIVER   Taurus, 1989, EP
EAT A BOWL OF TEA   Columbia, 1989,
   EP w/John K. Chan
SIGNS OF LIFE   Avenue, 1989, EP w/Cary Brokaw
BLOODHOUNDS OF BROADWAY   Columbia, 1989, EP
LONGTIME COMPANION   Samuel Goldwyn Company,
   1990, EP
STRAIGHT OUT OF BROOKLYN   Samuel Goldwyn
   Company, 1991, EP w/Ira Deutchman
DAUGHTERS OF THE DUST   American Playhouse
   Theatrical Films, 1991, EP

JOHN LAWRENCE
THE INCREDIBLE TWO-HEADED TRANSPLANT
   AIP, 1971
THE THING WITH TWO HEADS   AIP, 1972, EP

MEL LAWRENCE
POWAQQATSI (FD)   Cannon, 1988, w/Godfrey Reggio &
   Lawrence Taub

ROBERT LAWRENCE
Business: Robert Lawrence Productions, c/o 20th Century
   Fox, 10201 W. Pico Blvd., Los Angeles, CA 90035,
   310/203-1069, Fax: 310/203-1398

S*P*Y*S   20th Century Fox, 1974, AP
IT TAKES TWO   United Artists, 1988
A KISS BEFORE DYING   Universal, 1991

GORDON C. LAYNE
(credit w/Mike Henry)

THE ZEBRA KILLER   General Film, 1974
ABBY   AIP, 1974, w/William Girdler

JOE LAYTON
Business: Radio City Music Hall Productions, 1260
   Avenue of the Americas, New York, NY 10020,
   212/632-4000
Personal Manager: Roy Gerber Associates, 9200 Sunset
   Blvd., Suite 620, Los Angeles, CA 90069, 310/550-0100

ANNIE   Columba, 1982, EP

IRVING PAUL LAZAR
Business: 211 S. Beverly Dr., Beverly Hills, CA 90212,
   310/275-6153; One East 66th St., New York, NY,10021,
   212/355-1177

NEIGHBORS   Columbia, 1981, EP w/Bernie Brillstein

PAUL N. LAZARUS III
WESTWORLD   MGM, 1973
EXTREME CLOSE-UP   National General, 1973
FUTUREWORLD   AIP, 1976, w/James T. Aubrey &
   Richard T. Heffron
CAPRICORN ONE   Warner Bros., 1978
HANOVER STREET   Columbia, 1979
BARBAROSA   Universal/AFD, 1982

HEINZ LAZEK
A LITTLE NIGHT MUSIC   New World, 1978, EP

DAVID LAZER
Business: Jim Henson Productions, 117 East 69th Street,
   New York, NY 10021, 212/794-2400

THE MUPPET MOVIE   AFD, 1979, CP
THE GREAT MUPPET CAPER   Universal/AFD, 1981,
   w/Frank Oz
THE DARK CRYSTAL   Universal/AFD, 1982, EP
THE MUPPETS TAKE MANHATTAN   TriStar, 1984
LABYRINTH   TriStar, 1986, SP

LARRY LEAHY
THE LAWLESS LAND   Concorde, 1988,
   w/Tony Cinciripini

Le

FILM
PRODUCERS,
STUDIOS,
AGENTS AND
CASTING
DIRECTORS
GUIDE

F
I
L
M

P
R
O
D
U
C
E
R
S

Le

FILM
PRODUCERS,
STUDIOS,
AGENTS AND
CASTING
DIRECTORS
GUIDE

F
I
L
M

P
R
O
D
U
C
E
R
S

NORMAN LEAR
Business: Act III Communications, c/o Sunset-Gower Studios, 1438 N. Gower, Box 27, Los Angeles, CA 90028, 213/460-7388; Fax: 213/460-7636

COME BLOW YOUR HORN   Paramount, 1963, w/Bud Yorkin
NEVER TOO LATE   Warner Bros., 1965
DIVORCE AMERICAN STYLE   Columbia, 1967
THE NIGHT THEY RAIDED MINSKY'S   United Artists, 1968
START THE REVOLUTION WITHOUT ME   Warner Bros., 1970, EP
COLD TURKEY   United Artists, 1971
THE PRINCESS BRIDE   20th Century Fox, 1987, EP

VICKI LEBENBAUM
SIDEWALK STORIES   Island Pictures, 1989, EP w/Howard M. Brickner

STEVEN LEBER
BEATLEMANIA   American Cinema, 1981, w/David Krebs, Edie Landau & Ely Landau

LARRY J. LEBOW
CAGE   New Century/Vista, 1989, EP

ROBERT S. LECKY
TAPEHEADS   Avenue, 1988, CP
KEYS TO FREEDOM   RPB Pictures/Queens Cross Productions, 1989, w/Stuart Rose

RICHARD LEDERER
EXORCIST II: THE HERETIC   Warner Bros., 1977, w/John Boorman

PATRICE LEDOUX
THE BIG BLUE   WEG/Columbia, 1988, EP

L. W. LEDWELL
THE LEGEND OF BOGGY CREEK   Halco, 1973, EP

DAMIAN LEE
(credit w/David Mitchell)
Business: Rose & Ruby Productions, Inc., 33 Howard St., Toronto, M4X 1J6, 416/961-0555; Fax: 416/961-5575

BUSTED UP   Shapiro Entertainment, 1987
WATCHERS   TriStar, 1988
FOOD OF THE GODS II   Concorde, 1989

LORA LEE
CAREER OPPORTUNITIES   Universal, 1991, EP

SPIKE LEE
Business: 40 Acres & A Mule Filmworks, 124 DeKalb Ave., Brooklyn, NY 11217, 718/624-3703; Fax: 718/624-2008

JOE'S BED-STUY BARBERSHOP: WE CUT HEADS   First Run Features, 1983
SHE'S GOTTA HAVE IT   Island Pictures, 1986
SCHOOL DAZE   Columbia, 1988
DO THE RIGHT THING   Universal, 1989
MO' BETTER BLUES   Universal, 1990
JUNGLE FEVER   Universal, 1991
MALCOLM X   Warner Bros., 1992

VIVIENNE LEEBOSH
TICKET TO HEAVEN   United Artists Classics, 1981
SPEED ZONE   Orion, 1989, CP

TOM LEETCH
Contact: Directors Guild of America - Los Angeles, 213/289-2000

SCANDALOUS JOHN   Buena Vista, 1971, AP
NAPOLEON AND SAMANTHA   Buena Vista, 1972, AP
SNOWBALL EXPRESS   Buena Vista, 1972, AP
ONE LITTLE INDIAN   Buena Vista, 1973, AP
FREAKY FRIDAY   Buena Vista, 1977, AP
THE NORTH AVENUE IRREGULARS   Buena Vista, 1979, CP
THE APPLE DUMPLING GANG RIDES AGAIN   Buena Vista, 1979, CP
THE WATCHER IN THE WOODS   Buena Vista, 1980, CP
NIGHT CROSSING   Buena Vista, 1982

ERNEST LEHMAN
Business Manager: Henry J. Bamberger, 2049 Century Park East, Los Angeles, CA 90067, 310/553-0581
Agent: The Gersh Agency - Beverly Hills, 310/274-6611

WHO'S AFRAID OF VIRGINIA WOOLF? ★   Warner Bros., 1966
HELLO, DOLLY! ★   20th Century Fox, 1969
PORTNOY'S COMPLAINT   Warner Bros., 1972

ARNOLD LEIBOVIT
Business: Talking Rings Entertainment, P.O. Box 2019, Beverly Hills, CA 90213, 310/306-1909

THE PUPPETOON MOVIE   Expanded Entertainment, 1987

LEO LEICHTER
Contact: 213/837-2269

THE BIKINI SHOP   *THE MALIBU BIKINI SHOP*   International Film Marketing, 1987, CP
KANDYLAND   New World, 1988, CP w/Richard Hahn

JERRY LEIDER
Business: Fred Silverman Company, 11661 San Vicente Blvd., Suite 901, Los Angeles, CA 90049, 310/820-3161; Fax: 310/820-4323

TRENCHCOAT   Buena Vista, 1983

MICHAEL W. LEIGHTON
Contact: Noble Entertainment Group, 1801 Avenue of the Stars, Suite 1225, Los Angeles, CA 90067, 310/788-9177; Fax: 310/788-9170

THE KILLER INSIDE ME   Warner Bros., 1976

MATT LEIPZIG
Business: Columbia Pictures, 10202 W. Washington Blvd., Culver City, CA 90232, 310/280-8000

BIG BAD MAMA II   Concorde, 1987, AP
STRIPPED TO KILL   Concorde, 1987, w/Mark Byers & Andy Ruben
THE DRIFTER   Concorde, 1988, CP

DOUGLAS LEITERMAN
MILLENNIUM   20th Century Fox, 1989

RUSTY LEMORANDE
Contact: Directors Guild of America - Los Angeles, 213/289-2000

YENTL   MGM/UA, 1983, CP
ELECTRIC DREAMS   MGM/UA, 1984, w/Larry De Waay
GETTING IT RIGHT   MCEG, 1989, EP

C. H. LEHENHOF
JULIA HAS TWO LOVERS   South Gate Entertainment, 1991, EP w/Randall Davis

JOHN THOMAS LENOX
Agent: The Agency - Los Angeles, 310/551-3000
Contact: Directors Guild of America - Los Angeles, 213/289-2000

SPLASH   Buena Vista, 1984, EP

TERRY LENS
THE HUMAN FACTOR   Bryanston, 1975, EP

MALCOLM LEO
Business: Malcolm Leo Productions, 6536 Sunset Blvd., Hollywood, CA 90028, 213/464-4448; Fax: 213/856-8755
Agent: William Morris Agency - Beverly Hills, 310/274-7451

THIS IS ELVIS (FD)   Warner Bros., 1981, w/Andrew Solt

MICHAEL C. LEONE
DOGS   R.C. Riddell, 1977, EP
ACAPULCO GOLD   R.C. Riddell, 1978, EP
THE GREAT SMOKEY ROADBLOCK   THE LAST OF THE COWBOYS   Dimension, 1978, EP
A DIFFERENT STORY   Avco Embassy, 1978, EP
GO TELL THE SPARTANS   Avco Embassy, 1978, EP
GOOD GUYS WEAR BLACK   American Cinema, 1978, EP
DIRT   American Cinema, 1979, EP w/Roger Riddell
THE LATE GREAT PLANET EARTH (FD)   Pacific International, 1979, EP
A FORCE OF ONE   American Cinema, 1979, EP
THE OCTAGON   American Cinema, 1980, EP w/Alan Belkin
CHARLIE CHAN AND THE CURSE OF THE DRAGON QUEEN   American Cinema, 1981, EP w/Alan Belkin
I, THE JURY   20th Century Fox, 1982, EP w/Andrew D.T. Pfeffer
THE ENTITY   20th Century Fox, 1983, EP w/Andrew D.T. Pfeffer
TOUGH ENOUGH   20th Century Fox, 1983, w/Andrew D.T. Pfeffer

STRATTON LEOPOLD
Contact: Directors Guild of America - Los Angeles, 213/289-2000

THE ADVENTURES OF BARON MUNCHAUSEN   Columbia, 1989, SP

JEAN FRANCOIS LEPETIT
THREE MEN AND A CRADLE   Samuel Goldwyn Company, 1986
THREE MEN AND A BABY   Buena Vista, 1987, EP
RIO NEGRO   Yavita Film/Flach Film, 1990
THREE MEN AND A LITTLE LADY   Buena Vista, 1990, EP

EUGENE LEPICIER
(credit w/Denis Heroux)

THE LITTLE GIRL WHO LIVES DOWN THE LANE   AIP, 1977, CP w/Leland Nolan
VIOLETTE   Gaumont/New Yorker, 1978, EP

OSCAR S. LERMAN
YESTERDAY'S HERO   EMI, 1979, w/Ken Regan

AVI LERNER
AMERICAN NINJA 2   Cannon, 1987, EP
DRAGONARD   Cannon, 1987, EP
ALLAN QUATERMAIN AND THE LOST CITY OF GOLD   Cannon, 1987, EP
OUTLAW OF GOR   Cannon, 1988, w/Harry Alan Towers
HOWLING IV...THE ORIGINAL NIGHTMARE   Allied Entertainment, 1988, EP w/Steven Lane, Robert Pringle & Edward Simons
ALIEN FROM L.A.   Cannon, 1988, EP
AMERICAN NINJA 3: BLOOD HUNT   Cannon, 1989, EP
RIVER OF DEATH   Cannon, 1989, w/Harry Alan Towers
TEN LITTLE INDIANS   Cannon, 1989, EP
JOURNEY TO THE CENTER OF THE EARTH   Cannon, 1989, EP w/Adam Fields & Tom Udell
MASTER OF DRAGONARD HILL   Cannon, 1989, EP
AMERICAN NINJA 4: THE ANNIHILATION   Cannon, 1991, EP

DAVID V. LESTER
Contact: Directors Guild of America - Los Angeles, 213/289-2000

BULL DURHAM   Orion, 1988, EP
BLAZE   Buena Vista, 1989, EP w/Don Miller
LORD OF THE FLIES   Columbia, 1990, CP
WHITE MEN CAN'T JUMP   20th Century Fox, 1991, w/Don Miller

MARK L. LESTER
Agent: The Chasin Agency - Beverly Hills, 213/278-7805
Contact: Directors Guild of America - Los Angeles, 213/289-2000
Business: Original Pictures, 1900 S. Sepulveda Blvd., 3rd Floor, Los Angeles, CA 90025, 310/473-6999, Fax: 310/473-7967

STEEL ARENA   L-T Films, 1973, w/Peter Traynor
TRUCK STOP WOMEN   L-T Films, 1974
BOBBIE JO AND THE OUTLAW   AIP, 1976
THE FUNHOUSE   Universal, 1981, EP w/Mace Neufeld
CLASS OF 1999   Taurus, 1990

RICHARD LESTER
Business: Twickenham Film Studios, St. Margarets, Middlesex, England
Agent: CAA - Beverly Hills, 310/288-4545

HOW I WON THE WAR   United Artists, 1967
THE BED-SITTING ROOM   United Artists, 1969, w/Oscar Lewenstein
FINDERS KEEPERS   Warner Bros., 1984, EP

ROBERT LeTET
DOGS IN SPACE   Skouras Pictures, 1987, EP w/Dennis Wright

Le

FILM
PRODUCERS,
STUDIOS,
AGENTS and
CASTING
DIRECTORS
GUIDE

F
I
L
M

P
R
O
D
U
C
E
R
S

MICHAEL LEVEE
THE BLACK BIRD   Columbia, 1975, w/Lou Lombardo
SLOW DANCING IN THE BIG CITY   United Artists,
  1978, w/John G. Avildsen
CASEY'S SHADOW   Columbia, 1978, EP

HAROLD LEVENTHAL
BOUND FOR GLORY ★   United Artists, 1976,
  w/Robert F. Blumofe

JAMES B. LEVERT, JR.
BELIZAIRE THE CAJUN   Skouras Pictures, 1986, EP

WILLIAM A. LEVEY
Business: The American Moving Picture Company, 838
  Doheny Dr., Suite 904, Los Angeles, CA 90069,
  310/273-3838

THE HAPPY HOOKER GOES TO WASHINGTON
  Cannon, 1977
SKATETOWN U.S.A.   Columbia, 1979, w/Lorin Dreyfuss

DON LEVIN
(credit w/Mel Pearl)

LOVE LETTERS   New World, 1983, EP
HAMBONE AND HILLIE   New World, 1984, EP
THE BOYS NEXT DOOR   New World, 1985, EP
MAXIMUM OVERDRIVE   DEG, 1986, EP
THE SUPERNATURALS   Republic Entertainment,
  1987, EP
TWO MOON JUNCTION   Lorimar, 1988, EP
ANGEL III: THE FINAL CHAPTER   New World,
  1988, EP
SCISSORS   DDM Film Corp., 1991, w/Hal Polaire

IRVING H. LEVIN
TO LIVE AND DIE IN L.A.   New Century, 1985

LLOYD LEVIN
Business: Largo Entertainment, c/o 20th Century Fox,
  10201 W. Pico Blvd., Los Angeles, CA 90035,
  310/203-3600; Fax: 310/203-4133

DIE HARD 2   20th Century Fox, 1990,
  EP w/Michael Levy
THE ROCKETEER   Buena Vista, 1991,
  w/Charles Gordon & Lawrence Gordon

STEPHEN J. LEVIN
ALMOST YOU   20th Century Fox, 1984, EP w/Sandy
  Climan & Charles C. Thieriot

SY LEVIN
FLOWERS IN THE ATTIC   New World, 1987,
  w/Thomas Fries

JOEL LEVINE
Contact: Gibraltar Entertainment, 14101 Valleyheart Dr.,
  Suite 205, Sherman Oaks, CA 91423, 818/501-2076;
  Fax: 818/501-5138

HEADHUNTER   Academy Entertainment, 1989, EP
MORTAL PASSIONS   MGM/UA, 1990, EP w/Wayne
  Crawford & Andrew Lane
THE SERVANTS OF TWILIGHT   Trimark, 1991,
  EP w/Mark Amin, Wayne Crawford, Andrew Lane

RICHARD P. LEVINE
(credit w/Joseph E. Levine)
Business: Joseph E. Levine Presents, Inc., 165 W. Putnam
  Ave., Greenwich, CT 06830, 203/622-0814;
  Fax: 203/622-4098

A BRIDGE TOO FAR   United Artists, 1977
MAGIC   20th Century Fox, 1978
TATTOO   20th Century Fox, 1981

ROBERT F. LEVINE
THAT CHAMPIONSHIP SEASON   Cannon, 1982, EP

ART LEVINSON
Agent: The Gersh Agency - Beverly Hills, 310/274-6611
Contact: Directors Guild of America - Los Angeles,
  213/289-2000

BREAKING AWAY   20th Century Fox, 1979, AP
MY FAVORITE YEAR   MGM/UA, 1982, AP
MR. MOM   20th Century Fox, 1983, AP
RACING WITH THE MOON   Paramount, 1984, AP
THE MONEY PIT   Universal, 1986, w/Kathleen
  Kennedy & Frank Marshall
MANNEQUIN   20th Century Fox, 1987
LITTLE NIKITA   Columbia, 1988, CP
MY STEPMOTHER IS AN ALIEN   WEG/Columbia, 1988,
  EP w/Laurence Mark
STOP OR MY MOTHER WILL SHOOT   Universal,
  1991, AP

BARRY LEVINSON
Business: Baltimore Pictures, 10201 W. Pico Blvd.,
  Suite 12, Los Angeles, CA 90035, 310/203-2525;
  Fax: 310/203-3806
Agent: CAA - Beverly Hills, 310/288-4545

AVALON   TriStar, 1990, w/Mark Johnson
BUGSY   TriStar, 1991, w/Mark Johnson &
  Warren Beatty

BARRY LEVINSON
THE INTERNECINE PROJECT   Allied Artists, 1974

MARK LEVINSON
(credit w/Scott Rosenfelt)
Business: Levinson-Rosenfelt Productions, 1639 11th St.,
  Santa Monica, CA 90404, 310/399-1844; 310/399-8241
Agent: Triad Artists, Inc. - Los Angeles, 310/556-2727

WALTZ ACROSS TEXAS   Atlantic, 1983, AP*
ROADHOUSE 66   Atlantic, 1984
TEEN WOLF   Atlantic, 1985
REMOTE CONTROL   New Century/Vista, 1988
STRANDED   New Line, 1987
RUSSKIES   New Century/Vista, 1987
MYSTIC PIZZA   Samuel Goldwyn Company, 1988
BIG MAN ON CAMPUS   Vestron, 1989, CP
HOME ALONE   20th Century Fox, 1990, EP

MALCOLM LEVINTHAL
THE EVIL   New World, 1978, EP w/Paul A. Joseph

ABE LEVITOW
THE PHANTOM TOLLBOOTH (AF)   MGM, 1970,
  CP w/Les Goldman

ZANE W. LEVITT

Business: Zeta Entertainment, Ltd., 814 N. Highland Ave., Hollywood, CA 90038, 213/466-8066; Fax: 213/466-0322

OUT OF THE DARK   CineTel Films, 1989
LIQUID DREAMS   1991, w/Diane Firestone

ARIEL LEVY

Agent: The Agency - Los Angeles, 310/551-3000
Contact: Directors Guild of America - Los Angeles, 213/289-2000

HYPER SAPIEN   TriStar, 1986, CP

FRANKLIN R. LEVY

Business: Catalina Production Group, 8327 Santa Monica Blvd., Los Angeles, CA 90069, 213/650-0689; Fax: 213/650-8383

NIGHTHAWKS   Universal, 1981, EP w/Michael Wise
MY STEPMOTHER IS AN ALIEN   WEG/Columbia, 1988, w/Ronald Parker

GENE LEVY

Contact: Directors Guild of America - Los Angeles, 213/289-2000

HYSTERICAL   Embassy, 1983
STREETS OF FIRE   Universal, 1984, EP
BREWSTER'S MILLIONS   Universal, 1985, EP

JEFERY LEVY

ROCKULA   Cannon, 1990

JULES LEVY

(credit w/Arthur Gardner)
Business: Levy-Gardner-Laven Productions, 9595 Wilshire Blvd., Suite 610, Beverly Hills, CA 90212, 310/278-9820; Fax: 310/278-2632

THE McKENZIE BREAK   United Artists, 1970
UNDERGROUND   United Artists, 1970
THE HUNTING PARTY   United Artists, 1971, EP
THE HONKERS   United Artists, 1972
KANSAS CITY BOMBER   MGM, 1972, EP
WHITE LIGHTNING   United Artists, 1973
McQ   Warner Bros., 1974
BRANNIGAN   United Artists, 1975
GATOR   United Artists, 1976

MARK C. LEVY

YOUR THREE MINUTES ARE UP   Cinerama, 1973, w/Jerry Gershwin

MICHAEL LEVY

Business: Silver Pictures, 4000 Warner Blvd., Bldg. 90, Burbank, CA 91522, 818/954-4490; Fax: 818/954-3237

FORD FAIRLANE   20th Century Fox, 1990, EP
DIE HARD 2   20th Century Fox, 1990, EP w/Lloyd Levin
THE LAST BOY SCOUT   Warner Bros., 1991, w/Steve Perry & Joel Silver
RICOCHET   Warner Bros., 1991, w/Joel Silver

MICHAEL I. LEVY

Business: The Gruskoff-Levy Company, 8737 Clifton Way, Beverly Hills, CA 90211, 310/550-7302

GOTCHA!   Universal, 1985, EP
GARDENS OF STONE   TriStar, 1987, w/Francis Ford Coppola
MASQUERADE   MGM/UA, 1988
PRELUDE TO A KISS   20th Century Fox, 1991, w/Michael Gruskoff

ROBERT L. LEVY

Contact: Tapestry Films, c/o Writers Bldg. #12, 1041 N. Formosa Ave., West Hollywood, CA 90046, 213/850-3591; Fax: 213/850-3571

THE TODD KILLINGS   National General, 1971, AP
SMOKEY & THE BANDIT   Universal, 1977, EP
RAD   TriStar, 1986
THE KILLING TIME   New World, 1987, w/Peter Abrams

SANDRA LEVY

HIGH TIDE   TriStar, 1987

OSCAR LEWENSTEIN

THE KNACK - AND HOW TO GET IT   United Artists, 1965
THE BED-SITTING ROOM   United Artists, 1969, w/Richard Lester
RED, WHITE AND ZERO   Entertainment Marketing, 1979
RITA, SUE & BOB TOO!   Orion Classics, 1987, EP

ARTHUR LEWIS

LOOT   Cinevision, 1972
BAXTER   National General, 1973
THE KILLER ELITE   United Artists, 1975, w/Martin Baum
BRASS TARGET   United Artists, 1978

EDWARD LEWIS

SPARTACUS   Universal, 1960
THE LAST SUNSET   Universal, 1961, w/Eugene Frenke
THE LIST OF ADRIAN MESSENGER   Universal, 1963
SECONDS   Paramount, 1966
THE EXTRAORDINARY SEAMAN   MGM, 1968
THE GYPSY MOTHS   MGM, 1969, EP
I WALK THE LINE   Columbia, 1970, EP
THE HORSEMEN   Columbia, 1971
THE ICEMAN COMETH   American Film Theatre, 1973, EP
EXECUTIVE ACTION   National General, 1973
LOST IN THE STARS   American Film Theatre, 1974, EP
RHINOCEROS   American Film Theatre, 1974, EP
THE BLUE BIRD   20th Century Fox, 1976, EP
BROTHERS   Warner Bros., 1977, w/Mildred Lewis
MISSING ★   Universal, 1982, w/Mildred Lewis
CRACKERS   Universal, 1984, w/Robert Cortes
THE RIVER   Universal, 1984, w/Robert Cortes

MARILYN LEWIS

SUPERSTAR (FD)   Marilyn Lewis Entertainment Ltd., 1990, EP w/Peter English Nelson

MILDRED LEWIS

(credit w/Edward Lewis)

HAROLD & MAUDE   Paramount, 1971, EP*
BROTHERS   Warner Bros., 1977
MISSING ★   Universal, 1982

Le

FILM
PRODUCERS,
STUDIOS,
AGENTS AND
CASTING
DIRECTORS
GUIDE

F
I
L
M

P
R
O
D
U
C
E
R
S

PAUL LEWIS
Contact: Directors Guild of America - Los Angeles,
    213/289-2000

GETTING STRAIGHT   Columbia, 1970, AP
THE LAST MOVIE   Universal, 1971
WEREWOLVES ON WHEELS   Fanfare, 1971
THIS IS A HIJACK   Fanfare, 1973
PHANTOM OF THE PARADISE   20th Century Fox,
    1974, AP
THE VAN   Crown International, 1977
OUT OF THE BLUE   Discovery, 1982
THE HITCHER   TriStar, 1986, CP
THE HOT SPOT   Orion, 1990
CATCHFIRE   1991, LP

RICHARD LEWIS
PIGEONS   *SIDELONG GLANCES OF A PIGEON
    KICKER*   MGM, 1970
THE HAPPINESS CAGE   Cinerama, 1972, EP

RICHARD B. LEWIS
Business: Trilogy Entertainment Group, c/o Sony Studios,
    10202 W. Washington Blvd., Culver City, CA 90232,
    310/204-3133; Fax: 310/204-1160
Agent: William Morris Agency - Beverly Hills,
    310/274-7451

THE ZOO GANG   New World, 1985, CP
THE KISS   TriStar, 1988, EP
BACKDRAFT   Universal, 1991, w/Pen Densham &
    John Watson
ROBIN HOOD: PRINCE OF THIEVES   Warner Bros.,
    1991, w/Pen Densham & John Watson

ROBERT LLOYD LEWIS
Agent: ICM - Los Angeles, 310/550-4461

SUPERSTITION   Almi Releasing, 1983
HAMBURGER: THE MOTION PICTURE   FM
    Entertainment, 1986, CP w/Donald Ross

ROGER LEWIS
SHAFT'S BIG SCORE!   MGM, 1972, w/Ernest Tidyman
SHAFT IN AFRI CA   MGM, 1973

SIMON R. LEWIS
Contact: 16002 Meadowcrest, Sherman Oaks, CA 91403,
    818/906-7677; Fax: 818/906-2836

SLIPPING INTO DARKNESS   MCEG, 1988,
    CP w/Don Schain
THE CHOCOLATE WAR   MCEG, 1988, CP

ELLIOTT LEWITT
Business: Elliott Lewitt Productions, 3000 Olympic Blvd.,
    Suite 1426, Santa Monica, CA 90404, 310/315-4702;
    Fax: 310/315-4736

AT CLOSE RANGE   Orion, 1986, w/Don Guest
ZELLY AND ME   Columbia, 1988, EP w/Tina Rathborne
SHADOW OF CHINA   New Line, 1991, w/Don Guest

ROBERT LIBERMAN
DEADLY HERO   Avco Embassy, 1976,
    EP w/Stan Plotnick

GLENNIS LIBERTY
Business: The Liberty Company, 10845 Lindbrook, Suite 200,
    Los Angeles, CA 90024, 310/824-7937; Fax: 310/824-4933

CADENCE   New Line, 1991, CP

ANDREW LICHT
(credit w/Jeffrey Mueller)
Business: Licht-Mueller Film Corporation, 2121 Avenue of
    the Stars, Suite 2900, Los Angeles, CA 90067,
    310/551-2262; Fax: 310/556-3760

LICENSE TO DRIVE   20th Century Fox, 1988
LITTLE MONSTERS   MGM/UA, 1989, w/John A. Davis

PAUL LICHTMAN
(credit w/Arnold Fishman)

TRANSYLVANIA 6-5000   New World, 1985, EP
OUT OF CONTROL   New World, 1985, EP

J. MICHAEL LIDDLE
GETTING EVEN   American Distribution Group, 1986

A. MICHAEL LIEBERMAN
RED SONJA   MGM/UA, 1985, EP

SANFORD LIEBERSON
Business: Pathe Entertainment, 76 Hammersmith Rd.,
    London, W14 8YR, England, 071/603-4555;
    Fax: 071/603-5616

PERFORMANCE   Warner Bros., 1970
THE PIED PIPER   Paramount, 1972, w/David Puttnam
SWASTIKA (FD)   Cinema 5, 1974, w/David Puttnam
THAT'LL BE THE DAY   EMI, 1974, w/David Puttnam
THE LAST DAYS OF MAN ON EARTH   *THE FINAL
    PROGRAMME*   New World, 1974, w/John Goldstone
MAHLER   Mayfair, 1974, EP w/David Puttnam
STARDUST   Columbia, 1975, w/David Puttnam
LISZTOMANIA   Warner Bros., 1975, EP
BROTHER, CAN YOU SPARE A DIME? (FD)   Dimension,
    1975, w/David Puttnam
ALL THIS AND WORLD WAR II (FD)   20th Century Fox,
    1976, w/Martin J. Machat
JABBERWOCKY   Cinema 5, 1977
RITA, SUE & BOB TOO!   Orion Classics, 1987
STARS & BARS   Columbia, 1988
THE MIGHTY QUINN   MGM/UA, 1989, w/Ed Elbert &
    Marion Hunt

LEONARD LIGHTSTONE
THE MAN WHO HAD POWER OVER WOMEN   Avco
    Embassy, 1971, EP

GARY R. LINDBERG
THAT WAS THEN...THIS IS NOW   Paramount, 1985,
    w/John M. Ondov

GEORGE LINDER
THE RUNNING MAN   TriStar, 1987, w/Tim Zinnemann

LESLIE LINDER
(credit w/Martin Ransohoff)

HAMLET   Columbia, 1969, EP
10 RILLINGTON PLACE   Columbia, 1971
SEE NO EVIL   Columbia, 1971

ANDRE LINK
(credit w/John Dunning)
Business: Cinepix Inc., 8275 Mayrand St., Montreal, H4P 2C8, 514/342-2340; Fax: 514/342-1922

THEY CAME FROM WITHIN   Trans-America, 1976, w/Alfred Pariser
THE HOUSE BY THE LAKE   AIP, 1977, EP
RABID   New World, 1977, EP w/Ivan Reitman*
BLACKOUT   New World, 1978, EP w/Ivan Reitman & John Vidette*
MEATBALLS   Paramount, 1979, EP
MY BLOODY VALENTINE   Paramount, 1981, w/Stephen Miller
HAPPY BIRTHDAY TO ME   Columbia, 1981
SPACEHUNTER: ADVENTURES IN THE FORBIDDEN ZONE   Columbia, 1983, w/Don Carmody
MEATBALLS III   Moviestore, 1986, EP w/Lawrence Nesis*
SNAKE EATER   Moviestore, 1990, EP*
WHISPERS   ITC, 1990, EP*

RICHARD LINKLATER
SLACKER   Orion Classics, 1991

HERB LINSEY
RICH GIRL   Studio Three, 1991, LP

ART LINSON
Business: Art Linson Productions, 4000 Warner Blvd., Bldg. 66, Rm. 12, Burbank, CA 91522, 818/954-3385; Fax: 818/954-3776

RAFFERTY AND THE GOLD DUST TWINS   Warner Bros., 1975, w/Michael Gruskoff
CAR WASH   Universal, 1976, w/Gary Stromberg
AMERICAN HOT WAX   Paramount, 1978
WHERE THE BUFFALO ROAM   Universal, 1980
MELVIN AND HOWARD   Universal, 1980, w/Don Phillips
FAST TIMES AT RIDGEMONT HIGH   Universal, 1982, w/Irving Azoff
THE WILD LIFE   Universal, 1984, w/Cameron Crowe
THE UNTOUCHABLES   Paramount, 1987
SCROOGED   Paramount, 1988, w/Richard Donner
CASUALTIES OF WAR   Columbia, 1989
WE'RE NO ANGELS   Paramount, 1989
DICK TRACY   Buena Vista, 1990, EP w/Floyd Mutrux & Barrie M. Osborne
SINGLES   Warner Bros., 1992, EP

KLAUS LINTSCHINGER
MINDWALK   Mindwalk Productions, 1990, EP

MARK LIPSKY
Business: Paramount Pictures, 5555 Melrose Ave., Los Angeles, CA 90038, 213/956-4545; Fax: 213/956-8602

COMING TO AMERICA   Paramount, 1988, EP w/Leslie Belzberg
HARLEM NIGHTS   Paramount, 1989, w/Robert D. Wachs
ANOTHER 48 HOURS   Paramount, 1990, EP w/Ralph S. Singleton

MARK LIPSON
Business: 350 Bleecker St., Suite 4E, New York, NY 10014, 212/691-4305

CHILDREN OF THE CORN   New World, 1984, AP

ALMOST YOU   20th Century Fox, 1985
THE THIN BLUE LINE (FD)   Miramax, 1988

HOWARD LIPSTONE
Business: The Landsburg Company, 11811 W. Olympic Blvd., Los Angeles, CA 90064, 310/478-7878; Fax: 310/477-7166

JAWS 3-D   Universal, 1983, EP w/Alan Landsburg

LYNNE LITTMAN
Agent: William Morris Agency - Beverly Hills, 310/274-7451
Contact: Directors Guild of America - Los Angeles, 213/289-2000

TESTAMENT   Paramount, 1983, w/Jonathan Bernstein

ROBERT LITTMAN
Business: The Robert Littman Company, 409 N. Camden Dr., Suite 105, Beverly Hills, CA 90210, 310/278-1572

SALOME'S LAST DANCE   Vestron, 1988, CP
WICKED STEPMOTHER   MGM/UA, 1989

GEORGE LITTO
Business: George Litto Productions, 5345 Encino Ave., Encino, CA 91316, 818/986-4590; Fax: 818/986-9873

THIEVES LIKE US   United Artists, 1974, EP
OBSESSION   Columbia, 1976, w/Harry N. Blum
DRIVE-IN   Columbia, 1976, EP
OVER THE EDGE   Orion/Warner Bros., 1979
DRESSED TO KILL   Filmways, 1980
BLOW OUT   Filmways, 1981
KANSAS   Trans World, 1988
NIGHT GAME   Trans World, 1989

SI LITVINOFF
WALKABOUT   20th Century Fox, 1971
A CLOCKWORK ORANGE ★   Warner Bros., 1971, EP w/Max L. Raab
ALL THE RIGHT NOISES   20th Century Fox, 1973, w/Max L. Raab
THE MAN WHO FELL TO EARTH   Cinema 5, 1976, EP

MORT LITWACK
WHITE LINE FEVER   Columbia, 1975, EP w/Gerald Schneider

LUIS LLOSA
Agent: CAA - Beverly Hills, 310/288-4545

HOUR OF THE ASSASSIN   Concorde, 1987
CRIME ZONE   Concorde, 1988
FULL FATHOM FIVE   Concorde, 1990
CRACKDOWN   Concorde, 1991

EUAN LLOYD
Business: Euan Lloyd Productions, Ltd., c/o Nicholas Morrris, 81 Piccadilly, London W1V 0JH England, 071/493-8811; Fax: 071/491-2094

THE MAN CALLED NOON   National General, 1973
PAPER TIGER   Joseph E. Levine, 1975
THE WILD GEESE   Allied Artists, 1978

LI

FILM
PRODUCERS,
STUDIOS,
AGENTS AND
CASTING
DIRECTORS
GUIDE

F
I
L
M

P
R
O
D
U
C
E
R
S

LAUREN LLOYD
(credit w/Wallis Nicita)
Business: Nicita-Lloyd Productions, Paramount Pictures,
5555 Melrose Ave., Los Angeles, CA 90035,
213/956-8514; Fax: 213/956-2007

MERMAIDS   Orion, 1990, w/Patrick Palmer
FIRES WITHIN   Pathe, 1990

MICHAEL LLOYD
LOVELINES   TriStar, 1984, w/Hal Taines
THE GARBAGE PAIL KIDS MOVIE   Atlantic, 1987,
CP w/Melinda Palmer

MICHAEL LOBELL
Business: Lobell-Bergman Productions, 9336 W.
Washington Blvd., Culver City, CA 90230,
310/202-3362; Fax: 310/202-3238

DREAMER   20th Century Fox, 1979
WINDOWS   United Artists, 1980
SO FINE   Warner Bros., 1981
THE JOURNEY OF NATTY GANN   Buena Vista, 1985
CHANCES ARE   TriStar, 1989
THE FRESHMAN   TriStar, 1990
WHITE FANG   Buena Vista, 1991,
EP w/Andrew Bergman

PETER LOCKE
Business: The Kushner-Locke Company, 11601 Wilshire
Blvd., 21st Floor, Los Angeles, CA 90025,
310/445-1111; Fax: 310/445-1191

YOU'VE GOT TO WALK IT LIKE YOU TALK IT OR
YOU'LL LOSE THAT BEAT   JER, 1971
THE HILLS HAVE EYES   Vanguard, 1977
THE HILLS HAVE EYES II   Castle Hill, 1985,
w/Barry Cahn
NUTCRACKER   Atlantic, 1986, w/Willard Carroll,
Donald Kushner & Thomas L. Wilhite
POUND PUPPIES & THE LEGEND OF BIG PAW (AF)
TriStar, 1988, w/Donald Kushner

WARREN LOCKHART
THE MOUSE AND HIS CHILD (AF)   Sanrio, 1978,
EP w/Shintaro Tsuji

MAURIZIO LODI-FE
THE CONFORMIST   Paramount, 1971

HAROLD LOEB
SOLDIER BLUE   Avco Embassy, 1970, w/Gabriel Katzka

JOSEPH LOEB III
(credit w/Matthew Weisman)
Agent: CAA - Beverly Hills, 310/288-4545

BURGLAR   Warner Bros., 1987, CP

VICTOR LOEWY
Business: Alliance Entertainment Corporation, 8439
Sunset Blvd., Suite 404, Los Angeles, CA 90069,
213/654-9488; Fax: 213/654-9786;
920 Yonge Street, Ste 400, Toronto, Ontario M4W 3C7,
Canada, 416/967-1174; Fax: 416/960-0971

EDDIE & THE CRUISERS II: EDDIE LIVES   Scotti Bros.,
1989, EP w/Denis Héroux, James L. Stewart &
William Stuart

RAYMOND LOFARO
STUNTS   New Line, 1977, w/William N. Panzer

CHRIS LOFVEN
20TH CENTURY OZ   Inter-Planetary, 1977, w/Lyne Helms

LOU LOMBARDO
Contact: Directors Guild of America - Los Angeles,
213/289-2000

THE BLACK BIRD   Columbia, 1975, w/Michael Levee
UP IN SMOKE   Paramount, 1978, w/Lou Adler
LADIES AND GENTLEMEN...THE FABULOUS STAINS
Paramount, 1982, EP

MARK LOMBARDO
MISUNDERSTOOD   MGM/UA, 1984, AP
PIRATES   Cannon, 1986, EP w/Thom Mount

MICHAEL B. LONDON
RICH GIRL   Studio Three, 1991

RICHARD LORBER
Business: Fox/Lorber Associates, 419 Park Ave. South,
New York, NY 10016, 212/686-6777; Fax: 212/685-2625

PRAYER OF THE ROLLERBOYS   Academy Entertainment,
1991, EP w/Robert Baruc, Tetsu Fujimara & Martin F. Gold

LYNN LORING
Business: MGM Television, 10202 W. Washington Blvd.,
Culver City, CA 90232, 310/280-6161

MR. MOM   20th Century Fox, 1983,
w/Lauren Shuler-Donner

GAVRIK LOSEY
AGATHA   Warner Bros., 1979, w/Jarvis Astaire

PATRICK LOUBERT
(credit w/Michael Hirsh & Clive A. Smith)
Business: Nelvana Ltd., 32 Atlantic Ave., Toronto, M6K 1X8,
416/588-5571; Fax: 416/588-5588; 9000 Sunset Blvd.,
Suite 911, Los Angeles, CA 90069, 310/278-8466;
Fax: 310/278-4872

ROCK & RULE (AF)   MGM/UA, 1985, w/Michael Hirsh*
THE CARE BEARS MOVIE (AF)   Samuel Goldwyn
Company, 1985
CARE BEARS MOVIE II: A NEW GENERATION (AF)
Columbia, 1986
THE CARE BEARS ADVENTURE IN WONDERLAND (AF)
Cineplex Odeon, 1987
BABAR: THE MOVIE (AF)   New Line, 1989

DAVID LOUCKA
Agent: UTA - Beverly Hills, 310/273-6700
Contact: Writers Guild of America - Los Angeles,
310/550-1000

THE DREAM TEAM   Universal, 1989, CP w/Jon Connolly

DAVID LOUGHERY
Agent: UTA - Beverly Hills, 310/273-6700
Contact: Writers Guild of America - Los Angeles,
310/550-1000

FLASHBACK   Paramount, 1990, CP

Lu

FILM
PRODUCERS,
STUDIOS,
AGENTS AND
CASTING
DIRECTORS
GUIDE

R. J. LOUIS
Contact: Directors Guild of America - Los Angeles, 213/289-2000

THE KARATE KID   Columbia, 1984, EP
THE KARATE KID PART II   Columbia, 1986, EP
MAC AND ME   Orion, 1988

GUY J. LOUTHAN
Contact: Highland Films, 8747 Bonner Dr., West Hollywood, CA 90048, 310/652-5111; Fax: 310/652-7951

GENUINE RISK   I.R.S., 1990, w/William Ewart & Larry J. Rattner

DYSON LOVELL
THE CHAMP   United Artists, 1979
ENDLESS LOVE   Universal, 1981
THE COTTON CLUB   Orion, 1984, EP
HAMLET   Warner Bros., 1990

KENT C. LOVELL
(credit w/Dennis Wright)

BACKSTAGE   Hoyts, 1988, EP
GROUND ZERO   Avenue Pictures, 1988, EP w/John Kearney

PATRICIA LOVELL
PICNIC AT HANGING ROCK   Atlantic, 1979, EP
GALLIPOLI   Paramount, 1981, w/Robert Stigwood

LAWRENCE LOVENTHAL
THE FIRST TIME   New Line, 1982, EP w/Robert Shaye

DAVID LOWE
FIGHTING BACK   Paramount, 1982, CP w/Alex DeBenedetti

VICTOR LOWNES
MACBETH   Columbia, 1971, EP w/Hugh M. Hefner
AND NOW FOR SOMETHING COMPLETELY DIFFERENT   Columbia, 1972, EP

HUNT LOWRY
Contact: Directors Guild of America - Los Angeles, 213/289-2000

AIRPLANE!   Paramount, 1980, AP
HUMANOIDS FROM THE DEEP   New World, 1980, w/Martin B. Cohen
GET CRAZY   Embassy, 1983
TOP SECRET!   Paramount, 1984, w/Jon Davison
BAJA OKLAHOMA   HBO Pictures, 1988, EP
WILDFIRE   Cinema Group, 1988, CP
REVENGE   Columbia, 1990, w/Stanley Rubin
CAREER OPPORTUNITIES   Universal, 1991, w/John Hughes
ONLY THE LONELY   20th Century Fox, 1991, w/John Hughes
THE LAST OF THE MOHICANS   20th Century Fox, 1991, w/Michael Mann

GEORGE LUCAS
Business: Lucasfilm, Ltd., P.O. Box 2009, San Rafael, CA 94912, 415/662-1800

MORE AMERICAN GRAFFITI   Universal, 1979, EP
THE EMPIRE STRIKES BACK   20th Century Fox, 1980, EP
RAIDERS OF THE LOST ARK ★   Paramount, 1981, EP w/Howard Kazanjian
TWICE UPON A TIME   Warner Bros., 1983, EP
RETURN OF THE JEDI   20th Century Fox, 1983, EP
INDIANA JONES AND THE TEMPLE OF DOOM   Paramount, 1984, EP w/Frank Marshall
MISHIMA: A LIFE IN FOUR CHAPTERS   Warner Bros., 1985, EP w/Francis Ford Coppola
LABYRINTH   TriStar, 1986, EP
HOWARD THE DUCK   Universal, 1986, EP
WILLOW   MGM/UA, 1988, EP
TUCKER: THE MAN AND HIS DREAM   Paramount, 1988, EP
THE LAND BEFORE TIME (AF)   Universal, 1988, EP w/Kathleen Kennedy, Frank Marshall & Steven Spielberg
INDIANA JONES AND THE LAST CRUSADE   Paramount, 1989, EP w/Kathleen Kennedy & Frank Marshall

TOM LUDDY
Business: Zoetrope Studios, Sentinel Bldg., 916 Kearny St., San Francisco, CA 94133, 415/789-7500; Fax: 415/989-7910

MISHIMA: A LIFE IN FOUR CHAPTERS   Warner Bros., 1985, w/Mata Yamamoto
BARFLY   Cannon, 1987, w/Fred Roos & Barbet Schroeder
TOUGH GUYS DON'T DANCE   Cannon, 1987, EP w/Francis Coppola
KING LEAR   Cannon, 1988, AP
POWAQQATSI (FD)   Cannon, 1988, LP w/Marcel Kahn
WAIT UNTIL SPRING, BANDINI   Orion, 1990, w/Erwin Provoost & Fred Roos

JOYCE LUKOW
HANG TOUGH   Moviestore Entertainment, 1990, EP

SIDNEY LUMET
Agent: ICM - New York, 212/556-5600
Contact: Directors Guild of America - New York, 212/581-0370

THE DEADLY AFFAIR   Columbia, 1967
BYE BYE BRAVERMAN   Warner Bros./7 Arts, 1968
THE SEA GULL   Warner Bros./7 Arts, 1968
LAST OF THE MOBILE HOT-SHOTS   Warner Bros., 1970
JUST TELL ME WHAT YOU WANT   Warner Bros., 1980, w/Jay Presson Allen
DANIEL   Paramount, 1983, EP w/E. L. Doctorow

JAN ERIK LUNDE
BROTHERS IN ARMS   Ablo, 1988, EP w/Andre Boissier

NEIL C. LUNDELL
BULLETPROOF   CineTel Films, 1987, CP

GUY LUONGO
LADY LIBERTY   United Artists, 1972, EP

MARTIN LUPEZ
MUTANT ON THE BOUNTY   Skouras Pictures, 1989, w/Robert Torrance

JEFFREY LURIE
Business: Chestnut Hill Prods., 9320 Wilshire Blvd., Beverly Hills, CA 90212, 310/247-3900; Fax: 310/247-3919

SWEET HEARTS DANCE   TriStar, 1988
I LOVE YOU TO DEATH   TriStar, 1990, w/Ron Moler

Ly

FILM
PRODUCERS,
STUDIOS,
AGENTS AND
CASTING
DIRECTORS
GUIDE

F
I
L
M

P
R
O
D
U
C
E
R
S

DAVID LYNCH
Business: Lynch/Frost Productions, 7700 Balboa Blvd.,
Van Nuys, CA 91406, 818/909-7900
Agent: CAA - Beverly Hills, 310/288-4545

ERASERHEAD   Independent, 1977

VICTOR LYNDON
THE OPTIMISTS   Paramount, 1973, w/Adrian Gaye

KANE W. LYNN
BEAST OF BLOOD   Marvin, 1971, EP

NELSON LYON
Contact: Writers Guild of America - New York,
213/245-6180

SPIKE OF BENSONHURST   FilmDallas, 1989,
w/David Weisman

JOSEPH LYTTLE
DEATH PLAY   New Line, 1976, EP

SHEL LYTTON
BODY SLAM   DEG, 1987, w/Mike Curb

COLIN MacCABE
Business: British Film Institute, 29 Rathbone Street, London
W1P1AG England, 071/636-5587; Fax: 071/580-9456

CARAVAGGIO   Cinevista, 1986, EP

HOLLY MACCONKEY
Contact: 213/883-6252

BODY PARTS   Raedon Entertainment, 1990,
w/Matt Devlen

SIMON MacCORKINDALE
Agent: APA - Los Angeles, 310/273-0744
Contact: Directors Guild of America - Los Angeles,
213/289-2000
Business: Amy International Prods., 2a Park Avenue,
Wraysbury, Middlesex TW19 5ET, 0784/483-131;
Fax: 0784/483-812

STEALING HEAVEN   Scotti Bros., 1989,
w/Andros Epaminondas

MICHAEL MacDONALD
ONE MAGIC CHRISTMAS   Buena Vista, 1985, AP
SHORT CIRCUIT II   TriStar, 1988, EP

PETER MacDONALD
Contact: Directors Guild of America - Los Angeles,
213/289-2000

TANGO AND CASH   Warner Bros., 1989, EP
GRAFFITI BRIDGE   Warner Bros., 1990, EP

PETER MacGREGOR-SCOTT
Contact: Directors Guild of America - Los Angeles,
213/289-2000

THE JERK   Universal, 1979, AP
THE PRISONER OF ZENDA   Universal, 1979, AP
CHEECH AND CHONG'S NEXT MOVIE   Universal,
1980, AP
THE BEST LITTLE WHOREHOUSE IN TEXAS
Universal, 1982, CP
CHEECH AND CHONG'S STILL SMOKIN'
Paramount, 1983
CHEECH AND CHONG'S THE CORSICAN BROTHERS
Orion, 1984
REVENGE OF THE NERDS   20th Century Fox, 1984, CP
GOTCHA!   Universal, 1985, SP
THE WHOOPEE BOYS   Paramount, 1986,
w/Adam Fields
BORN IN EAST L.A.   Universal, 1987
TROOP BEVERLY HILLS   WEG/Columbia, 1989,
CP w/Martin Mickelson
MARKED FOR DEATH   20th Century Fox, 1990, CP
LITTLE VEGAS   I.R.S., 1990
OUT FOR JUSTICE   Warner Bros., 1991, CP

MARTIN J. MACHAT
ALL THIS AND WORLD WAR II (FD)   20th Century Fox,
1976, w/Sandy Lieberson

NEIL A. MACHLIS
Contact: Directors Guild of America - Los Angeles,
213/289-2000

CAN'T STOP THE MUSIC   AFD, 1980, AP
MOMMIE DEAREST   Paramount, 1981, AP
GREASE 2   Paramount, 1982, AP
JOHNNY DANGEROUSLY   20th Century Fox, 1984, AP
2010   MGM/UA, 1984, AP w/Jonathan A. Zimbert
THE MONSTER SQUAD   TriStar, 1987, CP
PLAINS, TRAINS AND AUTOMOBILES   Paramount, 1987,
EP w/Michael Chinich
CHANCES ARE   TriStar, 1989, EP w/Andrew Bergman
AN INNOCENT MAN   Buena Vista, 1989, CP
POSTCARDS FROM THE EDGE   Columbia, 1990,
EP w/Robert Greenhut
THREE MEN AND A LITTLE LADY   Buena Vista,
1990, CP

EARLE MACK
Business: Precision Films, 110 E. 59th St., Suite 1405,
New York, NY 10022, 212/319-3030

THE CHILDREN OF THEATER STREET (FD)
Peppercorn-Wormser, 1977
SHE DANCES ALONE   Continental, 1982,
w/Federico De Laurentiis

KAREN MACK
Business: Republic Pictures, 350 S. Beverly Dr., Beverly
Hills, CA 90212, 310/552-7100; Fax: 310/552-7121

IN THE MOOD   Lorimar, 1987, w/Gary Adelson

WILLIAM MacKINNON
SWEETIE   Avenue Pictures, 1990, w/John Maynard

ROBERT MacLEAN
CRIMINAL LAW   Hemdale, 1989, w/Hilary Heath

DAVID L. MacLEOD
REDS ★   Paramount, 1981, AP
ISHTAR   Columbia, 1987, AP w/Nigel Wooll
THE PICK-UP ARTIST   20th Century Fox, 1987

MICHAEL MacREADY
COUNT YORGA, VAMPIRE   AIP, 1970
THE RETURN OF COUNT YORGA   AIP, 1971

MARIANNE MADDALENA
Business: Wes Craven Productions, c/o MGM-UA TV,
   10000 W. Washington Blvd., Suite 3016, Culver City,
   CA 90232, 310/280-6033; Fax: 310/558-5964

SHOCKER   Universal, 1989, w/Barin Kumar

DAVID MADDEN
Business: Interscope Communications, 10900 Wilshire
   Blvd., Ste. 1400, Los Angeles, CA 90024, 310/208-8525

RELENTLESS   Universal, 1989
BLIND FURY   TriStar, 1990, EP w/Robert W. Cort
THE FIRST POWER   Orion, 1990
EVE OF DESTRUCTION   Orion, 1991
THE HAND THAT ROCKS THE CRADLE   Buena
   Vista, 1991

LEE MADDEN
ANGEL UNCHAINED   AIP, 1970

BRENT MADDOCK
Agent: Gorfaine/Schwartz/Roberts - Beverly Hills,
   310/275-9384
Contact: Writers Guild of America - Los Angeles,
   310/550-1000

TREMORS   Universal, 1990, w/S.S. Wilson

BEN MADDOW
(credit w/Joseph Strick)

THE SAVAGE EYE   Trans-Lux, 1959,
   w/Sidney Meyers
THE BALCONY   Continental, 1963

GUY MAGAR
Business: 8033 Sunset Blvd., Suite 1102, Los Angeles,
   CA 90046, 213/466-0786
Contact: Directors Guild of America - Los Angeles,
   213/289-2000

RETRIBUTION   Taurus Entertainment, 1988

CHARLES H. MAGUIRE
Business: Lucasfilm, Ltd., P.O. Box 2009, San Rafael, CA
   94912, 415/662-1800
Contact: Directors Guild of America - Los Angeles,
   213/289-2000

FAIL SAFE   Columbia, 1964, AP
I LOVE YOU, ALICE B. TOKLAS   Warner Bros., 1968
THE ARRANGEMENT   Warner Bros./7 Arts, 1969, AP
FUZZ   United Artists, 1972, AP
HEAVEN CAN WAIT   Paramount, 1978,
   EP w/Howard W. Koch, Jr.
DOWNTOWN   20th Century Fox, 1990

DEZSO MAGYAR
Agent: Paul Kohner, Inc. - Los Angeles, 310/550-1060
Contact: Directors Guild of America - Los Angeles,
   213/289-2000

STREETS OF GOLD   20th Century Fox, 1986,
   CP w/Patrick McCormick

MICHAEL MAIELLO
NAKED TANGO   Scotia International, 1990,
   CP w/Milena Canonero

ROBERT MAIER
Contact: Directors Guild of America - Los Angeles,
   213/289-2000

POLYESTER   New Line, 1981, LP
HAIRSPRAY   New Line, 1988, LP

LEE MAJORS
Agent: William Morris Agency - Beverly Hills, 310/274-7451
Personal Manager: 818/783-3713
Contact: Directors Guild of America - Los Angeles,
   213/289-2000

STEEL   World Northal, 1980, EP

BORIS MALDEN
FRATERNITY VACATION   New World, 1985,
   w/Christopher Nelson & Robert C. Peters

TERRENCE MALICK
Agent: Ziegler & Associates - Los Angeles, 310/278-0070

BADLANDS   Warner Bros., 1974

AMIR J. MALIN
Business: Cinecom Entertainment, 850 Third Ave.,
   New York, NY 10022, 212/319-5000

SWIMMING TO CAMBODIA   Cinecom, 1987, EP w/Lewis
   Allen, Ira Deutchman & Peter Newman
MATEWAN   Cinecom, 1987, EP w/Mark Balsam &
   Jerry Silva
MILES FROM HOME   Cinecom, 1988, EP
SCENES FROM THE CLASS STRUGGLE IN BEVERLY
   HILLS   Cinecom, 1989, EP w/Ira Deutchman

HOWARD MALIN
SEBASTIAN   Discopat, 1977, w/James Whaley
JUBILEE   Cinegate, 1979, w/James Whaley
ENID IS SLEEPING   Vestron, 1990, w/John A. Davis

JOHN MALKOVICH
Agent: William Morris Agency - Los Angeles, 310/274-7451

THE ACCIDENTAL TOURIST ★   Warner Bros., 1988, EP
   w/Phyllis Carlyle

LOUIS MALLE
Business Manager: Gelfand, Rennert, Feldman - New York,
   212/682-0234
Agent: ICM - New York, 212/556-5600

LACOMBE LUCIEN   20th Century Fox, 1974
BLACK MOON   20th Century Fox, 1975, EP
HUMAIN, TROP HUMAIN (FD)   New Yorker, 1975
PRETTY BABY   Paramount, 1978
ALAMO BAY   TriStar, 1985, w/Vincent Malle

Ma

FILM
PRODUCERS,
STUDIOS,
AGENTS AND
CASTING
DIRECTORS
GUIDE

F
I
L
M

P
R
O
D
U
C
E
R
S

127

Ma

FILM
PRODUCERS,
STUDIOS,
AGENTS AND
CASTING
DIRECTORS
GUIDE

F
I
L
M

P
R
O
D
U
C
E
R
S

VINCENT MALLE
SWEET MOVIE   Biograph, 1975, w/Richard Helman
ALAMO BAY   TriStar, 1985, w/Louis Malle

JEFFREY B. MALLIAN
MOB BOSS   Vidmark Entertainment, 1990, LP

RENÉ MALO
Business: The Image Organization, 9000 Sunset Blvd.,
   Suite 915, Los Angeles, CA 90069, 310/278-8751,
   Fax: 310/278-3967; 1207 rue St. Andre, Montreal,
   H2L 3S8, 514/844-4555, Fax: 514/844-1471

INTERNAL AFFAIRS   Paramount, 1990, EP w/Pierre
   David & David Streit

GEORGE MANASSE
JOE   Cannon, 1970, AP
JUMP   Cannon, 1971, AP
WHO KILLED MARY WHAT'S 'ERNAME?   Cannon, 1971
BLADE   Joseph Green, 1973

CLAUDIO MANCINI
DUCK, YOU SUCKER!   United Artists, 1972, AP
MY NAME IS NOBODY   Universal, 1974
ONCE UPON A TIME IN AMERICA   The Ladd Company/
   Warner Bros., 1984, EP

FRANK MANCUSO, JR.
Business: Hometown Films, Paramount Pictures, 5555
   Melrose Ave., Los Angeles, CA 90038, 213/956-5955;
   Fax: 213/956-8676

FRIDAY THE 13TH PART 2   Paramount, 1981, AP
FRIDAY THE 13TH PART 3   Paramount, 1982
OFF THE WALL   Jensen Farley Pictures, 1983
THE MAN WHO WASN'T THERE   Paramount, 1983
FRIDAY THE 13TH - THE FINAL CHAPTER
   Paramount, 1984
FRIDAY THE 13TH PART V - A NEW BEGINNING
   Paramount, 1985, EP
APRIL FOOL'S DAY   Paramount, 1986
BACK TO THE BEACH   Paramount, 1987
PERMANENT RECORD   Paramount, 1988
INTERNAL AFFAIRS   Paramount, 1990
HE SAID, SHE SAID   Paramount, 1991
BODY PARTS   Paramount, 1991

YORAM MANDEL
PARTING GLANCES   Cinecom, 1986,
   w/Arthur Silverman

GABRIELLE MANDELIK
SWEET HEARTS DANCE   TriStar, 1988, EP w/Robert
   Greenwald & Lauren Weissman

LUIS MANDOKI
Agent: ICM - Los Angeles, 310/550-4000
Contact: 100 Universal Plaza, Bldg. 507, Room 3F,
   Universal City, CA 91608, 818/777-6975

GABY - A TRUE STORY   TriStar, 1987, CP

JOSEPH MANDUKE
A NEW LEAF   Paramount, 1971
CORNBREAD, EARL AND ME   AIP, 1975
THE GUMSHOE KID   Skouras, 1990

FRITZ MANES
Agent: APA - Los Angeles, 310/273-0744
Contact: Directors Guild of America - Los Angeles,
   213/289-2000

THE ENFORCER   Warner Bros., 1976, AP
THE OUTLAW JOSEY WALES   Warner Bros., 1976, AP
THE GAUNTLET   Warner Bros., 1977, AP
EVERY WHICH WAY BUT LOOSE   Warner Bros.,
   1978, AP
ESCAPE FROM ALCATRAZ   Paramount, 1979, AP
BRONCO BILLY   Warner Bros., 1980, AP
ANY WHICH WAY YOU CAN   Warner Bros., 1980, EP
HONKY TONK MAN   Warner Bros., 1982, EP
FIREFOX   Warner Bros., 1982, EP
SUDDEN IMPACT   Warner Bros., 1983, EP
TIGHTROPE   Warner Bros., 1984, w/Clint Eastwood
CITY HEAT   Warner Bros., 1984
PALE RIDER   Warner Bros., 1985, EP
RATBOY   Warner Bros., 1986
HEARTBREAK RIDGE   Warner Bros., 1986, EP

MICHAEL MANHEIM
Business: The Manheim Company, c/o NBC Productions,
   330 Bob Hope Dr., Burbank, CA 91523, 818/840-7546;
   Fax: 818/840-7795
Agent: UTA - Beverly Hills, 310/273-6700

PLAIN CLOTHES   Paramount, 1988, w/Richard Wechsler

JOSEPH L. MANKIEWICZ
Agent: ICM - New York, 212/556-5600

THREE GODFATHERS   *MIRACLE IN THE SAND*
   MGM, 1936
FURY   MGM, 1936
THE GORGEOUS HUSSY   MGM, 1936
LOVE ON THE RUN   MGM, 1936
THE BRIDE WORE RED   MGM, 1937
DOUBLE WEDDING   MGM, 1937
MANNEQUIN   MGM, 1937
THREE COMRADES   MGM, 1938
THE SHOPWORN ANGEL   MGM, 1938
THE SHINING HOUR   MGM, 1938
A CHRISTMAS CAROL   MGM, 1938
STRANGE CARGO   MGM, 1940
THE PHILADELPHIA STORY   MGM, 1940
THE WILD MAN OF BORNEO   MGM, 1941
THE FEMININE TOUCH   MGM, 1941
WOMAN OF THE YEAR   MGM, 1942
REUNION IN FRANCE   MGM, 1942
THE KEYS OF THE KINGDOM   20th Century Fox, 1944
THE BAREFOOT CONTESSA   United Artists, 1954, EP
THE QUIET AMERICAN   United Artists, 1958
THE HONEY POT   *IT COMES UP MURDER*   United
   Artists, 1967, w/Charles K. Feldman
THERE WAS A CROOKED MAN   Warner Bros., 1970

TOM MANKIEWICZ
Agent: ICM - Los Angeles, 310/550-4000
Contact: Writers Guild of America - Los Angeles,
   310/550-1000

MOTHER, JUGS & SPEED   20th Century Fox, 1976,
   w/Peter Yates

WOLF MANKOWITZ
THE HERO   Avco Embassy, 1972, w/John Heyman

MICHAEL MANLEY
AMERICAN GOTHIC   Vidmark Entertainment, 1988,
    EP w/Ray Homer & George Walker

MICHAEL MANN
Business: ZZY, Inc., 9200 Sunset Blvd., Suite 1005, Los
    Angeles, CA 90069, 310/273-9802; Fax: 310/273-9767
Agent: ICM - Los Angeles, 310/550-4000

BAND OF THE HAND   TriStar, 1986, EP
THE LAST OF THE MOHICANS   20th Century Fox,
    1991, w/Hunt Lowry

RICHARD MANN
RICH GIRL   Studio Three, 1991, AP w/Carol Kottenbrook

ROBERT W. MANN
MARTIAL LAW UNDERCOVER   Image, 1991,
    EP w/Pierre David

RON MANN
Business: Sphinx Productions, 24 Mercer St., Toronto,
    M5V 1H3, 416/971-9131
Agent: The Colbert Agency - Toronto, 416/964-3302

COMIC BOOK CONFIDENTIAL (FD)   Cinecom, 1989,
    w/Don Haig & Martin Harbury

STANLEY MANN
Agent: The Agency - Los Angeles, 310/551-3000

THE DEVIL'S WIDOW   *TAM LIN*   AIP, 1972,
    w/Alan Ladd, Jr.
THEATRE OF BLOOD   United Artists, 1973,
    w/John Kohn

TED MANN
Business: Ted Mann Productions, 5555 Melrose Ave.,
    Los Angeles, CA 90038, 213/956-6000

THE ILLUSTRATED MAN   Warner Bros., 1969,
    w/Howard B. Kreitsek
BUSTER & BILLIE   Columbia, 1974, EP
LIFEGUARD   Paramount, 1976
BRUBAKER   20th Century Fox, 1980, EP
KRULL   Columbia, 1983, EP

SAM MANNERS
Contact: Directors Guild of America - Los Angeles,
    213/289-2000

VALDEZ IS COMING   United Artists, 1971, AP
MISCHIEF   20th Century Fox, 1985, w/Michael Nolin
BAD MEDICINE   20th Century Fox, 1985, EP w/Michael
    Jaffe & Myles Osterneck

BOB MANNING
THE SLEEPING CAR   Vidmark, 1990, CP

MICHELLE MANNING
Business: Orion Pictures, 1888 Century Park East,
    Los Angeles, CA 90067, 310/282-0550
Contact: Directors Guild of America - Los Angeles,
    213/289-2000

SIXTEEN CANDLES   Universal, 1984, AP
THE BREAKFAST CLUB   Universal, 1985, CP

BRIAN C. MANOOGIAN
MOONTRAP   Shapiro-Glickenhaus Entertainment, 1989,
    EP w/James A. Courtney & Alan M. Solomon

PETER MANOOGIAN
DEADLY WEAPON   Empire, 1988

DAVID MANSON
Business: Sarabande Productions, 10000 W. Washington
    Blvd., Suite 3012, Culver City, CA 90232, 310/280-6462;
    Fax: 310/836-1680

BIRDY   TriStar, 1984, EP
BRING ON THE NIGHT (FD)   Samuel Goldwyn Company, 1985

ALLAN MARCIL
Business: Stonehenge Productions, c/o Viacom,
    10 Universal Plaza, 32nd Floor, Universal City, CA
    91608, 818/505-7566

FRESH HORSES   WEG/Columbia, 1988, EP

ROBERT P. MARCUCCI
THE RAZOR'S EDGE   Columbia, 1984, w/Harry Benn

ALAN C. MARDEN
THE HAPPY HOOKER GOES TO WASHINGTON   Cannon,
    1977, EP

JAMES MARGELLOS
Contact: Directors Guild of America - Los Angeles,
    213/289-2000

SLIPSTREAM   Pacific Rim Films, 1974
PAPERBACK HERO   Runson, 1975, w/John F. Bassett
STRIKING BACK   Film Ventures International, 1981

IRWIN MARGULIES
DIGBY, THE BIGGEST DOG IN THE WORLD   Cinerama,
    1974, EP

STAN MARGULIES
Business: The Stan Margulies Company, 1440 S. Sepulveda
    Blvd., 3rd Floor, Los Angeles, CA 90025, 310/444-8264;
    Fax: 310/444-8428

40 POUNDS OF TROUBLE   Universal, 1962
THOSE MAGNIFICENT MEN IN THEIR FLYING MACHINES
    20th Century Fox, 1965
THE PINK JUNGLE   Universal, 1968
IF IT'S TUESDAY, THIS MUST BE BELGIUM   United
    Artists, 1969
I LOVE MY WIFE   Universal, 1970
WILLY WONKA & THE CHOCOLATE FACTORY
    Paramount, 1971, w/David L. Wolper
ONE IS A LONELY NUMBER   MGM, 1972
VISIONS OF EIGHT (FD)   Cinema 5, 1973

PETER MARIS
VIPER   Fries Entertainment, 1988
TRUE BLOOD   Fries Entertainment, 1989

LAURENCE MARK
Business: Walt Disney Pictures, 500 S. Buena Vista St.,
    Burbank, CA 91521, 818/560-6280

BLACK WIDOW   20th Century Fox, 1987, EP
MY STEPMOTHER IS AN ALIEN   WEG/Columbia, 1988,
    EP w/Art Levinson

FILM
PRODUCERS,
STUDIOS,
AGENTS AND
CASTING
DIRECTORS
GUIDE

FILM PRODUCERS

Ma

**FILM
PRODUCERS,
STUDIOS,
AGENTS** AND
**CASTING
DIRECTORS**
GUIDE

F
I
L
M

P
R
O
D
U
C
E
R
S

WORKING GIRL ★ 20th Century Fox, 1988,
EP w/Robert Greenhut
COOKIE Warner Bros., 1989
MR. DESTINY Buena Vista, 1990, EP
TRUE COLORS Paramount, 1991, w/Herbert Ross

TONY MARK
(credit w/Sue Jett)
Contact: Directors Guild of America - Los Angeles,
213/289-2000

BILLY GALVIN Vestron, 1986
ZELLY & ME Columbia, 1988
ROOFTOPS New Visions, 1989, CP w/Allan Goldstein

TONY MARKES
Contact: 213/315-5325

INVISIBLE MANIAC Republic Pictures, 1990,
w/Matt Devlen

PATRICK MARKEY
Contact: Directors Guild of America - Los Angeles,
213/289-2000

HOUSE New World, 1986, AP
STACKING Spectrafilm, 1987, CP w/Peter Burrell
DEEPSTAR SIX TriStar, 1989, w/Sean S. Cunningham

RUSSELL D. MARKOWITZ
Business: A Cut Above Productions, Inc., 11816 Chandler
Blvd., Suite 8, N. Hollywood, CA 91606, 818/985-2105

TIME OF THE BEAST Liberty Films, 1989

ARTHUR MARKS
Business Manager: Robert Brenner, Gibson, Hoffman &
Pancione, 1888 Century Park East, Suite 1777,
Los Angeles, CA 90067, 310/556-4660

DETROIT 9000 General, 1973
FRIDAY FOSTER AIP, 1975
THE MONKEY HUSTLE AIP, 1976
J.D.'S REVENGE AIP, 1976

HARRY MARKS
JOE COCKER/MAD DOGS AND ENGLISHMEN (FD)
MGM, 1971, w/Robert Abel & Pierre Adidge

J. DAVID MARKS
(credit w/Gabe Sumner)

TAKE THIS JOB AND SHOVE IT Embassy, 1981,
EP w/William J. Immerman*
SISTER SISTER New World, 1988, EP
MEMORIES OF ME MGM/UA, 1988, EP

RICHARD MARKS
JUMPIN' JACK FLASH 20th Century Fox, 1986, AP
SAY ANYTHING 20th Century Fox, 1989, CP

NEAL MARLENS
Business: The Black/Marlens Company, 17351 Sunset
Blvd., Suite 504, Pacific Palisades, CA 90272;
310/573-1717; Fax: 310/573-1704
Agent: UTA - Beverly Hills, 310/273-6700

SOUL MAN New World, 1986, CP w/Carol Black

WAYNE MARMORSTEIN
DEAD MEN DON'T DIE Trans Atlantic Pictures, 1990

ANDRAS MAROS
JOKES MY FOLKS NEVER TOLD ME New World,
1979, EP

SANDRA MARSH
(credit w/Terence Marsh)
Business: Sandra Marsh Management, 14930 Ventura Blvd.,
Suite 200, Sherman Oaks, CA 91403, 818/285-8303

FINDERS KEEPERS Warner Bros., 1984

TERENCE MARSH
(credit w/Sandra Marsh)
Agent: Sandra Marsh Management, 14930 Ventura Blvd.,
Suite 200, Sherman Oaks, CA 91403, 818/285-8303

THE WORLD'S GREATEST LOVER 20th Century Fox,
1977, CP w/Chris Greenbury
FINDERS KEEPERS Warner Bros., 1984

ALAN MARSHALL
Contact:: Lowe Howard Spink - London, 071/225-3434

BUGSY MALONE Paramount, 1976
MIDNIGHT EXPRESS ★ Columbia, 1978,
w/David Puttnam
FAME MGM/UA, 1980, w/David De Silva
SHOOT THE MOON MGM, 1982
PINK FLOYD - THE WALL MGM/UA, 1982
ANOTHER COUNTRY Orion Classics, 1984
BIRDY TriStar, 1984
ANGEL HEART TriStar, 1987, w/Elliott Kastner
LEONARD PART 6 Columbia, 1987, EP w/Steve Sohmer
HOMEBOY Homeboy Productions, 1990, w/Elliott Kastner
JACOB'S LADDER TriStar, 1990
BASIC INSTINCT TriStar, 1992

FRANK MARSHALL
Agent: CAA - Beverly Hills, 310/288-4545
Contact: Directors Guild of America - Los Angeles,
213/289-2000

PAPER MOON Paramount, 1973, AP
DAISY MILLER Paramount, 1974, AP
AT LONG LAST LOVE 20th Century Fox, 1975, AP
NICKELODEON Columbia, 1976, AP
THE LAST WALTZ (FD) United Artists, 1978, LP
THE DRIVER 20th Century Fox, 1978, AP
THE WARRIORS Paramount, 1979, EP
RAIDERS OF THE LOST ARK ★ Paramount, 1981
POLTERGEIST MGM, 1982, w/Steven Spielberg
TWILIGHT ZONE - THE MOVIE Warner Bros., 1983, EP
INDIANA JONES & THE TEMPLE OF DOOM Paramount,
1984, EP w/George Lucas
GREMLINS Warner Bros., 1984, EP w/Kathleen Kennedy
& Steven Spielberg
FANDANGO Warner Bros., 1985, EP w/Kathleen Kennedy
THE GOONIES Warner Bros., 1985, EP w/Kathleen
Kennedy & Steven Spielberg
BACK TO THE FUTURE Universal, 1985, EP w/Kathleen
Kennedy & Steven Spielberg
YOUNG SHERLOCK HOLMES Paramount, 1985,
EP w/Kathleen Kennedy & Steven Spielberg
THE COLOR PURPLE ★ Warner Bros., 1985,
w/Quincy Jones, Kathleen Kennedy & Steven Spielberg

AN AMERICAN TAIL (AF)   Universal, 1986,
  EP w/Kathleen Kennedy, David Kirschner &
  Steven Spielberg
THE MONEY PIT   Universal, 1986, EP w/Kathleen
  Kennedy & Art Levinson
INNERSPACE   Warner Bros., 1987, EP w/Peter Guber,
  Kathleen Kennedy, Jon Peters & Steven Spielberg
BATTERIES NOT INCLUDED   Universal, 1987,
  EP w/Kathleen Kennedy & Steven Spielberg
EMPIRE OF THE SUN   Warner Bros., 1987, w/Kathleen
  Kennedy & Steven Spielberg
WHO FRAMED ROGER RABBIT   Buena Vista, 1988,
  w/Robert Watts
THE LAND BEFORE TIME (AF)   Universal, 1988,
  EP w/Kathleen Kennedy, George Lucas &
  Steven Spielberg
INDIANA JONES & THE LAST CRUSADE   Paramount,
  1989, EP w/Kathleen Kennedy & George Lucas
DAD   Universal, 1989, EP w/Kathleen Kennedy &
  Steven Spielberg
BACK TO THE FUTURE PART II   Universal, 1989,
  EP w/Kathleen Kennedy & Steven Spielberg
ALWAYS   Universal, 1989, w/Kathleen Kennedy &
  Steven Spielberg
BACK TO THE FUTURE PART III   Universal, 1990,
  EP w/Kathleen Kennedy & Steven Spielberg
GREMLINS II   Warner Bros., 1990, EP w/Kathleen
  Kennedy & Steven Spielberg
JOE VERSUS THE VOLCANO   Warner Bros., 1990,
  EP w/Kathleen Kennedy & Steven Spielberg
ARACHNOPHOBIA   Buena Vista, 1990,
  EP w/Robert W. Cort, Ted Field & Steven Spielberg
CAPE FEAR   Universal, 1991, EP w/Kathleen
  Kennedy & Steven Spielberg
HOOK   TriStar, 1991, w/Kathleen Kennedy &
  Gerald R. Molen
NOISES OFF   Buena Vista, 1992, w/Steve Starkey

GARRY MARSHALL
Business: Henderson Productions, 500 S. Buena Vista St.,
  Burbank, CA 818/560-7826
Contact: Directors Guild of America - Los Angeles,
  213/289-2000

HOW SWEET IT IS!   National General, 1968,
  w/Jerry Belson
THE GRASSHOPPER   National General, 1979,
  w/Jerry Belson
YOUNG DOCTORS IN LOVE   20th Century Fox,
  1982, EP
FRANKIE AND JOHNNY   Paramount, 1991

NOEL MARSHALL
THE EXORCIST ★   Warner Bros., 1973, EP
THE HARRAD EXPERIMENT   Cinerama, 1973, EP
ROAR   1981
A NIGHT IN THE LIFE OF JIMMY REARDON   20th
  Century Fox, 1988, EP w/Mel Klein

PAUL MARSHALL
JACQUES BREL IS ALIVE AND WELL AND LIVING
  IN PARIS   American Film Theatre, 1975

PENNY MARSHALL
Agent: CAA - Beverly Hills, 310/288-4545
Business: Columbia, 10202 W. Washington Blvd., Culver
  City, CA 90232, 310/280-4474; Fax: 310/280-1474

AWAKENINGS ★   Columbia, 1990, EP w/Elliott
  Abbott & Arne L. Schmidt

WILLIAM MARSHALL
OUTRAGEOUS!   Cinema 5, 1977,
  w/Hendrick J. Van Der Kolk

KENNETH MARTEL
CALL ME   Vestron, 1988, w/John Quill

BONNIE BRUCKHEIMER-MARTELL
(see Bonnie BRUCKHEIMER-Martell)

PETER MARTHESHEIMER
DESPAIR   New Line, 1979

ERNEST MARTIN
(credit w/Cy Feuer)

A CHORUS LINE   Columbia, 1985

STEVE MARTIN
Agent: APA - Los Angeles, 310/273-0744
Contact: Writers Guild of America - Los Angeles,
  310/550-1000

THREE AMIGOS   Orion, 1986, EP
ROXANNE   Columbia, 1987, EP
L.A. STORY   TriStar, 1991, EP w/Mario Kassar

GABRIELLA MARTINELLI
NIGHTBREED   20th Century Fox, 1990

MIKE MARVIN
Agent: The Irv Schechter Company - Beverly Hills,
  310/278-8070

HOT DOG...THE MOVIE   MGM/UA, 1984, CP

JOZSEF MARX
BRADY'S ESCAPE   Satori, 1984, EP

TIMOTHY MARX
Contact: 3000 W. Olympic Blvd., Santa Monica, CA
  90404, 310/820-7313

SMOOTH TALK   Spectrafilm, 1985, AP
RACHEL RIVER   Taurus, 1989
PENN AND TELLER GET KILLED   Warner Bros.,
  1989, CP

SAMMY O. MASADA
CLASS OF NUKE 'EM HIGH PART II: SUBHUMANOID
  MELTDOWN   Troma, 1991, EP w/Masahiro Ebisawa &
  Tetsu Fujimura

ARTHUR H. MASLANSKY
Business: Bima Entertainment, Ltd., 2049 Century Park
  East, Suite 4050, Los Angeles, CA 90067,
  310/203-8488

GHOST WARRIOR   Empire, 1986, EP w/Albert Band,
  Efrem Harkham & Uri Harkham
SLIPSTREAM   Entertainment Films, 1989, EP w/William
  Braunstein & Nigel Green

Ma

FILM
PRODUCERS,
STUDIOS,
AGENTS AND
CASTING
DIRECTORS
GUIDE

F
I
L
M

P
R
O
D
U
C
E
R
S

Ma

FILM
PRODUCERS,
STUDIOS,
AGENTS AND
CASTING
DIRECTORS
GUIDE

F
I
L
M

P
R
O
D
U
C
E
R
S

PAUL MASLANSKY
Business: Paul Maslansky Productions, 1041 N. Formosa
Ave., Los Angeles, CA 90046, 213/850-2805;
Fax: 213/850-2806
Contact: The Howard Brandy Company, Inc. -
Los Angeles, 213/657-8320

SUDDEN TERROR   National General, 1971
RAW MEAT   AIP, 1973
HARD TIMES   Columbia, 1975, EP
RACE WITH THE DEVIL   20th Century Fox,
1975, EP
THE BLUE BIRD   20th Century Fox, 1976
DAMNATION ALLEY   20th Century Fox, 1977,
w/Jerome M. Zeitman
HOT STUFF   Columbia, 1979, EP
CIRCLE OF IRON   Avco Embassy, 1979,
w/Sandy Howard
WHEN YOU COMIN' BACK, RED RYDER   Columbia,
1979, CP
SCAVENGER HUNT   20th Century Fox, 1979, CP
THE VILLAIN   Columbia, 1979, EP
LOVE CHILD   The Ladd Company/Warner Bros., 1982
THE SALAMANDER   ITC, 1983
POLICE ACADEMY   The Ladd Company/Warner
Bros., 1984
RETURN TO OZ   Buena Vista, 1985
POLICE ACADEMY 2: THEIR FIRST ASSIGNMENT
Warner Bros., 1985
POLICE ACADEMY 3: BACK IN TRAINING
Warner Bros., 1986
POLICE ACADEMY 4: CITIZENS ON PATROL
Warner Bros., 1987
POLICE ACADEMY 5: ASSIGNMENT MIAMI BEACH
Warner Bros., 1988
POLICE ACADEMY 6: CITY UNDER SIEGE   Warner
Bros., 1989
SKI PATROL   Triumph Releasing, 1990, EP
HONEYMOON ACADEMY   Triumph, 1990,
EP w/Eric Ellenbogen
THE RUSSIA HOUSE   MGM/UA, 1990,
w/Fred Schepisi

JIMMY MASLON
BLOOD DINER   Lightning/Vestron, 1987

MORGAN MASON
Agent: William Morris Agency, 151 El Camino Dr.,
Beverly Hills, CA 90212, 310/274-7451

sex, lies & videotape   Miramax, 1989, EP w/Nancy
Tenenbaum & Nick Wechsler
TWENTY-ONE   Triton, 1991, w/John Hardy
NO SECRETS   I.R.S., 1991, w/John Hardy &
Shaun A. Shapiro

PAUL MASON
Business: Trans World Entertainment, 3330 W. Cahuenga
Blvd., Suite 500, Los Angeles, CA 90068, 213/969-2800

THE LADIES CLUB   New Line, 1986, w/Nick J. Mileti
THE WILD PAIR   Trans World, 1987,
w/Randall Torno
SEVEN HOURS TO JUDGMENT   Trans World
Entertainment, 1988, EP w/Helen Sarlui-Tucker
I, MADMAN   Trans World, 1989,
EP w/Helen Sarlui-Tucker

NICO MASTORAKIS
Business: Omega Entertainment, Ltd., 8760 Shoreham Dr.,
Ste 501, Los Angeles, CA 90069, 213/855-0516;
Fax: 213/650-0325

THE GREEK TYCOON   Universal, 1978,
CP w/Lawrence Myers
BLIND DATE   New Line, 1984

EDDY MATALON
BLACKOUT   New World, 1978, w/Nicole Boisvert &
John Dunning

TIM MATHESON
Agent: CAA - Beverly Hills, 310/288-4545

BLIND FURY   TriStar, 1990, w/Daniel Grodnik

HARVEY MATOFSKY
FACE TO THE WIND   Warner Bros., 1974
ZANDY'S BRIDE   Warner Bros., 1974

WALTER MATTHAU
Agent: William Morris Agency - Beverly Hills, 310/274-7451

LITTLE MISS MARKER   Universal, 1980, EP

BURNY MATTINSON
Business: Walt Disney Studios, 500 S. Buena Vista St.,
Burbank, CA 91521, 818/560-1000

THE GREAT MOUSE DETECTIVE (AF)   Buena Vista, 1986

MICHAEL MAURER
DIVING IN   Skouras, 1990, EP w/Mark Shaw

ISABEL MAXWELL
'68   New World, 1988, w/Dale Djerassi & Steven Kovacs

MITCHELL MAXWELL
KEY EXCHANGE   20th Century Fox, 1985, w/Paul Kurta

GAY MAYER
Business: Continental Film Group, Ltd., 321 W. 44th St.,
Suite 405, New York, NY 10036, 212/265-2530;
Fax: 212/245-6275; Park St., Sharon, PA 16146,
412/981-3456; Fax: 412/981-2668

TIGER WARSAW   Sony Pictures, 1988, EP w/Navin Desai
& Watson Warriner

LEE R. MAYES
F/X 2 — THE DEADLY ART OF ILLUSION   Orion, 1991,
EP w/Bryan Brown

LES MAYFIELD
HEARTS OF DARKNESS: A FILMMAKER'S APOCALYPSE
Avenue, 1991, w/George Zaloom

JOHN MAYNARD
Business: Z.M. Productions, 100 Universal Plaza, M.T. #27,
Universal City, CA 91608, 818/777-4664; Fax: 818/777-8870

THE NAVIGATOR: AN ODYSSEY ACROSS TIME   Circle
Releasing, 1989
SWEETIE   Avenue Pictures, 1990, w/William MacKinnon
AN ANGEL AT MY TABLE   Fine Line, 1991, CP

GEOFFREY MAYO
Business: UMP & Associates, Raleigh Studios,
    5300 Melrose Ave., Suite 411-E, Hollywood, CA 90038,
    213/960-4580

ROCKET GIBRALTAR   Columbia, 1988, EP w/Robert
    Fisher & Michael Ulick

MELANIE MAYRON
Agent: Triad Artists, Inc. - Los Angeles, 310/556-2727

STICKY FINGERS   Spectrafilm, 1988, w/Catlin Adams

PAULA MAZUR
Contact: Directors Guild of America - Los Angeles,
    213/289-2000

HOME OF THE BRAVE (FD)   Cinecom, 1986
THE SEARCH FOR SIGNS OF INTELLIGENT LIFE IN
    THE UNIVERSE (FD)   Orion Classics, 1991

PAUL MAZURSKY
Agent: ICM - Los Angeles, 310/550-4000
Contact: Directors Guild of America - Los Angeles,
    213/289-2000

I LOVE YOU, ALICE B. TOKLAS   Warner Bros., 1968,
    EP w/Larry Tucker
BLUME IN LOVE   Warner Bros., 1973
HARRY & TONTO   20th Century Fox, 1974
NEXT STOP, GREENWICH VILLAGE   20th Century Fox,
    1976, w/Tony Ray
AN UNMARRIED WOMAN ★   20th Century Fox, 1978,
    w/Tony Ray
WILLIE & PHIL   20th Century Fox, 1980, w/Tony Ray
TEMPEST   Columbia, 1982
MOSCOW ON THE HUDSON   Columbia, 1984
DOWN AND OUT IN BEVERLY HILLS   Buena Vista, 1986
MOON OVER PARADOR   Universal, 1988
ENEMIES, A LOVE STORY   20th Century Fox, 1989
TAKING CARE OF BUSINESS   Buena Vista, 1990, EP
SCENES FROM A MALL   Buena Vista, 1991

EUGENE MAZZOLA
Agent: Gray/Goodman, Inc. - Beverly Hills, 310/276-7070
Contact: Directors Guild of America - Los Angeles,
    213/289-2000

JOYRIDE   AIP, 1977, CP
ALOHA SUMMER   Spectrafilm, 1987
CLASS OF 1999   Taurus, 1990, CP

CHERYL McCALL
STREETWISE   Angelika, 1985

RICK McCALLUM
Contact: Directors Guild of America - Los Angeles,
    213/289-2000
Agent: ICM - Duncan Heath, 071/439-1471

PENNIES FROM HEAVEN   MGM, 1981, EP
I OUGHT TO BE IN PICTURES   20th Century Fox,
    1982, AP
DREAMCHILD   Universal, 1985, w/Kenith Trodd
LINK   Cannon, 1986, CP
CASTAWAY   Cannon, 1987
TRACK 29   Island Pictures, 1988
STRAPLESS   Miramax, 1990

PETER McCARTHY
REPO MAN   Universal, 1984, w/Jonathan Wacks
SID & NANCY   Samuel Goldwyn Company, 1986, CP
TAPEHEADS   Avenue, 1988
I'M GONNA GIT YOU SUCKA   MGM/UA, 1989,
    w/Carl Craig

RICKY McCARTNEY
ICE HOUSE   Upfront Films, 1989, EP

KIRBY McCAULEY
Business: 432 Park Ave. South, Suite 1509, New York, NY
    10016, 212/628-9729

CHRISTINE   Columbia, 1983, EP w/Mark Tarlov

KEVIN McCLORY
THUNDERBALL   United Artists, 1965
NEVER SAY NEVER AGAIN   Warner Bros., 1983, EP

KEVIN McCORMICK
Business: Fogwood Films, 825 S. Barrington, Suite 204, Los
    Angeles, CA 90049, 310/820-3443; Fax: 310/820-2227

SATURDAY NIGHT FEVER   Paramount, 1977, EP
MOMENT BY MOMENT   Universal, 1978, EP
TIMES SQUARE   AFD, 1980, EP w/John Nicolella
THE FAN   Paramount, 1981, EP
BURGLAR   Warner Bros., 1987, w/Michael Hirsh
DYING YOUNG   20th Century Fox, 1991, w/Sally Field

PATRICK McCORMICK
Contact: Directors Guild of America - New York,
    212/581-0370

WISE GUYS   MGM/UA, 1986, AP
STREETS OF GOLD   20th Century Fox, 1986,
    CP w/Dezso Magyar
MORGAN STEWART'S COMING HOME   New Century/
    Vista, 1987, AP
LAST RITES   MGM/UA, 1988, w/Donald Bellisario
AND GOD CREATED WOMAN   Vestron, 1988, SP
A SHOCK TO THE SYSTEM   Corsair, 1990
SCENES FROM A MALL   Buena Vista, 1991,
    CP w/Pato Guzman

IAN McDOUGALL
CLEARCUT   Alliance, 1991, w/Stephen J. Roth

RODDY McDOWALL
Agent: Badgley-Conner - Los Angeles, 310/278-9313
Business: Foxboro Entertainment, 8222 Melrose Ave.,
    Suite 301, Los Angeles, CA 90046, 213/966-4371;
    Fax: 213/966-4385

OVERBOARD   MGM/UA, 1987, EP

HAL McELROY
(credit w/James McElroy)
Contact: Australian Film Commission, 9229 Sunset Blvd.,
    Los Angeles, CA 90069, 310/275-7074

THE CARS THAT EAT PEOPLE   *THE CARS THAT ATE
    PARIS*   New Line, 1976
THE LAST WAVE   World Northal, 1978
PICNIC AT HANGING ROCK   Atlantic, 1979
RAZORBACK   Warner Bros., 1985*

Mc

FILM
PRODUCERS,
STUDIOS,
AGENTS AND
CASTING
DIRECTORS
GUIDE

F
I
L
M

P
R
O
D
U
C
E
R
S

Mc

FILM
PRODUCERS,
STUDIOS,
AGENTS AND
CASTING
DIRECTORS
GUIDE

F
I
L
M

P
R
O
D
U
C
E
R
S

JAMES McELROY
(credit w/Hal McElroy)
Contact: Australian Film Commission, 9229 Sunset Blvd.,
Los Angeles, CA 90069, 310/275-7074

THE CARS THAT EAT PEOPLE   *THE CARS THAT
ATE PARIS*   New Line, 1976
THE LAST WAVE   World Northal, 1978
PICNIC AT HANGING ROCK   Atlantic, 1979
THE YEAR OF LIVING DANGEROUSLY
MGM/UA, 1983*

WILLIAM E. McEUEN
THE JERK   Universal, 1979, w/David V. Picker
DEAD MEN DON'T WEAR PLAID   Universal, 1979,
w/David V. Picker
THE MAN WITH TWO BRAINS   Warner Bros., 1983,
w/David V. Picker
THE LONELY GUY   Universal, 1984,
EP w/C. O. Erickson
PEE-WEE'S BIG ADVENTURE   Warner Bros.,
1985, EP
PULSE   Columbia, 1988, EP
BIG TOP PEE-WEE   Paramount, 1988,
EP w/Richard Gilbert Abramson
THE BIG PICTURE   Columbia, 1989,
EP w/Richard Gilbert Abramson

TIMOTHY McGINN
SPACE AVENGER   Manley, 1990, EP w/Richard
Albert & David Smith

DARRELL McGOWAN
Contact: 825 S. Barrington, Suite 204, Los Angeles, CA
90049, 310/820-3443; Fax: 310/820-2227

THE BILLION DOLLAR HOBO   International Picture
Show, 1977, EP w/Lloyd N. Adams, Jr.

THOMAS J. McGRATH
DEADLY HERO   Avco Embassy, 1976

HUGH McGRAW
FUNNYMAN   New Yorker, 1967,
w/Stephen Schmidt

PAUL McGUINNESS
U2: RATTLE & HUM   Paramount, 1988, EP

DOUG McHENRY
Contact: Jackson-McHenry, 4000 Warner Blvd.,
Burbank, CA 91522, 818/954-3221

KRUSH GROOVE   Warner Bros., 1985,
w/Michael Schultz
NEW JACK CITY   Warner Bros., 1991,
w/George A. Jackson

PETER R. McINTOSH
Contact: Directors Guild of America - New York,
212/581-0370

MONKEY SHINES   Orion, 1988, AP
THE HARD WAY   Universal, 1991, CP

ANDREW V. McLAGLEN
Business: Stanmore Productions, Inc., 1900 Avenue of the
Stars, Ste. 2270, Los Angeles, CA 90067, 310/277-1900
Agent: The Chasin Agency - Beverly Hills, 310/278-7505

SOMETHING BIG   National General, 1971, AP
FOOLS' PARADE   Columbia, 1971, AP

MARY McLAGLEN
COLD FEET   Avenue, 1989, CP

VINCE McMAHON
Business: World Wrestling Federation, P.O. Box 3857,
Stamford, CT 06905

NO HOLDS BARRED   New Line, 1989, EP w/Richard
Glover & Hulk Hogan

JOHN McNAB
CARAVAN TO VACCARES   Bryanston, 1976, EP

JOHN McNAUGHTON
Business: UTA - Beverly Hills, 310/273-6700

HENRY: PORTRAIT OF A SERIAL KILLER   Greycat Films,
1990, w/Lisa Dedmond

PETER A. McRAE
EDGE OF SANITY   Millimeter Films, 1989, EP

JOHN McTIERNAN
Agent: William Morris Agency - Beverly Hills, 310/274-7451
Business: 2308 Broadway, Santa Monica, CA 90404,
310/859-0331
Contact: Directors Guild of America - Los Angeles,
213/289-2000

FLIGHT OF THE INTRUDER   Paramount, 1990,
EP w/Brian Frankish

JOSEPH MEDAWAR
(credit w/Nabeel Zahid)
Business: Ion Pictures, 3122 Santa Monica Blvd., Suite 300,
Santa Monica, CA 90404, 310/453-4466

PRETTY SMART   New World, 1987, EP*
CHAMPIONS FOREVER (FD)   Ion, 1989
THE CLOSER   Ion, 1991

ROY MEDAWAR
Business: Ion Pictures, 3122 Santa Monica Blvd., Suite 300,
Santa Monica, CA 90404, 310/453-4466

THE CLOSER   Ion, 1991, EP w/Mitchell Calder, Tony
Conforti & George Pappas

JOE MEDJUCK
(credit w/Michael C. Gross)
Business: Ivan Reitman Productions, 100 Universal Plaza,
415B, Universal City, CA 91608, 818/777-8080;
Fax: 818/777-0689

STRIPES   Columbia, 1981, AP*
GHOSTBUSTERS   Columbia, 1984, AP
LEGAL EAGLES   Universal, 1986, EP
BIG SHOTS   20th Century Fox, 1987
TWINS   Universal, 1988, EP

GHOSTBUSTERS II   Columbia, 1989,
   EP w/Bernie Brillstein
KINDERGARTEN COP   Universal, 1990, EP
BEETHOVEN   UNIVERSAL, 1991
STOP OR MY MOTHER WILL SHOOT   Universal, 1991,
   w/Ivan Reitman

MICHAEL MEDWIN
GUMSHOE   Columbia, 1972
O LUCKY MAN!   Warner Bros., 1973,
   w/Lindsay Anderson
LAW AND DISORDER   Columbia, 1974,
   EP w/Edgar J. Scherick

CHARLES R. MEEKER
(credit w/Edward S. Feldman)
Business: F/M Entertainment, 9454 Wilshire Blvd.,
   Suite 701, Beverly Hills, CA 90212, 310/859-7050

THE HITCHER   TriStar, 1986, EP
HAMBURGER: THE MOTION PICTURE
   FM Entertainment, 1986
THE GOLDEN CHILD   Paramount, 1986,
   EP w/Richard Tienken*
NEAR DARK   DEG, 1987, EP
WIRED   Taurus, 1989

GARY MEHLMAN
Business: Viacom Pictures, 10 Universal Plaza, Universal
   City, CA 91608, 818/505-7700; Fax: 818/505-7755

YOU'VE GOT TO WALK IT LIKE YOU TALK IT OR YOU'LL
   LOSE THAT BEAT   JER, 1971, AP
CIRCLE OF POWER   Televicine International, 1984
THE BIKINI SHOP   *THE MALIBU BIKINI SHOP*
   International Film Marketing, 1987, w/J. Kenneth Rotcop
THE NEW ADVENTURES OF PIPPI LONGSTOCKING
   Columbia, 1988, w/Walter Moshay

CHRIS MELEDANDRI
(credit w/Mark R. Gordon)
Business: Steel Pictures, c/o Walt Disney Pictures, 500 S.
   Buena Vista St., Burbank, CA 91521, 818/560-7877;
   Fax: 818/560-7889

QUICKSILVER   Columbia, 1986, AP*
BROTHERS IN ARMS   Ablo, 1988
OPPORTUNITY KNOCKS   Universal, 1990

BILL MELENDEZ
(credit w/Lee Mendelson)
Business: Bill Melendez Productions, 439 N. Larchmont
   Blvd., Los Angeles, CA 90004, 213/463-4101

A BOY NAMED CHARLIE BROWN (AF)   National
   General, 1968
SNOOPY, COME HOME (AF)   National General, 1972
RACE FOR YOUR LIFE, CHARLIE BROWN (AF)
   Paramount, 1977
BON VOYAGE, CHARLIE BROWN (AND DON'T COME
   BACK!) (AF)   Paramount, 1980

DANIEL MELNICK
Business: IndieProd, c/o Carolco, 8800 Sunset Blvd.,
   5th Floor, Los Angeles, CA 90069, 310/289-7100;
   Fax: 310/652-2165

STRAW DOGS   Cinerama, 1971
THAT'S ENTERTAINMENT (FD)   MGM/UA, 1974, EP

THAT'S ENTERTAINMENT, PART 2 (FD)   MGM/UA, 1976,
   w/Saul Chaplin
ALL THAT JAZZ   20th Century Fox, 1979, EP
ALTERED STATES   Warner Bros., 1980, EP
FIRST FAMILY   Warner Bros., 1980
MAKING LOVE   20th Century Fox, 1982, w/Allen Adler
UNFAITHFULLY YOURS   20th Century Fox, 1984, EP
FOOTLOOSE   Paramount, 1984, EP
QUICKSILVER   Columbia, 1986, w/Michael Rachmil
ROXANNE   Columbia, 1987, w/Michael Rachmil
PUNCHLINE   Columbia, 1988, w/Michael Rachmil
AIR AMERICA   TriStar, 1990
MOUNTAINS OF THE MOON   TriStar, 1990
L.A. STORY   TriStar, 1991, w/Michael Rachmil

BENJAMIN MELNIKER
(credit w/Michael Uslan)
Business: Bat Film Productions, 123 W. 44th St., Suite 10-K,
   New York, NY 10036, 212/302-2688

MITCHELL   Allied Artists, 1975, EP*
SWAMP THING   Embassy, 1982
BATMAN   Warner Bros., 1989, EP
THE RETURN OF SWAMP THING   Miramax, 1989

MICHAEL MELTZER
Business: 1219 Sunset Plaza Drive, Los Angeles, CA 90069,
   310/289-0701; Fax: 310/289-0436

UP THE CREEK   Orion, 1984
THE HIDDEN   New Line, 1987, w/Gerald T. Olson &
   Robert Shaye
DEAD HEAT   New World, 1988, w/David Helpern

JULIAN MELZACK
THE HAUNTING OF JULIA   Discovery, 1981, EP
ANGELA   Embassy, 1984, w/Claude Héroux

JANA SUE MEMEL
Business: Chanticleer Films, 6525 Sunset Blvd., 6th Floor,
   Los Angeles, CA 90028, 213/462-4705;
   Fax: 213/462-1603

TOUGH GUYS   Buena Vista, 1986,
   CP w/Richard Hashimoto
DICE RULES   SEVEN ARTS, 1991, EP w/J.R. Guterman

LEE MENDELSON
(credit w/Bill Melendez)
Business: Lee Mendelson Film Productions, Inc., 1408
   Chapin Ave., Burlingame, CA 94010, 415/342-8284;
   Fax: 415/342-6170

A BOY NAMED CHARLIE BROWN (AF)   National
   General, 1968
COME TO YOUR SENSES   National General, 1971, EP*
SNOOPY, COME HOME (AF)   National General, 1972
RACE FOR YOUR LIFE, CHARLIE BROWN (AF)
   Paramount, 1977
BON VOYAGE, CHARLIE BROWN (AND DON'T COME
   BACK!) (AF)   Paramount, 1980

FRANK MENKE
MARVIN & TIGE   Castle Hill, 1985, EP

JERRY MENKIN
TORN APART   Castle Hill, 1990, w/Danny Fisher

Me

FILM
PRODUCERS,
STUDIOS,
AGENTS AND
CASTING
DIRECTORS
GUIDE

F
I
L
M

P
R
O
D
U
C
E
R
S

Me

FILM
PRODUCERS,
STUDIOS,
AGENTS AND
CASTING
DIRECTORS
GUIDE

F
I
L
M

P
R
O
D
U
C
E
R
S

BRYCE MENZIES
MALCOLM   Vestron, 1986, EP
RIKKY AND PETE   MGM/UA, 1988, EP

BOB MERCER
SLAYGROUND   Universal, 1984, EP

ISMAIL MERCHANT
Business: Merchant Ivory Productions, 250 West 57th St.,
   Suite 1913-A, New York, NY 10019, 212/582-8049;
   Fax: 212/459-9201; 46 Lexington Street, London W1
   England, 071/437-1200; Fax: 071/734-1579

THE HOUSEHOLDER   Royal Films International, 1963
SHAKESPEARE WALLAH   Continental, 1966
THE GURU   20th Century Fox, 1969
BOMBAY TALKIE   Dia Films, 1970
SAVAGES   Angelika, 1972
THE WILD PARTY   AIP, 1975
ROSELAND   Cinema Shares International, 1977
HULLABALOO OVER GEORGIA & BONNIE'S PICTURES
   Corinth, 1979
THE EUROPEANS   Levitt-Pickman, 1979
JANE AUSTEN IN MANHATTAN   Contemporary, 1980
QUARTET   New World, 1981
HEAT AND DUST   Universal Classics, 1983
THE BOSTONIANS   Almi Pictures, 1984
A ROOM WITH A VIEW ★   Cinecom, 1986
MAURICE   Cinecom, 1987
MY LITTLE GIRL   Hemdale, 1987, EP
THE DECEIVERS   Cinecom, 1988
SLAVES OF NEW YORK   TriStar, 1989,
   w/Gary J. Hendler
MR. & MRS. BRIDGE   Miramax, 1990
THE BALLAD OF THE SAD CAFE   Angelika, 1991
HOWARD'S END   Orion Classics, 1992

TOM MERCHANT
HOLLYWOOD BOULEVARD II   Concorde, 1991,
   w/Chris Beckman

NEIL MERON
Business: Storyline Productions, c/o Spectacor Films,
   7920 Sunset Blvd., 4th Floor, Los Angeles, CA 90046,
   213/851-8425; Fax: 213/871-2963

SING   TriStar, 1989, CP
IF LOOKS COULD KILL   Warner Bros., 1991,
   w/Craig Zadan

DAVID MERRICK
CHILD'S PLAY   Paramount, 1973
THE GREAT GATSBY   Paramount, 1974
SEMI-TOUGH   United Artists, 1977
ROUGH CUT   Paramount, 1980

KEITH MERRILL
Contact: Directors Guild of America - Los Angeles,
   213/289-2000

THE GREAT AMERICAN COWBOY (FD)   Sun
   International, 1974
TAKE DOWN   Buena Vista, 1979

MARK METCALF
CHILLY SCENES OF WINTER   *HEAD OVER HEELS*
   United Artists, 1979, w/Griffin Dunne & Amy Robinson

JACQUES METHE
THE LAST BUTTERFLY   1991, w/Boudjemaa Dahmane,
   Patrick Dromgoole

ANDREW MEYER
THE SKY PIRATE   FilmMakers, 1970
THE BREAKFAST CLUB   Universal, 1985,
   EP w/Gil Friesen
BETTER OFF DEAD   Warner Bros., 1985,
   EP w/Gil Friesen
BRING ON THE NIGHT   Samuel Goldwyn Company, 1985,
   EP w/Gil Friesen
ONE CRAZY SUMMER   Warner Bros., 1986,
   EP w/Gil Friesen
PROMISED LAND   Vestron, 1988, EP w/Robert Redford
BREAKING IN   Samuel Goldwyn Company, 1989,
   EP w/Sarah Ryan Black

IRWIN MEYER
Business: Ventura Motion Pictures, 9150 Wilshire Blvd.,
   #205, Beverly Hills, CA 90212, 310/285-0400;
   Fax: 310/281-2585

DEADLY ILLUSION   CineTel Films, 1987

PATRICIA MEYER
Business: c/o Von Zerneck-Sertner, 12001 Ventura Place,
   #400, Studio City, CA 91604, 818/766-2610;
   Fax: 818/766-7423

THIS IS MY LIFE   20th Century Fox, 1991,
   EP w/Carole Isenberg

JANET MEYERS
Business: c/o Imagine Films, 1925 Century Park East,
   Los Angeles, CA 90067-2734, 310/277-1665;
   Fax: 310/785-0107

CLOSET LAND   Universal, 1991

NANCY MEYERS
Agent: ICM - Los Angeles, 310/550-4000

PRIVATE BENJAMIN   Warner Bros., 1980, w/Harvey Miller
   & Charles Shyer
BABY BOOM   MGM/UA, 1987
FATHER OF THE BRIDE   Buena Vista, 1991, w/Carol
   Baum & Howard Rosenman

SIDNEY MEYERS
THE SAVAGE EYE   Trans-Lux, 1959, w/Ben Maddow &
   Joseph Strick

JOEL B. MICHAELS
THE PEACE KILLERS   Transvue, 1971
PRISONERS   American Films Ltd., 1975, AP
BITTERSWEET LOVE   Avco Embassy, 1976, w/Gene
   Slott & Joseph Zappala
THE SILENT PARTNER   EMC Film/Aurora, 1979,
   w/Stephen Young
THE CHANGELING   AFD, 1980, w/Garth Drabinsky
TRIBUTE   20th Century Fox, 1980, w/Garth Drabinsky
THE AMATEUR   20th Century Fox, 1981,
   w/Garth Drabinsky
LOSIN' IT   Embassy, 1983, EP w/Garth Drabinsky
THE PHILADELPHIA EXPERIMENT   New World, 1984,
   w/Douglas Curtis
BLACK MOON RISING   New World, 1986,
   w/Douglas Curtis

LORNE MICHAELS

Business: Broadway Video, c/o Paramount Studios,
5555 Melrose, Dressing Room # 305, Los Angeles,
CA 90038-3197, 213/956-5729; Fax: 213/956-8605

MR. MIKE'S MONDO VIDEO   New Line, 1979, EP
GILDA LIVE (FD)   Warner Bros., 1980
NOTHING LASTS FOREVER   MGM/UA, 1984
THREE AMIGOS   Orion, 1986, w/George Folsey Jr.

MARTIN MICKELSON

Business: Itsbinso Long, Inc., c/o Imagine Entertainment,
1925 Century Park East, 23rd Floor, Los Angeles, CA
90067-2734, 310/277-1665; Fax: 310/785-0107

HELLO AGAIN   Buena Vista, 1987, CP w/G. Mac Brown,
Thomas Folino & Susan Isaacs
OUTRAGEOUS FORTUNE   Buena Vista, 1987,
CP w/Peter V. Herald & Scott Kroopf
TROOP BEVERLY HILLS   WEG/Columbia, 1989,
CP w/Peter MacGregor-Scott

ROBERT MICKELSON

HARD CHOICES   Lorimar, 1986
PRAYER OF THE ROLLERBOYS   Academy
Entertainment, 1991

BETTE MIDLER

Business: All-Girl Pictures, Walt Disney Pictures, 500 S.
Buena Vista St., Burbank, CA 91521, 818/560-6547;
Fax: 818/560-1930

BEACHES   Buena Vista, 1988, w/Bonnie Bruckheimer
Martell & Margaret Jennings South
FOR THE BOYS   Buena Vista, 1991, w/Bonnie
Bruckheimer Martell & Margaret Jennings South

MICHAEL R. MIHALICH

Business: MJR Theatres, Inc., 13671 W. Eleven Mile Rd.,
Oak Park, MI 48237, 313/548-8282

THE ROSARY MURDERS   New Line, 1987, EP

ARNON MILCHAN

Business: New Regency Films, 4000 Warner Blvd., Bldg. 66,
Burbank, CA 91522, 818/954-3044; Fax: 818/954-3295

BLACK JOY   Hemdale, 1977, w/Elliott Kastner
THE MEDUSA TOUCH   Warner Bros., 1978,
EP w/Lew Grade & Elliott Kastner
THE KING OF COMEDY   20th Century Fox, 1983
ONCE UPON A TIME IN AMERICA   The Ladd Co./
Warner Bros., 1984
BRAZIL   Universal, 1985
LEGEND   Universal, 1986
STRIPPER (FD)   20th Century Fox, 1986, EP
MAN ON FIRE   TriStar, 1987
WHO'S HARRY CRUMB?   TriStar, 1989
BIG MAN ON CAMPUS   Vestron, 1989
THE WAR OF THE ROSES   20th Century Fox, 1989,
w/James L. Brooks
Q&A   TriStar, 1990, w/Burtt Harris
PRETTY WOMAN   Buena Vista, 1990, w/Steven Reuther
GUILTY BY SUSPICION   Warner Bros., 1991
MEMOIRS OF AN INVISIBLE MAN   Warner Bros.,
1991, EP
THE MAMBO KINGS   Warner Bros., 1991,
w/Arnold Glimcher
JFK   Warner Bros., 1991, EP

JULIA MILES

FOUR FRIENDS   Filmways, 1981,
EP w/Michael Tolan

NICK J. MILETI

STREAMERS   United Artists Classics, 1983,
w/Robert Altman
THE LADIES CLUB   New Line, 1986, w/Paul Mason

JOHN MILIUS

Business: Paramount Pictures, 5555 Melrose Ave.,
Los Angeles, CA 90038, 213/956-5738
Agent: ICM - Los Angeles, 310/550-4000

1941   Universal, 1979, EP
HARDCORE   Columbia, 1979, EP
USED CARS   Columbia, 1980, EP w/Steven Spielberg
UNCOMMON VALOR   Paramount, 1983,
w/Buzz Feitshans

EDWARD K. MILKIS

(credit w/Thomas L. Miller)
Contact: Directors Guild of America - Los Angeles,
213/289-2000

SILVER STREAK   20th Century Fox, 1976
FOUL PLAY   Paramount, 1978
THE BEST LITTLE WHOREHOUSE IN TEXAS   Universal,
1982, w/Robert L. Boyett

SCOTT MILLANEY

STRAIGHT TO HELL   Island Pictures, 1988,
EP w/Cary Brokaw

STUART MILLAR

Contact: Directors Guild of America - New York,
212/581-0370

THE YOUNG DOCTORS   United Artists, 1961,
w/Lawrence Turman
I COULD GO ON SINGING   United Artists, 1963,
w/Lawrence Turman
THE BEST MAN   United Artists, 1964,
w/Lawrence Turman
PAPER LION   United Artists, 1968
LITTLE BIG MAN   National General, 1970
WHEN THE LEGENDS DIE   20th Century Fox, 1972
SHOOT THE MOON   MGM/UA, 1982,
EP w/Edgar J. Scherick

DON MILLER

BLAZE   Buena Vista, 1989, EP w/David V. Lester
WHITE MEN CAN'T JUMP   20th Century Fox, 1991,
w/David V. Lester

GEORGE MILLER

Business Manager: Gang, Tyre & Brown, 6400 Sunset Blvd.,
Los Angeles, CA 90028
Business: Kennedy Miller Productions, 30 Orwell St.,
Kings Cross, Sydney, Australia

MAD MAX BEYOND THUNDERDOME   Warner
Bros., 1985
DEAD CALM   Warner Bros., 1989, w/Terry Hayes &
Doug Mitchell

Mi

FILM
PRODUCERS,
STUDIOS,
AGENTS AND
CASTING
DIRECTORS
GUIDE

F
I
L
M

P
R
O
D
U
C
E
R
S

Mi

FILM
PRODUCERS,
STUDIOS,
AGENTS AND
CASTING
DIRECTORS
GUIDE

F
I
L
M

P
R
O
D
U
C
E
R
S

HARVEY MILLER
Business: 5538 Calhoun Ave., Van Nuys, CA 91401,
818/997-6760
Agent: ICM - Los Angeles, 310/550-4000

PRIVATE BENJAMIN Warner Bros., 1980, w/Nancy
Meyers & Charles Shyer
STUDENT BODIES Paramount, 1981, EP w/Jerry Belson

JENNIFER MILLER
Contact: Directors Guild of America - Los Angeles,
213/289-2000

HEARTS OF FIRE Lorimar, 1988, w/Jennifer Alward &
Richard Marquand

MARVIN MILLER
MAN & BOY Levitt-Pickman, 1972

RON MILLER
MOON PILOT Buena Vista, 1962, AP
BON VOYAGE! Buena Vista, 1962, AP w/Bill Walsh
SON OF FLUBBER Buena Vista, 1963, AP w/Bill Walsh
SUMMER MAGIC Buena Vista, 1963, AP
THE MISADVENTURES OF MERLIN JONES Buena
Vista, 1964, AP
THE MONKEY'S UNCLE Buena Vista, 1965, CP
THAT DARN CAT! Buena Vista, 1965, CP w/Bill Walsh
LT. ROBIN CRUSOE, USN Buena Vista, 1966,
CP w/Bill Walsh
MONKEYS, GO HOME! Buena Vista, 1967, CP
NEVER A DULL MOMENT Buena Vista, 1968
THE BOATNIKS Buena Vista, 1970
THE WILD COUNTRY Buena Vista, 1971
NOW YOU SEE HIM, NOW YOU DON'T Buena
Vista, 1972
SNOWBALL EXPRESS Buena Vista, 1972
THE CASTAWAY COWBOY Buena Vista, 1974,
w/Winston Hibler
ESCAPE TO WITCH MOUNTAIN Buena Vista, 1975, EP
NO DEPOSIT, NO RETURN Buena Vista, 1976
RIDE A WILD PONY Buena Vista, 1976, EP
GUS Buena Vista, 1976
TREASURE OF MATECUMBE Buena Vista, 1976, EP
THE SHAGGY D.A. Buena Vista, 1976, EP
FREAKY FRIDAY Buena Vista, 1977
THE LITTLEST HORSE THIEVES ESCAPE FROM THE
DARK Buena Vista, 1977
THE RESCUERS (AF) Buena Vista, 1977, EP
HERBIE GOES TO MONTE CARLO Buena Vista, 1977
PETE'S DRAGON Buena Vista, 1977,
w/Jerome Courtland
THE CAT FROM OUTER SPACE Buena Vista, 1978
HOT LEAD AND COLD FEET Buena Vista, 1978
CANDLESHOE Buena Vista, 1978
RETURN FROM WITCH MOUNTAIN Buena Vista,
1978, w/Jerome Courtland
THE NORTH AVENUE IRREGULARS Buena Vista, 1979
THE APPLE DUMPLING GANG RIDES AGAIN
Buena Vista, 1979
UNIDENTIFIED FLYING ODDBALL Buena Vista, 1979
THE BLACK HOLE Buena Vista, 1979
MIDNIGHT MADNESS Buena Vista, 1980
THE LAST FLIGHT OF NOAH'S ARK Buena Vista, 1980
HERBIE GOES BANANAS Buena Vista, 1980
THE DEVIL AND MAX DEVLIN Buena Vista, 1981, EP
THE WATCHER IN THE WOODS Buena Vista, 1981
CONDORMAN Buena Vista, 1981, EP
THE FOX AND THE HOUND (AF) Buena Vista, 1981, EP
NIGHT CROSSING Buena Vista, 1982, EP

TRON Buena Vista, 1982, EP
TEX Buena Vista, 1982, EP
NEVER CRY WOLF Buena Vista, 1983, EP
THE BLACK CAULDRON (AF) Buena Vista, 1985, EP

STEPHEN MILLER
THE WEREWOLF OF WASHINGTON Diplomat, 1973, AP
HOG WILD Avco Embassy, 1980, EP w/Pierre David &
Victor Solnicki
MY BLOODY VALENTINE Paramount, 1981,
w/John Dunning & Andre Link

THOMAS L. MILLER
(credit w/Edward K. Milkis)
Business: Miller-Boyett Productions, 3970 Overland Av.,
TriStar Bldg., Suite 211, Culver City, CA 90232,
310/280-8700

SILVER STREAK 20th Century Fox, 1976
FOUL PLAY Paramount, 1978
THE BEST LITTLE WHOREHOUSE IN TEXAS Universal,
1982, w/Robert L. Boyett

ROSS E. MILLOY
ALAMO BAY TriStar, 1985, EP
1918 Cinecom, 1985, w/Lillian V. Foote
ON VALENTINE'S DAY Angelika, 1986, EP w/Lewis Allen,
Lindsay Law & Peter Newman
MISS FIRECRACKER Corsair, 1989, EP w/Lewis Allen
LORD OF THE FLIES Castle Rock/Columbia, 1990

PETER B. MILLS
THE FARMER Columbia, 1977, EP

GERALD MILTON
TWISTED JUSTICE Seymour Borde & Associates, 1990,
EP w/Arnie Lakeyn & S. Leigh Savidge

STEVE MINER
Business: 1137 Second St., Suite 103, Santa Monica, CA
90403, 310/393-0291
Agent: The Gersh Agency - Los Angeles, 310/274-6611

HERE COME THE TIGERS AIP, 1978,
w/Sean S. Cunningham
FRIDAY THE 13TH PART 2 Paramount, 1981
WARLOCK Trimark, 1991

MARVIN MINOFF
Business: Farrell-Minoff Productions, 14755 Ventura Blvd.,
Suite 203, Sherman Oaks, CA 91403, 818/789-5766;
Fax: 818/789-7459

DOMINICK AND EUGENE Orion, 1988, w/Mike Farrell

WILLIAM MINOT
(credit w/Howard L. Baldwin)

BILLY GALVIN Vestron, 1986, EP w/Stuart Benjamin &
Lindsay Law
FROM THE HIP DEG, 1987, EP w/Brian Russell

HOWARD G. MINSKY
LOVE STORY ★ Paramount, 1970

LEON MIRELL
WATERMELON MAN Columbia, 1970, EP
OUTSIDE IN Robbins International, 1972, EP

STACEY! New World, 1973
THE KILLING KIND Media Trend, 1974, EP

MARVIN MIRISCH
Business: The Mirisch Corporation, 100 Universal City
  Plaza, Universal City, CA 91608, 818/777-1271;
  Fax: 818/777-0668

DRACULA Universal, 1979, EP
ROMANTIC COMEDY MGM/UA, 1983, EP

WALTER MIRISCH
Business: The Mirisch Corporation, 100 Universal City
  Plaza, Universal City, CA 91608, 818/777-1271;
  Fax: 818/777-0668

FLAT TOP Allied Artists, 1952
THE ROSE BOWL STORY Monogram, 1952
WICHITA Allied Artists, 1955
AN ANNAPOLIS STORY Allied Artists, 1956
THE FIRST TEXAN Allied Artists, 1956
MAN OF THE WEST United Artists, 1958
THE MAGNIFICENT SEVEN United Artists, 1960
BY LOVE POSSESSED United Artists, 1961
TOYS IN THE ATTIC United Artists, 1962
TWO FOR THE SEESAW United Artists, 1962
HAWAII United Artists, 1966
IN THE HEAT OF THE NIGHT ★★ United Artists, 1967
FITZWILLY United Artists, 1968
SOME KIND OF NUT United Artists, 1969
SINFUL DAVEY United Artists, 1969, EP
HALLS OF ANGER United Artists, 1970, EP
THE HAWAIIANS United Artists, 1970
THEY CALL ME MISTER TIBBS United Artists, 1970, EP
THE ORGANIZATION United Artists, 1971
SCORPIO United Artists, 1973
MR. MAJESTYK United Artists, 1974
THE SPIKES GANG United Artists, 1974
MIDWAY Universal, 1976
GRAY LADY DOWN Universal, 1978
SAME TIME, NEXT YEAR Universal, 1978,
  w/Morton Gottlieb
DRACULA Universal, 1979
THE PRISONER OF ZENDA Universal, 1979
ROMANTIC COMEDY MGM/UA, 1983, w/Morton Gottlieb

ROBERT MISIOROWSKI
Business: Cinergi Productions, 2308 Broadway, Santa
  Monica, CA 90404, 310/315-6000; Fax: 310/828-0443

FOOD OF THE GODS II Concorde, 1989,
  EP w/Andras Hamori

RENEE MISSEL
(credit w/Howard Rosenman)
Business: 2174 Canyon Drive, Los Angeles, CA 90068,
  213/464-8560; Fax: 213/957-2060

THE MAIN EVENT Warner Bros., 1979, EP
RESURRECTION Universal, 1980

CHARLES MITCHELL
(credit w/Tom Kuhn)
Business: Lightyear Entertainment, 350 5th Ave.,
  Suite 5101, New York, NY 10118

HEAVEN (FD) Island Pictures, 1987,
  EP w/Arlyne Rothberg
ARIA Miramax, 1988, EP

THE RETURN OF SWAMP THING Miramax, 1989, EP
THE LEMON SISTERS Miramax, 1990,
  EP w/Arnold J. Holland

DAVID MITCHELL
(credit w/Damian Lee)
Business: Rose & Ruby Productions, Inc., 33 Howard St.,
  Toronto, M4X 1J6, 416/961-0555; Fax: 416/961-5575

BUSTED UP Shapiro Entertainment, 1987
WATCHERS Universal, 1988
FOOD OF THE GODS II Concorde, 1989

DOUG MITCHELL
(credit w/Terry Hayes)
Business: Kennedy Miller Productions, 30 Orwell St.,
  Kings Cross, Sydney, Australia

MAD MAX BEYOND THUNDERDOME Warner Bros.,
  1985, CP
DEAD CALM Warner Bros., 1989, w/George Miller

J. TERRANCE MITCHELL
Agent: The Agency - Los Angeles, 310/551-3000

GET ROLLIN' Aquarius, 1981

RON MITCHELL
Contact: Directors Guild of America - Los Angeles,
  213/289-2000

WITCHBOARD Cinema Group, 1987, SP

MORTON J. MITOSKY
AARON LOVES ANGELA Columbia, 1975, EP

YOSUKE MIZUNO
TOO MUCH Cannon, 1987, LP

ALEXANDRE MNOUCHKINE
(credit w/Georges Dancigers)

THAT MAN FROM RIO Lopert, 1964
LOVE IS A FUNNY THING United Artists, 1970
THE CROOK United Artists, 1971*
MONEY, MONEY, MONEY Cinerama, 1973, EP*
STAVISKY Cinemation, 1974, EP
TOUCH AND GO Libra, 1975
A PAIN IN THE A... Corwin-Mahler, 1975
ANOTHER MAN, ANOTHER CHANCE United Artists, 1977
DEAR DETECTIVE DEAR INSPECTOR Cinema 5, 1978
JUPITER'S THIGH Quartet, 1981
LA BALANCE Spectrafilm, 1983
THE NAME OF THE ROSE 20th Century Fox, 1986,
  CP w/Franco Cristaldi*

MICHAEL MODER
Business: Viacom Productions, 10 Universal City Plaza,
  Universal City, CA 91608, 818/505-7500
Contact: Directors Guild of America - Los Angeles,
  213/289-2000

JEREMIAH JOHNSON Warner Bros., 1972, AP
MIXED COMPANY United Artists, 1974, AP
THEY ALL LAUGHED United Artists Classics, 1982, EP
SUMMER LOVERS Filmways, 1982
SONGWRITER TriStar, 1984, EP
BEVERLY HILLS COP Paramount, 1984, EP

Mo

FILM
PRODUCERS,
STUDIOS,
AGENTS AND
CASTING
DIRECTORS
GUIDE

F
I
L
M

P
R
O
D
U
C
E
R
S

Mo

FILM
PRODUCERS,
STUDIOS,
AGENTS AND
CASTING
DIRECTORS
GUIDE

F
I
L
M

P
R
O
D
U
C
E
R
S

LEONARD MOGEL
HEAVY METAL (AF)   Columbia, 1981, EP

GERALD R. MOLEN
Business: Amblin Entertainment, Universal Studios,
   100 Universal Plaza, Bungalow 477, Universal City,
   CA 91608, 818/777-4600
Contact: Directors Guild of America - Los Angeles,
   213/289-2000

BATTERIES NOT INCLUDED   Universal, 1987, AP
RAIN MAN ★★   MGM/UA, 1988, CP
BRIGHT LIGHTS, BIG CITY   MGM/UA, 1988, EP
DAYS OF THUNDER   Paramount, 1990, EP
ONE CUP OF COFFEE   Miramax, 1991, CP
HOOK   TriStar, 1991, w/Kathleen Kennedy &
   Frank Marshall

RON MOLER
Business: UMP & Associates, Raleigh Studios,
   5300 Melrose Ave., Suite 411-E, Hollywood, CA
   90038 213/960-4580

BACHELOR PARTY   20th Century Fox, 1984,
   w/Robert Israel
I LOVE YOU TO DEATH   TriStar, 1990, w/Jeffrey Lurie

MARIANNE MOLONEY
CLARA'S HEART   Warner Bros., 1988, EP

PAUL MONASH
Business: Red Bank Films, Inc., 415 N. Crescent Dr.,
   Suite 300, Beverly Hills, CA 90210, 310/859-3374
Contact: Directors Guild of America - Los Angeles,
   213/289-2000

BUTCH CASSIDY AND THE SUNDANCE KID ★
   20th Century Fox, 1969, EP
SLAUGHTERHOUSE FIVE   Universal, 1972
THE FRIENDS OF EDDIE COYLE   Paramount, 1973
THE FRONT PAGE   Universal, 1974
CARRIE   United Artists, 1976
BIG TROUBLE IN LITTLE CHINA   20th Century Fox,
   1986, EP w/Keith Barish

E. C. MONELL
HIGHLANDER   20th Century Fox, 1986, EP

JUDITH MONTELL
FOREVER ACTIVISTS (FD)   Tara Releasing, 1991

MONTY MONTGOMERY
(credit w/Steven Golin & Sigurjon Sighvatsson)
Business: Propaganda Films, 940 N. Mansfield Ave.,
   Los Angeles, CA 90038, 213/462-6400

DADDY'S DYIN'...WHO'S GOT THE WILL?
   MGM/UA, 1990
WILD AT HEART   Samuel Goldwyn Company, 1990

PATRICK MONTGOMERY
Business: Archive Film Productions, 530 W. 25th St.,
   New York, NY 10001, 212/620-3955

THE COMPLEAT BEATLES (FD)   TeleCulture, 1984,
   w/Stephanie Bennett

EDWARD L. MONTORO
DAY OF THE ANIMALS   Film Ventures International, 1977
THE DARK   Film Ventures International, 1979,
   w/Dick Clark

HANK MOONJEAN
Contact: Directors Guild of America - Los Angeles,
   213/289-2000

THE SECRET LIFE OF AN AMERICAN WIFE   20th Century
   Fox, 1968, AP
WUSA   Paramount, 1970, AP
CHILD'S PLAY   Paramount, 1972, AP
THE GREAT GATSBY   Paramount, 1974, AP
THE FORTUNE   Columbia, 1975, EP
THE END   United Artists, 1978, EP
HOOPER   Warner Bros., 1978
SMOKEY AND THE BANDIT PART II   Universal, 1980
THE INCREDIBLE SHRINKING WOMAN   Universal, 1981
PATERNITY   Paramount, 1981, w/Lawrence Gordon
SHARKY'S MACHINE   Orion/Warner Bros., 1981
STROKER ACE   Universal, 1983
STEALING HOME   Warner Bros., 1988, w/Thom Mount
DANGEROUS LIAISONS ★   Warner Bros., 1988,
   w/Norma Heyman

MICHAEL MOORCOCK
THE LAST DAYS OF MAN ON EARTH   *THE FINAL
   PROGRAMME*   New World, 1974, EP w/Roy Baird &
   David Puttnam

ALVY MOORE
THE BROTHERHOOD OF SATAN   Columbia, 1971,
   w/L.Q. Jones
A BOY AND HIS DOG   LQJaf, 1975

DEBORAH MOORE
Business: New Line Productions, 116 N. Robertson Blvd.,
   Los Angeles, CA 90048, 310/854-5811

LUCKY STIFF   New Line, 1988, LP

DEMI MOORE
Business: Rufglen Films, c/o TriStar, 1453 Third St. #420,
   Santa Monica, CA 90401, 310/576-0577;
   Fax: 310/576-0527

MORTAL THOUGHTS   Columbia, 1991, CP

DUDLEY MOORE
Agent: ICM - Los Angeles, 310/550-4000

ARTHUR 2 ON THE ROCKS   Warner Bros., 1988, EP

MICHAEL MOORE
ROGER & ME (FD)   Warner Bros., 1989

TERRY MOORE
Contact: Screen Actors Guild - Los Angeles, 213/465-4600

BEVERLY HILLS BRATS   Taurus, 1989, w/Jerry Rivers

TIM MOORE
Business: Perry Penguin Pictures, 818/848-1800;
   Fax: 818/841-6500

ROADHOUSE   United Artists, 1989, EP w/Steve Perry

Mo

FILM
PRODUCERS,
STUDIOS,
AGENTS AND
CASTING
DIRECTORS
GUIDE

ADAM MOOS
GUILTY AS CHARGED   I.R.S., 1991, CP

PHILIPPE MORA
Agent: The Marion Rosenberg Office - Los Angeles,
   213/653-7383
Contact: Directors Guild of America - Los Angeles,
   213/289-2000

HOWLING III: THE MARSUPIALS   Square Pictures,
   1987, w/Charles Waterstreet
COMMUNION   New Line, 1989, w/Dan Allingham &
   Whitley Strieber

JACQUES MORALI
CAN'T STOP THE MUSIC   AFD, 1980, w/Henri Belolo &
   Allan Carr

FRANK MORENO
SWITCHBLADE SISTERS   Centaur, 1975,
   EP w/Jeff Begun

GEORGE MORFOGEN
THEY ALL LAUGHED   United Artists Classics, 1982,
   w/Blaine Novak
ILLEGALLY YOURS   DEG, 1988

ANDRE MORGAN
(credit w/Al Ruddy)
Business: Ruddy-Morgan Productions, 9300 Wilshire Blvd.,
   #508, Beverly Hills, CA 90212, 310/271-7698;
   Fax: 310/278-9978

THE AMSTERDAM KILL   Columbia, 1978*
THE BOYS IN COMPANY C   Columbia, 1978*
LASSITER   Warner Bros., 1984, EP w/Raymond Chow
FAREWELL TO THE KING   Orion, 1989
SPEED ZONE   Orion, 1989, EP
IMPULSE   Warner Bros., 1990

LESLIE MORGAN
A SHOCK TO THE SYSTEM   Corsair, 1990, EP

PETER MORGAN
Business: MG Entertainment, c/o New Line Cinema,
   116 N. Robertson Blvd., #401, Los Angeles, CA 90048,
   818/891-6325

POISON IVY   New Line, 1992, EP w/Melissa Goddard

SEYMOUR MORGENSTERN
TOO MUCH SUN   New Line, 1990, EP w/Paul
   Hertzberg & Al Schwartz

LOU MORHEIM
THE HUNTING PARTY   United Artists, 1971

TSUNEYUKI MORISHIMA
SOLAR CRISIS   NHK, 1990, w/James Nelson

ERROL MORRIS
Agent: CAA - Beverly Hills, 310/288-4545

THE GATES OF HEAVEN (FD)   1978
VERNON, FLORIDA (FD)   1981

REDMOND MORRIS
THE MIRACLE   Miramax, 1991, w/Stephen Woolley

RICHARD MORRIS-ADAMS
CARAVAN TO VACCARES   Bryanston, 1976,
   w/Geoffrey Reeve

**GLORIA BARTHOLOMEW
MORRISON**
Business: Unistar International Pictures, 6363 Sunset Blvd.,
   #930C, Los Angeles, CA 90028, 213/462-7991;
   Fax: 213/462-3752

MIDNIGHT   SVS Films, 1989, w/Norman Thaddeus Vane

PATRICIA MORRISON
THE INDIAN RUNNER   1991, CP

STEVE MORRISON
Business: Granada, 36 Golden Square, London W1R 4AH
   England, 071/734-8080; Fax: 071/494-6360

WONDERLAND   Vestron, 1988
MY LEFT FOOT ★   Miramax, 1989, EP w/Paul Heller
THE FIELD   Avenue Pictures, 1990, EP

TERRY MORSE
RETURN OF A MAN CALLED HORSE   United
   Artists, 1976
SKY RIDERS   20th Century Fox, 1976
TEENAGE MUTANT NINJA TURTLES II: THE SECRET
   OF THE OOZE   New Line, 1991, CP

FULVIO MORSELLA
DUCK, YOU SUCKER!   United Artists, 1972
MY NAME IS NOBODY   Universal, 1974, EP

GARY MORTON
Contact: Screen Actors Guild - Los Angeles, 213/465-4600

ALL THE RIGHT MOVES   20th Century Fox, 1983, EP

LAWRENCE MORTORFF
(formerly Lawrence Taylor-Mortorff)
Business: International Sales Organization, 10880 Wilshire
   Blvd., Suite 1000, Los Angeles, CA 90024, 310/470-0804

MARIA'S LOVERS   Cannon, 1984, w/Bosko Djordjevic
HE'S MY GIRL   Scotti Bros., 1987,
   w/Angela P. Schapiro
LADY BEWARE   Scotti Bros., 1987, w/Tony Scotti
ROMERO   Four Seasons Entertainment, 1989,
   EP w/John Sacret Young

SANDRA MOSBACHER
IN A SHALLOW GRAVE   Skouras Pictures, 1988, CP

BEN MOSES
Agent: Writers & Artists Agency - Los Angeles,
   310/820-2240
Contact: Directors Guild of America - Los Angeles,
   213/289-2000

GOOD MORNING, VIETNAM   Buena Vista, 1987,
   CP w/Harry Benn

FILM
PRODUCERS,
STUDIOS,
AGENTS AND
CASTING
DIRECTORS
GUIDE

WALTER MOSHAY
THE NEW ADVENTURES OF PIPPI LONGSTOCKING
  Columbia, 1988, w/Gary Mehlman

LAURA MOSKOWITZ
CHILD'S PLAY 2   Universal, 1990, CP
CHILD'S PLAY 3   Universal, 1991, w/Robert Latham
  Brown & David Kirschner

CHARLES B. MOSS, JR.
LET'S SCARE JESSICA TO DEATH   Paramount, 1971

HAJNA O. MOSS
DEF BY TEMPTATION   Troma, 1990,
  CP w/Kervin Simms

JERRY MOSS
Business: A & M Films, 1416 La Brea Ave., Hollywood,
  CA 90028, 213/469-2411

JOE COCKER/MAD DOGS AND ENGLISHMEN (FD)
  MGM, 1971, EP

THOM MOUNT
Business: The Mount Co., 3723 W. Olive Ave., Burbank,
  CA 91505, 818/846-1500; Fax: 818/846-7059

PIRATES   Cannon, 1986, EP w/Mark Lombardo
CAN'T BUY ME LOVE   Buena Vista, 1987
STEALING HOME   Warner Bros., 1988,
  w/Hank Moonjean
BULL DURHAM   Orion, 1988, w/Mark Burg
TEQUILA SUNRISE   Warner Bros., 1988
FRANTIC   Warner Bros., 1988, w/Tim Hampton
FRANKENSTEIN UNBOUND   20th Century Fox, 1990,
  w/Roger Corman & Kabi Jaeger
THE INDIAN RUNNER   1991, EP w/Stephon K.
  Bannon & Mark Bisgeier

P. GAEL MOURANT
MILLENNIUM   20th Century Fox, 1989, EP w/Freddie
  Fields, John Foreman & Louis M. Silverstein

CAROLINE MOURIS
BEGINNERS LUCK   New World, 1986

JEFFREY A. MUELLER
(credit w/Andrew Licht)
Business: Licht-Mueller Film Corporation, 2121 Avenue
  of the Stars, Suite 2900, Los Angeles, CA 90067,
  310/551-2262; Fax: 310/556-3760

LICENSE TO DRIVE   20th Century Fox, 1988
LITTLE MONSTERS   MGM/UA, 1989,
  w/John A. Davis

EDWARD MUHL
THE LOST MAN   Universal, 1969, w/Melville Tucker

LEE MUHL
HEARTBREAKERS   Orion, 1985, EP w/Harry Cooper &
  Joseph Franck
THE HIDDEN   New Line, 1987, EP w/Stephen Diener,
  Dennis Harris & Jeffrey Klein

MARTIN MULL
Agent: APA - Los Angeles, CA 90069,
  310/273-0744
Contact: Writers Guild of America - Los Angeles,
  310/550-1000

RENTED LIPS   Cine World Enterprises, 1988,
  w/Mort Engleberg

ROBERT MULLIGAN
Business: Boardwalk Productions, 5150 WilshireBlvd.,
  Suite 505, Los Angeles, CA 90036, 213/938-0109
Agent: UTA - Beverly Hills, 310/273-6700

THE OTHER   20th Century Fox, 1972
THE NICKEL RIDE   20th Century Fox, 1974
KISS ME GOODBYE   20th Century Fox, 1982

CHARLES B. MULVEHILL
Contact: Directors Guild of America - Los Angeles,
  213/289-2000

HAROLD AND MAUDE   Paramount, 1971,
  w/Colin Higgins
THE LAST DETAIL   Columbia, 1973, AP
BOUND FOR GLORY   United Artists, 1976, AP
BEING THERE   United Artists, 1979, AP
THE POSTMAN ALWAYS RINGS TWICE   Paramount,
  1981, w/Bob Rafelson
FRANCES   Universal, 1982, AP
SWING SHIFT   Warner Bros., 1984, AP
SWEET DREAMS   TriStar, 1985, CP
CREATOR   Universal, 1985, AP
EIGHT MILLION WAYS TO DIE   TriStar,
  1986, CP
THE MILAGRO BEANFIELD WAR   Universal,
  1988, CP
IN COUNTRY   Warner Bros., 1989, EP
THE GODFATHER PART III ★   Paramount, 1990,
  CP w/Gray Frederickson & Fred Roos
FRANKIE AND JOHNNY   Paramount, 1991,
  EP w/Alex Rose

ROBERT L. MUNGER
BORN AGAIN   Avco Embassy, 1978, EP

MICHAEL S. MURPHEY
(credit w/Joel Soisson)
Business: Soisson Murphey Productions, 9060 Santa
  Monica Blvd., Suite 210, Los Angeles, CA 90069,
  310/273-3157; Fax: 310/271-5581

HAMBONE & HILLIE   New World, 1984, AP
THE BOYS NEXT DOOR   New World, 1985, AP
AVENGING ANGEL   New World, 1985, AP
A NIGHTMARE ON ELM STREET, PART 2: FREDDY'S
  REVENGE   New Line, 1985, LP
KGB: THE SECRET WAR   Cinema Group,
  1986, AP
TRICK OR TREAT   DEG, 1986
THE SUPERNATURALS   Republic Entertainment, 1987
BILL & TED'S EXCELLENT ADVENTURE   Orion,
  1989, w/Scott Kroopf
MODERN LOVE   Triumph, 1990, EP
BLUE DESERT   Neo Films, 1991, EP

DENNIS MURPHY
Agent: Shapiro/Lichtman Talent Agency - Los Angeles,
    310/859-8877
Contact: Directors Guild of America - Los Angeles,
    213/289-2000

CHEERLEADERS' BEACH PARTY   Cannon, 1978,
    w/Alex E. Goitein
FRIDAY THE 13TH PART 2   Paramount, 1981, CP
MY BEST FRIEND IS A VAMPIRE   Kings Road, 1988
BLIND FURY   TriStar, 1990, AP

EDDIE MURPHY
Business: Paramount Pictures, 5555 Melrose Ave., Los
    Angeles, CA 90038, 213/956-4545; Fax: 213/956-8602
Agent: ICM - Los Angeles, 310/550-4000
Contact: Writers Guild of America - Los Angeles
    310/550-1000

EDDIE MURPHY RAW   Paramount, 1987,
    EP w/Richard Tienken
HARLEM NIGHTS   Paramount, 1989, EP

KAREN MURPHY
Business: Interscope Communications, 10900 Wilshire
    Blvd., Suite 1400, Los Angeles, CA 90024,
    310/208-8525; Fax: 310/208-1764

THIS IS SPINAL TAP   Embassy, 1984
TRUE STORIES   Warner Bros., 1986, CP
DRUGSTORE COWBOY   Avenue Pictures, 1989,
    w/Nick Wechsler
THE CUTTING EDGE   MGM, 1991, w/Robert Cort &
    Dean O'Brien

MICHAEL TIMOTHY MURPHY
Business: Davis-Panzer Productions, 1438 N. Gower St.,
    Suite 401, Los Angeles, CA 90028, 213/463-2343

ROSELAND   Cinema Shares International, 1977,
    EP w/Ottomar Rudolf
ST. HELENS   Parnell, 1981
O'HARA'S WIFE   Enfield, 1984, EP

ROGER MURPHY
TOGETHER (FD)   Hallmark, 1971,
    w/Sean S. Cunningham

BILL MURRAY
Agent: CAA - Beverly Hills, 310/288-4545
Contact: Writers Guild of America - New York,
    212/245-6180

QUICK CHANGE   Warner Bros., 1990,
    w/Robert Greenhut

DON MURRAY
Agenr: Camden Artists - Los Angeles, 213/556-2022

ANNIE'S COMING OUT   Film Australia, 1984
A TEST OF LOVE   Universal, 1985

FORREST MURRAY
Contact: Directors Guild of America - New York,
    212/581-0370

FIVE CORNERS   Cineplex Odeon, 1988, w/Tony Bill

RICK MURRAY
CRACKING UP   AIP, 1977, w/C.D. Taylor

TOM MUSCA
Agent: ICM - Los Angeles, 310/550-4000
Contact: Writers Guild of America - Los Angeles,
    310/550-1000

STAND AND DELIVER   Warner Bros., 1988

MICHAEL MUSCAL
BRIDE OF RE-ANIMATOR   50th St. Films, 1991, CP

JOHN MUSKER
THE LITTLE MERMAID (AF)   Buena Vista, 1989,
    w/Howard Ashman

FLOYD MUTRUX
Agent: William Morris Agency - Beverly Hills, 310/274-7451
Contact: Directors Guild of America - Los Angeles,
    213/289-2000

THE CHRISTIAN LICORICE STORE   National General,
    1971, w/Michael S. Laughlin
FREEBIE & THE BEAN   Warner Bros., 1974, EP
DICK TRACY   Buena Vista, 1990, EP w/Art Linson &
    Barrie M. Osborne

NANCYLEE MYATT
little secrets   1991, w/Mark Sobel

LAWRENCE MYERS
THE GREEK TYCOON   Universal, 1978,
    CP w/Nico Mastorakis

LYNDA MYLES
Business: British Broadcasting Corporation, Woodlands,
    80 Wood Lane, London W12 7RJ, 081/576-7014
Contact: Pandora Productions, 83 Highbury Hill,
    London N5 1SX England

DEFENSE OF THE REALM   Hemdale, 1987,
    w/Robin Douet

BEN MYRON
Business: Lightmotive Inc., 662 N. Robertson Blvd., Los
    Angeles, CA 90069, 310/659-6200; Fax: 310/659-6688

SIGNAL 7   One Pass Pictures, 1986, w/Don Taylor
CHECKING OUT   Warner Bros., 1989
ONE FALSE MOVE   1991

My

FILM
PRODUCERS,
STUDIOS,
AGENTS AND
CASTING
DIRECTORS
GUIDE

F
I
L
M

P
R
O
D
U
C
E
R
S

Na

FILM
PRODUCERS,
STUDIOS,
AGENTS AND
CASTING
DIRECTORS
GUIDE

F
I
L
M

P
R
O
D
U
C
E
R
S

N

JOSEPH T. NAAR
BLACULA   AIP, 1972
SCREAM, BLACULA, SCREAM!   AIP, 1973
THE ALL-AMERICAN BOY   Warner Bros., 1973,
   w/Saul Krugman

DIANE NABATOFF
Business: Fair Dinkum Prods., 5555 Melrose Ave., Los
   Angeles, CA 90038, 213/956-5700; Fax: 213/956-8593

HIDER IN THE HOUSE   Vestron, 1989,
   EP w/Steven Reuther

JEAN NACHBAUR
Business: Kaufman & Nachbaur, 100 Merrick Rd.,
   Rockville Centre, NY, 516/536-5760

IMPROMPTU   Hemdale, 1991, EP

MIRA NAIR
Business: Mirabai Films, 6 Rivington St., New York, NY
   10002, 212/254-7826

SALAAM BOMBAY!   Cinecom, 1988

STEVEN NALEVANSKY
Business: Paramount Television, 5555 Melrose Ave.,
   Los Angeles, CA 90038, 213/956-5519

BLOOD BEACH   Jerry Gross Organization, 1981

FRANK DARIUS NAMEI
(credit w/Robert Resnikoff)
Business: Paramount Pictures, 5555 Melrose Ave.,
   Los Angeles, CA 90038, 213/956-4302
Agent: BBMW - Los Angeles, 310/247-5500

COLLISION COURSE   DEG, 1988, CP

HERBERT S. NANAS
Business: Moress-Nanas-Golden Entertainment,
   12424 Wilshire Blvd., #840, Los Angeles, CA
   90025, 310/820-9897; Fax: 310/820-7375

ROCKY III   MGM/UA, 1982, EP
FIRST BLOOD   Orion, 1982, CP
LOST IN AMERICA   Warner Bros., 1985, EP
EYE OF THE TIGER   Scotti Bros., 1986,
   EP w/Ben Scotti
DEFENDING YOUR LIFE   Geffen/Warner Bros.,
   1991, EP

MICHAEL NANKIN
Agent: ICM - Los Angeles, 310/550-4000
Contact: Writers Guild of America - Los Angeles,
   310/550-1000

MIDNIGHT MADNESS   Buena Vista, 1980,
   CP w/David Wechter

GARY NARDINO
Business: Gary Nardino Productions, c/o Lorimar TV,
   300 Lorimar Plaza, Producers Bldg. 8, #109, Burbank,
   CA 91505, 818/954-4535

STAR TREK III: THE SEARCH FOR SPOCK   Paramount,
   1984, EP
FIRE WITH FIRE   Paramount, 1986

JOHN NARTMANN
HARD COUNTRY   AFD, 1981, CP

MARCIA NASATIR
Business: The Haft-Nasatir Company, c/o 20th Century Fox,
   P.O. Box 900, Beverly Hills, CA 90213, 310/203-2974,
   Fax: 310/788-9753

THE BIG CHILL ★   Columbia, 1983,
   EP w/Lawrence Kasdan
IRONWEED   TriStar, 1987, w/Keith Barish
HAMBURGER HILL   Paramount, 1987,
   w/Jim Carabatsos

JULES R. NASSO
Business: Steamroller Productions, Warner Brothers, 4000
   Warner Blvd., Burbank, CA 91522, 818/954-4267;
   Fax; 818/954-4128

OUT FOR JUSTICE   Warner Bros., 1991, EP

RICK NATHANSON
THE ARROGANT   Cannon, 1987, LP
HALLOWEEN 5: THE REVENGE OF MICHAEL MYERS
   Galaxy, 1989, LP

CHRISTOPHER NEAME
Agent: Hutton Management, 200 Fulham Road, London
   SW10 9PN England, 071/352-4825; Fax: 071/351-4560

THE BEAST IN THE CELLAR   Cannon, 1971, AP
FOREIGN BODY   Orion, 1986, EP
BELLMAN AND TRUE   Island Pictures, 1987,
   w/Michael Wearing

CHRIS D. NEBE
THE NAKED CAGE   Cannon, 1986

GARY A. NEILL
BAT 21   TriStar, 1988, w/Michael Balson & David Fisher

CHRISTOPHER NELSON
Contact: Directors Guild of America - Los Angeles,
   213/289-2000

FRATERNITY VACATION   New World, 1985, w/Boris
   Malden & Robert C. Peters

JAMES NELSON
Contact: Directors Guild of America - Los Angeles,
   213/289-2000

BORDERLINE   AFD, 1980
SOLAR CRISIS   NHK, 1990, w/Tsuneyuki Morishima

JEFFREY NELSON
LIANNA   United Artists Classics, 1983, w/Maggie Renzi

Ne

FILM
PRODUCERS,
STUDIOS,
AGENTS AND
CASTING
DIRECTORS
GUIDE

F
I
L
M

P
R
O
D
U
C
E
R
S

PETER NELSON
Agent: APA - Los Angeles, 310/273-0744

SMORGASBORD   Warner Bros., 1985, w/Arnold Orgolini

PETER NELSON
Contact: Writers Guild of America - Los Angeles,
310/550-1000

THE LONELY PASSION OF JUDITH HEARNE   Island
Pictures, 1987, w/Richard Johnson

PETER ENGLISH NELSON
SUPERSTAR (FD)   Marilyn Lewis Entertainment Ltd.,
1990, EP w/Marilyn Lewis

TERRY NELSON
Business: Having Had Productions, Universal Pictures,
100 Universal City Plaza, Bldg. 507, #2E, Universal
City, CA 91608, 818/777-1128; Fax: 818/777-6481
Contact: Directors Guild of America - Los Angeles,
213/289-2000

PART 2, SOUNDER   Gamma III, 1976
MELVIN AND HOWARD   Universal, 1980, AP
RAGGEDY MAN   Universal, 1981, AP
MISSING ★   Universal, 1982, AP
CROSS CREEK   Universal, 1983, CP
GHOST DAD   Universal, 1990

WILLIE NELSON
Agent: ICM - Los Angeles, 310/550-4000

RED HEADED STRANGER   Alive Films, 1986,
w/William D. Wittliff

LAWRENCE NESIS
CITY ON FIRE   Avco Embassy, 1979, AP
MEATBALLS   Paramount, 1979, AP
HEAVY METAL (AF)   Columbia, 1981,
AP w/Michael Gross
MY BLOODY VALENTINE   Paramount, 1981, AP
ATLANTIC CITY ★   Paramount, 1981, AP
HAPPY BIRTHDAY TO ME   Columbia, 1981, AP
VIDEODROME   Universal, 1983, AP
COVERGIRL   Paramount, 1979, AP
MEATBALLS III   Moviestore, 1986, EP w/Andre Link
BUSTED UP   Shapiro Entertainment, 1987, EP

MICHAEL NESMITH
Business: Pacific Arts, 11858 LaGrange Av., Los Angeles,
CA 90025, 310/820-0991; Fax: 310/826-4779
Agent: William Morris Agency - Beverly Hills, 310/274-7451

TIMERIDER: THE ADVENTURE OF LYLE SWANN
Jensen Farley, 1983, EP
REPO MAN   Universal, 1984, EP
TAPEHEADS   Avenue Pictures, 1988, EP

AMY NESS
STATIC   MCEG, 1988

STEPHEN J. NETBURN
Contact: Directors Guild of America - Los Angeles,
213/289-2000

TERROR IN THE AISLES   Universal, 1984,
w/Andrew J. Kuehn

GEOFFREY NETHERCOTT
MERRY CHRISTMAS, MR. LAWRENCE   Universal, 1983,
EP w/Terry Glinwood, Masato Hara & Eiko Oshima

DOUGLAS NETTER
MR. RICCO   United Artists, 1975
THE WILD GEESE   Allied Artists, 1978, CP

GIL NETTER
Contact: Zucker Brothers Productions, 11777 San Vicente
Blvd., #640, Los Angeles, CA 90049, 310/826-1333;
Fax: 310/826-3493

THE NAKED GUN 2 1/2: THE SMELL OF FEAR
Paramount, 1991, EP w/Jerry Zucker & Jim Abrahams

MACE NEUFELD
Business: Neufeld/Rehme Productions, Paramount Pictures,
5555 Melrose Ave., Dressing #112, Los Angeles, CA
90038, 213/956-4816; Fax: 213/956-2571

THE OMEN   20th Century Fox, 1976, EP
THE FRISCO KID   Warner Bros., 1979
THE FUNHOUSE   Universal, 1981, EP w/Mark Lester
THE FINAL CONFLICT   20th Century Fox, 1981, AP
THE AVIATOR   MGM/UA, 1985, w/Thomas H. Brodek
TRANSYLVANIA 6-5000   New World, 1985,
w/Thomas H. Brodek
NO WAY OUT   Orion, 1987, EP
THE HUNT FOR RED OCTOBER   Paramount, 1990
FLIGHT OF THE INTRUDER   Paramount, 1991
NECESSARY ROUGHNESS   Paramount, 1991,
w/Robert Rehme

EDWARD NEUMEIER
Agent: UTA - Beverly Hills, 310/273-6700
Contact: Writers Guild of America - Los Angeles,
310/550-1000

ROBOCOP   Orion, 1987, CP

PAUL NEWMAN
Agent: CAA - Beverly Hills, 310/288-4545
Contact: Directors Guild of America - Los Angeles,
213/289-2000

RACHEL, RACHEL ★   Warner Bros., 1968
WUSA   Paramount, 1970, w/John Foreman
THEY MIGHT BE GIANTS   Universal, 1971,
w/John Foreman
THE EFFECT OF GAMMA RAYS ON MAN-IN-THE- MOON
MARIGOLDS   20th Century Fox, 1972
HARRY AND SON   Orion, 1984, w/Ronald L. Buck

PETER NEWMAN
Business: Peter Newman Productions, 1500 Broadway
#2011, New York, NY 10036, 212/221-2400;
Fax: 212/221-2415

COME BACK TO THE 5 & DIME JIMMY DEAN,
JIMMY DEAN   Cinecom, 1982, AP
1918   Cinecom, 1985, EP w/Lewis Allen
ON VALENTINE'S DAY   Angelika, 1986, EP w/Lewis Allen,
Lindsay Law & Ross E. Milloy
SWIMMING TO CAMBODIA   Cinecom, 1987, EP w/Lewis
Allen, Ira Deutchman & Amir J. Malin
END OF THE LINE   Orion Classics, 1987, w/Lewis Allen
O. C. AND STIGGS   MGM, 1987, w/Robert Altman
LORD OF THE FLIES   Castle Rock/Columbia, 1990,
w/Lewis Allen

Ne

FILM
PRODUCERS,
STUDIOS,
AGENTS AND
CASTING
DIRECTORS
GUIDE

F
I
L
M

P
R
O
D
U
C
E
R
S

ROBERT NEWMYER

Business: Outlaw Productions, 12103 Maxwellton Rd.,
   Studio City, CA 91604, 818/509-7953; Fax: 818/506-0983

sex, lies & videotape   Miramax, 1989, w/John Hardy
DON'T TELL MOM THE BABYSITTER'S DEAD   Warner
   Bros., 1991, w/Brian Reilly & Jeffrey Silver

MIKE NICHOLS

Attorney: Marvin B. Meyer, Rosenfeld, Meyer & Susman,
   Beverly Hills, CA, 310/858-7700
Agent: Sam Cohn, ICM - New York, 212/556-5600

CARNAL KNOWLEDGE   Avco Embassy, 1971
THE FORTUNE   Columbia, 1975, w/Don Devlin
SILKWOOD   20th Century Fox, 1983,
   w/Michael Hausman
HEARTBURN   Paramount, 1986, w/Robert Greenhut
THE LONGSHOT   Orion, 1986, EP
POSTCARDS FROM THE EDGE   Columbia, 1990,
   w/John Calley
REGARDING HENRY   Paramount, 1991, w/Scott Rudin

JACK NICHOLSON

Business Manager: Guild Management Corporation,
   Los Angeles, 310/277-9711
Agent: Sandy Bresler, Bresler, Kelly & Kipperman -
   Encino, 818/905-3210

RIDE IN THE WHIRLWIND   Favorite/Jack H. Harris,
   1966, w/Monte Hellman
THE SHOOTING   Favorite/Jack H. Harris, 1966,
   w/Monte Hellman
HEAD   Columbia, 1968, w/Bob Rafelson
DRIVE, HE SAID   Columbia, 1971, w/Steve Blauner

WALLIS NICITA

(credit w/Lauren Lloyd)
Business: Nicita-Lloyd Productions, Paramount Pictures,
   5555 Melrose Ave., Los Angeles, CA 90035,
   213/956-8514; Fax: 213/956-2007

MERMAIDS   Orion, 1990, w/Patrick Palmer
FIRES WITHIN   Pathe, 1990

DAVID A. NICKSAY

Business: Morgan Creek Productions, 1875 Century Park
   East, Suite 200, Los Angeles, CA 90067, 310/284-8884;
   Fax: 310/282-8794

I'M DANCING AS FAST AS I CAN   Paramount, 1982, AP
MRS. SOFFEL   MGM/UA, 1984, w/Scott Rudin &
   Edgar J. Scherick
LUCAS   20th Century Fox, 1986
YOUNG GUNS II   20th Century Fox, 1990, EP w/Gary
   Barber, John Fusco, James G. Robinson & Joe Roth
PACIFIC HEIGHTS   20th Century Fox, 1990,
   EP w/Gary Barber, James G. Robinson & Joe Roth
ROBIN HOOD: PRINCE OF THIEVES   Warner Bros.,
   1991, EP w/Gary Barber & James G. Robinson
FREEJACK   Warner Bros., 1991, EP w/Gary Barber &
   James G. Robinson

STEVE NICOLAIDES

(credit w/Jeffrey Stott)
Business: Castle Rock Entertainment, 335 N. Maple Dr.,
   Suite 135, Beverly Hills, CA 90210, 310/285-2300
Contact: Directors Guild of America - Los Angeles,
   213/289-2000

THE PRINCESS BRIDE   20th Century Fox, 1987, AP
IT TAKES TWO   United Artists, 1988, EP*
WHEN HARRY MET SALLY...   Castle Rock/Columbia,
   1989, CP
MISERY   Castle Rock/Columbia, 1990, CP
BOYZ IN THE HOOD   Columbia, 1991*

JOHN NICOLELLA

Agent: William Morris Agency - Beverly Hills, 310/274-7451
Contact: Directors Guild of America - Los Angeles,
   213/289-2000

LAST EMBRACE   United Artists, 1979, AP
WINDOWS   United Artists, 1980, AP
TIMES SQUARE   AFD, 1980, EP w/Kevin McCormick
THE FAN   Paramount, 1981, AP w/Bill Oakes
EASY MONEY   Orion, 1983
A RAGE IN HARLEM   Miramax, 1991,
   CP w/Forest Whitaker

ROB NILSSON

Business: Snowball Productions, 415/567-4404
Agent: Sanford-Skouras-Gross - Los Angeles, 310/208-2100

NORTHERN LIGHTS   Cine Manifest, 1979,
   w/John Hanson
ON THE EDGE   Skouras Pictures, 1986, w/Jeffrey Hayes

LEONARD NIMOY

Business: Rumbleseat Productions, c/o Walt Disney Studios,
   500 S. Buena Vista St., Burbank, CA 91521-0001,
   818/560-7010; Fax: 818/843-5714

STAR TREK VI: THE UNDISCOVERED COUNTRY
   Paramount, 1991, EP

DAVID NIVEN, JR.

THE EAGLE HAS LANDED   Columbia, 1977,
   w/Jack Winer
ESCAPE TO ATHENA   AFD, 1979, w/Jack Winer
MONSIGNOR   20th Century Fox, 1982, w/Frank Yablans
BETTER LATE THAN NEVER   Warner Bros., 1983,
   w/Jack Haley, Jr.
KIDCO   20th Century Fox, 1984, w/Frank Yablans
THAT'S DANCING (FD)   MGM, 1985, w/Jack Haley Jr.

ROBERT NIXON

Agent: William Morris Agency - Beverly Hills, 310/274-7451
Contact: Directors Guild of America - Los Angeles,
   213/289-2000

GORILLAS IN THE MIST   Universal, 1988,
   CP w/Judy Kessler

LELAND NOLAN

THE LITTLE GIRL WHO LIVES DOWN THE LANE   AIP,
   1977, CP w/Denis Heroux & Eugene Lepicier

O'b

FILM
PRODUCERS,
STUDIOS,
AGENTS and
CASTING
DIRECTORS
GUIDE

F
I
L
M

P
R
O
D
U
C
E
R
S

MICHAEL NOLIN
Business: Alliance Entertainment Corporation, 8439 Sunset Blvd., #404, Los Angeles, CA 90069, 213/654-9488 or 920 Yonge Street, Suite 400, Toronto, Ontario, M4W 3C7, Canada, 416/967-1174

MISCHIEF   20th Century Fox, 1985, w/Sam Manners
STRIPPER (FD)   20th Century Fox, 1986, CP w/Thom Tyson
THE STRANGER   Columbia, 1987, EP
84 CHARLIE MOPIC   New Century/Vista, 1989

RON NORMAN
Business: Horizons Productions, 1134 N. Ogden Dr., West Hollywood, CA 90046, 213/654-6911

LOVERS   Horizons Productions, 1984
STRANGERS IN PARADISE   New West, 1985

DON NORMANN
GRUNT! THE WRESTLING MOVIE   New World, 1985, w/Anthony Randell

STEVEN NORTH
Business: 100 Blvd. Sebastopol, Paris, 75003, 40/279660
Contact: London Film Prods., 44a Floral Street, London WC2E 9DA England, 071/379-3366; Fax: 071/240-7065
Contact: Writers Guild of America - Los Angeles, 213/289-2000

HOMER   National General, 1970
SHANKS   Paramount, 1974
WELCOME TO ARROW BEACH   Warner Bros., 1974, w/John H. Cushingham
THE BOY IN BLUE   20th Century Fox, 1986, EP
THE LAST BUTTERFLY   1991

F. RICHARD NORTHCOTT
Business: Nelson Entertainment, Inc., 335 N. Maple Dr., Suite 350, Beverly Hills, CA 90210, 310/285-6150; Fax: 310/285-6190

9 1/2 WEEKS   MGM/UA, 1986, EP w/Keith Barish & Frank Konigsberg

BLAINE NOVAK
Agent: The Chasin Agency - Beverly Hills, 310/278-7505
Contact: Writers Guild of America - New York, 212/245-6180

THEY ALL LAUGHED   United Artists Classics, 1982, w/George Morfogen

MICHAEL NOZIK
Contact: Directors Guild of America - New York, 212/581-0370

CHINA GIRL   Vestron, 1987
CROSSING DELANCEY   Warner Bros., 1988
SALAAM BOMBAY!   Cinecom, 1988, EP w/Gabriel Auer, Cherie Rodgers & Anil Tejani

GINNY NUGENT
MUNCHIES   Concorde, 1987, CP
BAD DREAMS   20th Century Fox, 1988, AP
TREMORS   Universal, 1990, LP

GRAFTON NUNES
THE LOVELESS   Atlantic, 1984, w/A. Kitman Ho

BILL OAKES
Business: RSO Films, 1041 N. Formosa Ave., Los Angeles, CA 90046, 213/850-2601

SGT. PEPPER'S LONELY HEARTS CLUB BAND Universal, 1978, AP
THE FAN   Paramount, 1981, AP w/John Nicolella
GREASE 2   Paramount, 1982, EP
STAYING ALIVE   Paramount, 1983, EP

HERBERT L. OAKES
EDUCATING RITA   Columbia, 1983, EP
NOT QUITE PARADISE   New World, 1986, EP

PETER O'BRIAN
Business: Independent Pictures Inc., 111 Gore Vale Ave., Toronto, M6J 2R5, 416/363-5155; Fax: 416/363-1021

OUTRAGEOUS!   Cinema 5, 1977, AP
LOVE AT FIRST SIGHT   Movietime, 1978
THE GREY FOX   United Artists Classics, 1983
ONE MAGIC CHRISTMAS   Buena Vista, 1985
MY AMERICAN COUSIN   Spectrafilm, 1986
JOHN AND THE MISSUS   Cinema Group, 1987, EP w/S. Howard Rosen

DEAN O'BRIEN
THELMA & LOUISE   MGM-PATHE, 1991, CP W/Callie Khouri
THE CUTTING EDGE   MGM, 1991, w/Robert W. Cort & Karen Murphy

DENIS O'BRIEN
(credit w/George Harrison)
Business: HandMade Films, Ltd., 26 Cadogan Square, London SW1X 0JP, England, 071/581-1265, 071/581-8345; Fax: 071/584-7338

MONTY PYTHON'S LIFE OF BRIAN   Orion/Warner Bros., 1979, EP
TIME BANDITS   Avco Embassy, 1981, EP
THE MISSIONARY   Columbia, 1982, EP
PRIVATES ON PARADE   Orion Classics, 1984, EP
SCRUBBERS   Orion Classics, 1984, EP
BULLSHOT   Island Alive, 1985, EP
A PRIVATE FUNCTION   Island Alive, 1985, EP
MONA LISA   Island Pictures, 1986, EP
SHANGHAI SURPRISE   MGM, 1986, EP
WATER   Atlantic, 1986, EP
WITHNAIL & I   Cineplex Odeon, 1987, EP
THE LONELY PASSION OF JUDITH HEARNE   Island Pictures, 1987, EP
BELLMAN & TRUE   Island Pictures, 1987, EP w/Johnny Goodman & John Hambley
FIVE CORNERS   Cineplex Odeon, 1988, EP
TRACK 29   Island Pictures, 1988, EP
THE RAGGEDY RAWNEY   Four Seasons Entertainment, 1989, EP
POWWOW HIGHWAY   Warner Bros., 1989, EP
CHECKING OUT   Warner Bros., 1989, EP

O'b

**FILM
PRODUCERS,
STUDIOS,
AGENTS AND
CASTING
DIRECTORS
GUIDE**

F
I
L
M

P
R
O
D
U
C
E
R
S

HOW TO GET AHEAD IN ADVERTISING   Warner Bros.,
   1989, EP
NUNS ON THE RUN   20th Century Fox, 1990, EP

FRANCIS O'BRIEN
GALLIPOLI   Paramount, 1981, EP

LORENZO O'BRIEN
Business: 9505 W. Washington Blvd., Culver City,
   CA 90230, 310/841-2301; Fax: 310/559-5529

WALKER   Universal, 1987, w/Angel Flores-Marini

REBECCA O'BRIEN
HIDDEN AGENDA   Hemdale, 1990, CP

JEFFREY OBROW
Agent: Triad Artists, Inc. - Los Angeles, 310/556-2727

THE POWER   Film Ventures International, 1982
PRANKS   *THE DORM THAT DRIPPED BLOOD*   New
   Image, 1983
THE KINDRED   FM Entertainment, 1987
THE SERVANTS OF TWILIGHT   Trimark, 1991,
   w/Venetia Stevenson

DAVID OBST
(credit w/Jeff Buhai & Steve Zacharias)
Agent: UTA - Beverly Hills, 310/273-6700

REVENGE OF THE NERDS   20th Century Fox, 1984,
   EP w/Peter Bart*
THE WHOOPEE BOYS   Paramount, 1986, EP
JOHNNY BE GOOD   Orion, 1988, EP

LYNDA OBST
(credit w/Debra Hill)
Business: Lynda Obst Productions, Columbia Pictures,
   10202 W. Washington Blvd., TriStar Bldg. #206, Culver
   City, CA 90232-3195, 310/280-5221; Fax: 310/280-1721

FLASHDANCE   Paramount, 1983, AP w/Tom Jacobson*
ADVENTURES IN BABYSITTING   Buena Vista, 1987
HEARTBREAK HOTEL   Buena Vista, 1988
THE FISHER KING   TriStar, 1991
THIS IS MY LIFE   20th Century Fox, 1991*

RICHARD L. O'CONNOR
Contact: Directors Guild of America - Los Angeles,
   213/289-2000

DISTANT THUNDER   Paramount, 1988, EP

DENIS O'DELL
A HARD DAY'S NIGHT   United Artists, 1964, AP
HOW I WON THE WAR   United Artists, 1967, AP
THE DEADLY AFFAIR   Columbia, 1967, AP
PETULIA   United Artists, 1968, AP
THE MAGIC CHRISTIAN   Commonwealth United, 1970
THE OFFENCE   United Artists, 1973
JUGGERNAUT   United Artists, 1974, AP
ROYAL FLASH   20th Century Fox, 1975,
   w/David V. Picker
ROBIN AND MARIAN   Columbia, 1976
THE RITZ   Warner Bros., 1976
CUBA   United Artists, 1979, EP

LYNN O'DONNELL
LIVING ON TOKYO TIME   Skouras Pictures, 1987,
   w/Dennis Hayashi

MICHAEL O'DONOGHUE
Agent: William Morris Agency - New York, 212/586-5100
Contact: Writers Guild of America - New York, 212/245-6180

MR. MIKE'S MONDO VIDEO   New Line, 1979

DANNY O'DONOVAN
GOLDENGIRL   Avco Embassy, 1979
ABSOLUTION   Trans World, 1988, w/Elliott Kastner

CHRISTINE OESTRICHER
Business: Flamingo Pictures, 47 Lonsdale Square, London
   N1 1EW England, 071/607-9958; Fax: 071/609-7669

STRIKE IT RICH   Millimeter, 1990, w/Graham Easton

GERALD OFFSAY
Business: ABC Productions, 2040 Avenue of the Stars,
   Los Angeles, CA 90067, 310/557-7777

HAMBURGER HILL   Paramount, 1987, EP w/David Korda
EIGHT MEN OUT   Orion, 1988, EP w/Barbara Boyle
NARROW MARGIN   TriStar, 1990, CP
THE SHRIMP ON THE BARBIE   Unity Pictures, 1990, EP
FALSE IDENTITY   RKO, 1990, EP w/Ted Hartley &
   Daniel Sarnoff

JENNIFER OGDEN
Contact: Directors Guild of America - New York,
   212/581-0370

GARBO TALKS   MGM/UA, 1984, AP
THE MANHATTAN PROJECT   20th Century Fox, 1986,
   w/Marshall Brickman
SUSPECT   TriStar, 1987, AP
COOKIE   Warner Bros., 1989, CP
FAMILY BUSINESS   TriStar, 1989, EP w/Burtt Harris
PRELUDE TO A KISS   20th Century Fox, 1991, EP

TAKASHI OHASHI
HIGH VELOCITY   First Asian, 1977

BERTIL OHLSSON
Business: Sandrews, Floragatan 4, Box 5612, S-114 86
   Stockholm, Sweden, 08/23-47-00

AMADEUS   Orion, 1984, EP w/Michael Hausman
THE UNBEARABLE LIGHTNESS OF BEING   Orion,
   1988, EP

KIP OHMAN
THE FLY   20th Century Fox, 1986, CP w/Marc Boyman
THE HITCHER   TriStar, 1986, w/David Bombyk

STUART OKEN
Business: Morgan Creek Productions, 1875 Century Park
   East, Los Angeles, CA 90067, 310/284-8884;
   Fax: 310/282-8794

ABOUT LAST NIGHT...   TriStar, 1986, w/Jason Brett
QUEENS LOGIC   Seven Arts, 1991, w/Russ Smith
IMPROMPTU   Hemdale, 1991, w/Daniel A. Sherkow
FREEJACK   Warner Bros., 1991, w/Ronald Shusett

CHARLES OKUN
(credit w/Michael Grillo)
Business: 650 N. Bronson Ave., Room 306, Hollywood,
CA 90004

LOVESICK   Warner Bros., 1983*
SILVERADO   Columbia, 1985, EP
CROSS MY HEART   Universal, 1987, CP
THE ACCIDENTAL TOURIST ★   Warner Bros., 1988,
w/Lawrence Kasdan
I LOVE YOU TO DEATH   TriStar, 1990, EP
GRAND CANYON   20th Century Fox, 1991,
w/Lawrence Kasdan

TORU OKUYAMA
RHAPSODY IN AUGUST   1991, EP

S. RODGER OLENICOFF
ICE CASTLES   Columbia, 1978, CP

CORINNE OLIVO
BLOODMATCH   21st Century, 1991, w/Rick Blumenthal

JONATHAN OLSBERG
Business: Glinwood Films Ltd., Swan House,
52 Poland St., London W1V 3DF, 071/437-1181

STICKY FINGERS   Spectrafilm, 1988, EP
TOKYO POP   Spectrafilm, 1988, EP

DANA OLSEN
Agent: InterTalent Agency - Los Angeles, 310/858-6200

THE 'BURBS   Universal, 1989, CP

GERALD T. OLSON
Business: New Line, 116 N. Robertson Blvd., Suite 808,
Los Angeles, CA 90048, 310/854-5811
Contact: Directors Guild of America - Los Angeles,
213/289-2000

REPO MAN   Universal, 1984, AP
QUIET COOL   New Line, 1986, w/Robert Shaye
BLOODY BIRTHDAY   Judica Productions, 1986
THE HIDDEN   New Line, 1987, w/Michael Meltzer &
Robert Shaye
LUCKY STIFF   New Line, 1988
HOUSE PARTY   New Line, 1990, EP

JASON O'MALLEY
BACKSTREET DREAMS   Vidmark, 1990,
w/Lance H. Robbins

JOHN M. ONDOV
THAT WAS THEN...THIS IS NOW   Paramount, 1985,
w/Gary R. Lindberg

TERENCE O'NEILL
MOMMIE DEAREST   Paramount, 1981,
EP w/David Koontz

IRVING ONG
Business: Davis Entertainment, 20th Century Fox, 10201
W. Pico Blvd., Los Angeles, CA 90035, 310/203-3540

SALVATION!   Circle Releasing, 1987,
EP w/Michel Duval & Ned Richardson

MARILYN ONG
DRIVING FORCE   J&M Entertainment, 1990,
EP w/Antony I. Ginnane

MARCEL OPHULS
Agent: InterTalent Agency - Los Angeles, 310/858-6200

THE SORROW AND THE PITY (FD)   Cinema 5, 1972
A SENSE OF LOSS (FD)   Cinema 5, 1972
THE MEMORY OF JUSTICE (FD)   Paramount, 1976
HOTEL TERMINUS: THE LIFE AND TIMES OF KLAUS
BARBIE (FD)   Samuel Goldwyn Company, 1988

PEER J. OPPENHEIMER
THE GAMES GIRLS PLAY   General Film, 1975
NASHVILLE GIRL   New World, 1976
NEW GIRL IN TOWN   New World, 1977
KEY EXCHANGE   20th Century Fox, 1985,
EP w/Michael Pochna & Ronald Winston

BARRY OPPER
(credit w/Rupert Harvey)
Business: Sho Films, 2300 Duane St., Suite 9, Los Angeles,
CA 90039, 213/665-9088; Fax: 213/665-7087

ANDROID   Island Alive, 1984, EP
CITY LIMITS   Atlantic, 1985
SLAMDANCE   Island Pictures, 1987

KERRY ORENT
Business: P.O. Box 543, Northport, NY 11768,
516/754-4886

THE PRINCE OF PENNSYLVANIA   New Line, 1988, CP

ARNOLD ORGOLINI
Business: Go Entertainment, Raleigh Studios, 650 N.
Bronson, Suite 134, Los Angeles, CA 90004,
213/465-4650

MOLLY AND LAWLESS JOHN   Producers Distributing
Corp., 1972, EP
EMBRYO   Cine Artists, 1976, w/Anita Doohan
METEOR   AIP, 1979, w/Theodore R. Parvin
SMORGASBORD   Warner Bros., 1985, w/Peter Nelson
HOLLYWOOD VICE SQUAD   Cinema Group, 1986,
w/Sandy Howard
ANGEL III: THE FINAL CHAPTER   New World, 1988

CHARLES ORME
ZARDOZ   20th Century Fox, 1974, AP
THE MAN WITH THE GOLDEN GUN   United Artists,
1974, AP
EXORCIST II: THE HERETIC   Warner Bros., 1977, AP
DAMIEN - OMEN II   20th Century Fox, 1978, CP

JAMES C. O'ROURKE
SCHLOCK   *BANANA MONSTER*   Jack H. Harris
Enterprises, 1973

JAMES ORR
Business: Orr & Cruickshank Productions, c/o Walt Disney
Studios, 500 S. Buena Vista St., Animation 2G11,
Burbank, CA 91521, 818/560-6423; Fax: 818/566-7310
Agent: William Morris Agency - Beverly Hills, 310/274-7451

MR. DESTINY   Buena Vista, 1990, w/Jim Cruickshank
FATHER OF THE BRIDE   1991, Buena Vista, EP w/Jim
Cruickshank & Sandy Gallin

Or

FILM
PRODUCERS,
STUDIOS,
AGENTS AND
CASTING
DIRECTORS
GUIDE

F
I
L
M

P
R
O
D
U
C
E
R
S

Os

FILM
PRODUCERS,
STUDIOS,
AGENTS AND
CASTING
DIRECTORS
GUIDE

F
I
L
M

P
R
O
D
U
C
E
R
S

BARRIE M. OSBORNE
Contact: Directors Guild of America - Los Angeles,
213/289-2000

THE BIG CHILL ★   Columbia, 1983, AP
THE COTTON CLUB   Orion, 1984,
   LP w/Joseph Cusumano
FANDANGO   Warner Bros., 1985, AP w/Pat Kehoe
PEGGY SUE GOT MARRIED   TriStar, 1986, EP
CHILD'S PLAY   MGM/UA, 1988, EP w/Elliott Geisinger
DICK TRACY   Buena Vista, 1990, EP w/Art Linson &
   Floyd Mutrux

WILLIAM OSCO
NIGHT PATROL   New World, 1984

EIKO OSHIMA
MERRY CHRISTMAS, MR. LAWRENCE   Universal,
   1983, EP w/Terry Glinwood, Masato Hara &
   Geoffrey Nethercott

IRVING OSHMAN
PRIVATE LESSONS   Jensen Farley, 1981, CP

CLAUDE OSSARD
THE ARROWTOOTH WALTZ   Warner Bros., 1991,
   w/Cedomir Kolar

MYLES OSTERNECK
BAD MEDICINE   20th Century Fox, 1985,
   EP w/Michael Jaffe & Sam Manners

RANDY OSTROW
(credit w/Ned Dowd)
Business: 496 LaGuardia Place, Suite 353, New York,
   NY 10012, 212/533-5318

LET IT RIDE   Paramount, 1989, CP
STATE OF GRACE   Orion, 1990, w/Ron Rotholz

STANLEY O'TOOLE
THE LAST OF SHEILA   Warner Bros., 1973, EP
OPERATION DAYBREAK   Warner Bros., 1975, AP
THE SEVEN PERCENT SOLUTION   Universal,
   1976, AP
THE SQUEEZE   Warner Bros., 1977
THE BOYS FROM BRAZIL   20th Century Fox, 1978,
   w/Martin Richards
NIJINSKY   Paramount, 1980, w/Nora Kaye
OUTLAND   The Ladd Company/Warner Bros., 1981, EP
SPHINX   Orion/Warner Bros., 1981
ENEMY MINE   20th Century Fox, 1985, EP
LIONHEART   Orion, 1987, w/Talia Shire
QUIGLEY DOWN UNDER   Pathe/MGM/UA, 1990,
   w/Alex Rose

JEAN-PAUL OUELLETTE
Contact: Yankee Classic Pictures, 4072 Inglewood Blvd.,
   Suite 2, Los Angeles, CA 90066, 310/397-0587

THE UNNAMEABLE   Vidmark Entertainment, 1988,
   w/Dean Ramser

ALISON OWEN
Contact: Working Title Films, 1 Water Lane, Kentish Town
   Lane, London NW1 8NZ England, 071/911-6100;
   Fax: 071/911-6150

HEAR MY SONG   Miramax, 1992

FRANK OZ
Business: Orion Pictures, 1888 Century Park East,
   Los Angeles, CA 90067, 310/282-2956
Agent: CAA - Beverly Hills, 310/288-4545
Contact: Directors Guild of America - Los Angeles,
   213/289-2000

THE GREAT MUPPET CAPER   Universal/AFD, 1981,
   w/David Lazer

P

AMADEO PAGANI
WAIT UNTIL SPRING, BANDINI   Orion, 1990,
   EP w/Christian Charret, Cyril de Rouvre & Giorgio Silvago

JAMES PAINTEN
ABC Productions, 2020 Avenue of the Stars, 5th Floor,
   Los Angeles, CA 90067, 310/557-7777

THE GRIFTERS   Miramax, 1990, w/Robert Harris &
   Martin Scorsese

ALAN J. PAKULA
Business: Pakula Productions, Inc., 330 West 58th St.,
   New York, NY 10019, 212/664-0640
Agent: William Morris Agency - Beverly Hills, 310/274-7451

FEAR STRIKES OUT   Paramount, 1957
TO KILL A MOCKINGBIRD ★   Universal, 1962
LOVE WITH THE PROPER STRANGER   Paramount, 1963
BABY, THE RAIN MUST FALL   Columbia, 1965
INSIDE DAISY CLOVER   Warner Bros., 1965
UP THE DOWN STAIRCASE   Warner Bros., 1967
THE STALKING MOON   National General, 1968
THE STERILE CUCKOO   Paramount, 1969
KLUTE   Warner Bros., 1971
LOVE & PAIN & the whole damn thing   Columbia, 1973
THE PARALLAX VIEW   Paramount, 1974
STARTING OVER   Paramount, 1979, w/James L. Brooks
SOPHIE'S CHOICE   Universal, 1982, w/Keith Barish
DREAM LOVER   MGM/UA, 1986, w/Jon Boorstin
ORPHANS   Lorimar, 1987
SEE YOU IN THE MORNING   Warner Bros., 1989,
   w/Susan Solt

JULIA PALAU
Business: J & M Entertainment, 1289 Sunset Plaza Dr.,
   Los Angeles, CA 90069, 213/652-7733; 2 Dorset Square,
   London NW1 6PU, 071/723-6544; Fax: 071/724-7541

PLAYING FOR KEEPS   Universal, 1986,
   EP w/Michael Ryan & Patrick Wachsberger

Pa

FILM
PRODUCERS,
STUDIOS,
AGENTS and
CASTING
DIRECTORS
GUIDE

BONNIE PALEF
Business: 375 Greenwich St., 5th Floor, New York, NY
10013, 212/941-3888; Fax: 212/941-3997
Business: Snapdragon Productions, 7135 Hollywood Blvd.,
Suite 1203, Los Angeles, CA 90046, 213/850-5946

AGNES OF GOD Columbia, 1985, AP
MOONSTRUCK ★ MGM, 1987, AP
PARENTS Vestron, 1989

MAX PALEVSKY
(credit w/Peter Bart)

MARJOE (FD) Cinema 5, 1972, EP
A SENSE OF LOSS (FD) Cinema 5, 1972, EP
FUN WITH DICK & JANE Columbia, 1977
ISLANDS IN THE STREAM Paramount, 1977

MICHAEL PALIN
Business: Prominent Features Ltd., 68A Delancey St.,
London NW1 7RY, England, 071/284-0242;
Fax: 071/284-1004

THE MISSIONARY Columbia, 1982,
w/Neville C. Thompson

JOHN PALMER
CIAO! MANHATTAN Maron, 1973, w/David Weisman

MELINDA PALMER
Contact: Writers Guild of America - Los Angeles,
310/550-1000

THE GARBAGE PAIL KIDS MOVIE Atlantic
Entertainment, 1987, CP w/Michael Lloyd

PATRICK PALMER
Business: Patrick Palmer Productions, c/o Orion Producers
Bldg., 11500 Tennessee Av., Los Angeles, CA 90064,
310/444-7540; Fax: 310/312-2085
Contact: Directors Guild of America - Los Angeles,
213/289-2000

THE LANDLORD United Artists, 1970, AP
FIDDLER ON THE ROOF United Artists, 1971, AP
JESUS CHRIST SUPERSTAR Universal, 1973, AP
BILLY TWO HATS United Artists, 1972,
w/Norman Jewison
ROLLERBALL United Artists, 1975, AP
F.I.S.T. United Artists, 1978, AP
...AND JUSTICE FOR ALL Columbia, 1979,
w/Norman Jewison
THE DOGS OF WAR United Artists, 1981,
EP w/Norman Jewison
BEST FRIENDS Warner Bros., 1982, w/Norman Jewison
ICEMAN Universal, 1984, w/Norman Jewison
A SOLDIER'S STORY ★ Columbia, 1984,
w/Norman Jewison & Ronald L. Schwary
AGNES OF GOD Columbia, 1985, w/Norman Jewison
CHILDREN OF A LESSER GOD ★ Paramount, 1986,
w/Burt Sugarman
MOONSTRUCK ★ MGM /UA, 1987, w/Norman Jewison
STANLEY & IRIS MGM/UA, 1990, EP
MERMAIDS Orion, 1990, w/Lauren Lloyd & Wallis Nicita
PARADISE Buena Vista, 1991, w/Scott Kroopf

NANCY PALOIAN
WAXWORK II: LOST IN TIME Seven Arts/Live, 1991

BRUCE PALTROW
Attorney: Ken Meyer, Rosenfeld, Meyer & Susman,
9601 Wilshire Blvd., Beverly Hills, CA, 310/858-7700
Business: The Paltrow Group, Pier 62, 3rd Floor, West 23rd
St. & Hudson River, New York, NY 10011, 212/633-1313;
Fax: 212/741-0851

A LITTLE SEX Universal, 1982, w/Robert DeLaurentis

WILLIAM N. PANZER
(credit w/Peter Davis)
Business: Davis-Panzer Productions, 1754 N. Serrano, #401,
Hollywood, CA 90028, 213/463-2343; Fax: 213/465-0948

DEATH COLLECTOR Epoh, 1976*
STUNTS New Line, 1977, w/Raymond Lofaro*
FAMILY ENFORCER First American, 1978*
STEEL World Northal, 1980
ST. HELENS Parnell, 1981, AP
THE OSTERMAN WEEKEND 20th Century Fox, 1983
O'HARA'S WIFE Enfield, 1984
HIGHLANDER 20th Century Fox, 1986
FREEWAY New World, 1988

GERALD S. PAONESSA
MONKEY SHINES Orion, 1988, EP w/Peter Grunwald

ROBERT A. PAPAZIAN
Business: Papazian-Hirsch Entertainment, 500 S. Sepulveda
Blvd., Suite 600, Los Angeles, CA 90049, 310/471-2332;
Fax: 310/471-3352

DILLINGER AIP, 1973, AP
COFFY AIP, 1973

GEORGE PAPPAS
Business: Cinema Seven Productions, 154 West 57th St.,
Suite 112, New York, NY 10019, 212/315-1060;
Fax: 212/315-1085; Winkast Programming Ltd., Pinewood
Studios, Iver Heath, Bucks., SL0 0NH, 0753/651-700;
Fax: 0753/652-525

COPS & ROBBERS United Artists, 1973, AP
JEREMY United Artists, 1973
92 IN THE SHADE United Artists, 1975
FAREWELL, MY LOVELY Avco Embassy, 1975,
w/Jerry Bruckheimer
THE FIRST DEADLY SIN Filmways, 1980,
w/Mark Shanker
NOMADS Atlantic, 1986, w/Cassian Elwes
HEAT New Century/Vista, 1987, w/Keith Rotman
THE CLOSER Ion, 1991, EP w/Mitchell Calder,
Tony Conforti & Roy Medawar

ALFRED PARISER
Business: Edward R. Pressman Film Corporation, 4000
Warner Blvd., Prod. 5, Room 114, Burbank, CA 91522,
818/954-3315

BREAKING POINT 20th Century Fox, 1976,
EP w/Harold Greenberg
THE LITTLE GIRL WHO LIVES DOWN THE LANE AIP,
1977, EP w/Harold Greenberg
THEY CAME FROM WITHIN Trans-America, 1977,
EP w/John Dunning & Andre Link
THE HAUNTING OF JULIA Discovery, 1981,
w/Peter Fetterman
IMPROPER CHANNELS Crown International, 1981,
w/Morrie Ruvinsky

Pa

**FILM
PRODUCERS,
STUDIOS,
AGENTS AND
CASTING
DIRECTORS GUIDE**

F
I
L
M

P
R
O
D
U
C
E
R
S

MICHAEL D. PARISER
MARTIANS GO HOME   Taurus, 1990
WHORE   Trimark, 1991, LP

DAVID PARKER
(credit w/Nadia Tass)
Agent: CAA - Beverly Hills, 310/288-4545

MALCOLM   Vestron, 1986
RIKKY & PETE   MGM/UA, 1988

DON LeROY PARKER
CHINA CRY   Penland, 1990, EP

FRANCINE PARKER
Agent: Shapiro-Lichtman Agency - Los Angeles,
   310/859-8877

F.T.A.   AIP, 1972, w/Jane Fonda & Donald Sutherland

LAURIE PARKER
THE RAPTURE   Fine Line, 1991, EP

RONALD PARKER
Contact: Writers Guild of America - Los Angeles,
   310/550-1000

MY STEPMOTHER IS AN ALIEN   WEG/Columbia, 1988,
   w/Franklin R. Levy

STEVEN H. PARKER
RICH GIRL   Studio Three, 1991, EP w/Mark Hoffman

WALTER F. PARKES
(credit w/Lawrence Lasker)
Agent: CAA - Beverly Hills, 310/288-4545

THE CALIFORNIA REICH (FD)   Intercontinental, 1976,
   w/Keith Critchlow
VOLUNTEERS   TriStar, 1985, w/Richard Shepherd*
PROJECT X   20th Century Fox, 1987
TRUE BELIEVER   Columbia, 1989
AWAKENINGS ★   Columbia, 1990

JAY PARSLEY
THE TEXAS CHAINSAW MASSACRE   Bryanston,
   1974, EP

CLIVE PARSONS
(credit w/Davina Belling)
Business: Film & General Productions, Ltd., 1362 N.
   Wetherly Drive, Los Angeles, CA 90069, 310/274-4773;
   Fax: 310/274-7947; 10 Pembridge Place, London
   W2 4XB, 071/221-1141; Fax: 071/792-1167

INSERTS   United Artists, 1976
THAT SUMMER   Columbia, 1979
SCUM   Berwick Street Films, 1979
BREAKING GLASS   Paramount, 1980
BRITANNIA HOSPITAL   United Artists Classics, 1982
GREGORY'S GIRL   Samuel Goldwyn Company, 1982
COMFORT AND JOY   Universal, 1984

LINDSLEY PARSONS, JR.
Contact: Directors Guild of America - Los Angeles,
   213/289-2000

THE WIZARD   Universal, 1989, EP

THEODORE R. PARVIN
Agent: The Artists Agency - Los Angeles, 213/828-1003
Contact: Directors Guild of America - Los Angeles,
   213/289-2000

VOLUNTEERS   TriStar, 1985, AP
HOT PURSUIT   Paramount, 1987, w/Pierre David

UMBERTO PASOLINI
Business: Enigma Productions, Ltd., 15 Queen's Gate Place
   Mews, London SW7 5BG, England, 071/581-0238;
   Fax: 071/584-1799

MEETING VENUS   Warner Bros., 1991, w/David Puttnam

ANDY PATERSON
Business: Oxford Film Company, 2 Mountfort Terrace,
   London N1 1JJ England, 071/607-8200;
   Fax: 071/607-4037

RESTLESS NATIVES   Orion Classics, 1986, CP

IAIN PATERSON
SWEET LORRAINE   Angelika Films, 1987, LP
FRIDAY THE 13TH, PART VII - THE NEW BLOOD
   Paramount, 1988

MICHAEL PATTINSON
Contact: Australian Film Commission, 9229 Sunset Blvd.,
   Los Angeles, CA 90069, 310/275-7074

GROUND ZERO   Avenue, 1988

BART PATTON
Contact: Directors Guild of America - Los Angeles,
   213/289-2000

THE RAIN PEOPLE   Warner Bros., 1969, w/Ronald Colby

DOROTHY KOSTER PAUL
Business: Paul Entertainment, Inc., 517A Wilshire Blvd.,
   Santa Monica, CA 90401, 310/319-3562

ETERNITY   Triax, 1990, EP w/Hank Paul

HANK PAUL
Business: Paul Entertainment, Inc., 517A Wilshire Blvd.,
   Santa Monica, CA 90401, 310/319-3562

ETERNITY   Triax, 1990, EP w/Dorothy Koster Paul

STEVEN PAUL
Business: Paul Entertainment, Inc., 517A Wilshire Blvd.,
   Santa Monica, CA 90401, 310/319-3562

ETERNITY   Triax, 1990

STUART PAUL
Business: Paul Entertainment, Inc., 517A Wilshire Blvd.,
   Santa Monica, CA 90401, 310/319-3562

ETERNITY   Triax, 1990, CP

WILLIAM PAUL
THE NINTH CONFIGURATION   *TWINKLE, TWINKLE,
   "KILLER" KANE*   Warner Bros., 1979, EP

Pe

FILM
PRODUCERS,
STUDIOS,
AGENTS AND
CASTING
DIRECTORS
GUIDE

F
I
L
M

P
R
O
D
U
C
E
R
S

DAN PAULSON
Business: 4000 Warner Blvd., Burbank, CA 91522,
818/954-3320; Fax: 818/954-6728

COMES A HORSEMAN   United Artists, 1978,
   w/Gene Kirkwood
CATCHFIRE   1991, w/Dick Clark

CLIFF PAYNE
THE LADY IN WHITE   New Century/Vista, 1988,
   EP w/Charles M. LaLoggia

GREG PEAD
(see Yahoo SERIOUS)

CHRISTOPHER PEARCE
(credit w/Yoram Globus)
Business: Cannon Productions, 8200 Wilshire Blvd.,
   Beverly Hills, CA 90212, 213/966-5600;
   Fax: 213/653-5485
Contact: Directors Guild of America - Los Angeles,
   213/289-2000

THE ROSE GARDEN   Cannon, 1989, EP
A MAN CALLED SARGE   Cannon, 1990, EP
DELTA FORCE 2   Cannon, 1990
ROCKULA   Cannon, 1990, EP
AMERICAN NINJA 4: THE ANNIHILATION   Cannon,
   1991, EP

MEL PEARL
(credit w/Don Levin)

LOVE LETTERS   New World, 1983, EP
HAMBONE & HILLIE   New World, 1984, EP
THE BOYS NEXT DOOR   New World, 1985, EP
MAXIMUM OVERDRIVE   DEG, 1986, EP
THE SUPERNATURALS   Republic Entertainment,
   1987, EP
WEEDS   DEG, 1987, EP w/Billy Cross*
TWO MOON JUNCTION   Lorimar, 1988, EP
ANGEL III: THE FINAL CHAPTER   New World,
   1988, EP
SCISSORS   DDM Film Corp., 1991, w/Hal Polaire

BARRY PEARSON
PLAGUE   Group I, 1979, w/Ed Hunt

MICHAEL PEARSON
VANISHING POINT   20th Century Fox, 1971, EP

NOEL PEARSON
MY LEFT FOOT ★   Miramax, 1989
THE FIELD   Avenue Pictures, 1990

GREGORY PECK
Agent: Triad Artists, Inc. - Los Angeles, 310/556-2727

THE TRIAL OF THE CATONSVILLE NINE
   Cinema 5, 1972
THE DOVE   Paramount, 1974

M. J. PECKOS
BURNING SECRET   Vestron, 1988,
   EP w/William J. Quigley
PAPERHOUSE   Vestron, 1989, EP w/Dan Ireland

JIM PEDAS
BARTON FINK   20th Century Fox, 1991, EP w/Ted Pedas,
   Ben Barenholtz & Bill Durkin

TED PEDAS
BARTON FINK   20th Century Fox, 1991,
   EP w/Ben Barenholtz, Jim Pedas & Bill Durkin

WILLIAM PEIFFER
TEXASVILLE   Columbia, 1990, EP w/Jake Eberts

YORAM PELMAN
Business: South Gate Entertainment, 7080 Hollywood Blvd.,
   Suite 307, Hollywood, CA 90028, 213/962-8530

COMMANDO SQUAD   Trans World, 1987, EP

ARTHUR PENN
Business: Florin Productions, 1860 Broadway, New York, NY
   10023, 310/585-1470
Agent: ICM - New York, 212/556-5600

FOUR FRIENDS   Filmways, 1981, w/Gene Lasko
PENN AND TELLER GET KILLED   Warner Bros., 1989

EAGLE PENNELL
Attorney: Tom Garvin, Ervin, Cohen & Jessup, 9401
   Wilshire Blvd., Beverly Hills, CA 90212, 310/273-6333

THE WHOLE SHOOTIN' MATCH   Cinema
   Perspectives, 1979
LAST NIGHT AT THE ALAMO   Cinecom, 1984,
   w/Kim Henkel

JON PENNINGTON
THE MOUSE THAT ROARED   Columbia, 1959,
   w/Walter Shenson
ALF 'N' FAMILY   Sherpix, 1972

GEORGE PEPPARD
Agent: David Shapira & Associates - Sherman Oaks,
   818/906-0322

FIVE DAYS FROM HOME   Universal, 1979

PAUL PEPPERMAN
PHANTASM   Avco Embassy, 1979, CP

LAURENCE P. PEREIRA
PREDATOR   20th Century Fox, 1987, EP w/Jim Thomas

JOSEPH PEREZ
PERSONAL CHOICE   Moviestore Entertainment, 1989

ANDRE PERGAMENT
ENIGMA   Embassy, 1983, w/Ben Arbeid & Peter Shaw

FRANK RAY PERILLI
(credit w/Albert Band)

DRACULA'S DOG   Crown International, 1978
SHE CAME TO THE VALLEY   R&V Pictures, 1979

Pe

FILM
PRODUCERS,
STUDIOS,
AGENTS AND
CASTING
DIRECTORS
GUIDE

F
I
L
M

P
R
O
D
U
C
E
R
S

GEORGE W. PERKINS
Business: Motor Av., Los Angeles, CA 90064,
310/839-8583
Agent: Jerry Adler, 818/761-9850

EXTREMITIES   Atlantic, 1986, LP w/Scott Rosenfelt

ARNOLD PERL
MALCOLM X (FD)   Warner Bros., 1972, w/Marvin Worth

LAURIE PERLMAN
Business: Perlman Productions, 20th Century Fox, 10201
W. Pico Blvd., Trailer 78, Los Angeles, CA 90035,
310/203-3482; Fax: 310/203-2651

LUCKY STIFF   New Line, 1988, EP w/Miles Copeland,
Derek Power & Pat Proft
VITAL SIGNS   20th Century Fox, 1990,
w/Cathleen Summers

DAVID M. PERLMUTTER
THE NEPTUNE FACTOR   20th Century Fox, 1973,
EP w/Harold Greenberg
LOVE AT FIRST SIGHT   Movietime, 1978,
EP w/John Trent

SAM PERLMUTTER
THE FOURTH WAR   Warner Bros., 1990,
EP w/William Stuart

DAVID PERMUT
Business: Permut Presentations, Inc., 116 N. Robertson
Blvd., Suite 710, Los Angeles, CA 90048, 310/967-6640;
Fax: 310/289-8313

FIGHTING BACK   Paramount, 1982, EP w/Mark Travis
BLIND DATE   TriStar, 1987, EP w/Gary Hendler &
Jonathan D. Krane
DRAGNET   Universal, 1987, w/Robert K. Weiss
THE MARRYING MAN   Buena Vista, 1991
BUDDY COPS   TriStar, 1991

RUPERT A. L. PERRIN
BEVERLY HILLS BRATS   Taurus, 1989, EP

E. LEE PERRY
MEAN STREETS   Warner Bros., 1973, EP

FRANK PERRY
Agent: ICM - New York, 212/556-5600

DIARY OF A MAD HOUSEWIFE   Universal, 1970
DOC   United Artists, 1971
PLAY IT AS IT LAYS   Universal, 1972
COMPROMISING POSITIONS   Paramount, 1985
HELLO AGAIN   Buena Vista, 1987

PINCHAS PERRY
Business: Pinchas Perry Productions, 8200 Wilshire Blvd.,
Beverly Hills, CA 90211, 213/658-3028

GABY - A TRUE STORY   TriStar, 1987, EP

SIMON PERRY
Business: British Screen, 37-39 Oxford St., London W1R
1RE, 071/434-0291; Fax: 071/434-9933

ANOTHER TIME, ANOTHER PLACE   Samuel Goldwyn
Company, 1984
1984   Atlantic, 1985
NANOU   Umbrella/Arion, 1986
WHITE MISCHIEF   Columbia, 1988
THE PLAYBOYS   Goldwyn, 1991

STEVE PERRY
Business: Silver Pictures, 4000 Warner Blvd., Burbank, CA
91522, 818/954-4490
Contact: Directors Guild of America - Los Angeles,
213/289-2000

ACTION JACKSON   Lorimar, 1988, AP
LETHAL WEAPON 2   Warner Bros., 1989,
CP w/Jennie Lew Tugend
ROADHOUSE   MGM/UA, 1989, EP w/Tim Moore
FORD FAIRLANE   20th Century Fox, 1990, w/Joel Silver
DIE HARD 2   20th Century Fox, 1990, CP
THE LAST BOY SCOUT   Warner Bros., 1991,
w/Michael Levy & Joel Silver

LESTER PERSKY
Business: Lester Persky Productions, Inc., 935 Bel Air Rd.,
Los Angeles, CA 90077, 310/476-9697;
Fax: 310/476-6665
Contact: 150 Central Park South, New York, NY 10019,
212/246-7700

FORTUNE & MEN'S EYES   MGM, 1971, w/Lewis Allen
EQUUS   United Artists, 1977, w/Elliott Kastner
HAIR   United Artists, 1979, w/Michael Butler
YANKS   Universal, 1979, w/Joseph Janni

LUCIANO PERUGIA
DEAF SMITH AND JOHNNY EARS   MGM, 1973,
w/Joseph Janni

BROCK PETERS
Agent: Gores-Fields Agency - Los Angeles, 310/277-4400

FIVE ON THE BLACK HAND SIDE   United Artists,
1973, w/Michael Tolan

DAVID ANDREW PETERS
BLUE DESERT   Neo Films, 1991

JON PETERS
(credit w/Peter Guber)
Business: Columbia Pictures, 10202 W. Washington Blvd.,
Culver City, CA 90232, 310/280-8000

A STAR IS BORN   Warner Bros., 1976*
EYES OF LAURA MARS   Columbia, 1978*
THE MAIN EVENT   Warner Bros., 1979,
w/Barbra Streisand*
CADDYSHACK   Orion, 1980, EP*
DIE LAUGHING   Orion, 1980, EP*
AN AMERICAN WEREWOLF IN LONDON   Universal,
1981, EP
SIX WEEKS   Universal, 1982, EP
MISSING ★   Universal, 1982, EP
FLASHDANCE   Paramount, 1983, EP
D.C. CAB   Universal, 1983, EP

Ph

FILM
PRODUCERS,
STUDIOS,
AGENTS AND
CASTING
DIRECTORS
GUIDE

VISION QUEST   Warner Bros., 1985
THE LEGEND OF BILLIE JEAN   TriStar, 1985, EP
HEAD OFFICE   TriStar, 1985, EP
THE COLOR PURPLE ★   Warner Bros., 1985, EP
CLUE   Paramount, 1985, EP w/George Folsey Jr. &
   John Landis
THE CLAN OF THE CAVE BEAR   Warner Bros., 1986,
   EP w/Mark Damon, John Hyde & Sidney Kimmel
YOUNGBLOOD   MGM/UA, 1986, EP
THE WITCHES OF EASTWICK   Warner Bros., 1987,
   w/Neil Canton
INNERSPACE   Warner Bros., 1987, EP w/Kathleen
   Kennedy, Frank Marshall & Steven Spielberg
WHO'S THAT GIRL   Warner Bros., 1987,
   EP w/Roger Birnbaum
GORILLAS IN THE MIST   Universal, 1988, EP
RAIN MAN ★★   MGM/UA, 1988, EP
CADDYSHACK II   Warner Bros., 1988, w/Neil Canton
BATMAN   Warner Bros., 1989
TANGO & CASH   Warner Bros., 1989
MISSING LINK   Universal, 1989, EP
THE BONFIRE OF THE VANITIES   Warner Bros.,
   1990, EP

ROBERT C. PETERS
Business: New World Pictures, 1440 S. Sepulveda Blvd.,
   Los Angeles, CA 90025, 310/444-8222;
   Fax: 310/444-8407

FRATERNITY VACATION   New World, 1985, w/Boris
   Malden & Christopher Nelson
WANTED DEAD OR ALIVE   New World, 1987

JO PETERSON
FROM HOLLYWOOD TO DEADWOOD   Island
   Pictures, 1989

DANIEL PETRIE
Agent: CAA - Beverly Hills, 310/288-4545
Contact: Directors Guild of America - Los Angeles,
   213/289-2000

SQUARE DANCE   *HOME IS WHERE THE HEART IS*
   Island Pictures, 1987

DANIEL PETRIE, JR.
Business: Walt Disney Pictures, 500 S. Buena Vista St.,
   Animation 2-B-5, Burbank, CA 91521, 818/560-6450;
   Fax: 818/560-1930
Agent: The Richland/Wunsch/Hohman Agency -
   Los Angeles, 310/278-1955

SHOOT TO KILL   Buena Vista, 1988, w/Ron Silverman
TURNER & HOOCH   Buena Vista, 1989,
   EP w/Michael Hertzberg

GIANCARLO PETTINI
THE CASSANDRA CROSSING   Avco Embassy,
   1977, EP

MIKE PETZOLD
Business: Rafaella Productions, Universal Pictures, 100
   Universal City Plaza, Bungalow 121-C, Universal City, CA
   91608, 818/777-2655

PRANCER   Orion, 1989, CP w/Greg Taylor

JOHN PEVERALL
THE DEER HUNTER ★★   Universal, 1978, w/Michael
   Cimino, Michael Deeley & Barry Spikings
McVICAR   Crown International, 1982, AP

MICHAEL PEYSER
Business: Peyser & Alexander, 500 Fifth Avenue, 28th Floor,
   New York, NY 10110, 212/823-3755
Contact: Directors Guild of America - Los Angeles,
   213/289-2000

A MIDSUMMER NIGHT'S SEX COMEDY   Orion/Warner
   Bros., 1982, AP
BROADWAY DANNY ROSE   Orion, 1984, AP
THE PURPLE ROSE OF CAIRO   Orion, 1985, AP
DESPERATELY SEEKING SUSAN   Orion, 1985, EP
F/X   Orion, 1986, EP
RUTHLESS PEOPLE   Buena Vista, 1986
BIG BUSINESS   Buena Vista, 1988, w/Steve Tisch

ANDREW D. T. PFEFFER
(credit w/Michael C. Leone)
Business: Epic Productions, 3330 W. Cahuenga Blvd.,
   Suite 500, Los Angeles, CA 90068, 213/969-2800;
   Fax: 213/969-8211

I, THE JURY   20th Century Fox, 1982, EP
TOUGH ENOUGH   20th Century Fox, 1983, EP
THE ENTITY   20th Century Fox, 1983, EP
STONE COLD   Columbia, 1991, CP w/Nick Grillo

CAROLYN PFEIFFER
Business: Alive Films, 8912 Burton Way, Beverly Hills, CA
   90211, 310/247-7800; Fax: 310/247-7823

ROADIE   United Artists, 1980
ENDANGERED SPECIES   MGM/UA, 1982
RETURN ENGAGEMENT   Island Alive, 1983
CHOOSE ME   Island Alive, 1984, w/David Blocker
TROUBLE IN MIND   Alive Films, 1985, w/David Blocker
THE WHALES OF AUGUST   Alive Films, 1987,
   w/Mike Kaplan
FAR NORTH   Alive Films, 1988, w/Malcolm R. Harding
THE MODERNS   Alive Films, 1988, w/David Blocker
A TIME OF DESTINY   Columbia, 1988, EP w/Shep Gordon

STUART W. PHELPS
THE FIRST NUDIE MUSICAL   Paramount, 1976,
   EP w/Peter S. Brown

BRANDON K. PHILLIPS
THAT WAS THEN...THIS IS NOW   Paramount, 1985,
   EP w/Alan Belkin

DON PHILLIPS
CAR WASH   Universal, 1976, AP
MELVIN & HOWARD   Universal, 1980, w/Art Linson
THE WILD LIFE   Universal, 1984, CP
THE INDIAN RUNNER   1991

JULIA PHILLIPS
(credit w/Michael Phillips)

STEELYARD BLUES   Warner Bros., 1973, w/Tony Bill
THE STING ★★   Universal, 1973, w/Tony Bill
THE BIG BUS   Paramount, 1976, EP
TAXI DRIVER ★   Columbia, 1976
CLOSE ENCOUNTERS OF THE THIRD KIND
   Columbia, 1977

Ph

**FILM
PRODUCERS,
STUDIOS,
AGENTS** AND
**CASTING
DIRECTORS** GUIDE

F
I
L
M

P
R
O
D
U
C
E
R
S

THE BEAT   Vestron, 1988, w/Jon Kilik & Nick Wechsler*
DON'T TELL MOM THE BABYSITTER'S DEAD
   Warner Bros., 1991, EP

LLOYD PHILLIPS
(credit w/Robert Whitehouse)
Agent: ICM - Duncan Heath, 071/439-1471

WARLORDS OF THE 21ST CENTURY   *BATTLE TRUCK*
   New World, 1982
NATE & HAYES   Paramount, 1983

MICHAEL PHILLIPS
(credit w/Julia Phillips)
Business: 120 El Camino Drive #212, Beverly Hills, CA
   90212, 310/859-4923; Fax: 310/859-7511

STEELYARD BLUES   Warner Bros., 1973, w/Tony Bill
THE STING ★★   Universal, 1973, w/Tony Bill
THE BIG BUS   Paramount, 1976, EP
TAXI DRIVER ★   Columbia, 1976
CLOSE ENCOUNTERS OF THE THIRD KIND
   Columbia, 1977
HEARTBEEPS   Universal, 1981*
CANNERY ROW   MGM/UA, 1982*
THE FLAMINGO KID   20th Century Fox, 1984*
MOM AND DAD SAVE THE WORLD   Warner Bros.,
   1991, w/Mike Erwin

RANDY PHILLIPS
GRAFFITI BRIDGE   Warner Bros., 1990, w/Arnold Stiefel

MARK PICK
ELENI   Warner Bros., 1985, w/Nicholas Gage &
   Nick Vanoff

DAVID V. PICKER
Business: Two Roads Productions, 711 5th Ave.,
   Suite 401, New York, NY 10022, 212/702-6480

LENNY ★   United Artists, 1974, EP
JUGGERNAUT   United Artists, 1974, EP
SMILE   United Artists, 1975, EP w/Marion Dougherty
ROYAL FLASH   20th Century Fox, 1975, w/Denis O'Dell
WON TON TON, THE DOG WHO SAVED HOLLYWOOD
   Paramount, 1976, w/Arnold Schulman & Michael Winner
OLIVER'S STORY   Paramount, 1978
THE ONE & ONLY   Paramount, 1978, w/Steve Gordon
SIDNEY SHELDON'S BLOODLINE   Paramount, 1979,
   w/Sidney Beckerman
THE JERK   Universal, 1979, w/William E. McEuen
DEAD MEN DON'T WEAR PLAID   Universal, 1982,
   w/William E. McEuen
THE MAN WITH TWO BRAINS   Warner Bros., 1983,
   w/William E. McEuen
BEAT STREET   Orion, 1984, w/Harry Belafonte
THE GOODBYE PEOPLE   Embassy, 1984
LEADER OF THE BAND   New Century/Vista, 1988
STELLA   Samuel Goldwyn Company/Buena Vista,
   1990, EP

CHARLES B. PIERCE
THE LEGEND OF BOGGY CREEK   Halco, 1973
BOOTLEGGERS   Howco International, 1974
WINTER HAWK   Howco International, 1975
THE WINDS OF AUTUMN   Howco International, 1976
GRAYEAGLE   AIP, 1977
THE TOWN THAT DREADED SUNDOWN   AIP, 1977

THE NORSEMAN   AIP, 1978
THE EVICTORS   AIP, 1979

MARK PIERSON
ELVIRA, MISTRESS OF THE DARK   New World, 1988,
   w/Eric Gardner

SIR WILLIAM PIGGOTT-BROWN
FIGURES IN A LANDSCAPE   National General, 1971, EP

LYDIA DEAN PILCHER
Business: 61 Eastern Parkway, Suite 4-G, Brooklyn, NY
   11238, 718/230-9489

SLIPPING INTO DARKNESS   MCEG, 1988, LP
THE KILL-OFF   Cabriolet, 1990
LONGTIME COMPANION   Samuel Goldwyn Company,
   1990, CP

SARAH PILLSBURY
(credit w/Midge Sanford)
Business: Sanford-Pillsbury Productions, 20th Century Fox,
   10201 W. Pico Blvd., Bldg. 50, Los Angeles, CA 90035,
   310/203-1847; Fax: 310/203-4142

DESPERATELY SEEKING SUSAN   Orion, 1985
RIVER'S EDGE   Island Pictures, 1987
EIGHT MEN OUT   Orion, 1988
IMMEDIATE FAMILY   Columbia, 1989

HOWARD PINE
STRAIGHT TIME   Warner Bros., 1978, EP
THE COMPETITION   Columbia, 1980, EP
THE SURVIVORS   Columbia, 1983, EP

ERNEST PINTOFF
Agent: Contemporary Artists - Beverly Hills, 310/278-8250

DYNAMITE CHICKEN   EYR, 1972
BLADE   Joseph Green, 1973, EP

GLEN PITRE
Business: Louisiana Office of Film & Video, P.O. Box 94361,
   Baton Rouge, LA, 70804, 504/342-8150;
   Fax: 504-342-3207
Agent: William Morris Agency - Beverly Hills, 310/274-7451

BELIZAIRE THE CAJUN   Skouras Pictures, 1986,
   w/Allan L. Durand

ANGELO PIZZO
Agent: ICM - Los Angeles, 310/550-4000
Contact: Writers Guild of America - Los Angeles,
   310/550-1000

HOOSIERS   Orion, 1986, w/Carter De Haven

GRAHAM PLACE
Contact: Directors Guild of America - Los Angeles,
   213/289-2000

MILLER'S CROSSING   20th Century Fox, 1990, LP
BARTON FINK   20th Century Fox, 1991, CP
THE ADDAMS FAMILY   Orion, 1991, EP

Po

FILM
PRODUCERS,
STUDIOS,
AGENTS AND
CASTING
DIRECTORS
GUIDE

F
I
L
M

P
R
O
D
U
C
E
R
S

OTTO PLASCHKES
Business: Ariel Productions, 93 Wardour Street, London
    W1V 3TE England, 071/494-2169; Fax: 071/494-2695

A SEPARATE PEACE   Paramount, 1972,
    w/Robert A. Goldston
THE HOMECOMING   American Film Theatre, 1973, EP
BUTLEY   American Film Theatre, 1974, EP
GALILEO   American Film Theatre, 1975, EP
IN CELEBRATION   American Film Theatre, 1975, EP
HOPSCOTCH   Avco Embassy, 1980, EP
THE HOLCROFT COVENANT   Universal, 1985, CP
SHADEY   Skouras Pictures, 1987

ADAM PLATNICK
Business: New Regency Films, 4000 Warner Blvd.,
    Bldg. 66, Burbank, CA 91522

ENID IS SLEEPING   Vestron, 1990,
    EP w/Dori Berinstein & Mitchell Cannold

MARC E. PLATT
Business: Orion Pictures, 1888 Century Park East,
    Los Angeles, CA 90067-1728, 310/282-0550

CAMPUS MAN   Paramount, 1987, EP w/Barbara Boyle

POLLY PLATT
Business: Gracie Films, 20th Century Fox, 10201 W. Pico
    Blvd., Los Angeles, CA 90035, 310/280-4222;
    Fax: 310/203-3770
Contact: Writers Guild of America - Los Angeles,
    310/550-1000

BROADCAST NEWS   20th Century Fox, 1987, EP
SAY ANYTHING   20th Century Fox, 1989
THE WAR OF THE ROSES   20th Century Fox, 1989,
    EP w/Doug Claybourne

HENRY G. PLITT
SATAN'S PRINCESS   Sun Heat Pictures, 1990

MIKE PLOTKIN
PERSONAL CHOICE   Moviestore Entertainment,
    1989, EP

STAN PLOTNICK
DEADLY HERO   Avco Embassy, 1976,
    EP w/Robert Liberman
GET ROLLIN'   Aquarius, 1981, EP w/Irwin Young

MICHAEL POCHNA
KEY EXCHANGE   20th Century Fox, 1985,
    EP w/Peer J. Oppenheimer & Ronald Winston

STEPHEN POE
MEATBALLS PART II   TriStar, 1984, w/Tony Bishop

WILLIAM POHLAD
OLD EXPLORERS   Taurus, 1991, w/David
    Herbert & Tom Jenz

HAL W. POLAIRE
(credit w/Joe Eszterhas)
Business: The Polaire Production Company, 13437 Ventura
    Blvd., Suite 102, Sherman Oaks, CA 91423,
    818/501-8871
Contact: Directors Guild of America - Los Angeles,
    213/289-2000

BETRAYED   MGM/UA, 1988, EP
MUSIC BOX   TriStar, 1989, EP
SCISSORS   DDM Film Corp., 1991,
    w/Don Levin & Mel Pearl*

MICHAEL POLAIRE
Contact: Directors Guild of America - Los Angeles,
    213/289-2000

YOU TALKIN' TO ME?   MGM/UA, 1987

MIMI POLK-SOTELA
Business: Percy Main Productions, c/o Carolco Pictures,
    8439 Sunset Blvd., Suite 103, Los Angeles, CA
    90069-1909, 213/654-4417; Fax: 213/654-8936

THELMA & LOUISE   MGM-Pathe, 1991, w/Ridley Scott

MARTIN POLL
Business: Hollane Corporation, 8961 Sunset Blvd., Suite E,
    Los Angeles, CA 90069, 310/285-9808;
    Fax: 310/285-9530

LOVE IS A BALL   United Artists, 1963
SYLVIA   Paramount, 1964
THE LION IN WINTER ★   Avco Embassy, 1968
THE APPOINTMENT   MGM, 1968
THE MAGIC GARDEN OF STANLEY SWEETHEART
    MGM, 1970
NIGHT WATCH   Avco Embassy, 1973,
    w/George W. George
THE MAN WHO LOVED CAT DANCING   MGM, 1973,
    w/Eleanor Perry
LOVE & DEATH   United Artists, 1975, EP
THE SAILOR WHO FELL FROM GRACE WITH THE SEA
    Avco Embassy, 1976
SOMEBODY KILLED HER HUSBAND   Columbia, 1978
NIGHTHAWKS   Universal, 1981
GIMME AN F   20th Century Fox, 1984
HAUNTED SUMMER   Cannon, 1988
MY HEROES HAVE ALWAYS BEEN COWBOYS   Samuel
    Goldwyn Company, 1991, w/E. K. Gaylord II

SYDNEY POLLACK
Business: Mirage Enterprises, Universal Studios, 100
    Universal City Plaza, Universal City, CA 91608-1085,
    818/777-2000; Fax: 818/777-5416
Agent: CAA - Beverly Hills, 310/288-4545

THEY SHOOT HORSES, DON'T THEY?   Cinerama
    Releasing Corporation, 1969, w/Robert
    Chartoff & Irwin Winkler
THE YAKUZA   Warner Bros., 1975
BOBBY DEERFIELD   Columbia, 1977
HONEYSUCKLE ROSE   Warner Bros., 1980, EP
ABSENCE OF MALICE   Columbia, 1981
TOOTSIE ★   Columbia, 1982, w/Dick Richards
SONGWRITER   TriStar, 1984
OUT OF AFRICA ★★   Universal, 1985
BRIGHT LIGHTS, BIG CITY   MGM/UA, 1988,
    w/Mark Rosenberg

THE FABULOUS BAKER BOYS   20th Century Fox, 1989, EP
PRESUMED INNOCENT   Warner Bros., 1990, w/Mark Rosenberg
WHITE PALACE   Universal, 1990, EP
HAVANA   Universal, 1990, w/Richard Roth
KING RALPH   Universal, 1991, EP w/Mark Rosenberg
LEAVING NORMAL   Universal, 1991, EP

DALE POLLOCK
(credit w/Gil Friesen)
Business: A & M Films, 1416 La Brea Ave., Hollywood, CA 90028, 213/469-2411; Fax: 213/856-2740

THE BEAST   Columbia, 1988, EP
THE MIGHTY QUINN   MGM/UA, 1989, EP
WORTH WINNING   20th Century Fox, 1989
BLAZE   Buena Vista, 1989
CROOKED HEARTS   MGM, 1991, w/Rick Stevenson & Gil Friesen
A MIDNIGHT CLEAR   Interstar, 1991, w/Bill Borden*

PATSY POLLOCK
Contact: Wizzo, 071/736-5425

RITA, SUE & BOB TOO!   Orion Classics, 1987, CP

JOHN POMEROY
(credit w/Don Bluth & Gary Goldman)
Business: Sullivan/Bluth Studios, 2501 W. Burbank Blvd., Suite 201, Burbank, CA 91505, 818/840-9446; Fax: 818/840-0487

THE SECRET OF N.I.M.H. (AF)   MGM/UA, 1982
AN AMERICAN TAIL (AF)   Universal, 1986
THE LAND BEFORE TIME (AF)   Universal, 1988
ALL DOGS GO TO HEAVEN (AF)   Universal, 1989

LYLE S. PONCHER
Business: Great River Productions, 11611 San Vicente Blvd., Suite 800, Los Angeles, CA 90049, 310/820-4680

THE CHALLENGE   Embassy, 1982, EP

PAUL PONPIAN
STREET GIRLS   New World, 1975, w/Jeff Begun

ALEX PONTI
OSCAR   Buena Vista, 1991, EP w/Joseph S. Vecchio

CARLO PONTI
THE TENTH VICTIM   Avco Embassy, 1965
DR. ZHIVAGO   MGM, 1966
ZABRISKIE POINT   MGM, 1970
LADY LIBERTY   United Artists, 1972
WHITE SISTER   Columbia, 1973
MASSACRE IN ROME   National General, 1973
WHAT?   Avco Embassy, 1973
TORSO   Joseph Brenner, 1974
ANDY WARHOL'S DRACULA   Bryanston, 1974, w/Andrew Braunsberg & Jean Pierre Rassam
ANDY WARHOL'S FRANKENSTEIN   Bryanston, 1974, w/Andrew Braunsberg & Jean Pierre Rassam
THE PASSENGER   United Artists, 1975
THE CASSANDRA CROSSING   Avco Embassy, 1977
A SPECIAL DAY   Cinema 5, 1977
POOPSIE   Cougar, 1978
DOWN AND DIRTY   New Line, 1979

RANDY POPE
HANGFIRE   Motion Picture Corp. of America, 1991, CP

NIKOLA POPOVIC
HEY BABU RIBA   Orion Classics, 1987, w/Dragoljub Popovich

DRAGOLJUB POPOVICH
HEY BABU RIBA   Orion Classics, 1987, w/Nikola Popovic

PHILIP PORCELLA
THE WIZARD OF LONELINESS   Skouras Pictures, 1988, w/Thom Tyson

DENNIS POTTER
Contact: Writers Guild of America - Los Angeles, 310/550-1000

DREAMCHILD   Universal, 1985, EP w/Verity Lambert

MARYKAY POWELL
Business: Rastar Productions, c/o Maple Plaza, 335 N. Maple Drive, Suite 356, Beverly Hills, CA 90210, 310/247-0130; Fax: 310/247-9120

VIOLETS ARE BLUE   Columbia, 1986
BAJA OKLAHOMA   HBO Pictures, 1988
BILOXI BLUES   Universal, 1988, EP w/Joseph M. Carraciolo
LISTEN TO ME   WEG/Columbia, 1989
WHITE FANG   Buena Vista, 1991

MELISSA POWELL
LISTEN UP: THE LIVES OF QUINCY JONES (FD)   Warner Bros., 1990, LP

NIK POWELL
Business: Palace Pictures, 16/17 Wardour Mews, London W1V 3FF, England, 071/734-7060; Fax: 071/437-3248; 8170 Beverly Blvd., Suite 203, Los Angeles, CA 90048, 213/655-1114; Fax: 213/655-1195

THE COMPANY OF WOLVES   Cannon, 1985, EP
ABSOLUTE BEGINNERS   Orion, 1986, EP w/Al Clark & Robert Devereux
SIESTA   Lorimar, 1987, EP w/Julio Caro & Zalman King
HIGH SPIRITS   TriStar, 1988, CP w/Selwyn Roberts
SHAG: THE MOVIE   Hemdale, 1989, EP w/John Daly & Derek Gibson
SCANDAL   Miramax, 1989, EP w/Joe Boyd, Bob Weinstein & Harvey Weinstein
HARDWARE   Miramax, 1990, EP w/Bob Weinstein, Harvey Weinstein, Stephen Woolley, & Trix Worrell
A RAGE IN HARLEM   Miramax, 1991, EP w/Terry Glinwood, William Horberg, Bob Weinstein & Harvey Weinstein
THE MIRACLE   Miramax, 1991, EP

DEREK POWER
THE DARK   Film Ventures International, 1979, EP
THE FUNHOUSE   Universal, 1981, w/Steven Bernhardt
LUCKY STIFF   New Line, 1988, EP w/Miles Copeland, Laurie Perlman & Pat Proft
THE HOT SPOT   Orion, 1990, EP w/Steve Ujlaki & Bill Gavin

CHARLES A. PRATT
BEN   Cinerama, 1972, EP
YOU'LL LIKE MY MOTHER   Universal, 1972, EP
WALKING TALL   Cinerama, 1973, EP
TERROR IN THE WAX MUSEUM   Cinerama, 1973, EP
"W"   Cinerama, 1974, EP
PART 2 WALKING TALL   AIP, 1975
THE REINCARNATION OF PETER PROUD   AIP, 1975, EP
SPECIAL DELIVERY   AIP, 1976, EP
FINAL CHAPTER - WALKING TALL   AIP, 1977
THE GREAT SANTINI   *THE ACE*   Orion/Warner Bros., 1979

RON PREISSMAN
THE FURY   20th Century Fox, 1978, EP

NORM PRESCOTT
JOURNEY BACK TO OZ (AF)   Filmation, 1974, w/Lou Scheimer
PINOCCHIO & THE EMPEROR OF NIGHT

EDWARD R. PRESSMAN
Business: Edward R. Pressman Film Corporation, 445 N. Bedford Drive, Penthouse, Beverly Hills, CA 90210; 310/271-8383; Fax: 310/271-9497
Agent: CAA - Beverly Hills, 310/288-4545

OUT OF IT   United Artists, 1970
THE REVOLUTIONARY   United Artists, 1970
DEALING   Warner Bros., 1972
SISTERS   AIP, 1973
BADLANDS   Warner Bros., 1974, EP
PHANTOM OF THE PARADISE   20th Century Fox, 1974
PARADISE ALLEY   Universal, 1978, EP
DESPAIR   New Line, 1979, EP w/Lutz Hengst
OLD BOYFRIENDS   Avco Embassy, 1979, w/Michele Rappaport
HEART BEAT   Orion, 1980, EP w/William Tepper
THE HAND   Orion, 1981
DAS BOOT   Columbia, 1982, EP w/Mark Damon & John Hyde
CONAN THE BARBARIAN   Universal, 1982, EP w/D. Constantine Conte
THE PIRATES OF PENZANCE   Universal, 1983, EP
PLENTY   20th Century Fox, 1985, w/Joseph Papp
CRIMEWAVE   Embassy, 1986, EP w/Irvin Shapiro
HALF MOON STREET   20th Century Fox, 1986, EP w/David Korda
TRUE STORIES   Warner Bros., 1986, EP
GOOD MORNING BABYLON   Vestron, 1987, EP
WALKER   Universal, 1987, EP
WALL STREET   20th Century Fox, 1987
MASTERS OF THE UNIVERSE   Cannon, 1987, EP
CHERRY 2000   Orion, 1988, w/Caldecot Chubb
TALK RADIO   Universal, 1988, w/A. Kitman Ho
PARIS BY NIGHT   Cineplex Odeon, 1990, EP
WAITING FOR THE LIGHT   Triumph Releasing, 1990, EP
TO SLEEP WITH ANGER   Samuel Goldwyn Company, 1990, EP w/Danny Glover & Harris E. Tulchin
REVERSAL OF FORTUNE   Warner Bros., 1990, w/Oliver Stone
MARTIANS GO HOME   Taurus, 1990, EP
BLUE STEEL   MGM/UA, 1990, w/Oliver Stone
IRON MAZE   Trans-Tokyo, 1991, EP w/Katsumi Kimura, Oliver Stone & Hidenori Taga
HOMICIDE   Triumph, 1991, w/Michael Hausman
STORYVILLE   20th Century Fox, 1992, w/David Roe

MICHAEL PRESSMAN
Agent: Broder-Kurland-Webb-Uffner Agency - Los Angeles, 213/656-9262
Contact: Directors Guild of America - Los Angeles, 213/289-2000

THOSE LIPS, THOSE EYES   United Artists, 1980, w/Steven Charles Jaffe

STEVE PREVIN
THE BATTLE OF NERETVA   AIP, 1971, EP w/Anthony B. Unger & Henry Weinstein

NORMAN PRIGGEN
SECRET CEREMONY   Universal, 1968, AP
THE GO-BETWEEN   Columbia, 1971, w/John Heyman
BLACK GUNN   Columbia, 1972, w/John Heyman
THE ASSASSINATION OF TROTSKY   Cinerama, 1972, w/Joseph Losey
TALES THAT WITNESS MADNESS   Paramount, 1973

RICHARD PRINCE
THE LEMON SISTERS   Miramax, 1990, CP

ROBERT PRINGLE
HOWLING II...YOUR SISTER IS A WEREWOLF   Thorn EMI, 1986, AP
HOWLING III: THE MARSUPIALS   Square Pictures, 1987, EP w/Steven Lane & Edward Simons
HOWLING IV...THE ORIGINAL NIGHTMARE   Allied Entertainment, 1988, EP w/Steven Lane, Avi Lerner & Edward Simons

JOHN PRIZER
DEADHEAD MILES   Paramount, 1971, AP
UNHOLY ROLLERS   AIP, 1972, w/Jack Bohrer
THE SWINGING CHEERLEADERS   Centaur, 1974
SWITCHBLADE SISTERS   Centaur, 1975

PAT PROFT
Agent: InterTalent Agency - Los Angeles, 310/858-6200
Contact: Writers Guild of America - Los Angeles, 310/550-1000

MOVING VIOLATIONS   20th Century Fox, 1985, EP w/Doug Draizin
LUCKY STIFF   New Line, 1988, EP w/Miles Copeland, Laurie Perlman & Derek Power
HOT SHOTS!   20th Century Fox, 1991, EP

CHIP PROSER
Attorney: Samantha Shad, 9465 Wilshire Blvd., Suite 920, Beverly Hills, CA 90212, 310/276-7017
Contact: Writers Guild of America - Los Angeles, 310/550-1000

INNERSPACE   Warner Bros., 1987, CP

ERWIN PROVOOST
WAIT UNTIL SPRING, BANDINI   Orion, 1990, w/Tom Luddy & Fred Roos

RICHARD PRYOR
Business: Indigo Productions, 1900 S. Bundy #808PH, Los Angeles, CA 90025, 310/442-3510; Fax: 310/442-3569
Attorney: Bloom & Dekom, Los Angeles, 310/278-8622
Agent: ICM - Los Angeles, 310/550-4000

BUSTIN' LOOSE   Universal, 1981, w/Michael S. Glick
RICHARD PRYOR LIVE ON THE SUNSET STRIP
   Columbia, 1982
JO JO DANCER, YOUR LIFE IS CALLING
   Columbia, 1986

ALBERTO PUGLIESE
WIFEMISTRESS   Quartet Films, 1979, EP

EVELYN PURCELL
Business Manager: Barbara Carswell Management, 321 S. Beverly Dr., Suite M, Beverly Hills, CA 90212, 310/556-0563
Agent: William Morris Agency - Beverly Hills, 310/274-7451

CAGED HEAT   New World, 1974
FIGHTING MAD   20th Century Fox, 1976, CP

DAVID PUTTNAM
Business: Enigma Productions, Ltd., 15 Queen's Gate Place Mews, London SW7 5BG, England, 071/581-0238; Fax: 071/584-1799

MELODY   Levitt-Pickman, 1971
THE PIED PIPER   Paramount, 1972, w/Sandy Lieberson
SWASTIKA (FD)   Cinema 5, 1974, w/Sandy Lieberson
THAT'LL BE THE DAY   EMI, 1974, w/Sandy Lieberson
MAHLER   Mayfair, 1974, EP w/Sandy Lieberson
THE LAST DAYS OF MAN ON EARTH   *THE FINAL PROGRAMME*   New World, 1974, EP w/Roy Baird & Michael Moorcock
STARDUST   Columbia, 1975, w/Sandy Lieberson
BROTHER, CAN YOU SPARE A DIME? (FD)   Dimension, 1975, w/Sandy Lieberson
LISZTOMANIA   Warner Bros., 1975, w/Roy Baird
BUGSY MALONE   Paramount, 1976, EP
THE DUELLISTS   Paramount, 1978
MIDNIGHT EXPRESS ★   Columbia, 1978, w/Alan Marshall
FOXES   United Artists, 1980, w/Gerald Ayres
CHARIOTS OF FIRE ★★   The Ladd Company/Warner Bros., 1981
LOCAL HERO   Warner Bros., 1983
EXPERIENCE PREFERRED...BUT NOT ESSENTIAL
   Samuel Goldwyn Company, 1983
SECRETS   Samuel Goldwyn Company, 1984
KIPPERBANG   *P'TANG YANG, KIPPERBANG*   MGM/United Artists Classics, 1984, EP
THE KILLING FIELDS ★   Warner Bros., 1984
CAL   Warner Bros., 1984, w/Stuart Craig
THE FROG PRINCE   Warner Bros., 1985, EP
KNIGHTS & EMERALDS   Warner Bros., 1986, EP
MR. LOVE   Warner Bros., 1986, EP
SHARMA & BEYOND   Cinecom, 1986, EP
FOREVER YOUNG   Cinecom, 1986, EP
THOSE GLORY, GLORY DAYS   Cinecom, 1986, EP
WINTER FLIGHT   Cinecom, 1986, EP
ARTHUR'S HALLOWED GROUND   Cinecom, 1986, EP
THE MISSION ★   Warner Bros., 1986, w/Fernando Ghia
DEFENSE OF THE REALM   Hemdale, 1987, EP
MEMPHIS BELLE   Warner Bros., 1990, w/Catherine Wyler
MEETING VENUS   Warner Bros., 1991, w/Uberto Pasolini

Q

JEAN-PIERRE QUENET
DUCK TALES: THE MOVIE - TREASURE OF THE LOST LAMP (AF)   Buena Vista, 1990, CP w/Robert Taylor

JOHN QUESTED
Business: Goldcrest Films & Television Ltd., 1240 Olive, Los Angeles, CA 90069, 213/650-4551; Fax: 213/650-3581 or 36-44 Brewer St., London W1R 3HP, England, 071/437-8696; Fax: 071/437-4448

LEOPARD IN THE SNOW   New World, 1979, w/Chris Harrop
THE PASSAGE   United Artists, 1979
SUNBURN   Paramount, 1979, EP w/Jay Bernstein
THE RETURN OF THE SOLDIER   European Classics, 1985, EP w/J. Gordon Arnold & Edward Simons
AMERICAN GOTHIC   Vidmark Entertainment, 1988

ROBERTO A. QUEZADA
PHANTASM II   Universal, 1988
SURVIVAL QUEST   MGM/UA, 1990

WILLIAM J. QUIGLEY
THE DEAD   Vestron, 1987, EP
STEEL DAWN   Vestron, 1987, EP w/Larry Sugar
SALOME'S LAST DANCE   Vestron, 1987
THE UNHOLY   Vestron, 1988
THE LAIR OF THE WHITE WORM   Vestron, 1988, EP w/Dan Ireland
WAXWORK   Vestron, 1988, EP w/Gregory Cascante, Dan Ireland & Mario Sotela
BURNING SECRET   Vestron, 1988, EP w/MJ Peckos
THE RAINBOW   Vestron, 1989, EP w/Dan Ireland
TWISTER   Vestron, 1990, EP w/Dan Ireland

JOHN QUILL
NATURAL ENEMIES   Cinema 5, 1979
CALL ME   Vestron, 1988, w/Kenneth Martel

ANTHONY QUINN
Agent: BBMW - Los Angeles, 310/247-5500

ACROSS 110th STREET   United Artists, 1972, EP w/Barry Shear

GENE QUINTANO
Business: Trans World, 3330 W. Cahuenga Blvd., Suite 500, Los Angeles, CA 90068, 213/969-2800
Agent: ICM - Los Angeles, 310/550-4000

MAKING THE GRADE   MGM/UA/Cannon, 1984

R

MAX L. RAAB
(credit w/Si Litvinoff)

END OF THE ROAD   Allied Artists, 1970, EP
WALKABOUT   20th Century Fox, 1971, EP*
A CLOCKWORK ORANGE ★   Warner Bros., 1971, EP
ALL THE RIGHT NOISES   20th Century Fox, 1973

DAVID RABE
Agent: UTA - Beverly Hills, 310/273-6700
Contact: Writers Guild of America - New York, 212/245-6180

I'M DANCING AS FAST AS I CAN   Paramount, 1982, EP

STEVE RABINER
Business: Concorde/New Horizons, 11600 San Vicente
   Blvd., Los Angeles, CA 90049, 310/820-6733;
   Fax: 310/207-6816

FORCED EXPOSURE   Concorde, 1991

HERB RABINOWITZ
PERMANENT RECORD   Paramount, 1988, CP

MICHAEL RACHMIL
Contact: Directors Guild of America - Los Angeles,
   213/289-2000

WESTWORLD   MGM, 1973, AP
EXTREME CLOSE-UP   National General, 1973, AP
CAPRICORN ONE   Warner Bros., 1978, AP
TOM HORN   Warner Bros., 1980,
   AP w/Sandra Weintraub
DEAD & BURIED   Avco Embassy, 1981, AP
RUNAWAY   TriStar, 1984
QUICKSILVER   Columbia, 1986, w/Daniel Melnick
ROXANNE   Columbia, 1987, w/Daniel Melnick
ELVIRA, MISTRESS OF THE DARK   New World,
   1988, EP
PUNCHLINE   Columbia, 1988, w/Daniel Melnick
NO HOLDS BARRED   New Line, 1989
HARD TO KILL   Warner Bros., 1990, EP w/Lee Rich
FLATLINERS   Columbia, 1990, EP w/Peter Filardi &
   Scott Rudin
L.A. STORY   TriStar, 1991, w/Daniel Melnick

MARK RADCLIFFE
ONLY THE LONELY   20th Century Fox, 1991, CP

SARAH RADCLYFFE
Business: 1416 N. La Brea, Hollywood, CA 90028,
   213/856-2779; Fax: 213/856-2615
Contact: Working Title Films, 1 Water Lane, Kentish Town
   Lane, London NW1 8NZ England, 071/911-6100;
   Fax: 071/911-6150

MY BEAUTIFUL LAUNDRETTE   Orion Classics, 1986,
   w/Tim Bevan
CARAVAGGIO   Cinevista, 1986

WISH YOU WERE HERE   Atlantic, 1987
SAMMY & ROSIE GET LAID   Cinecom, 1987,
   w/Tim Bevan
A WORLD APART   Atlantic, 1988
PAPERHOUSE   Vestron, 1989, w/Tim Bevan
FOOLS OF FORTUNE   New Line, 1990
HEAR MY SONG   Miramax, 1992

PAUL RADIN
LIVING FREE   Columbia, 1972
PHASE IV   Paramount, 1974

ROBERT B. RADNITZ
Business: Robert Radnitz Productions, 10182 1/2 Culver
   Blvd., Culver City, CA 90230, 310/837-0422

A DOG OF FLANDERS   20th Century Fox, 1959
MISTY   20th Century Fox, 1961
ISLAND OF BLUE DOLPHINS   Universal, 1964
MY SIDE OF THE MOUNTAIN   Paramount, 1968
THE LITTLE ARK   National General, 1972
SOUNDER ★   20th Century Fox, 1972
WHERE THE LILIES BLOOM   United Artists, 1974
PART 2, SOUNDER   Gamma III, 1976, EP
BIRCH INTERVAL   Gamma III, 1976
A HERO AIN'T NOTHIN' BUT A SANDWICH   New
   World, 1977
CROSS CREEK   Universal, 1983

BOB RAFELSON
Business: Marmont Productions, c/o Carolco, 8800 Sunset
   Blvd., 2nd Floor, Los Angeles, CA 90069, 310/855-7261
Contact: Directors Guild of America - Los Angeles,
   213/289-2000

HEAD   Columbia, 1968, w/Jack Nicholson
FIVE EASY PIECES ★   Columbia, 1970,
   w/Richard Wechsler
THE KING OF MARVIN GARDENS   Columbia, 1972
STAY HUNGRY   United Artists, 1976, w/Harold Schneider
THE POSTMAN ALWAYS RINGS TWICE   Paramount,
   1981, w/Charles Mulvehill

ALEXANDRA RAFFE
Business: Vos Productions Inc., 152 John St., Suite 502,
   Toronto, M5V 2T2, 416/971-9401; Fax: 416/971-9605

I'VE HEARD THE MERMAIDS SINGING   Miramax, 1987,
   w/Patricia Rozema
THE WHITE ROOM   Alliance, 1990

KEVIN RAFFERTY
BLOOD IN THE FACE (FD)   First Run Features, 1991,
   w/Anne Bohlen & James Ridgeway

JOSEPH C. RAFFILL
THE SEA GYPSIES   Warner Bros., 1978
THE GIANT OF THUNDER MOUNTAIN   Castle Hill, 1991

SAMUEL M. RAIMI
Business: Renaissance Motion Pictures, Inc., 28 East 10th
   St., New York, NY 10003, 212/477-0432
Business: 6381 Hollywood Blvd., #680, Los Angeles, CA
   90028, 213/463-9965; Fax: 213/969-8509
Agent: InterTalent Agency - Los Angeles, 310/858-6200

THE EVIL DEAD   New Line, 1983, EP w/Bruce Campbell

Ra

FILM
PRODUCERS,
STUDIOS,
AGENTS AND
CASTING
DIRECTORS
GUIDE

F
I
L
M

P
R
O
D
U
C
E
R
S

Ra

FILM
PRODUCERS,
STUDIOS,
AGENTS and
CASTING
DIRECTORS
GUIDE

F
I
L
M

P
R
O
D
U
C
E
R
S

PEGGY RAJSKI
Business: 306 W. 38th St., Suite 1002, New York, NY
10018, 212/239-0521

THE BROTHER FROM ANOTHER PLANET   Cinecom,
1984, w/Maggie Renzi
MATEWAN   Cinecom, 1987, w/Maggie Renzi
EIGHT MEN OUT   Orion, 1988, CP
THE GRIFTERS   Miramax, 1990, CP

FRANCISCO RAMALHO, JR.
KISS OF THE SPIDER WOMAN ★   Island Alive, 1985, EP

HAROLD RAMIS
Business: Ocean Pictures, 2821 Main St., Santa Monica, CA
90405, 310/399-9271
Agent: CAA - Beverly Hills, 310/288-4545

BACK TO SCHOOL   Orion, 1986, EP w/Estelle Endler &
Michael Endler

PHIL RAMONE
BODY ROCK   New World, 1984, EP w/Jon Feltheimer &
Charles J. Weber

DEAN RAMSER
THE UNNAMEABLE   Vidmark Entertainment, 1988,
w/Jean Paul Ouellette

ROGER RANDALL-CUTLER
Business: First Film Company, 38 Great Windmill Street,
London W1V 7PA, 071/439-1640; Fax: 071/437-2062

DANCE WITH A STRANGER   Samuel Goldwyn
Company, 1985

ANTHONY RANDELL
GRUNT! THE WRESTLING MOVIE   New World, 1985,
w/Don Normann

PAUL RANNAM
VALMONT   Orion, 1989, w/Michael Hausman

MORT RANSEN
FALLING OVER BACKWARDS   Astral Films, 1990,
w/Stewart Harding

MARTIN RANSOHOFF
Business: Albacore Films, 9350 Wilshire Blvd., Suite 219,
Beverly Hills, CA 90212, 310/274-4585;
Fax: 310/276-3093

THE AMERICANIZATION OF EMILY   MGM, 1964
THE SANDPIPER   MGM, 1965
THE CINCINNATI KID   MGM, 1965
ICE STATION ZEBRA   MGM, 1968, w/John Calley
CASTLE KEEP   Columbia, 1969, w/John Calley
HAMLET   Columbia, 1969, EP w/Leslie Linder
CATCH 22   Paramount, 1970, w/John Calley
THE MOONSHINE WAR   MGM, 1970
10 RILLINGTON PLACE   Columbia, 1971, w/Leslie Linder
SEE NO EVIL   Columbia, 1971, w/Leslie Linder
THE WHITE DAWN   Paramount, 1974
SILVER STREAK   20th Century Fox, 1976,
EP w/Frank Yablans
THE WANDERERS   Orion/Warner Bros., 1979
NIGHTWING   Columbia, 1979

THE MOUNTAIN MEN   Columbia, 1980, w/Andrew
Scheinman & Martin Shafer
A CHANGE OF SEASONS   20th Century Fox, 1980
AMERICAN POP (AF)   Paramount, 1981, w/Ralph Bakshi
HANKY PANKY   Columbia, 1982
CLASS   Orion, 1983
JAGGED EDGE   Columbia, 1985
THE BIG TOWN   Columbia, 1987
SWITCHING CHANNELS   TriStar, 1988
PHYSICAL EVIDENCE   Columbia, 1989
WELCOME HOME   Columbia, 1989

PAUL RAPHAEL
Contact: 10 Star Field Road, London W12 9SW England

PASCALI'S ISLAND   Avenue Entertainment, 1988, CP
THE RACHEL PAPERS   MGM/UA, 1989, CP

NEIL RAPP
Contact: Directors Guild of America - Los Angeles,
213/289-2000

INDEPENDENCE DAY   Unifilm, 1977, w/Bobby Roth

PAUL RAPP
AVALANCHE   New World, 1978, EP

MICHELE RAPPAPORT
Business: Carliner-Rappaport Productions, 11700
Laurelwood Dr., Studio City, CA 91604, 818/763-4783

OLD BOYFRIENDS   Avco Embassy, 1979,
w/Edward R. Pressman
WHITE MEN CAN'T JUMP   20th Century Fox, 1991, EP

DANIEL RASKOV
Business: I.R.S. World Media, 3939 Lankershim Blvd.,
Universal City, CA 91604, 818/505-0555;
Fax: 818/505-1318

A SINFUL LIFE   New Line, 1989

TINA RATHBORNE
ZELLY AND ME   Columbia, 1988, EP w/Elliott Lewitt

LARRY J. RATTNER
GENUINE RISK   I.R.S., 1990, w/William Ewart &
Guy J. Louthan

ERIC RATTRAY
Contact: 59 Botley Road, Chesham, Bucks HP5 1XG,
0494/783-248

THE GREEK TYCOON   Universal, 1978, AP
DRAGONSLAYER   Paramount, 1981, AP
BETRAYAL   20th Century Fox International Classics, 1983
LABYRINTH   TriStar, 1986
MEMPHIS BELLE   Warner Bros., 1990, AP

MICHAEL JAY RAUCH
Contact: Directors Guild of America - Los Angeles,
213/289-2000

BAND OF THE HAND   TriStar, 1986
APPRENTICE TO MURDER   New World, 1988, EP
BLUE STEEL   MGM/UA, 1990, CP
REVERSAL OF FORTUNE   Warner Bros., 1990, EP

TAMARA RAWITT
Business: Ivory Way Productions, c/o KTTV, 5746 Sunset
    Blvd., Hollywood, CA 90028-8588, 213/856-1190;
    Fax: 213/462-7382

I'M GONNA GIT YOU SUCKA   MGM/UA, 1989,
    CP w/Eric Barrett

PETER RAWLEY
Agent: ICM - Los Angeles, 310/550-4000

THE TERRORISTS   20th Century Fox, 1975

FRED OLEN RAY
BIOHAZARD   21st Century, 1985
THE TOMB   Trans World, 1986, w/Ronnie Hadar
ARMED RESPONSE   Cinetel, 1986, CP
COMMANDO SQUAD   Trans World, 1987, CP
MOB BOSS   Vidmark Entertainment, 1990

TONY RAY
Contact: Directors Guild of America - Los Angeles,
    213/289-2000

ALEX IN WONDERLAND   MGM, 1970, AP
BLUME IN LOVE   Warner Bros., 1973, AP
FREEBIE & THE BEAN   Warner Bros., 1974, AP
HARRY AND TONTO   20th Century Fox, 1974, AP
NEXT STOP, GREENWICH VILLAGE   20th Century Fox,
    1976, w/Paul Mazursky
AN UNMARRIED WOMAN ★   20th Century Fox, 1978,
    w/Paul Mazursky
THE ROSE   20th Century Fox, 1979, EP
WILLIE & PHIL   20th Century Fox, 1980,
    w/Paul Mazursky

MICHELE RAY-GAVRAS
HANNA K.   Universal, 1983, EP

WANDA S. RAYLE
MIDNIGHT CROSSING   Vestron, 1988, EP w/Gary
    Barber, Gregory Cascante & Doug Ireland

THOMAS A. RAZZANO
Contact: Directors Guild of America - New York,
    212/581-0370

A RAGE IN HARLEM   Miramax, 1991, LP

PETER W. REA
GRANDVIEW, U.S.A.   Warner Bros., 1984,
    w/William Warren Blaylock

ERIC RED
Agent: UTA - Beverly Hills, 310/273-6700

NEAR DARK   DEG, 1987, CP

JACK N. REDDISH
LE MANS   National General, 1971

ROBERT REDFORD
Business: Wildwood Enterprises, 1223 Wilshire Blvd.,
    Suite 412, Santa Monica, CA 90403, 310/395-5155
Agent: CAA - Beverly Hills, 310/288-4545

THE CANDIDATE   Warner Bros., 1972,
    EP w/Michael Ritchie

PROMISED LAND   Vestron, 1988, EP w/Andrew Meyer
SOME GIRLS   MGM/UA, 1988, EP
THE MILAGRO BEANFIELD WAR   Universal, 1988,
    w/Moctesuma Esparza

ROBERT REDLIN
AFTER DARK, MY SWEET   Avenue Pictures, 1990,
    w/Ric Kidney

PAUL REDSHAW
COMMUNION   New Line, 1989, EP w/Gary Barber

JERRY REED
Business: Jerry Reed Enterprises - Nashville, 615/256-4770
Contact: Directors Guild of America - Los Angeles,
    213/289-2000

WHAT COMES AROUND   W.O. Associates, 1986, EP
BAT 21   TriStar, 1988, EP

GEOFFREY REEVE
CARAVAN TO VACCARES   Bryanston, 1976,
    w/Richard Morris-Adams
THE SHOOTING PARTY   European Classics, 1985
HALF MOON STREET   20th Century Fox, 1986
THE WHISTLE BLOWER   Hemdale, 1987

JAMES REEVE
THE WHISTLE BLOWER   Hemdale, 1987, EP

JACK REEVES
DARKER THAN AMBER   National General, 1970,
    w/Walter Seltzer
THE FIRST NUDIE MUSICAL   Paramount, 1976

KEN REGAN
YESTERDAY'S HERO   EMI, 1979, w/Oscar S. Lerman

RUSS REGAN
ALL THIS AND WORLD WAR II (FD)   20th Century Fox,
    1976, EP

GODFREY REGGIO
POWAQQATSI (FD)   Cannon, 1988, w/Mel Lawrence &
    Lawrence Taub

ROBERT REHME
Business: Neufeld/Rehme Productions, Paramount Pictures,
    5555 Melrose Ave., Dressing #112, Los Angeles, CA
    90038, 213/956-4816; Fax: 213/956-2571

AN EYE FOR AN EYE   Avco Embassy, 1981, EP
VICE SQUAD   Avco Embassy, 1982, EP w/Frank Capra Jr.
    & Sandy Howard
NECESSARY ROUGHNESS   Paramount, 1991,
    w/Mace Neufeld

STEVEN REICH
Business: IRS Media, 3939 Lankershim Blvd., Universal City,
    CA 91604, 818/505-0555; Fax: 818/505-1318

CIRCUITRY MAN   Skouras, 1990, w/John Schouweiler

STEPHANE REICHEL
EDDIE & THE CRUISERS II: EDDIE LIVES   Scotti
    Bros., 1989

Re

**FILM
PRODUCERS,
STUDIOS,
AGENTS** AND
**CASTING
DIRECTORS
GUIDE**

F
I
L
M

P
R
O
D
U
C
E
R
S

FRANCOIS REICHENBACH
Business: Films du Prisme, 72 bis Rue de la Tour, 75016 Paris, 04/504-4229

MEDICINE BALL CARAVAN (FD)   Warner Bros., 1971, w/Tom Donahue

ANDREW REICHSMAN
SIGNS OF LIFE   Avenue, 1989, w/Marcus Viscidi

SHELLEY E. REID
Business: Monarch Pictures, 10000 W. Washington Blvd., #224N, Culver City, CA 90232-2792, 310/287-0484; Fax: 310/575-3229

NIGHT VISITOR   MGM/UA, 1989, EP w/Tom Broadbridge

KEVIN REIDY
Business: IRS Media, 3939 Lankershim Blvd., Universal City, CA 91604, 818/505-0555; Fax: 818/505-1318

CRACKDOWN   Concorde, 1991, EP

BRIAN REILLY
Business: Outlaw Productions, 12103 Maxwellton Rd., Studio City, CA 91604, 818/509-7953; Fax: 818/506-0983

DON'T TELL MOM THE BABYSITTER'S DEAD   Warner Bros.   1991, w/Robert Newmyer & Jeffrey Silver

CARL REINER
Business Manager: George Shapiro, Shapiro-West, 141 El Camino Dr., Beverly Hills, CA 90212, 310/278-8896
Agent: William Morris Agency - Beverly Hills, 310/274-7451

THE COMIC   Columbia, 1969, w/Aaron Ruben

ROB REINER
(credit w/Andrew Scheinman)
Business: Castle Rock Entertainment, 335 N. Maple Dr., Suite 135, Beverly Hills, CA 90210, 310/285-2300; Fax: 310/285-2345
Agent: CAA - Beverly Hills, 310/288-4545

THE PRINCESS BRIDE   20th Century Fox, 1987
WHEN HARRY MET SALLY...   Castle Rock/ Columbia, 1989
MISERY   Castle Rock/Columbia, 1990

JONATHON REISS
Contact: 213/935-0173

LOVE IS LIKE THAT   Boomerang Pictures, 1991, w/Matt Devlen

IVAN REITMAN
Business: Ivan Reitman Productions, 100 Universal Plaza, Universal City, CA 91608-1085, 818/777-8080; Fax: 818/777-0689
Agent: CAA - Beverly Hills, 310/288-4545

FOXY LADY   Cinepix, 1971
CANNIBAL GIRLS   AIP, 1973, EP
THEY CAME FROM WITHIN   Trans-America, 1976
THE HOUSE BY THE LAKE   AIP, 1977
RABID   New World, 1977, EP w/Andre Link
BLACKOUT   New World, 1978, EP w/Andre Link & John Vidette

NATIONAL LAMPOON'S ANIMAL HOUSE   Universal, 1978, w/Matty Simmons
STRIPES   Columbia, 1981, w/Dan Goldberg
HEAVY METAL (AF)   Columbia, 1981
SPACEHUNTER: ADVENTURES IN THE FORBIDDEN ZONE   Columbia, 1983, EP
GHOSTBUSTERS   Columbia, 1984
LEGAL EAGLES   Universal, 1986
BIG SHOTS   20th Century Fox, 1987, EP
CASUAL SEX?   Universal, 1988, EP
FEDS   Warner Bros., 1988, EP
TWINS   Universal, 1988
GHOSTBUSTERS II   Columbia, 1989
KINDERGARTEN COP   Universal, 1990, w/Brian Grazer
BEETHOVEN   Universal, 1992, EP
STOP OR MY MOTHER WILL SHOOT   Universal, 1992, w/Michael C. Gross & Joe Medjuck

SIMON RELPH
Business: Skreba Films, 5a Noel Street, London W1V 3RB England, 071/437-6492; Fax: 071/437-0644

REDS ★   Paramount, 1981, EP w/Dede Allen
PRIVATES ON PARADE   Orion Classics, 1984
THE PLOUGHMAN'S LUNCH   Samuel Goldwyn Company, 1984, w/Ann Scott
WETHERBY   MGM/UA Classics, 1985
SECRET PLACES   20th Century Fox, 1985, w/Ann Skinner
THE RETURN OF THE SOLDIER   European Classics, 1985, w/Ann Skinner

ROBERT E. RELYEA
Business: Paramount Pictures, 5555 Melrose Ave., Hollywood, CA 90038, 213/956-5512
Contact: Directors Guild of America - Los Angeles, 213/289-2000

BULLITT   Warner Bros., 1968, EP
THE REIVERS   National General, 1969, EP
ADAM AT SIX A.M.   National General, 1970, EP
LE MANS   National General, 1971, EP
THE DAY OF THE DOLPHIN   Avco Embassy, 1973
THE SAVAGE IS LOOSE   Campbell Devon, 1974, EP
BLAME IT ON RIO   20th Century Fox, 1984, AP

MAGGIE RENZI
LIANNA   United Artists Classics, 1983, w/Jeffrey Nelson
THE BROTHER FROM ANOTHER PLANET   Cinecom, 1984, w/Peggy Rajski
MATEWAN   Cinecom, 1987, w/Peggy Rajski
CITY OF HOPE   Samuel Goldwyn Company, 1991, w/Sarah Green

ROBERT D. RESNIKOFF
(credit w/Frank Darius Namei)
Business: Paramount Pictures, 5555 Melrose Ave., Los Angeles, CA 90038, 213/956-4302
Agent: UTA - Beverly Hills, 310/273-6700

COLLISION COURSE   DEG, 1988, CP

PAUL REUBENS
(Pee-Wee Herman)
Business: Paramount Pictures, 5555 Melrose Ave., Los Angeles, CA 90038, 213/956-4504
Contact: Michael McLean - 818/505-0945

BIG TOP PEE-WEE   Paramount, 1988, w/Debra Hill

Ri

FILM
PRODUCERS,
STUDIOS,
AGENTS AND
CASTING
DIRECTORS
GUIDE

STEVEN REUTHER
(credit w/Mitchell Cannold)
Business: New Regency Films, 4000 Warner Blvd.,
    Burbank, CA 91522, 818/954-3044; Fax: 818/954-3295

DIRTY DANCING   Vestron, 1987, EP
CHINA GIRL   Vestron, 1987, EP
AND GOD CREATED WOMAN   Vestron, 1988,
    EP w/Ruth Vitale
CALL ME   Vestron, 1988, EP w/Ruth Vitale
BIG MAN ON CAMPUS   Vestron, 1989, EP
PARENTS   Vestron, 1989, EP
HIDER IN THE HOUSE   Vestron, 1989,
    EP w/Diane Nabatoff*
PRETTY WOMAN   Buena Vista, 1990, w/Arnon Milchan*
GUILTY BY SUSPICION   Warner Bros., 1991, EP*
CATCHFIRE   1991, EP
THE MAMBO KINGS   Warner Bros., 1991, EP

DON REYNOLDS
THE AMAZING DOBERMANS   Golden, 1977, EP

PHILLIP RHEE
BEST OF THE BEST   Taurus, 1989, w/Peter E. Strauss

JOSEPH RHODES
SOME OF MY BEST FRIENDS ARE...   AIP, 1971, EP

MIKE RHODES
Contact: Directors Guild of America - Los Angeles,
    213/289-2000

ROMERO   Four Seasons Entertainment, 1989, SP

CRAIG RICE
GRAFFITI BRIDGE   Warner Bros., 1990, CP

WAYNE RICE
LOVE STINKS   Live Entertainment, 1991,
    w/Morrie Eisenman

LEE RICH
Business: Lee Rich Productions, 4000 Warner Blvd.,
    Burbank, CA 91522, 818/954-3556; Fax: 818/954-4176

THE SPORTING CLUB   Avco Embassy, 1971
THE MAN   Paramount, 1972
WHO IS KILLING THE GREAT CHEFS OF EUROPE?
    Warner Bros., 1972, EP w/Merv Adelson
THE CHOIRBOYS   Universal, 1977, w/Merv Adelson
THE BIG RED ONE   United Artists, 1980,
    EP w/Merv Adelson
HARD TO KILL   Warner Bros., 1990,
    EP w/Michael Rachmil

MATTY RICH
Agent: William Morris Agency - New York, 212/586-5100

STRAIGHT OUT OF BROOKLYN   Samuel Goldwyn
    Company, 1991

RON RICH
GHOST FEVER   Miramax, 1987, w/Edward Coe

JEF RICHARD
HIT LIST   New Line, 1989, CP

DICK RICHARDS
Agent: Triad Artists, Inc. - Los Angeles, 310/556-2727
Contact: Directors Guild of America - Los Angeles,
    213/289-2000

MARCH OR DIE   Columbia, 1977, w/Jerry Bruckheimer
TOOTSIE ★   Columbia, 1982, w/Sydney Pollack

MARTIN RICHARDS
Business: Producers Circle, 1350 Avenue of the Americas,
    New York, NY 10019, 212/765-6760

SOME OF MY BEST FRIENDS ARE...   AIP, 1971,
    w/John Lauricella
FUN AND GAMES   Audubon, 1973, w/Gill Champion
THE BOYS FROM BRAZIL   20th Century Fox, 1978,
    w/Stanley O'Toole
FORT APACHE, THE BRONX   20th Century Fox, 1981,
    w/Tom Fiorello

SUSAN RICHARDS
WINTER FLIGHT   Cinecom, 1986, w/Robin Douet
MR. LOVE   Warner Bros., 1986, w/Robin Douet
KNIGHTS AND EMERALDS   Warner Bros., 1986,
    w/Raymond Day
STARS AND BARS   Columbia, 1988, CP

NED RICHARDSON
SALVATION!   Circle Releasing, 1987, EP w/Michel Duval &
    Irving Ong

TONY RICHARDSON
Business: Woodfall Ltd., Hill House,1 Little New St., London
    EC4A 3TR, England or 1478 N. Kings Rd., Los Angeles,
    CA 90069, 213/656-5314
Contact: Directors Guild of America - Los Angeles,
    213/289-2000

TOM JONES ★★   United Artists, 1963

ALAN RICHE
Business: TriStar Pictures, 10202 W. Washington Blvd.,
    Culver City, CA 90232-3195, 310/280-7861

MESSIAH OF EVIL   *DEAD PEOPLE*   International
    Cinefilm, 1975, w/Willard Huyck, EP
YOUNGBLOOD   AIP, 1978, w/Nick Grillo

WILLIAM RICHERT
Agent: The Gersh Agency - Beverly Hills, 310/274-6611

DERBY (FD)   Cinerama, 1971
FIRST POSITION (FD)   Roninfilm, 1973
LAW AND DISORDER   Columbia, 1974

W. D. RICHTER
Business: Granite Pictures, 335 N. Maple Dr., #135,
    Beverly Hills, CA 90210, 310/285-6426
Agent: Shapiro-Lichtman, Inc. - Los Angeles, 310/859-8877

SLITHER   MGM, 1973, AP
THE ADVENTURES OF BUCKAROO BANZAI ACROSS
    THE EIGHTH DIMENSION   20th Century Fox, 1984,
    w/Neil Canton

BRUCE RICKER
THELONIOUS MONK: STRAIGHT, NO CHASER (FD)
    Warner Bros., 1988, w/Charlotte Zwerin

Ri

FILM
PRODUCERS,
STUDIOS,
AGENTS AND
CASTING
DIRECTORS
GUIDE

F
I
L
M

P
R
O
D
U
C
E
R
S

ROGER RIDDELL
DIRT   American Cinema, 1979,
  EP w/Michael C. Leone

JAMES RIDGEWAY
Business: The Village Voice, 842 Broadway, New York,
  NY 10003, 212/475-3300

BLOOD IN THE FACE (FD)   First Run Features, 1991,
  w/Anne Bohlen & Kevin Rafferty

RICHARD R. RIMMEL
KAMA SUTRA   Trans America, 1971, w/Kobi Jaeger

JEFF RINGLER
Business: SVS, Inc., 1700 Broadway, New York, NY
  10019, 212/757-4990; Fax: 212/956-3792

BEST OF THE BEST   Taurus, 1989, EP w/Frank
  Giustra & Michael Holzman

SARA RISHER
Business: New Line, 116 N. Robertson Blvd., Los Angeles,
  CA 90048, 310/854-5811

POLYESTER   New Line, 1981, AP
THE FIRST TIME   New Line, 1982, AP
A NIGHTMARE ON ELM STREET   New Line, 1984, CP
A NIGHTMARE ON ELM STREET 2: FREDDY'S
  REVENGE   New Line, 1985, CP
QUIET COOL   New Line, 1986, AP
A NIGHTMARE ON ELM STREET 3: DREAM WARRIORS
  New Line, 1987, CP
MY DEMON LOVER   New Line, 1987, CP
THE PRINCE OF PENNSYLVANIA   New Line, 1988,
  EP w/Robert Shaye
HAIRSPRAY   New Line, 1988, EP w/Robert Shaye
A NIGHTMARE ON ELM STREET 4: THE DREAM
  MASTER   New Line, 1988, EP w/Stephen Diener
A NIGHTMARE ON ELM STREET PART 5: THE DREAM
  CHILD   New Line, 1989, EP w/Jon Turtle
PUMP UP THE VOLUME   New Line, 1990, EP w/Syd
  Cappe & Nicolas Stiliadis

EDWARD L. RISSIEN
CASTLE KEEP   Columbia, 1969, AP
SNOW JOB   Warner Bros., 1972
THE CRAZY WORLD OF JULIUS VROODER
  20th Century Fox, 1974, w/Arthur Hiller
SAINT JACK   New World, 1979, EP w/Hugh Hefner

DANTON RISSNER
A SUMMER STORY   Atlantic, 1988

MICHAEL RITCHIE
Business: Miracle Pictures, 22 Miller Ave., Mill Valley, CA
  94941, 415/383-2564
Agent: ICM - New York, 212/556-5600

THE CANDIDATE   Warner Bros., 1972,
  EP w/Robert Redford
SMILE   United Artists, 1975
THE BAD NEWS BEARS GO TO JAPAN
  Paramount, 1978
DIVINE MADNESS (FD)   The Ladd Company/Warner
  Brothers, 1980

JERRY RIVERS
BEVERLY HILLS BRATS   Taurus Entertainment, 1989,
  w/Terry Moore

ANGELO RIZZOLI
EVERYBODY'S FINE   Miramax, 1991
THE COMFORT OF STRANGERS   Skouras, 1991

DAVID ROACH
YOUNG EINSTEIN   Warner Bros., 1989, w/Warwick Ross
  & Yahoo Serious

JOHN F. ROACH
Business: Force Ten Productions, 587 Perugia Way, Bel Air,
  CA 90077, 310/471-0691; Fax: 310/471-6482

PARADISE ALLEY   Universal, 1978, w/Ronald A. Suppa
JAKE SPEED   New World, 1986, EP
THE IN CROWD   Orion, 1988, EP w/Jeff Franklin

JILL ROBB
CAREFUL, HE MIGHT HEAR YOU   20th Century Fox, 1984

LANCE H. ROBBINS
Business: Saban Entertainment, 4000 W. Alameda Av.,
  5th Floor, Burbank, CA 91505, 818/972-4800;
  Fax: 818/972-4895

BACKSTREET DREAMS   Vidmark, 1990, w/Jason O'Malley

MATTHEW ROBBINS
Agent: ICM - Los Angeles, 310/550-4000
Contact: Directors Guild of America - Los Angeles,
  213/289-2000

WARNING SIGN   20th Century Fox, 1985, EP

BOBBY ROBERTS
(credit w/Hal Landers)

THE GYPSY MOTHS   MGM, 1969
MONTE WALSH   National General, 1970
THE HOT ROCK   20th Century Fox, 1972
THE BANK SHOT   United Artists, 1974
DEATH WISH   Paramount, 1974
DAMNATION ALLEY   20th Century Fox, 1977, EP
JOYRIDE   AIP, 1977, EP
DEATH WISH II   Filmways, 1982, EP

SELWYN ROBERTS
HIGH SPIRITS   TriStar, 1988, CP w/Nik Powell

WILLIAM ROBERTS
THE LAST AMERICAN HERO   *HARD DRIVER*   20th
  Century Fox, 1973, w/John Cutts

CLIFF ROBERTSON
Agent: ICM - Los Angeles, 310/550-4000

J. W. COOP   Columbia, 1972

ROBBIE ROBERTSON
Personal Manager: Nick Wechsler, Addis-Wechsler & Assoc.,
  8444 Wilshire Blvd., 5th Flr, Beverly Hills, CA 90211,
  213/653-8867

THE LAST WALTZ (FD)   United Artists, 1978
CARNY   United Artists, 1980

STANLEY ROBERTSON
Business: JillChris Productions, 100 Universal Plaza, 507/3B, Universal City, CA 91608, 818/777-3142

GHOST DAD   Universal, 1990, EP

AMY ROBINSON
(credit w/Griffin Dunne)
Business: Double Play Productions, 445 Park Avenue, 8th Floor, New York, NY 10022, 212/605-2722

CHILLY SCENES OF WINTER   *HEAD OVER HEELS*
United Artists, 1979, w/Mark Metcalf
BABY IT'S YOU   Paramount, 1983
AFTER HOURS   Geffen/Warner Bros., 1985,
w/Robert F. Colesberry
RUNNING ON EMPTY   Warner Bros., 1988
WHITE PALACE   Universal, 1990, w/Mark Rosenberg
ONCE AROUND   Universal, 1991

DON ROBINSON
Business: Paragon Arts International, 6777 Hollywood Blvd., Suite 700, Hollywood, CA 90028, 213/465-5355

NIGHT OF THE DEMONS   IFM, 1988, LP

JAMES G. ROBINSON
Business: Morgan Creek Productions, 1875 Century Park East, Suite 200, Los Angeles, CA 90067, 310/284-8884; Fax: 310/282-8794

THE STONE BOY   20th Century Fox, 1984, EP
GRUNT! THE WRESTLING MOVIE   New World, 1985, EP
WHERE THE RIVER RUNS BLACK   MGM, 1986, EP
YOUNG GUNS   20th Century Fox, 1988,
EP w/John Fusco
SKIN DEEP   20th Century Fox, 1989, EP w/Joe Roth
RENEGADES   Universal, 1989, EP w/Robert W. Cort, Ted Field & Joe Roth
ENEMIES, A LOVE STORY   20th Century Fox, 1989, EP w/Joe Roth
NIGHTBREED   20th Century Fox, 1990, EP w/Joe Roth
THE EXORCIST III   20th Century Fox, 1990, EP w/Joe Roth
COUPE DE VILLE   Universal, 1990, EP
YOUNG GUNS II   20th Century Fox, 1990, EP w/Gary Barber, John Fusco, David Nicksay & Joe Roth
PACIFIC HEIGHTS   20th Century Fox, 1990, EP w/Gary Barber, David Nicksay & Joe Roth
ROBIN HOOD: PRINCE OF THIEVES   Warner Bros., 1991, EP w/Gary Barber & David Nicksay
FREEJACK   Warner Bros., 1991, EP w/Gary Barber & David Nicksay

MATT ROBINSON
SAVE THE CHILDREN (FD)   Paramount, 1973
AMAZING GRACE   United Artists, 1974

PHIL ALDEN ROBINSON
Business: Universal Pictures, 100 Universal Plaza, Universal City, CA 91608-1085, 818/777-5055; Fax: 818/777-0490
Agent: William Morris Agency - Beverly Hills, 310/274-7451
Contact: Directors Guild of America - Los Angeles, 213/289-2000

ALL OF ME   Universal, 1984, AP

MARC ROCCO
Business: Yankee Entertainment Group, 2919 W. Burbank Blvd. #C, Burbank, CA 91505, 818/954-0780; Fax: 818/954-0964

DREAM A LITTLE DREAM   Vestron, 1989,
w/D. E. Eisenberg

DON ROCHAMBEAU
THE WIZARD OF SPEED AND TIME   Shapiro-Glickenhaus Entertainment, 1989, EP

FRANC RODDAM
Agent: ICM - Los Angeles, 310/550-4000
Contact: Directors Guild of America - Los Angeles, 213/289-2000

WAR PARTY   Hemdale, 1989, EP w/Chris Chesser

CHERIE RODGERS
SALAAM BOMBAY!   Cinecom, 1988, EP w/Gabriel Auer, Michael Nozik & Anil Tejani

DAVID ROE
STORYVILLE   20TH Century Fox, 1991,
w/Edward R. Pressman

JAMES T. ROE III
THE RACHEL PAPERS   United Artists, 1989,
EP w/Eric Fellner

LUC ROEG
Contact: Vivid Productions, 1st Floor, Centro House, 23 Mandeka Street, London NW1 0DY England, 071/388-4559; Fax: 071/388-7489

BIG TIME (FD)   Island Pictures, 1988
LET HIM HAVE IT   1992

NICOLAS ROEG
Agent: The Robert Littman Company - Beverly Hills, 310/278-1572

WITHOUT YOU I'M NOTHING   MCEG, 1990, EP

MICHAEL ROEMER
(credit w/Robert M. Young)
Business: Yale School of Art, Box 1605-A Yale Station, New Haven, CT 06520, 203/432-2600

NOTHING BUT A MAN   Cinema 5, 1965
THE PLOT AGAINST HARRY   New Yorker Films, 1990

GEORGE J. ROEWE III
Business: Propaganda Films, 940 N. Mansfield Ave., Los Angeles, CA 90038, 213/462-6400

KILL ME AGAIN   MGM/UA, 1989, LP
DADDY'S DYIN'...WHO'S GOT THE WILL?   MGM/UA, 1990, CP

OTHON ROFFIEL
Business: Accent Entertainment, 8439 Sunset Blvd., Suite 302, Los Angeles, CA 90069, 213/654-0231

THE BLUE IGUANA   Paramount, 1988,
CP w/Angel Flores-Marini

Ro

FILM
PRODUCERS,
STUDIOS,
AGENTS AND
CASTING
DIRECTORS
GUIDE

F
I
L
M

P
R
O
D
U
C
E
R
S

JIM ROGERS
SPONTANEOUS COMBUSTION   Taurus, 1990

PHILLIP ROGERS
SHOOT TO KILL   Buena Vista, 1988, EP

STAN ROGOW
Business: NBC Productions, 330 Bob Hope Dr., Burbank,
   CA 91523, 818/840-7558

THE CLAN OF THE CAVE BEAR   Warner Bros.,
   1986, CP

GUNTER ROHRBACH
DAS BOOT   Columbia, 1982
THE NEVERENDING STORY   Warner Bros., 1984, CP

SANDRA WEINTRAUB ROLAND
(formerly Sandra Weintraub)
Business: Fred Weintraub Productions, 1900 Avenue of
   the Stars, #1500, Los Angeles, CA 90067,
   310/788-9380; Fax: 310/788-0476
Agent: J. Michael Bloom & Associates - Los Angeles,
   310/275-6800

ALICE DOESN'T LIVE HERE ANYMORE   Warner Bros.,
   1975, AP
TOM HORN   Warner Bros., 1980, AP w/Michael Rachmil
THE PRINCESS ACADEMY   Empire, 1987

JACK ROLLINS
(credit w/Charles H. Joffe)
Business: Rollins-Joffe Productions, 300 S. Lorimar Plaza,
   Rm. 1016, Burbank, CA 91505, 818/954-7036;
   Fax: 818/954-7874

SLEEPER   United Artists, 1973, EP
STARDUST MEMORIES   United Artists, 1980, EP
ZELIG   Orion, 1983, EP
HANNAH AND HER SISTERS ★   Orion, 1986, EP
RADIO DAYS   Orion, 1987, EP
SEPTEMBER   Orion, 1987, EP
ANOTHER WOMAN   Orion, 1988, EP
NEW YORK STORIES   Buena Vista, 1989, EP
CRIMES AND MISDEMEANORS   Orion, 1989, EP
ALICE   Orion, 1990, EP

LAWRENCE ROMAN
McQ   Warner Bros., 1974, CP

RIC R. ROMAN
BUCKTOWN   AIP, 1975, EP
SENIORS   Cinema Shares Inernational, 1978, EP

LENKE ROMANSZKY
THE TEACHER   Crown International, 1974, EP

EDDIE ROMERO
THE BIG DOLL HOUSE   New World, 1971, EP
BEAST OF BLOOD   Marvin, 1971

GEORGE A. ROMERO
Agent: The Gersh Agency - Beverly Hills, 310/274-6611

NIGHT OF THE LIVING DEAD   Columbia, 1990,
   EP w/Ami Artzi & Menahem Golan

NANCY ROMERO
HUNGRY WIVES   Jack H. Harris, 1973

FRED ROOS
Business: F.R. Productions, 2980 Beverly Glen Circle,
   Suite 203, Los Angeles, CA 90077, 310/470-9212;
   Fax: 310/470-4905

DRIVE, HE SAID   Columbia, 1971, AP
THE CONVERSATION   Paramount, 1974, CP
THE GODFATHER - PART II ★★   Paramount, 1974,
   CP w/Gray Frederickson
THE BLACK STALLION   United Artists, 1979,
   w/Tom Sternberg
APOCALYPSE NOW ★   United Artists, 1979,
   CP w/Gray Frederickson & Tom Sternberg
ONE FROM THE HEART   Columbia, 1982,
   w/Gray Frederickson
THE ESCAPE ARTIST   Orion/Warner Bros., 1982,
   EP w/Francis Ford Coppola
HAMMETT   Orion/Warner Bros., 1982, w/Ronald Colby &
   Don Guest
THE BLACK STALLION RETURNS   MGM/UA, 1983,
   w/Doug Claybourne & Tom Sternberg
THE OUTSIDERS   Warner Bros., 1983,
   w/Gray Frederickson
RUMBLE FISH   Universal, 1983, w/Doug Claybourne
THE COTTON CLUB   Orion, 1984, CP w/Sylvio Tabet
SEVEN MINUTES IN HEAVEN   Warner Bros., 1986
GARDENS OF STONE   TriStar, 1987, EP w/Jay Emmett,
   David Valdes & Stan Weston
BARFLY   Cannon, 1987, w/Tom Luddy & Barbet Schroeder
TUCKER - THE MAN & HIS DREAM   Paramount, 1988,
   w/Fred Fuchs
NEW YORK STORIES   "Life Without Zoe"   Buena Vista,
   1989, w/Fred Fuchs
WAIT UNTIL SPRING, BANDINI   Orion, 1990, w/Tom
   Luddy & Erwin Provoost
THE GODFATHER PART III ★   Paramount, 1990,
   CP w/Gray Frederickson & Charles Mulvehill
HEARTS OF DARKNESS: A FILMMAKER'S APOCALYPSE
   Avenue, 1991, EP w/Doug Claybourne

TOM ROPELEWSKI
Agent: ICM - Los Angeles, 310/550-4000

LOVERBOY   TriStar, 1989, EP w/Leslie Dixon

ALEXANDRA (ALEX) ROSE
Business: Alex Rose Productions, 8291 Presson Place, Los
   Angeles, CA 90069, 213/654-8662; Fax: 213/654-0196

DRIVE-IN   Columbia, 1976, w/Tamara Asseyev
BIG WEDNESDAY   Warner Bros., 1978,
   EP w/Tamara Asseyev
I WANNA HOLD YOUR HAND   Universal, 1978,
   w/Tamara Asseyev
NORMA RAE ★   20th Century Fox, 1979,
   w/Tamara Asseyev
NOTHING IN COMMON   TriStar, 1986
OVERBOARD   MGM/UA, 1987, w/Anthea Sylbert
QUIGLEY DOWN UNDER   Pathe/MGM/UA, 1990,
   w/Stanley O'Toole
FRANKIE AND JOHNNY   Paramount, 1991,
   EP w/Chuck Mulvehill

JACK ROSE
STARHOPS   First American, 1978, EP w/Daniel Grodnik &
   Robert Sharpe

MEGAN ROSE
Business: Alex Rose Productions, 1630 S. Greenfield Ave., Los Angeles, CA 90025

QUIGLEY DOWN UNDER   Pathe/MGM/UA, 1990, CP

REGINALD ROSE
Agent: Preferred Artists,- Encino, 818/990-0305
Contact: Writers Guild of America - Los Angeles, 310/550-1000

TWELVE ANGRY MEN ★   United Artists, 1957, w/Henry Fonda

SEYMOUR ROSE
KEYS TO FREEDOM   RPB Pictures/Queens Cross Productions, 1989, EP

SI ROSE
PUFNSTUF   Universal, 1970

STUART ROSE
KEYS TO FREEDOM   RPB Pictures/Queens Cross Productions, 1989, w/Robert S. Lecky

SYDNEY ROSE
Business: Slade Square/Gibb-Rose, 9145 Sunset Blvd., #220, Los Angeles, CA 90069, 310/471-5357

THE KIDS ARE ALRIGHT (FD)   New World, 1979, EP

EDWARD ROSEN
THE DEADLY TRACKERS   Warner Bros., 1973, EP
ALOHA, BOBBY AND ROSE   Columbia, 1975, EP
AMERICATHON   United Artists, 1979, EP

MARTIN ROSEN
Business: 305 San Anselmo Ave., San Anselmo, CA 94960, 415/456-1414

WOMEN IN LOVE   United Artists, 1970, CP
WATERSHIP DOWN (AF)   Avco Embassy, 1978
BURNOUT   Crown International, 1979
SMOOTH TALK   Spectrafilm, 1985
THE PLAGUE DOGS (AF)   Nepenth Productions, 1985
STACKING   Spectrafilm, 1987

ROBERT L. ROSEN
Attorney: Marty Weiss, 12301 Wilshire Blvd., Suite 203, Los Angeles, CA 90025, 310/820-8872
Contact: Directors Guild of America - Los Angeles, 213/289-2000

TOGETHER BROTHERS   20th Century Fox, 1974
THE FRENCH CONNECTION II   20th Century Fox, 1975
BLACK SUNDAY   Paramount, 1977, EP
PROPHECY   Paramount, 1979
GOING APE!   Paramount, 1981
THE CHALLENGE   Embassy, 1982, w/Ron Beckman
RAW COURAGE   *COURAGE*   New World, 1984, w/Ronny Cox
PORKY'S REVENGE   20th Century Fox, 1985
WORLD GONE WILD   Lorimar, 1988
DEAD BANG   Warner Bros., 1989, EP
THE FOURTH WAR   Warner Bros., 1990, LP

S. HOWARD ROSEN
Business: Nova Motion Pictures Ltd., 1200 Bay St., Suite 703, Toronto, Ontario M5R 2A5, Canada, 416/923-9230

JOHN AND THE MISSUS   Cinema Group, 1987, EP w/Peter O'Brian

JEFFREY M. ROSENBAUM
FIREWALKER   Cannon, 1986, EP w/Norman Aladjem

FRANK P. ROSENBERG
THE STEAGLE   Avco Embassy, 1971, EP
THE REINCARNATION OF PETER PROUD   AIP, 1975

KAREN ROSENBERG
LOOKING UP   Levitt-Pickman, 1977, CP

MARK ROSENBERG
Business: Spring Creek Productions, 4000 Warner Blvd., Producers Bldg. 7, #8, Burbank, CA 91522, 818/954-1210; Fax: 818/954-2737

BRIGHT LIGHTS, BIG CITY   MGM/UA, 1988, w/Sydney Pollack
MAJOR LEAGUE   Paramount, 1989, EP
THE FABULOUS BAKER BOYS   20th Century Fox, 1989, w/Paula Weinstein
PRESUMED INNOCENT   Warner Bros., 1990, w/Sydney Pollack
WHITE PALACE   Universal, 1990, w/Griffin Dunne & Amy Robinson
KING RALPH   Universal, 1991, EP w/Sydney Pollack

MAX ROSENBERG
(credit w/Milton Subotsky)

THE DEADLY BEES   Paramount, 1967
SCREAM AND SCREAM AGAIN   AIP, 1969
THE MIND OF MR. SOAMES   Columbia, 1970
THE HOUSE THAT DRIPPED BLOOD   Cinerama, 1971
WHAT BECAME OF JACK AND JILL   20th Century Fox, 1972
ASYLUM   Cinerama, 1972
TALES FROM THE CRYPT   Cinerama, 1972, CP*
THE VAULT OF HORROR   Cinerama, 1973
AND NOW THE SCREAMING STARTS   Cinerama, 1973
THE BEAST MUST DIE   Cinerama, 1974
I, MONSTER   Cannon, 1974
MADHOUSE   AIP, 1974
FROM BEYOND THE GRAVE   Howard Mahler, 1975
PRIMARY MOTIVE   Hemdale, 1991, EP w/Don Carmody

RICK ROSENBERG
(credit w/Robert Christiansen)
Business: Chris-Rose Productions, 4000 Warner Blvd., Producers 2, #1104-A, Burbank, CA 91522, 818/954-1748; Fax: 818/954-4822

ADAM AT SIX A.M.   National General, 1970
HIDE IN PLAIN SIGHT   MGM/UA, 1980

STUART ROSENBERG
Agent: William Morris Agency - Beverly Hills, 310/274-7451

THE LAUGHING POLICEMAN   20th Century Fox, 1973

FILM PRODUCERS

Ro

FILM
PRODUCERS,
STUDIOS,
AGENTS AND
CASTING
DIRECTORS
GUIDE

F
I
L
M

P
R
O
D
U
C
E
R
S

TOM ROSENBERG
Business: Beacon Pictures, 1041 N. Formosa Av.,
    Hollywood, CA 90046-6798, 213/850-2651;
    Fax: 213/850-2613

A MIDNIGHT CLEAR   Interstar, 1991, EP w/Marc
    Abraham & Armyan Bernstein

MICHAEL ROSENBLATT
(credit w/Thomas Coleman)

THE DAY THE MUSIC DIED (FD)   Atlantic, 1977, EP
VALLEY GIRL   Atlantic, 1983, EP
ROADHOUSE 66   Atlantic, 1984, EP
ALPHABET CITY   Atlantic, 1984, EP
TEEN WOLF   Atlantic, 1985, EP
THE MEN'S CLUB   Atlantic, 1986, EP w/John Harada
EXTREMITIES   Atlantic, 1986, EP
NUTCRACKER   Atlantic, 1986, EP
SUMMER HEAT   Atlantic, 1987, EP
STEEL JUSTICE   Atlantic, 1987, EP
WILD THING   Atlantic, 1987, EP
THE GARBAGE PAIL KIDS MOVIE   Atlantic, 1987, EP
TEEN WOLF TOO   Atlantic, 1987, EP
COP   Atlantic, 1988, EP
PATTY HEARST   Atlantic, 1988, EP

DALE ROSENBLOOM
Business: 211 S. Beverly Drive #105, Beverly Hills, CA
    90212, 310/859-9800; Fax: 310/859-0422

INSTANT KARMA   MGM, 1990, w/George Edwards &
    Bruce A. Taylor

RICHARD ROSENBLOOM
Business: 15860 Dartford Way, Sherman Oaks, CA 91403,
    818/789-0331; Fax: 818/789-7560

CATCH MY SOUL   Cinerama, 1974, w/Jack Good

MARVIN J. ROSENBLUM
1984   Atlantic, 1985, EP

RALPH ROSENBLUM
Agent: The Gersh Agency - Beverly Hills, 310/274-6611

BANANAS   United Artists, 1971, AP
THE GREAT BANK HOAX   *SHENANIGANS*   Warner
    Bros., 1979, w/Joseph Jacoby

MIKE ROSENFELD
(credit w/Charles Fries)
Business: Kenwood Productions, P.O. Box 217, Kenwood,
    CA 95452, 707/833-2829

THRASHIN'   Fries Entertainment, 1986
OUT OF BOUNDS   Columbia, 1986

SCOTT M. ROSENFELT
(credit w/Mark Levinson)
Business: Levinson-Rosenfelt Productions, 1639 11th St.,
    Santa Monica, CA 90404, 310/399-1844;
    Fax: 310/399-8241
Agent: Triad Artists, Inc. - Los Angeles, CA 90067,
    310/556-2727

WALTZ ACROSS TEXAS   Atlantic, 1983, CP*
ROADHOUSE 66   Atlantic, 1984
TEEN WOLF   Atlantic, 1985

EXTREMITIES   Atlantic, 1986, LP w/George W. Perkins*
REMOTE CONTROL   New Century/Vista, 1988
STRANDED   New Line, 1987
RUSSKIES   New Century/Vista, 1987
MYSTIC PIZZA   Samuel Goldwyn Company, 1988
BIG MAN ON CAMPUS   Vestron, 1989, CP
HOME ALONE   20th Century Fox, 1990, EP

JAMES ROSENFIELD
WAVELENGTH   New World, 1983

LOIS ROSENFIELD
BANG THE DRUM SLOWLY   Paramount, 1973,
    w/Maurice Rosenfield

MAURICE ROSENFIELD
BANG THE DRUM SLOWLY   Paramount, 1973,
    w/Lois Rosenfield
WAVELENGTH   New World, 1983, EP

HOWARD ROSENMAN
Business: Sandollar Productions, 8730 Sunset Blvd.,
    Penthouse, Los Angeles, CA 90069, 310/659-5933;
    Fax: 310/659-0433

SPARKLE   Warner Bros., 1976
THE MAIN EVENT   Warner Bros., 1979,
    EP w/Renee Missel
RESURRECTION   Universal, 1980, w/Renee Missel
LOST ANGELS   Orion, 1989, w/Thomas Baer
GROSS ANATOMY   Buena Vista, 1989, w/Debra Hill
FATHER OF THE BRIDE   1991, Buena Vista, w/Carol
    Baum & Nancy Meyers

MARK D. ROSENTHAL
Business: Konner-Rosenthal Productions, Paramount
    Pictures, 5555 Melrose Ave., Los Angeles, CA 90038,
    213/956-5909
Agent: CAA - Beverly Hills, 310/288-4545

THE LEGEND OF BILLIE JEAN   TriStar, 1985,
    CP w/Lawrence Konner

BARNEY ROSENZWEIG
Business: The Rosenzweig Company, 130 S. Hewitt St., Los
    Angeles, CA 90012, 213/680-3737; Fax: 213/680-1597

MORITURI   CODE NAME "MORITURI"   20th Century Fox,
    1965, AP
DO NOT DISTURB   20th Century Fox, 1965, AP
WHO FEARS THE DEVIL   *THE LEGEND OF HILLBILLY
    JOHN*   Jack H. Harris, 1974

COURTNEY SALE ROSS
LISTEN UP: THE LIVES OF QUINCY JONES (FD)   Warner
    Bros., 1990

DONALD H. ROSS
Agent: The Cooper Agency - Los Angeles, 310/277-8422

HAMBURGER: THE MOTION PICTURE   FM
    Entertainment, 1986, CP w/Robert Lloyd Lewis

GARY A. ROSS
Agent: CAA - Beverly Hills, 310/288-4545
Contact: Writers Guild of America - Los Angeles,
    310/550-1000

BIG   20th Century Fox, 1988, CP w/Anne Spielberg

Ro

**FILM
PRODUCERS,
STUDIOS,
AGENTS** and
**CASTING
DIRECTORS
GUIDE**

**F
I
L
M

P
R
O
D
U
C
E
R
S**

HERBERT ROSS

Business: c/o Paramount Communications, 15 Columbus
    Circle, Guest Ofc. #6, 29th Floor, New York, NY 10023,
    212/373-7672; Fax: 212/373-7875
Agent: CAA - Beverly Hills, 310/288-4545

THE LAST OF SHEILA   Warner Bros., 1973
THE SEVEN-PERCENT SOLUTION   Universal, 1976
THE TURNING POINT ★   20th Century Fox, 1977,
    w/Arthur Laurents
PENNIES FROM HEAVEN   MGM, 1981, w/Nora Kaye
I OUGHT TO BE IN PICTURES   20th Century Fox, 1982,
    w/Neil Simon
MAX DUGAN RETURNS   20th Century Fox, 1983,
    w/Neil Simon
THE SECRET OF MY SUCCESS   Universal, 1987
MY BLUE HEAVEN   Warner Bros., 1990,
    w/Anthea Sylbert
TRUE COLORS   Paramount, 1991, w/Laurence Mark
SOAPDISH   Paramount, 1991, EP

LYNN ROSS

BOBBIE JO AND THE OUTLAW   AIP, 1976,
    CP w/Steve Brodie

MONTY ROSS

Business: 40 Acres & A Mule Filmworks, 124 DeKalb
    Ave., Brooklyn, NY 11217, 718/624-3703;
    Fax: 718/624-2008

SCHOOL DAZE   Columbia, 1988,
    CP w/Loretha C. Jones
DO THE RIGHT THING   Universal, 1989, CP
MO' BETTER BLUES   Universal, 1990, CP
JUNGLE FEVER   Universal, 1991, CP
MALCOLM X   Warner Bros., 1992

WARWICK ROSS

YOUNG EINSTEIN   Warner Bros., 1989, w/David
    Roach & Yahoo Serious

CAROL M. ROSSI

CARTEL   Shapiro Glickenhaus, 1990, EP

PETER ROSTEN

TRUE BELIEVER   Columbia, 1989, EP

J. KENNETH ROTCOP

Agent: Barry Perelman Agency - Los Angeles,
    310/274-5999
Contact: Writers Guild of America - Los Angeles,
    310/550-1000

THE BIKINI SHOP   *THE MALIBU BIKINI SHOP*
    International Film Marketing, 1987, w/Gary Mehlman

ANNA ROTH

Business: 2255 Beverly Glen Place, Los Angeles, CA,
    90077, 310/475-8673

UNDER FIRE   Orion, 1983, AP
THE EXPENDABLES   Concorde, 1988,
    w/Christopher Santiago
DADDY'S BOYS   Concorde, 1988, AP
DANCE OF THE DAMNED   Concorde, 1989,
    CP w/Reid Shane

BOBBY ROTH

Business: 7469 Melrose Ave., Suite 35, Los Angeles, CA
    90046, 213/651-0288
Contact: Directors Guild of America - Los Angeles,
    213/289-2000

INDEPENDENCE DAY   Unifilm, 1977, w/Neil Rapp
HEARTBREAKERS   Orion, 1985, w/Bob Weis

JOE ROTH

Business: 20th Century Fox, 10201 W. Pico Blvd.,
    Los Angeles, CA 90035, 310/277-2211
Contact: Directors Guild of America - Los Angeles,
    213/289-2000

TUNNELVISION   World Wide, 1976
CRACKING UP   AIP, 1977, EP
OUR WINNING SEASON   AIP, 1978
AMERICATHON   United Artists, 1979
LADIES AND GENTLEMEN...THE FABULOUS STAINS
    Paramount, 1982
THE FINAL TERROR   Aquarius, 1984
THE STONE BOY   20th Century Fox, 1984, w/Ivan Bloch
BACHELOR PARTY   20th Century Fox, 1984, EP
MOVING VIOLATIONS   20th Century Fox, 1985,
    w/Harry Ufland
STREETS OF GOLD   20th Century Fox, 1986,
    w/Harry Ufland
OFF BEAT   Buena Vista, 1986, w/Harry Ufland
WHERE THE RIVER RUNS BLACK   MGM, 1986,
    w/Harry Ufland
P.K. & THE KID   Castle Hill, 1987
REVENGE OF THE NERDS II: NERDS IN PARADISE
    20th Century Fox, 1987, EP
YOUNG GUNS   20th Century Fox, 1988,
    w/Christopher Cain
DEAD RINGERS   20th Century Fox, 1988
RENEGADES   Universal, 1989, EP w/Robert W. Cort,
    Ted Field & James G. Robinson
SKIN DEEP   20th Century Fox, 1989,
    EP w/James G. Robinson
ENEMIES, A LOVE STORY   20th Century Fox, 1989,
    EP w/James G. Robinson
NIGHTBREED   20th Century Fox, 1990,
    EP w/James G. Robinson
THE EXORCIST III   20th Century Fox, 1990,
    EP w/James G. Robinson
YOUNG GUNS II   20th Century Fox, 1990, EP w/Gary
    Barber, John Fusco, David Nicksay & James G. Robinson
PACIFIC HEIGHTS   20th Century Fox, 1990, EP w/Gary
    Barber, David Nicksay & James G. Robinson

RICHARD ROTH

Business: 1017 N. LaCienega Blvd., Los Angeles, CA 90069,
    310/658-7070; Fax: 310/658-6717

THE WAY WE WERE   Columbia, 1973, AP
JULIA ★   20th Century Fox, 1977
BLUE VELVET   DEG, 1986, EP
MANHUNTER   DEG, 1986
IN COUNTRY   Warner Bros., 1989, w/Norman Jewison
HAVANA   Universal, 1990, w/Sydney Pollack

RICHARD A. ROTH

SUMMER OF '42   Warner Bros., 1971
OUR TIME   Warner Bros., 1974
THE ADVENTURE OF SHERLOCK HOLMES' SMARTER
    BROTHER   20th Century Fox, 1975
OUTLAND   The Ladd Company/Warner Bros., 1981

Ro

FILM
PRODUCERS,
STUDIOS,
AGENTS AND
CASTING
DIRECTORS
GUIDE

F
I
L
M

P
R
O
D
U
C
E
R
S

STEPHEN J. ROTH
(credit w/Robert Lantos)
Business: Cinexus/Famous Players Films, Inc.,
129 Yorkville Ave., 4th Floor, Toronto, M5R 1C4,
416/968-1222; Fax: 416/927-0725

IN PRAISE OF OLDER WOMEN   Avco Embassy, 1979,
EP w/Harold Greenberg*
SUZANNE   RSL/Ambassador, 1980, EP*
AGENCY   Jensen Farley, 1981
PARADISE   Embassy, 1982
HEAVENLY BODIES   MGM/UA, 1985
JOSHUA THEN & NOW   20th Century Fox, 1985
SEPARATE VACATIONS   RSK Entertainmet, 1986
BEDROOM EYES   Aquarius Releasing, 1986
CLEARCUT   Alliance, 1991, w/Ian McDougall

STEVE ROTH
Business: Steve Roth Productions, c/o TriStar Bldg. #220,
10202 W. Washington Blvd., Culver City, CA
90232-3195, 310/280-4210; Fax: 310/280-1367

SECRET ADMIRER   Orion, 1985
EIGHT MILLION WAYS TO DIE   TriStar, 1986
SCROOGED   Paramount, 1988, EP
DEAD BANG   Warner Bros., 1989
GLADIATOR   Columbia, 1991
MOBSTERS   Universal, 1991

ARLYNE ROTHBERG
Business: 213/276-2214

CRIMES OF THE HEART   DEG, 1986, CP w/Bill Gerber
HEAVEN (FD)   Island Pictures, 1987, EP w/Tom Kuhn &
Charles Mitchell

JEFFREY ROTHBERG
Business: Locomotion Pictures, c/o New World
Entertainment, 1440 S. Sepulveda, Los Angeles,
CA 90025-3400, 310/444-8269; Fax: 310/444-8101
Contact: Writers Guild of America - Los Angeles,
310/550-1000

HIDING OUT   DEG, 1987

KEITH ROTHMAN
BROKEN ENGLISH   Lorimar, 1981, w/Bert Schneider
HEAT   New Century/Vista, 1987, w/George Pappas

MOSES ROTHMAN
ffolkes   Universal, 1980, EP

TOM ROTHMAN
Business: The Samuel Goldwyn Company, 10203 Santa
Monica Blvd., Los Angeles, CA 90067, 310/552-2255;
Fax: 310/284-8493

DOWN BY LAW   Island Pictures, 1986, CP w/Jim Stark

RON ROTHOLZ
Business: Cinehaus, 245 W. 55th St., Suite 1011,
New York, NY 10019, 212/245-9060

STATE OF GRACE   Orion, 1990, w/Ned Dowd &
Randy Ostrow
HOMICIDE   Triumph, 1991, EP

RICHARD ROTHSTEIN
Business: Sovereign Pictures, 11845 Olympic Blvd., #1055,
Los Angeles, CA 90064, 310/312-1001;
Fax: 310/478-7707
Agent: ICM - Los Angeles, 310/550-4000
Contact: Directors Guild of America - Los Angeles,
213/289-2000

DEATH VALLEY   Universal, 1982, CP w/Stanley Beck

WILLIAM J. ROUHANA, JR.
SLIPPING INTO DARKNESS   MCEG, 1988, EP

YVES ROUSSET-ROUARD
Business: Trincara Pictures, France

EMMANUELLE   Columbia, 1974
A LITTLE ROMANCE   Orion/Warner Bros., 1979,
w/Robert L. Crawford

CHARLES ROVEN
Business: Roven-Cavallo Entertainment, Raleigh Studios,
650 Bronson Ave., Suite 218 West, Los Angeles, CA
90038, 213/960-4921

HEART LIKE A WHEEL   20th Century Fox, 1983
MADE IN U.S.A.   TriStar, 1988
JOHNNY HANDSOME   TriStar, 1989
THE BLOOD OF HEROES   New Line, 1990
CADILLAC MAN   Orion, 1990, w/Roger Donaldson
FINAL ANALYSIS   Warner Bros., 1991, w/Tony Thomas &
Paul Junger Witt

GLENYS ROWE
DOGS IN SPACE   Skouras Pictures, 1987

PATRICIA ROZEMA
Business: Vos Productions Inc., 152 John St., Suite 502,
Toronto, M5V 2T2, 416/971-9401; Fax: 416/971-9605

I'VE HEARD THE MERMAIDS SINGING   Miramax, 1987,
w/Alexandra Raffe
THE WHITE ROOM   Alliance, 1990, EP

AL RUBAN
Contact: Directors Guild of America - New York,
212/581-0370

FACES   Continental, 1968, AP
HUSBANDS   Columbia, 1970
MINNIE & MOSKOWITZ   Universal, 1971
THE KILLING OF A CHINESE BOOKIE   Faces
Distribution, 1976
OPENING NIGHT   Faces Distribution, 1979
LOVE STREAMS   Cannon, 1984, EP
HAPPY NEW YEAR   Columbia, 1987, EP
TEXASVILLE   Columbia, 1990, CP

JANINE RUBEIZ
DEATHWATCH   Quartet, 1982, w/Gabriel Boustani

AARON RUBEN
Agent: Robinson, Weintraub, Gross, Inc. - Los Angeles,
213/653-5802
Contact: Writers Guild of America - Los Angeles,
310/550-1000

THE COMIC   Columbia, 1969, w/Carl Reiner

ANDY RUBEN
Business: Concorde Films, 11600 San Vicente Blvd.,
   Los Angeles, CA 90049, 310/820-6733

STRIPPED TO KILL   Concorde, 1987, w/Mark Byers &
   Matt Leipzig
DANCE OF THE DAMNED   Concorde, 1989
STRIPPED TO KILL 2   Concorde, 1989
STREETS   Concorde, 1990
POISON IVY   New Line, 1991

JOSEPH RUBEN
Agent: UTA - Beverly Hills, 310/273-6700
Contact: Directors Guild of America - Los Angeles,
   213/289-2000

THE SISTER-IN-LAW   Crown International, 1975,
   w/Jonathan Krivine
THE POM POM GIRLS   Crown International, 1976

BRUCE JOEL RUBIN
Agent: Sanford-Skouras-Gross - Los Angeles,
   310/208-2100
Contact: Writers Guild of America - Los Angeles,
   310/550-1000

DIONYSUS IN '69   Sigma III, 1970, w/Brian DePalma &
   Robert Fiore
GHOST ★   Paramount, 1990, AP
JACOB'S LADDER   TriStar, 1990, AP

RICK RUBIN
Business: Def American Records, c/o Geffen Records,
   9130 Sunset Blvd., Los Angeles, CA 90069,
   310/278-9010

TOUGHER THAN LEATHER   New Line, 1988,
   EP w/Russell Simmons

STANLEY RUBIN
Agent: Triad Artists, Inc. - Los Angeles, 310/556-2727
Contact: Writers Guild of America - Los Angeles,
   310/550-1000

THE PRESIDENT'S ANALYST   Paramount, 1967
THE TAKE   Columbia, 1974, EP
REVENGE   Columbia, 1990, w/Hunt Lowry
WHITE HUNTER, BLACK HEART   Warner Bros.,
   1990, CP

KEITH RUBINSTEIN
Business: Badham-Cohen Group, 100 Universal City Plaza,
   Bldg. 82, Universal City, CA 91608, 818/777-3477;
   Fax: 818/777-8226

THE BOYS NEXT DOOR   New World, 1985,
   w/Sandy Howard
AVENGING ANGEL   New World, 1985, w/Sandy Howard
KGB: THE SECRET WAR   Cinema Group, 1986,
   w/Sandy Howard
ODD JOBS   TriStar, 1986
THE IN CROWD   Orion, 1988, w/Lawrence Konner
THE HARD WAY   Universal, 1991, AP

RICHARD P. RUBINSTEIN
Business: Laurel Entertainment, Inc., 928 Broadway, 12th Flr.,
   New York, NY 10010, 212/674-3800; Fax: 212/777-6426

MARTIN   Libra, 1978
DAWN OF THE DEAD   United Film Distribution, 1979
KNIGHTRIDERS   United Film Distribution, 1981
CREEPSHOW   Warner Bros., 1982
DAY OF THE DEAD   United Film Distribution, 1985
PET SEMATARY   Paramount, 1989
TALES FROM THE DARKSIDE: THE MOVIE   Paramount,
   1990, w/Mitchell Galin

ALBERT S. RUDDY
Business: Ruddy-Morgan Productions, 9300 Wilshire Blvd.,
   Suite 508, Beverly Hills, CA 90212, 310/271-7698;
   Fax: 310/278-9978

THE WILD SEED   Universal, 1965
LITTLE FAUSS & BIG HALSY   Paramount, 1970
MAKING IT   20th Century Fox, 1971
THE GODFATHER ★★   Paramount, 1972
THE LONGEST YARD   Paramount, 1974
COONSKIN (AF)   Bryanston, 1975
MATILDA   AIP, 1978
THE CANNONBALL RUN   20th Century Fox, 1981
DEATH HUNT   20th Century Fox, 1981,
   EP w/Raymond Chow
MEGAFORCE   20th Century Fox, 1982
LASSITER   Warner Bros., 1984
THE CANNONBALL RUN II   Warner Bros., 1984
FAREWELL TO THE KING   Orion, 1989, w/Andre Morgan
SPEED ZONE   Orion, 1989, EP w/Andre Morgan
IMPULSE   Warner Bros., 1990, w/Andre Morgan

SCOTT RUDIN
Business: Paramount Pictures, 5555 Melrose Ave., Los
   Angeles, CA 90038, 213/956-4600; Fax: 213/956-4738

I'M DANCING AS FAST AS I CAN   Paramount, 1982,
   w/Edgar G. Scherick
MRS. SOFFEL   MGM/UA, 1984, w/David A. Nicksay &
   Edgar G. Scherick
RECKLESS   MGM/UA, 1984, w/Edgar G. Scherick
FLATLINERS   Columbia, 1990, EP w/Peter Filardi &
   Michael Rachmil
PACIFIC HEIGHTS   20th Century Fox, 1990,
   w/William Sackheim
REGARDING HENRY   Paramount, 1991, w/Mike Nichols
THE ADDAMS FAMILY   Orion, 1991
WHITE SANDS   Warner Bros., 1991, w/William Sackheim

OTTOMAR RUDOLF
ROSELAND   Cinema Shares International, 1977,
   EP w/Michael Timothy Murphy

JOSEPH RUFFALO
(credit w/Robert Cavallo & Steven Fargnoli)

PURPLE RAIN   Warner Bros., 1984
UNDER THE CHERRY MOON   Warner Bros., 1986
SIGN O' THE TIMES   Cineplex Odeon, 1987

LORD ANTHONY RUFUS ISAACS
Business: New Galactic Films, 8737 Clifton Way,
   Beverly Hills, CA 90211, 310/273-5642

THE BLOCKHOUSE   Cannon, 1974,
   w/Edgar Bronfman, Jr.
9 1/2 WEEKS   MGM/UA, 1986, w/Zalman King
COHEN & TATE   Hemdale, 1989, w/Jeff Young

Ru

FILM
PRODUCERS,
STUDIOS,
AGENTS and
CASTING
DIRECTORS
GUIDE

F
I
L
M

P
R
O
D
U
C
E
R
S

Ru

**FILM
PRODUCERS,
STUDIOS,
AGENTS** AND
**CASTING
DIRECTORS**
GUIDE

F
I
L
M

P
R
O
D
U
C
E
R
S

ED RUGOFF
Agent: Jim Preminger Agency - Los Angeles, 310/475-9491
Contact: Writers Guild of America - Los Angeles,
310/550-1000

MANNEQUIN   20th Century Fox, 1987,
EP w/Joseph Farrell
MANNEQUIN TWO: ON THE MOVE   20th Century
Fox, 1991

RICHARD RUSH
Agent: CAA - Beverly Hills, 310/288-4545
Contact: Directors Guild of America - Los Angeles,
213/289-2000

TOO SOON TO LOVE   Universal, 1959
GETTING STRAIGHT   Columbia, 1970
FREEBIE & THE BEAN   Warner Bros., 1974
THE STUNT MAN   20th Century Fox, 1980

SUSAN RUSKIN
Business: Pal-Mel Productions, 9350 Wilshire Blvd.,
Suite 316, Beverly Hills, CA 90212, 310/859-0497;
Fax: 310/859-7327

HAUNTED HONEYMOON   Orion, 1986

BRIAN RUSSELL
FROM THE HIP   DEG, 1987, EP w/Howard L. Baldwin &
William Minot
SPELLBINDER   MGM/UA, 1988, w/Joe Wizan

CHUCK RUSSELL
Agent: UTA - Beverly Hills, 310/273-6700
Contact: Writers Guild of America - Los Angeles,
310/550-1000

CHEERLEADERS' WILD WEEKEND   Dimension, 1979
HELL NIGHT   Aquarius, 1981, EP w/Joseph Wolf
THE SEDUCTION   Avco Embassy, 1982, EP w/Frank
Capra Jr. & Joseph Wolf
BODY ROCK   New World, 1984, AP
DREAMSCAPE   20th Century Fox, 1984, AP
GIRLS JUST WANT TO HAVE FUN   New World, 1985
BACK TO SCHOOL   Orion, 1986

KEN RUSSELL
Agent: The Robert Littman Company - Beverly Hills,
310/278-1572
Contact: Directors Guild of America - Los Angeles,
213/289-2000

THE MUSIC LOVERS   United Artists, 1971
THE DEVILS   Warner Bros., 1971, w/Robert H. Solo
THE BOY FRIEND   MGM, 1971
SAVAGE MESSIAH   MGM, 1972
TOMMY   Columbia, 1975, w/Robert Stigwood
THE LAIR OF THE WHITE WORM   Vestron, 1988
THE RAINBOW   Vestron, 1989

AARON RUSSO
Business: Oasis Films, 9000 Sunset Blvd., #814,
Los Angeles, CA 90069, 310/273-5813;
Fax: 310/273-1352

THE ROSE   20th Century Fox, 1979, w/Marvin Worth
PARTNERS   Paramount, 1982
TRADING PLACES   Paramount, 1983

TEACHERS   MGM/UA, 1984
WISE GUYS   MGM/UA, 1986
RUDE AWAKENING   Orion, 1989

IRWIN RUSSO
WISE GUYS   MGM/UA, 1986, EP

JOHN A. RUSSO
THERE'S ALWAYS VANILLA   *THE AFFAIR*   Cambist,
1972, w/Russell W. Streiner
NIGHT OF THE LIVING DEAD   Columbia, 1990

MARDI RUSTAM
TOM   Four Star International, 1973, EP w/Robert Brown
PSYCHIC KILLER   Avco Embassy, 1975
THE BAD BUNCH   Dimension, 1976,
EP w/Robert Brown
EATEN ALIVE   Virgo International, 1977

MOHAMMED RUSTAM
PSYCHIC KILLER   Avco Embassy, 1975, EP
EATEN ALIVE   Virgo International, 1977, EP

MORRIE RUVINSKY
Contact: Writers Guild of America - Los Angeles,
310/550-1000

IMPROPER CHANNELS   Crown International, 1981,
w/Alfred Pariser

JOHN RYAN
STICKY FINGERS   Spectrafilm, 1988, LP

MICHAEL RYAN
Business: J & M Entertainment, 1289 Sunset Plaza Dr.,
Los Angeles, CA 90069, 213/652-7733 or 2 Dorset Sq.,
London NW1 6PU, 071/723-6544; Fax: 071/724-7541

PLAYING FOR KEEPS   Universal, 1986, EP w/Julia
Palau & Patrick Wachsberger

MARK RYDELL
Business: Concourse Productions, c/o Warner Hollywood,
1041 N. Formosa Av., Formosa Bldg., Los Angeles, CA
90046-6798, 213/850-2550; Fax: 213/850-2540
Agent: ICM - Los Angeles, 310/550-4000

THE COWBOYS   Warner Bros., 1972
CINDERELLA LIBERTY   20th Century Fox, 1973
FOR THE BOYS   20th Century Fox, 1991, EP

S

PETER SABISTON
HELL UP IN HARLEM   AIP, 1973, EP
BLACK CAESAR   AIP, 1973, EP
IT'S ALIVE   Warner Bros., 1974, EP

ALEXANDER SACHS
GINGER ALE AFTERNOON   Skouras Pictures, 1989, EP

MONROE SACHSON
THE MCMASTERS   Chevron, 1970
SLAUGHTER   AIP, 1972
SLAUGHTER'S BIG RIPOFF   AIP, 1973

WILLIAM SACKHEIM
Business: Universal Studios, 100 Universal City Plaza,
   Universal City, CA 91608, 818/777-1000
Contact: Writers Guild of America - Los Angeles,
   310/550-1000

THE IN-LAWS   Warner Bros., 1979, w/Arthur Hiller
THE COMPETITION   Columbia, 1980
THE SURVIVORS   Columbia, 1983
NO SMALL AFFAIR   Columbia, 1984
PACIFIC HEIGHTS   20th Century Fox, 1990,
   w/Scott Rudin
THE HARD WAY   Universal, 1991, w/Rob Cohen
WHITE SANDS   Warner Bros., 1991, w/Scott Rudin

ALAN SACKS
Business: Heritage Entertainment, 7920 Sunset Blvd.,
   Suite 200, Los Angeles, CA 90046, 213/850-5858;
   Fax: 213/851-1177

THRASHIN'   Fries Entertainment, 1986

DAVID M. SACKS
THE NEW YORK EXPERIENCE (FD)   Trans-Lux,
   1973, EP

TAKEHITO SADAMURA
SOLAR CRISIS   NHK, 1990, EP w/Takeshi Kawata

FOUAD SAID
ACROSS 110th STREET   United Artists, 1972,
   w/Ralph Serpe
HICKEY AND BOGGS   United Artists, 1972
THE DEADLY TRACKERS   Warner Bros., 1973
ALOHA, BOBBY AND ROSE   Columbia, 1975

WAFIC SAID
THE FOURTH PROTOCOL   Lorimar, 1987,
   EP w/Michael Caine & Frederick Forsyth

OTTO SALAMON
Contact: Directors Guild of America - New York,
   212/581-0370

BASIC TRAINING   Moviestore, 1985, w/Gilbert Adler

RONALD SALAND
THE AMITYVILLE HORROR   AIP, 1979, w/Elliott Geisinger

ANGELIKA SALEH
Business: Angelika Films, 110 Greene St., Suite 1102,
   New York, NY 10012, 212/274-1990; Fax: 212/966-4957

SWEET LORRAINE   Angelika Films, 1987,
   EP w/Joseph Saleh

JOSEPH SALEH
Business: Angelika Films, 110 Greene St., New York, NY
   10012, 212/274-1990

SWEET LORRAINE   Angelika Films, 1987,
   EP w/Angelika Saleh

ALEXANDER SALKIND
BLUEBEARD   Cinerama, 1972
KILL KILL KILL   Cinerama, 1974, w/Ilya Salkind
THE THREE MUSKETEERS   20th Century Fox, 1974
THE FOUR MUSKETEERS   20th Century Fox, 1975,
   w/Michael Salkind

ILYA SALKIND
BLUEBEARD   Cinerama, 1972, EP
KILL KILL KILL   Cinerama, 1974, w/Alexander Salkind
THE THREE MUSKETEERS   20th Century Fox, 1974,
   EP w/Pierre Spengler
THE FOUR MUSKETEERS   20th Century Fox, 1975,
   EP w/Pierre Spengler
CROSSED SWORDS   20th Century Fox, 1978, EP
SUPERMAN   Warner Bros., 1978, EP
SUPERMAN II   Warner Bros., 1981, EP
SUPERMAN III   Warner Bros., 1983, EP
SUPERGIRL   Warner Bros., 1984, EP
SANTA CLAUS - THE MOVIE   TriStar, 1985,
   w/Pierre Spengler

MICHAEL SALKIND
THE FOUR MUSKETEERS   20th Century Fox, 1975,
   w/Alexander Salkind

ROBERT SALLIN
Contact: Directors Guild of America - Los Angeles,
   213/289-2000

STAR TREK II: THE WRATH OF KHAN   Paramount, 1982

HARRY SALTZMAN
THE IRON PETTICOAT   MGM, 1956
LOOK BACK IN ANGER   Warner Bros., 1958
THE ENTERTAINER   Continental, 1960, EP
SATURDAY NIGHT & SUNDAY MORNING   Continental,
   1961, EP
DR. NO   United Artists, 1962, w/Albert R. Broccoli
CALL ME BWANA   United Artists, 1963,
   w/Albert R. Broccoli
FROM RUSSIA WITH LOVE   United Artists, 1963,
   w/Albert R. Broccoli
GOLDFINGER   United Artists, 1964, w/Albert R. Broccoli
THE IPCRESS FILE   Universal, 1965
FUNERAL IN BERLIN   Paramount, 1966
YOU ONLY LIVE TWICE   United Artists, 1967,
   w/Albert R. Broccoli
BILLION DOLLAR BRAIN   United Artists, 1967
BATTLE OF BRITAIN   United Artists, 1969,
   w/S. Benjamin Fisz

Sa

FILM
PRODUCERS,
STUDIOS,
AGENTS and
CASTING
DIRECTORS
GUIDE

F
I
L
M

P
R
O
D
U
C
E
R
S

Sa

FILM
PRODUCERS,
STUDIOS,
AGENTS AND
CASTING
DIRECTORS
GUIDE

F
I
L
M

P
R
O
D
U
C
E
R
S

PLAY DIRTY   United Artists, 1969
ON HER MAJESTY'S SECRET SERVICE   United Artists,
   1969, w/Albert R. Broccoli
DIAMONDS ARE FOREVER   United Artists, 1971,
   w/Albert R. Broccoli
LIVE & LET DIE   United Artists, 1973,
   w/Albert R. Broccoli
THE MAN WITH THE GOLDEN GUN   United Artists,
   1974, w/Albert R. Broccoli
NIJINSKY   Paramount, 1980, EP

COKE SAMS
ERNEST SAVES CHRISTMAS   Buena Vista, 1988,
   CP w/Justis Greene
ERNEST GOES TO JAIL   Buena Vista, 1990, CP

RON SAMUELS
Business: Ron Samuels Productions, Inc., 120 El Camino
   Dr., Beverly Hills, CA 90212, 310/273-8964

IRON EAGLE   TriStar, 1986, w/Joe Wizan

PETER SAMUELSON
(credit w/Ted Field)
Business: New Era Productions, 10401 Wyton Dr., Los
   Angeles, CA 90024, 310/208-1000; Fax: 310/208-2809

A MAN, A WOMAN, AND A BANK   Avco Embassy, 1979,
   w/John B. Bennett
REVENGE OF THE NERDS   20th Century Fox, 1984
TURK 182   20th Century Fox, 1985, EP w/Robert Cort

DAN SANDBURG
Q   UFD, 1982, EP

IAN SANDER
(credit w/Laura Ziskin)

D.O.A.   Buena Vista, 1988
EVERYBODY'S ALL-AMERICAN   Warner Bros., 1988,
   w/Taylor Hackford

JACK FROST SANDERS
Contact: Directors Guild of America - Los Angeles,
   213/289-2000

KING OF THE MOUNTAIN   Universal, 1981
THE WOMAN IN RED   Orion, 1984, EP
THE MAN WITH ONE RED SHOE   20th Century Fox,
   1985, AP
SOLARBABIES   MGM/UA, 1986, w/Irene Walzer

KEN SANDERS
BLOOD SALVAGE   Paragon Arts International, 1990,
   w/Martin J. Fischer

BARRY SANDLER
Agent: Harris & Goldberg - Los Angeles, 310/553-5200
Contact: Writers Guild of America - Los Angeles,
   310/550-1000

MAKING LOVE   20th Century Fox, 1982, AP
CRIMES OF PASSION   New World, 1984

EDWARD SANDS
A PASSAGE TO INDIA   Columbia, 1984, CP

MIDGE SANFORD
(credit w/Sarah Pillsbury)
Business: Sanford-Pillsbury Productions, 20th Century Fox,
   10201 W. Pico Blvd., Bldg. 50, Los Angeles, CA 90035,
   310/203-1847; Fax: 310/203-4142

DESPERATELY SEEKING SUSAN   Orion, 1985
RIVER'S EDGE   Island Pictures, 1987
EIGHT MEN OUT   Orion, 1988
IMMEDIATE FAMILY   Columbia, 1989

JONATHAN SANGER
Business: Chanticleer Films, 6525 Sunset Blvd., 6th Floor,
   Los Angeles, CA 90028, 213/462-4705;
   Fax: 213/462-1603
Contact: Directors Guild of America - Los Angeles,
   213/289-2000

A FORCE OF ONE   American Cinema, 1979, AP
FATSO   20th Century Fox, 1980, AP
THE ELEPHANT MAN ★   Paramount, 1980
FRANCES   Universal, 1982
THE DOCTOR & THE DEVILS   20th Century Fox, 1985
CODE NAME: EMERALD   MGM/UA, 1985,
   CP w/Howard Alston
FLIGHT OF THE NAVIGATOR   Buena Vista, 1986,
   EP w/Mark Damon, Malcolm R. Harding & John Hyde

JIMMY SANGSTER
THE HORROR OF FRANKENSTEIN   American
   Continental, 1971
FEAR IN THE NIGHT   International Co-Productions, 1974

ANTHONY SANTA CROCE
Contact: Ascato Entertainment, 6650 Santa Monica Blvd.,
   Hollywood, CA 90038, 213/463-2393; Fax: 213/469-1864

MARTIANS GO HOME   Taurus, 1990,
   CP w/Ted Bafaloukos

CHRISTOPHER SANTIAGO
THE EXPENDABLES   Concorde, 1988, w/Anna Roth

HENRY G. SAPERSTEIN
Business: 14101 Valleyheart Dr., Suite 200, Sherman Oaks,
   CA 91423, 818/990-3800; Fax: 818/990-4854

GAY PURR-EE (AF)   Warner Bros., 1962, EP
WHAT'S UP TIGER LILY?   AIP, 1966, EP

PETER SAPHIER
Business: Paramount Pictures, 5555 Melrose Ave.,
   Los Angeles, CA 90038, 213/956-4506

EDDIE MACON'S RUN   Universal, 1983, EP
SCARFACE   Universal, 1983, CP

DERAN SARAFIAN
Agent: Triad Artists, Inc. - Los Angeles, 310/556-2727

ALIEN PREDATOR   Trans World, 1987, w/Carlos Aured

JOSEPH SARGENT
Agent: Shapiro-Lichtman, Inc. - Los Angeles, 310/859-8877
Contact: Joseph Sargent Productions, c/o Hearst
   Entertainment, 1640 S. Sepulveda Blvd., Los Angeles, CA
   90025, 310/478-1700

JAWS THE REVENGE   Universal, 1987

ARTHUR M. SARKISSIAN
QUIET COOL   New Line, 1986, EP w/Pierre David &
   Larry Thompson
WANTED DEAD OR ALIVE   New World, 1988, EP
SPONTANEOUS COMBUSTION   Taurus, 1990,
   EP w/Henry Bushkin

EDUARD SARLUI
(credit w/Moshe Diamant)
Business: Epic Productions, Inc., 3330 W. Cahuenga Blvd.,
   Suite 500, Los Angeles, CA 90068, 213/969-2800;
   Fax: 213/969-8211

ALIEN PREDATOR   Trans World, 1987,
   EP w/Helen Sarlui-Tucker
HIGH SPIRITS   TriStar, 1988, EP
FULL MOON IN BLUE WATER   Trans World
   Entertainment, 1988, EP
TEEN WITCH   Trans World, 1989, EP
NIGHT GAME   Trans World, 1989, EP

HELEN SARLUI-TUCKER
Business: Epic Productions, Inc., 3330 W. Cahuenga Blvd.,
   Suite 500, Los Angeles, CA 90068, 213/969-2800;
   Fax: 213/969-8211

ALIEN PREDATOR   Trans World, 1987,
   EP w/Eduard Sarlui
THE WILD PAIR   Trans World, 1987, EP
SEVEN HOURS TO JUDGMENT   Trans World
   Entertainment, 1988, EP w/Paul Mason
I, MADMAN   Trans World, 1989, EP w/Paul Mason

DANIEL SARNOFF
FALSE IDENTITY   RKO, 1990, EP w/Ted Hartley &
   Gerald Offsay

JEFFREY W. SASS
Business: Troma, Inc., 733 Ninth Ave., New York, NY
   10019, 212/757-4555; Fax: 212/399-9885

CLASS OF NUKE 'EM HIGH PART II: SUBHUMANOID
   MELTDOWN   Troma, 1991, LP

DAVID SAUNDERS
Contact: Guber-Peters Entertainment Co., 10202 W.
   Washington, Thalberg Bldg., 3rd Floor, Culver City, CA
   90232, 310/280-5262; Fax: 310/280-1366

HELLRAISER   New World, 1987, EP w/Mark
   Armstrong & Christopher Webster
HIGH SPIRITS   TriStar, 1988, w/Stephen Woolley
BAT 21   TriStar, 1988, CP w/Mark Damon
UNDER THE BOARDWALK   New World, 1989, EP
WILD ORCHID   Triumph Releasing, 1990,
   EP w/James Dyer
I COME IN PEACE   Triumph, 1990, EP w/Mark Damon

JAN SAUNDERS
GIRLFRIENDS   Warner Bros., 1978, CP

JEREMY SAUNDERS
THE SHOOTING PARTY   European Classics, 1985, EP

LAWRENCE D. SAVADOVE
THE OUTER SPACE CONNECTION (FD)   Sunn Classic,
   1975, EP

S. LEIGH SAVIDGE
Business: Xenon Entertainment, 211 Arizona Ave.,
   Suite 25, Santa Monica, CA 90401, 310/451-5510;
   Fax: 310/395-4058

TWISTED JUSTICE   Seymour Borde & Associates, 1990,
   EP w/Arnie Lakeyn & Gerald Milton

LEE SAVIN
BLACK GIRL   Cinerama, 1972
BROTHERS   Warner Bros., 1977, EP

EDWARD SAXON
Business: Clinica Estetico Ltd., 1600 Broadway, Suite 503,
   New York, NY 10019, 212/262-2777

SWIMMING TO CAMBODIA   Cinecom, 1987, AP
SOMETHING WILD   Orion, 1987, EP
MARRIED TO THE MOB   Orion, 1988, w/Kenneth Utt
MIAMI BLUES   Orion, 1990, EP w/Fred Ward
THE SILENCE OF THE LAMBS   Orion, 1991,
   w/Ron Bozman & Kenneth Utt

GIULIO SBARIGIA
A MATTER OF TIME   AIP, 1976, EP w/Samuel Z. Arkoff
SALON KITTY   *MADAME KITTY*   AIP, 1976,
   w/Ermanno Donati

T. CARLYLE SCALES
THE GREAT BANK HOAX   *SHENANIGANS*   Warner Bros.,
   1979, EP w/Richard F. Bridges & Laurence Klausner

ROBERT L. SCHAFFEL
Business: Paramount Pictures, 5555 Melrose Ave.,
   Los Angeles, CA 90038, 213/956-5000

GORDON'S WAR   20th Century Fox, 1973
SUNNYSIDE   AIP, 1979
LOOKIN' TO GET OUT   Paramount, 1982
TABLE FOR FIVE   Warner Bros., 1983
AMERICAN ANTHEM   Columbia, 1986, w/Doug Chapin
DISTANT THUNDER   Paramount, 1988
JACKNIFE   Cineplex Odeon, 1989, w/Carol Baum

JANE SCHAFFER
ANGELS DIE HARD   New World, 1970,
   EP w/James Tannenbaum
THE BIG DOLL HOUSE   New World, 1971
THE BIG BIRD CAGE   New World, 1972

DON SCHAIN
Contact: Directors Guild of America - Los Angeles,
   213/289-2000

H.O.T.S.   Derio, 1979, w/W. Terry Davis
SLIPPING INTO DARKNESS   MCEG, 1988,
   CP w/Simon R. Lewis

JAMES SCHAMUS
Business: Independent Feature Project East, NYC

POISON   Zeitgeist, 1991, EP w/Brian Greenbaum

ANGELA P. SCHAPIRO
Business: 9600 Kirkside Rd., Los Angeles, CA 90035,
   213/558-0531

HE'S MY GIRL   Scotti Bros., 1987, w/Lawrence Mortorff
THE IRON TRIANGLE   Scotti Bros., 1989, w/Tony Scotti

Sc

FILM
PRODUCERS,
STUDIOS,
AGENTS AND
CASTING
DIRECTORS
GUIDE

F
I
L
M

P
R
O
D
U
C
E
R
S

Sc

FILM
PRODUCERS,
STUDIOS,
AGENTS AND
CASTING
DIRECTORS
GUIDE

F
I
L
M

P
R
O
D
U
C
E
R
S

JERRY SCHATZBERG
Agent: ICM - Los Angeles, 310/550-4000
Contact: Directors Guild of America - Los Angeles,
213/289-2000

SWEET REVENGE   United Artists, 1976

JEFF SCHECHTMAN
Business: Filmstar Inc., 12301 Wilshire Blvd., Suite 505,
Los Angeles, CA 90025, 310/207-6331;
Fax: 310/207-3195

PIRANHA   New World, 1978, EP w/Roger Corman
PIRANHA II: THE SPAWNING   Saturn International,
1983, w/Chako van Leuwen
BODY ROCK   New World, 1984

LOU SCHEIMER
Contact: Lou Scheimer Productions, 21300 Victory Blvd.,
Suite 670, Woodland Hills, CA 91367, 818/884-2810;
Fax: 818/884-1824

JOURNEY BACK TO OZ (AF)   Filmation, 1974,
w/Norm Prescott
PINOCCHIO & THE EMPEROR OF NIGHT?
HAPPILY EVER AFTER (AF)   Kel-Air Entertainment, 1990

ANDREW SCHEINMAN
Business: Castle Rock Entertainment, 335 N. Maple Dr.,
Suite 135, Beverly Hills, CA 90210, 310/285-2300;
Fax: 310/285-2345

THE MOUNTAIN MEN   Columbia, 1980, w/Martin
Shafer & Martin Ransohoff
THE AWAKENING   Orion, 1980, w/Robert H. Solo &
Martin Shafer
MODERN ROMANCE   Columbia, 1981, w/Martin Shafer
THE SURE THING   Embassy, 1985, CP
STAND BY ME   Columbia, 1986, w/Bruce A. Evans &
Raynold Gideon
THE PRINCESS BRIDE   20th Century Fox, 1987,
w/Rob Reiner
WHEN HARRY MET SALLY...   Castle Rock/Columbia,
1989, w/Rob Reiner
MISERY   Castle Rock/Columbia, 1990, w/Rob Reiner

MAXIMILIAN SCHELL
Agent: ICM - Los Angeles, 310/550-4000

THE PEDESTRIAN   Cinerama, 1974, CP
END OF THE GAME   20th Century Fox, 1976,
w/Arlene Sellers

FRED SCHEPISI
Agent: ICM - New York, 212/556-5600

THE DEVIL'S PLAYGROUND   Entertainment
Marketing, 1979
THE CHANT OF JIMMIE BLACKSMITH   New Yorker
Films, 1980
THE RUSSIA HOUSE   MGM/UA, 1990, w/Paul Maslansky

EDGAR J. SCHERICK
Business: Saban-Scherick Productions, 4000 W. Alameda
Blvd., Burbank, CA 91505, 818/972-4870;
Fax: 818/972-4892

THE BIRTHDAY PARTY   Continental, 1968, EP
FOR LOVE OF IVY   Cinerama, 1968, w/Jay Weston

THANK YOU ALL VERY MUCH   Columbia, 1969, EP
RING OF BRIGHT WATER   Cinerama, 1969, EP
HOMER   National General, 1970, EP
JENNY   Cinerama, 1970
WHAT BECAME OF JACK AND JILL   20th Century Fox,
1972, EP
TO KILL A CLOWN   20th Century Fox, 1972, EP
THE DARWIN ADVENTURE   20th Century Fox,
1972, EP
THE HEARTBREAK KID   20th Century Fox, 1972
GORDON'S WAR   20th Century Fox, 1973, EP
LAW AND DISORDER   Columbia, 1974,
EP w/Michael Medwin
THE TAKING OF PELHAM 1-2-3   United Artists, 1974,
w/Gabriel Katzka
THE STEPFORD WIVES   Columbia, 1975
I NEVER PROMISED YOU A ROSE GARDEN   New World,
1977, EP w/Roger Corman
SUCCESS   *THE AMERICAN SUCCESS COMPANY*
Columbia, 1979, w/Daniel H. Blatt
SHOOT THE MOON   MGM/UA, 1982, EP w/Stuart Millar
I'M DANCING AS FAST AS I CAN   Paramount, 1982,
w/Scott Rudin
RECKLESS   MGM/UA, 1984, w/Scott Rudin
MRS. SOFFEL   MGM/UA, 1984, w/David A. Nicksay &
Scott Rudin

ELLIOT SCHICK
Agent: The Gersh Agency - Beverly Hills, 310/274-6611
Contact: Directors Guild of America - Los Angeles,
213/289-2000

SUGAR HILL   AIP, 1974
RETURN TO MACON COUNTY   AIP, 1975
MARIE   MGM/UA, 1985, EP
MASTERS OF THE UNIVERSE   Cannon, 1987, CP
CHERRY 2000   Orion, 1988, CP
IF LOOKS COULD KILL   Warner Bros., 1991, EP

G. DAVID SCHINE
THE FRENCH CONNECTION ★★   20th Century Fox,
1971, EP

PAUL SCHIFF
Business: Paul Schiff Productions, c/o 20th Century-Fox,
10201 W. Pico Blvd., Bldg. 15, Room 1, Los Angeles, CA
90035, 310/203-3434; Fax: 310/203-1445

REVENGE OF THE NERDS II: NERDS IN PARADISE
20th Century Fox, 1987, AP
YOUNG GUNS   20th Century Fox, 1988,
CP w/Irby Smith
RENEGADES   Universal, 1989, CP
COUPE DE VILLE   Universal, 1990, w/Larry Brezner
YOUNG GUNS II   20th Century Fox, 1990, w/Irby Smith

REENE SCHISGAL
POWER   20th Century Fox, 1986, w/Mark Tarlov

GEORGE SCHLATTER
Business: George Schlatter Productions, 8321 Beverly
Blvd., Los Angeles, CA 90048, 213/655-1400;
Fax: 213/852-1640
Agent: William Morris Agency - Beverly Hills,
310/274-7451

NORMAN...IS THAT YOU?   MGM/UA, 1976

Sc

FILM
PRODUCERS,
STUDIOS,
AGENTS AND
CASTING
DIRECTORS
GUIDE

F
I
L
M

P
R
O
D
U
C
E
R
S

JOHN SCHLESINGER
Agent: ICM - Los Angeles, 310/550-4000
Contact: Directors Guild of America - Los Angeles,
213/289-2000

THE FALCON & THE SNOWMAN   Orion, 1985,
w/Gabriel Katzka
THE BELIEVERS   Orion, 1987, w/Beverly J. Camhe &
Michael Childers

JULIAN SCHLOSSBERG
Business: Castle Hill Productions, 1414 Avenue of the
Americas, New York, NY 10019, 212/888-0080;
Fax: 212/644-0956 or 116 N. Robertson Blvd.,
Suite 701, Los Angeles, CA 90048, 310/652-5254

TEN FROM YOUR SHOW OF SHOWS   Continental,
1973, EP
NO NUKES (FD)   Warner Bros., 1980,
w/Danny Goldberg
IN THE SPIRIT   Castle Hill, 1990, w/Beverly Irby

ARNE L. SCHMIDT
Business: 2501 Banyon Dr., Los Angeles, CA 90049
Contact: Directors Guild of America - Los Angeles,
213/289-2000

HEART LIKE A WHEEL   20th Century Fox, 1983, AP
ROBOCOP   Orion, 1987
THROW MOMMA FROM THE TRAIN   Orion,
1987, EP
THE GREAT OUTDOORS   Universal, 1988
THE PACKAGE   Orion, 1989, EP
AWAKENINGS ★   Columbia, 1990, EP w/Elliot Abbott &
Penny Marshall

MARLENE SCHMIDT
Business: Hickmar, 4000 Warner Blvd., Producers 4,
Burbank, CA 91522, 818/954-5104

DR. MINX   Dimension, 1975. EP
THE SPECIALIST   Crown International, 1975, EP
SCORCHY   AIP, 1976, EP

STEPHEN SCHMIDT
CRAZY QUILT   Farallon, 1965
FUNNYMAN   New Yorker, 1967, w/Hugh McGraw
RIVERRUN   Columbia, 1970

WOLF SCHMIDT
Business: Kodiak Films, Inc., 11075 Santa Monica Blvd.,
Suite 200, Los Angeles, CA 90025, 310/479-8575;
Fax: 310/473-8555

THE PASSOVER PLOT   Atlas, 1977
RIDING THE EDGE   Trans World, 1989
THE FOURTH WAR   Warner Bros., 1990

RICHARD SCHMIECHEN
Business: 213/657-9131

THE TIMES OF HARVEY MILK (FD)
Teleculture, 1984

GARY SCHMOELLER
BLACK MAGIC WOMAN   Trimark, 1991, LP

CHARLES H. SCHNEER
Business: Morningside Pictures Corporation, c/o Robert H.
Montgomery, Jr., 1285 Ave. of the Americas, New York, NY
10019, 212/373-3000

IT CAME FROM BENEATH THE SEA   Columbia, 1955
TWENTY MILLION MILES TO EARTH   Columbia, 1957
THE SEVENTH VOYAGE OF SINBAD   Columbia, 1958
THE THREE WORLDS OF GULLIVER   Columbia, 1960
MYSTERIOUS ISLAND   Columbia, 1961
JASON AND THE ARGONAUTS   Columbia, 1963
FIRST MEN IN THE MOON   Columbia, 1964
HALF A SIXPENCE   Paramount, 1967
THE VALLEY OF GWANGI   Warner Bros., 1969
THE EXECUTIONER   Columbia, 1970
THE GOLDEN VOYAGE OF SINBAD   Columbia, 1974,
w/Ray Harryhausen
SINBAD AND THE EYE OF THE TIGER   Columbia, 1977,
w/Ray Harryhausen

BERT SCHNEIDER
EASY RIDER   Columbia, 1969, EP
FIVE EASY PIECES ★   Columbia, 1970, EP
THE LAST PICTURE SHOW   Columbia, 1971, EP
DRIVE, HE SAID   Columbia, 1970, EP
A SAFE PLACE   Columbia, 1971, EP
HEARTS & MINDS (FD)   Warner Bros./Columbia,
1975, EP
TRACKS   Castle Hill Productions, 1976, EP
THE GENTLEMAN TRAMP (FD)   Tinc, 1978
DAYS OF HEAVEN   Paramount, 1978, w/Harold Schneider
BROKEN ENGLISH   Lorimar, 1981, w/Keith Rothman

GERALD SCHNEIDER
THE APPRENTICESHIP OF DUDDY KRAVITZ   Paramount,
1974, EP
WHITE LINE FEVER   Columbia, 1975, EP w/Mort Litwack

HAROLD SCHNEIDER
Business Manager: Fred Altman, F. Altman & Co., 9255
Sunset Blvd., Suite 901, Los Angeles, CA 90069,
310/278-4201
Contact: Directors Guild of America - Los Angeles,
213/289-2000

FIVE EASY PIECES ★   Columbia, 1970, AP
THE LAST PICTURE SHOW   Columbia, 1971, AP
THE KING OF MARVIN GARDENS   Columbia, 1972, AP
STEELYARD BLUES   Warner Bros., 1973, AP
STAY HUNGRY   United Artists, 1976, w/Bob Rafelson
DAYS OF HEAVEN   Paramount, 1978, w/Bert Schneider
GOIN' SOUTH   Paramount, 1978, w/Harry Gittes
THE ENTITY   20th Century Fox, 1983
WARGAMES   MGM/UA, 1983
THE HOUSE OF GOD   United Artists, 1984,
w/Charles H. Joffe
BLACK WIDOW   20th Century Fox, 1987
SOMEONE TO WATCH OVER ME   Columbia, 1987,
w/Thierry De Ganay
THE TWO JAKES   Paramount, 1990, w/Robert Evans

ROBERT SCHNITZER
Contact: Movicorp, 9887 Santa Monica Blvd., Beverly Hills,
CA 90212, 310/553-4300; Fax: 310/553-1159

KANDYLAND   New World, 1988, EP

Sc

FILM
PRODUCERS,
STUDIOS,
AGENTS and
CASTING
DIRECTORS
GUIDE

F
I
L
M

P
R
O
D
U
C
E
R
S

JOHN D. SCHOFIELD
THE NAKED GUN 2 1/2: THE SMELL OF FEAR
Paramount, 1991, CP

JOHN SCHOUWEILER
CIRCUITRY MAN   Skouras, 1990, w/Steven Reich
TRANCERS II   1991, LP w/David DeCoteau

PAUL SCHRADER
Agent: ICM - Los Angeles, 310/550-4000
Contact: Directors Guild of America - New York,
212/581-0370

OLD BOYFRIENDS   Avco Embassy, 1989, EP

SHELDON SCHRAGER
Business: Columbia Pictures, 10202 W. Washington Blvd.,
Culver City, CA 90232
Contact: Directors Guild of America - Los Angeles,
213/289-2000

SHANKS   Paramount, 1974, AP
THE DAY OF THE LOCUST   Paramount, 1975, EP
PROMISES IN THE DARK   Orion/Warner Bros.,
1979, EP
STARS AND BARS   Columbia, 1988, EP
THE KARATE KID PART III   Columbia, 1989, EP

BARBET SCHROEDER
Business: Les Films du Losange, 26 Avenue Pierre de
Serbie, Paris 75116, France, 04/472-5412
Agent: CAA - Beverly Hills, 310/288-4545
Contact: Directors Guild of America - Los Angeles,
213/289-2000

MY NIGHT AT MAUD'S   Pathe, 1970,
w/Pierre Cottrell
LA COLLECTIONNEUSE   Pathe, 1971,
w/Georges de Beauregard
PERCEVAL   Gaumont/New Yorker, 1978, EP
CELINE & JULIE GO BOATING   New Yorker Films,
1978, EP
BARFLY   Cannon, 1987, w/Tom Luddy & Fred Roos

THOMAS SCHUHLY
Business: Via Tuscolana, 1055, 00100 Rome, Italy,
722/93489; Fax: 722/2443

VERONIKA VOSS   United Artists Classics, 1982
OUT OF ORDER   Sandstar Releasing, 1985,
w/Matthias Deyle
THE NAME OF THE ROSE   20th Century Fox, 1986,
EP w/Jake Eberts
THE ADVENTURES OF BARON MUNCHAUSEN
Columbia, 1989

SANDRA SCHULBERG
Business: American Playhouse Abroad, Markgraf-
Albrechtstrasse 14, 1000 Berlin 31, 4930/323-7085;
Fax: 4930/324-0841

NORTHERN LIGHTS   Cine Manifest, 1979, AP
WILDROSE   Troma, 1985
BELIZAIRE THE CAJUN   Skouras Pictures,
1986, LP
WAITING FOR THE MOON   Skouras Pictures, 1987

ARNOLD SCHULMAN
Agent: CAA - Beverly Hills, 310/288-4545
Business Manager: Starr & Co., 350 Park Ave., New York,
NY 10022, 212/759-6556

WON TON TON, THE DOG WHO SAVED HOLLYWOOD
Paramount, 1976, w/David V. Picker & Michael Winner
PLAYERS   Paramount, 1979, EP

NINA SCHULMAN
THE WEREWOLF OF WASHINGTON   Diplomat, 1973

SAMUEL SCHULMAN
TO LIVE & DIE IN L.A.   New Century, 1985, EP

TOM SCHULMAN
THE LAST DAYS OF EDEN   Buena Vista, 1991, w/Donna
Dubrow & Andrew Vajna

BARBARA SCHULTZ
ALAMBRISTA!   Bobwin/Film Haus, 1979, EP

CHIZ SCHULTZ
Business: Fireside Entertainment Corporation, 1650
Broadway, Suite 1001, New York, NY 10019,
212/489-8160

THE ANGEL LEVINE   United Artists, 1970
GANJA & HESS   *BLOOD COUPLE*   Kelly- Jordan, 1973

MICHAEL SCHULTZ
Business: Crystalite Productions, P.O. Box 1940,
Santa Monica, CA 90406
Agent: ICM - Los Angeles, 310/550-4000

KRUSH GROOVE   Warner Bros., 1985,
w/Doug McHenry
DISORDERLIES   Warner Bros., 1987, w/George A.
Jackson & Michael Jaffe

WIELAND SCHULZ-KEIL
UNDER THE VOLCANO   Universal, 1984,
w/Moritz Borman
THE DEAD   Vestron, 1987, w/Chris Sievernich
TWISTER   Vestron, 1990
THE KING'S WHORE   J&M, 1990, w/Maurice Bernart &
Paolo Zaccaria

MARTHA SCHUMACHER
Business: De Laurentiis Communications, 8670 Wilshire
Blvd., 3rd Floor, Beverly Hills, CA 90211, 310/289-6100

FIRESTARTER   Universal, 1984, AP
STEPHEN KING'S SILVER BULLET   Paramount, 1985
STEPHEN KING'S CAT'S EYE   *CAT'S EYE*
MGM/UA, 1985
RAW DEAL   DEG, 1986
MAXIMUM OVERDRIVE   DEG, 1986
KING KONG LIVES   DEG, 1986
THE BEDROOM WINDOW   DEG, 1987
DATE WITH AN ANGEL   DEG, 1987
THE DESPERATE HOURS   MGM/UA, 1990, EP

THOMAS SCHUMACHER
THE RESCUERS DOWN UNDER (AF)   Buena
Vista, 1990

MARTIN C. SCHUTE
MACHO CALLAHAN   Avco Embassy, 1970,
   w/Bernard L. Kowalski
WHOSE LIFE IS IT ANYWAY?   MGM, 1981,
   EP w/Ray Cooney
SCANDALOUS   Orion, 1984, CP

AARON SCHWAB
Business: MMA Inc., 8484 Wilshire Blvd., Suite 235,
   Beverly Hills, CA 90211, 213/852-1956

CHATTAHOOCHEE   Hemdale, 1990, EP

FAYE SCHWAB
Business: MMA Inc., 8484 Wilshire Blvd., Suite 235,
   Beverly Hills, CA 90211, 213/852-1956

THE MORNING AFTER   20th Century Fox, 1986, EP
CHATTAHOOCHEE   Hemdale, 1990

AL SCHWARTZ
Contact: Dick Clark Productions, 3003 W. Olive Ave.,
   Burbank, CA 91510, 818/841-3003; Fax: 818/954-8609

TOO MUCH SUN   New Line, 1990, EP w/Paul
   Hertzberg & Seymour Morgenstern

ALBERT SCHWARTZ
(credit w/Michael S. Landes)
Business: The Almi Group, 1900 Broadway, New York, NY
   10023, 212/769-6400; Fax: 212/769-9295

THE BIG SCORE   Almi, 1983
I AM THE CHEESE   Almi, 1983, EP w/Jack Schwartzman
THE BOSTONIANS   Almi, 1984, EP

BERNARD SCHWARTZ
Business: Bernard Schwartz Productions, 1900 Avenue
   of the Stars, Suite 1700, Los Angeles, CA 90067,
   310/277-3700; 310/785-9189

EYE OF THE CAT   Universal, 1969, w/Phillip Hazelton
JENNIFER ON MY MIND   United Artists, 1971
HAMMER   United Artists, 1972, EP w/Phillip Hazelton
THAT MAN BOLT   Universal, 1973
BUCKTOWN   AIP, 1975
TRACKDOWN   United Artists, 1976
COAL MINER'S DAUGHTER ★   Universal, 1980
ROAD GAMES   Avco Embassy, 1981, EP
PSYCHO II   Universal, 1983, EP
ST. ELMO'S FIRE   Columbia, 1985, EP w/Ned Tanen
SWEET DREAMS   TriStar, 1985

BILL SCHWARTZ
Contact: Zacs Productions, c/o Warner Bros. TV,
   4063 Radford Ave., Suite 201E, Studio City, CA 91604,
   818/762-1588

WHERE DOES IT HURT?   Cinerama, 1972,
   w/Rod Amateau

IRVING SCHWARTZ
(credit w/Harry Hurwitz)

THE ROSEBUD BEACH HOTEL   *THE BIG LOBBY*
   Almi, 1984
THAT'S ADEQUATE   That's Adequate Company, 1986

MARVIN SCHWARTZ
WELCOME HOME, SOLDIER BOYS   20th Century
   Fox, 1972
KID BLUE   20th Century Fox, 1973

ROBERT SCHWARTZ
OLD EXPLORERS   Taurus, 1991, CP

RUSSELL SCHWARTZ
Business: HBO Independent Productions, 2049 Century Park
   East, Suite 4100, Los Angeles, CA 90067, 310/201-9300;
   Fax: 310/201-9293

THEY ALL LAUGHED   United Artists Classics, 1982, AP
A NIGHT IN THE LIFE OF JIMMY REARDON   20th Century
   Fox, 1988

TERI SCHWARTZ
Agent: ICM - Los Angeles, 310/550-4000
Contact: Directors Guild of America - Los Angeles,
   213/289-2000

HOLLYWOOD BOULEVARD   New World, 1977, AP
THE BEES   New World, 1978, AP
NUTS   Warner Bros., 1987, EP w/Cis Corman
BEACHES   Buena Vista, 1988, EP
JOE VERSUS THE VOLCANO   Warner Bros., 1990
DECEIVED   Buena Vista, 1991, EP w/Anthea Sylbert

JACK SCHWARTZMAN
BEING THERE   United Artists, 1979, EP
NEVER SAY NEVER AGAIN   Warner Bros., 1983
I AM THE CHEESE   Almi, 1983, EP w/Michael S. Landes &
   Albert Schwartz
RAD   TriStar, 1986, EP
HYPER SAPIEN   TriStar, 1986
LIONHEART   Orion, 1987, EP w/Francis Ford Coppola

RONALD L. SCHWARY
Business: Schwary Enterprises, Inc., c/o Stan Karp, 10350
   Santa Monica Blvd., Suite 200, Los Angeles, CA 90025,
   310/277-0711
Contact: Directors Guild of America - Los Angeles,
   213/289-2000

SHADOW OF THE HAWK   Columbia, 1976, AP
CALIFORNIA SUITE   Columbia, 1978, AP
ORDINARY PEOPLE ★★   Paramount, 1980
ABSENCE OF MALICE   Columbia, 1981, EP
TOOTSIE ★   Columbia, 1982, EP
LET'S SPEND THE NIGHT TOGETHER   Embassy, 1983
A SOLDIER'S STORY ★   Columbia, 1984, w/Norman
   Jewison & Patrick Palmer
BATTERIES NOT INCLUDED   Universal, 1987
HAVANA   Universal, 1990, EP

KENNETH SCHWENKER
Business: Cabriolet Films, Inc., 34 W. 13th St., New York,
   NY 10011

ICE HOUSE   Upfront Films, 1989, CP

ALDEN SCHWIMMER
HARRY IN YOUR POCKET   United Artists, 1973, EP

RALPH SCOBIE
HOME IS WHERE THE HART IS   Atlantic, 1987,
   EP w/Richard Strafehl

Sc

FILM
PRODUCERS,
STUDIOS,
AGENTS AND
CASTING
DIRECTORS
GUIDE

F
I
L
M

P
R
O
D
U
C
E
R
S

Sc

FILM
PRODUCERS,
STUDIOS,
AGENTS AND
CASTING
DIRECTORS
GUIDE

F
I
L
M

P
R
O
D
U
C
E
R
S

MICHAEL A. P. SCORDING
OUT OF SIGHT, OUT OF MIND   Spectrum Entertainment,
1990, EP

MARTIN SCORSESE
Agent: CAA - Beverly Hills, 310/288-4545
Business: Tribeca Film Center, 375 Greenwich St.,
New York, NY 10013

MEDICINE BALL CARAVAN (FD)   Warner Bros.,
1971, AP
THE GRIFTERS   Miramax, 1990, w/Robert Harris &
James Painten

ALLAN SCOTT
Agent: The Robert Littman Company - Beverly Hills,
310/278-1572
Contact: Writers Guild of America - Los Angeles,
310/550-1000

TAFFIN   MGM/UA, 1988, EP

ANN SCOTT
Business: Greenpoint Films, 5a Noel Street, London
W1V 3RB England, 071/437-6492; Fax: 071/437-0644

THE PLOUGHMAN'S LUNCH   Samuel Goldwyn
Company, 1984, w/Simon Relph

DARIN SCOTT
Agent: Irene Robinson Group - Los Angeles,
213/274-5101

STEPFATHER II   Millimeter, 1989, w/William Burr
TO SLEEP WITH ANGER   Samuel Goldwyn Company,
1990, w/Thomas S. Byrnes & Caldecot Chubb

GEORGE C. SCOTT
Agent: Jane Deacy Agency - New York, 914/941-1414
Business Manager: Becker & London - New York,
212/541-7070

THE SAVAGE IS LOOSE   Campbell Devon, 1974

JANE SCOTT
Business: Paramount Pictures, 5555 Melrose Ave.,
Hollywood, CA 90067, 213/956-5796

20TH CENTURY OZ   Inter-Planetary, 1977, AP
CROCODILE DUNDEE   Paramount, 1986, LP
CROCODILE DUNDEE II   Paramount, 1988,
w/John Cornell

MARTHA SCOTT
Agent: The Barry Freed Company - Los Angeles,
310/274-6898

FIRST MONDAY IN OCTOBER   Paramount, 1981,
w/Paul Heller

PIPPA SCOTT
Business: Linden Productions, 10850 Wilshire Blvd.,
Suite 250, Los Angeles, CA 90024, 310/474-2234;
Fax: 310/474-8773

MEET THE HOLLOWHEADS   Moviestore, 1989, EP

RIDLEY SCOTT
Business: Percy Main Prods., c/o Carolco, 8439 Sunset
Blvd., Suite 103, Los Angeles, CA 90069, 213/654-4417;
Fax: 213/654-8936
Agent: CAA - Beverly Hills, 310/288-4545

SOMEONE TO WATCH OVER ME   Columbia, 1987, EP
THELMA & LOUISE   MGM-PATHE, 1991, w/Mimi Polk

WILLIAM P. SCOTT
THE LAST OF THE FINEST   Orion, 1990, CP

BEN SCOTTI
(credit w/Fred Scotti)
Business: Scotti Brothers Pictures, Inc., 2114 Pico Blvd.,
Santa Monica, CA 90405, 310/452-4040;
Fax: 310/452-9053

EYE OF THE TIGER   Scotti Bros., 1986,
EP w/Herb Nanas
LADY BEWARE   Scotti Bros., 1987, EP
THE IRON TRIANGLE   Scotti Bros., 1989, EP

FRED SCOTTI
(credit w/Ben Scotti)
Business: Scotti Brothers Pictures, Inc., 2114 Pico Blvd.,
Santa Monica, CA 90405, 310/452-4040;
Fax: 310/452-9053

LADY BEWARE   Scotti Bros., 1987, EP
THE IRON TRIANGLE   Scotti Bros., 1989, EP

TONY SCOTTI
Business: All American Television, 6277 Selma Ave.,
Hollywood, CA 90028, 213/466-1006; Fax: 213/463-1584

EYE OF THE TIGER   Scotti Bros., 1986
LADY BEWARE   Scotti Bros., 1987,
w/Lawrence Mortorff
THE IRON TRIANGLE   Scotti Bros., 1989,
w/Angela P. Schapiro

BODO SCRIBA
THE NEVERENDING STORY II: THE NEXT CHAPTER
Warner Bros., 1991, CP

STEVEN SEAGAL
Business: Seagal-Feder-Nasso Productions, Warner
Brothers, 4000 Warner Blvd., Burbank, CA 91522,
818/954-4267
Agent: CAA - Beverly Hills, 310/288-4545

ABOVE THE LAW   Warner Bros., 1988, w/Andrew Davis
MARKED FOR DEATH   20th Century Fox, 1990,
w/Michael Grais & Mark Victor
OUT FOR JUSTICE   Warner Bros., 1991,
w/Steven Seagal

GEORGE SEGAL
Contact: Screen Actors Guild - Los Angeles, 213/465-4600

THE BLACK BIRD   Columbia, 1975, EP

RAY SEGER
PROM NIGHT III; THE LAST KISS   Norstar, 1990,
w/Peter Simpson

SUSAN SEIDELMAN
Business Manager: Shedler & Shedler, 225 W. 34th St.,
New York, NY 10122, 212/564-6656
Agent: ICM - New York, 212/556-5600

SMITHEREENS   New Line, 1982
MAKING MR. RIGHT   Orion, 1987, EP w/Dan Enright
COOKIE   Warner Bros., 1989, EP w/Alice Arlen &
Nora Ephron
SHE-DEVIL   Orion, 1989, w/Jonathan Brett

W. JOHN SEIG
PRISONERS   American Films Ltd., 1975,
w/Lewis M. Horwitz

MARK SEILER
PLENTY   20th Century Fox, 1985, EP

WILLIAM SELF
(credit w/M. J. Frankovich)
Contact: Self Productions, 975 Somera Dr., Los Angeles,
CA 90077, 310/476-2404; Fax: 310/476-3205

THE SHOOTIST   Paramount, 1976
FROM NOON TILL THREE   United Artists, 1976

JOANNE SELLAR
HARDWARE   Miramax, 1990, w/Paul Trybits

ARLENE SELLERS
(credit w/Alex Winitsky)
Business: Lantana Productions, 3000 Olympic Blvd.,
Suite 1300, Santa Monica, CA 90404, 310/315-4777;
Fax: 310/315-4778

THE SEVEN-PERCENT SOLUTION   Universal, 1976, EP
END OF THE GAME   20th Century Fox, 1976,
w/Maximilian Schell*
CROSS OF IRON   Avco Embassy, 1977
SILVER BEARS   Columbia, 1978
BREAKTHROUGH   *SERGEANT STEINER*   Maverick
Pictures International, 1978
HOUSE CALLS   Universal, 1978
THE LADY VANISHES   Rank, 1979,
EP w/Michael Carreras
CUBA   United Artists, 1979
BLUE SKIES AGAIN   Warner Bros., 1983
SWING SHIFT   Warner Bros., 1984, EP
SCANDALOUS   Orion, 1984
IRRECONCILABLE DIFFERENCES   Warner Bros., 1984
BAD MEDICINE   20th Century Fox, 1985
STANLEY & IRIS   MGM/UA, 1990

CHARLES E. SELLIER, JR.
Agent: The Schallert Agency - Beverly Hills, 310/276-2044

THE BROTHERS O'TOOLE   CVD, 1973
THE LIFE AND TIMES OF GRIZZLY ADAMS   Sun
International, 1974
THE MYSTERIOUS MONSTERS (FD)   Sunn
Classic, 1976
GUARDIAN OF THE WILDERNESS   Sunn Classic, 1976
IN SEARCH OF NOAH'S ARK (FD)   Sunn Classic, 1976
THE ADVENTURES OF FRONTIER FREMONT   Sunn
Classic, 1976
THE AMAZING WORLD OF PSYCHIC PHENOMENA (FD)
Sunn Classic, 1976

THE LINCOLN CONSPIRACY (FD)   Sunn Classic, 1977,
w/Raylan D. Jensen
BEYOND & BACK (FD)   Sunn Classic, 1978
THE BERMUDA TRIANGLE (FD)   Sunn Classic, 1979,
w/James L. Conway
THE LEGEND OF SLEEPY HOLLOW   Sunn Classic,
1979, w/James L. Conway
THE FALL OF THE HOUSE OF USHER   Sunn
Classic, 1979
IN SEARCH OF HISTORIC JESUS (FD)   Sunn Classic,
1979, w/James L. Conway
BEYOND DEATH'S DOOR (FD)   Sunn Classic, 1979, EP
LEGEND OF THE WILD   Jensen Farley, 1981
THE BOOGENS   Jensen Farley, 1982

JERRY SELTZER
FIRST POSITION (FD)   Roninfilm, 1973, EP

WALTER SELTZER
DARKER THAN AMBER   National General, 1970,
w/Jack Reeves
THE OMEGA MAN   Warner Bros., 1971
SKYJACKED   MGM, 1972
SOYLENT GREEN   MGM, 1973, w/Russell Thacher
THE LAST HARD MEN   20th Century Fox, 1976,
w/Russell Thacher

LORENZO SEMPLE, JR.
Agent: CAA - Beverly Hills, 310/288-4545
Contact: Writers Guild of America - Los Angeles,
310/550-1000

HURRICANE   Paramount, 1979, EP

DANIEL SENATORE
IN SEARCH OF GREGORY   Universal, 1970,
w/Joseph Janni

YAHOO SERIOUS
(Greg Pead)
Contact: Australian Film Commission, 9229 Sunset Blvd.,
Los Angeles, CA 90069, 310/275-7074

YOUNG EINSTEIN   Warner Bros., 1989, w/David Roach &
Warwick Ross

JOHN SERONG
THE GARBAGE PAIL KIDS MOVIE   Atlantic Entertainment,
1987, SP

RALPH SERPE
THE DESERTER   Paramount, 1971, w/Norman Baer
LOLA   AIP, 1971, AP w/Norman Thaddeus Vane
ACROSS 110th STREET   United Artists, 1972,
w/Fouad Said
MANDINGO   Paramount, 1975, EP
DRUM   United Artists, 1976
THE BRINK'S JOB   Universal, 1978

ALEX SESSA
Business: Arles International, S.A., Lavalle 1710-60-11,
1048 Buenos Aires, Argentina, 54-1-814-3859

WIZARDS OF THE LOST KINGDOM   Concorde, 1985,
w/Frank Isaac
BARBARIAN QUEEN   Concorde, 1985, w/Frank Isaac
COCAINE WARS   Concorde, 1985, w/Roger Corman

Se

FILM
PRODUCERS,
STUDIOS,
AGENTS and
CASTING
DIRECTORS
GUIDE

F I L M   P R O D U C E R S

Se

**FILM
PRODUCERS,
STUDIOS,
AGENTS AND
CASTING
DIRECTORS GUIDE**

F
I
L
M

P
R
O
D
U
C
E
R
S

JOHN SEXTON
PHAR LAP   20th Century Fox, 1984
BURKE AND WILLS   Hemdale, 1987, w/Graeme Clifford

JULIAN SEYMOUR
ANOTHER COUNTRY   Orion Classics, 1984,
   EP w/Robert Fox

LENNY SHABES
CINDERELLA   Group I, 1977, EP w/Ronald Domont

SUSAN SHADBURNE
Business: Millennium Pictures, Inc., 2580 N.W. Upshur,
   Portland, OR 97210, 503/227-7041

THE ADVENTURES OF MARK TWAIN   Atlantic
   Entertainment, 1986, AP
SHADOW PLAY   New World, 1986, w/Dan Biggs &
   Will Vinton

MARTIN SHAFER
(credit w/Andrew Scheinman)
Business: Castle Rock Entertainment, 335 N. Maple Dr.,
   Suite 135, Beverly Hills, CA 90210, 310/285-2300;
   Fax: 310/285-2345

THE MOUNTAIN MEN   Columbia, 1980,
   w/Martin Ransohoff
THE AWAKENING   Orion/Warner Bros., 1980,
   w/Robert H. Solo
MODERN ROMANCE   Columbia, 1981

RENEE A. SHAFRANSKY
Agent: ICM - Los Angeles, 310/550-4000
Contact: Writers Guild of America - New York,
   212/245-6180

VARIETY   Horizon Films, 1985
SWIMMING TO CAMBODIA   Cinecom, 1987

JOSEF SHAFTEL
Business: Crystal Entertainment, London

THE LAST GRENADE   Cinerama, 1970
SAY HELLO TO YESTERDAY   Cinerama, 1971
THE STATUE   Cinerama, 1971
THE ASSASSINATION OF TROTSKY   Cinerama,
   1972, EP
ALICE'S ADVENTURES IN WONDERLAND   American
   National, 1972, EP
WHERE DOES IT HURT?   Cinerama, 1972, EP

ROBERT SHAFTER
TIME WALKER   New World, 1982, EP

STEVE SHAGAN
Agent: William Morris Agency - Beverly Hills, 310/274-7451
Contact: Writers Guild of America - Los Angeles,
   310/550-1000

SAVE THE TIGER   Paramount, 1973
W.W. AND THE DIXIE DANCEKINGS   20th Century Fox,
   1975, EP
THE FORMULA   MGM/UA, 1980

ASH R. SHAH
Business: Imperial Entertainment Corp., 4640 Lankershim
   Blvd., North Hollywood, CA 91602, 818/762-0005;
   Fax: 818/762-0006

ANGEL TOWN   Taurus, 1990, w/Eric Karson

SUNDIP R. SHAH
Business: Imperial Entertainment Corp., 4640 Lankershim
   Blvd., North Hollywood, CA 91602, 818/762-0005;
   Fax: 818/762-0006

ANGEL TOWN   Taurus, 1990, EP w/Anders P. Jensen &
   Sunil R. Shah

SUNIL R. SHAH
(credit w/Moshe Barkat & Moshe Diamant)
Business: Imperial Entertainment Corp., 4640 Lankershim
   Blvd., North Hollywood, CA 91602, 818/762-0005;
   Fax: 818/762-0006

PRAY FOR DEATH   American Distribution Group,
   1986, EP
RAGE OF HONOR   Trans World, 1987, EP
ANGEL TOWN   Taurus, 1990, EP w/Anders P. Jensen &
   Sundip R. Shah

MICHAEL SHAMBERG
Business: Ocean Pictures, 2821 Main St., Santa Monica,
   CA 90405, 310/399-9271

HEART BEAT   Orion/Warner Bros., 1980,
   w/Alan Greisman
MODERN PROBLEMS   20th Century Fox, 1981,
   w/Alan Greisman
THE BIG CHILL ★   Columbia, 1983
CLUB PARADISE   Warner Bros., 1986
SALVATION!   Circle Releasing, 1987, w/Beth B
A FISH CALLED WANDA   MGM/UA, 1988
HOW I GOT INTO COLLEGE   20th Century Fox, 1989

REID SHANE
THE TERROR WITHIN   Concorde, 1989,
   CP w/Rodman Flender
DANCE OF THE DAMNED   Concorde, 1989,
   CP w/Anna Roth

JOHN HERMAN SHANER
Agent: Robinson, Weintraub, Gross, Inc. - Los Angeles,
   213/653-5802
Contact: Writers Guild of America - Los Angeles,
   310/550-1000

THE LAST MARRIED COUPLE IN AMERICA   Universal,
   1980, w/Edward S. Feldman

MARK SHANKER
THE FIRST DEADLY SIN   Filmways, 1980,
   w/George Pappas

ALLEN SHAPIRO
Contact: The Indieprod Company, 8800 Sunset Blvd.,
   5th Floor, Los Angeles, CA 90069, 310/289-7100;
   Fax: 310/652-2165

AIR AMERICA   TriStar, 1990, CP w/John Eskow

Sh

FILM
PRODUCERS,
STUDIOS,
AGENTS AND
CASTING
DIRECTORS
GUIDE

F
I
L
M

P
R
O
D
U
C
E
R
S

GEORGE SHAPIRO
Business: Shapiro/West, 151 El Camino Dr., Beverly Hills,
  CA 90210, 310278-8896

THE LAST REMAKE OF BEAU GESTE   Universal, 1977,
  EP w/Howard West
IN GOD WE TRUST   Universal, 1980, w/Howard West
SUMMER RENTAL   Paramount, 1985
SUMMER SCHOOL   Paramount, 1987, w/Howard West
BERT RIGBY, YOU'RE A FOOL   Warner Bros., 1989

IRVIN SHAPIRO
CRIMEWAVE   Embassy, 1986, EP w/Edward R. Pressman

LEONARD SHAPIRO
Business: Shapiro-Glickenhaus Entertainment, 1619
  Broadway, New York, NY 10019, 212/265-1150;
  12001 Ventura Pl., Suite 404, Studio City, CA 91604,
  818/766-8500; Fax: 818/766-7873

SHAKEDOWN   Universal, 1988, EP w/Alan M. Solomon

MICHAEL SHAPIRO
DEADLY ILLUSION   CineTel Films, 1987,
  EP w/Rodney Sheldon

ROBERT SHAPIRO
Business: Robert Shapiro Productions, c/o Warner
  Hollywood Studios, 1041 N. Formosa Ave., Hollywood,
  CA 90046, 213/850-3975; Fax: 213/850-3917

PEE-WEE'S BIG ADVENTURE   Warner Bros., 1985,
  w/Richard Gilbert Abramson
EMPIRE OF THE SUN   Warner Bros., 1987, EP
ARTHUR 2 ON THE ROCKS   Warner Bros., 1988

RON SHAPIRO
TRUCKIN' BUDDY MCCOY   Bedford Entertainment,
  1984, EP
KANDYLAND   New World, 1988, AP

SHAUNA SHAPIRO
NO SECRETS   I.R.S., 1991, w/Morgan Mason &
  John Hardy

STUART S. SHAPIRO
MONDO NEW YORK   4th & Broadway, 1988
COMEDY'S DIRTIEST DOZEN   4th & Broadway, 1989

SUSAN HILLARY SHAPIRO
Business: Neo Modern Entertainment, 8033 Sunset Blvd.,
  Suite 640, Los Angeles, CA 90046, 213/650-1642

GINGER ALE AFTERNOON   Skouras Pictures, 1989,
  w/Rafal Zielinski

TED SHAPIRO
TRACKS   Castle Hill Productions, 1976,
  w/Norman I. Cohen & Howard Zucker

BRUCE SHARMAN
Agent: London Management - London, 071/493-1610

HENRY V   Samuel Goldwyn Company, 1989

HARVE SHARMAN
SHOOT   Avco Embassy, 1976

CLIVE SHARP
LOLA   *TWINKY*   AIP, 1973

JAN SHARP
THE GOOD WIFE   Atlantic, 1987

ROBERT SHARPE
STARHOPS   First American, 1978, EP w/Daniel Grodnik &
  Jack Rose

MELVILLE SHAVELSON
Agent: William Morris Agency - Beverly Hills, 310/274-7451
Contact: Writers Guild of America - Los Angeles,
  310/550-1000

TROUBLE ALONG THE WAY   Warner Bros., 1953
THE PIGEON THAT TOOK ROME   Paramount, 1962
A NEW KIND OF LOVE   Paramount, 1963
CAST A GIANT SHADOW   United Artists, 1966
MIXED COMPANY   United Artists, 1974

JAMES SHAVICK
FALSE IDENTITY   RKO, 1990

LARRY SHAW
WATTSTAX (FD)   Columbia, 1973, w/Mel Stuart

MARK SHAW
DIVING IN   Skouras, 1990, EP w/Michael Maurer

PETER SHAW
Business: UBA, Pinewood Studios, Iver Heath, Bucks SL0
  0NH England, 0753/651-700; Fax: 0753/656-844

ENIGMA   Embassy, 1983, w/Ben Arbeid &
  Andre Pergament
CHAMPIONS   Embassy, 1984
CASTAWAY   Cannon, 1987, EP w/Richard Johnson
TAFFIN   MGM/UA, 1988

RUN RUN SHAW
(credit w/Gustave Berne)

CANNONBALL   New World, 1976, EP
THE STRANGER AND THE GUNFIGHTER
  Columbia, 1976

SAM SHAW
HUSBANDS   Columbia, 1970, AP
A WOMAN UNDER THE INFLUENCE   Faces
  International, 1974
OPENING NIGHT   Faces International, 1979, EP
GLORIA   Columbia, 1980, EP

TOM SHAW
Contact: Directors Guild of America - Los Angeles,
  213/289-2000

FACE TO THE WIND   Warner Bros., 1974, AP
THE NINTH CONFIGURATION   *TWINKLE,*
  TWINKLE,"KILLER" KANE   Warner Bros., 1979, AP
MR. NORTH   Samuel Goldwyn Company, 1988, CP
TEQUILA SUNRISE   Warner Bros., 1988, EP

Sh

**FILM
PRODUCERS,
STUDIOS,
AGENTS AND
CASTING
DIRECTORS**
GUIDE

F
I
L
M

P
R
O
D
U
C
E
R
S

ROBERT SHAYE
Business: New Line, 116 N. Robertson Blvd., Los Angeles,
    CA 90048, 310/854-5811

STUNTS   New Line, 1977, EP w/Peter S. Davis
POLYESTER   New Line, 1981, EP
ALONE IN THE DARK   New Line, 1982
THE FIRST TIME   New Line, 1982,
    EP w/Lawrence Loventhal
XTRO   New Line, 1983, EP
A NIGHTMARE ON ELM STREET   New Line, 1984, EP
A NIGHTMARE ON ELM STREET 2: FREDDY'S
    REVENGE   New Line, 1985
CRITTERS   New Line, 1986, EP
QUIET COOL   New Line, 1986, w/Gerald T. Olson
A NIGHTMARE ON ELM STREET 3: DREAM WARRIORS
    New Line, 1987
MY DEMON LOVER   New Line, 1987
STRANDED   New Line, 1987, EP
THE HIDDEN   New Line, 1987, w/Michael Meltzer &
    Gerald T. Olson
THE PRINCE OF PENNSYLVANIA   New Line, 1988,
    EP w/Sara Risher
CRITTERS 2: THE MAIN COURSE   New Line
    Cinema, 1988
HAIRSPRAY   New Line, 1988, EP w/Sara Risher
A NIGHTMARE ON ELM STREET 4: THE DREAM
    MASTER   New Line, 1988, w/Rachel Talalay
A NIGHTMARE ON ELM STREET 5: THE DREAM CHILD
    New Line, 1989, w/Rupert Harvey
LEATHERFACE: THE TEXAS CHAINSAW MASSACRE III
    New Line, 1990, EP
HEART CONDITION   New Line, 1990, EP

BASHAR SHBIB
JULIA HAS TWO LOVERS   South Gate
    Entertainment, 1991

RONALD SHEDLO
Contact: Weissmann, Wolff, Bergman, Coleman &
    Silverman, 9665 Wilshire Blvd., Suite 900, Beverly Hills,
    CA 90209, 310/858-7888

THE WHISPERERS   United Artists, 1967,
    w/Michael S. Laughlin
THE RECKONING   Columbia, 1971
BACK ROADS   Warner Bros., 1981
THE DRESSMAKER   Euro-American Classics, 1988

MARTIN SHEEN
(credit w/William R. Greenblatt)
Business: Symphony Pictures, 5711 W. Slauson Blvd.,
    Suite 226, Culver City, CA 90230, 310/649-3668
Agent: William Morris Agency - Beverly Hills, 310/274-7451
Contact: Glynnis Liberty, The Liberty Company -
    Los Angeles, 213/824-7937

JUDGMENT IN BERLIN   New Line, 1988,
    EP w/Jeffrey Auerbach
DA   FilmDallas, 1988, EP w/Sam Grogg

CRAIG SHEFFER
INSTANT KARMA   MGM, 1990, EP w/Steven J. Bratter

ERIC F. SHEFFER
JEZEBEL'S KISS   Shapiro Glickenhaus, 1990

JON SHEINBERG
Business: Lee Rich Productions, 4000 Warner Blvd.,
    Burbank, CA 91522, 818/954-3556

HARD TO KILL   Warner Brothers, 1990, CP

CAROLYN SHELBY
Agent: UTA - Beverly Hills, 310/273-6700
Business: North Beach Productions, 818/591-2222

CLASS ACTION   20th Century Fox, 1991,
    CP w/Christopher Ames

RODNEY SHELDON
DEADLY ILLUSION   CineTel Films, 1987,
    EP w/Michael Shapiro

BRUCE SHELLY
THE HAZING   Miraleste, 1978, w/Douglas Curtis

WALTER SHENSON
Business: Shenson Films, 120 El Camino Dr., Suite 200,
    Beverly Hills, CA 90212, 310/275-6886

THE MOUSE THAT ROARED   Columbia, 1959,
    w/Jon Pennington
A MATTER OF WHO   MGM, 1962, w/Milton Holmes
THE MOUSE ON THE MOON   United Artists, 1963
A HARD DAY'S NIGHT   United Artists, 1964
HELP!   United Artists, 1965
30 IS A DANGEROUS AGE, CYNTHIA   Columbia, 1968
WELCOME TO THE CLUB   Columbia, 1971
DIGBY, THE BIGGEST DOG IN THE WORLD
    Cinerama, 1974
THE CHICKEN CHRONICLES   Avco Embassy, 1977
REUBEN, REUBEN   20th Century Fox International
    Classics, 1983
ECHO PARK   Atlantic, 1986

PETER SHEPHERD
Business: Cannon Productions, 5757 Wilshire Blvd.,
    Suite 721, Los Angeles, CA 90036, 213/965-0901

LAMBADA   Warner Bros., 1990

RICHARD SHEPHERD
Agent: The Artists Agency, 10000 Santa Monica Blvd.,
    Suite 305, Los Angeles, CA 90067, 310/277-7779

THE HANGING TREE   Warner Bros., 1959,
    w/Martin Jurow
THE FUGITIVE KIND   United Artists, 1960, w/Martin Jurow
BREAKFAST AT TIFFANY'S   Paramount, 1961,
    w/Martin Jurow
ROBIN AND MARIAN   Columbia, 1976, EP
ALEX AND THE GYPSY   20th Century Fox, 1976
THE HUNGER   MGM/UA, 1983
VOLUNTEERS   TriStar, 1985, w/Walter F. Parkes

JACK SHER
SLITHER   MGM, 1973

VICTOR SHER
POSITIVE I.D.   Universal, 1987, EP

DANIEL A. SHERKOW
Contact: Dick Clark Productions, 3003 W. Olive Ave.,
   Burbank, CA 91510, 818/841-3003; Fax: 818/954-8609

SUSPECT   TriStar, 1987
RACE TO GLORY   New Century/Vista, 1989,
   w/Jon Gordon
IMPROMPTU   Hemdale, 1991, w/Stuart Oken

JERRY SHERLOCK
CHARLIE CHAN & THE CURSE OF THE DRAGON
   QUEEN   American Cinema, 1981
THE HUNT FOR RED OCTOBER   Paramount, 1990,
   EP w/Larry De Waay

GARY A. SHERMAN
Agent: Camden Artists, Ltd. - Los Angeles, 213/556-2022
Contact: Directors Guild of America - Los Angeles,
   213/289-2000

POLTERGEIST III   MGM/UA, 1988, EP

ROBERT M. SHERMAN
SCARECROW   Warner Bros., 1973
NIGHT MOVES   Warner Bros., 1975
THE MISSOURI BREAKS   United Artists, 1976,
   w/Elliott Kastner
CONVOY   United Artists, 1978
OH, GOD! YOU DEVIL   Warner Bros., 1984
DEADLY FRIEND   Warner Bros., 1986

NED SHERRIN
THE VIRGIN SOLDIERS   Columbia, 1970, w/Leslie Gilliat
UP POMPEII   MGM/EMI, 1974
THINK DIRTY   Quartet, 1978
THE NATIONAL HEALTH   Columbia, 1979,
   w/Terry Glinwood

TERI SHIELDS
SAHARA   MGM/UA, 1984, EP

BARRY SHILS
THE STUFF   New World, 1985, AP
VAMPIRE'S KISS   Hemdale, 1989, w/Barbara Zitwer

JOHN SHIPP
THE STUDENT BODY   Surrogate, 1976, EP

TALIA SHIRE
HYPER SAPIEN   TriStar, 1986, EP
LIONHEART   Orion, 1987, w/Stanley O'Toole

MARK SHIVAS
Business: British Broadcasting Corporation, Woodlands,
   80 Wood Lane, London W12 7RJ, 081/743-8000

HENRY VIII AND HIS SIX WIVES   Anglo EMI, 1973, EP
RICHARD'S THINGS   New World, 1981
MOONLIGHTING   Universal, 1982, w/Jerzy Skolimowski
A PRIVATE FUNCTION   Island Alive, 1985
THE WITCHES   Warner Bros., 1990

MARC SHMUGER
Contact: Writers Guild of America - Los Angeles,
   310/550-1000

DEAD OF WINTER   MGM/UA, 1987,
   w/John Bloomgarden

SIG SHORE
SUPER FLY   Warner Bros., 1972
SUPER FLY T.N.T.   Paramount, 1973
THAT'S THE WAY OF THE WORLD   *SHINING STAR*
   United Artists, 1975
THE RETURN OF SUPERFLY   Triton, 1990,
   w/Anthony Wisdom

DEL SHORES
Business: Warner Bros. TV, 4000 Warner Blvd., Burbank,
   CA 91522, 818/954-3135
Agent: Artists Circle Entertainment - Los Angeles,
   310/275-6330

DADDY'S DYIN'...WHO'S GOT THE WILL?   MGM/UA,
   1990, EP w/Bobbie Edrick, Michael Kuhn & Nigel Sinclair

SKIP SHORT
FLASHPOINT   TriStar, 1984

MURRAY SHOSTAK
Agent: Camden Artists, Ltd. - Los Angeles, 213/556-2022

CHILD UNDER A LEAF   Cinema National, 1975,
   w/Robert Baylis
DEATH HUNT   20th Century Fox, 1981
SILENCE OF THE NORTH   Universal, 1982
MARIA CHAPDELAINE   Moviestore, 1986,
   w/Robert Baylis
LOVE SONGS   Spectrafilm, 1986,
   EP w/Marie-Christine Chouraqui
SPEED ZONE   Orion, 1989

LAUREN SHULER-DONNER
(formerly Lauren Shuler)
Business: Shuler-Donner Productions, Warner Brothers,
   4000 Warner Blvd., Burbank, CA 91522, 818/954-3611;
   Fax: 818/954-3475

MR. MOM   20th Century Fox, 1983, w/Lynn Loring
LADYHAWKE   Warner Bros., 1985, w/Richard Donner
ST. ELMO'S FIRE   Columbia, 1985
PRETTY IN PINK   Paramount, 1986
THREE FUGITIVES   Buena Vista, 1989

RONALD SHUSETT
Agent: Triad Artists, Inc. - Los Angeles, 310/556-2727
Contact: Writers Guild of America - Los Angeles,
   310/550-1000

ALIEN   20th Century Fox, 1979, EP
DEAD AND BURIED   Avco Embassy, 1981,
   w/Robert Fentress
KING KONG LIVES   DEG, 1986, EP
TOTAL RECALL   TriStar, 1990, w/Buzz Feitshans
FREEJACK   Warner Bros., 1991, w/Stuart Oken

CHARLES SHYER
Agent: ICM - Los Angeles, 310/550-4000
Contact: Directors Guild of America - Los Angeles,
   213/289-2000

PRIVATE BENJAMIN   Warner Bros., 1980,
   w/Nancy Meyers & Harvey Miller

Sh

FILM
PRODUCERS,
STUDIOS,
AGENTS AND
CASTING
DIRECTORS
GUIDE

F
I
L
M

P
R
O
D
U
C
E
R
S

Si

**FILM
PRODUCERS,
STUDIOS,
AGENTS and
CASTING
DIRECTORS
GUIDE**

F
I
L
M

P
R
O
D
U
C
E
R
S

ANDY SIDARIS
Business: Malibu Bay Films, 8560 Sunset Blvd., 2nd Floor,
Los Angeles, CA 90069, 310/278-5056

SEVEN   AIP, 1979, EP

ARLENE SIDARIS
Business: Malibu Bay Films, 8560 Sunset Blvd., 2nd Floor,
Los Angeles, CA 90069, 310/278-5056

MALIBU EXPRESS   Malibu Bay Films, 1984
HARD TICKET TO HAWAII   Malibu Bay Films, 1987
PICASSO TRIGGER   Malibu Bay Films, 1988
SAVAGE BEACH   Malibu Bay Films, 1989

STEVEN SIEBERT
Contact: Lighthouse Entertainment, 19744 Pacific Coast
Highway, Malibu, CA 90265, 310/456-1946;
Fax: 310/456-9854

THE ROOKIE   Warner Bros., 1990, w/Howard Kazanjian
& David Valdes

STAN SIEGEL
THE LEGEND OF SLEEPY HOLLOW   Sunn Classic,
1979, AP
BEYOND DEATH'S DOOR (FD)   Sunn Classic, 1979

STEVEN JAY SIEGEL
Agent: UTA - Beverly Hills, 310/273-6700
Contact: Writers Guild of America - Los Angeles,
310/550-1000

K-9   Universal, 1989, CP

CHRIS SIEVERNICH
Business: Delta Films, 853 Broadway, Suite 1711,
New York, NY 10003, 212/473-3600

LIGHTNING OVER WATER   Gray City, 1981
THE STATE OF THINGS   Gray City, 1983
PARIS, TEXAS   20th Century Fox, 1984, EP
THE DEAD   Vestron, 1987, w/Wieland Schulz-Keil

SIGURJON SIGHVATSSON
(credit w/Steven Golin)
Business: Propaganda Films, 940 N. Mansfield Ave.,
Los Angeles, CA 90038, 213/462-6400;
Fax: 213/463-7874

PRIVATE INVESTIGATIONS   MGM, 1987
THE BLUE IGUANA   Paramount, 1988
FEAR, ANXIETY AND DEPRESSION   Samuel Goldwyn
Company, 1989, w/Stanley Wlodkowski
KILL ME AGAIN   MGM/UA, 1989, w/David W. Warfield
DADDY'S DYIN'...WHO'S GOT THE WILL?   MGM/UA,
1990, w/Monty Montgomery
WILD AT HEART   Samuel Goldwyn Company, 1990,
w/Monty Montgomery

SERGE SILBERMAN
AND HOPE TO DIE   20th Century Fox, 1972
THE DISCREET CHARM OF THE BOURGEOISIE
20th Century Fox, 1972
THE PHANTOM OF LIBERTY   20th Century Fox, 1974
THAT OBSCURE OBJECT OF DESIRE   First Artists,
1977, EP
EXPOSED   MGM/UA, 1983, EP
RAN   Orion Classics, 1985, w/Masato Hara

STIRLING SILLIPHANT
Agent: CAA - Beverly Hills, 310/288-4545
Contact: Writers Guild of America - Los Angeles,
310/550-1000

A WALK IN THE SPRING RAIN   Columbia, 1970
CATCH THE HEAT   Trans World, 1987,
EP w/Moshe Diamant

TEDDY B. SILLS
TO KILL A CLOWN   20th Century Fox, 1972

JERRY SILVA
Business: Double Helix Films, Inc., 275 Seventh Ave.,
Suite 2003, New York, NY 10001, 212/727-2000

FUNLAND   Double Helix, 1987, EP w/Kirk Smith &
Stan Wakefield
MATEWAN   Cinecom, 1987, EP w/Mark Balsam &
Amir J. Malin
FAST FOOD   Fries Entertainment, 1989, EP
ELLIOT FAUMAN, PH.D.   Taurus, 1990,
EP w/Stan Wakefield

GIORGIO SILVAGO
WAIT UNTIL SPRING, BANDINI   Orion, 1990,
EP w/Christian Charret, Cyril de Rouvre & Amadeo Pagani

ALAIN SILVER
Business: Pendragon Film Ltd., 9336 Washington Blvd.,
Culver City, CA 90230, 310/559-0346
Contact: Directors Guild of America - Los Angeles,
213/289-2000

NIGHT VISITOR   MGM/UA, 1989

DIANE SILVER
Contact: Writers Guild of America - Los Angeles,
213.550-1000

NATIVE SON   Cinecom, 1986

DINA SILVER
Business: Midwest Film Productions, 600 Madison Avenue,
New York, NY 10022, 212/355-0282

OLD ENOUGH   Orion Classics, 1984
A WALK ON THE MOON   Skouras Pictures, 1987

JEFFREY SILVER
Business: Outlaw Productions, 12103 Maxwellton Rd.,
Studio City, CA 91604, 818/509-7953; Fax: 818/506-0983
Contact: Directors Guild of America - Los Angeles,
213/289-2000

RAPPIN'   Cannon, 1985, AP
SHAG: THE MOVIE   Hemdale, 1989, LP
DON'T TELL MOM THE BABYSITTER'S DEAD   Warner
Bros., 1991, w/Robert Newmyer & Brian Reilly

JOAN MICKLIN SILVER
Business: Midwest Film Productions, 600 Madison Avenue,
New York, NY 10022, 212/355-0282
Agent: Broder/Kurland/Webb/Uffner - Los Angeles,
213/656-9262

ON THE YARD   Midwest Film Productions, 1979

JOEL SILVER
Business: Silver Pictures, 4000 Warner Blvd., Burbank, CA
91522, 818/954-4490; Fax: 818/954-3237

THE WARRIORS   Paramount, 1979, AP
XANADU   Universal, 1980, CP
48 HOURS   Paramount, 1982, w/Lawrence Gordon
JEKYLL & HYDE...TOGETHER AGAIN   Paramount,
1982, EP
STREETS OF FIRE   Universal, 1984, w/Lawrence Gordon
BREWSTER'S MILLIONS   Universal, 1985,
w/Lawrence Gordon
WEIRD SCIENCE   Universal, 1985
COMMANDO   20th Century Fox, 1985
JUMPIN' JACK FLASH   20th Century Fox, 1986,
w/Lawrence Gordon
LETHAL WEAPON   Warner Bros., 1987, w/Richard Donner
PREDATOR   20th Century Fox, 1987, w/John Davis &
Lawrence Gordon
ACTION JACKSON   Lorimar, 1988
DIE HARD   20th Century Fox, 1988, w/Lawrence Gordon
LETHAL WEAPON 2   Warner Bros., 1989,
w/Richard Donner
ROADHOUSE   MGM/UA, 1989
FORD FAIRLANE   20th Century Fox, 1990, w/Steve Perry
DIE HARD 2   20th Century Fox, 1990,
w/Charles Gordon & Lawrence Gordon
HUDSON HAWK   TriStar, 1991
THE LAST BOY SCOUT   Warner Bros., 1991,
w/Michael Levy & Steve Perry
RICOCHET   Warner Bros., 1991, w/Michael Levy

RAPHAEL D. SILVER
Business: Midwest Film Productions, 600 Madison Avenue,
New York, NY 10022, 212/355-0282
Contact: Directors Guild of America - New York,
213/581-0370

HESTER STREET   Midwest Film Productions, 1975
BETWEEN THE LINES   Midwest Film Productions, 1977
CROSSING DELANCEY   Warner Bros., 1988, EP

TIMOTHY SILVER
Contact: Directors Guild of America - Los Angeles,
213/289-2000

FRIDAY THE 13TH PART V - A NEW BEGINNING
Paramount, 1985

ARTHUR SILVERMAN
PARTING GLANCES   Cinecom, 1986, w/Yoram Mandel

JACK SILVERMAN
CRACK HOUSE   Cannon, 1989, EP

JIM SILVERMAN
CRACK HOUSE   Cannon, 1989

RON SILVERMAN
Agent: Triad Artists, Inc. - Los Angeles, 310/556-2727

BUSTER AND BILLIE   Columbia, 1974
LIFEGUARD   Paramount, 1976, EP
BRUBAKER   20th Century Fox, 1980
KRULL   Columbia, 1983
THE LAST INNOCENT MAN (CTF)   HBO Pictures/
Maurice Singer Productions, 1987
SHOOT TO KILL   Buena Vista, 1988, w/Daniel Petrie Jr.

ELLIOT SILVERSTEIN
Agent: The Gersh Agency - Beverly Hills, 310/274-6611

THE CAR   Universal, 1977, w/Marvin Birdt

FRED SILVERSTEIN
DICE RULES   Seven Arts, 1991

LOUIS M. SILVERSTEIN
STRANGE BREW   MGM/UA, 1983
MILLENNIUM   20th Century Fox, 1989, EP w/Freddie
Fields, John Foreman & P. Gael Mourant

ALAN SIMMONDS
TICKET TO HEAVEN   United Artists Classics, 1981, CP

MATTY SIMMONS
Business: National Lampoon Films, 3619 Motor Ave.,
Suite 300, Los Angeles, CA 90034, 310/204-6270
Contact: Writers Guild of America - Los Angeles,
310/550-1000

NATIONAL LAMPOON'S ANIMAL HOUSE   Universal,
1978, w/Ivan Reitman
NATIONAL LAMPOON'S MOVIE MADNESS   United
Artists, 1981
NATIONAL LAMPOON'S CLASS REUNION   20th
Century Fox, 1982
NATIONAL LAMPOON'S VACATION   Warner Bros., 1983
NATIONAL LAMPOON'S EUROPEAN VACATION
Warner Bros., 1985
NATIONAL LAMPOON'S CHRISTMAS VACATION
Warner Bros., 1989, EP

RUDD SIMMONS
LASERMAN   Peter Wang Films/Film Workshop, 1988, AP
MYSTERY TRAIN   Orion Classics, 1989, LP

RUSSELL SIMMONS
Business: Def Jam Records, 652 Broadway, 3rd Floor,
New York, NY 10012, 212/979-2610

KRUSH GROOVE   Warner Bros., 1985, CP
TOUGHER THAN LEATHER   New Line, 1988,
EP w/Rick Rubin

KERVIN SIMMS
DEF BY TEMPTATION   Troma, 1990,
CP w/Hajna O. Moss

JOEL SIMON
(credit w/Bill Todman Jr.)
Business: Todman-Simon Productions, 300 S. Lorimar Plaza,
Bldg. 137, Room 1107, Burbank, CA 91505,
818/954-7582; Fax: 818/954-7874

MARRIED TO THE MOB   Orion, 1988, EP
HARD TO KILL   Warner Bros., 1990, w/Gary Adelson

MELVIN SIMON
SCAVENGER HUNT   20th Century Fox, 1979, EP
WHEN YOU COMIN' BACK, RED RYDER?   Columbia,
1979, EP
WHEN A STRANGER CALLS   Columbia, 1979,
EP w/Barry Krost
THE RUNNER STUMBLES   20th Century Fox, 1979, EP
SEVEN   AIP, 1979, EP

Si

FILM
PRODUCERS,
STUDIOS,
AGENTS AND
CASTING
DIRECTORS
GUIDE

F
I
L
M

P
R
O
D
U
C
E
R
S

Si

**FILM
PRODUCERS,
STUDIOS,
AGENTS** AND
**CASTING
DIRECTORS
GUIDE**

F
I
L
M

P
R
O
D
U
C
E
R
S

TILT   Warner Bros., 1979, EP
MY BODYGUARD   20th Century Fox, 1980, EP
THE STUNT MAN   20th Century Fox, 1980, EP
THE MAN WITH BOGART'S FACE   *SAM MARLOW,
PRIVATE EYE*   20th Century Fox, 1980, EP
CHU CHU & THE PHILLY FLASH   20th Century Fox,
1981, EP
PORKY'S   20th Century Fox, 1982,
EP w/Harold Greenberg
PORKY'S II: THE NEXT DAY   20th Century Fox,
1983, EP w/Harold Greenberg & Alan Landsburg
PORKY'S REVENGE   20th Century Fox, 1985,
EP w/Milton Goldstein
UFORIA   Universal, 1985, EP w/Barry Krost

NEIL SIMON
Personal Manager: Albert DaSilva - Los Angeles,
213/752-9323
Contact: Writers Guild of America - Los Angeles,
310/550-1000

ONLY WHEN I LAUGH   Columbia, 1981,
w/Roger M. Rothstein
I OUGHT TO BE IN PICTURES   20th Century Fox, 1982,
w/Herbert Ross
MAX DUGAN RETURNS   20th Century Fox, 1983,
w/Herbert Ross

ROBERT SIMONDS
Contact: Universal Pictures, 100 Universal City Plaza,
Universal City, CA 91608, 818/777-5445;
Fax: 818/777-7670

PROBLEM CHILD   Universal, 1990
PROBLEM CHILD II   Universal, 1991
SHOUT!   Universal, 1991

EDWARD SIMONS
THE STUD   Trans-American, 1979, EP
THE RETURN OF THE SOLDIER   European Classics,
1985, EP w/J. Gordon Arnold & John Quested
HOWLING III: THE MARSUPIALS   Square Pictures,
1987, EP w/Steven Lane & Robert Pringle
HOWLING IV...THE ORIGINAL NIGHTMARE   Allied
Entertainment, 1988, EP w/Steven Lane, Avi Lerner &
Robert Pringle
EDGE OF SANITY   Millimeter Films, 1989,
w/Harry Alan Towers
COMMUNION   New Line, 1989, CP

M. H. SIMONSONS
Business: International Rainbow Pictures, 9165 Sunset
Blvd., Penthouse, Los Angeles, CA 90069,
310/271-0202

SOMEONE TO LOVE   International Rainbow/
Castle Hill, 1987

DON SIMPSON
(credit w/Jerry Bruckheimer)
Business: Simpson-Bruckheimer Productions, Walt Disney
Studios, 500 S. Buena Vista St., Burbank, CA 91521,
818/560-7711

FLASHDANCE   Paramount, 1983
BEVERLY HILLS COP   Paramount, 1984
THIEF OF HEARTS   Paramount, 1984
TOP GUN   Paramount, 1986
BEVERLY HILLS COP II   Paramount, 1987
DAYS OF THUNDER   Paramount, 1990

MICHAEL A. SIMPSON
Business: Double Helix Films, Inc., 275 Seventh Ave.,
Suite 2003, New York, NY 10001, 212/727-2000

FUNLAND   Double Helix, 1987, w/William VanDerKloot
FAST FOOD   Fries Entertainment, 1989, w/Stan Wakefield

PETER R. SIMPSON
Business: Norstar Entertainment, 86 Bloor St., Toronto,
Ontario, 416/961-6278; Fax: 416/961-5608

THE SEA GYPSIES   Warner Bros., 1978, EP
BULLIES   Universal, 1986
HELLO MARY LOU: PROM NIGHT II   Samuel Goldwyn
Company, 1987
PROM NIGHT III; THE LAST KISS   Norstar, 1990,
w/Ray Seger

GREG H. SIMS
(credit w/Lee Caplin)
Business: Arrowhead Entertainment, 20th Century Fox,
10201 W. Pico Blvd., Los Angeles, CA 90035,
310/203-2790

TO DIE FOR   Skouras Pictures, 1989, EP
SON OF DARKNESS: TO DIE FOR II   Trimark, 1991, EP

FRANK SINATRA
Business Manager: Nathan Golden, 8501 Wilshire Blvd.,
Suite 250, Beverly Hills, CA 90211, 310/855-0850
Contact: Directors Guild of America - Los Angeles,
213/289-2000

THE FIRST DEADLY SIN   Filmways, 1980,
EP w/Elliott Kastner

JOSHUA SINCLAIR
JUDGMENT IN BERLIN   New Line, 1988,
w/Ingrid Windlisch

NIGEL SINCLAIR
(credit w/Michael Kuhn)
Business: Propaganda Films, 940 N. Mansfield Ave.,
Los Angeles, CA 90038, 213/462-6400

THE BLUE IGUANA   Paramount, 1988, EP
FEAR, ANXIETY & DEPRESSION   Samuel Goldwyn
Company, 1989, EP
KILL ME AGAIN   MGM/UA, 1989, EP
DADDY'S DYIN'...WHO'S GOT THE WILL?   MGM/UA,
1990, EP w/Bobbie Edrick & Del Shores

ROBERT SINGER
(credit w/Daniel H. Blatt)
Business: Daniel H. Blatt Productions, 10202 W. Washington
Blvd., Culver City, CA 90230, 310/280-5170

BURNT OFFERINGS   United Artists, 1976, AP*
INDEPENDENCE DAY   Warner Bros., 1983
CUJO   Warner Bros., 1983
LET'S GET HARRY   TriStar, 1986

ANANT SINGH
Business: Distant Horizon, 52 Crescent Ave., St. George,
Staten Island, NY 10301, 718/816-6732 or 5-6 Portman
Mews South, London W1H 9AU, 071/493-1625

TERMINAL BLISS   Distant Horizon, 1990, EP

JOAN V. SINGLETON
Business: R.S. Singleton Productions, c/o Perry & Neidorf, 9720 Wilshire Blvd., 3rd Floor, Beverly Hills, CA 90212, 310/550-1254; Fax: 310/550-2039

STEPHEN KING'S GRAVEYARD SHIFT   Paramount, 1990, AP

RALPH S. SINGLETON
Business: R.S. Singleton Productions, c/o Perry & Neidorf, 9720 Wilshire Blvd., 3rd Floor, Beverly Hills, CA 90212, 310/550-1254; Fax: 310/550-2039

PET SEMATARY   Paramount, 1989, AP
HARLEM NIGHTS   Paramount, 1989, CP
ANOTHER 48 HOURS   Paramount, 1990,
   EP w/Mark Lipsky
STEPHEN KING'S GRAVEYARD SHIFT   Paramount, 1990, w/William J. Dunn
PET SEMATARY II   Paramount, 1992

CALVIN SKAGGS
ON VALENTINE'S DAY   Angelika, 1986,
   w/Lillian V. Foote
THE WASH   Skouras Pictures, 1988

ANN SKINNER
(credit w/Simon Relph)
Business: Skreba Films, 5a Noel Street, London W1V 3RB England, 071/437-6492; Fax: 071/437-0644

SECRET PLACES   20th Century Fox, 1985
THE RETURN OF THE SOLDIER   European Classics, 1985
THE GOOD FATHER   Skouras Pictures, 1987*

JACK H. SKIRBALL
A MATTER OF TIME   AIP, 1976, w/J. Edmund Grainger

DANIEL SKLAR
RED SCORPION   Shapiro Glickenhaus, 1989,
   EP w/Robert Abramoff & Paul Erickson

WILLIAM D. SKLAR
(credit w/Peter S. Traynor)

THE ULTIMATE THRILL   General Cinema, 1974
BOGARD   L-T Films, 1975
BLACK STREETFIGHTER   New Line, 1976

JERZY SKOLIMOWSKI
Agent: ICM - Los Angeles, 310/550-4000
Contact: Directors Guild of America - Los Angeles, 213/289-2000

MOONLIGHTING   Universal, 1982, w/Mark Shivas

DIMITRI T. SKOURAS
BLIND DATE   New Line, 1984, EP

JOSEPH SKRZYNSKI
HIGH TIDE   TriStar, 1987, EP w/Antony I. Ginnane

JON SLAN
Business: Paragon Entertainment Corp., 260 Richmond Street W., Suite 405, Toronto, M5V 1W5, 416/977-2929; Fax: 416/977-0489; 2211 Corinth Ave., Suite 305, Los Angeles, CA 90064, 310/478-7272; Fax: 310/479-2314

HIGH-BALLIN'   AIP, 1978
FISH HAWK   Avco Embassy, 1981
THRESHOLD   20th Century Fox International Classics, 1983, w/Michael Burns

JOHN R. SLOAN
FRAGMENT OF FEAR   Columbia, 1971
THE ODESSA FILE   Columbia, 1974, CP
FORCE 10 FROM NAVARONE   Columbia, 1978,
   CP w/Anthony Unger
NO SEX PLEASE - WE'RE BRITISH   Columbia, 1979

JOHN SLOSS
CITY OF HOPE   Samuel Goldwyn Company, 1991,
   EP w/Harold Welb

GENE SLOTT
(credit w/Joseph Zappala)

BITTERSWEET LOVE   Avco Embassy, 1976,
   w/Joel B. Michaels
LAS VEGAS LADY   Crown International, 1976

DAVID A. SMITAS
RESCUE ME   Cannon, 1991, EP w/Jere Henshaw

ANNICK SMITH
HEARTLAND   Levitt-Pickman, 1979, EP

BUD SMITH
Agent: UTA - Beverly Hills, 310/273-6700
Contact: Directors Guild of America - Los Angeles, 213/289-2000

SORCERER   Paramount/Universal, 1977, AP
THE KARATE KID   Columbia, 1984, AP
TO LIVE AND DIE IN L.A.   New Century, 1985, CP

CLIVE A. SMITH
(credit w/Michael Hirsh & Patrick Loubert)
Business: Nelvana Ltd., 32 Atlantic Ave., Toronto, M6K 1X8, 416/588-5571; Fax: 416/588-5588; 9000 Sunset Blvd., Suite 911, Los Angeles, CA 90069, 310/278-8466

THE CARE BEARS MOVIE (AF)   Samuel Goldwyn Company, 1985
CARE BEARS MOVIE II: A NEW GENERATION (AF)   Columbia, 1986
THE CARE BEARS ADVENTURE IN WONDERLAND (AF)   Cineplex Odeon, 1987
BABAR: THE MOVIE (AF)   New Line, 1989

DAVID SMITH
SPACE AVENGER   Manley, 1990, EP w/Richard Albert & Timothy McGinn

Sm

FILM
PRODUCERS,
STUDIOS,
AGENTS AND
CASTING
DIRECTORS
GUIDE

F
I
L
M

P
R
O
D
U
C
E
R
S

DONNA SMITH
Contact: Universal City Studios, 100 Universal Plaza,Bldg.
500, 11th Floor, Universal City, CA 91608, 818/777-4272

SOUL MAN   New World, 1986, LP
NIGHT OF THE CREEPS   TriStar, 1986, AP
K-9   Universal, 1989, EP

GREG SMITH
CONFESSIONS OF A WINDOW CLEANER
Columbia, 1974

HOWARD SMITH
MARJOE (FD)   Cinema 5, 1972, w/Sarah Kernochan
GIZMO (FD)   New Line, 1977
RHINESTONE   20th Century Fox, 1984, w/Marvin Worth
PUMPKINHEAD   United Artists, 1988,
w/Richard C. Weinman
RELENTLESS   New Line, 1989

IAIN SMITH
Business: Applecross Productions, The Old House,
Shepperton Studios, Studios Road, Shepperton,
Middlesex TW17 0QD England, 0932/562-611;
Fax: 0932/568-240

LOCAL HERO   Warner Bros., 1983, AP
THE KILLING FIELDS ★   Warner Bros., 1984, AP
THE FROG PRINCE   Warner Bros., 1985
THE MISSION ★   Warner Bros., 1986, AP
HEARTS OF FIRE   Lorimar, 1988, CP
CITY OF JOY   TriStar, 1991, AP

IRA N. SMITH
AMITYVILLE II: THE POSSESSION   Orion, 1982,
w/Stephen R. Greenwald

IRBY SMITH
Business: Morgan Creek Productions, 1875 Century Park
East, Suite 200, Los Angeles, CA 90067, 310/284-8884;
Fax: 310/282-8794
Contact: Directors Guild of America - Los Angeles,
213/289-2000

YOUNG GUNS   20th Century Fox, 1988, CP w/Paul Schiff
MAJOR LEAGUE   Paramount, 1989, w/Chris Chesser
ENEMIES, A LOVE STORY   20th Century Fox, 1989,
CP w/Pato Guzman
YOUNG GUNS II   20th Century Fox, 1990, w/Paul Schiff
CITY SLICKERS   Columbia, 1991

JACK SMITH
NEITHER THE SEA NOR THE SAND   International
Amusement Corp., 1974, w/Peter Fetterman

JOHN TEMPLE-SMITH
(see John TEMPLE-Smith)

KIRK SMITH
FUNLAND   Double Helix, 1987, EP w/Jerry Silva &
Stan Wakefield

MAURICE SMITH
CYCLE SAVAGES   Trans American, 1970
DELINQUENT SCHOOLGIRLS   *CARNAL MADNESS*
Rainbow, 1975
HOW COME NOBODY'S ON OUR SIDE?   American
Films Ltd., 1975

P. MICHAEL SMITH
WIRED   Taurus, 1989, EP w/Paul Carran

RODNEY CARR-SMITH
(see Rodney CARR-Smith)

RUSS SMITH
QUEENS LOGIC   Seven Arts, 1991, w/Stuart Oken

THOMAS G. SMITH
Business: Walt Disney Studios, 500 S. Buena Vista St.,
Burbank, CA 91521, 818/560-3200; Fax: 818/567-0435

HONEY, I SHRUNK THE KIDS   Buena Vista, 1989, EP

PETER SNELL
Business: British Lion Screen Entertainment, Pinewood
Studios, Pinewood Rd., Iver, Bucks., SL0 0NH,
0753/651-700; Fax: 0753/656-391

ANTONY AND CLEOPATRA   Rank, 1973
HENNESSY   AIP, 1975
THE WICKER MAN   Warner Bros., 1975
TURTLE DIARY   Samuel Goldwyn Company, 1986, EP
LADY JANE   Paramount, 1986
A PRAYER FOR THE DYING   Samuel Goldwyn
Company, 1987

HAROLD SOBEL
MASSACRE AT CENTRAL HIGH   Brian, 1976
DANGEROUSLY CLOSE   Cannon, 1986

MARK SOBEL
little secrets   1991, w/Nancylee Myatt

RAINER SOEHNLEIN
Agent: ICM - Los Angeles, 310/550-4000

THE LIGHTSHIP   Castle Hill, 1986, EP

STEVE SOHMER
Contact: Directors Guild of America - Los Angeles,
213/289-2000

LEONARD PART 6   Columbia, 1987, EP w/Alan Marshall

JOEL SOISSON
(credit w/Michael S. Murphey)
Business: Soisson Murphey Productions, 9060 Santa Monica
Blvd., Suite 210, Los Angeles, CA 90069, 310/273-3157;
Fax: 310/271-5581

HAMBONE & HILLIE   New World, 1984, AP
THE BOYS NEXT DOOR   New World, 1985, AP
AVENGING ANGEL   New World, 1985, AP
A NIGHTMARE ON ELM STREET, PART 2: FREDDY'S
REVENGE   New Line, 1985, LP
KGB: THE SECRET WAR   Cinema Group, 1986, AP
TRICK OR TREAT   DEG, 1986
THE SUPERNATURALS   Republic Entertainment, 1987
BILL & TED'S EXCELLENT ADVENTURE   Orion, 1989,
w/Scott Kroopf
MODERN LOVE   Triumph, 1990, EP
BLUE DESERT   Neo Films, 1991, EP

Sp

FILM
PRODUCERS,
STUDIOS,
AGENTS AND
CASTING
DIRECTORS
GUIDE

F
I
L
M

P
R
O
D
U
C
E
R
S

VICTOR SOLNICKI
(credit w/Pierre David)
Business: Jillian Film & Investment Corp., 344 Dupont St.,
    Suite 201, Toronto, M5R 1V9, 416/922-3168;
    Fax: 416/922-2502

THE BROOD   New World, 1979, EP
HOG WILD   Avco Embassy, 1980, EP w/Stephen Miller
SCANNERS   Avco Embassy, 1981, EP
GAS   Paramount, 1981, EP
DIRTY TRICKS   Avco Embassy, 1981,
    EP w/Arnold Kopelson
VISITING HOURS   20th Century Fox, 1982, EP
VIDEODROME   Universal, 1983, EP
COVERGIRL   New World, 1984, EP

ROBERT H. SOLO
Business: The SoloFilm Company, c/o Orion Pictures,
    1888 Century Park East, Los Angeles, CA 90067,
    90067, 310/282-2795; Fax: 310/785-1800

SCROOGE   National General, 1970
THE DEVILS   Warner Bros., 1971, w/Ken Russell
INVASION OF THE BODY SNATCHERS   United
    Artists, 1978
THE AWAKENING   Orion/Warner Bros., 1980,
    w/Andrew Scheinman & Martin Shafer
I, THE JURY   20th Century Fox, 1982
BAD BOYS   Universal, 1983
COLORS   Orion, 1988
ABOVE THE LAW   Warner Bros., 1988, EP
WINTER PEOPLE   Columbia, 1989

ALAN M. SOLOMON
Business: Shapiro-Glickenhaus Entertainment, 1619
    Broadway, New York, NY 10019, 212/265-1150 or
    12001 Ventura Pl., Suite 404, Studio City, CA 91604,
    818/766-8500; Fax: 818/766-7873

SHAKEDOWN   Universal, 1988, EP w/Leonard Shapiro
MOONTRAP   Shapiro-Glickenhaus Entertainment, 1989,
    EP w/James A. Courtney & Brian C. Manoogian

JOE SOLOMON
EVEL KNIEVEL   Fanfare, 1971, w/George Hamilton
THIS IS A HIJACK   Fanfare, 1973, EP
A SMALL TOWN IN TEXAS   AIP, 1976

KEN SOLOMON
PRETTY SMART   New World, 1987, w/Jeff Begun

HERBERT F. SOLOW
Contact: Directors Guild of America - Los Angeles,
    213/289-2000

GET CRAZY   Embassy, 1983, EP
SAVING GRACE   Embassy, 1986

ANDREW SOLT
Business: Andrew Solt Productions, 9121 Sunset Blvd.,
    Los Angeles, CA 90069, 310/276-9522;
    Fax: 310/276-0242
Agent: William Morris Agency - Beverly Hills, 310/274-7451

THIS IS ELVIS (FD)   Warner Bros., 1981, w/Malcolm Leo
IMAGINE: JOHN LENNON (FD)   Warner Bros., 1988,
    w/David L. Wolper

SUSAN SOLT
Business: Pakula Productions, Inc., 330 West 58th St.,
    New York, NY 10019, 212/664-0640

DREAM LOVER   MGM/UA, 1986, AP
ORPHANS   Lorimar, 1987, CP
SEE YOU IN THE MORNING   Warner Bros., 1989,
    w/Alan J. Pakula
PRESUMED INNOCENT   Warner Bros., 1990, EP

MARY ROSE SOLTI
BILLY JACK   Warner Bros., 1971

F. DANIEL SOMRACK
Business: Ion Pictures, 3122 Santa Monica Blvd.,
    Santa Monica, CA 90404, 310/453-4466

THE CLOSER   Ion, 1991, SP w/Michel Kossak

MARIO SOTELA
Business: Sotela Pictures, Ltd., 9000 Sunset Blvd., Suite
    1000, Los Angeles, CA 90069, 310/271-5858;
    Fax: 310/273-5566

WAXWORK   Vestron, 1988, EP w/Gregory Cascante,
    Dan Ireland & William J. Quigley
WAXWORK II: LOST IN TIME   Seven Arts/Live, 1991, EP

MICHAEL SOURAPAS
Business: SPI Entertainment, 279 South Beverly Dr.,
    Penthouse, Beverly Hills, CA 90212, 310/827-4229

ALIEN PREDATOR   Trans World, 1987, CP

MARGARET JENNINGS SOUTH
Business: All-Girl Pictures, Walt Disney Pictures,
    500 S. Buena Vista St., Burbank, CA 91521, 818/560-5000

BEACHES   Buena Vista, 1988, w/Bonnie Bruckheimer &
    Bette Midler
FOR THE BOYS   20th Century Fox, 1991,
    w/Bonnie Bruckheimer & Bette Midler

TERRY SOUTHERN
Contact: Writers Guild of America - Los Angeles,
    310/550-1000

END OF THE ROAD   Allied Artists, 1970,
    w/Stephen Kesten

CAROLINE SPACK
LETTER TO BREZHNEV   Circle Releasing, 1986, CP

LARRY G. SPANGLER
THE LAST REBEL   Columbia, 1971
THE LEGEND OF NIGGER CHARLEY   Paramount, 1972
THE SOUL OF NIGGER CHARLEY   Paramount, 1973

TERRY SPAZEK
Contact: The Disney Channel, 3800 W. Alameda Ave.,
    Burbank, CA 91505, 818/569-7500; Fax: 818/566-1358

THE DREAM TEAM   Universal, 1989, SP

ARMAND SPECA
LOVE AT STAKE   TriStar, 1988, CP

Sp

FILM
PRODUCERS,
STUDIOS,
AGENTS AND
CASTING
DIRECTORS
GUIDE

F
I
L
M

P
R
O
D
U
C
E
R
S

AARON SPELLING
(credit w/Alan Greisman)
Business: Aaron Spelling Productions, 5700 Wilshire Blvd.,
  Los Angeles, CA 90036, 213/965-5800;
  Fax: 213/965-5808

CALIFORNIA SPLIT   Columbia, 1974,
  EP w/Leonard J. Goldberg*
BABY BLUE MARINE   Columbia, 1976,
  w/Leonard J. Goldberg*
MR. MOM   20th Century Fox, 1983, EP*
'NIGHT, MOTHER   Universal, 1986
CROSS MY HEART   Universal, 1987, EP
SURRENDER   Warner Bros., 1987
THREE O'CLOCK HIGH   Universal, 1987, EP
SATISFACTION   20th Century Fox, 1988
LOOSE CANNONS   TriStar, 1990
SOAPDISH   Paramount, 1991, w/Alan Greisman

NORMAN SPENCER
Agent: MacNaughton Lowe Representation - London

VANISHING POINT   20th Century Fox, 1971
CRY FREEDOM   Universal, 1987, CP w/John Briley

PIERRE SPENGLER
THE THREE MUSKETEERS   20th Century Fox, 1974,
  EP w/Ilya Salkind
THE FOUR MUSKETEERS   20th Century Fox, 1975,
  EP w/Ilya Salkind
CROSSED SWORDS   Warner Bros., 1978
SUPERMAN   Warner Bros., 1978
SUPERMAN II   Warner Bros., 1981
SUPERMAN III   Warner Bros., 1983
SANTA CLAUS - THE MOVIE   TriStar, 1985,
  w/Ilya Salkind
THE RETURN OF THE MUSKETEERS   Universal, 1990

ELAINE SPERBER
Contact: HBO, 2049 Century Park East, Suite 4100,
  Los Angeles, CA 90067, 310/201-9200;
  Fax: 310/201-9293

BLUE HEAVEN   Vestron/Shapiro Entertainment, 1985

STEPHANE SPERRY
BABAR: THE MOVIE (AF)   New Line, 1989,
  EP w/Yannick Bernard & Pierre Bertrand-Jaume

PENELOPE SPHEERIS
Agent: William Morris Agency - Beverly Hills, 310/274-7451

REAL LIFE   Paramount, 1979

LARRY SPIEGEL
Business: Appledown Films, Inc., 9687 Olympic Blvd.,
  Beverly Hills, CA 90291, 310/552-1833

DEATH GAME   Levitt-Pickman, 1977,
  EP w/Peter Traynor
PHOBIA   Paramount, 1979
REMO WILLIAMS: THE ADVENTURE BEGINS...
  Orion, 1985
FIELDS OF HONOR   Pathe, 1990

ANNE SPIELBERG
Agent: CAA - Beverly Hills, 310/288-4545
Contact: Writers Guild of America - Los Angeles,
  310/550-1000

BIG   20th Century Fox, 1988, CP w/Gary Ross

MICHAEL SPIELBERG
Contact: Monument Pictures, 8271 Melrose Ave., Suite 105,
  Los Angeles, CA 90046, 213/852-1275;
  Fax: 213/852-1279

LITTLE NOISES   Monument Pictures, 1991, w/Brad Gilbert

STEVEN SPIELBERG
Business: Amblin Entertainment, Universal Studios, 100
  Universal Plaza, Bungalow 477, Universal City, CA
  91608, 818/777-4600
Contact: Directors Guild of America - Los Angeles,
  213/289-2000

I WANNA HOLD YOUR HAND   Universal, 1978, EP
USED CARS   Columbia, 1980, EP w/John Milius
CONTINENTAL DIVIDE   Universal, 1981,
  EP w/Bernie Brillstein
POLTERGEIST   MGM, 1982, w/Frank Marshall
E.T. THE EXTRA-TERRESTRIAL ★   Universal, 1982,
  w/Kathleen Kennedy
TWILIGHT ZONE - THE MOVIE   Warner Bros., 1983,
  w/John Landis
GREMLINS   Warner Bros., 1984, EP w/Kathleen Kennedy
  & Frank Marshall
THE GOONIES   Warner Bros., 1985, EP w/Kathleen
  Kennedy & Frank Marshall
BACK TO THE FUTURE   Universal, 1985, EP w/Kathleen
  Kennedy & Frank Marshall
YOUNG SHERLOCK HOLMES   Paramount, 1985,
  EP w/Kathleen Kennedy & Frank Marshall
THE COLOR PURPLE ★   Warner Bros., 1985, w/Quincy
  Jones, Kathleen Kennedy & Frank Marshall
AN AMERICAN TAIL (AF)   Universal, 1986, EP w/Kathleen
  Kennedy, David Kirschner & Frank Marshall
THE MONEY PIT   Universal, 1986, EP w/David Giler
INNERSPACE   Warner Bros., 1987, EP w/Peter Guber,
  Kathleen Kennedy, Frank Marshall & Jon Peters
BATTERIES NOT INCLUDED   Universal, 1987,
  EP w/Kathleen Kennedy & Frank Marshall
EMPIRE OF THE SUN   Warner Bros., 1987,
  w/Kathleen Kennedy & Frank Marshall
WHO FRAMED ROGER RABBIT   Buena Vista, 1988,
  EP w/Kathleen Kennedy
THE LAND BEFORE TIME (AF)   Universal, 1988,
  EP w/Kathleen Kennedy, George Lucas & Frank Marshall
DAD   Universal, 1989, EP w/Kathleen Kennedy &
  Frank Marshall
BACK TO THE FUTURE II   Universal, 1989,
  EP w/Kathleen Kennedy & Frank Marshall
ALWAYS   Paramount, 1989, w/Kathleen Kennedy &
  Frank Marshall
BACK TO THE FUTURE III   Universal, 1990,
  EP w/Kathleen Kennedy & Frank Marshall
JOE VERSUS THE VOLCANO   Warner Bros., 1990,
  EP w/Kathleen Kennedy & Frank Marshall
ARACHNOPHOBIA   Buena Vista, 1990,
  EP w/Robert W. Cort, Ted Field & Frank Marshall
CAPE FEAR   Universal, 1991, EP w/Kathleen Kennedy &
  Frank Marshall

St

FILM
PRODUCERS,
STUDIOS,
AGENTS AND
CASTING
DIRECTORS
GUIDE

F
I
L
M

P
R
O
D
U
C
E
R
S

BARRY SPIKINGS
(credit w/Michael Deeley)
Business: Nelson Entertainment, Inc., 335 N. Maple Dr.,
Suite 350, Beverly Hills, CA 90210, 310/285-6150;
Fax: 310/285-6190

CONDUCT UNBECOMING   Allied Artists, 1975
THE MAN WHO FELL TO EARTH   Cinema 5, 1976
THE DEER HUNTER ★★   Universal, 1978,
w/Michael Cimino & John Peverall
CONVOY   United Artists, 1978, EP
TEXASVILLE   Columbia, 1990, w/Peter Bogdanovich

SUSAN SPINKS
UFORIA   Universal, 1985, CP

RICHARD M. SPITALNY
RHINESTONE   20th Century Fox, 1984, CP w/Bill Blake

ROGER SPOTTISWOODE
Agent: InterTalent Agency - Los Angeles, 310/858-6200
Contact: Directors Guild of America - Los Angeles,
213/289-2000

BABY...SECRET OF THE LOST LEGEND   Buena Vista,
1985, EP

PETER J. SPRAGUE
STEPPENWOLF   D/R Films, 1974, EP

MARC SPRINGER
BLACK MAGIC WOMAN   Trimark, 1991,
w/Deryn Warren

VITTORIA SQUILLANTE
KING OF NEW YORK   Seven Arts, 1990,
EP w/Jay Julien

STEVEN STABLER
(credit w/Brad Krevoy)
Business: Motion Picture Corporation of America, 1401
Ocean Ave., 3rd. Floor, Santa Monica, CA 90401,
310/319-9500; Fax: 310/319-9501

SWEET REVENGE   Concorde, 1987
DANGEROUS LOVE   Motion Picture Corp. of
America, 1988
PURPLE PEOPLE EATER   Concorde, 1988
MEMORIAL VALLEY MASSACRE   Nelson
Entertainment, 1989
MINISTRY OF VENGEANCE   Motion Picture Corp. of
America, 1989
THINK BIG   Concorde, 1990
BACK TO BACK   Concorde, 1990
HANGFIRE   Motion Picture Corp. of America, 1991

PAUL STADER
Contact: Directors Guild of America - Los Angeles,
213/289-2000

IT'S ALIVE III: ISLAND OF THE ALIVE   Warner
Bros., 1987

NIGEL STAFFORD-CLARK
Business: Zenith Productions, Ltd., 43-45 Dorset St.,
London W1H 4AB, 071/224-2440; Fax: 071/224-3194

STORMY MONDAY   Atlantic, 1988

PATRICIA STALLONE
SUMMER HEAT   Atlantic, 1987, LP
PULSE   Columbia, 1988

SYLVESTER STALLONE
Business: White Eagle Enterprises, 2308 Broadway,
Santa Monica, CA 90404, 310/828-8988
Agent: CAA - Beverly Hills, 310/288-4545
Contact: Directors Guild of America - Los Angeles,
213/289-2000

STAYING ALIVE   Paramount, 1983, w/Robert Stigwood

CHRISTOPHER STAMP
TOMMY   Columbia, 1975, EP w/Beryl Vertue

MICHAEL STANLEY-EVANS
A BRIDGE TOO FAR   United Artists, 1977, CP
GANDHI ★★   Columbia, 1982, EP

MARTIN STARGER
Business: Marstar Productions, 20th Century Fox,
10201 W. Pico Blvd., Los Angeles, CA 90035,
310/203-3843; Fax: 310/203-2576

NASHVILLE ★   Paramount, 1975, EP w/Jerry Weintraub
THE DOMINO PRINCIPLE   Avco Embassy, 1977, EP
MOVIE MOVIE   Warner Bros., 1978, EP
AUTUMN SONATA   New World, 1978
THE MUPPET MOVIE   AFD, 1979, EP
RAISE THE TITANIC   AFD, 1980, EP
FROM THE LIFE OF THE MARIONETTES   Universal/AFD,
1980, EP w/Lew Grade
BORDERLINE   AFD, 1980, EP
SATURN 3   AFD, 1980, EP
HARD COUNTRY   AFD, 1981, EP
THE LEGEND OF THE LONE RANGER   Universal/AFD,
1981, EP
THE GREAT MUPPET CAPER   Universal/AFD, 1981, EP
BARBAROSA   Universal/AFD, 1982, EP
SOPHIE'S CHOICE   Universal, 1982, EP
CODE NAME: EMERALD   MGM/UA, 1985
MASK   Universal, 1985

JIM STARK
DOWN BY LAW   Island Pictures, 1986,
CP w/Tom Rothman
CANDY MOUNTAIN   International Film Exchange, 1987
MYSTERY TRAIN   Orion Classics, 1989

RAY STARK
Business: Rastar Productions, Inc., 335 N. Maple Dr.,
Beverly Hills, CA 90210, 310/247-0130;
Fax: 310/247-9120

THE WORLD OF SUZIE WONG   Paramount, 1960
FUNNY GIRL ★   Columbia, 1968
THE OWL & THE PUSSYCAT   Columbia, 1970
FAT CITY   Columbia, 1972
THE WAY WE WERE   Columbia, 1973
FUNNY LADY   Columbia, 1975
THE SUNSHINE BOYS   United Artists, 1975

MURDER BY DEATH   Columbia, 1976
ROBIN AND MARIAN   Columbia, 1976, EP
THE GOODBYE GIRL ★   Warner Bros., 1977
CASEY'S SHADOW   Columbia, 1978
THE CHEAP DETECTIVE   Columbia, 1978
CALIFORNIA SUITE   Columbia, 1978
CHAPTER TWO   Columbia, 1979
THE ELECTRIC HORSEMAN   Columbia, 1979
SEEMS LIKE OLD TIMES   Columbia, 1980
ANNIE   Columbia, 1982
THE SLUGGER'S WIFE   Columbia, 1985
BRIGHTON BEACH MEMOIRS   Universal, 1986
NOTHING IN COMMON   TriStar, 1986, EP
PEGGY SUE GOT MARRIED   TriStar, 1986, EP
BILOXI BLUES   Universal, 1988
STEEL MAGNOLIAS   TriStar, 1989

WILBUR STARK
Business: 3712 Barham Blvd., C-203, Los Angeles, CA
   90068, 213/851-0572

MY LOVER, MY SON   MGM, 1970
VAMPIRE CIRCUS   20th Century Fox, 1972
THE THING   Universal, 1982, EP

STEVE STARKEY
NOISES OFF   Buena Vista, 1991, w/Frank Marshall

RINGO STARR
(Richard Starkey)

SON OF DRACULA   Cinemation, 1974

GAIL STAYDEN
I COULD NEVER HAVE SEX WITH ANY MAN WHO HAS
   SO LITTLE REGARD FOR MY HUSBAND   Cinema 5,
   1973, w/Martin Stayden

MARTIN STAYDEN
I COULD NEVER HAVE SEX WITH ANY MAN WHO HAS
   SO LITTLE REGARD FOR MY HUSBAND   Cinema 5,
   1973, w/Gail Stayden

MARY STEENBURGEN
Agent: ICM - Los Angeles, 310/550-4000

END OF THE LINE   Orion Classics, 1987, EP

KEN STEIN
Business: Concorde Films, 11600 San Vicente Blvd.,
   Los Angeles, CA 90049, 310/820-6733

THE DRIFTER   Concorde, 1988
THE RAIN KILLER   Concorde, 1990, EP

JOEL STEINBERGER
GLASS HOUSES   Columbia, 1972, EP

IRA STEINER
VALDEZ IS COMING   United Artists, 1971

HERBERT R. STEINMANN
THE PAWNBROKER   Allied Artists, 1965, w/Ely Landau

ELLEN STELOFF
(credit w/Lawrence Kasanoff)
Business: Gibson Lefebure Gartner, 2980 Beverly Glen
   Circle, Suite 203, Los Angeles, CA 90077, 310/474-2665;
   Fax: 310/470-4905

BLOOD DINER   Lightning/Vestron, 1987, EP
YOU CAN'T HURRY LOVE   Vestron, 1988,
   w/Jonathan D. Krane
DREAM A LITTLE DREAM   Vestron, 1989, EP
FAR FROM HOME   Vestron, 1989, EP
CLASS OF 1999   Taurus, 1990, EP

SKIP STELOFF
Business: Heritage Entertainment, 7920 Sunset Blvd.,
   Suite 200, Los Angeles, CA 90048, 213/850-5858;
   Fax: 213/851-1177

SHARK   Excelsior, 1970, w/Marc Cooper
THE ISLAND OF DR. MOREAU   AIP, 1977,
   w/John Temple-Smith
MR. NORTH   Samuel Goldwyn Company, 1988,
   w/Steven Haft

RICHARD STENTA
Contact: Directors Guild of America - Los Angeles,
   213/289-2000

ACROSS 110th STREET   United Artists, 1972, AP
LET IT RIDE   Paramount, 1989, EP
FLASHBACK   Paramount, 1990, EP

ROBERT STERLING
WINTER KILLS   Avco Embassy, 1979,
   EP w/Leonard J. Goldberg

DAVID G. STERN
RACE TO GLORY   New Century/Vista, 1989, EP
ALL'S FAIR   Moviestore Entertainment, 1989, EP

JOSEPH STERN
NO MAN'S LAND   Orion, 1987, w/Dick Wolf
DAD   Universal, 1989, w/Gary David Goldberg

SANDY STERN
Contact: SC Entertainment Group, 1326 Londonderry View,
   Los Angeles, CA 90069, 310/854-0337;
   Fax: 310/854-0737

PUMP UP THE VOLUME   New Line, 1990,
   w/Rupert Harvey

TOM STERN
CLAY PIGEON   MGM, 1971

TOM STERNBERG
THE BLACK STALLION   United Artists, 1979, w/Fred Roos
APOCALYPSE NOW ★   United Artists, 1979,
   CP w/Gray Frederickson & Fred Roos
THE BLACK STALLION RETURNS   MGM/UA, 1983,
   w/Doug Claybourne & Fred Roos
DIM SUM: A LITTLE BIT OF HEART   Orion Classics, 1985,
   w/Wayne Wang & Danny Yung
EAT A BOWL OF TEA   Columbia, 1989

CHARLES STETTLER
DISORDERLIES   Warner Bros., 1987,
   EP w/Joseph E. Zynczak

ANDREW STEVENS
Agent: Shapiro & Associates - Sherman Oaks,
   818/906-0322
Manager: Joseph, Rix, Ubell & Malis - Los Angeles

NIGHT EYES   Amritraj-Baldwin Entertainment, 1990, SP

DAVE STEVENS
THE ROCKETEER   Buena Vista, 1991, CP

DENNIS F. STEVENS
THE HARRAD EXPERIMENT   Cinerama, 1973
THE HARRAD SUMMER   Cinerama, 1974

LESLIE STEVENS
Agent: CAA - Beverly Hills, 310/288-4545

BATTLESTAR GALACTICA   Universal, 1979, SP
BUCK ROGERS IN THE 25TH CENTURY   Universal,
   1979, SP

ROY STEVENS
Business: Paravision (UK), 114 The Chambers, Chelsea
   Harbour, London SW10 0XF England, 071/351-7070;
   Fax: 071/352-3645
Agent: Sandra Marsh Management - Sherman Oaks,
   818/905-6961

THE BED SITTING ROOM   United Artists, 1969, AP
RYAN'S DAUGHTER   MGM, 1970, AP
LION OF THE DESERT   UFD, 1981, AP
PLENTY   20th Century Fox, 1985, AP
A CRY IN THE DARK   Warner Bros., 1988, LP

RICK STEVENSON
Agent: William Morris Agency - Beverly Hills, 310/274-7451
Business: Oxford Film Company, 2 Mountfort Terrace,
   London N1 1JJ England, 071/607-8200;
   Fax: 071/607-4037

PRIVILEGED   New Yorker, 1983
RESTLESS NATIVES   Orion Classics, 1986
PROMISED LAND   Vestron, 1988
SOME GIRLS   MGM/UA, 1988
CROOKED HEARTS   MGM, 1991,
   w/Gil Friesen & Dale Pollock

VENETIA STEVENSON
THE SERVANTS OF TWILIGHT   Trimark, 1991,
   w/Jeffrey Obrow

DAVID A. STEWART
DEEP BLUES   1991, EP

JAMES L. STEWART
Business: Aurora Productions, Inc., 8642 Melrose Ave.,
   Suite 200, Los Angeles, CA 90069, 310/854-5742

WHY WOULD I LIE?   MGM/UA, 1980, EP w/Rich Irvine
HEART LIKE A WHEEL   20th Century Fox, 1983,
   EP w/Rich Irvine
MAXIE   Orion, 1985, EP w/Rich Irvine
THE ALLNIGHTER   Universal, 1987, EP
EDDIE & THE CRUISERS II: EDDIE LIVES   Scotti Bros.,
   1989, EP w/Denis Héroux, Victor Loewy &
   William Stewart

JOHN STEWART
DEEP BLUES   1991, w/Eileen Gregory

ARNOLD STIEFEL
Business: Arnold Stiefel Company, 9200 Sunset Blvd.,
   Suite 415, Los Angeles, CA 90069, 310/274-7510

THAT WAS THEN, THIS IS NOW?
STOP MAKING SENSE?
ABOUT LAST NIGHT...   TriStar, 1986, EP
GRAFFITI BRIDGE   Warner Bros., 1990, w/Randy Phillips

ROBERT STIGWOOD
Business: RSO Films, Walt Disney Studios, 500 S. Buena
   Vista St., Burbank, CA 91521, 818/560-6537 or The
   Robert Stigwood Organization, Ltd., 118-120 Wardour St.,
   London, England, 071/437-2512; Fax: 071/437-3674

JESUS CHRIST SUPERSTAR   Universal, 1973,
   w/Norman Jewison
TOMMY   Columbia, 1975, w/Ken Russell
SATURDAY NIGHT FEVER   Paramount, 1977
SGT. PEPPER'S LONELY HEARTS CLUB BAND
   Universal, 1978
GREASE   Paramount, 1978, w/Allan Carr
MOMENT BY MOMENT   Universal, 1978
TIMES SQUARE   AFD, 1980, w/Jacob Brackman
THE FAN   Paramount, 1981
GALLIPOLI   Paramount, 1981, w/Patricia Lovell
GREASE 2   Paramount, 1982, w/Allan Carr
STAYING ALIVE   Paramount, 1983, w/Sylvester Stallone

NICOLAS STILIADIS
(credit w/Syd Cappe)
Contact: SC Entertainment Group, 1326 Londonderry View,
   Los Angeles, CA 90069, 310/854-0337;
   Fax: 310/854-0737

FRIENDS, LOVERS, AND LUNATICS   Fries
   Entertainment, 1989
PUMP UP THE VOLUME   New Line, 1990,
   EP w/Sara Risher

WHIT STILLMAN
Agent: William Morris Agency - New York, 212/586-5100

METROPOLITAN   New Line, 1990

MARC STIRDIVANT
Agent: Daniel Ostroff Agency - Los Angeles, 310/278-2020
Contact: Writers Guild of America - Los Angeles,
   310/550-1000

NIGHT CROSSING   Buena Vista, 1982, AP
WITHOUT A CLUE   Orion, 1988

RICHARD R. ST. JOHNS
Business: Cinevent Corporation, 5200 Longridge Ave.,
   Sherman Oaks, CA 91401, 818/788-1133

MATILDA   AIP, 1978, EP
THE WANDERERS   Orion/Warner Bros., 1979, EP
NIGHTWING   Columbia, 1979, EP
A CHANGE OF SEASONS   20th Century Fox, 1980, EP
THE FINAL COUNTDOWN   United Artists, 1980, EP
THE MOUNTAIN MEN   Columbia, 1980, EP
AMERICAN POP (AF)   Paramount, 1981, EP
DEAD & BURIED   Avco Embassy, 1981, EP

St

FILM
PRODUCERS,
STUDIOS,
AGENTS AND
CASTING
DIRECTORS
GUIDE

F
I
L
M

P
R
O
D
U
C
E
R
S

St

FILM
PRODUCERS,
STUDIOS,
AGENTS AND
CASTING
DIRECTORS
GUIDE

F
I
L
M

P
R
O
D
U
C
E
R
S

VENOM   Paramount, 1982, EP w/Louis A. Stroller
FIRE & ICE (AF)   20th Century Fox, 1983,
   EP w/John Hyde

ANDREW STONE
Contact: Directors Guild of America - Los Angeles,
   213/289-2000

MY BLUE HEAVEN   Warner Bros., 1990,
   EP w/Nora Ephron & Goldie Hawn

OLIVER STONE
Business: Ixtlan, Inc., 3110 Main St., 3rd Floor, Santa
   Monica, CA 90405, 310/399-2550; Fax: 310/399-1561
Agent: CAA - Beverly Hills, 310/288-4545
Contact: Directors Guild of America - Los Angeles,
   213/289-2000

SUGAR COOKIES   General Film, 1973, AP
SALVADOR   Hemdale, 1986, w/Gerald Green
BORN ON THE FOURTH OF JULY ★   Universal, 1989,
   w/A. Kitman Ho
BLUE STEEL   MGM/UA, 1990, w/Edward R. Pressman
REVERSAL OF FORTUNE   Warner Bros., 1990,
   w/Edward R. Pressman
IRON MAZE   Trans-Tokyo, 1991, EP w/Katsumi Kimura,
   Edward R. Pressman & Hidenori Taga
JFK   Warner Bros., 1991, w/A. Kitman Ho

ROBERT J. STONE
NECROMANCY   Cinerama, 1972,
   EP w/Sidney L. Caplan

RAY STOREY
THE HOUSE ON SKULL MOUNTAIN   20th
   Century-Fox, 1974

JEFFREY STOTT
(credit w/Steve Nicolaides)
Business: Castle Rock Entertainment, 335 N. Maple Dr.,
   Suite 135, Beverly Hills, CA 90210, 310/285-2300;
   Fax: 310/285-2345

THE PRINCESS BRIDE   20th Century Fox, 1987, AP
WHEN HARRY MET SALLY...   Castle Rock/Columbia,
   1989, CP
MISERY   Castle Rock/Columbia, 1990, CP

RICHARD STRAFEHL
HOME IS WHERE THE HART IS   Atlantic, 1987,
   EP w/Ralph Scobie

GREG STRANGIS
(credit w/Sam Strangis)
Business: Ten Four Productions, 11300 W. Olympic Blvd.,
   Suite 870, Los Angeles, CA 90064, 310/473-4747;
   Fax: 310/477-9279

TALK RADIO   Universal, 1988, EP

SAM STRANGIS
(credit w/Greg Strangis)
Business: Ten Four Productions, 11300 W. Olympic Blvd.,
   Suite 870, Los Angeles, CA 90064, 310/473-4747;
   Fax: 310/477-9279
Contact: Directors Guild of America - Los Angeles,
   213/289-2000

TALK RADIO   Universal, 1988, EP

BARNARD STRAUS
NIGHT WATCH   Avco Embassy, 1973, w/George W.
   George & Martin Poll

HELEN M. STRAUSS
MR. QUILP   Avco Embassy, 1975
THE INCREDIBLE SARAH   Readers Digest, 1976

PETER E. STRAUSS
Business: The Movie Group, 1900 Avenue of the Stars,
   Suite 1425, Los Angeles, CA 90067, 310/556-2830;
   Fax: 310/277-1490

SKATETOWN U.S.A.   Columbia, 1979, EP
BUSTER   TriStar, 1988, EP w/Frank Giustra
BEST OF THE BEST   Taurus, 1989, w/Phillip Rhee
CADENCE   New Line, 1991, EP w/Timothy Gamble &
   Frank Giustra

RUSSELL W. STREINER
NIGHT OF THE LIVING DEAD   Continental, 1968,
   w/Karl Hardman
THERE'S ALWAYS VANILLA   *THE AFFAIR*   Cambist,
   1972, w/John A. Russo

BARBRA STREISAND
Business: Barwood Films, 75 Rockefeller Plaza, 18th Floor,
   New York, NY 10019, 212/484-7300
Agent: CAA - Beverly Hills, 310/288-4545

A STAR IS BORN   Warner Bros., 1976, EP
THE MAIN EVENT   Warner Bros., 1979, w/Jon Peters
YENTL   MGM/UA, 1983
NUTS   Warner Bros., 1987

DAVID STREIT
Business: 8489 W. Third St., Suite 1104, Los Angeles, CA
   90048, 213/655-0295; Fax: 213/655-6207
Contact: Directors Guild of America - Los Angeles,
   213/289-2000

ALAMBRISTA!   Bobwin/Film Haus, 1977, AP
ROCKERS   New Yorker, 1979, AP
DEEP IN THE HEART   *HANDGUN*   Warner Bros.,
   1984, CP
RIVER'S EDGE   Island Pictures, 1987, CP
PASS THE AMMO   New Century/Vista, 1988, LP
INTERNAL AFFAIRS   Paramount, 1990, EP w/Pierre
   David & René Malo
FIRES WITHIN   MGM, 1991, AP
THE MARRYING MAN   Buena Vista, 1991, CP

JOSEPH STRICK
Agent: David Dworski & Associates - Los Angeles,
   310/273-6173
Contact: Directors Guild of America - Los Angeles,
   213/289-2000

THE SAVAGE EYE   Trans-Lux, 1959, w/Ben Maddow &
   Sidney Meyers
THE BALCONY   Continental, 1963, w/Ben Maddow
ULYSSES   Continental, 1967
RING OF BRIGHT WATER   Cinerama, 1969
TROPIC OF CANCER   Paramount, 1970
ROAD MOVIE   Grove Press, 1974
NEVER CRY WOLF   Buena Vista, 1983, w/Lewis Allen &
   Jack Couffer

WHITLEY STRIEBER
Agent: CAA - Beverly Hills, 310/288-4545
Contact: Writers Guild of America - New York, 212/245-6180

COMMUNION   New Line, 1989, w/Dan Allingham &
   Philippe Mora

DAN STRIEPEKE
Sssssssss   Universal, 1973

LOUIS A. STROLLER
Business: Martin Bregman Productions, 100 Universal City
   Plaza, Universal City, CA 91608, 818/777-4950
Contact: Directors Guild of America - Los Angeles,
   213/289-2000

BADLANDS   Warner Bros., 1974, AP
CARRIE   United Artists, 1976, AP
THE SEDUCTION OF JOE TYNAN   Universal, 1979, EP
SIMON   Orion/Warner Bros., 1980, EP
THE FOUR SEASONS   Universal, 1981, EP
VENOM   Paramount, 1982, EP w/Richard R. St. Johns
EDDIE MACON'S RUN   Universal, 1983
SCARFACE   Universal, 1983, EP
SWEET LIBERTY   Universal, 1986, EP
REAL MEN   MGM/UA, 1987, EP
A NEW LIFE   Paramount, 1988, EP
SEA OF LOVE   Universal, 1989, w/Martin Bregman
BETSY'S WEDDING   Buena Vista, 1990,
   w/Martin Bregman

GARY STROMBERG
CAR WASH   Universal, 1976, w/Art Linson
THE FISH THAT SAVED PITTSBURGH   United Artists,
   1979, w/David Dashev

JOHN STRONG
STEEL JUSTICE   Atlantic, 1987
A SHOW OF FORCE   Paramount, 1990

RAYMOND STROSS
I WANT WHAT I WANT   Cinerama, 1972
GOOD LUCK, MISS WYCKOFF   Bel Air/Gradison, 1979

CHARLES STROUD
DETROIT 9000   General Film Corp., 1973, AP
THE ROOM MATES   General Film Corp., 1973
BONNIE'S KIDS   General Film Corp., 1973
THE CENTERFOLD GIRLS   General Film Corp., 1974
FRIDAY FOSTER   AIP, 1975, EP

ALEXANDER STUART
INSIGNIFICANCE   Island Alive, 1985, EP

MALCOLM STUART
A CAPTIVE IN THE LAND   1991, w/John Berry

MARVIN STUART
SHORT EYES   Paramount, 1977, EP

MEL STUART
Contact: Directors Guild of America - Los Angeles,
   213/289-2000

WATTSTAX (FD)   Columbia, 1973, w/Larry Shaw

WALKER STUART
Business: Lewis Allen Productions, 1500 Broadway,
   New York, NY 10036, 212/221-2400
Contact: Directors Guild of America - Los Angeles,
   213/289-2000

SHORT EYES   Paramount, 1977, AP
NEVER CRY WOLF   Buena Vista, 1983, AP
1918   Cinecom, 1985, CP
END OF THE LINE   Orion Classics, 1987, CP
LORD OF THE FLIES   Castle Rock/Columbia, 1990, AP

WILLIAM STUART
Business: Aurora Productions, Inc., 8642 Melrose Ave.,
   Suite 200, Los Angeles, CA 90069, 310/854-6900;
   Fax: 310/854-0583

EDDIE & THE CRUISERS II: EDDIE LIVES   Scotti Bros.,
   1989, EP w/Denis Héroux, Victor Loewy &
   James L. Stewart
THE FOURTH WAR   Warner Bros., 1990,
   EP w/Sam Perlmutter

JOHN V. STUCKMEYER
TOO MUCH SUN   New Line, 1990, CP w/Joe Bilella

GORDON STULBERG
A CHORUS LINE   Columbia, 1985, EP

PEGGY ANN STULBERG
GET ROLLIN'   Aquarius, 1981, CP

LAWRENCE STURHAHN
Contact: Directors Guild of America - Los Angeles,
   213/289-2000

THX 1138   Warner Bros., 1971

MICHAEL STYLE
(credit w/Harry Fine)

VAMPIRE LOVERS   AIP, 1970
MONIQUE   Avco Embassy, 1970*
LUST FOR A VAMPIRE   American Continental, 1971
TWINS OF EVIL   Universal, 1972

MILTON SUBOTSKY
(credit w/Max Rosenberg)
Business: Amicus Productions, Ltd., 20 Stradella Rd.,
   London SE24 9HA England, 071/274-3205

IT'S TRAD, DAD   *RING-A-DING RHYTHM*   Columbia,
   1962, EP*

Su

FILM
PRODUCERS,
STUDIOS,
AGENTS AND
CASTING
DIRECTORS
GUIDE

F
I
L
M

P
R
O
D
U
C
E
R
S

THE DEADLY BEES   Paramount, 1967
SCREAM AND SCREAM AGAIN   AIP, 1969
THE MIND OF MR. SOAMES   Columbia, 1970
THE HOUSE THAT DRIPPED BLOOD   Cinerama, 1971
WHAT BECAME OF JACK AND JILL   20th
   Century-Fox, 1972
ASYLUM   Cinerama, 1972
TALES FROM THE CRYPT   Cinerama, 1972*
THE VAULT OF HORROR   Cinerama, 1973
AND NOW THE SCREAMING STARTS   Cinerama, 1973
THE VAULT OF HORROR   Cinerama, 1973
MADHOUSE   AIP, 1974
THE BEAST MUST DIE   Cinerama, 1974
I, MONSTER   Cannon, 1974
FROM BEYOND THE GRAVE   Howard Mahler, 1975
STEPHEN KING'S CAT'S EYE   *CAT'S EYE*   MGM/UA,
   1985, CP*
MAXIMUM OVERDRIVE   DEG, 1986, CP*

HIDEAKI SUDA
MYSTERY TRAIN   Orion Classics, 1989,
   EP w/Kunjiro Hirata

BONNIE SUGAR
Business: Sugar Entertainment Inc., 15821 Ventura Blvd.,
   Suite 290, Encino, CA 91436, 818/789-6555;
   Fax: 818/789-6658

GRAVEYARD SHIFT   Paramount, 1990,
   EP w/Larry Sugar

LARRY SUGAR
Business: Sugar Entertainment Inc., 15821 Ventura Blvd.,
   Suite 290, Encino, CA 91436, 818/789-6555;
   Fax: 818/789-6658

STEEL DAWN   Vestron, 1987, EP w/William J. Quigley
GRAVEYARD SHIFT   Paramount, 1990,
   EP w/Bonnie Sugar

BURT SUGARMAN
Business: 150 El Camino Dr., Suite 303, Beverly Hills, CA
   90212, 310/273-0900

EXTREMITIES   Atlantic, 1986
CRIMES OF THE HEART   DEG, 1986, EP
CHILDREN OF A LESSER GOD ★   Paramount, 1986,
   w/Patrick Palmer

MORRIS F. SULLIVAN
Business: Sullivan/Bluth Studios, 2501 W. Burbank Blvd.,
   Suite 201, Burbank, CA 91505, 818/840-9446;
   Fax: 818/840-0487

ALL DOGS GO TO HEAVEN (AF)   Universal, 1989,
   EP w/George A. Walker

ROBERT SULLIVAN
SEXTETTE   Crown International, 1979, w/Daniel Briggs

CATHLEEN SUMMERS
Business: Summers-Quaid Productions, c/o TriStar, 10202
   W. Washington Blvd., Culver City, CA 90232,
   310/280-7942

CLASS   Orion, 1983, EP
STAKEOUT   Buena Vista, 1987, w/Jim Kouf
D.O.A.   Buena Vista, 1988, CP w/Andrew J. Kuehn
VITAL SIGNS   20th Century Fox, 1990, w/Laurie Perlman

GABE SUMNER
Business: Odyssey Film Partners, Ltd., 6500 Wilshire Blvd.,
   Suite 400, Los Angeles, CA 90048, 213/655-9335

THE HEAVENLY KID   Orion, 1985,
   EP w/Stephen G. Cheikes
MEMORIES OF ME   MGM/UA, 1988, EP w/J. David Marks

SHIRLEY SUN
A GREAT WALL   Orion Classics, 1986
IRON & SILK   Prestige, 1991

RAY SUNDLIN
SPACE AVENGER   Manley, 1990, w/Robert Harris

RONALD A. SUPPA
Contact: 3737 Ventura Canyon Ave., Sherman Oaks, CA
   91423, 818/784-6369

PARADISE ALLEY   Universal, 1978, w/John F. Roach

DONALD SUTHERLAND
Agent: CAA - Beverly Hills, 310/288-4545

F.T.A.   AIP, 1972, w/Jane Fonda & Francine Parker
STEELYARD BLUES   Warner Bros., 1973, EP

TED SWANSON
Contact: Directors Guild of America - Los Angeles,
   213/289-2000

NOBODY'S PERFEKT   Columbia, 1981, EP

HERBERT SWARTZ
SOMETHING SHORT OF PARADISE   AIP, 1979,
   EP w/Michael Ingber

JOHN K. SWENSSON
FIRE BIRDS   Buena Vista, 1990, CP w/Dale Dye

EZRA SWERDLOW
Business: Swerdlow/Schindler Prods., 110 W. 57th Street,
   Suite 401, New York, NY 10019, 212/265-7760;
   Fax: 212/581-3617
Contact: Directors Guild of America - New York,
   212/581-0370

SPACEBALLS   MGM/UA, 1987, CP
RADIO DAYS   Orion, 1987, AP
THE JANUARY MAN   MGM/UA, 1989, w/Norman Jewison
EVERYBODY WINS   Orion, 1990, CP
LIFE STINKS   MGM, 1991, EP

SAUL SWIMMER
(credit w/Tony Anthony)

COMETOGETHER   Allied Artists, 1971
BLINDMAN   20th Century Fox, 1972

ANTHEA SYLBERT
Business: Hawn/Sylbert Productions, Hollywood Pictures,
   500 S. Buena Vista St., Animation Bldg. 1-D-6, Burbank,
   CA 91521, 818/560-6101; Fax: 818/566-4141

PROTOCOL   Warner Bros., 1984
WILDCATS   Warner Bros., 1986
OVERBOARD   MGM/UA, 1987, w/Alexandra Rose

MY BLUE HEAVEN   Warner Bros., 1990,
   w/Herbert Ross
DECEIVED   Buena Vista, 1991, EP w/Teri Schwartz

DUSTY SYMONDS
Agent: London Management - London, 071/493-1610

FINDERS KEEPERS   Warner Bros., 1984, AP
WITCHES   Warner Bros., 1989, LP

T

SYLVIO TABET
FADE TO BLACK   American Cinema, 1980,
   EP w/Irwin Yablans
THE COTTON CLUB   Orion, 1984, CP w/Fred Roos
DEAD RINGERS   20th Century Fox, 1988,
   EP w/Carol Baum

HIDENORA TAGA
IRON MAZE   Trans-Tokyo, 1991, EP w/Katsumi Kimura,
   Edward R. Pressman & Oliver Stone

VINCENT TAI
DIM SUM: A LITTLE BIT OF HEART   Orion Classics,
   1985, EP

HAL TAINES
LOVELINES   TriStar, 1984, w/Michael Lloyd

RACHEL TALALAY
Business: New Line, 116 N. Robertson Blvd., Los Angeles,
   CA 90048, 213/854-5811

A NIGHTMARE ON ELM STREET 3: DREAM WARRIORS
   New Line, 1987, LP
HAIRSPRAY   New Line, 1988
A NIGHTMARE ON ELM STREET 4: THE DREAM
   MASTER   New Line, 1988, w/Robert Shaye
CRY-BABY   Universal, 1990
BOOK OF LOVE   New Line, 1990

WILLIAM TALMADGE
THE DARK BACKWARD   RCA/Columbia, 1991,
   EP w/Randolf Turrow

FLAVIO R. TAMBELLINI
WHERE THE RIVER RUNS BLACK   MGM, 1986,
   LP w/Bruno Barreto

NED TANEN
Business: Channel Productions, c/o Paramount Pictures,
   5555 Melrose Ave., Los Angeles, CA 90038,
   213/956-5050; Fax: 213/956-3472

SIXTEEN CANDLES   Universal, 1984, EP
THE BREAKFAST CLUB   Universal, 1985,
   w/John Hughes
ST. ELMO'S FIRE   Columbia, 1985,
   EP w/Bernard Schwartz

MICHAEL TANNEN
ONE-TRICK PONY   Warner Bros., 1980
THE SQUEEZE   TriStar, 1987, w/Rupert Hitzig

JAMES TANNENBAUM
ANGELS DIE HARD   New World, 1970,
   EP w/Jane Schaffer

MARK M. TANZ
INSIDE MOVES   AFD, 1980, w/Richard W. Goodwin

ROBERT G. TAPERT
Business: Renaissance Motion Pictures, Inc., 28 East 10th
   St., New York, NY 10003, 212/477-0432; 6381 Hollywood
   Blvd., Suite 680, Los Angeles, CA 90028, 213/969-9795;
   Fax: 213/969-8509

THE EVIL DEAD   New Line, 1983
CRIMEWAVE   Embassy, 1986
EVIL DEAD 2: DEAD BY DAWN   DEG, 1987
EASY WHEELS   Fries Entertainment, 1989,
   EP w/Bruce Campbell
DARKMAN   Universal, 1990
ARMY OF DARKNESS   1991

JONATHAN T. TAPLIN
Business: Trans Pacific Films, 3000 W. Olympic Blvd.,
   Suite 1410, Santa Monica, CA 90404, 310/315-4701;
   Fax: 310/315-4729

MEAN STREETS   Warner Bros., 1973
GRAVY TRAIN   Columbia, 1974
THE LAST WALTZ   United Artists, 1978, EP
CARNY   United Artists, 1980, EP
UNDER FIRE   Orion, 1983
GRANDVIEW, U.S.A.   Warner Bros., 1984,
   EP w/Andrew Gellis
BABY...SECRET OF THE LOST LEGEND   Buena
   Vista, 1985
MY SCIENCE PROJECT   Buena Vista, 1985

MARK TARLOV
Business: Addis-Wechsler & Associates, 955 S. Carillo Dr.,
   Suite 300, Los Angeles, CA 90048, 213/954-9000;
   Fax: 213/954-0990

CHRISTINE   Columbia, 1983, EP w/Kirby McCauley
POWER   20th Century Fox, 1986, w/Reene Schisgal
WHITE WATER SUMMER   Columbia, 1987
SECOND SIGHT   Warner Bros., 1989
TUNE IN TOMORROW...   Cinecom, 1990, w/John Fiedler
MORTAL THOUGHTS   Columbia, 1991, w/John Fiedler

JOHN TARNOFF
Business: Village Roadshow Pictures, 2121 Avenue of the
   Stars, 22nd Floor, Los Angeles, CA 90067, 310/282-8964

OUT OF BOUNDS   Columbia, 1986, EP w/Ray Hartwick

NADIA TASS
(credit w/David Parker)
Agent: CAA - Beverly Hills, 310/288-4545

MALCOLM   Vestron, 1986
RIKKY & PETE   MGM/UA, 1988

Ta

FILM
PRODUCERS,
STUDIOS,
AGENTS and
CASTING
DIRECTORS
GUIDE

FILM PRODUCERS

Ta

FILM
PRODUCERS,
STUDIOS,
AGENTS AND
CASTING
DIRECTORS
GUIDE

F
I
L
M

P
R
O
D
U
C
E
R
S

TOM TATUM
WINNERS TAKE ALL   Apollo, 1987,
   w/Christopher W. Knight

LAWRENCE TAUB
POWAQQATSI (FD)   Cannon, 1988, w/Mel Lawrence &
   Godfrey Reggio

BARBI TAYLOR
ROAD GAMES   Avco Embassy, 1981, CP

BRUCE A. TAYLOR
INSTANT KARMA   MGM, 1990, w/George Edwards &
   Dale Rosenbloom

C. D. TAYLOR
CRACKING UP   AIP, 1977, w/Rick Murray

DELORES TAYLOR
BILLY JACK GOES TO WASHINGTON
   Taylor-Laughlin, 1978

DON TAYLOR
SIGNAL 7   One Pass Pictures, 1986, w/Ben Myron

GEOFFREY TAYLOR
MOSCOW ON THE HUDSON   Columbia, 1984, AP
DOWN AND OUT IN BEVERLY HILLS   Buena Vista,
   1986, AP
MOON OVER PARADOR   Universal, 1988,
   CP w/Pato Guzman
TAKING CARE OF BUSINESS   Buena Vista, 1990

GREG TAYLOR
PRANCER   Orion, 1989, CP w/Mike Petzold

JEFFREY TAYLOR
Business: Centre Entertainment PLC, 118 Cleveland
   Street, London W1P 5DN England, 071/387-4045;
   Fax: 071/388-0408

A HANDFUL OF DUST   New Line, 1988,
   EP w/Kent Walwin

LAWRENCE TAYLOR-MORTORFF
(see Lawrence MORTORFF)

MICHAEL TAYLOR
Business: Precision Films, 110 East 59th St., Suite 1405,
   New York, NY 10022, 212/319-3030

LAST EMBRACE   United Artists, 1979, w/Dan Wigutow
THE PURSUIT OF D. B. COOPER   Universal, 1981,
   w/Dan Wigutow
HIDER IN THE HOUSE   Vestron, 1989, w/Edward Teets

ROBERT TAYLOR
DUCK TALES: THE MOVIE - TREASURE OF THE
   LOST LAMP (AF)   Buena Vista, 1990,
   CP w/Jean-Pierre Quenet

EDWARD TEETS
Contact: Directors Guild of America - Los Angeles,
   213/289-2000

SHARKY'S MACHINE   Orion/Warner Bros., 1981, AP
LOOKIN' TO GET OUT   Paramount, 1982, AP

UNDER FIRE   Orion, 1983, EP
THE FALCON AND THE SNOWMAN   Orion, 1985, CP
JUST BETWEEN FRIENDS   Orion, 1986, w/Allan Burns
THE BELIEVERS   Orion, 1987, EP
THREE MEN AND A BABY   Buena Vista, 1987, CP
HIDER IN THE HOUSE   Vestron, 1989, w/Michael Taylor

IRVING TEITELBAUM
SINGING THE BLUES IN RED   Angelika, 1988, EP

MIGUEL TEJADA-FLORES
Agent: Harris & Goldberg - Los Angeles, 310/553-5200
Contact: Writers Guild of America - Los Angeles,
   310/550-1000

DUDES   New Century/Vista, 1988, w/Herb Jaffe

ANIL TEJANI
SALAAM BOMBAY!   Cinecom, 1988, EP w/Gabriel Auer,
   Michael Nozik & Cherie Rodgers

JOHN TEMPLE-SMITH
THE ISLAND OF DR. MOREAU   AIP, 1977, w/Skip Steloff

NANCY TENENBAUM
sex, lies & videotape   Miramax, 1989, EP w/Morgan Mason
   & Nick Wechsler
THE RAPTURE   Fine Line, 1991, w/Nick Wechsler &
   Karen Koch

TIM TENNANT
Agent: Gorfaine/Schwartz/Roberts - Beverly Hills,
   310/275-9384
Contact: Directors Guild of America - Los Angeles,
   213/289-2000

HOT DOG...THE MOVIE   MGM/UA, 1984, AP
GHOST TOWN   Trans World, 1988

WILLIAM TENNANT
CLEOPATRA JONES   Warner Bros., 1973
CLEOPATRA JONES AND THE CASINO OF GOLD
   Warner Bros., 1975
THE PURSUIT OF D. B. COOPER   Universal, 1981,
   EP w/Donald Kranze
KING OF THE MOUNTAIN   Universal, 1981, EP
SUMMER HEAT   Atlantic, 1987

ALBERT J. TENSER
HARRY TRACY   Quartet/Films, 1983, EP w/Marty Krofft &
   Sid Krofft

MARILYN TENSER
Business: Crown International Pictures, 8701 Wilshire Blvd.,
   Beverly Hills, CA 90211, 310/657-6700; Fax: 310/657-4489

POLICEWOMEN   Crown International, 1974, EP
THE POM POM GIRLS   Crown International, 1976, EP
VAN NUYS BLVD.   Crown International, 1979

TONY TENSER
Business: Crown International Pictures, 8701 Wilshire Blvd.,
   Beverly Hills, CA 90211, 310/657-6700; Fax: 310/657-4489

MONIQUE   Avco Embassy, 1970, EP
THE CRIMSON CULT   AIP, 1970, EP
THE BLOOD ON SATAN'S CLAW   Cannon, 1971, EP
THE BODY STEALERS   Allied Artists, 1971

WHAT'S GOOD FOR THE GOOSE   National
    Showmanship, 1972
HANNIE CAULDER   Paramount, 1972, EP
NEITHER THE SEA NOR THE SAND   International
    Amusement Corp., 1974, EP w/Peter J. Thompson

BERT TENZER
THE DAY THE MUSIC DIED   Atlantic, 1977

WILLIAM TEPPER
Contact: Writers Guild of America - Los Angeles,
    310/550-1000

HEART BEAT   Orion, 1980, EP w/Edward R. Pressman

RUSSELL THACHER
(credit w/Walter Seltzer)

SOYLENT GREEN   MGM, 1973
THE LAST HARD MEN   20th Century Fox, 1976

CHARLES C. THIERIOT
(credit w/Sandy Climan)

ALMOST YOU   20th Century Fox, 1984,
    EP w/Stephen J. Levin
3:15 THE MOMENT OF TRUTH   Dakota Entertainment,
    1986, EP w/Andrew Bullians & Jean Bullians
THE BIKINI SHOP   *THE MALIBU BIKINI SHOP*
    International Film Marketing, 1987, EP w/Andrew
    Bullians & Jean Bullians

ANNA THOMAS
Agent: ICM - Los Angeles, 310/550-4000
Contact: Writers Guild of America - Los Angeles,
    310/550-1000

THE HAUNTING OF M   Nu-Image, 1981
EL NORTE   Cinecom/Island Alive, 1984
A TIME OF DESTINY   Columbia, 1988

DAVID C. THOMAS
Business: Zeta Entertainment, Ltd., 6565 Sunset Blvd.,
    Suite 321, Hollywood, CA 90028, 213/461-7332
Contact: Directors Guild of America - Los Angeles,
    213/289-2000

STAND ALONE   New World, 1985, CP
WELCOME TO 18   American Distribution Group, 1986
OUT OF THE DARK   Cinetel, 1989, CP

GARTH THOMAS
CHECKING OUT   Warner Bros., 1989, CP

JEREMY THOMAS
Business: The Recorded Picture Company Ltd.,
    8-12 Broadwick Street, London W1V 1FH England,
    071/439-0607; Fax: 071/434-1192

MAD DOG MORGAN   Cinema Shares International, 1976
THE SHOUT   Films Inc., 1979
THE GREAT ROCK 'N' ROLL SWINDLE (FD)
    Kendon Films, 1980
EUREKA   UA Classics, 1984
MERRY CHRISTMAS, MR. LAWRENCE   Universal, 1983
INSIGNIFICANCE   Island Alive, 1985
THE HIT   Island Alive, 1985
GOOD TO GO   Island Pictures, 1986,
    EP w/Chris Blackwell

THE LAST EMPEROR ★★   Columbia, 1987
EVERYBODY WINS   Orion, 1990
THE SHELTERING SKY   Warner Bros., 1990
NAKED LUNCH   20th Century Fox, 1991

JIM THOMAS
Agent: InterTalent Agency, Inc. - Los Angeles, 310/858-6200
Contact: Writers Guild of America - Los Angeles,
    310/550-1000

PREDATOR   20th Century Fox, 1987,
    EP w/Laurence P. Pereira
THE RESCUE   Buena Vista, 1988, CP w/John Thomas

JOHN THOMAS
Agent: InterTalent Agency, Inc. - Los Angeles, 310/858-6200
Contact: Writers Guild of America - Los Angeles,
    310/550-1000

THE RESCUE   Buena Vista, 1988, CP w/Jim Thomas

PETER THOMAS
FROGS   AIP, 1972, w/George Edwards

RAMSEY THOMAS
Agent: Stone-Manners - Los Angeles, 310/275-9599
Contact: Directors Guild of America - Los Angeles,
    213/289-2000
Business: Trancas International, 9229 Sunset Blvd.,
    Suite 415, Los Angeles, CA 90069, 310/657-7670;
    Fax: 310/271-4156

A MAN CALLED DAGGER   MGM, 1968, AP
THE AROUSERS   *SWEET KILL*   New World, 1970, AP
SOME CALL IT LOVING   Cine Globe, 1973, AP
BLUE SUNSHINE   Cinema Shares International, 1979, AP
HALLOWEEN 5: THE REVENGE OF MICHAEL MYERS
    Galaxy, 1989

TONY THOMAS
(credit w/Paul Junger Witt)
Business: Witt-Thomas Prods., 846 N. Cahuenga Blvd., Los
    Angeles, CA 90038, 213/464-1333; Fax: 213/960-1837

FIRSTBORN   Paramount, 1984
DEAD POETS SOCIETY ★   Buena Vista, 1989,
    w/Steven Haft
FINAL ANALYSIS   Warner Bros., 1991, w/Charles Roven

JOHN THOMPSON
HERCULES   Cannon, 1983, EP
THE ASSISI UNDERGROUND   Cannon, 1985, AP
DETECTIVE SCHOOL DROPOUTS   *DUMB DICKS*
    Cannon, 1986, AP
OTELLO   Cannon, 1986, EP
DANCERS   Cannon, 1987, AP
THE BARBARIANS   Cannon, 1987
HAUNTED SUMMER   Cannon, 1988, AP
THE COMFORT OF STRANGERS   Skouras, 1990, AP

LARRY THOMPSON
Business: The Larry A. Thompson Org., 345 N. Maple Dr.,
    Suite 183, Beverly Hills, CA 90210, 310/288-0700;
    Fax: 310/288-0711

QUIET COOL   New Line, 1986, EP w/Pierre David &
    Arthur Sarkissian
MY DEMON LOVER   New Line, 1987, EP w/Pierre David

Th

FILM
PRODUCERS,
STUDIOS,
AGENTS and
CASTING
DIRECTORS
GUIDE

F
I
L
M

P
R
O
D
U
C
E
R
S

Th

FILM
PRODUCERS,
STUDIOS,
AGENTS AND
CASTING
DIRECTORS
GUIDE

F
I
L
M

P
R
O
D
U
C
E
R
S

NEVILLE C. THOMPSON
THE MISSIONARY   Columbia, 1982, w/Michael Palin

PETER J. THOMPSON
NEITHER THE SEA NOR THE SAND   International
   Amusement Corp., 1974, EP w/Tony Tenser

TOMMY THOMPSON
Contact: Directors Guild of America - Los Angeles,
   213/289-2000

IMAGES   Columbia, 1972
A WEDDING   20th Century Fox, 1978, EP
QUINTET   20th Century Fox, 1979, EP
A PERFECT COUPLE   20th Century Fox,
   1979, EP
HEALTH   20th Century Fox, 1980, EP

JOEL THURM
Business: NBC Entertainment, 3000 W. Alameda Ave.,
   Burbank, CA 91523, 818/840-4444

ELVIRA, MISTRESS OF THE DARK   New World,
   1988, SP

RICHARD TIENKEN
Business: Paramount Pictures, 5555 Melrose Ave.,
   Los Angeles, CA 90038, 213/956-4545

THE GOLDEN CHILD   Paramount, 1986,
   EP w/Charles R. Meeker
BEVERLY HILLS COP II   Paramount, 1987,
   w/Robert D. Wachs
EDDIE MURPHY RAW   Paramount, 1987,
   EP w/Eddie Murphy

ERIC TILL
Contact: Directors Guild of America - Los Angeles,
   213/289-2000

IF YOU COULD SEE WHAT I HEAR   Jensen Farley
   Pictures, 1982

HUGH TIRRELL
THE ADVENTURES OF MARK TWAIN (AF)   Atlantic
   Entertainment, 1986, EP

STEVE TISCH
Business: The Steve Tisch Company, 3815 Hughes Ave.,
   Culver City, CA 90232, 310/838-2500;
   Fax: 310/204-2713

OUTLAW BLUES   Warner Bros., 1977
ALMOST SUMMER   Universal, 1978, EP
COAST TO COAST   Paramount, 1980, w/Jon Avnet
RISKY BUSINESS   Geffen/Warner Bros., 1983,
   w/Jon Avnet
DEAL OF THE CENTURY   Warner Bros., 1983,
   EP w/Jon Avnet & Paul Brickman
SOUL MAN   New World, 1976
HOT TO TROT   Warner Bros., 1988
BIG BUSINESS   Buena Vista, 1988,
   w/Michael Peyser
HEART OF DIXIE   Orion, 1989
HEART CONDITION   New Line, 1990
BAD INFLUENCE   Triumph, 1990

JAMES TOBACK
Business Manager: David Kaufman, Kaufman & Nachbaur,
   100 Merrick Rd., Rockville Centre, NY, 516/536-5760
Agent: ICM - Los Angeles, 310/550-4000

LOVE AND MONEY   Paramount, 1982
EXPOSED   MGM/UA, 1983

MARC TOBEROFF
ZOMBIE HIGH   Cinema Group, 1987, w/Aziz Ghazal

MICHAEL TODD, JR.
THE BELL JAR   Avco Embassy, 1979, w/Jerrold Brandt, Jr.

BILL TODMAN, JR.
(credit w/Joel Simon)
Business: Todman-Simon Productions, 300 S. Lorimar
   Plaza, Bldg. 137, Room 1107, Burbank, CA 91505,
   818/954-7508; Fax: 818/954-7874

MARRIED TO THE MOB   Orion, 1988, EP
HARD TO KILL   Warner Bros., 1990, w/Gary Adelson

JERRY TOKOFSKY
Business: Zupnik Enterprises, Inc., 9229 Sunset Blvd.,
   Suite 818, Los Angeles, CA 90069, 310/273-9125

WHERE'S POPPA   United Artists, 1970, w/Marvin Worth
BORN TO WIN   United Artists, 1971, EP
PATERNITY   Paramount, 1981, EP
DREAMSCAPE   20th Century Fox, 1984, CP
FEAR CITY   Chevy Chase Distribution, 1985, CP
WILDFIRE   Cinema Group, 1988

MICHAEL TOLAN
FIVE ON THE BLACK HAND SIDE   United Artists, 1973,
   w/Brock Peters
FOUR FRIENDS   Filmways, 1981, EP w/Julia Miles

FRANK D. TOLIN
SURF II   International Films, 1984, EP w/Lou George

MICHAEL TOLKIN
THE PLAYER   Avenue, 1991, w/David Brown &
   Nick Wechsler

DAVID TOMBLIN
THE ADVENTURES OF BARON MUNCHAUSEN
   Columbia, 1989, LP

LILY TOMLIN
THE SEARCH FOR SIGNS OF INTELLIGENT LIFE IN
   THE UNIVERSE (FD)   Orion Classics, 1991,
   EP w/Jane Wagner

KEN TOPOLSKY
THE WIZARD   Universal, 1989, w/David Chisholm

BURT TOPPER
Contact: Directors Guild of America - Los Angeles,
   213/289-2000

FIREBALL 500   AIP, 1966, CP
THE HARD RIDE   AIP, 1971, EP
THE DAY THE LORD GOT BUSTED   American
   Films, 1976
C.H.O.M.P.S.   Orion, 1979, CP

JEFF TORNBERG
ANDY WARHOL'S BAD   New World, 1977

RANDALL TORNO
THE WILD PAIR   Trans World, 1987, w/Paul Mason

ROBERT TORRANCE
MUTANT ON THE BOUNTY   Skouras Pictures, 1989,
   w/Martin Lupez

WARNER G. TOUB
SEXTETTE   Crown International, 1979, EP

HARRY ALAN TOWERS
(Peter Welbeck)
Business: 21st Century Film Corporation, 8200 Wilshire
   Blvd., Beverly Hills, CA 90211, 213/658-3000

TEN LITTLE INDIANS   7 Arts, 1965
THE BRIDES OF FU MANCHU   7 Arts, 1966,
   w/Oliver Unger
THE VENGEANCE OF FU MANCHU   Warner Bros./
   7 Arts, 1967
HOUSE OF 1000 DOLLS   AIP, 1967
THE MILLION EYES OF SU-MURU   AIP, 1967
PSYCHO-CIRCUS   AIP, 1967
KISS AND KILL   Commonwealth United, 1968
THE CASTLE OF FU MANCHU   International
   Cinema, 1968
FIVE GOLDEN DRAGONS   Warner Bros., 1968
99 WOMEN   Commonwealth United, 1969
EUGENIE...THE STORY OF HER JOURNEY INTO
   PERVERSION   Distinction, 1969
VENUS IN FURS   AIP, 1970
DORIAN GRAY   AIP, 1970
COUNT DRACULA   World Entertainment, 1971
NIGHT OF THE BLOOD MONSTER   AIP, 1972
TREASURE ISLAND   National General, 1972
TEN LITTLE INDIANS   Avco Embassy, 1975
THE CASTLE OF FU MANCHU   International
   Cinema, 1975
THE SHAPE OF THINGS TO COME   Film Ventures,
   1979, EP
LIGHTNING - THE WHITE STALLION
   Cannon, 1986
WARRIOR QUEEN   *POMPEII*   Seymour Borde &
   Associates, 1987
DRAGONARD   Cannon, 1987
OUTLAW OF GOR   Cannon, 1988, w/Avi Lerner
AMERICAN NINJA 3: BLOOD HUNT
   Cannon, 1989
RIVER OF DEATH   Cannon, 1989, w/Avi Lerner
TEN LITTLE INDIANS   Cannon, 1989
EDGE OF SANITY   Millimeter Films, 1989,
   w/Edward Simons
THE PHANTOM OF THE OPERA   21st Century Film
   Corporation, 1989
MASTER OF DRAGONARD HILL   Cannon, 1989

ROBERT TOWNE
Agent: ICM - Los Angeles, 310/550-4000
Contact: Directors Guild of America - Los Angeles,
   213/289-2000

PERSONAL BEST   Warner Bros., 1982
THE BEDROOM WINDOW   DEG, 1987, EP

ROGER TOWNE
Business: Rolling Hills Productions, 204 South Beverly Dr.,
   #166, Beverly Hills, CA 90212, 310/275-0872
Agent: ICM - Los Angeles, 310/550-4000

THE NATURAL   TriStar, 1984,   EP w/Philip M. Breen

ROBERT TOWNSEND
Agent: UTA - Beverly Hills, 310/273-6700
Contact: Directors Guild of America - Los Angeles,
   213/289-2000
Business: Tinsel Townsend, 8033 Sunset Blvd., Suite 890,
   Los Angeles, CA, 213/962-2240

HOLLYWOOD SHUFFLE   Samuel Goldwyn
   Company, 1987
THE FIVE HEARTBEATS   20th Century Fox, 1991, EP

PETE TOWNSHEND
Business: Faber & Faber Publishers, Ltd., 3 Queen Square,
   London WC1 N3AU, 071/278-6881; Fax: 071/465-0034

QUADROPHENIA   World Northal, 1979, EP w/Roger
   Daltrey, John Entwistle & Keith Moon

MARC TRABULUS
Business: GMS, 7025 Santa Monica Blvd., Hollywood, CA
   90038, 213/856-4848

SUMMER SCHOOL   Paramount, 1987, EP

J. MARK TRAVIS
(credit w/Del Jack)

RICHARD PRYOR LIVE IN CONCERT (FD)   Special Event
   Entertainment, 1979
SAMMY STOPS THE WORLD   Special Event
   Entertainment, 1979

MARK TRAVIS
FIGHTING BACK   Paramount, 1982, EP w/David Permut

PETER S. TRAYNOR
STEEL ARENA   L-T Films, 1973, w/Mark L. Lester
TRUCK STOP WOMEN   L-T Films, 1974, EP
THE ULTIMATE THRILL   General Cinema, 1974,
   w/William D. Sklar
BOGARD   L-T Films, 1975, w/William D. Sklar
BLACK STREETFIGHTER   New Line, 1976,
   w/William D. Sklar
DEATH GAME   Levitt-Pickman, 1977, EP w/Larry Spiegel

JOHN TRENT
DEAD OF NIGHT   Europix International, 1974,
   EP w/Peter James
LOVE AT FIRST SIGHT   Movietime, 1978,
   EP w/David Perlmutter

MICHAEL TRIKILIS
STACEY!   New World, 1973, EP
SIX PACK   20th Century Fox, 1982

KENITH TRODD
Business: Pennies From Heaven, 83 Eastbourne Mews,
   London W2 England, 071/402-0051

BRIMSTONE AND TREACLE   United Artists Classics, 1982
DREAMCHILD   Universal, 1985, w/Rick McCallum

Tr

FILM
PRODUCERS,
STUDIOS,
AGENTS AND
CASTING
DIRECTORS
GUIDE

FILM PRODUCERS

Tr

FILM
PRODUCERS,
STUDIOS,
AGENTS AND
CASTING
DIRECTORS
GUIDE

F
I
L
M

P
R
O
D
U
C
E
R
S

BOET TROSKIE
THE GODS MUST BE CRAZY II   WEG/Columbia, 1990

DOUGLAS TRUMBULL
Business: Showscan Film Corporation, 3939 Landmark St.,
   Culver City, CA 90230, 310/558-0150
Business Manager: Larry Goldberg, Nagler & Schneider,
   9460 Wilshire Blvd., Suite 410, Beverly Hills, CA 90212,
   310/274-8201

BRAINSTORM   MGM/UA, 1983

PAUL TRYBITS
Business: Wicked Films & Television Ltd., 3-6 Winnett St.,
   London W1V 7HS, 071/494-0909; Fax: 071/287-5618

HARDWARE   Miramax, 1990, w/Joanne Sellar

SHINTARO TSUJI
THE MOUSE AND HIS CHILD (AF)   Sanrio, 1978,
   EP w/Warren Lockhart

JOEL TUBER
Contact: Directors Guild of America - New York,
   212/581-0370

SILKWOOD   20th Century Fox, 1983, AP
MAKING MR. RIGHT   Orion, 1987, w/Michael Wise
TOKYO POP   Spectrafilm, 1988, w/Kaz Kuzui

HELEN SARLUI-TUCKER
(see Helen SARLUI-Tucker)

LARRY TUCKER
Contact: Writers Guild of America - Los Angeles,
   310/550-1000

I LOVE YOU, ALICE B. TOKLAS   Warner Bros., 1968,
   EP w/Paul Mazursky
BOB & CAROL & TED & ALICE   Columbia, 1969
ALEX IN WONDERLAND   MGM, 1970

MELVILLE TUCKER
THE LOST MAN   Universal, 1969, w/Edward Muhl
A WARM DECEMBER   National General, 1973
UPTOWN SATURDAY NIGHT   Warner Bros., 1974
LET'S DO IT AGAIN   Warner Bros., 1975
A PIECE OF THE ACTION   Warner Bros., 1977
STIR CRAZY   Columbia, 1980, EP
HANKY PANKY   Columbia, 1982, EP
FAST FORWARD   Columbia, 1985, EP

MARTIN TUDOR
HIDING OUT   DEG, 1987, EP

CHRIS TUFTY
BLOODY BIRTHDAY   Judica Productions, 1986, EP

JENNIE LEW TUGEND
(formerly Jennie Lew)

LETHAL WEAPON   Warner Bros., 1987, AP
SCROOGED   Paramount, 1988, AP
LETHAL WEAPON 2   Warner Bros., 1989,
   CP w/Steve Perry

HARRIS E. TULCHIN
TO SLEEP WITH ANGER   Samuel Goldwyn Company,
   1990, EP w/Danny Glover & Edward R. Pressman

JOHN TURMAN
Business: The Turman-Foster Company, 3400 Riverside Dr.,
   11th Floor, Burbank, CA 91505, 818/972-7774

FULL MOON IN BLUE WATER   Trans World, 1988,
   w/David Foster & Lawrence Turman

LAWRENCE TURMAN
(credit w/David Foster)
Business: The Turman-Foster Company, c/o Warner
   Hollywood Studios, 1041 N. Formosa, Formosa Bldg., Los
   Angeles, CA 90046, 213/850-3151; Fax: 213/850-3181
Contact: Directors Guild of America - Los Angeles,
   213/289-2000

THE YOUNG DOCTORS   United Artists, 1961,
   w/Stuart Millar*
I COULD GO ON SINGING   United Artists, 1963,
   w/Stuart Millar*
THE BEST MAN   United Artists, 1964, w/Stuart Millar*
THE GRADUATE ★   Embassy, 1967*
THE FLIM-FLAM MAN   20th Century Fox, 1967*
PRETTY POISON   20th Century Fox, 1968, EP*
THE GREAT WHITE HOPE   20th Century Fox, 1970*
THE MARRIAGE OF A YOUNG STOCKBROKER   20th
   Century Fox, 1971*
THE NICKEL RIDE   20th Century Fox, 1974, EP
THE DROWNING POOL   Warner Bros., 1975
FIRST LOVE   Paramount, 1977
HEROES   Universal, 1977
WALK PROUD   Universal, 1979*
TRIBUTE   20th Century Fox, 1980, EP w/Richard S. Bright
CAVEMAN   United Artists, 1981
THE THING   Universal, 1982
SECOND THOUGHTS   Universal, 1983
MASS APPEAL   Universal, 1984
THE MEAN SEASON   Orion, 1985
SHORT CIRCUIT   TriStar, 1986
RUNNING SCARED   MGM/UA, 1986
FULL MOON IN BLUE WATER   Trans World Entertainment,
   1988, w/John Turman
SHORT CIRCUIT II   TriStar, 1988, w/Gary Foster
GLEAMING THE CUBE   20th Century Fox, 1989

RANDOLF TURROW
THE DARK BACKWARD   RCA/Columbia, 1991,
   EP w/William Talmadge

JON TURTLE
A NIGHTMARE ON ELM STREET 5: THE DREAM CHILD
   New Line, 1989, EP w/Sara Risher
I COME IN PEACE   Triumph, 1990, CP w/Rafael Eisenman

NORMAN TWAIN
LEAN ON ME   Warner Bros., 1989

THOM TYSON
Business: Knight-Tyson Prods., 127 Broadway, Suite 220, Santa
   Monica, CA 90401, 310/395-7100; Fax: 310/395-7099
Contact: Directors Guild of America - Los Angeles,
   213/289-2000

STRIPPER   20th Century Fox, 1986, CP w/Michael Nolin
THE WIZARD OF LONELINESS   Skouras Pictures, 1988,
   w/Philip Porcella

U

TOM UDELL
JOURNEY TO THE CENTER OF THE EARTH   Cannon, 1989, EP w/Adam Fields & Avi Lerner

HIDENORI UEKI
IRON MAZE   Trans-Tokyo, 1991, w/Ilona Herzberg

HARRY UFLAND
Business: Ufland Productions, 10000 W. Washington Blvd., Suite 3022, Culver City, CA 90232, 310/280-6499; Fax: 310/836-1680

MOVING VIOLATIONS   20th Century Fox, 1985, w/Joe Roth
STREETS OF GOLD   20th Century Fox, 1986, w/Joe Roth
OFF BEAT   Buena Vista, 1986, w/Joe Roth
WHERE THE RIVER RUNS BLACK   MGM, 1986, w/Joe Roth
THE LAST TEMPTATION OF CHRIST   Universal, 1988, EP
NOT WITHOUT MY DAUGHTER MGM, 1991, w/Mary Jane Ufland

MARY JANE UFLAND
Business: Ufland Productions, 10000 W. Washington Blvd., Suite 3022, Culver City, CA 90232, 310/280-6499; Fax: 310/836-1680

NOT WITHOUT MY DAUGHTER MGM, 1991, w/Harry J. Ufland

STEVE UJLAKI
Contact: Writers Guild of America - Los Angeles, 310/550-1000

COURAGE MOUNTAIN   Triumph, 1990
THE HOT SPOT   Orion, 1990, EP w/Bill Gavin & Derek Power

MICHAEL ULICK
Business: UMP & Associates, Raleigh Studios, 5300 Melrose Ave., Suite 411-E, Hollywood, CA 90038, 213/960-4580
Contact: Directors Guild of America - New York, 212/581-0370

ROCKET GIBRALTAR   Columbia, 1988, EP w/Robert Fisher & Geoffrey Mayo

ANTHONY B. UNGER
Business: Unger Productions, Inc., 131 N. Bundy Dr., Los Angeles, CA 90049, 310/471-9624; Fax: 310/440-2219

THE DESPERATE ONES   AIP, 1968, AP
THE MADWOMAN OF CHAILLOT   Warner Bros., 1969, AP
THE MAGIC CHRISTIAN   Commonwealth, 1970, EP w/Henry Weinstein

JULIUS CAESAR   AIP, 1970, EP w/Henry Weinstein
THE BATTLE OF NERETVA   AIP, 1971, EP w/Steve Previn & Henry Weinstein
THE DEVIL'S WIDOW   AIP, 1971, EP w/Henry Weinstein
DON'T LOOK NOW   Paramount, 1973, EP
FORCE 10 FROM NAVARONE   Columbia, 1978, CP w/John Sloan
THE UNSEEN   World Northal, 1981
SILENT RAGE   Columbia, 1982

KURT UNGER
POPE JOAN   Columbia, 1972
PUPPET ON A CHAIN   Cinerama, 1972

OLIVER A. UNGER
THE BRIDES OF FU MANCHU   7 Arts, 1966, w/Harry Alan Towers
FORCE 10 FROM NAVARONE   Columbia, 1978

MICHAEL USLAN
(credit w/Benjamin Melniker)

SWAMP THING   Embassy, 1982
THE RETURN OF SWAMP THING   Miramax, 1989
BATMAN   Warner Bros., 1989, EP

KENNETH UTT
Contact: Directors Guild of America - New York, 212/581-0370

THE SUBJECT WAS ROSES   MGM, 1968, AP
MIDNIGHT COWBOY   United Artists, 1969, AP
THE BOYS IN THE BAND   National General, 1970, AP
THE PEOPLE NEXT DOOR   Avco Embassy, 1970, AP
THE FRENCH CONNECTION   20th Century Fox, 1971, AP
GODSPELL   Columbia, 1973, AP
THE SEVEN-UPS   20th Century Fox, 1973, EP w/Barry Weitz
ALL THAT JAZZ   20th Century Fox, 1979, AP w/Wolfgang Glattes
EYEWITNESS   20th Century Fox, 1981, AP
STILL OF THE NIGHT   MGM/UA, 1982, AP w/Wolfgang Glattes
STAR 80   The Ladd Company/Warner Bros., 1983, w/Wolfgang Glattes
HEAVEN HELP US   TriStar, 1985, AP
POWER   20th Century Fox, 1986, AP w/Wolfgang Glattes
SOMETHING WILD   Orion, 1987, w/Jonathan Demme
MARRIED TO THE MOB   Orion, 1988, w/Edward Saxon
MIAMI BLUES   Orion, 1990, CP w/Ron Bozman
THE SILENCE OF THE LAMBS   Orion, 1991, w/Ron Bozman & Edward Saxon
GLADIATOR   Columbia, 1992, EP

Va

FILM
PRODUCERS,
STUDIOS,
AGENTS AND
CASTING
DIRECTORS
GUIDE

F
I
L
M

P
R
O
D
U
C
E
R
S

V

CHRISTINE VACHON
Business: Apparatus, Inc., New York

POISON   Zeitgeist, 1991

HELENE VAGAR
SWEET MOVIE   Biograph, 1975, EP

STEVEN A. VAIL
SCAVENGER HUNT   20th Century Fox, 1979
JOKES MY FOLKS NEVER TOLD ME   New World,
   1979, w/Ted Woolery

ANDREW VAJNA
(credit w/Mario Kassar)
Business: Cinergi Productions, 2308 Broadway, Santa
   Monica, CA 90404, 310/315-6000; Fax: 310/828-0443

THE AMATEUR   20th Century Fox, 1981, EP
FIRST BLOOD   Orion, 1982
SUPERSTITION   Almi Pictures, 1985
RAMBO: FIRST BLOOD PART II   TriStar, 1985, EP
EXTREME PREJUDICE   TriStar, 1987, EP
ANGEL HEART   TriStar, 1987, EP
RAMBO III   TriStar, 1988
RED HEAT   TriStar, 1988, EP
DEEPSTAR SIX   TriStar, 1989, EP
JOHNNY HANDSOME   TriStar, 1989, EP
NARROW MARGIN   TriStar, 1990, EP
TOTAL RECALL   TriStar, 1990, EP
AIR AMERICA   TriStar, 1990, EP
JACOB'S LADDER   TriStar, 1990, EP
MOUNTAINS OF THE MOON   TriStar, 1990, EP
THE LAST DAYS OF EDEN   Buena Vista, 1991,
   w/Donna Dubrow & Tom Schulman*

DAVID VALDES
Business: Malpaso Productions, 4000 Warner Blvd.,
   Burbank, CA 91522, 818/954-2567
Agent: UTA - Beverly Hills, 310/273-6700

PALE RIDER   Warner Bros., 1985, AP
RATBOY   Warner Bros., 1986, AP
LIKE FATHER, LIKE SON   TriStar, 1987, w/Brian Grazer
GARDENS OF STONE   TriStar, 1987, EP w/Jay
   Emmett, Fred Roos & Stan Weston
BIRD   Warner Bros., 1988, EP
THE DEAD POOL   Warner Bros., 1988
PINK CADILLAC   Warner Bros., 1989
WHITE HUNTER, BLACK HEART   Warner Bros.,
   1990, EP
THE ROOKIE   Warner Bros., 1990, w/Howard
   Kazanjian & Steven Siebert

RENEE VALENTE
Business: 13601 Ventura Blvd., Suite 194, Sherman
   Oaks, CA 91423, 818/340-3305

LOVING COUPLES   20th Century Fox, 1980

DON Van ATTA
Agent: Broder/Kurland/Webb/Uffner - Los Angeles,
   213/656-9262
Contact: Directors Guild of America - Los Angeles,
   213/289-2000

PRAY FOR DEATH   American Distribution Group, 1986
CATCH THE HEAT   Trans World, 1987
RAGE OF HONOR   Trans World, 1987

WILLIAM VANDERKLOOT
Business: Double Helix Films, Inc., 303 W. 76th St., Suite B,
   New York, NY 10023, 212/769-0202

FUNLAND   Double Helix, 1987, w/Michael A. Simpson

HENDRICK J. Van Der KOLK
OUTRAGEOUS!   Cinema 5, 1977, w/William Marshall

NORMAN THADDEUS VANE
Business: Screen Writers Productions, 1411 N. Harper Ave.,
   Los Angeles, CA 90046, 213/656-9260
Contact: Writers Guild of America - Los Angeles,
   310/550-1000

LOLA   AIP, 1971, AP w/Ralph Serpe
CLUB LIFE   *KING OF THE CITY*   Troma, 1986
MIDNIGHT   SVS Films, 1989, w/Gloria J. Morrison

RICHARD VANE
THE BOY WHO COULD FLY   Lorimar, 1986, CP
HARRY & THE HENDERSONS   Universal, 1987,
   w/William Dear
TAP   TriStar, 1989, w/Gary Adelson
ALWAYS   Universal, 1989, CP
ARACHNOPHOBIA   Buena Vista, 1990,
   w/Kathleen Kennedy
DUTCH   20th Century Fox, 1991, w/John Hughes

GREGORY VANGER
HOTEL OKLAHOMA   1991, w/Terry Kahn & Ed Elbert

LAWRENCE VANGER
Business: Eagle Entertainment, Inc., 1554 S. Sepulveda
   Blvd., Suite 102, Los Angeles, CA 90025, 310/478-3355;
   Fax: 310/478-0576

BASIC TRAINING   Moviestore, 1985, EP w/Paul Klein
CERTAIN FURY   New World, 1985, EP
HOTEL OKLAHOMA   1991, EP w/Martin Barab

KELLY Van HORN
ALMOST AN ANGEL   Paramount, 1990, LP

CHAKO Van LEUWEN
PIRANHA   New World, 1978, CP
PIRANHA II: THE SPAWNING   Saturn International, 1983,
   w/Jeff Schechtman

MELVIN Van PEEBLES
SWEET SWEETBACK'S BAADASSSSS SONG
   Cinemation, 1971

TIM Van RELLIM
EAT THE RICH   New Line, 1987
THE DECEIVERS   Cinecom, 1988, CP

ED VANSTON
BENJI THE HUNTED   Buena Vista, 1987, EP

STERLING Van WAGENEN
THE TRIP TO BOUNTIFUL   Island Pictures, 1985,
   w/Horton Foote

MICHAEL VARHOL
Agent: ICM - Los Angeles, 310/550-4000
Contact: Directors Guild of America - Los Angeles,
   213/289-2000

BANJOMAN   Blue Pacific, 1975, w/Richard Gilbert
   Abramson & Robert French
THE BIG PICTURE   Columbia, 1989

CARLOS VASALLO
CRYSTAL HEART   New World, 1987
FISTFIGHTER   Taurus, 1989

RONALDO VASCONCELLOS
Business: M.L. International Pictures, 6413 Colgate
   Avenue, Los Angeles, CA 90048, 213/954-0932;
   Fax: 213/954-0933

THE LAIR OF THE WHITE WORM   Vestron, 1988, LP
THE RAINBOW   Vestron, 1989, LP
WHORE   Trimark, 1991, w/Dan Ireland

BEN VAUGHN
FOR THE LOVE OF BENJI   Mulberry Square, 1977
BENJI THE HUNTED   Buena Vista, 1987

FRANCIS VEBER
Agent: CAA - Beverly Hills, 310/288-4545
Contact: Directors Guild of America - Los Angeles,
   213/289-2000

PARTNERS   Paramount, 1982, EP
THREE FUGITIVES   Buena Vista, 1989, EP

JOSEPH S. VECCHIO
Contact: Joseph S. Vecchio Productions, 3565 Beverly
   Glen Terrace, Sherman Oaks, CA 91423,
   310/859-0999; Fax: 818/788-9900

OSCAR   Buena Vista, 1991, EP w/Alex Ponti

JOHN VEITCH
Business: TriStar Pictures, 1875 Century Park East,
   Los Angeles, CA 90067, 310/282-0870

FAST FORWARD   Columbia, 1985
SUSPECT   TriStar, 1987, EP

ROBERT VELAISE
THE GO-BETWEEN   Columbia, 1971, EP

STEPHEN F. VERONA
Agent: David Shapira & Associates - Sherman Oaks,
   818/906-0322
Contact: Directors Guild of America - Los Angeles,
   213/289-2000

THE LORDS OF FLATBUSH   Columbia, 1974
PIPE DREAMS   Avco Embassy, 1976

BERYL VERTUE
Contact: Hartswood Films, Shepperton Studios, Studios
   Road, Shepperton, Middlesex TW17 0QD, 0932/562-611;
   Fax: 0932/568-989

TOMMY   Columbia, 1975, EP w/Christopher Stamp
SPARKLE   Warner Bros., 1976, EP w/Peter Brown

MARK VICTOR
(credit w/Michael Grais)
Agent: APA - Los Angeles, 310/273-0744
Contact: Writers Guild of America - Los Angeles,
   310/550-1000

POLTERGEIST II: THE OTHER SIDE   MGM, 1986
GREAT BALLS OF FIRE!   Orion, 1989, EP
MARKED FOR DEATH   20th Century Fox, 1990,
   w/Steven Seagal

JOSE VICUNA
OPEN SEASON   Columbia, 1974
RUSTLER'S RHAPSODY   Paramount, 1985, EP

JOHN VIDETTE
BLACKOUT   New World, 1978, EP w/Andre Link &
   Ivan Reitman

DIMITRI VILLARD
(credit w/Robby Wald)
Business: Dimitri Villard Productions, 8721 Santa Monica
   Blvd., Suite 100, Los Angeles, CA 90069, 310/854-4442;
   Fax: 310/854-6044

TIME WALKER   New World, 1982, w/Jason Williams*
ONCE BITTEN   Samuel Goldwyn Company, 1985,
   w/Frank E. Hildebrand
FLIGHT OF THE NAVIGATOR   Buena Vista, 1986
DEATH OF AN ANGEL   20th Century Fox, 1986,
   EP w/Charles J. Weber
PURGATORY   New Star Entertainment, 1989, EP
EASY WHEELS   Fries Entertainment, 1989

ROBERT VINCE
MILLENNIUM   20th Century Fox, 1989, CP

LUCIANO VINCENZONI
ORCA   Paramount, 1977

JESSE VINT
BLACK OAK CONSPIRACY   New World, 1977,
   w/Tom Clark
HOMETOWN U.S.A.   Film Ventures International, 1979,
   w/Roger Camras

WILL VINTON
Business: Will Vinton Productions, Inc., 1400 NW 22nd St.,
   Portland, OR 97210, 503/225-1130

THE ADVENTURES OF MARK TWAIN (AF)
   Atlantic, 1986
SHADOW PLAY   New World, 1986, w/Dan Biggs &
   Susan Shadburne
WILL VINTON'S FESTIVAL OF CLAYMATION (AF)
   Expanded Entertainment, 1987

Vi

FILM
PRODUCERS,
STUDIOS,
AGENTS AND
CASTING
DIRECTORS
GUIDE

F
I
L
M

P
R
O
D
U
C
E
R
S

Vi

FILM
PRODUCERS,
STUDIOS,
AGENTS AND
CASTING
DIRECTORS
GUIDE

F
I
L
M

P
R
O
D
U
C
E
R
S

JOE VIOLA

Contact: Directors Guild of America - Los Angeles,
213/289-2000

ANGELS HARD AS THEY COME   New World, 1972,
w/Jonathan Demme

MARCUS VISCIDI

Contact: Directors Guild of America - New York,
212/581-0370

ROCKET GIBRALTAR   Columbia, 1988, CP
SIGNS OF LIFE   Avenue, 1989,
w/Andrew Reichsman

FRANK VITALE

THE BATTLE OF LOVE'S RETURN   Standard, 1971,
w/Lloyd Kaufman
CRY UNCLE   Cambist, 1971, AP

RUTH VITALE

Business: UBU Productions, 5555 Melrose Ave.,
Los Angeles, CA 90038, 213/956-8625

THE BEAT   Vestron, 1988, EP w/Lawrence Kasanoff
CALL ME   Vestron, 1988, EP w/Mitchell Cannold &
Steven Reuther
AND GOD CREATED WOMAN   Vestron, 1988,
EP w/Mitchell Cannold & Steven Reuther

DAVID E. VOGEL

Contact: Walt Disney Studios, 500 S. Buena Vista St.,
Burbank, CA 91521, 818/560-5151

THREE O'CLOCK HIGH   Universal, 1987

SUSAN VOGELFANG

BIG MAN ON CAMPUS   Vestron, 1989, LP
ENID IS SLEEPING   Vestron, 1990, LP

RAY VOLPE

POUND PUPPIES & THE LEGEND OF BIG PAW (AF)
TriStar, 1988, EP w/Edd Griles

ANTON VON KASSEL

THE JERUSALEM FILE   MGM, 1972

ALESSANDRO VON NORMANN

THE PASSENGER   United Artists, 1975, EP

ROBERT D. WACHS

Business: Robert D. Wachs Company, 345 N. Maple Dr.,
Suite 179, Beverly Hills, CA 90212, 310/276-1123;
Fax: 310/276-5572
Contact: Writers Guild of America - Los Angeles,
310/550-1000

THE GOLDEN CHILD   Paramount, 1986,
w/Edward S. Feldman
BEVERLY HILLS COP II   Paramount, 1987,
EP w/Richard Tienken
EDDIE MURPHY RAW   Paramount, 1987,
w/Keenen Ivory Wayans
COMING TO AMERICA   Paramount, 1988,
w/George Folsey Jr.
HARLEM NIGHTS   Paramount, 1989, w/Mark Lipsky

NAT WACHSBERGER
(credit w/Patrick Wachsberger)

KILLER FORCE   AIP, 1975
STARCRASH   New World, 1979

PATRICK WACHSBERGER

Business: Odyssey, 6500 Wilshire Blvd., Suite 400, Los
Angeles, CA 90048, 213/655-9335; Fax: 213/655-1928

KILLER FORCE   AIP, 1975, w/Nat Wachsberger
STARCRASH   New World, 1979, w/Nat Wachsberger
PLAYING FOR KEEPS   Universal, 1986, EP w/Julia Palau
& Michael Ryan
Q & A   TriStar, 1990, EP

JONATHAN WACKS

Agent: UTA - Beverly Hills, 310/273-6700

REPO MAN   Universal, 1984, w/Peter McCarthy

PHILIP WADDILOVE

THE BUTTERCUP CHAIN   Columbia, 1971,
w/John Whitney

JANE WAGNER

Agent: ICM - Los Angeles, 310/550-4000
Contact: Writers Guild of America - Los Angeles,
310/550-1000

THE INCREDIBLE SHRINKING WOMAN   Universal,
1981, EP
THE SEARCH FOR SIGNS OF INTELLIGENT LIFE IN THE
UNIVERSE (FD)   Orion Classics, 1991, EP w/Lily Tomlin

RAYMOND WAGNER

PETULIA   Warner Bros./7 Arts, 1968
LOVING   Columbia, 1970, EP
CODE OF SILENCE   Orion, 1985
HERO AND THE TERROR   Cannon, 1988
RENT-A-COP   Kings Road, 1988
TURNER & HOOCH   Buena Vista, 1989
RUN   Buena Vista, 1991

RICHARD WAGNER
(credit w/Joanna Lancaster)

LITTLE TREASURE   TriStar, 1985, EP
RUTHLESS PEOPLE   Buena Vista, 1986,
   EP w/Walter Yetnikoff

STAN WAKEFIELD
Business: Double Helix Films, Inc., 275 Seventh Ave.,
   Suite 2003, New York, NY 10001, 212/727-2000

FUNLAND   Double Helix, 1987, EP w/Jerry Silva &
   Kirk Smith
FAST FOOD   Fries Entertainment, 1989,
   w/Michael A. Simpson
ELLIOT FAUMAN, PH.D.   Taurus, 1990,
   EP w/Jerry Silva

GILLIAN RICHARDSON WALAS
THE VAGRANT   MGM, 1991

ROBBY WALD
(credit w/Dimitri Villard)
Business: Dimitri Villard Productions, 8721 Santa Monica
   Blvd., Suite 100, Los Angeles, CA 90069, 310/854-4442;
   Fax: 310/854-6044

ONCE BITTEN   Samuel Goldwyn Company, 1985,
   w/Frank E. Hildebrand
FLIGHT OF THE NAVIGATOR   Buena Vista, 1986
DEATH OF AN ANGEL   20th Century Fox, 1986,
   EP w/Charles J. Weber
PURGATORY   New Star Entertainment, 1989, EP
EASY WHEELS   Fries Entertainment, 1989

RUTH WALDBURGER
CANDY MOUNTAIN   International Film Exchange, 1988

KEN WALES
Business: Ken Wales Productions, 856 Yale St., Santa
   Monica, CA 90403, 310/828-0405
Contact: Directors Guild of America - Los Angeles,
   213/289-2000

THE PARTY   United Artists, 1967, AP
WATERHOLE #3   Paramount, 1968, AP
PETER GUNN   Paramount, 1968, AP
DARLING LILI   Paramount, 1970, AP
WILD ROVERS   MGM, 1971, w/Blake Edwards
THE TAMARIND SEED   Avco Embassy, 1974
ISLANDS IN THE STREAM   Paramount, 1977, AP
REVENGE OF THE PINK PANTHER   MGM/UA,
   1978, AP
THE PRODIGAL   World Wide Pictures, 1984
DOOR TO DOOR   Castle Hill Productions, 1984

GEORGE WALKER
AMERICAN GOTHIC   Vidmark Entertainment, 1988,
   EP w/Ray Homer & Michael Manley

GEORGE A. WALKER
ALL DOGS GO TO HEAVEN (AF)   Universal, 1989,
   EP w/Morris F. Sullivan

WILLIAM WALKER
MUSTANG: THE HOUSE THAT JOE BUILT (FD)   RG
   Productions, 1978, EP

GARY WALKOW
Agent: The Chasin Agency - Beverly Hills, 310/278-7505
Attorney: Frank Gruber - Los Angeles, 310/274-5638

THE TROUBLE WITH DICK   Fever Dream, 1989,
   w/Bob Augur

JOSEPHINE WALLACE
BAIL JUMPER   Angelika Films, 1990, EP

TREVOR WALLACE
THE GROUNDSTAR CONSPIRACY   Universal, 1972

KEITH WALLEY
BRIDE OF RE-ANIMATOR   50th St. Films, 1991,
   EP w/Hidetaka Konno & Paul White

JOSEPH WALSH
Contact: Writers Guild of America - Los Angeles,
   310/550-1000

CALIFORNIA SPLIT   Columbia, 1974, w/Robert Altman

MARTIN WALTERS
NIGHTSTICK   Production Distribution Company, 1987
BLUE MONKEY   Spectrafilm, 1987
PRETTYKILL   Spectrafilm, 1987, w/John R. Bowey

KENT WALWIN
Business: Centre Entertainment PLC, 118 Cleveland
   Street, London W1P 5DN England, 071/387-4045;
   Fax: 071/388-0408

A HANDFUL OF DUST   New Line, 1988,
   EP w/Jeffrey Taylor

IRENE WALZER
TO BE OR NOT TO BE   20th Century Fox, 1983, AP
SOLARBABIES   MGM/UA, 1986, w/Jack Frost Sanders

WAYNE WANG
Business: C.I.M. Productions, 665 Bush St., San Francisco,
   CA 94108, 415/433-2342
Agent: William Morris Agency - Beverly Hills,
   310/274-7451

CHAN IS MISSING   New Yorker, 1982
DIM SUM: A LITTLE BIT OF HEART   Orion Classics,
   1985, w/Tom Sternberg & Danny Yung
LIFE IS CHEAP...BUT TOILET PAPER IS EXPENSIVE
   Silverlight, 1990, EP w/John K. Chan

GEOFFREY WANSELL
WHEN THE WHALES CAME   20th Century Fox,
   1989, EP

FRED WARD
Agent: STE Representation, Ltd. - Beverly Hills,
   310/550-3982

MIAMI BLUES   Orion, 1990, EP w/Edward Saxon

DAVID W. WARFIELD
KILL ME AGAIN   MGM/UA, 1989, w/Steven Golin &
   Sigurjon Sighvatsson

Wa

FILM
PRODUCERS,
STUDIOS,
AGENTS AND
CASTING
DIRECTORS
GUIDE

F I L M   P R O D U C E R S

FILM
PRODUCERS,
STUDIOS,
AGENTS AND
CASTING
DIRECTORS GUIDE

F
I
L
M

P
R
O
D
U
C
E
R
S

ROB WARR
Business: Vivid Productions, 1st Floor, Centro House,
23 Mandela Street, London NW1 0DY England,
071/388-4559; Fax: 071/388-7489

LET HIM HAVE IT   1992

DERYN WARREN
BLACK MAGIC WOMAN   Trimark, 1991, w/Marc Springer

WATSON WARRINER
Business: Continental Film Group, Ltd., 321 W. 44th St.,
Suite 405, New York, NY 10036, 212/265-2530;
Fax: 212/245-6275 or Park St., Sharon, PA 16146,
412/981-3456; Fax: 412/981-2668

TIGER WARSAW   Sony Pictures, 1988, EP w/Navin
Desai & Gay Mayer

DORI B. WASSERMAN
LITTLE MONSTERS   United Artists, 1989,
EP w/Mitchell Cannold

JOHN WATERS
Agent: InterTalent Agency - Los Angeles, 310/858-6200

MONDO TRASHO   Filmmakers, 1970
PINK FLAMINGOS   Saliva Films, 1974
FEMALE TROUBLE   New Line, 1975
DESPERATE LIVING   New Line, 1977
POLYESTER   New Line, 1981
HAIRSPRAY   New Line, 1988, CP w/Stanley F. Buchthal

CHARLES WATERSTREET
HOWLING III: THE MARSUPIALS   Square Pictures,
1987, w/Philippe Mora

GREG WATKINS
A LITTLE STIFF   1991, w/Caveh Zahedi

JOHN WATSON
(credit w/Pen Densham)
Business: Trilogy Entertainment Group, c/o Sony Studios,
10202 West Washington Blvd., Culver City, CA 90232,
310/204-3133; Fax: 310/204-1160
Agent: William Morris Agency - Beverly Hills, 310/274-7451

THE ZOO GANG   New World, 1985
THE KISS   TriStar, 1988
BACKDRAFT   Universal, 1991, w/Richard B. Lewis
ROBIN HOOD: PRINCE OF THIEVES   Warner Bros.,
1991, w/Richard B. Lewis

MIKE WATTS
Business: Virgin Vision Ltd., 328 Kensal Rd., London
W10 5XJ, England, 081/968-8888; Fax: 081/968-8537

ARIA   Miramax, 1988, CP w/Al Clark & Robert Devereux

ROBERT WATTS
Agent: Duncan Heath Associates, Paramount House,
162/170 Wardour St., London W1V 4AB, England

THE EMPIRE STRIKES BACK   20th Century Fox, 1980,
AP w/Jim Bloom
RAIDERS OF THE LOST ARK ★   Paramount, 1981, AP
RETURN OF THE JEDI   20th Century Fox, 1983,
CP w/Jim Bloom

INDIANA JONES AND THE TEMPLE OF DOOM
Paramount, 1984
WHO FRAMED ROGER RABBIT   Buena Vista, 1988,
w/Frank Marshall
INDIANA JONES AND THE LAST CRUSADE
Paramount, 1989

ROY WATTS
ANGEL   New World, 1984, w/Donald P. Borchers

KEENEN IVORY WAYANS
Business: Ivory Way Productions, c/o KTTV, 5746 Sunset
Blvd., Hollywood, CA 90028, 213/856-1190;
Fax: 213/462-7382
Agent: InterTalent Agency - Los Angeles, 310/858-6200

EDDIE MURPHY RAW   Paramount, 1987,
w/Robert D. Wachs

MICHAEL A. WAYNE
Business: Batjac Productions, Inc., 9570 Wilshire Blvd.,
Suite 400, Beverly Hills, CA 90212, 310/278-9870;
Fax: 310/272-7381

McLINTOCK!   United Artists, 1963
CAST A GIANT SHADOW   United Artists, 1966, CP
THE GREEN BERETS   Warner Bros., 1968
CHISUM   Warner Bros., 1970, EP
BIG JAKE   National General, 1971
CAHILL, UNITED STATES MARSHAL   Warner
Bros., 1973
THE TRAIN ROBBERS   Warner Bros., 1973
McQ   Warner Bros., 1974, EP
BRANNIGAN   United Artists, 1975, EP

MICHAEL WEARING
Business: British Broadcasting Corporation, Woodlands,
80 Wood Lane, London W12 7RJ, 081/743-8000

BELLMAN AND TRUE   Island Pictures, 1987,
w/Christopher Neame

CASSIUS VERNON WEATHERSBY
D.C. CAB   Universal, 1983, CP

GORDON A. WEBB
Agent: Gray/Goodman, Inc. - Beverly Hills, 310/276-7070
Contact: Directors Guild of America - Los Angeles,
213/289-2000

TRAIN RIDE TO HOLLYWOOD   Taylor-Laughlin, 1975
BRUBAKER   20th Century Fox, 1980, AP
FLETCH   Universal, 1985, AP
WILDCATS   Warner Bros., 1986, AP
THE GOLDEN CHILD   Paramount, 1986, AP
THE COUCH TRIP   Orion, 1988, CP
GHOSTBUSTERS II   Columbia, 1989, AP w/Sheldon Kahn
KINDERGARTEN COP   Universal, 1990,
AP w/Sheldon Kahn

MONICA WEBB
Business: Westwind Productions, 1746 1/2 Westwood Blvd.,
Los Angeles, CA 90024, 310/470-6949;
Fax: 310/470-1832

PARTY LINE   SVS Films, 1988, CP

We

FILM
PRODUCERS,
STUDIOS,
AGENTS and
CASTING
DIRECTORS
GUIDE

F
I
L
M

P
R
O
D
U
C
E
R
S

WILLIAM WEBB
Business: Westwind Productions, 1746 1/2 Westwood
Blvd., Los Angeles, CA 90024, 310/470-6949;
Fax: 310/470-1832

PARTY LINE   SVS Films, 1988, w/Kurt Anderson &
Thomas S. Byrnes
MARTIAL LAW UNDERCOVER   Image, 1991

BRUCE WEBER
Business: Little Bear Films, 135 Watts St., New York, NY
10012, 212/226-0814; Fax: 212/334-5180
Contact: Directors Guild of America - New York,
212/581-0370

LET'S GET LOST (FD)   Zeitgeist, 1989

CHARLES J. WEBER
BODY ROCK   New World, 1984, EP w/Jon Feltheimer &
Phil Ramone
CHILDREN OF THE CORN   New World, 1984,
EP w/Earl Glick
DEATH OF AN ANGEL   20th Century Fox, 1986,
EP w/Dimitri Villard & Robby Wald

CHRISTOPHER WEBSTER
Contact: Fangoria Films, 475 Park Ave. South, New York,
NY 10016, 212/689-2830; Fax: 212/889-7933

HELLRAISER   New World, 1987, EP w/Mark
Armstrong & David Saunders
HELLBOUND: HELLRAISER II   New World, 1988,
EP w/Clive Barker
HEATHERS   New World, 1989, EP
MEET THE APPLEGATES   Triton, 1991,
EP w/Steve White

PAUL WEBSTER
Contact: Working Title Films, 1416 N. La Brea Ave.,
Hollywood, CA 90028, 213/856-2779;
Fax: 213/856-2615

THE TALL GUY   Miramax, 1990
DROP DEAD FRED   NEW LINE, 1991

NICK WECHSLER
Business: Addis-Wechsler & Associates, 955 S. Carillo Dr.,
Suite 300, Los Angeles, CA 90048, 213/954-9000;
Fax: 213/954-0990

THE BEAT   Vestron, 1988, w/Jon Kilik & Julia Phillips
sex, lies & videotape   Miramax, 1989, EP w/Morgan
Mason & Nancy Tenenbaum
DRUGSTORE COWBOY   Avenue, 1989,
w/Karen Murphy
THE RAPTURE   Fine Line, 1991, w/Nancy
Tenenbaum & Karen Koch
THE PLAYER   Avenue, 1991, w/David Brown &
Michael Tolkin

RICHARD WECHSLER
FIVE EASY PIECES ★   Columbia, 1970, w/Bob Rafelson
PLAIN CLOTHES   Paramount, 1988, w/Michael Manheim

DAVID WECHTER
Agent: William Morris Agency - Beverly Hills, 310/274-7451

MIDNIGHT MADNESS   Buena Vista, 1980,
CP w/MichaelNankin

JOAN WEIDMAN
CRACK HOUSE   Cannon, 1989, CP
THE GIANT OF THUNDER MOUNTAIN   Castle Hill, 1991,
LP w/Von Bernuth

HERMAN WEIGEL
Business: Neue Constantin Film, GmbH & Co Verleih KG,
Kaiserstraße 39, D-8000 München 40, West Germany,
38-60-90

LAST EXIT TO BROOKLYN   Cinecom, 1990, CP

CLAUDIA WEILL
Agent: William Morris Agency - Beverly Hills, 310/274-7451
Contact: Directors Guild of America - Los Angeles,
213/289-2000

GIRLFRIENDS   Warner Bros., 1978

ROBERT D. WEINBACH
THE MUTATIONS   Columbia, 1974

RICHARD C. WEINMAN
Contact: Directors Guild of America - Los Angeles,
213/289-2000

PUMPKINHEAD   United Artists, 1988, w/Howard Smith
SON OF DARKNESS: TO DIE FOR II   Trimark, 1991

BOB WEINSTEIN
(credit w/Harvey Weinstein)
Business: Miramax Films, 375 Greenwich St., New York, NY
10013, 212/941-3800; Fax: 212/941-3949

PLAYING FOR KEEPS   Universal, 1986, w/Alan Brewer
SCANDAL   Miramax, 1989, EP w/Joe Boyd & Nik Powell
STRIKE IT RICH   Milliimeter, 1990, EP
HARDWARE   Miramax, 1990, EP w/Nik Powell, Stephen
Woolley & Trix Worrell
A RAGE IN HARLEM   Miramax, 1991, EP w/Terry
Glinwood, William Horberg & Nik Powell

HARVEY WEINSTEIN
(credit w/Bob Weinstein)
Business: Miramax Films, 375 Greenwich St., New York, NY
10013, 212/941-3800; Fax: 212/941-3949
Contact: Directors Guild of America - New York,
212/581-0370

PLAYING FOR KEEPS   Universal, 1986, w/Alan Brewer
SCANDAL   Miramax, 1989, EP w/Joe Boyd & Nik Powell
STRIKE IT RICH   Milliimeter, 1990, EP
HARDWARE   Miramax, 1990, EP w/Nik Powell, Stephen
Woolley & Trix Worrell
A RAGE IN HARLEM   Miramax, 1991, EP w/Terry
Glinwood, William Horberg & Nik Powell

HENRY T. WEINSTEIN
Contact: The Howard Brandy Company, Inc., Los Angeles,
CA 90069, 213/657-8320; 75 Rockfeller Plaza,
Suite 1706, New York, NY 10019
Business: Cine-Source, 10 Universal City Plaza,
Suite 1950, Universal City, CA 91608, 818/509-7330;
Fax: 818/505-2856

CERVANTES   *THE YOUNG REBEL*   AIP, 1969, EP
THE MADWOMAN OF CHAILLOT   Warner Bros.,
1969, EP

THE MAGIC CHRISTIAN   Commonwealth United, 1970,
     EP w/Anthony Unger
JULIUS CAESAR   AIP, 1970, EP w/Anthony Unger
THE BATTLE OF NERETVA   AIP, 1971,
     EP w/Anthony Unger
THE DEVIL'S WIDOW   *TAM LIN*   AIP, 1972,
     EP w/Anthony Unger
A DELICATE BALANCE   American Film Theatre,
     1973, AP
THE ICEMAN COMETH   American Film Theatre,
     1973, AP
THE HOMECOMING   American Film Theatre, 1973, AP
BUTLEY   American Film Theatre, 1974, AP
LUTHER   American Film Theatre, 1974, AP
RHINOCEROS   American Film Theatre, 1974, AP
LOST IN THE STARS   American Film Theatre, 1974, AP
IN CELEBRATION   American Film Theatre, 1975, AP
GALILEO   American Film Theatre, 1975, AP
THE MAN IN THE GLASS BOOTH   American Film
     Theatre, 1975, AP
RUNAWAY TRAIN   Cannon, 1985, EP w/Robert A.
     Goldston & Robert Whitmore
52 PICK-UP   Cannon, 1986, EP
TEXASVILLE   Columbia, 1990, SP w/Robert Whitmore

LISA WEINSTEIN
GHOST ★   Paramount, 1990

PAULA WEINSTEIN
Business: Spring Creek Productions, 4000 Warner Blvd.,
     Producers Bldg. 7, Room 8, Burbank, CA 91522,
     818/954-1210; Fax: 818/954-2737

AMERICAN FLYERS   Warner Bros., 1985,
     w/Gareth Wigan
A DRY WHITE SEASON   MGM/UA, 1989
THE FABULOUS BAKER BOYS   20th Century Fox, 1989,
     w/Mark Rosenberg

FRED WEINTRAUB
(credit w/Paul Heller)
Business: Fred Weintraub Productions, 1900 Avenue of
     the Stars, Suite 1500, Los Angeles, CA 90067,
     310/788-9380; Fax: 310/788-0476

RAGE   Warner Bros., 1972*
ENTER THE DRAGON   Warner Bros., 1973
BLACK BELT JONES   Warner Bros., 1974
INVASION OF THE BEE GIRLS   Centaur, 1974*
TRUCK TURNER   AIP, 1974
GOLDEN NEEDLES   AIP, 1974
THE ULTIMATE WARRIOR   Warner Bros., 1976
DIRTY KNIGHTS' WORK   Gamma III, 1976
IT'S SHOWTIME (FD)   United Artists, 1976
HOT POTATO   Warner Bros., 1976
OUTLAW BLUES   Warner Bros., 1977, EP
THE PACK   Warner Bros., 1978
CHECKERED FLAG OR CRASH   Universal, 1978
THE PROMISE   Universal, 1979
TOM HORN   Warner Bros., 1980, EP*
FORCE: FIVE   American Cinema, 1981*
HIGH ROAD TO CHINA   Warner Bros., 1983*
GYMKATA   MGM/UA, 1985*
OUT OF CONTROL   New World, 1985,
     w/Daniel Grodnik*
THE WOMEN'S CLUB   Lightning, 1987*
THE PRINCESS ACADEMY   Empire, 1987, EP*
A SHOW OF FORCE   Paramount, 1990, CP*

JERRY WEINTRAUB
Business: 4000 Warner Blvd., Bungalow 1, Burbank, CA
     91522, 818/954-2500; Fax: 818/954-1399

NASHVILLE ★   Paramount, 1975, EP w/Martin Starger
OH, GOD!   Warner Bros., 1977
9/30/55   Universal, 1978
CRUISING   United Artists, 1980
ALL NIGHT LONG   Universal, 1981,   w/Leonard Goldberg
DINER   MGM/UA, 1982
THE KARATE KID   Columbia, 1984
HAPPY NEW YEAR   Columbia, 1987
THE KARATE KID PART II   Columbia, 1986
THE KARATE KID PART III   Columbia, 1989

SANDRA WEINTRAUB ROLAND
(see Sandra Weintraub ROLAND)

PETER WEIR
Agent: CAA - Beverly Hills, 310/288-4545

GREEN CARD   Buena Vista, 1990

BOB WEIS
HEARTBREAKERS   Orion, 1985, w/Bobby Roth
THE RAGGEDY RAWNEY   Four Seasons
     Entertainment, 1989

GARY WEIS
Contact: Directors Guild of America - Los Angeles,
     213/289-2000

JIMI HENDRIX (FD)   Warner Bros., 1973, w/Joe Boyd &
     John Head

LEE D. WEISEL
LOOSE SHOES   *COMING ATTRACTIONS*
     National-American, 1979, EP w/Byron H. Lasky

DOUGLAS J. WEISER
Contact: Writers Guild of America - Los Angeles,
     310/550-1000

MIDNIGHT CROSSING   Vestron, 1988, CP

DAVID WEISMAN
CIAO! MANHATTAN   Maron, 1973, w/John Palmer
KISS OF THE SPIDER WOMAN ★   Island Alive, 1985
SPIKE OF BENSONHURST   FilmDallas, 1989,
     w/Nelson Lyon
NAKED TANGO   Scotia International, 1990

MATTHEW WEISMAN
(credit w/Joseph Loeb III)
Agent: CAA - Beverly Hills, 310/288-4545
Contact: Writers Guild of America - Los Angeles,
     310/550-1000

BURGLAR   Warner Bros., 1987, CP

BRUCE WEISS
Contact: True Fiction Pictures, 12 W. 27th Street, 10th Floor,
     New York, NY 10001, 212/684-4284; Fax: 212/686-6109

THE UNBELIEVABLE TRUTH   Miramax, 1990,
     w/Hal Hartley

We

FILM
PRODUCERS,
STUDIOS,
AGENTS AND
CASTING
DIRECTORS
GUIDE

F
I
L
M

P
R
O
D
U
C
E
R
S

JEFF WEISS
ROCKET GIBRALTAR   Columbia, 1988

ROBERT K. WEISS
Business: Universal Studios, Bldg. 157, Rm. 209,
   100 Universal City Plaza, Universal City, CA 91608,
   818/777-1281
Contact: Directors Guild of America - Los Angeles,
   213/289-2000

THE KENTUCKY FRIED MOVIE   UFD, 1977
THE BLUES BROTHERS   Universal, 1980
DOCTOR DETROIT   Universal, 1983
AMAZON WOMEN ON THE MOON   Universal, 1987
DRAGNET   Universal, 1987, w/David Permut
THE NAKED GUN: FROM THE FILES OF POLICE
   SQUAD   Paramount, 1988
CRAZY PEOPLE   Paramount, 1990, EP
NOTHING BUT TROUBLE   Warner Bros., 1991
THE NAKED GUN 2 1/2: THE SMELL OF FEAR
   Paramount, 1991

STANLEY A. WEISS
THE HIRED HAND   Universal, 1971, EP

BURT WEISSBOURD
HAUNTS   Intercontinental, 1977, w/Herb Freed
GHOST STORY   Universal, 1981
RAGGEDY MAN   Universal, 1981, w/William D. Wittliff

LAUREN WEISSMAN
Contact: Danika Productions, 14755 Ventura Blvd.,
   Suite 1802, Sherman Oaks, CA 91403, 818/995-8095;
   Fax: 818/995-3589

SWEET HEARTS DANCE   TriStar, 1988,
   EP w/Robert Greenwald & Gabrielle Mandelik
I LOVE YOU TO DEATH   TriStar, 1990,
   CP w/Patrick C. Wells

ROBERT M. WEITMAN
THE ANDERSON TAPES   Columbia, 1971
SHAMUS   Columbia, 1973

BARRY WEITZ
Contact: Barry Weitz Film, c/o Multimedia TV Productions,
   8439 Sunset Blvd., Suite 200, Los Angeles, CA 90069,
   213/656-9756; Fax: 213/656-1693

THE SEVEN-UPS   20th Century Fox, 1973,
   EP w/Kenneth Utt

HAROLD WELB
Business: I.R.S. World Media, 3939 Lankershim Blvd.,
   Universal City, CA 91604, 818/505-0555;
   Fax: 818/505-1318

LITTLE VEGAS   I.R.S., 1990, EP
BLOOD AND CONCRETE   I.R.S., 1991, EP w/Paul
   Colichman & Miles A. Copeland III
CITY OF HOPE   Samuel Goldwyn Company, 1991,
   EP w/John Sloss

BO WELCH
THE ACCIDENTAL TOURIST   Warner Bros., 1988, EP

JOHN WELLS
NICE GIRLS DON'T EXPLODE   New World, 1987,
   w/Douglas Curtis

PATRICK C. WELLS
Business: Patrick C. Wells Associates, Inc., 2415 Vado
   Drive, Los Angeles, CA 90046, 213/650-8544

THE PERSONALS   New World, 1982
SPACE RAGE   Vestron, 1985, AP
YOUNGBLOOD   MGM/UA, 1986, w/Peter Bart
I LOVE YOU TO DEATH   TriStar, 1990,
   CP w/Lauren Weissman
HONOR BOUND   MGM/UA, 1990, AP
THE CELLAR   Moviestore, 1990, w/Steven E. Burman &
   John Woodward

WIM WENDERS
WINGS OF DESIRE   Orion Classics, 1988,
   w/Anatole Dauman

GORDON WESCOURT
THE HOUSE THAT DRIPPED BLOOD   Cinerama, 1971,
   EP w/Paul Ellsworth

CHARLES WESSLER
COLD FEET   Cinecom, 1984

DONALD WEST
Business: Paul Maslansky Productions, 4000 Warner Blvd.,
   Burbank, CA 91522, 818/954-3811

POLICE ACADEMY 3: BACK IN TRAINING   Warner Bros.,
   1986, AP
POLICE ACADEMY 4: CITIZENS ON PATROL   Warner
   Bros., 1987, AP
POLICE ACADEMY 5: ASSIGNMENT MIAMI BEACH
   Warner Bros., 1988, CP
POLICE ACADEMY 6: CITY UNDER SIEGE   Warner Bros.,
   1989, CP
SKI PATROL   Triumph Releasing, 1990,
   w/Phillip B. Goldfine

HOWARD WEST
(credit w/George Shapiro)
Business: Shapiro/West, 151 El Camino Dr., Beverly Hills,
   CA 90210, 310/278-8896

THE LAST REMAKE OF BEAU GESTE   Universal,
   1977, EP
IN GOD WE TRUST   Universal, 1980
SUMMER SCHOOL   Paramount, 1987

JAY WESTON
Business: Jay Weston Productions, 10390 Wilshire Blvd.,
   Suite 403, Los Angeles, CA 90024, 310/278-2900;
   Fax: 310/285-0033

FOR LOVE OF IVY   Cinerama, 1968, w/Edgar J. Scherick
LADY SINGS THE BLUES   Paramount, 1972,
   w/James S. White
W.C. FIELDS & ME   Universal, 1976
NIGHT OF THE JUGGLER   Columbia, 1980
CHU CHU & THE PHILLY FLASH   20th Century
   Fox, 1981
BUDDY BUDDY   MGM/UA, 1981
UNDERGROUND ACES   Filmways, 1981
SIDEOUT   TriStar, 1990, EP

ROBERT R. WESTON
THE BETSY   Allied Artists, 1978

We

FILM
PRODUCERS,
STUDIOS,
AGENTS AND
CASTING
DIRECTORS
GUIDE

F
I
L
M

P
R
O
D
U
C
E
R
S

STAN WESTON
VISION QUEST   Warner Bros., 1985, EP w/Adam Fields
GARDENS OF STONE   TriStar, 1987, EP w/Jay Emmett,
   Fred Roos & David Valdes

HANS WETH
CHRISTIANE F.   New World, 1982, w/Bernd Eichinger

JAMES WHALEY
(credit w/Howard Malin)

SEBASTIAN   Discopat, 1977
JUBILEE   Cinegate, 1979

JIM WHEAT
(credit w/Ken Wheat)
Agent: The Gersh Agency - Beverly Hills, 310/274-6611
Contact: Writers Guild of America - Los Angeles,
   310/550-1000

SILENT SCREAM   American Cinema, 1979
AFTER MIDNIGHT   MGM/UA, 1989, w/Richard Arlook &
   Peter Greene

KEN WHEAT
(credit w/Jim Wheat)
Agent: The Gersh Agency - Beverly Hills, 310/274-6611
Contact: Writers Guild of America - Los Angeles,
   310/550-1000

SILENT SCREAM   American Cinema, 1979
AFTER MIDNIGHT   MGM/UA, 1989, w/Richard Arlook &
   Peter Greene

FOREST WHITAKER
Agent: InterTalent Agency, Inc. - Beverly Hills,
   310/858-6200

A RAGE IN HARLEM   Miramax, 1991,
   CP w/John Nicolella

JAMES S. WHITE
LADY SINGS THE BLUES   Paramount, 1972,
   w/Jay Weston

MICHAEL WHITE
Business: Michael White Productions, 13 Duke Street,
   London SW1Y 6DB England, 071/839-3971;
   Fax: 071/839-3836

THE ROCKY HORROR PICTURE SHOW   20th Century
   Fox, 1975
THE HOUND OF THE BASKERVILLES   Atlantic, 1979,
   EP w/Andrew Braunsberg
SHOCK TREATMENT   20th Century Fox, 1981,
   EP w/Lou Adler
URGH! A MUSIC WAR (FD)   Lorimar, 1982
STRANGERS KISS   Orion Classics, 1984, EP
WHITE MISCHIEF   Columbia, 1988, EP
THE DECEIVERS   Cinecom, 1988, EP
NUNS ON THE RUN   20th Century Fox, 1990

PAUL WHITE
Business: Wild Street Pictures, 6525 Sunset Blvd., 8th Floor,
   Hollywood, CA 90028, 213/466-1230; Fax: 213/466-0871

THE UNNAMEABLE   Vidmark Entertainment, 1988, EP
BRIDE OF RE-ANIMATOR   50th St. Films, 1991,
   EP w/Hidetaka Konno & Keith Walley

STEVE WHITE
Business: Steve White Productions, 7920 Sunset Blvd.,
   4th Floor, Los Angeles, CA 90046, 213/962-1923;
   Fax: 213/871-2963

MEET THE APPLEGATES   Triton, 1991,
   EP w/Christopher Webster

VICTORIA WHITE
STEEL MAGNOLIAS   TriStar, 1989, EP
SOAPDISH   Paramount, 1991, CP w/Joel Freeman

ROB WHITEHOUSE
(credit w/Lloyd Phillips)

WARLORDS OF THE 21ST CENTURY   *BATTLE TRUCK*
   New World, 1982
NATE & HAYES   Paramount, 1983

KAREN J. WHITFIELD
THE CALIFORNIA REICH (FD)   Intercontinental, 1976,
   EP w/Marshall C. Whitfield

MARSHALL C. WHITFIELD
THE CALIFORNIA REICH (FD)   Intercontinental, 1976,
   EP w/Karen J. Whitfield

ROBERT WHITMORE
Business: Cine-Source, 10 Universal City Plaza,
   Suite 1950, Universal City, CA 91608, 818/509-7330;
   Fax: 818/505-2856

RUNAWAY TRAIN   Cannon, 1985, EP w/Robert A.
   Goldston & Henry T. Weinstein
TEXASVILLE   Columbia, 1990, SP w/Henry T. Weinstein

JOHN WHITNEY
THE BUTTERCUP CHAIN   Columbia, 1971,
   w/Philip Waddilove

CHRISTIAN WHITTAKER
CALIFORNIA DREAMING   AIP, 1979

HOLLISTER WHITWORTH
CHAMPIONS FOREVER (FD)   Ion, 1989,
   EP w/Tom Bellagio

GARY WICHARD
STONE COLD   Columbia, 1991, EP w/Walter Doniger

DOUGLAS WICK
Business: Red Wagon Productions, Tri-Star, 10202 W.
   Washington Blvd., Suite 212, Culver City, CA 90232,
   310/280-4466; Fax: 310/280-1480

STARTING OVER   Paramount, 1979, AP
WORKING GIRL ★   20th Century Fox, 1988

JACK WIENER
OLD DRACULA   AIP, 1975
THE EAGLE HAS LANDED   Columbia, 1977,
   w/David Niven, Jr.
ESCAPE TO ATHENA   AFD, 1979, w/David Niven, Jr.
F/X   Orion, 1986, w/Dodi Fayed
F/X 2 — THE DEADLY ART OF ILLUSION   Orion, 1991,
   EP w/Dodi Fayed

Wi

FILM
PRODUCERS,
STUDIOS,
AGENTS AND
CASTING
DIRECTORS
GUIDE

F
I
L
M

P
R
O
D
U
C
E
R
S

JAN WIERINGA
POWWOW HIGHWAY   Warner Bros., 1989

SAM WIESENTHAL
THE KREMLIN LETTER   20th Century Fox, 1970,
w/Carter De Haven

GARETH WIGAN
Business: Columbia Pictures, 10202 W. Washington Blvd.,
Culver City, CA 90232, 310/280-8111

UNMAN, WITTERING AND ZIGO   Paramount, 1971
AMERICAN FLYERS   Warner Bros., 1985,
w/Paula Weinstein

DENIS WIGMAN
THE COOK, THE THIEF, HIS WIFE & HER LOVER
Miramax, 1990, CP w/Pascale Dauman &
Daniel Toscan duPlantier

LIONEL WIGRAM
Business: Alive Films, 8912 Burton Way, Beverly Hills, CA
90211, 310/247-7800; Fax: 310/247-7823

NEVER ON TUESDAY   Palisades Entertainment, 1987,
w/Brad Wyman
COOL BLUE   Cinema Corporation of America, 1990
WARM SUMMER RAIN   Trans World, 1990,
w/Cassian Elwes

DAN WIGUTOW
LAST EMBRACE   United Artists, 1979, w/Michael Taylor
THE PURSUIT OF D. B. COOPER   Universal, 1981,
w/Michael Taylor
HEAVEN HELP US   TriStar, 1985, w/Mark Carliner

MAGGIE WILDE
Contact: Gere Productions, 10202 W. Washington Blvd.,
Metro #2062, Culver City, CA 90232, 310/280-8410;
Fax: 310/280-1598

FINAL ANALYSIS   Warner Bros., 1991,
EP w/Richard Gere

BILLY WILDER
Agent: Paul Kohner, Inc. - Los Angeles, 310/550-1060
Contact: Directors Guild of America - Los Angeles,
213/289-2000

ACE IN THE HOLE   *THE BIG CARNIVAL*
Paramount, 1951
STALAG 17   Paramount, 1953
SABRINA   Paramount, 1954
THE SEVEN YEAR ITCH   20th Century Fox, 1955,
w/Charles K. Feldman
LOVE IN THE AFTERNOON   Allied Artists, 1957
SOME LIKE IT HOT   United Artists, 1959
THE APARTMENT ★★   United Artists, 1960
ONE, TWO, THREE   United Artists, 1961
IRMA LA DOUCE   United Artists, 1963
KISS ME, STUPID   United Artists, 1964
THE FORTUNE COOKIE   United Artists, 1966
THE PRIVATE LIFE OF SHERLOCK HOLMES   United
Artists, 1970
AVANTI!   United Artists, 1972
FEDORA   United Artists, 1979

GENE WILDER
Agent: CAA - Beverly Hills, 310/288-4545
Business: Pal-Mel Productions, 9350 Wilshire Blvd.,
Suite 316, Beverly Hills, CA 90212, 310/859-0497;
Fax: 310/859-7327
Contact: Directors Guild of America - Los Angeles,
213/289-2000

THE WORLD'S GREATEST LOVER   20th Century
Fox, 1977

MARTIN WILEY
DIVING IN   Skouras, 1990

THOMAS L. WILHITE
Business: Hyperion Entertainment, 837 Traction Ave.,
Suite 402, Los Angeles, CA 90013, 213/625-2921;
Fax: 213/687-4955

NUTCRACKER   Atlantic, 1986, w/Willard Carroll,
Donald Kushner & Peter Locke

SETH M. WILLENSON
JEZEBEL'S KISS   Shapiro Glickenhaus, 1990, EP
DELUSION   Cineville, 1991, EP w/Christoph Henkel

BERNARD WILLIAMS
Contact: Peter Grossman, 9665 Wilshire Blvd., Suite 900,
Beverly Hills, CA 90212, 310/858-7888

A CLOCKWORK ORANGE ★   Warner Bros., 1971, AP
LADY CAROLINE LAMB   United Artists, 1973, AP
BARRY LYNDON   Warner Bros., 1975, AP
THE LAST REMAKE OF BEAU GESTE   20th Century Fox,
1977, AP
THE BIG SLEEP   United Artists, 1978, AP
FLASH GORDON   Universal, 1980, EP
RAGTIME   Paramount, 1981, EP w/Michael Hausman
AMITYVILLE II: THE POSSESSION   Orion, 1982, EP
THE BOUNTY   Orion, 1984
MIRACLES   Orion, 1986
MANHUNTER   DEG, 1986, EP
WISDOM   20th Century Fox, 1986
WHO'S THAT GIRL   Warner Bros., 1987, w/Rosilyn Heller
DIRTY ROTTEN SCOUNDRELS   Orion, 1988
WAR PARTY   Hemdale, 1989, w/John Daly &
Derek Gibson
WHAT ABOUT BOB?   Buena Vista, 1991, CP

DWIGHT WILLIAMS
Contact: Directors Guild of America - New York,
212/581-0370

THE WHITE GIRL   Tony Brown Productions, 1990, LP

ELMO WILLIAMS
Contact: Directors Guild of America - Los Angeles,
213/289-2000

THE LONGEST DAY   20th Century Fox, 1962, AP
THE BLUE MAX   20th Century Fox, 1966, EP
TORA! TORA! TORA!   20th Century Fox, 1970
SIDEWINDER ONE   Avco Embassy, 1977
CARAVANS   Universal, 1978
SOGGY BOTTOM U.S.A.   Gaylord, 1982
MAN, WOMAN & CHILD   Paramount, 1983,
w/Elliott Kastner
ERNEST GOES TO CAMP   Buena Vista, 1987,
EP w/Martin Erlichman

JAN WILLIAMS
HERBIE GOES TO MONTE CARLO   Buena Vista, 1977, AP
THE CAT FROM OUTER SPACE   Buena Vista, 1978, AP
THE LAST FLIGHT OF NOAH'S ARK   Buena Vista, 1980, CP
CONDORMAN   Buena Vista, 1981

JASON WILLIAMS
TIME WALKER   New World, 1982, w/Dimitri Villard

LEON WILLIAMS
STAND ALONE   New World, 1985

STACY WILLIAMS
Contact: Directors Guild of America - Los Angeles, 213/289-2000

ERNEST GOES TO CAMP   Buena Vista, 1987
ERNEST SAVES CHRISTMAS   Buena Vista, 1988, w/Doug Claybourne
ERNEST GOES TO JAIL   Buena Vista, 1990

WAYNE S. WILLIAMS
Business: Wayne S. Williams Productions, c/o Davis Entertainment, 2121 Ave. of the Stars, Suite 2800, Los Angeles, CA 90067, 310/551-2258; Fax: 310/556-3760

TOY SOLDIERS   TriStar, 1991, w/Jack E. Freedman & Patricia Herskovic

FRED WILLIAMSON
BOSS NIGGER   Dimension, 1975, w/Jack Arnold
NO WAY BACK   Atlas, 1976
ADIOS AMIGO   Atlas, 1976
MEAN JOHNNY BARROWS   Atlas, 1976
MR. MEAN   Lone Star & Po'Boy, 1977

JEFF WILLIAMSON
NO WAY BACK   Atlas, 1976, EP

GEORGE WILLOUGHBY
OUTBACK   United Artists, 1972
BOARDWALK   ARC, 1979

DANIEL WILSON
THE HANDMAID'S TALE   Cinecom, 1989

JIM WILSON
Business: Tig Productions, 4000 Warner Blvd., Burbank, CA 91522, 818/954-4500; Fax: 818/954-4882
Agent: CAA - Beverly Hills, 310/288-4545

DANCES WITH WOLVES ★★   Orion, 1990, w/Kevin Costner

JOHN G. WILSON
Business: 818/501-0771
Contact: Directors Guild of America - Los Angeles, 213/289-2000

THE OUTLAW JOSEY WALES   Warner Bros., 1976, AP
JO JO DANCER, YOUR LIFE IS CALLING   Columbia, 1986, AP
ABOVE THE LAW   Warner Bros., 1988, CP
FRESH HORSES   WEG/Columbia, 1988, AP
SHE'S OUT OF CONTROL   WEG/Columbia, 1989, CP

LARRY WILSON
Agent: CAA - Beverly Hills, 310/288-4545
Contact: Writers Guild of America - Los Angeles, 310/550-1000

BEETLEJUICE   Warner Bros., 1988, w/Michael Bender & Richard Hashimoto

MICHAEL G. WILSON
Business: Warfield Productions, 10000 W. Washington Blvd., Culver City, CA 90232, 310/280-6565
Contact: Writers Guild of America - Los Angeles, 310/550-1000

MOONRAKER   United Artists, 1979, EP
FOR YOUR EYES ONLY   United Artists, 1981
OCTOPUSSY   MGM/UA, 1983, EP
A VIEW TO A KILL   MGM/UA, 1985, w/Albert R. Broccoli
THE LIVING DAYLIGHTS   MGM/UA, 1987, w/Albert R. Broccoli
LICENCE TO KILL   MGM/UA, 1989, w/Albert R. Broccoli

SANDY WILSON
Agent: Writers & Artists Agency - Los Angeles, 310/820-2240

MY AMERICAN COUSIN   Spectrafilm, 1986, CP

S. S. WILSON
Agent: Gorfaine/Schwartz/Roberts - Beverly Hills, 310/275-9384
Contact: Writers Guild of America - Los Angeles, 310/550-1000

TREMORS   Universal, 1990, w/Brent Maddock

WILLIAM P. WILSON
PIGEONS   *SIDELONG GLANCES OF A PIGEON KICKER*   MGM, 1970, EP

DAVID WIMBURY
Business: HandMade Films, Ltd., 26 Cadogan Square, London SW1X 0JP, England, 071/584-8345 or 7400 Beverly Blvd., #210, Los Angeles, CA 90036, 213/936-8050
Agent: ICM - Duncan Heath, 071/439-1471

BULLSHOT   Island Alive, 1985, AP
ABSOLUTE BEGINNERS   Orion, 1986, AP
WATER   Atlantic, 1986, CP
WITHNAIL AND I   Cineplex Odeon, 1987, CP
A HANDFUL OF DUST   New Line, 1988, AP
HOW TO GET AHEAD IN ADVERTISING   Warner Bros., 1989

SIMON WINCER
Agent: CAA - Beverly Hills, 310/288-4545
Contact: Directors Guild of America - Los Angeles, 213/289-2000

THE MAN FROM SNOWY RIVER   20th Century Fox, 1983, EP w/Michael Edgley

INGRID WINDISCH
JUDGMENT IN BERLIN   New Line, 1988, w/Joshua Sinclair
SINGING THE BLUES IN RED   Angelika, 1988, AP
WINGS OF DESIRE   Orion Classics, 1988, EP

JONATHAN WINFREY
Business: Concorde Films, 11600 San Vicente Blvd.,
    Los Angeles, CA 90049, 310/820-6733

THE UNBORN   Califilm, 1991, LP
DEAD SPACE   Califilm, 1991, AP

ALEX WINITSKY
(credit w/Arlene Sellers)
Business: Lantana Productions, 3000 Olympic Blvd.,
    Suite 1300, Santa Monica, CA 90404, 310/315-4777;
    Fax: 310/315-4778

THE SEVEN-PERCENT SOLUTION   Universal, 1976, EP
END OF THE GAME   20th Century Fox, 1976, EP*
CROSS OF IRON   Avco Embassy, 1977
SILVER BEARS   Columbia, 1978
BREAKTHROUGH   SERGEANT STEINER   Maverick
    Pictures International, 1978
HOUSE CALLS   Universal, 1978
THE LADY VANISHES   Rank, 1979,
    EP w/Michael Carreras
CUBA   United Artists, 1979
BLUE SKIES AGAIN   Warner Bros., 1983
SWING SHIFT   Warner Bros., 1984, EP
SCANDALOUS   Orion, 1984
IRRECONCILABLE DIFFERENCES   Warner Bros., 1984
BAD MEDICINE   20th Century Fox, 1985
STANLEY & IRIS   MGM, 1990

HENRY WINKLER
Business: Fair Dinkum Prods., 5555 Melrose Ave., Los
    Angeles, CA 90038, 213/956-5700; Fax: 213/956-8593
Agent: ICM - Los Angeles, 310/550-4000

THE SURE THING   Embassy, 1985, EP

IRWIN WINKLER
(credit w/Robert Chartoff)
Agent: CAA - Beverly Hills, 310/288-4545
Contact: Directors Guild of America - Los Angeles,
    213/289-2000

DOUBLE TROUBLE   MGM, 1967, w/Judd Bernard*
BLUE   Paramount, 1968, w/Judd Bernard*
THE SPLIT   MGM, 1968
THEY SHOOT HORSES, DON'T THEY?   Cinerama,
    1969, w/Sydney Pollack
LEO THE LAST   United Artists, 1970
THE STRAWBERRY STATEMENT   MGM, 1970
BELIEVE IN ME   MGM, 1971
THE GANG THAT COULDN'T SHOOT STRAIGHT
    MGM, 1971
THE MECHANIC   United Artists, 1972,
    w/Lewis John Carlino
THE NEW CENTURIONS   Columbia, 1972
THUMB TRIPPING   Avco Embassy, 1972
UP THE SANDBOX   National General, 1972
BUSTING   United Artists, 1974
S*P*Y*S   20th Century Fox, 1974
BREAKOUT   Columbia, 1975
THE GAMBLER   Paramount, 1974
PEEPER   20th Century Fox, 1976
NICKELODEON   Columbia, 1976
ROCKY ★★   United Artists, 1976
NEW YORK, NEW YORK   United Artists, 1977
VALENTINO   United Artists, 1977
COMES A HORSEMAN   United Artists, 1978, EP
UNCLE JOE SHANNON   United Artists, 1978

ROCKY II   United Artists, 1979
RAGING BULL ★   United Artists, 1980
TRUE CONFESSIONS   United Artists, 1981
ROCKY III   MGM/UA, 1982
AUTHOR! AUTHOR!   20th Century Fox, 1982*
THE RIGHT STUFF ★   The Ladd Company/Warner
    Bros., 1983
ROCKY IV   MGM/UA, 1985
REVOLUTION   Warner Bros., 1985*
ROUND MIDNIGHT   Warner Bros., 1986*
BETRAYED   MGM/UA, 1988*
MUSIC BOX   TriStar, 1989*
GOOD FELLAS ★   Warner Bros., 1990*
ROCKY V   MGM/UA, 1990

LEE B. WINKLER
ADIOS AMIGO   Atlas, 1976, EP
MEAN JOHNNY BARROWS   Atlas, 1976, EP

MICHAEL WINNER
Business: Scimitar Films, Ltd., 6-8 Sackville St., London
    W1X 1DD, 071/603-7272; Fax: 071/603-5606
Contact: Directors Guild of America - Los Angeles,
    213/289-2000

LAWMAN   United Artists, 1971
CHATO'S LAND   United Artists, 1972
THE NIGHTCOMERS   United Artists, 1972
THE STONE KILLER   Columbia, 1973
DEATH WISH   Paramount, 1974, CP
WON TON TON, THE DOG WHO SAVED HOLLYWOOD
    Paramount, 1976, w/David V. Picker & Arnold Schulman
THE SENTINEL   Universal, 1977, w/Jeffrey Konvitz
THE BIG SLEEP   United Artists, 1978, w/Elliott Kastner
FIREPOWER   AFD, 1979
SCREAM FOR HELP   Lorimar, 1984
DEATH WISH 3   Cannon, 1985, CP
A CHORUS OF DISAPPROVAL   South Gate
    Entertainment, 1989

RONALD WINSTON
KEY EXCHANGE   20th Century Fox, 1985, EP w/Peer J.
    Oppenheimer & Michael Pochna

RALPH WINTER
Business: Paramount Pictures, 5555 Melrose Ave., Los
    Angeles, CA 90038, 213/956-5797; Fax: 213/956-8642

STAR TREK IV: THE VOYAGE HOME   Paramount,
    1986, EP
STAR TREK V: THE FINAL FRONTIER   Paramount,
    1989, EP
FLIGHT OF THE INTRUDER   Paramount, 1991,
    EP w/Brian Frankish
STAR TREK VI: THE UNDISCOVERED COUNTRY
    Paramount, 1991, w/Steven-Charles Jaffe

DAVID WINTERS
Business: Action International Pictures, 10726 McCune Ave.,
    Los Angeles, CA 90034, 310/559-8805;
    Fax: 310/559-8849

FIREHEAD   Pyramid, 1991, EP w/Marc Winters
RAW NERVE   Pyramid, 1991, EP w/Marc Winters

LOREN WINTERS
(credit w/Paul Winters)

THE FREEWAY MANIAC   Cannon, 1988

Wi

FILM
PRODUCERS,
STUDIOS,
AGENTS AND
CASTING
DIRECTORS
GUIDE

F
I
L
M

P
R
O
D
U
C
E
R
S

Wi

FILM
PRODUCERS,
STUDIOS,
AGENTS AND
CASTING
DIRECTORS
GUIDE

F
I
L
M

P
R
O
D
U
C
E
R
S

MARC WINTERS
FIREHEAD   Pyramid, 1991, EP w/David Winters
RAW NERVE   Pyramid, 1991, EP w/David Winters

PAUL WINTERS
(credit w/Loren Winters)

THE FREEWAY MANIAC   Cannon, 1988

ANTHONY WISDOM
THE RETURN OF SUPERFLY   Triton, 1990, w/Sig Shore

MICHAEL WISE
NIGHTHAWKS   Universal, 1981, EP w/Franklin R. Levy
MAKING MR. RIGHT   Orion, 1987, w/Joel Tuber

ROBERT WISE
Business: Robert Wise Productions, 315 S. Beverly Dr.,
   Suite 214, Beverly Hills, CA 90212, 310/284-7932;
   Fax: 310/284-8127
Agent: Phil Gersh, The Gersh Agency - Beverly Hills,
   310/274-6611

ODDS AGAINST TOMORROW   United Artists, 1959
WEST SIDE STORY ★★   United Artists, 1961
THE HAUNTING   MGM, 1963
THE SOUND OF MUSIC ★★   20th Century Fox, 1965
THE SAND PEBBLES ★   20th Century Fox, 1966
THE ANDROMEDA STRAIN   Universal, 1971
TWO PEOPLE   Universal, 1973
WISDOM   20th Century Fox, 1986, EP

DAVID WISNIEVITZ
Contact: Directors Guild of America - Los Angeles,
   213/289-2000

THE BALLAD OF GREGORIO CORTEZ   Embassy,
   1983, AP
VALENTINO RETURNS   Skouras Pictures, 1989,
   w/Peter Hoffman
OLD GRINGO   Columbia, 1989, EP
GHOST DAD   Universal, 1989, AP

PAUL JUNGER WITT
(credit w/Tony Thomas)
Business: Witt-Thomas Productions, 846 N. Cahuenga
   Blvd., Los Angeles, CA 90038, 213/464-1333;
   Fax: 213/960-1837
Agent: CAA - Beverly Hills, 310/288-4545

FIRSTBORN   Paramount, 1984
DEAD POETS SOCIETY ★   Buena Vista, 1989,
   w/Steven Haft
FINAL ANALYSIS   Warner Bros., 1991, w/Charles Roven

DAVID G. WITTER
FOREPLAY   Cinema National, 1975, w/Benni Korzen

WILLIAM D. WITTLIFF
Business: 510 Baylor, Austin, TX 78703, 512/476-6821;
   Fax: 512/476-9393
Agent: ICM - Los Angeles, 310/550-4000

RAGGEDY MAN   Universal, 1981, w/Burt Weissbourd
BARBAROSA   Universal/AFD, 1982, CP
COUNTRY   Buena Vista, 1984, w/Jessica Lange
RED HEADED STRANGER   Alive Films, 1986,
   w/Willie Nelson

TED WITZER
SIX PACK   20th Century Fox, 1982,
   EP w/Edward S. Feldman

JOE WIZAN
Business: Wizan/Black Films, 11999 San Vicente Blvd.,
   Suite 450, Los Angeles, CA 90049, 310/472-6133;
   Fax: 310/471-9074

JUNIOR BONNER   Cinerama, 1972
JEREMIAH JOHNSON   Warner Bros., 1972
PRIME CUT   National General, 1972
THE LAST AMERICAN HERO   *HARD DRIVER*   20th
   Century Fox, 1973, EP
99 & 44/100 PERCENT DEAD   20th Century Fox, 1974
AUDREY ROSE   United Artists, 1977, w/Frank De Felitta
VOICES   United Artists, 1979
...AND JUSTICE FOR ALL   Columbia, 1979, EP
BEST FRIENDS   Warner Bros., 1982, EP
TWO OF A KIND   20th Century Fox, 1983,
   w/Roger M. Rothstein
UNFAITHFULLY YOURS   20th Century Fox, 1984,
   w/Marvin Worth
IRON EAGLE   TriStar, 1986, w/Ron Samuels
TOUGH GUYS   Buena Vista, 1986
SPELLBINDER   MGM/UA, 1988, w/Brian Russell
SPLIT DECISION   New Century/Vista, 1988
THE GUARDIAN   Universal, 1990
SHORT TIME   20th Century Fox, 1990,
   EP w/Mickey Borofsky
STOP OR MY MOTHER WILL SHOOT   Universal, 1992,
   EP w/Todd Black

STEVE WIZAN
REPOSSESSED   New Line, 1990

STAN WLODKOWSKY
Business: 24 W. 96th St., #2F, New York, NY 10025,
   212/749-1676

FEAR, ANXIETY & DEPRESSION   Samuel Goldwyn
   Company, 1989, w/Steve Golin & Sigurjon Sighvatsson
LONGTIME COMPANION   Samuel Goldwyn
   Company, 1990

DICK WOLF
Contact: Writers Guild of America - Los Angeles,
   310/550-1000

NO MAN'S LAND   Orion, 1987, w/Joseph Stern

GORDON WOLF
Business: Wolf Films, Inc., 100 Universal City Plaza,
   Bldg. 69, Universal City, CA 91608, 818/777-3131
Contact: Directors Guild of America - Los Angeles,
   213/289-2000

UFORIA   Universal, 1985
DUDES   New Century/Vista, 1987, LP

JOSEPH WOLF
Business: Ascot Entertainment Group, 9000 Sunset Blvd.,
   Suite 1010, Los Angeles, CA 90069, 310/273-9501

HIGH VELOCITY   First Asian, 1977, EP
ROLLER BOOGIE   United Artists, 1979, AP
HELL NIGHT   Aquarius, 1981, EP w/Chuck Russell
HALLOWEEN II   Universal, 1981, EP w/Irwin Yablans

HALLOWEEN III: SEASON OF THE WITCH   Universal,
   1982, EP w/Irwin Yablans
PARASITE   Embassy, 1982, EP w/Irwin Yablans
THE SEDUCTION   Avco Embassy, 1982, EP w/Frank
   Capra Jr. & Chuck Russell
A NIGHTMARE ON ELM STREET   New Line, 1984,
   EP w/Stanley Dudelson

MICHAEL B. WOLF
S.O.B.   Lorimar/Paramount, 1981, EP

RICHARD A. WOLF
SKATEBOARD   Universal, 1978, w/Harry N. Blum

JUDITH WOLINSKY
Business: International Rainbow Pictures, 9165 Sunset
   Blvd., Penthouse 300, Los Angeles, CA 90069,
   310/271-0202; Fax: 310/271-2753

ALWAYS   Samuel Goldwyn Company, 1985, AP
SOMEONE TO LOVE   International Rainbow/Castle Hill,
   1987, AP
NEW YEAR'S DAY   International Rainbow, 1989
EATING   International Rainbow, 1990

RON WOLOTZKY
IN A SHALLOW GRAVE   Skouras Pictures, 1988, LP

DAVID L. WOLPER
Business: David L. Wolper Productions, Inc., Warner Bros.,
   4000 Warner Blvd., Burbank, CA 91522, 818/954-1707;
   Fax: 818/954-4380

THE BRIDGE AT REMAGEN   United Artists, 1969
IF IT'S TUESDAY, THIS MUST BE BELGIUM   United
   Artists, 1969, EP
I LOVE MY WIFE   Universal, 1970, EP
WILLY WONKA AND THE CHOCOLATE FACTORY
   Paramount, 1971, w/Stan Margulies
THE HELLSTROM CHRONICLE   Cinema 5, 1971, EP
ONE IS A LONELY NUMBER   MGM, 1972, EP
KING, QUEEN, KNAVE   Avco Embassy, 1972,
   w/Lutz Hengst
VISIONS OF EIGHT (FD)   Cinema 5, 1973, EP
WATTSTAX (FD)   Columbia, 1973, EP w/Al Bell
THE MAN WHO SAW TOMORROW (FD)   Warner Bros.,
   1981, EP
THIS IS ELVIS (FD)   Warner Bros., 1981, EP
IMAGINE: JOHN LENNON (FD)   Warner Bros., 1988,
   w/Andrew Solt

WALTER WOOD
THE TODD KILLINGS   National General, 1971, EP

JAMES WOODS
Agent: CAA - Beverly Hills, 310/288-4545
Business: Breakheart Films, 100 Universal City Plaza,
   Bungalow 82, Universal City, CA 91608, 818/777-3414;
   Fax: 818/777-8226

COP   Atlantic, 1988, w/James B. Harris

JOHN WOODWARD
THE CELLAR   Moviestore, 1990, w/Patrick C. Wells &
   Steven E. Burman

TED WOOLERY
JOKES MY FOLKS NEVER TOLD ME   New World, 1979,
   w/Steven A. Vail

DENNIS WOOLF
Business: Dennis Woolf Productions, Silver House, 31-35
   Beak Street, London W1R 3LD England, 071/494-4060;
   Fax: 071/287-6366

RETURN TO WATERLOO   New Line, 1985

SIR JOHN WOOLF
Business: Romulus Films, Ltd., 214 The Chambers,
   Chelsea Harbour, London, SW10 0XF, 071/376-3791;
   Fax: 071/352-7457

ROOM AT THE TOP ★   Continental, 1959, w/James Woolf
THE L-SHAPED ROOM   Columbia, 1963,
   w/Richard Attenborough
LIFE AT THE TOP   Columbia, 1965
OLIVER! ★★   Columbia, 1968
THE DAY OF THE JACKAL   Universal, 1973
THE ODESSA FILE   Columbia, 1974

NIGEL WOOLL
Agent: Sandra Marsh Management - Beverly Hills,
   310/285-0303

THE DRESSER ★   Columbia, 1983, AP
ELENI   Warner Bros., 1985, AP
ISHTAR   Columbia, 1987, AP w/David L. MacLeod
WILLOW   MGM/UA, 1988
SHIPWRECKED   Buena Vista, 1991

STEPHEN WOOLLEY
Business: Palace Pictures, 16/17 Wardour Mews, London
   W1V 3FF England, 071/437-3248

THE COMPANY OF WOLVES   Cannon, 1985,
   w/Chris Brown
ABSOLUTE BEGINNERS   Orion, 1986, w/Chris Brown
MONA LISA   Island Pictures, 1986, w/Patrick Cassavetti
HIGH SPIRITS   TriStar, 1988, w/David Saunders
SCANDAL   Miramax, 1989
SHAG: THE MOVIE   Hemdale, 1989, w/Julia Chasman
HARDWARE   Miramax, 1990, EP w/Nik Powell, Bob
   Weinstein, Harvey Weinstein & Trix Worrell
A RAGE IN HARLEM   Miramax, 1991, w/Kerry Boyle
THE MIRACLE   Miramax, 1991, w/Redmond Morris

CHUCK WORKMAN
Business: Calliope Films, 195 S. Beverly Dr., Suite 414,
   Beverly Hills, CA 90212, 310/271-0964
Agent: APA - Los Angeles, 310/273-0744

THE MONEY   Coliseum, 1976
SUPERSTAR (FD)   Marilyn Lewis Entertainment Ltd., 1990

TRIX WORRELL
Business: Wicked Films & Television Ltd., 3-6 Winnett Street,
   London W1V 7HS, 071/494-0909; Fax: 071/287-5618
Agent: Tessa Sayle Agency, 11 Jubilee Place, London SW3
   3TE England, 071/823-3883; Fax: 071/823-3363

HARDWARE   Miramax, 1990, EP w/Nik Powell, Bob
   Weinstein, Harvey Weinstein & Stephen Woolley

HOWARD WORTH
Contact: Directors Guild of America - Los Angeles,
   213/289-2000

WILD ORCHID   Triumph Releasing, 1990, CP

Wo

FILM
PRODUCERS,
STUDIOS,
AGENTS AND
CASTING
DIRECTORS
GUIDE

F
I
L
M

P
R
O
D
U
C
E
R
S

Wo

FILM
PRODUCERS,
STUDIOS,
AGENTS AND
CASTING
DIRECTORS
GUIDE

F
I
L
M

P
R
O
D
U
C
E
R
S

MARVIN WORTH
Business: Paramount Pictures, 5555 Melrose Ave., Los
   Angeles, CA 90038, 213/956-5788; Fax: 213/956-2307

WHERE'S POPPA?   United Artists, 1970,
   w/Jerry Tokofsky
MALCOLM X (FD)   Warner Bros., 1972, w/Arnold Perl
LENNY ★   United Artists, 1974
FIRE SALE   20th Century Fox, 1977
THE ROSE   20th Century Fox, 1979, w/Aaron Russo
MAD MAGAZINE PRESENTS UP THE ACADEMY
   Warner Bros., 1980, w/Danton Rissner
SOUP FOR ONE   Warner Bros., 1982
UNFAITHFULLY YOURS   20th Century Fox, 1984,
   w/Joe Wizan
RHINESTONE   20th Century Fox, 1984, w/Howard Smith
FALLING IN LOVE   Paramount, 1984
PATTY HEARST   Atlantic, 1988
SEE NO EVIL, HEAR NO EVIL   TriStar, 1989
FLASHBACK   Paramount, 1990, w/David Loughery
MALCOLM X   Warner Bros., 1992

NICHOLAS WOWCHUCK
THE INCREDIBLE TWO-HEADED TRANSPLANT   AIP,
   1971, EP

DENNIS WRIGHT
(credit w/Kent C. Lovell)

DOGS IN SPACE   Skouras Pictures, 1987,
   EP w/Robert Le Tet*
BACKSTAGE   Hoyts, 1988, EP
GROUND ZERO   Avenue, 1988, EP w/John Kearney

ROBERT S. WUNSCH
Business: Richland/Wunsch/Hohman Agency, 9220 Sunset
   Blvd., Los Angeles, CA 90069, 310/278-1955

SLAP SHOT   Universal, 1977, w/Stephen J. Friedman
DEFIANCE   AIP, 1980, EP

CATHERINE WYLER
Business: 310/271-8681

MEMPHIS BELLE   Warner Bros., 1990, w/David Puttnam

BRAD WYMAN
Business: Palisades Pictures, 1875 Century Park East,
   3rd Floor, Los Angeles, CA 90067, 310/785-3100

WHITE OF THE EYE   Palisades Entertainment, 1987,
   w/Cassian Elwes
NEVER ON TUESDAY   Palisades Entertainment, 1987,
   w/Lionel Wigram
DISTURBED   Live Entertainment/Odyssey, 1990
THE DARK BACKWARD   RCA/Columbia, 1991,
   w/Cassian Elwes

FRANK YABLANS
SILVER STREAK   20th Century Fox, 1976,
   EP w/Martin Ransohoff
THE OTHER SIDE OF MIDNIGHT   20th Century
   Fox, 1977
THE FURY   20th Century Fox, 1978
NORTH DALLAS FORTY   Paramount, 1979
MOMMIE DEAREST   Paramount, 1981
MONSIGNOR   20th Century Fox, 1982,
   w/David Niven Jr.
THE STAR CHAMBER   20th Century Fox, 1983
KIDCO   20th Century Fox, 1984, w/David Niven Jr.
BUY AND CELL   Empire, 1989
LISA   MGM/UA, 1990

IRWIN YABLANS
THE EDUCATION OF SONNY CARSON
   Paramount, 1974
HALLOWEEN   Compass International, 1978, EP
ROLLER BOOGIE   United Artists, 1979, EP
FADE TO BLACK   American Cinema, 1980,
   EP w/Sylvio Tabet
HALLOWEEN II   Universal, 1981, EP w/Joseph Wolf
HELL NIGHT   Aquarius, 1981, w/Bruce Cohn Curtis
PARASITE   Embassy, 1982, EP w/Joseph Wolf
HALLOWEEN III: SEASON OF THE WITCH   Universal,
   1982, EP w/Joseph Wolf
THE SEDUCTION   Avco Embassy, 1982,
   w/Bruce Cohn Curtis
TANK   Universal, 1984
SCREAM FOR HELP   Lorimar, 1984, EP
PRISON   Empire, 1988
WHY ME?   Triumph, 1990, EP
MEN AT WORK   Triumph, 1990, EP w/Moshe Diamant

MATA YAMAMOTO
MISHIMA: A LIFE IN FOUR CHAPTERS   Warner
   Bros., 1985, w/Tom Luddy

GEORGE YANEFF
THE TRIP TO BOUNTIFUL   Island Pictures, 1985,
   EP w/Sam Grogg

MARIE YATES
FRANCES   Universal, 1982, CP

PETER YATES
Agent: CAA - Beverly Hills, 310/288-4545
Contact: Directors Guild of America - New York,
   212/581-0370

MOTHER, JUGS & SPEED   20th Century Fox, 1976,
   w/Tom Mankiewicz
BREAKING AWAY ★   20th Century Fox, 1979
EYEWITNESS   20th Century Fox, 1981
THE DRESSER ★   Columbia, 1983
THE HOUSE ON CARROLL STREET   Orion, 1988,
   w/Robert F. Colesberry
THE YEAR OF THE COMET   Columbia, 1991

WILLIAM ROBERT YATES
AMY   Buena Vista, 1981, EP

LINDA YELLEN
Agent: William Morris Agency - Beverly Hills,
   310/274-7451
Business: The Linda Yellen Company, c/o Aaron Spelling,
   5700 Wilshire Blvd., Suite 575, Los Angeles, CA 90036,
   213/965-5943; Fax: 213/965-5840
Contact: Directors Guild of America - New York,
   212/581-0370

LOOKING UP   Levitt-Pickman, 1977
EVERYBODY WINS   Orion, 1990,
   EP w/Terry Glinwood

BILL YELLIN
THE WORLD OF HANS CHRISTIAN ANDERSEN (AF)
   United Artists, 1971, EP w/Herb Gelbspan

LOREES YERBY
RICHARD   Billings Associates, 1972, w/Harry Hurwitz

RON YERXA
JACK THE BEAR   20th Century Fox, 1991, EP

WALTER YETNIKOFF
RUTHLESS PEOPLE   Buena Vista, 1986, EP w/JoAnna
   Lancaster & Richard Wagner

BUD YORKIN
Business: Bud Yorkin Productions, 132 South Rodeo Dr.,
   Suite 300, Beverly Hills, CA 90212, 310/274-8111;
   Fax: 310/274-4155
Agent: CAA - Beverly Hills, 310/288-4545

COME BLOW YOUR HORN   Paramount, 1963,
   w/Norman Lear
THE NIGHT THEY RAIDED MINSKY'S   United Artists,
   1968, EP
START THE REVOLUTION WITHOUT ME   Warner
   Bros., 1970
COLD TURKEY   United Artists, 1971, EP
THE THIEF WHO CAME TO DINNER   Warner
   Bros., 1973
DEAL OF THE CENTURY   Warner Bros., 1983
TWICE IN A LIFETIME   Bud Yorkin
   Company, 1985
LOVE HURTS   Vestron, 1990, w/Doro Bachrach

DIANA YOUNG
AARON LOVES ANGELA   Columbia, 1975, CP

ERIC TYNAN YOUNG
ONE CUP OF COFFEE   Miramax, 1991,
   w/Robin B. Armstrong

IRWIN YOUNG
Business: DuArt Film Laboratories, 245 W. 55th St.,
   New York, NY 10019, 212/757-4580

ALAMBRISTA!   Bobwin/Film Haus, 1979,
   w/Michael Hausman
GET ROLLIN'   EP w/Stan Plotnick

JEFF YOUNG
Contact: Directors Guild of America - Los Angeles,
   213/289-2000

SPLIT IMAGE   Orion, 1982, EP
COHEN & TATE   Hemdale, 1989,
   w/Lord Anthony Rufus Isaacs
I COME IN PEACE   Triumph, 1990

JOHN SACRET YOUNG
Agent: ICM - Los Angeles, 310/550-4000

ROMERO   Four Seasons Entertainment, 1989,
   EP w/Lawrence Mortorff

ROBERT M. YOUNG
(credit w/Michael Roemer)
Agent: APA - Los Angeles, 310/273-0744
Contact: Directors Guild of America - Los Angeles,
   213/289-2000

NOTHING BUT A MAN   Cinema 5, 1965
THE PLOT AGAINST HARRY   New Yorker Films, 1990

STEPHEN YOUNG
THE SILENT PARTNER   EMC Film/Aurora, 1979,
   w/Joel B. Michaels

NG SEE YUEN
NO RETREAT, NO SURRENDER II   Shapiro Glickenhaus,
   1989, EP

PETER YUVAL
Business: Action International Pictures, 10726 McCune
   Ave., Los Angeles, CA 90034, 310/559-8805;
   Fax: 310/559-8849

FIREHEAD   Pyramid, 1991

BRIAN YUZNA
RE-ANIMATOR   Empire, 1985
FROM BEYOND   Empire, 1986
DOLLS   Empire, 1987
BRIDE OF RE-ANIMATOR   50th St. Films, 1991

Yu

FILM
PRODUCERS,
STUDIOS,
AGENTS AND
CASTING
DIRECTORS
GUIDE

FILM PRODUCERS

Za

FILM
PRODUCERS,
STUDIOS,
AGENTS AND
CASTING
DIRECTORS
GUIDE

F
I
L
M

P
R
O
D
U
C
E
R
S

Z

PAOLO ZACCARIA
THE KING'S WHORE   J&M, 1990, w/Maurice Bernart &
   Wieland Schulz-Keil

ALFREDO ZACHARIAS
THE BEES   New World, 1978

MICHEL ZACHARIAS
THE BEES   New World, 1978, EP

STEVE ZACHARIAS
(credit w/Jeff Buhai & David Obst)
Agent: UTA - Beverly Hills, 310/273-6700
Contact: Writers Guild of America - Los Angeles,
   310/550-1000

THE WHOOPEE BOYS   Paramount, 1986, EP
JOHNNY BE GOOD   Orion, 1988, EP

CRAIG ZADAN
Business: Storyline Productions, c/o Spectacor Films,
   7920 Sunset Blvd., 4th Floor, Los Angeles, CA 90046,
   213/851-8425; Fax: 213/871-2963

FOOTLOOSE   Paramount, 1984, w/Michael Rachmil
SING   TriStar, 1989
IF LOOKS COULD KILL   Warner Bros., 1991,
   w/Neil Meron

SAUL ZAENTZ
Business: The Saul Zaentz Company, 2600 Tenth St.,
   Berkeley, CA 94710, 415/549-1528;
   Fax: 415/486-2115

ONE FLEW OVER THE CUCKOO'S NEST ★★
   United Artists, 1975, w/Michael Douglas
THREE WARRIORS   Fantasy Films, 1977,
   w/Sy Gomberg
LORD OF THE RINGS   United Artists, 1978
AMADEUS ★★   Orion, 1984
THE MOSQUITO COAST   Warner Bros., 1986, EP
THE UNBEARABLE LIGHTNESS OF BEING
   Orion, 1988
AT PLAY IN THE FIELDS OF THE LORD
   Universal, 1991

CAVEH ZAHEDI
A LITTLE STIFF   1991, w/Greg Watkins

NABEEL ZAHID
(credit w/Joseph Medawar)
Business: Ion Pictures, 3122 Santa Monica Blvd.,
   Suite 300, Santa Monica, CA 90404, 310/453-4466

CHAMPIONS FOREVER (FD)   Ion, 1989
THE CLOSER   Ion, 1991

GEORGE ZALOOM
Business: Z.M. Productions, c/o Universal Studios, 100
   Universal City Plaza, M.T. #27, Universal City, CA 91608,
   818/777-4664; Fax: 818/777-8870

HEARTS OF DARKNESS: A FILMMAKER'S
   APOCALYPSE   Avenue, 1991, w/Les Mayfield

JOHN ZANE
Contact: Directors Guild of America - Los Angeles,
   213/289-2000

SIDEOUT   TriStar, 1990, CP

LILI FINI ZANUCK
(credit w/Richard D. Zanuck)
Business: The Zanuck Company, 202 N. Canon Dr.,
   Beverly Hills, CA 90210, 310/274-0261

COCOON   20th Century Fox, 1985, w/David Brown
COCOON: THE RETURN   20th Century Fox, 1988,
   w/David Brown
DRIVING MISS DAISY ★★   Warner Bros., 1989

RICHARD D. ZANUCK
(credit w/David Brown)
Business: The Zanuck Company, 202 N. Canon Dr.,
   Beverly Hills, CA 90210, 310/274-0261;
   Fax: 310/273-9217

SSSSSSSS   Universal, 1973, EP
WILLIE DYNAMITE   Universal, 1974
THE SUGARLAND EXPRESS   Universal, 1974
THE GIRL FROM PETROVKA   Universal, 1974
THE BLACK WINDMILL   Universal, 1974
THE EIGER SANCTION   Universal, 1975, EP
JAWS ★   Universal, 1975
MACARTHUR   Universal, 1977, EP
JAWS II   Universal, 1978
THE ISLAND   Universal, 1980
NEIGHBORS   Columbia, 1981
THE VERDICT ★   20th Century Fox, 1982
COCOON   20th Century Fox, 1985,
   w/Lili Fini Zanuck
TARGET   Warner Bros., 1985
COCOON: THE RETURN   20th Century Fox, 1988,
   w/Lili Fini Zanuck
DRIVING MISS DAISY ★★   Warner Bros., 1989,
   w/Lili Fini Zanuck*
RUSH   MGM, 1991*

JOSEPH ZAPPALA
(credit w/Gene Slott)

BITTERSWEET LOVE   Avco Embassy, 1976,
   w/Joel B. Michaels
LAS VEGAS LADY   Crown International, 1976

CHRIS ZARPAS
Business: Island World L.A., 8920 Sunset Blvd.,
   2nd Floor, Los Angeles, CA 90069, 310/632-3456;
   Fax: 310/271-7840

TOY SOLDIERS   TriStar, 1991, EP w/Mark Burg

Zu

FILM
PRODUCERS,
STUDIOS,
AGENTS AND
CASTING
DIRECTORS
GUIDE

F
I
L
M

P
R
O
D
U
C
E
R
S

GEORGE ZECEVIC
Business: Smart Egg Pictures, 7080 Hollywood Blvd.,
    Suite 518, Hollywood, CA 90028, 213/463-8937

HEY BABU RIBA   Orion Classics, 1987,
    EP w/Petar Jankovic
OMEGA SYNDROME   New World, 1987, EP
DOUBLE REVENGE   Smart Egg Releasing, 1988,
    EP w/Luigi Cingolani
CAMERON'S CLOSET   SVS Films, 1989, EP
SPACED INVADERS   Buena Vista, 1990, EP

JEROME M. ZEITMAN
DAMNATION ALLEY   20th Century Fox, 1977,
    w/Paul Maslansky
JUST YOU AND ME, KID   Columbia, 1979, w/Irving Fein
HOW TO BEAT THE HIGH COST OF LIVING   AIP,
    1980, w/Robert Kaufman

RAFAL ZIELINSKI
Business: Neo Modern Entertainment, 8033 Sunset Blvd.,
    Suite 640, Los Angeles, CA 90046, 213/650-1642

GINGER ALE AFTERNOON   Skouras Pictures, 1989,
    w/Susan Hillary Shapiro

JONATHAN A. ZIMBERT
Business: Morgan Creek Productions, 1875 Century Park
    East, Suite 200, Los Angeles, CA 90067, 310/284-8884;
    Fax: 310/282-8794

THE STAR CHAMBER   20th Century Fox, 1983, AP
2010   MGM/UA, 1984, AP w/Neil A. Machlis
RUNNING SCARED   MGM, 1986, AP
THE MONSTER SQUAD   TriStar, 1987
THE PRESIDIO   Paramount, 1988, EP
NARROW MARGIN   TriStar, 1990

VERNON ZIMMERMAN
Business: P.O. Box 900, Beverly Hills, CA 90213,
    310/203-3394
Business Manager: Eric Weissmann, Weissmann, Wolff,
    Bergman, Coleman & Schulman, 9665 Wilshire Blvd.,
    Suite 900, Beverly Hills, CA 90212, 310/858-7888

DEADHEAD MILES   Paramount, 1971, w/Tony Bill

FRED ZINNEMANN
Business: 128 Mount St., London W1, England,
    071/499-8810
Agent: William Morris Agency - Beverly Hills,
    310/274-7451

THE SUNDOWNERS ★   Warner Bros., 1960
BEHOLD A PALE HORSE   Columbia, 1964
A MAN FOR ALL SEASONS ★★   Columbia, 1966
FIVE DAYS ONE SUMMER   The Ladd Company/Warner
    Bros., 1982

TIM ZINNEMANN
Agent: ICM - Los Angeles, 310/550-4000
Contact: Directors Guild of America - Los Angeles,
    213/289-2000

THE COWBOYS   Warner Bros., 1972, AP
SMILE   United Artists, 1975, AP
STRAIGHT TIME   Warner Bros., 1978, w/Stanley Back
A SMALL CIRCLE OF FRIENDS   United Artists, 1980

THE LONG RIDERS   United Artists, 1980
TEX   Buena Vista, 1982
IMPULSE   20th Century Fox, 1984
FANDANGO   Warner Bros., 1985
CROSS ROADS   Columbia, 1986, EP
THE RUNNING MAN   TriStar, 1987, w/George Linder
PET SEMATARY   Paramount, 1989, EP

LAURA ZISKIN
Business: Laura Ziskin Productions, 10202 W. Washington
    Blvd., Thalberg Bldg., Suite 3527, Culver City, CA 90232,
    310/280-8360; Fax: 310/280-1365

EYES OF LAURA MARS   Columbia, 1978, AP
MURPHY'S ROMANCE   Columbia, 1985
NO WAY OUT   Orion, 1987, w/Robert Garland
D.O.A.   Buena Vista, 1988, w/Ian Sander
EVERYBODY'S ALL-AMERICAN   Warner Bros., 1988,
    w/Taylor Hackford & Ian Sander
THE RESCUE   Buena Vista, 1988
PRETTY WOMAN   Buena Vista, 1990, EP
WHAT ABOUT BOB?   Buena Vista, 1991

DAVID ZITO
BREAKIN'   Cannon, 1984, w/Allen DeBevoise

BARBARA ZITWER
Business: Montauk Pictures, 300 E. 54th St., #29E,
    New York, NY 10022

VAMPIRE'S KISS   Hemdale, 1989, w/Barry Shils

FREDERICK ZOLLO
Business: Zollo Productions, 226 W. 47th Street, New York,
    NY 10036, 212/944-1717

MILES FROM HOME   Cinecom, 1988, w/Paul Kurta
MISSISSIPPI BURNING ★   Orion, 1988,
    w/Robert F. Colesberry

DAVID ZUCKER
(credit w/Jim Abrahams & Jerry Zucker)
Business: 11777 San Vicente Blvd., Suite 640, Los Angeles,
    CA 90049, 310/826-1333; Fax: 310/826-3493
Agent: CAA - Beverly Hills, 310/288-4545

AIRPLANE!   Paramount, 1980, EP
THE NAKED GUN: FROM THE FILES OF POLICE
    SQUAD   Paramount, 1988, EP

HOWARD ZUCKER
TRACKS   Castle Hill Productions, 1976,
    w/Norman I. Cohen & Ted Shapiro

JERRY ZUCKER
(credit w/Jim Abrahams & David Zucker)
Business: 11777 San Vicente Blvd., Suite 640, Los Angeles,
    CA 90049, 310/826-1333
Agent: CAA - Beverly Hills, 310/288-4545

AIRPLANE!   Paramount, 1980, EP
THE NAKED GUN: FROM THE FILES OF POLICE SQUAD
    Paramount, 1988, EP
THE NAKED GUN 2 1/2: THE SMELL OF FEAR
    Paramount, 1991, EP w/Jim Abrahams & Gil Netter

Zu

FILM
PRODUCERS,
STUDIOS,
AGENTS AND
CASTING
DIRECTORS
GUIDE

STANLEY R. ZUPNIK
Business: Zupnik Enterprises, 9229 Sunset Blvd.,
Suite 818, Los Angeles, CA 90069, 310/273-9125;
Fax: 310/273-5076

DREAMSCAPE   20th Century Fox, 1984,
EP w/Tom Curtis
WILDFIRE   Jody Ann Productions, 1989,
EP w/Irvin Kershner

RON ZWANG
NAKED OBSESSION   Concorde, 1991

A. MARTIN ZWEIBACK
(credit w/Adrienne Zweiback)
Agent: APA - Los Angeles, 310/273-0744
Contact: Writers Guild of America - Los Angeles,
310/550-1000

GRACE QUIGLEY   *THE ULTIMATE SOLUTION OF
GRACE QUIGLEY*   MGM/UA/Cannon, 1984, EP

ADRIENNE ZWEIBACK
(credit w/A. Martin Zweiback)

GRACE QUIGLEY   *THE ULTIMATE SOLUTION OF
GRACE QUIGLEY*   MGM/UA/Cannon, 1984, EP

CHARLOTTE ZWERIN
Contact: Directors Guild of America - New York,
212/581-0370

THELONIOUS MONK: STRAIGHT, NO CHASER   (FD)
Warner Bros., 1988, w/Bruce Ricker

JOSEPH E. ZYNCZAK
DISORDERLIES   Warner Bros., 1987,
EP w/Charles Stettler

★ ★ ★ ★

FILM PRODUCERS

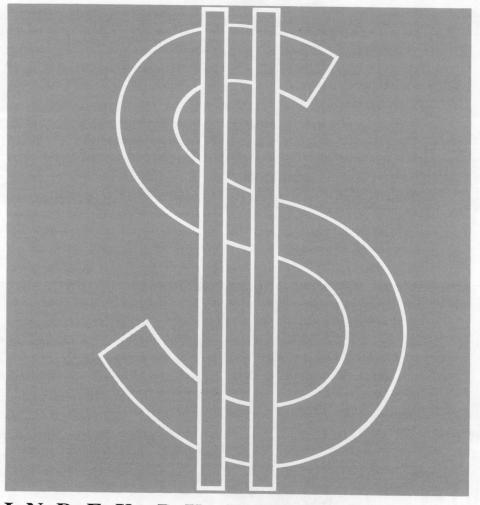

INDEX BY FILM TITLE

INDEX OF FILM TITLES

3:15-AI

FILM
PRODUCERS,
STUDIOS,
AGENTS AND
CASTING
DIRECTORS
GUIDE

Note: This is not an index of all films,
only those listed in this book
† = deceased

Al-Ap

FILM
PRODUCERS,
STUDIOS,
AGENTS AND
CASTING
DIRECTORS

GUIDE

I
N
D
E
X

O
F

F
I
L
M

T
I
T
L
E
S

Bi-Bl

FILM
PRODUCERS,
STUDIOS,
AGENTS AND
CASTING
DIRECTORS
GUIDE

INDEX OF FILM TITLES

233

BI-Bu

FILM
PRODUCERS,
STUDIOS,
AGENTS AND
CASTING
DIRECTORS

GUIDE

I
N
D
E
X

O
F

F
I
L
M

T
I
T
L
E
S

Bu-Ca

FILM
PRODUCERS,
STUDIOS,
AGENTS AND
CASTING
DIRECTORS
GUIDE

C

Ca-Ci

FILM
PRODUCERS,
STUDIOS,
AGENTS and
CASTING
DIRECTORS
GUIDE

I
N
D
E
X

O
F

F
I
L
M

T
I
T
L
E
S

Co-Da

FILM
PRODUCERS,
STUDIOS,
AGENTS AND
CASTING
DIRECTORS
GUIDE

INDEX OF FILM TITLES

D

De-Dr

FILM
PRODUCERS,
STUDIOS,
AGENTS AND
CASTING
DIRECTORS
GUIDE

I
N
D
E
X

O
F

F
I
L
M

T
I
T
L
E
S

Dr-En

FILM
PRODUCERS,
STUDIOS,
AGENTS AND
CASTING
DIRECTORS
GUIDE

En-Fe

FILM
PRODUCERS,
STUDIOS,
AGENTS and
CASTING
DIRECTORS
GUIDE

I
N
D
E
X

O
F

F
I
L
M

T
I
T
L
E
S

Fe-Fo

FILM
PRODUCERS,
STUDIOS,
AGENTS AND
CASTING
DIRECTORS
GUIDE

I N D E X   O F   F I L M   T I T L E S

Fo-Ga

FILM
PRODUCERS,
STUDIOS,
AGENTS and
CASTING
DIRECTORS
GUIDE

I
N
D
E
X

O
F

F
I
L
M

T
I
T
L
E
S

Ga-Gr

FILM
PRODUCERS,
STUDIOS,
AGENTS AND
CASTING
DIRECTORS
GUIDE

I
N
D
E
X

O
F

F
I
L
M

T
I
T
L
E
S

Gr-Ha

FILM
PRODUCERS,
STUDIOS,
AGENTS AND
CASTING
DIRECTORS
GUIDE

I
N
D
E
X

O
F

F
I
L
M

T
I
T
L
E
S

Ha-He

FILM
PRODUCERS,
STUDIOS,
AGENTS AND
CASTING
DIRECTORS
GUIDE

I N D E X   O F   F I L M   T I T L E S

He-Ho

FILM
PRODUCERS,
STUDIOS,
AGENTS and
CASTING
DIRECTORS

GUIDE

I N D E X   O F   F I L M   T I T L E S

I

Ho-In

FILM
PRODUCERS,
STUDIOS,
AGENTS AND
CASTING
DIRECTORS
GUIDE

INDEX OF FILM TITLES

In-Ji

FILM
PRODUCERS,
STUDIOS,
AGENTS and
CASTING
DIRECTORS
GUIDE

I
N
D
E
X

O
F

F
I
L
M

T
I
T
L
E
S

Ji-Ki

FILM
PRODUCERS,
STUDIOS,
AGENTS AND
CASTING
DIRECTORS
GUIDE

INDEX OF FILM TITLES

251

I N D E X O F F I L M T I T L E S

Lo-Ma

FILM
PRODUCERS,
STUDIOS,
AGENTS AND
CASTING
DIRECTORS
GUIDE

I
N
D
E
X

O
F

F
I
L
M

T
I
T
L
E
S

M

Me-Mo

FILM
PRODUCERS,
STUDIOS,
AGENTS and
CASTING
DIRECTORS
GUIDE

I
N
D
E
X

O
F

F
I
L
M

T
I
T
L
E
S

Mo-Na

FILM
PRODUCERS,
STUDIOS,
AGENTS and
CASTING
DIRECTORS
GUIDE

Na-Ni

FILM
PRODUCERS,
STUDIOS,
AGENTS and
CASTING
DIRECTORS
GUIDE

I
N
D
E
X

O
F

F
I
L
M

T
I
T
L
E
S

O

Ni-Op

FILM
PRODUCERS,
STUDIOS,
AGENTS and
CASTING
DIRECTORS

GUIDE

I
N
D
E
X

O
F

F
I
L
M

T
I
T
L
E
S

Op-Pe

FILM
PRODUCERS,
STUDIOS,
AGENTS AND
CASTING
DIRECTORS
GUIDE

P

Po-Qu

FILM
PRODUCERS,
STUDIOS,
AGENTS and
CASTING
DIRECTORS

GUIDE

I
N
D
E
X

O
F

F
I
L
M

T
I
T
L
E
S

Qu-Re

FILM
PRODUCERS,
STUDIOS,
AGENTS AND
CASTING
DIRECTORS
GUIDE

I
N
D
E
X

O
F

F
I
L
M

T
I
T
L
E
S

263

Re-Ro

FILM
PRODUCERS,
STUDIOS,
AGENTS and
CASTING
DIRECTORS
GUIDE

INDEX OF FILM TITLES

Ro-Se

FILM
PRODUCERS,
STUDIOS,
AGENTS AND
CASTING
DIRECTORS

GUIDE

I
N
D
E
X

O
F

F
I
L
M

T
I
T
L
E
S

Se-Sh

FILM
PRODUCERS,
STUDIOS,
AGENTS and
CASTING
DIRECTORS
GUIDE

I
N
D
E
X

O
F

F
I
L
M

T
I
T
L
E
S

FILM
PRODUCERS,
STUDIOS,
AGENTS and
CASTING
DIRECTORS
GUIDE

INDEX OF FILM TITLES

St-Su

FILM
PRODUCERS,
STUDIOS,
AGENTS AND
CASTING
DIRECTORS

GUIDE

I
N
D
E
X

O
F

F
I
L
M

T
I
T
L
E
S

269

Su-Te

FILM
PRODUCERS,
STUDIOS,
AGENTS AND
CASTING
DIRECTORS
GUIDE

I
N
D
E
X

O
F

F
I
L
M

T
I
T
L
E
S

Te-To

FILM
PRODUCERS,
STUDIOS,
AGENTS AND
CASTING
DIRECTORS
GUIDE

I N D E X   O F   F I L M   T I T L E S

271

To-Tw

FILM
PRODUCERS,
STUDIOS,
AGENTS and
CASTING
DIRECTORS
GUIDE

I
N
D
E
X

O
F

F
I
L
M

T
I
T
L
E
S

Tw-Vo

FILM
PRODUCERS,
STUDIOS,
AGENTS and
CASTING
DIRECTORS
GUIDE

INDEX OF FILM TITLES

W-Wh W

FILM
PRODUCERS,
STUDIOS,
AGENTS and
CASTING
DIRECTORS
GUIDE

I
N
D
E
X

O
F

F
I
L
M

T
I
T
L
E
S

Wo-Zo

FILM
PRODUCERS,
STUDIOS,
AGENTS AND
CASTING
DIRECTORS
GUIDE

★ ★ ★ ★

S T U D I O S

A

A & M FILMS, INC.
1416 N. La Brea Ave.
Hollywood, CA 90028
213/469-2411
Fax: 213/856-2740

President .... Dale Pollock
Vice President - Production .... Lianne Halfon
Executive in Charge of Development .... Ross Canter

ABC
CAPITAL CITIES/ABC, INC.
77 West 66th Street
New York, NY 10023
212/456-7777

Chairman .... Thomas S. Murphy
President & Chief Executive Officer .... Daniel B. Burke
President - ABC Communications .... Phillip J. Meek
Senior Vice President &
    Chief Financial Officer .... Ronald J. Doerfler
Senior Vice President &
    General Counsel .... David Westin
Senior Vice President -
    European Operations .... Richard Spinner
Vice President -
    Policy & Standards .... Alfred R. Schneider
Vice President - Corporate
    Communications .... Patricia J. Matson

ABC Network Division
77 West 66th Street
New York, NY 10023
212/887-7777

2040 Avenue of the Stars
Los Angeles, CA 90067-4785
310/557-7777

President .... John B. Sias
President - ABC Entertainment .... Robert A. Iger
Group President - ABC News & Sports/
    President - ABC News .... Roone Arledge
President - ABC Sports .... Dennis Swanson
President - ABC Television Network ..... Mark Mandala
President - Daytime, Children's &
    Late-Night Entertainment .... Michael Brockman
President - Broadcast
    Operations & Engineering .... Robert Siegenthaler
Senior Vice President -
    Network Group .... James J. Allegro
Senior Vice President -
    Affiliate Relations .... George M. Newi
Senior Vice President -Finance ...... Warren D. Schaub

Senior Vice President - Marketing &
    Research Services .... Alan Wurtzel
Senior Vice President - Sales .... H. Weller Keever
Vice President -Public Relations ... Richard J. Connelly
Vice President - Public Relations,
    West Coast .... Robert J. Wright
Vice President - Broadcast Standards
    & Practices, West Coast .... Brett A. White
Vice President - Eastern
    Division Sales .... William Harmond
Vice President - Western
    Division Sales .... Peter McCarthy
Vice President - Operations .... Mark Roth

ABC Broadcasting Division
President .... Michael P. Mallardi
President - Broadcast Operations &
    Engineering .... Julius Barnathan
President - ABC Video
    Enterprises .... Herbert A. Granath
President - Television
    Stations, East .... Lawrence J. Pollock
President - Television
    Stations, West .... Kenneth M. Johnson
President - ABC National
    Television Sales .... John B. Watkins
President - ABC Radio .... James B. Arcara
President - Radio Stations .... Don P. Bouloukos
President - Radio Networks .... Aaron M. Daniels

ABC Entertainment: West Coast
President .... Robert A. Iger
Executive Vice President -
    Primetime .... Stuart Bloomberg
Executive Vice President - Primetime .... Ted Harbert
Executive Vice President - Movies
    for Television/Miniseries .... Allen Sabinson
Vice President - Program
    Planning & Scheduling .... Alan Sternfeld
Vice President - Current
    Series Programs .... John L. Barber
Vice President -
    Promotion Projects .... Christopher Carlisle
Vice President - Comedy Series
    Development .... Kim Fleary
Vice President - Special Programs .... John Hamlin
Vice President - Tape Production .... Edgar Hirst
Vice President - Dramatic
    Series Development .... Gary Levine
Vice President - Mini-Series .... Judd Parkin
Vice President - Casting &
    Talent .... Donna L. Rosenstein
Executive Producer - Movies for TV ..Annette Handley
Director - Telefilms .... Maura Dunbar
Director - Current Series
    Programs .... Jackie Colden Lyons
Director - Comedy Series Development ....Dan Cohen
Director - Dramatic Series Development .... Rick Hull
Director - Current Series Programs .... Susan Leeper
Director - Dramatic
    Series Development .... Deborah Leoni
Director - Comedy Development .... Harvey Myman
Director - Program Administration .... Hank Miller

Ab

FILM
PRODUCERS,
STUDIOS,
AGENTS AND
CASTING
DIRECTORS
GUIDE

S
T
U
D
I
O
S

Director - Variety/
Late-Night Programs .... Launa Newman-Minson
Director - Casting .... Robin Stoltz Nassif
Director - Casting .... Nick Wilkinson
Associate Director -
Movies for TV .... Philippe Perebinosoff
Senior Vice President - Business
Affairs & Contracts .... Ronald B. Sunderland
Vice President - ABC Novels for
Television & Limited Series .... Christy Welker
Vice President - Production
Administration .... Deirdre A. Paulino
Vice President - Broadcast
Standards & Practices .... Christine Hikawa
Vice President - Business Affairs ...... Gavin B. Gordon
Vice President - Business
Affairs & Administration .... Ronald Pratz
Vice President - Children's
Programming .... Jennie Trias
Vice President - On-Air Promotion .... Stuart Brower
Vice President - Entertainment
Research .... Roy Rothstein
Vice President - Finance .... Thomas Van Schaick
Vice President - Marketing .... Mark Zakarin
Vice President - Program
Administration .... Stephen K. Nenno
Vice President - Program
Planning & Scheduling .... George Keramidas

ABC Entertainment: East Coast
Senior Vice President - Daytime
Programming .... Jo Ann Emmerich
Vice President - Early
Morning Programs .... Philip R. Beuth
Vice President - Motion Pictures
Post Production .... Andre De Szekely
Vice President & General Manager -
Broadcast Operations .... Joseph D. Giovanni

ABC Distribution
825 Seventh Ave.
New York, NY 10019

Senior Vice President .... Archie C. Purvis
Vice President - Worldwide Cable &
Home Video Marketing .... Michael Dragotto
Vice President - Program
Acquisitions & Development .... Paul Coss

ABC Productions
2020 Avenue of the Stars, 5th Floor
Los Angeles, CA 90067
310/557-7777

President .... Brandon Stoddard
Executive Vice President .... Jerry Offsay
Vice President, Development .... Amy Adelson
Vice President in Charge of Production .... Thomas Brodek
Vice President - Production .... Jim Painten
Vice President - Administration .... Deirdre A. Paulino
Executive Producer .... Ilene Berg
Director - Physical Production .... Dave Elliott
Director - Development .... Karey Nixon

ACT III COMMUNICATIONS INC.
c/o Sunset-Gower Studios
1438 N. Gower, Bldg. 35
Los Angeles, CA 90028-8306
213/460-7240
Fax: 213/460-7636

Chairman & Chief Executive Officer .... Norman Lear
President & Chief
Operating Officer .... Thomas B. McGrath
Senior Vice President &
General Counsel .... Michael E. Cahill
Vice President .... John DiLorenzo

Act III Productions
President .... Andrew Meyer
Senior Vice President .... Sarah Ryan Black
Senior Vice President - Production .... Nancy Klopper
Vice President, Business Affairs .... Tom Taylor

Act III Television
President .... Mark E. Pollack

ALLIANCE ENTERTAINMENT CORP.
8439 Sunset Blvd., Suite 404
Los Angeles, CA 90069-1909
213/654-9488
Fax: 213/654-9786

920 Yonge St., Suite 400
Toronto, Ontario, Canada M4W 3C7
416/967-1174

Chairman (Toronto) .... Robert Lantos
President .... Susan Cavan
Chief Financial Officer .... Jay Firestone
Senior Vice President - Television ..Michael Weisbarth
Vice President -
Development (Toronto) .... Steven DeNure
Vice President - Legal Affairs (Toronto) .... John Robinson
Director - Development .... Elisa Rothstein

Alliance Releasing Corporation
President .... Victor Loewy
Vice President & General Manager ..... Anthony Cianciotta
Director of Marketing .... Mary Pat Gleeson

AMBLIN ENTERTAINMENT
100 Universal Plaza, Bungalow 477
Universal City, CA 91608-1085
818/777-4600

Director & Executive Producer .... Steven Spielberg
President & Executive Producer ..... Kathleen Kennedy
President - Amblin TV .... Tony Thomopoulos
Senior Vice President -
Development .... Deborah Jelin-Newmyer
Vice President - Creative Affairs .... Sarah Bowman
Vice President - Amblin TV .... Philip Segal
Vice President - Marketing .... Brad Globe
Director - TV Programming .... Carol Monroe
Director - Animation .... Doug Wood
Director - Development .... Cathy Stewart

Literary Story Editor .... Anna DeRoy
Special Consultant .... Marvin J. Levy
Special Consultant .... Gerry Lewis

AMERICAN PLAYHOUSE
1776 Broadway, 9th Floor
New York, NY 10019-1990
212/757-4300
Fax: 212/333-7552

President & Chief Executive Officer ..... David M. Davis
Vice President - Business &
    Legal Affairs .... Roberta Lynn Tross
Executive Producer .... Lindsay Law
Director of Program Development .... Lynn Holst
Manager - Program Development .... Nicholas Gottlieb

ANGELIKA FILMS
110 Greene St., Suite1102
New York, NY 10012
212/274-1990
Fax: 212/966-4957

President & Chief Executive Officer ...... Joseph J.M. Saleh
Chairman .... Angelika Saleh
Vice President - Theatrical
    Distribution & Film Buyer .... Jeffrey Jacobs
Executive Vice President -
    International Marketing .... Alex Massis
Vice President - Foreign Sales .... Rafael Guadalupe
Vice President - Acquisitions .... Jessica Saleh-Hunt
Vics President - Creative Affairs .... Eva Saleh

APOLLO PICTURES
6071 Bristol Parkway
Culver City, CA 90230
310/568-8282
Fax: 310/641-5738

President .... David Smitas
Vice President - Physical Production ..... Robert Rosen
Production Executive .... Russell Chesley
Director of Creative Affairs .... Greg Johnson

AVENUE PICTURES
12100 Wilshire Blvd., Suite 1650
Los Angeles, CA 90025
310/442-2200
Fax: 310/207-1753

Chairman & Chief Executive Officer .... Cary Brokaw
Vice President - Finance &
    Administration .... Sheri Halfon
Executive Vice President &
    Chief Operations Officer .... Patrick Murray
Executive VicePresident -
    Marketing & Distribution .... Bingham Ray
Senior Vice President -
    Marketing & Distribution .... Yale Popowich
Vice President - Acquisitions &
    Co-Production .... Alison Brantley
Vice President - Production .... Claudia Lewis

B

STEVEN BOCHCO PRODUCTIONS
20th Century-Fox
10201 W. Pico Blvd.
Los Angeles, CA 90035
310/203-2400
Fax: 310/203-3236

Chairman & Chief Executive Officer .... Steven Bochco
President - TV Production .... Dayna Kalins Flanagan
President & Chief
    Financial Officer .... Franklin B. Rohner
Senior Vice President -
    Business Affairs .... Arnold Shane
Vice President - Administration .... Marilyn Fiebelkorn
Vice President - Business Affairs .... Wilton M. Haff
Vice President - Finance .... James A. Roach
Vice President - Production .... Phillip Goldfarb
Vice President - Public Relations ..... James A. Gordon

BUENA VISTA
(See Walt DISNEY Co.)

C

THE CANNELL STUDIOS
7083 Hollywood Blvd.
Los Angeles, CA 90028
213/465-5800
Fax: 213/463-4987

Chairman & Chief
    Executive Officer .... Stephen J. Cannell
President .... Michael Dubelko
Senior Vice President - Legal &
    Business Affairs .... Howard D. Kurtzman
Senior Vice President .... Jo Swerling Jr.
Senior Vice President & Chief
    Financial Officer .... Joe Kaczorowski
Vice President & Controller .... Andrew R. Hubsch

Stephen J. Cannell Productions, Inc.
President .... Peter Roth
Executive Vice President .... Mathew N. Herman
Vice President - Cannell Films, Ltd. .... Alex Beaton
Vice President - Talent & Casting .... Peter Golden
Vice President - Post Production .... Gary Winter
Vice President - Development .... Marilyn Osborn

Ca

FILM
PRODUCERS,
STUDIOS,
AGENTS AND
CASTING
DIRECTORS
GUIDE

S
T
U
D
I
O
S

Ca

FILM
PRODUCERS,
STUDIOS,
AGENTS AND
CASTING
DIRECTORS
GUIDE

S
T
U
D
I
O
S

CANNON PICTURES

8200 Wilshire Blvd.
Beverly Hills, CA 90212
213/966-5600
Fax: 213/653-5485

Executive President .... Christopher Pearce
Executive Vice President -
    Head of Production .... Jere Henshaw

CAROLCO PICTURES INC.

8800 Sunset Blvd.
Los Angeles, CA 90069-2105
310/850-8800
Fax: 310/657-1629

Chairman .... Mario Kassar
President, Producer &
    Chief Executive Officer .... Peter Hoffman
Executive Vice President -
    Business/Production Affairs .... Lynwood Spinks
Executive Vice President &
    Chief Financial Officer .... Louis Weiss
Senior Vice President - Production ..... Walter Coblenz
Senior Vice President -
    Creative Affairs .... Kathryn Sommer
Vice President - Production .... Cathy Rabin
Vice President - Production .... Doug Burdinsky
Associate Story Editor .... Janice Sirkin
Associate Story Editor .... Scott Sommer
President - Licensing .... Danny Simon
Executive Vice President -
    Foreign Sales .... Rocco Viglietta
Vice President & Head of Production .. Buzz Feitshans
Vice President & European
    Representative .... Gabriella Martin
Vice President - Business Affairs .. Barbara Zipperman
Vice President - Business Affairs .... Lorin Brennan
Vice President - Corporate
    Development .... Thomas Levine
Vice President - Finance .... Karen Taylor
Vice President - Music .... Steve Love
Vice President - Post Production ...... Michael R. Sloan
Vice President - Sales .... Chris Bialek

CASTLE ROCK ENTERTAINMENT

335 N. Maple Dr., Suite 135
Beverly Hills, CA 90210-3867
310/285-2300
Fax: 310/285-2345

Managing Partner & Co-Founder .... Alan Horn
Partner & Co Founder .... Glenn Padnick
Partner & Co Founder .... Rob Reiner
Partner & Co Founder .... Martin Shafer
Partner & Co Founder .... Andrew Scheinman
Chief Financial Officer .... Al Linton
Senior Vice President & General Counsel ... Greg Paul
Vice President - Development,
    Syndication & Cable .... Michael Binkow
Vice President - Business Affairs .... Jess Wittenberg

Vice President - Production .... Liz Glotzer
Vice President - Production .... Rachel Pfeffer
Vice President - Publicity & Promotion ..John DeSimio
Executive Story Editor .... Lisa Reeve
Vice President - Physical Production .... Jeffrey Stott
Vice President - Current Programs, TV ... Robin Green
Vice President - Legal Affairs .... Julia Bingham

CBS, INC.

7800 Beverly Blvd.
Los Angeles, CA 90036-2188
213/852-2345

51 W. 57th St.
New York, NY 10019
212/975-4321

President & Chief
    Executive Officer .... Laurence A. Tisch

CBS Broadcast Group
President - Broadcast Group .... Howard Stringer
President - Marketing Division .... Thomas F. Leahy
President - CBS Enterprises .... Jim Warner
President - CBS Entertainment .... Jeff Sagansky
President - CBS News .... David Burke
President - CBS Radio .... Nancy Widmann
President - CBS Sports .... Neal H. Pilson
President - CBS Television Stations .... Eric Ober
President - Affiliate
    Relations Division .... Anthony C. Malara
Senior Vice President -
    Communications .... George Schweitzer
Senior Vice President -
    Planning & Research .... David Poltrack
Vice President & Assistant
    to President .... Beth Waxman Bressan
Vice President - Creative Services ..... Jerold Goldberg
Vice President - Media Relations .... Ann Morfogen
Vice President - Publicity, West Coast .... Susan Tick

CBS Entertainment: Hollywood
President .... Jeff Sagansky
Executive Vice President .... Peter F. Tortorici
Vice President - Comedy
    Program Development .... Tim Flack
Vice President - Talent & Casting .... Lisa Freiberger
Vice President - Current Programs .... Maddy Horne
Vice President - Daytime Programs .... Lucy Johnson
Vice President - Dramatic
    Program Development .... Jonathan Levin
Vice President - Motion Pictures for
    TV and Miniseries .... John Matoian
Vice President - Creative Services &
    Artist Relations .... Madeline Peerce
Vice President - Late-Night Programs .... Rod Perth
Vice President - Children's Programs &
    Daytime Specials .... Judy Price
Vice President - Specials .... Susan Mischer
Vice President - Miniseries &
    Client Specials .... Larry Strichman

Co

FILM
PRODUCERS,
STUDIOS,
AGENTS AND
CASTING
DIRECTORS
GUIDE

S
T
U
D
I
O
S

Vice President - Program Planning .... Steve Warner
Senior Director - Casting .... Christopher Gorman
Director - Feature Films .... Joe Bowen
Director - Current Programs .... Jill Bowman
Director - Casting .... Tom Burke
Director - Current Programs .... Bill Coveny
Director - Dramatic Program
Development .... Marian Davis
Director - Motion Pictures for TV .... Joan Harrison
Director - Daytime
Programming (West Coast) .... Barbara Hunter
Director - Motion Pictures for TV .... Sunta Izzicupo
Director - Current Programs .... Dick Kirschner
Director - Current Programs .... Kristina Smith
Director - Current Programs .... Shirley Leeds
Director - Casting .... Margaret McSharry
Director - Late-Night Programs .... Kevin Stein
Director - Comedy Development .... Joe Voci
Director - Daytime Programs .... Margot Wain
Director - Motion Pictures for TV .... Trevor Walton
Director - Motion Pictures for TV .... Joan Yee
Senior Vice President -
Business Affairs .... William B. Klein
Vice President - Advertising &
Promotion .... Michael Mischler
Vice President - Affiliate
Advertising & Promotion .... Brad Crum
Vice President - Business
Affairs, Administration .... James F. McGowan
Vice President - Business Affairs,
Long Form Contracts & Acquisitions .... Sid Lyons
Vice President - Business Affairs,
Music Operations .... Harry Heitzer
Vice President - Business Affairs,
Talent & Guild Negotiations .... Leola Gorius
Vice President - Business Affairs,
West Coast .... Layne Britton
Vice President - Current
Programs .... Charles Schnebel
Vice President - Dramatic Specials ..... Marion Brayton
Vice President - Media Planning,
Advertising & Promotion .... Kathie Culleton
Vice President - Motion Pictures
for TV, Miniseries .... Steve Mills
Vice President - On-Air Promotion ..... Steve Jacobson
Vice President - Program Planning &
Current Programs .... Herbert Gross
Vice President - Talent &
Guild Negotiations .... Leola Govins

CBS Broadcast Group: Hollywood
Vice President - TV Research .... Arnold Becker
Vice President - Program Practices ...... Carol A. Altieri

CBS Entertainment Productions
Executive Vice President .... Andy Hill
Vice President .... Norman S. Powell
Vice President - Series Development .... Kelly Goode
Director .... Sandra Brice

CINECOM ENTERTAINMENT GROUP, INC.
850 Third Avenue
New York, NY 10022
212/319-5000
Fax: 212/245-4173

Chairman & Co-Chief
Executive Officer .... Stephen Swid
President & Co-Chief Executive Officer ...... Amir Malin
Executive Vice President .... Richard Abramowitz
Executive Vice President .... John Levy
Executive Vice President .... Bart Walker
Vice President - Productions &
Acquisitions .... Shelby Stone
Comptroller .... Dan Lieblein

CINETEL FILMS, INC.
3800 W. Alameda, Suite 825
Burbank, CA 91505-4398
818/955-9551
Fax: 818/955-9616

President & Chief Executive Officer ..... Paul Hertzberg
Executive Vice President .... Lisa Hansen
Senior Vice President - International
Distribution .... Mark Horowitz
Vice President - Business Affairs .... Judith Jecmen
Vice President - Creative Affairs .... Catalaine Knell
Chief Financial Officer .... Nick Gorenc

DICK CLARK PRODUCTIONS
3003 W. Olive Ave.
Burbank, CA 91510-7811
818/841-3003
Fax: 818/954-8609

President .... Dick Clark
President & COO .... Fran La Maina
Chief Financial Officer &
Vice President - Finance .... Ken Ferguson
Senior Vice President - Production .... Al Schwartz
Senior Vice President - Creative Affairs ... Neil Stearns
Vice President - TV Development .... Barry Adelman
Vice President - Business Affairs .... Aviva Bergman
Vice President - Entertainment
Programming .... Arthur Smith
Vice President - TV .... Gene Weed
Vice President - Production .... Don Wollman
Producer - Gameshow Deevlopment ..Ron Greenberg
Program Development .... Marilyn Wilson
Vice President - Creative Affairs .... Ellen Glick
Vice President & Chief
Labor Counsel .... Joel M. Grossman
Director of Development .... Pat Troise

COLUMBIA PICTURES
(See SONY Pictures Entertainment)

Co

FILM
PRODUCERS,
STUDIOS,
AGENTS AND
CASTING
DIRECTORS
GUIDE

S
T
U
D
I
O
S

CONCORDE PICTURES/NEW HORIZONS
11600 San Vicente Blvd.
Los Angeles, CA 90049
310/820-6733
Fax: 310/207-6816

President .... Roger Corman
Senior Vice President .... Julie Corman
Vice President -
    Ancillary Rights .... Pamela A. Abraham
Vice President - Finance .... Catherine Sanders
Vice President - Finance .... Dennis Manders
Vice President -
    Development & Operations .... Catherine Cyran
Vice President, Production .... Mike Elliott
Vice President - Marketing .... Jonathan Fernandez
Vice President - Southern Division ...Mary Lou Lanaux
Vice President - Creative Affairs .... Steven Rabiner
Director of Business Affairs .... Douglas Bull
Director of International Marketing &
    Services .... Pamela Vlastas
Director of Acquisitions .... Lynn Whitney
General Sales Manager .... Harry Gilg
Head of Development .... Rob kerchner

D

WALT DISNEY CO.
500 S. Buena Vista St.
Burbank, CA 91521
818/560-1000

Chairman of the Board & Chief
    Executive Officer .... Michael D. Eisner
President & Chief Operating Officer ..... Frank G. Wells
Vice Chairman of the Board .... Roy E. Disney
Senior Vice President/
    Chief Financial Officer .... Judson Green
Senior Vice President &
    General Counsel .... Sanford Litvack
Senior Vice President - Strategic
    Planning and Development ....Lawrence P. Murphy
Senior Vice President - Corporate
    Communications .... Erwin Okun
Senior Vice President - Administration, Worldwide
    Corporate Business Affairs .... Joe Shapiro
Vice President - Treasurer .... Richard D. Nanula
Vice President - Counsel .... Peter F. Nolan
Vice President - Counsel .... Joseph M. Santaniello
Vice President & Secretary .... Doris A. Smith
Corporate Vice President/Controller and
    Chief Accounting Officer .... Timothy V. Wolf

Walt Disney Studios
818/560-5151

Chairman .... Jeffrey Katzenberg
President .... Richard Frank
Executive Vice President .... Helene Hahn
Executive Vice President .... William E. Kerstetter
Executive Vice President - Finance & Chief
    Financial Officer .... Chris McGurk
Executive Vice President .... W. Randolph Reiss
Executive Vice President .... Marty Katz
Vice President - Studio
    Operations .... Harry Grossman
Vice President - New Technologies &
    Development .... Bob Lambert
Vice President - Controller ..... Lawrence R. Rutkowski

Walt Disney Pictures
818/560-5151

President .... David Hoberman
Executive Vice President -
    Production .... Donald De Line
Executive Vice President - Finance .... Chris McGurk
Executive Vice President -
    Production .... David E. Vogel
Senior Vice President - Motion Picture &
    Television Post Production.............. David McCann
Senior Vice President - Music .... Chris Montan
Senior Vice President - Production
    Finance - Motion Pictures .... Sandra Rabins
Senior Vice President - Feature
    Animation .... Peter Schneider
Vice President - Music Business &
    Legal Affairs .... Kevin Breen
Vice President - Participation &
    Residuals .... William Clark
Vice President - Information Services .... John Covas
Vice President - Business Affairs ...... Robert DeBitetto
Vice President - Feature Animation ...Maureen Donely
Vice President - Production
    Resources .... Scott Dorman
Vice President - Production & Finance
    (Feature Animation) .... Tim Engel
Vice President - Production .... Charles D. Fink
Vice President - Finance .... Susan Gelb
Vice President - Production .... Mireille Soria
Vice President - Labor Relations ... Robert W. Johnson
Vice President - Planning & Analysis .... Rob Moore
Vice President - Legal Affairs .... Katie O'Connell
Vice President - Business &
    Legal Affairs .... Robert Osher
Vice President - Casting .... Ilene Starger
Vice President - Production .... Michael Roberts
Creative Executive .... Todd Garner
Creative Executive .... Gaye Hirsch
Creative Executive .... Rick Phillips
Creative Executive .... Alexandra Schwartz
Creative Executive .... Brian Snedeker
Creative Executive .... Christina Steinberg
Creative Executive .... Steve Tao
Creative Executive .... Steven Mau

Creative Associate .... Robin Claire
Creative Associate .... Ann Milder
Director - Production .... Gail Lyon

Touchstone Pictures
818/560-1000

President .... David Hoberman
Executive Vice President - Motion Picture
    and Television Production .... Donald De Line
Executive Vice President - Finance .... Chris McGurk
Senior Vice President - Production ....Jane Goldenring
Senior Vice President - Motion Picture &
    Television Post Production .... David McCann
Senior Vice President - Music .... Chris Montan
Senior Vice President - Production
    Finance - Motion Pictures .... Sandra Rabins
Senior Vice President - Motion Picture
    Production .... Bruce Hendricks
Senior Vice President - Production .... Adam Leipzig
Vice President - Music Business &
    Legal Affairs .... Kevin Breen
Vice President - Participation &
    Residuals .... William Clark
Vice President - Information Services .... John Covas
Vice President - Production
    Resources .... Scott Dorman
Vice President - Production .... Patrick Faulstich
Vice President - Finance .... Susan Gelb
Vice President - Production .... Bridget Johnson
Vice President - Labor Relations ... Robert W. Johnson
Vice President - Planning & Analysis .... Rob Moore
Vice President - Casting .... Ilene Starger
Vice President - Controller ..... Lawrence R. Rutkowski
Director - Production .... Gail Lyon

Hollywood Pictures
818/560-1000

President - Production .... Ricardo Mestres
Executive Vice President - Finance .... Chris McGurk
Senior Vice President - Business &
    Legal Affairs .... Bernardine Brandis
Senior Vice President -
    Production .... Charles Hirschhorn
Senior Vice President - Production
    Finance - Motion Pictures .... Sandra Rabins
Vice President - Legal Affairs .... Steve Bardwill
Vice President - Music .... Christie Barnes
Vice President - Participation &
    Residuals .... William Clark
Vice President - Information Services .... John Covas
Vice President - Production
    Resources .... Scott Dorman
Vice President - Business Affairs .... Art Frazier
Vice President - Production .... Kathryn Galan
Vice President - Business Affairs .... Jane Garzilli
Vice President - Production .... Dan Halsted
Vice President - Production & Casting .... Paula Herold
Vice President - Production .... Chip Diggins
Vice President - Labor Relations ... Robert W. Johnson

Vice President - Motion Picture
    Production .... Sam Mercer
Vice President - Planning & Analysis .... Rob Moore
Vice President - Post Production .... Art Repola
Vice President - Controller ..... Lawrence R. Rutkowski
Vice President - Production Finance .... Paul Steinke
Vice President - Production .... Amanda Stern
Director - Post Production .... Bob Hacki
Story Editor .... Dominique Lett
Creative Assistant .... Larry Hymes
Director of Creative Affairs .... Scott Immergut
Director of Casting .... Leslee Feldman
Director of Creative Affairs .... Mike Stenson
Creative Executive .... Charles Gold
Creative Executive .... Henry Huang
Creative Executive .... Cheryl Hill
Creative Executive .... Jim Wedaa
Director - Creative Affairs .... Jay Stern

Buena Vista Productions
818/560-1989

Vice President -
    Programming .... Mark A. "Bruno" Cohen
Vice President - Production &
    Programming .... Mary Kellogg-Joslyn
Vice President - Programming -
    Europe (UK) .... David L. Simon
Vice President - International
    Programming .... David Snyder
Vice President -
    Production .... Hayma "Screech" Washington
Director - Programming .... Suzy Polse-Unger
Director - Programming .... Stephanie drachkovitz

Buena Vista Pictures Distribution
818/567-5000

President .... Richard W. Cook
Senior Vice President & General
    Sales Manager .... Phil Barlow
Vice President & General
    Counsel .... Robert Cunningham
Vice President - East/New York .... Phil Fortune
Vice President & Assistant General
    Sales Manager - West .... Roger Lewin
Vice President - Finance
    (Marketing & Distribution) .... Robert D. Murphy
Vice President - Southwest/Dallas .... Jim Nocella
Vice President - West/Los Angeles .... Pat Pade
Vice President - Non-Theatrical .... Linda Palmer
Vice President - Midwest/Chicago .... Rick Rice
Vice President - Southeast/Atlanta ...... Rod Rodriguez
Vice President & Assistant General
    Sales Manager - East & Canada ...... Charles Viane
Vice President - Operations .... Anne Waldeck
Managing Director - Canada .... Peter Wertelecky

Di

FILM
PRODUCERS,
STUDIOS,
AGENTS AND
CASTING
DIRECTORS
GUIDE

S
T
U
D
I
O
S

Di

**FILM
PRODUCERS,
STUDIOS,
AGENTS AND
CASTING
DIRECTORS
GUIDE**

S
T
U
D
I
O
S

Production Division
333 N. Glenoaks Blvd.
Suite 201
Burbank, CA 91501
818/955-6850

Vice President - Production .... Daniel Jason Heffner

Buena Vista Pictures Marketing
818/560-5151

President - Worldwide Marketing .... Robert B. Levin
Senior Vice President - Media .... Bobbi Blair
Senior Vice President -
    Creative Services .... Robert Jahn
Senior Vice President - Domestic
    Marketing .... Gary Kalkin
Vice President - Creative Film Services ..... Peter Adee
Vice President - Creative Film Services .... Oren Aviv
Vice President - Promotions .... Brett Dicker
Vice President - Special Marketing ...... Alan Dinwiddie
Vice President - Print Advertising .... Hy Levine
Vice President - Research .... Dana Lombardo
Vice President - Finance
    (Marketing & Distribution) .... Robert D. Murphy
Vice President - Publicity .... Terry Press

Buena Vista International
President - Theatrical Distribution &
    Worldwide Video .... William M. Mechanic
President - Worldwide Marketing .... Robert Levin
Senior Vice President - Theatrical
    Distribution & Marketing .... Kevin Hyson
Vice President - Publicity .... Hilary Clark
Vice President - Business Affairs ....Janet M. Johnson
Vice President - Finance &
    Administration .... Greg Probert

Buena Vista International Television
President - Television/London .... Etienne de Villiers
Vice President - Sales &
    Marketing/London .... Ed Borgerding
Vice President - Sales/Canada .... Orest Olijnyk

Buena Vista Productions - Foreign
Vice President - Programming - Europe ..David Simon
Vice President - Programming - Latin
    America, Far East & Australia .... David Snyder

Buena Vista Television
President .... Robert Jacquemin
Senior Vice President - Buena Vista
    Productions .... Jamie Bennett
Senior Vice President - Marketing - Buena
    Vista TV & Walt Disney TV .... Carole Black
Senior Vice President - Sales .... Mort Marcus
Senior Vice President - Ad Sales .... Mike Shaw
Senior Vice President - Business
    Affairs - Syndication .... Kenneth D. Werner
Senior Vice President & General
    Manager .... Mark Zoradi
Vice President & General
    Sales Manager - East .... Tom Cerio

Vice President - Programming .... Bruno Cohen
Vice President - Ad Sales/Midwest ....Jim Engleman
Vice President - Marketing .... Rick Haskins
Vice President & General Sales
    Manager - West Coast .... Rick Jacobson
Vice President - Production ....Mary Kellogg-Joslyn
Vice President - Ad Sales .... Howard Levy
Vice President & Western
    Regional Manager .... Janice Marinelli-Mazza
Vice President - Media Strategy .... Michael Mellon
Vice President - Creative Services .... Sal Sardo
Vice President & Eastern
    Regional Manager .... Ken Solomon
Vice President - Production .... Screech Washington

Walt Disney Television and Touchstone Television
President - Television Animation .... Gary Krisel
Executive Vice President -
    Network TV .... Dean Valentine
Senior Vice President -
    Television Production .... Mitch Ackerman
Senior Vice President - Marketing - Walt
    Disney TV & Buena Vista Television ... Carole Black
Senior Vice President - Current
    Programs & The Disney Hour ....John Fitzpatrick
Senior Vice President - Magical
    World of Disney .... John Litvak
Senior Vice President -
    Movies for Television .... Sheri Singer
Senior Vice President -
    Business Affairs .... Kenneth Werner
Senior Vice President - Business
    Affairs - Network TV .... Laurie Younger
Vice President - Casting .... Eugene Blythe
Vice President - Information Services .... John Covas
Vice President - Production
    Resources .... Scott Dorman
Vice President - Advertising/
    Publicity/Promotion .... Marion Effinger
Vice President - Pay Television
    Sales & Administration .... Wendy Ferren
Vice President - Network
    Legal Affairs .... Scottye Hedstrom
Vice President - Labor Relations ... Robert W. Johnson
Vice President - Post
    Production (WD TV) .... Grady Jones
Vice President - Network
    Legal Affairs .... Lawrence Kaplan
Vice President - Videotape Production .... Ted Kaye
Vice President - Planning & Analysis .... Rob Moore
Vice President -
    TV Production Finance .... Walter O'Neal
Vice President - Controller .....Lawrence R. Rutkowski
Vice President - Network Specials .... Amy Sacks
Vice President - Current
    Comedy Programs .... Lance Taylor
Vice President - Worldwide Production
    and Television Animation .... Michael Webster
Vice President - Business
    Affairs - Network Television .... Evan Weiss
Director of Production .... Tom Ruzicka
Director - International Production ....Lenora Hume

Creative Executive ....Bruce Cranston
Creative Executive - Series
    Development ....Greg Weisman
Manager - Current Comedy Programs ....Jordan Levin
Development Associate ....Ron Baham

The Disney Channel
818/569-7500
Fax: 818/566-1358

President ....John F. Cooke
Senior Vice President - Program
    Development ....Patrick Davidson
Senior Vice President - Original
    Programming ....Stephen D. Fields
Senior Vice President - Sales
    & Affiliate Marketing ....Mark Handler
Senior Vice President - Programming ..Bruce N. Rider
Senior Vice President - Business &
    Legal Affairs ....Frederick Kuperberg
Vice President -
    Creative Affairs ....Peggy J. Christianson
Vice President - Central Region/
    Chicago ....James R. Clark
Vice President - Production ....Edwin T. Lahti
Vice President - Production ....Terry Spazek
Vice President -
    Finance/Administration ....Patrick T. Lopker
Vice President - Original
    Programming ....Gary K. Marsh
Vice President - Southeast
    Region/Atlanta ....Michael J. Mason
Vice President - Southwest
    Region/Dallas ....Douglas K. Miller
Vice President - Creative
    Development ....Michael R. Nichols
Vice President - Affiliate
    Operations ....Charles A. Nooney
Vice President - Media Relations .....Cory J. O'Connor
Vice President - Western
    Region/Los Angeles ....Virginia A. Overbagh
Vice President - Engineering &
    Operations ....Vincent H. Roberts
Vice President - Creative Services ...Dea J. Shandera
Vice President - National Accounts ...Ann L. Swanson
Vice President - Eastern
    Region/New York ....Steven L. Wagner
Vice President - New Business
    Development ....Winifred B. Wechsler
Vice President -
    Consumer Marketing ....Thomas J. Wszalek
Vice President - Acquisitions ....Douglas J. Zwick
Executive Director - Feature
    Film Development ....Carol Rubin
Executive Director -
    Program Development ....Cathy Johnson
Director - Program Development ....Ellen Burditt
Director - Production ....Bob Holmes
Director - Program Development ....Victoria Fraser
Manager - Program
    Development ....Randie Laine Wiatt

Buena Vista Home Video
President - International Theatrical Distribution &
    Worldwide Video ....William M. Mechanic
Executive Vice President ....Richard B. Cohen
Senior Vice President -
    Domestic Marketing ....Ann Daly
Senior Vice President - International
    Home Video ....Michael Orlin Johnson
Senior Vice President -
    Domestic Sales ....Richard E. Longwell
Senior Vice President - Business &
    Legal Affairs ....John J. Reagan
Senior Vice President - Worldwide
    Pay TV ....Hal Richardson
Vice President - Brand Marketing -
    U.S. & Canada ....Kelley Avery
Vice President - Domestic & International
    Anti-Piracy ....Judy Denenholz
Vice President - Marketing Services ...Randy Erickson
Vice President - Business
    Affairs & Acquisitions ....Jere Hausfater
Vice President - Finance &
    Administration ....David C. Hendler
Vice President - Advertising &
    Research ....Mary Kincaid
Vice President - Worldwide
    Operations ....Craig Kornblau
Vice President - Publicity ....Tania Steele
Vice President - Latin America & The
    Caribbean/International Home Video ..Diego Lerner
Vice President - International
    Administration/Operations ....Chris Menosky
Vice President - International Marketing ....Chris Jay
Vice President/Executive
    Managing Director - Japan & Far
    East - International Home Video ....Bill Pfeiffer
Vice President - Business &
    Legal Affairs ....Diana Rivera
Vice President/Managing Director -
    Europe & United Kingdom/
    International Home Video ....Stuart Warrener

Buena Vista Visual Effects
Vice President (WDP) ....Harrison Ellenshaw
Vice President - Administration ....Ray Scalice

Buena Vista Worldwide Services
3900 Alameda Ave.
Tower Bldg.
Burbank, CA 91521-0021
818/567-5454

Vice President ....Jeffrey S. Miller

Di

FILM
PRODUCERS,
STUDIOS,
AGENTS AND
CASTING
DIRECTORS
GUIDE

S
T
U
D
I
O
S

287

Ep

FILM
PRODUCERS,
STUDIOS,
AGENTS and
CASTING
DIRECTORS
GUIDE

S
T
U
D
I
O
S

E

EPIC PRODUCTIONS INC.
3330 W. Cahuenga Blvd., Suite 500
Los Angeles, CA 90068
213/969-2800
Fax: 213/969-8211

Co-Chair .... Moshe Diamant
Co-Chair .... Eduard Sarlui
President & Chief
    Operating Officer .... Andrew D.T. Pfeffer
Senior Vice President -
    Production .... Avram "Butch" Kaplan
President - Marketing & Distribution .... Elliot Slutzky
President - Home Video .... Don Rosenberg
Chief Financial Officer .... Nancy Halloran
Senior Vice President - Advertising .... Andy Foster
Senior Vice President - Business
    Affairs & General Counsel .... Richard Reiner
Senior Vice President - Theatrical
    Distribution .... David Garber
Vice President - National Publicity .... Jeff Freedman

F

FRIES ENTERTAINMENT INC.
6922 Hollywood Blvd.
Los Angeles, CA 90028-6133
213/466-2266
Fax: 213/466-9407

Chairman & Chief Executive Officer &
    President .... Charles W. Fries
Senior Executive Vice President -
    Administration .... Charles M. Fries
Executive Vice President - Television ..... Gary Kessler
Senior Vice President - Production ... Clark Henderson
Chief Financial Officer .... Dennis Hamilton
Executive Director - Development ..... Natalie Lemberg
Executive Vice President - Corporate
    Development .... James A. Parsons
Executive Vice President -
    Business Affairs .... Robert L. Chasin
Executive Vice President -
    Fries Television .... Clifford Alsberg
Executive Vice President - Motion
    Picture Development .... Michael Rosenfeld
Executive Vice President - Theatrical
    Production & Acquisitions .... Henry Seggerman

Senior Vice President - Promotion &
    Marketing .... Tony Habeeb
Vice President - Administration .... William Roland
Vice President - Corporate
    Development .... Kent Cristensen
Vice President - Development .... Christopher Fries
Vice President - Development,
    TV Series .... Terry Allen
Vice President - Production .... Andrea Newman
Vice President - Production
    Supervision .... S. Bryan Hickox
Vice President - Production .... Tom Fries
Vice President - International .... Midge Barnett

Fries Theatrical
Executive Vice President - International
    Distribution .... Larry Friedricks
Executive Vice President .... Maurice Singer
Vice President - International
    Distribution .... Paula Fierman
Director of Foreign Distribution .... Tracy Levin

Fries Home Video
Vice President - Advertising &
    Publicity .... Cathy Mantegna
Vice President - Operations &
    Administration .... Keith Wood

Fries Distribution
Executive Vice President Distribution .... Ave Butensky
Executive Vice President .... James Dudelson
Senior Vice President & General
    Sales Manager .... Peter Schmid
Senior Vice President -
    Distribution .... Richard H. Askin Jr.
Vice President - Firstrun Syndication &
    Daytime Development .... Allan Schwartz
Vice President - Advertising &
    Promotion .... Lou Wexner
Director of Advertising & Promotion .... Terri Kilroy

G

GLADDEN ENTERTAINMENT CORPORATION
10100 Santa Monica Blvd., Suite 600
Los Angeles, CA 90067
310/282-7500
Fax: 310/282-8262

Chairman .... Bruce McNall
President & Chief Executive Officer ... David Begelman
Vice President & Chief Financial Officer .. Suzan Waks
Controller .... Patricia Linden
Vice President - Business Affairs .... Ezra J. Doner
Vice President - Post Production .. Norman Wallerstein
Director - Creative Affairs .... Courtney Silberberg
Marketing & Distribution Consultant .... Richard Kahn

Ho

FILM
PRODUCERS,
STUDIOS,
AGENTS AND
CASTING
DIRECTORS
GUIDE

S
T
U
D
I
O
S

THE SAMUEL GOLDWYN COMPANY
10203 Santa Monica Blvd.
Los Angeles, CA 90067
310/552-2255
Fax: 310/284-8493

Chairman & Chief
  Executive Officer .... Samuel Goldwyn Jr.
President & Chief
  Operating Officer .... Meyer Gottlieb
Director - TV Production &
  Development .... Julie Resh
Director - Acquisitions .... Betsy Spanbock
Story Editor .... Ellen Cockrill
Senior Vice President - Worldwide
  Marketing .... Ronald Wanless
Vice President -
  International Marketing .... Diana Hawkins
President - Worldwide
  Production .... Thomas Rothman
Senior Vice President - Business
  Affairs .... Norman Flicker
Senior Vice President -
  Theatrical Distribution .... Steve Rothenberg
Vice President - Publicity .... Leonie de Picciotto
Senior Vice President -
  Chief Financial Officer .... Hans Turner
Senior Vice President - International
  Theatrical Sales .... Andrew Milner
Senior Vice President - International &
  TV Operations .... J. Michael Byrd
Vice President - Asian & Latin
  American TV Sales .... Saralo MacGregor
Vice President - East Coast
  Creative Affairs .... Bonnie Solow
Vice President - Advertising .... Dan Gelfand
Vice President - Production &
  Acquisitions .... Howard Cohen
Vice President - Cable &
  Ancillary Sales .... Jeri Sacks

Television
President .... Dick Askin
Vice President - National
  Sales Manager .... Gary Perchick
Vice President - European
  Television Sales .... Gary Phillips

H

HEMDALE FILM CORPORATION
7966 Beverly Blvd.
Los Angeles, CA 90048
213/966-3700
Fax: 213/651-3107

Chairman .... John Daly
President .... Derek Gibson
Executive Vice President -
  Worldwide Marketing .... Martin Rabinovitch
Executive Vice President -
  International .... Kathy Morgan
Executive Vice President .... Terence Hustedt
Senior Vice President .... Steve Rothman
Vice President - Advertising .... Ed McKenna
Vice President - Aquisitions &
  Development .... Dorian Langdon
Director - Business Affairs .... Ron Aikin
Director - Creative Advertising .... David Zimmerman
Director - Foreign Sales &
  Acquisitions, London .... George Miller
Director - Publicity .... Amy Sexton
General Sales Manager .... Dick Miller
Acquisitions .... Ann Marie Gillen

Hemdale Releasing Corp.
Chairman .... John Daly
President - Worldwide Distribution .... Andy Gruenberg
Executive Vice President .... Derek Gibson

HOLLYWOOD PICTURES
(See Walt DISNEY Co.)

HOME BOX OFFICE, INC.
1100 Avenue of the Americas
New York, NY 10036
212/512-1000
Fax: 212/512-5517

2049 Century Park East, Suite 4100
Los Angeles, CA 90067-3215
310/201-9200
Fax: 310/201-9293

Chairman & Chief Executive Officer ..... Michael Fuchs
President & COO .... Jeff Bewkes
President - HBO Independent
  Productions .... Chris Albrecht
Executive Vice President -
  HBO Enterprises .... Lee DeBoer
Vice President - International
  Operations .... Larry Aidem
Vice President - East Coast Production .... Bill Chase
Vice President - Creative Affairs,
  Film Programming .... Bob Conte

Vice President & Executive Producer -
HBO Sports .... Ross Greenburg
Vice President - Sports Programming .. Bob Greenway
Vice President - Documentaries &
Family Programming .... Sheila Nevins
Vice President - Film Programming ... Perry Schneider
Vice President - Documentary
Development .... Cis Wilson
Vice President - Original
Programming .... Betty Bitterman
Executive Producer -
HBO Showcase .... Colin Callender
Executive Vice President - Affiliate
Sales & Operations .... Larry Carlson
Senior Vice President & Chief
Financial Officer .... Bill Nelson
Senior Vice President &
General Counsel .... John Redpath
Senior Vice President - Business
Affairs .... Harold Akselrad
Executive Vice President - Film
Programming & Home Video ... Stephen J. Scheffer
Senior Vice President - Film
Programming .... Leslie Jacobson
Senior Vice President - Marketing .... John Billick
Senior Vice PresidentOperations .... Bob Zitter
Senior Vice President - Original
Programming .... Bridget Potter
Vice President - Creative Affairs .... Lowell Mate
Vice President - Talent Relations &
Special Events .... Arthur Bedanas
Vice President - HBO Downtown
Productions .... Nancy Geller
Vice President - Corporate Affairs .... Jim Noonan
Vice President - Media Relations ...... Quentin Schaffer
Vice President - HBO International .. Steve Rosenberg
Vice President - Production,
East Coast .... Bill Chase
Vice President - Program Planning .... David Baldwin
Vice President - Program Promotion .... Kimball Howell
Vice President - Advertising .... Roberta Mell
Vice President - Reseach .... Bob Maxwell

HBO Pictures
Senior Vice President .... Robert Cooper
Senior Vice President - Business
Affairs .... Glenn Whitehead
Senior Vice President - Legal .... Horace Collins
Senior Vice President - Original
Programming .... Chris Albrecht
Director of Production .... Dennis Bishop
Vice President - Production .... Elaine Sperber
Vice President .... Richard Waltzer
Vice President .... Laurette Hayden
Associate Director - Original
Programming .... Susie Fitzgerald
Vice President - Business
Affairs .... Michael Lombardo
Vice President - Business
Affairs/Production .... Bruce Gelvetti
Vice President - Film Acquisitions .... Neil Brown

Vice President - Media Relations ...... Quentin Schaffer
Vice President - Media Relations,
West Coast .... Richard Licata
Vice President .... Susie Fitzgerald
Vice President - Program Publicity .... Ellen Rubin

HBO Video
President .... Eric Kessler
Senior Vice President - Marketing .... Tracy Dolgin
Vice President - Direct Marketing &
New Business Development .... Ellen Stolzman

Time Warner Sports
President .... Seth G. Abraham
Senior Vice President &
Chief Financial Officer .... MarkTaffet
Vice President - Production .... Linda Jackson
Vice President & General Counsel .... Lou diBella

Citadel Entertainment
President .... David Ginsberg
Senior Vice President -
Development & Production .... Tom Patricia

I

IMAGE ORGANIZATION INC.
9000 Sunset Blvd., Suite 915
Los Angeles, CA 90069
310/278-8751
Fax: 310/278-3967

Chairman & Chief Executive Officer .... Pierre David
Senior Vice President .... Lawrence Goebel
Vice President - Worldwide
Distribution .... Meyer Shwarzstein
Co-Chairman .... Rene Malo
Vice President - Production .... Noel Zanitsch
Controller .... Robert Hartstone
Director of Marketing .... Lee Matis

IMAGINE FILMS ENTERTAINMENT INC.
1925 Century Park East, Suite 2300
Los Angeles, CA 90067-2734
310/277-1665
Fax: 310/785-0107

Co-Chairman & Chief Executive Officer ... Ron Howard
Co-Chairman & Chief Executive Officer ..Brian Grazer
President - Production .... David Friendly
CFO & Senior Vice President - Finance ..Mike Meltzer
Senior Vice President -
Marketing .... Michael Rosenberg
Senior Vice President - Marketing .... Rich Cronin

Is

FILM
PRODUCERS,
STUDIOS,
AGENTS AND
CASTING
DIRECTORS
GUIDE

Senior Vice President -
New Business .... Anne Kreamer
Vice President -
Physical Production .... Michael Nelson
Executive in Charge of Production .... Bill Aikens
Executive in Charge of Production .... Terry Castle
Supervising Producer .... Roseanne Lopopolo
Director - Program Development .... Gwen Billings
Director - Talent Relations .... Michael Koegel
Director - Development .... Michael Bostick
Director - Development .... Devorah Moos
Senior Vice President - Business
Affairs .... Peter Bachman
Senior Vice President -
Motion Pictures .... Tova Laiter
Vice President - Controller .... Adene Walter
Vice President - Production Finance .... Jerry L. Rife
Vice President -
Motion Pictures .... Karen Kehela
Story Editor .... Diana Mack

Second City Entertainment
Andrew Alexander
Michael Rollens

THE INDIEPROD COMPANY
8800 Sunset Blvd., 5th Floor
Los Angeles, CA 90069-2105
310/289-7100
Fax: 310/652-2165

President .... Daniel Melnick
President - TV .... Bruce J. Sallan
Executive Vice President &COO .... Allen Shapiro
Vice President - Production .... Nancy Graham
Vice President .... Julie Bourne
Vice President .... Elizabeth Fox
Director - TV Development .... Andrew Burg
Production Executive .... Matt West

INTERSCOPE COMMUNICATIONS
10900 Wilshire Blvd., Suite 1400
Los Angeles, CA 90024
310/208-8525
Fax: 310/208-1764

President .... Robert W. Cort
Executive Vice President-
Television .... Patricia Clifford
Senior Vice President .... Michael Helfant
Senior Production Executive .... Scott Kroopf
Senior Production Executive .... David Madden
Vice President - TV .... Ed Gold
Production Executive .... Karen Murphy
Creative Executive .... Randy Castleman
Director - Television
Development .... Suzanne Welch
Production Executive .... Cynthia Sherman

ISLAND WORLD, INC.
8920 Sunset Blvd.
Second Floor
Los Angeles, CA 90069
310/276-4500
Fax: 310/271-7840

630 Fifth Avenue
Suite 1505
New York, NY 10111
212/632-3456
Fax: 212/632-3457

Chairman & Chief
Executive Officer .... John Heyman
President .... David Brown
Executive Vice President .... Jeff Dalla Betta (LA)
Senior Vice President .... Gary Lehman (LA)
Vice President - Business &
Legal Affairs .... Robert Chernoff (LA)

Island World Los Angeles, Inc.
Co-President .... Mark Burg
Co-President .... Chris Zarpas
Vice President - Production .... Todd Baker

Isalnd Pictures, Inc.
Chairman .... Chris Blackwell
Executive Vice President .... Dan Genetti

World Films, Inc.
President & Chief
Executive Officer .... Ann Dubinet
Vice President .... Nancy Lund

World Film Services, Inc.
1270 Avenue of the Americas
Suite 609
New York, NY 10020
212/632-3461
Fax: 212/632-3459

388 North Kentor Ave.
Los Angeles, CA 90069
310/471-7490
Fax: 310/471-8128

President .... David Brown
Executive Vice President .... Bill Gilmore
Vice President - Production .... Pamela Hedley (LA)

Islet, Inc.
153 Waverly Place
12th Floor
New York, NY 10014
212/620-9035
Fax: 212/645-1389

Managing Director .... John Pierson

Is

FILM
PRODUCERS,
STUDIOS,
AGENTS AND
CASTING
DIRECTORS
GUIDE

S
T
U
D
I
O
S

Island World, Ltd.
Pinewood Studios
Iver Heath
Bucks SL0 0NH, England
071/493-3045
Fax: 075/365-6475

Chairman .... John Heyman
Managing Director .... John Chambers
Production .... Richard Dalton

Island World Productions, Ltd.
12-14 Argyle Street
London W1V 1AB, England
071/734-3536
Fax: 071/734-3585

999 North Doheny
Suite 1001
Los Angeles, CA 90069
310/274-6539
Fax: 310/205-0776

Chief Executive Officer .... Tony Garnett
Chief Operating Officer .... Margaret Matheson
Head of International TV .... Michael Deeley
Development &
    Co-Productions .... Annette Kiely
Creative Affairs .... Katherine Haber (LA)

ITC ENTERTAINMENT GROUP
12711 Ventura Blvd.
Studio City, CA 91604
818/760-2110
Fax: 818/506-8189

115 E. 57th St.
New York, NY 10022
212/371-6660

President & Chief
    Executive Officer .... Chris Gorog
Executive Vice President -
    International .... James P. Marrinan
Senior Vice President - Worldwide
    Acquisitions .... Paul Almond

M

MANAGEMENT COMPANY ENTERTAINMENT GROUP, INC.
2121 Avenue of the Stars, Suite 2630
Los Angeles, CA 90067
310/282-0871

Chief Executive Officer .... John Hyde
President .... Raymond H. Godfrey, Jr.
Senior Executive Vice President .... William Tennant
Executive Vice President &
    Chief Financial Officer .... Mark Q. Huggins
Vice President - Corporate Controller &
    Chief Accounting Officer .... Kathryn E. Nielsen

MCA, INC.
(see UNIVERSAL Pictures)

MGM/PATHE COMMUNICATIONS COMPANY
10000 W. Washington Blvd.
Culver City, CA 90232
310/280-6000
Fax: 310/836-1680

Chairman .... Alan Ladd, Jr.
Chairman of Production .... Jay Kanter
Executive Vice President -
    Production Management .... Leonard Kroll
Vice President - Production .... David Ladd
Vice President - Production .... Rebecca Pollack
Vice President - Creative Affairs ...... Gregory A. Foster
Vice President - Creative Affairs ... Elizabeth Robinson

MIRAMAX
375 Greenwich St.
New York, NY 10013
212/941-3800
Fax: 212/941-3949

Co-Chairman .... Harvey Weinstein
Co-Chairman .... Bob Weinstein
Executive Vice President &
    Chief Financial Officer .... John Schmidt
Executive Vice President -
    Marketing .... Russell Schwartz
Executive Vice President -
    Distribution .... Martin Zeidman
Senior Vice President - Legal .... Ezra Doner

MORGAN CREEK PRODUCTIONS

1875 Century Park East, Suite 200
Los Angeles, CA 90067
310/284-8884
Fax: 310/282-8794

Chairman & Chief
    Executive Officer .... James G. Robinson
Chief Operating Officer .... Gary Barber
President .... David Nicksay
President - Marketing .... Gordon Armstrong
Vice President - Business
    Affairs - Finance .... Gary Stutman
Senior Vice President - Production .... Larry Katz
Vice President - Production .... Jonathan A. Zimbert
Vice President - Advertising .... Luke Adams
Vice President - Production Control .... Shelley Katz
Vice President - Post-Production .... Jody Levin
Senior Vice President - Morgan
    Creek International .... Julian Levin
Story Editor .... Scott Soloman

MTM ENTERPRISES, INC.

4024 Radford Ave.
Studio City, CA 91604
818/760-5942
Fax: 818/760-5826

President & Chief
    Executive Officer .... Robert Klosterman
President - International Programming ...... Tim Buxton
President - Distribution .... Kevin Tannehill
President - Television .... Peter Grad
Senior Executive Vice President &
    Chief Financial Officer .... Edward Bowen
Executive Vice President -
    General Counsel .... Ken Meyer
Executive Vice President - MTM TV .... Bill Allen
Executive Producer -
    Movies & Miniseries .... Bob Silberling
Vice President - Business &
    Legal Affairs .... Neil Strum
Vice President - Creative Affairs .... Bill Sheinberg
Vice President - Production .... Bernie Oseransky
Vice President - Creative Services .... Janet Bonifer
Vice President - Programming .... Bob George
Vice President - Operations .... Scott Higgins
Director - Post-Production/International
    Distribution .... Alicia Hirsch
Director - Production Estimating .... Robert J. Lewis
Director - West Coast Sales .... Tom Staszewski
Director - Research .... Tim McGowan

N

Nb

FILM
PRODUCERS,
STUDIOS,
AGENTS AND
CASTING
DIRECTORS
GUIDE

S
T
U
D
I
O
S

NBC

3000 W. Alameda Ave.
Burbank, CA 91523-0001
818/840-4444

30 Rockefeller Plaza

New York, NY 10020
212/664-4444

Chairman of the Board .... John Welch, Jr.
President & Chief Executive Officer .... Robert Wright

NBC Entertainment

President .... Warren Littlefield
Executive Vice President -
    Primetime Programs .... Perry Simon
Senior Vice President -
    Programs (East Coast) .... Lee Curlin
Senior Vice President - Specials & Variety
    Programs & Late-Night .... Richard Ludwin
Vice President - Current
    Comedy Programs .... Ted Frank
Vice President - Comedy Development ..... Leslie Lurie
Vice President - Production
    Business Affairs .... Lorna Bitensky
Vice President - Business Affairs .... Harold Brook
Vice President - Business Affairs .... Leslie Maskin
Vice President - Talent & Casting .... Lori Openden
Vice President - Drama Development .... Brian Pike
Vice President - Miniseries .... Ruth Slawson
Vice President - Daytime Programs .... Susan D. Lee
Vice President - Program &
    Media Planning .... Paul Wang
Vice President - Current
    Drama Programs .... Charisse McGhee
Director - Child & Family Programs .... Linda Pitt
Director - Daytime Development .... Michael Bevan
Director - Primetime Programs
    (East Coast) .... Danelle Black
Director - Story Department .... Geoffrey Harris
Director - Motion Pictures for TV .... Lisa Demberg
Director - Specials &
    Late-Night Programs .... Patti Grant
Director - Business Affairs .... Clay Lorinsky
Director - Business Affairs .... Stephen Grynberg
Director - Movies &
    Miniseries for TV .... Ricka Kanter Fisher
Director - Casting .... Jeff Meshel
Director - Motion Pictures for TV .... Michael Tenzer
Director - Drama Development .... Kevin Reilly
Director - Current Comedy Programs ..... Jeffrey Rowe
Director - Comedy Development .... Jamie Tarses
Director - Motion Pictures for TV .... Winifred Neisser
Director - Children's Programs .... Janice Souski

Nb

FILM
PRODUCERS,
STUDIOS,
AGENTS AND
CASTING
DIRECTORS
GUIDE

S
T
U
D
I
O
S

Director - Current
Comedy Programs .... David Zuckerman
Director - Miniseries & Novels for TV ... R. Mindy Green
Director - Current Comedy Programs .... Ken Mok
Director - Current Drama Programs .... Dona Cooper
Manager - Specials, Variety Programs &
Late-Night .... Jeremiah Bosgang
Manager - Daytime Programs .... Jonathan Littman

NBC Business Affairs
Senior Vice President .... Joseph Burges

NBC Productions
President .... John Agoglia
Senior Vice President & Executive in
Charge - Film Production .... Dennis A. Brown
Senior Vice President .... Todd P. Leavitt
Senior Vice President -
Production Operations .... Gary Considine
Vice President - Media Relations .... Gene Walsh
Vice President - Post-Production .... Dorothy Bailey
Vice President - Production & Marketing,
Business Affairs .... Albert Spevak
Director - Creative Affairs .... Sue Norris

NELSON ENTERTAINMENT
335 N. Maple Dr., Suite 350
Beverly Hills, CA 90210-3867
310/285-6000
Fax: 310/285-6199

8 Queen St.
London W1X 7PH

Chairman & Chief
Executive Officer .... Richard Northcott
President & COO .... Barry Spikings
President of Motion
Picture Production .... Rick Finkelstein
Executive Vice President .... Peter Graves
Vice President - Production .... Graham Henderson
Production Manager .... Bonnie Grossblatt
Director - Creative Affairs .... Susan Seletsky

Nelson International
President .... Massimo Graziosi

NEW LINE CINEMA
116 N. Robertson Blvd, 2nd Floor
Los Angeles, CA 90048
310/854-5811
Fax: 310/854-1824

575 8th Ave., 16th Floor
New York, NY 10018
212/239-8880
Fax: 212/239-9104

Chairman & Chief Executive Officer ...... Robert Shaye
President & COO .... Michael Lynne
Senior Vice President - Business Affairs .... Donna L.
Bascom
Vice President - Business Affairs .... Phillip Rosen

New Line Productions, Inc.
President .... Sarah Risher
Executive Vice President -
Production, East Coast .... Michael Harpster
Senior Vice President - Production ..... Deborah Moore
Vice President - Creative
Development .... Michael De Luca
Vice President - Post-Production .... Joseph Fineman
Vice President - Creative Affairs,
East Coast .... Janet Grillo
Vice President - Creative Affairs,
West Coast .... Marjorie Lewis
Vice President - Acquisitions &
Co-Production .... Tony Safford
Vice President - Production .... Cindy Hornickel
Vice President - Production .... Kevin Moreton
Vice President - Production .... Rachel Talalay
Creative Executive .... Aaron Meyerson
Director - Creative Affairs .... Nancy Moss
Director - Development, West Coast ..... Mark Ordesky
Director - Development,
East Coast .... Laurence Schwartz
Story Editor - East Coast .... Melanie Backer
Story Editor - West Coast .... Donna Hyams

O

ORION PICTURES CORPORATION
1888 Century Park East
Los Angeles, CA 90067-1728
310/282-0550

9 W. 57th St.
New York, NY 10019
212/980-1117

Founder & Chairman .... Arthur Krim
Chairman of the Board .... Eric Pleskow
President & Chief Executive Officer . William Bernstein
Executive Vice President .... David Forbes
Executive Vice President .... Marc E. Platt
Senior Vice President -
Post-Production .... Solomon Lomita
Vice President - Production .... John B. Carls
Vice President - Production .... Michelle Manning
Director - Creative Affairs .... Mark Protosevich
Story Editor .... Mike Karz

Orion Television Entertainment
Senior Vice President -
Production/Comedy .... Rick Rosen
Vice President -
Television Overhead .... Robert I. Sanitsky
Director - Development .... Nancy Perlman

P

PARAMOUNT PICTURES

5555 Melrose Ave.
Hollywood, CA 90038-3197
213/956-5000

Chairman .... Brandon Tartikoff
Executive Vice President &
    General Counsel .... A. Robert Pisano
Executive Vice President & Chief
    Financial Officer .... Patrick Purcell
Executive Vice President .... M. Kenneth Suddleson
Executive Vice President .... Richard Zimbert

Paramount Motion Picture Group
President .... David Kirkpatrick
President .... Barry London
Executive Vice President -
    Production .... John Goldwyn
Senior Vice President - Business
    Affairs & Acquisitions .... Richard Fowkes
Senior Vice President -
    Business Affairs .... Gregory Gelfan
Senior Vice President - Legal Affairs ..... Ralph Kamon
Vice President - Business Affairs .... Steven Bersch
Vice President - Legal Affairs .... Robert Cohen
Vice President - Acquisitions .... John Ferraro
Vice President - Music Legal Affairs .... Linda Wohl
Vice President - Creative Affairs .... Robert McMinn
Vice President - Music Business Affairs ... Kevin Koloff

Paramount Production Division
Senior Vice President .... Thomas Barad
Senior Vice President .... William Horberg
Senior Vice President .... Karen Rosenfelt
Senior Vice President -
    European Production (UK) .... Ileen Maisel
Senior Vice President - Feature
    Production Management .... Robert Relyea
Senior Vice President - Music .... Harlan Goodman
Vice President - Feature
    Production Management .... Larry Albucher
Vice President .... Don Granger
Vice President - Production Finance .... Frank Bodo
Vice President - Feature
    Production Administration .... Jeffery Coleman
Vice President - Post-Production .... Fred Chandler
Vice President - Production .... Mindy Farrell
Vice President - Casting .... Nancy Foy
Creative Executive .... Tony Smoller
Creative Executive .... Margaret Freanch
Creative Executive .... Jenny Mead
Creative Executive .... John Soriano
Director - Creative Affairs .... Doug Collins
Creative Director .... John-Michael Maas

Paramount Television Group
President .... Kerry McCluggage
Senior Vice President .... Jack Waterman
Vice President & Controller .... Alan C. Fels
Vice President - Operations .... Philip Murphy

Domestic Television Division
President .... Steven Goldman
Executive Vice President -
    Programming .... Frank Kelly
Senior Vice President - Business
    Affairs/Finance .... Robert Sheehan
Senior Vice President -
    Business Affairs .... Vance Van Petten
Vice President - Finance .... Emeline Davis
Vice President - Legal Affairs .... Thomas Fortuin
Vice President - Programming .... Carlotte Koppe
Vice President - Production .... Clifford Lachman
Vice President -
    Creative Affairs .... Steven Nalevansky
Vice President - Production .... Jack Wartlieb
Director - Program Development .... Barbara Bruce

Network Television Division
President .... John Pike
Executive Vice President -
    Business Affairs .... Cecelia Andrews
Executive Vice President -
    Network Programming .... John Symes
Senior Vice President - Legal Affairs ...Howard Barton
Senior Vice President - Development .... Dan Fauci
Vice President - Finance .... Gerald Goldman
Vice President -
    Current Programming .... Tim Iacofano
Vice President - Business Affairs ..... Ronald Jacobson
Vice President - Current Programming ..... Tom Mazza
Vice President - Talent & Casting .... Helen Mossler
Vice President - Advertising/
    Promotion/Publicity .... John A. Wentworth
Vice President - Business Affairs ...... Dirk van de Bunt
Director - Development .... Maria Crena

Paramount Video Division
President .... Robert Klingensmith
Executive Vice President .... Timothy Clott
Executive Vice President .... Eric Doctorow
Senior Vice President - Business
    Affairs & International .... James Gianopulos
Vice President - Legal Affairs .... Steven Madoff

Pa

FILM
PRODUCERS,
STUDIOS,
AGENTS AND
CASTING
DIRECTORS
GUIDE

S
T
U
D
I
O
S

Ra

FILM
PRODUCERS,
STUDIOS,
AGENTS AND
CASTING
DIRECTORS
GUIDE

S
T
U
D
I
O
S

R

S

RASTAR PRODUCTIONS

Maple Plaza
335 North Maple Dr., Suite 356
Beverly Hills, CA 90210
310/247-0130
Fax: 310/247-9120

Ray Stark .... Chairman
Vice Chairman .... William Nestel
Senior Vice President, Marketing .... Don Safran
Executive Vice President -
    Production .... MaryKay Powell
Vice President - Creative Affairs .... Tracey Barone

REPUBLIC PICTURES

12636 Beatrice St.
Los Angeles, CA 90066
310/306-4040
Fax: 310/301-0142

Chairman & Chief
    Executive Officer .... Russell Goldsmith
President -
    Domestic Distribution .... Charles W. Larsen
President - International Sales .... Joe Levinsohn
Senior Vice President -
    Acquisitions & Production .... Mel Layton
Senior Vice President & Chief Financial
    Officer .... David Kirchheimer
Senior Vice President - Marketing .... Glenn Ross
Senior Vice President -
    TV Comedy .... Ellen Endo-Dizon
Executive Vice President .... Steven Beeks
Vice President - Business
    Affairs & Legal .... Marty Kaplan
Vice President - Home Video .... Phil Kromnick
Vice President & National
    Sales Manager .... Gary Jones

SCOTTI BROTHERS ENTERTAINMENT

2114 Pico Blvd.
Santa Monica, CA 90405
310/452-4040
Fax: 310/452-9053

Co-Chairman & Chief Executive Officer ..... Tony Scotti
Co-Chairman .... Ben Scotti
Development .... Dan Watanabe

SHAPIRO GLICKENHAUS ENTERTAINMENT

12001 Ventura Pl., Suite 404
Studio City, CA 91604
818/766-8500
Fax: 818/766-7873

Chairman .... James Glickenhaus
President .... Leonard Shapiro
Executive Vice President .... Alan Solomon
Vice President, Worldwide Production ...... Frank Isaac

SONY PICTURES ENTERTAINMENT, INC.

10202 W. Washington Blvd.
Culver City, CA 90232-3195
310/280-8000

President - Columbia Pictures
    International TV .... Nicholas Bingham
President - RCA/Columbia
    Worldwide Video .... W. Patrick Campbell
President - Music
    Publishing Division .... Robert Holmes
Executive Vice President-
    Legal Affairs .... Jared Jussim
Vice President .... David Rosenfelt
Vice President - Regulatory Affairs ..... Vicki R. Solmon

Columbia Motion Picture Group
Chairman .... Peter Guber
President & COO .... Alan J. Levine
President - Motion Picture Groups .... Jonathan Dolgen
Chief Operating Officer .... Lewis J. Korman
Executive Vice President -
    Office of the Chairman .... Sid Ganis
Executive Vice President .... Paul Schaeffer
Executive Vice President .... David Matalon
Vice President - Columbia Tri-Star
    Film Distribution .... Marie M. Collins
Vice President -
    Office of the Chairmen .... Cary Woods

Columbia Pictures

Chairman .... Mark Canton
Executive Vice President .... Marvin Antonowsky
President - Production .... Michael Nathanson
Executive Production Consultant .... Gareth Wigan
Vice President - Production .... Stephanie Allain
Director - Development .... Jay Bernzweig
Creative Executive .... John Jashni
Creative Executive .... Robert Jaffe
Creative Executive .... Lizz Speed
Director - Operations .... Robert Romero
Executive Story Editor .... Eileen Stringer
Manager - Research .... Lea Goldbaum
Chief Financial Officer .... Lawrence J. Ruisi
President - Marketing .... Buffy Shutt
President - Domestic Distribution .... James Spitz
President - Production Administration .... Gary Martin
Executive Vice President .... Arnold W. Messer
Executive Vice President .... Roger Faxon
Executive Vice President .... Gary Schrager
Executive Vice President - Marketing ...... Kathy Jones
Executive Vice President -
   Operations .... David L. Kennedy
Executive Vice President - Production ..... Darris Hatch
Executive Vice President - Production ...... Amy Pascal
Executive Vice President - Production .... Teddy Zee
Executive Vice President - Worldwide
   Post Production .... Thomas McCarthy
Senior Vice President .... M. Jay Wilkingshaw
Senior Vice President - Advertising &
   Director of Creative Services .... Kenneth Stewart
Senior Vice President - Advertising .... William Loper
Senior Vice President - Business
   Affairs & Administration .... Christie Rothenberg
Senior Vice President -
   Business Affairs .... Lee N. Rosenbaum
Senior Vice President - Creative
   Advertising .... Howard Russo
Senior Vice President &
   General Counsel .... Ronald N. Jakobi
Senior Vice President &
   General Sales Manager .... Jerry Jorgensen
Senior Vice President - Legal Affairs .... Beth Burke
Senior Vice President - Legal Affairs &
   Assistant General Counsel .... Mark Resnick
Senior Vice President - Legal
   Affairs - Distribution .... Vicki R. Solmon
Senior Vice President - Marketing .... Eddie Egan
Senior Vice President - Media .... John Butkovich
Senior Vice President - Publicity,
   Promotion & Field Operations .... Edward Russell
Senior Vice President - Research .... Lenore Cantor
Senior Vice President - West
   Coast Administration .... Barbara Cline
Vice President - Advertising,
   Publicity & Promotion .... Janice E. Glaser
Vice President - Assistant
   Controller .... Richard Bengloff
Vice President - Assistant
   Treasurer .... Joseph W. Kraft
Vice President - Business
   Affairs Administration .... Thomas R. Stack

Vice President - Business
   Affairs, Music Group .... Keith C. Zajic
Vice President - Controller .... Edgar H. Howells Jr.
Vice President - Controller .... Jay M. Green
Vice President - East
   Coast Publicity .... Dennis Higgins
Vice President - Legal Affairs ...... Joan Salzman Grant
Vice President - Legal Affairs .... Phyllis Olmes
Vice President - Marketing &
   Distribution Administration .... Patrick D. Walters
Vice President - Music .... Bones Howe
Vice President - Operations .... Conrad K. Steely
Vice President - Operations .... David Holman
Vice President - Operations &
   Administration .... Mark Zucker
Vice President - Personnel .... Susan B. Ganelli
Vice President - Post Production .... Jim Honore
Vice President - Production .... Dennis Greene
Vice President - Production .... Barry Sabath
Vice President - Publicity &
   Special Events .... Hollace G. Davids
Vice President - Publicity .... Ann-Marie Stein
Vice President - Research .... Ariel Diaz
Vice President - Sales Planning .... Richard B. Elliott
Vice President - Studio Publicity .... Mark Gill
Vice President - Treasurer .... Kenneth S. Williams
Vice President - West Coast
   Administration .... Frederick J. Garcia
Vice President .... Claire Bisceglia
Executive Story Editor .... John B. Carls

Columbia Pictures Television
818/972-7000

Chairman & Chief Executive Officer .... Gary Lieberthal
President .... Scott Siegler
Senior Vice President -
   Talent & Casting .... Rick Jacobs
Senior Vice President -
   Business Affairs .... Jan Abrams
Senior Vice President - Corporate
   Communications & Publicity .... Don Demesquita
Senior Vice President - Drama
   Development .... Jeff Wachtel
Senior Vice President -
   Film Production .... William Phillips
Senior Vice President - Legal Affairs ... Gregory Boone
Senior Vice President - Marketing .... Michael Zucker
Senior Vice President - Research .... David Mumford
Senior Vice President .... Andrew J. Kaplan
Senior Vice President - Comedy
   Development .... Steven Mendelson
Vice President - Business
   Affairs Administration .... Stephanie Knauer
Vice President - Business Affairs .... Harvey Harrison
Vice President - Business Affairs .... Jeffrey S. Weiss
Vice President - Business Affairs .... Richard Frankie
Vice President - Comedy
   Development .... Lori Forte
Vice President - Current Comedy .... Jeanie Bradley
Vice President - Production .... Ed Lammi
Vice President - Production .... Mark Hufnail

So

FILM
PRODUCERS,
STUDIOS,
AGENTS AND
CASTING
DIRECTORS
GUIDE

S
T
U
D
I
O
S

So

**FILM
PRODUCERS,
STUDIOS,
AGENTS AND
CASTING
DIRECTORS
GUIDE**

**S
T
U
D
I
O
S**

Vice President -
  Videotape Operations .... David Holman
Director - Talent & Casting ...... Nancy McLeod Perkins
Director - Casting Administration .... Sonia Clyne
Director - Current Comedy .... Michael Hanel
Director - Comedy Development .... Ted Schachter
Director - Drama Development .... Jeff Kline
Manager - Comedy Development .... Allison Brecker
Program Executive .... Ellen Douglas
Program Executive .... Sheryl Rubinstein
Director - Talent & Casting .... Rick Millikan
Vice President - Research .... Douglas Roth

Columbia Pictures International Television
President .... Nicholas Bingham

RCA/Columbia Home Video Worldwide
President & Chief
  Executive Officer .... W. Patrick Campbell
Executive Vice President &
  Chief Financial Officer .... William Chardavoyne
Executive Vice President &
  Chief Operating Officer .... Paul Culberg
Executive Vice President - International
  Sales & Marketing .... Chris Deering
Executive Vice President .... James Tauber
Vice President - Worldwide
  Acquisitions & Business Affairs .... Gina Resnick
Vice President - Acquisitions &
  Programming .... Larry Estes
Vice President - Business &
  Legal Affairs .... Monica Lipkin

Trilogy Entertainment Group
10202 W. Washington Blvd.
Culver City, CA 90232

10100 Venice Blvd.
Turner Bldg., Suite 300
Culver City, CA 90232
310/204-3133
Fax: 310/204-1160

Partner .... Pen Densham
Partner .... Richard Lewis
Partner .... John Watson
Vice President - Development .... Christian L. Rehr
Vice President - Production .... Mark Stern

TriStar Pictures
10202 W. Washington Blvd.
Culver City, CA 90232
310/280-8000

Chairman .... Mike Medavoy
Executive Vice President - Production .... Alan Riche
Executive Vice President -
  Worldwide Production .... Stephen F. Randall
Senior Vice President - Production .... Richard Fischoff
Senior Vice President - Production .... Shelley Hochron
Senior Vice President - Production .... Kathy Lingg
Senior Vice President - Production .... Chris Lee

Director - Creative Affairs .... Stan Chervin
Senior Executive Vice President -
  Business Affairs .... Kenneth Lemberger
Executive Vice President -
  Domestic Distribution .... William Soady
Executive Vice President &
  General Counsel .... Leslie H. Jacobson
Senior Vice President &
  Production Controller .... Donald B. Miller
Senior Vice President -
  Creative Advertising .... Dallas Garred
Senior Vice President -
  General Sales Manager .... Robert Capps
Senior Vice President -
  Legal Affairs .... Lisbeth Aschenbrenner
Senior Vice President - National
  Advertising & Research .... Mark Kristol
Vice President - Production .... Kevin Misher
Vice President - Administration ..... Gerald Iannaccone
Vice President - Ancillary Markets .... Glen Meredith
Vice President & Assistant
  Controller - Theatrical .... Winston van Buitenen
Vice President - Business Affairs
  Administration .... Grant Gullickson
Vice President - Business Affairs .... John Sansone
Vice President - Creative
  Advertising .... Stephanie Allen
Vice President & Division
  Manager - Central .... Jack Simmons
Vice President & Division
  Manager - Eastern .... Howard Mahler
Vice President & Division
  Manager - Southern .... Joe Kennedy
Vice President & Division
  Manager - Western .... Rory Bruer
Vice President - Field Publicity &
  Promotion .... Ellen Kroner
Vice President - Legal Affairs .... Jon Gibson
Vice President - Legal Affairs .... Rebecca Nunberg
Vice President - Legal Affairs,
  Distribution & Marketing .... Surie Rudoff
Vice President - Management
  Information Systems .... James J. Dileo
Vice President - National Publicity .... Cara White
Vice President - National Publicity .... Marcy Granata
Vice President - Production
  Management .... Steven Saeta
Vice President & Treasurer .... Elizabeth Burnett
Assistant Story Editor .... Karen Moy
Literary Coordinator .... John Miller

Triumph Releasing
President .... J. Edward Shugrue
Executive Vice President -
  International .... S. Anthony Manna
Senior Vice President -
  Administration .... Milton Fishman
Senior Vice President -Marketing ...... Duncan C. Clark
Vice President - Administration .... Louis P. Mont
Vice President - Domestic
  Sales & Distribution .... Linda Ditrinco
Vice President - Legal Affairs .... Sherry E. Sherman
Vice President - Marketing .... Stephen Klein

SOVEREIGN PICTURES

11845 W. Olympic Blvd., Suite 1055
Los Angeles, CA 90064
310/312-1001
Fax: 310/478-7707

Chairman & Chief
    Executive Officer .... Ernst Goldschmidt
President .... Barbara Boyle
Production Executive .... Richard Rothstein
Story Editor .... Lisa Viola
Associate Production
    Executive .... Catherine Schulman

SPELLING PRODUCTIONS

5700 Wilshire Blvd., 5th Floor
Los Angeles, CA 90036-3696
213/965-5888
Fax: 213/965-5895

Chairman & Chief Executive Officer ..... Aaron Spelling
Vice Chairman .... E. Duke Vincent
President & COO .... Jules Haimovitz
Executive Vice President .... Ronald Lightstone
Executive Vice President & Senior
    Vice President - Creative Affairs .... Gary Randall
Senior Vice President & Chief
    Financial Officer .... John Brady
Senior Vice President, Business Affairs ..... Art Frankel
Vice President .... Renate Kamer
Vice President, Business Affairs .... Barbara Rubin
Vice President, Programming .... Marcia Basichis
Vice President - Development .... David Felser
Vice President, Talent .... Tony Shepherd
Vice President, TV MOWs &
    Miniseries .... Andy Siegel
Vice President, Production .... Gail Patterson
Vice President, Motion
    Picture Development .... Pam Bottaro
Director, TV Development .... Howard Rosenstein
Director, TV Series Development ...... Danielle Claman

T

TRILOGY ENTERTAINMENT GROUP
(See SONY Pictures Entertainment)

TRI-STAR PICTURES
(See SONY Pictures Entertainment)

TOUCHTONE PICTURES
(See Walt DISNEY Co.)

TURNER ENTERTAINMENT

One CNN Center
Box 105366
Atlanta, GA 30348
404/827-1500

1888 Century Park East
Loa Angeles, CA 90067
310/788-6800
Fax: 310/788-6825

Turner Entertainment Company
Chairman & Chief Executive Officer .... Ted Turner
President .... Roger Mayer

Turner Network Television
1888 Century Park East
Los Angeles, CA 90067
310/551-6300
Fax: 310-551-6344

President - Turner
    Entertainment Network .... Scott Sassa
Senior Vice President -
    Turner Pictures .... Neal Baseman
Executive Vice President - Operations ..... Bill Merriam
Executive Vice President - TNT .... Dennis A. Miller
Senior Vice President & General Manager -
    Acquisitions & Scheduling .... Terry Segal
Senior Vice President -
    Original Programming .... Linda Berman
Senior Vice President - Production ...... Nick Lombardo
Vice President - Development .... Gerald B. Clark
Vice President - Talent...................... Amy Kimmelman
Vice President - Movie Acquisitions &
    Scheduling .... Lisa Mateas
Vice President - Development .... Laurie Pozmantier
Director - Production .... Kim Long
Manager - Development .... Serena Misner
Director - Development .... Betsy Newman
Director - Production .... Jim Wilberger
Manager - Production .... Ralph Berge
Mamanger - Post-Production .... Candace Snyder

20TH CENTURY FOX

10201 W. Pico Blvd.
Los Angeles, CA 90035
310/277-2211

Mailing Address:
P.O. Box 900
Beverly Hills, CA 90213

40 W. 57th, 8th Floor
New York, NY 10019
212/977-5500

Owner .... Rupert Murdoch
Chairman & Chief ExecutiveOfficer .... Barry Diller

Motion Picture Production
Chairman .... Joe Roth
President & COO .... Strauss Zelnick

Tw

FILM
PRODUCERS,
STUDIOS,
AGENTS AND
CASTING
DIRECTORS
GUIDE

S
T
U
D
I
O
S

Tw

FILM
PRODUCERS,
STUDIOS,
AGENTS AND
CASTING
DIRECTORS
GUIDE

S
T
U
D
I
O
S

President - Worldwide Production ..... Roger Birnbaum
Executive Vice President -
    Production .... Tom Jacobson
Senior Vice President -
    Production .... Melissa Bachrach
Senior Vice President - Production ... Elizabeth Gabler
Senior Vice President -
    Feature Production .... John Landau
Senior Vice President - Production ..... Michael London
Senior Vice President - Acquisitions .... John Ruscin
Senior Vice President - Production ..... Margery Simkin
Senior Vice President - Production ... Michael R. Joyce
Senior Vice President - Production .... Susan Cartsonis
Senior Vice President -
    Production .... Riley Katheryn Ellis
Vice President - Creative
    Affair (NYC) .... Laurie Rosenfield
Feature Story Editor .... Juliette Schneider
Creative Executive .... Kit Cudahy
Director - Creative Development .... Jami Abell-Venit
Director - Creative Development .... Mitchell Levin

Marketing & Distribution
President - Marketing .... Joel Hochberg
Senior Vice President - Marketing ..... Geoffrey Ammer
Executive Vice President - Marketing ..... Cynthia Wick
President - Domestic Distribution .... Bruce Snyder

International Distribution
President .... Walter Senior
Vice President - International
    Advertising & Publicity .... Joel Coler
Senior Vice President - International
    Acquisitions .... Francesca Barra
Senior Vice President - Europe,
    Near East & Africa .... Jorge Canizares
Vice President - Latin America/
    International Operations .... Francisco Rodriquez
Vice President - Far East & Australia .... Jacob Shapiro
Vice President - International Division ...... Harold Mars
Vice President - Finance &
    Administration .... James Langsbard
Executive Vice President .... Melinda Benedek

Fox Broadcasting
President & COO .... Jamie Kellner
President - Fox Entertainment Group .... Peter Chernin
Executive Vice President - Fox
    Entertainment Group .... Sandy Grushow

FBC Entertainment
Senior Vice President - Programming &
    Development .... Rob Kenneally
Senior Vice President -
    Series Programming .... Lillah McCarthy
Vice President -
    Current Programs .... Christopher Davidson
Vice President - Creative Development ..... Joe Davola
Vice President - Talent & Casting .... Robert Harbin
Vice President -
    Film Acquisitions .... Suzanne Horenstein

20th Television
Chairman .... Lucille Salhany
President - TV Production .... Harris L. Katleman
Executive Vice President -
    Creative Affairs .... Stuart Sheslow
Executive Vice President -
    Production & Finance .... Charles Goldstein
Executive Vice President .... Leonard J. Grossi
Vice President - Programs ...... Shelly Raskov-Aronson
Vice President -
    Videotape Production .... Joel Hornstock
Vice President - Programs .... Jeffrey Kramer
Vice President -
    Production Management .... Robert Gros

20th Century Fox Domestic Television
President - Domestic Syndication ...... Michael Lambert
Vice President -
    Creative Services .... J. Mathy Wasserman

21ST CENTURY FILM CORPORATION
7000 W. 3rd St.
Los Angeles, CA 90048
213/658-3000
Fax: 213/658-3002

Chairman & Chief
    Executive Officer .... Menahem Golan
President .... Ami Artzi
Vice President - Creative Affairs .... Ed Rosen

U

UNIVERSAL PICTURES
100 Universal City Plaza
Universal City, CA 91608-1085
818/777-1000

445 Park Ave.
New York, NY 10022
212/759-7500

Matsushita Electric Industrial Corporation
1006 Oaza, Kadoma
Kadoma, Osaka
Japan 571
81/06-908-1121

President & Chief Executive Officer .... Akio Tanii
Executive Vice President .... Masahiko Hirata

MCA, Inc.
Chairman of the Board & Chief
    Executive Officer .... Lew Wasserman
President & COO .... Sidney J. Sheinberg
Executive Vice President .... Thomas Wertheimer

Vi

FILM
PRODUCERS,
STUDIOS,
AGENTS AND
CASTING
DIRECTORS
GUIDE

Vice President & Chief
  Financial Officer .... Richard E. Baker
Vice President & Chairman - Music &
  Entertainment Group .... Alvin N. Teller

MCA Motion Picture Group
Chairman .... Thomas Pollock
Senior Vice President .... Joseph Fischer
Senior Vice President .... Fredric I. Bernstein
Vice President .... C. Ann Busby

Universal Pictures
President .... Casey Silver
Executive Vice President -
  Production .... Joshua Donen
Senior Vice President - Production &
  Post-Production .... Donna N. Smith
Senior Vice President -
  Production .... Hal D. Lieberman
Senior Vice President - Music
  Creative Affairs .... Burt Berman
Senior Vice President - Legal &
  Business Affairs .... Jon Gumpert
Senior Vice President - Production .... Tom Craig
Vice President - Production .... Christopher Dorr
Vice President - Production .... Kathleen Barker
Vice President - Production .... Dan W. York
Vice President - Business Affairs .... Jerry Barton
Vice President - Finance .... Jim Burk
Vice President - Production .... Barry Isaacson
Vice President - Business Affairs .... Jeff Korchek
Vice President - Physical &
  Post Production .... Don Zepfel
Vice President - Music
  Creative Affairs .... Harry Garfield
Vice President - Production &
  Acquisitions .... Jim Jacks
Vice President -
  Production (East Coast) .... Julia Chasman
Vice President - Music
  Business Affairs .... Roxanne Lippel
Vice President - Casting .... Nancy Nayor

MCA Television Group
Chairman .... Alvin Rush
Executive Vice President -
  Children's Entertainment .... Jeff Segal
Executive Vice President -
  Administration .... Edward Masket
Vice President - Finance .... Jerome F. Clark

Universal Television
President .... Tom Thayer
Executive Vice President -
  Creative Affairs .... Ned Nalle
Executive Vice President .... Earl J. Bellamy
Executive Vice President -
  Administration .... Irv Sepkowitz
Senior Vice President -
  Longform Programming .... Charmaine Balian
Senior Vice President - TV
  Dramatic Development .... Dan Filie

Senior Vice President -
  Comedy Development .... Brad Johnson
Senior Vice President -
  Current Programming .... Garret Hart
Senior Vice President - Publicity,
  Promotion & Advertising .... Robert Crutchfield
Senior Vice President - Casting .... Joan Sittenfield
Vice President - Business Affairs ... Sheldon Mittelman
Vice President - Business Affairs .... James Brock
Vice President - Television
  Production .... Ralph Sariego
Vice President - Talent
  Development & Acquisition .... Peter Terranova

MCA Enterprises International
President .... Anthony J. Young
Executive Vice President .... Frank P. Stanek
Senior Vice President .... Robert Giovanettone

MCA Home Entertainment
Executive Vice President .... Sondra Berchin
Senior Vice President - Operations &
  Business Development .... Phil Pictaggi
Senior Vice President -
  Business & Administration .... Blair Westlake

MCA Home Video
President .... Robert Blattner
Executive Vice President .... Louis Feola

MCA Development
President .... Lawrence D. Spungin
Senior Vice President .... William E. Hickey
Senior Vice President .... James E. Hescox

V

VIACOM ENTERPRISES
10 Universal City Plaza
Universal City, CA 91608-1002
818/505-7700
Fax: 818/505-7755

1515 Broadway
New York, NY 10036

President - International Theatrical &
  Home Video Sales (NY) .... Arthur Kananack
President - First Run, International
  Distribution & Acquisitions (NY) ...... Michael Gerber
Vice President - Development &
  Production .... Julia Pistor
Vice President - Program
  Development (NY) .... Kim A. Schlotman
Director - Program Development &
  Production .... Charles Segars

Vi

FILM
PRODUCERS,
STUDIOS,
AGENTS AND
CASTING
DIRECTORS
GUIDE

S
T
U
D
I
O
S

Viacom Pictures

Chairman (NY) .... Neil Braun
President & Chief Executive Officer ...... Fred Schneier
Senior Vice President .... Paul Mason
Senior Vice President .... Barbara Title
Vice President - Production .... Gary Mehlman
Director - Creative Affairs .... Joan Boorstein
Director - Development .... Steve Schmidt
Manager - Production .... Lisa Niedenthal

Viacom Productions

818/505-7500

President .... Thomas D. Tannenbaum
Senior Vice President - Production .... Mike Moder
Senior Vice President - Comedy
    Development .... Richard Albarino
Senior Vice President - Drama
    Development .... Steve Gordon
Vice President - Post-Production .... Hal Harrison
Vice President - Comedy
    Development .... Mindy Schultheis
Director - Casting .... Beth Klein
Director - Public Relations .... George Fabern
Director - Production Administration ...... Janie Kleiman
Production Controller .... Victor Salant
Director - Drama Development .... James Waldron

W

WARNER BROS

4000 Warner Blvd.
Burbank. CA 91522-0001
818/954-6000
Fax: 818/905-1692

75 Rockefeller Plaza
New York, NY 10019
212/484-8000

Special Counsel .... Steve Ross
Chairman of the Board & Chief
    Executive Officer .... Robert A. Daly
President & COO .... Terry Semel
Executive Vice President .... Barry M. Meyer

Warner Bros. Production

President .... Bruce Berman
Executive Vice President .... Lucy Fisher
Senior Vice President .... Lance Young
Senior Vice President .... Bill Gerber
Senior Vice President .... Lisa Henson
Vice President .... Robert Brassel
Vice President - Creative
    Affairs (East Coast) .... Susan Dalsimer

Vice President .... Robert Guralnick
Vice President .... Tom Lassally
Vice President - Production .... Diana Rathbun
Vice President - Worldwide
    Production .... William L. Young
Production Executive .... Lorenzo DiBonaventura
Production Executive .... Courtenay Valenti
Production Associate .... Valerie Scoon
Production Associate .... Stacy Attanasio
Creative Assistant .... Phillippe Rousselet
West Coast Story Editor .... John Schimmel

Warner Bros. Advertising & Publicity

President .... Robert G. Friedman
Senior Vice President - Worldwide
    Creative Advertising .... Joel Wayne
Senior Vice President - Special Projects ...Joe Hyams
Vice President -
    Publicity & Promotion .... Charlotte Gee
Vice President - Media .... John Jacobs
Vice President - Worldwide
    Market Research .... Richard Del Belso
Vice President - Publicity .... John Dartigue
Vice President - National Publicity .... Carl Samrock
Vice President - Co-Operative
    Advertising .... Richard Kallet
Vice President - Worldwide Advertising &
    Publicity Services .... Lori Drazen

Warner Bros. International

President .... Richard J. Fox
Vice President - Sales .... Wayne Duband
Vice President - Advertising &
    Publicity .... Irving N. Ivers
Vice President - Administration .... Peter Howard
Vice President - Europe,
    Middle East & Africa .... Frank Pierce
Vice President - Far East Region .... Alex Ying
Vice President - Latin
    American Region .... Redo Farrah
Vice President - European Advertising &
    Publicity .... Julian Senior
Vice President - Business Affairs .... Eric Senat
Vice President - Theatrical
    Distribution .... Edward E. Frumkes

Warner Bros. Distribution

President .... D. Barry Reardon
Senior Vice President -
    General Sales Manager .... Daniel R. Fellman
Vice President -
    Branch Operations .... Howard Welinsky
Vice President & General Counsel .... Jane Goldman
Vice President - Sales Operations ..Don Tannenbaum
Vice President - Print Control .... Nancy Sams

Warner Bros. Television

President - Production .... Harvey Shephard
Senior Vice President - Production ..... Steve Papazian
Senior Vice President -
    Creative Affairs .... Norman Stephens

Senior Vice President -
    Current Programming .... David Sacks
Vice President -
    Special Projects .... Karen Cooper Minnicks
Vice President - Film &
    Tape Production .... Henry Johnson
Vice President - MOWs & Miniseries .... Greg Maday
Vice President - Comedy Development .... Pat Quinn
Vice President - Talent & Casting .... Marcia Ross
Vice President - Casting Administration ... Pat Hopkins
Vice President - Production &
    Operations .... Tom Treloggen
Vice President - Post-Production .... Karen Pingitore
Executive Production Manager .... John Rogers
Production Executive .... Rob Harland
Director - Current Programming .... Debra Langford
Director - Film & Tape Production .... Steve Reagan
Director - Drama Development .... Susan Reiner
Director - Talent & Casting .... John Levey
Manager - Creative Affairs .... Gerard Bocaccio

Warner Bros. Animation - Classics
3601 W. Olive Ave., Suite 450
Burbank, CA 91505-4603
818/954-3713

Vice President - Production &
    Administration .... Kathleen Helppie
Director - Operations .... Tad Marburg

Warner Bros. Animation - Creative Division
15303 Ventura Blvd., Suite 1100
Sherman Oaks, CA 91403
818/379-9401
Fax: 818/905-1692

Senior Vice President &
    General Manager .... Jean MacCurdy
Supervisor - Creative
    Development .... Christopher Keenan
Director - Programming
    (Writer's Liaison) .... Barbara Simon
Senior Producer .... Tom Ruegger

Wa

FILM
PRODUCERS,
STUDIOS,
AGENTS AND
CASTING
DIRECTORS
GUIDE

S
T
U
D
I
O
S

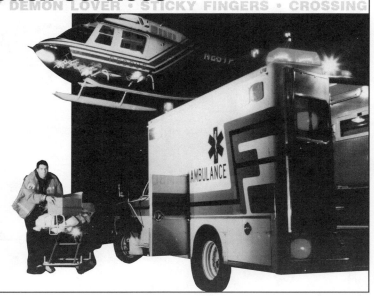

A G E N T S

FILM
PRODUCERS,
STUDIOS,
AGENTS and
CASTING
DIRECTORS
GUIDE

GUILDS

DIRECTORS GUILD OF AMERICA
7920 Sunset Blvd.
Los Angeles, CA 90046
213/289-2000
Fax: 213/289-2029

110 West 57th Street
New York, NY 10019
212/581-0370
Fax: 212/581-1441

520 North Michigan Avenue
Suite 1026
Chicago, IL 60611
312/644-5050

DIRECTORS GUILD OF GREAT BRITTAIN
56 Whitfield Street
London W1 England
71/880-9582

SCREEN ACTORS GUILD
7065 Hollywood Blvd.
Hollywood, CA 90028
213/465-4600

1515 Broadway
44th Floor
New York, NY 10036
212/944-1030

WRITERS GUILD OF AMERICA
8955 Beverly Blvd.
Los Angeles, CA 90048
310/550-1000

555 West 57th Street
New York, NY 10019
212/245-6180

WRITERS GUILD OF GREAT BRITTAIN
430 Edgeware Road
London W21 EH England
71/723-8074

AGENTS & MANAGERS

Ab-Am

FILM
PRODUCERS,
STUDIOS,
AGENTS and
CASTING
DIRECTORS
GUIDE

I
N
D
E
X

O
F

A
G
E
N
T
S

&

M
A
N
A
G
E
R
S

A

**ABRAMS ARTISTS &
ASSOCIATES, LTD.**
9200 Sunset Blvd., Suite 625
Los Angeles, CA 90069
310/859-0625
Fax: 310/276-6193

420 Madison Avenue
Suite 1400
New York, NY 10017
212/935-8980
Fax: 212/935-2862

Harry Abrams
Neal Altman
Robert Attermann
Alissa Begell
Toni Benson
Meg Bloom
Cesca Cecilio
Tina Devries
Doug Ely
Tracey Goldblum
Janey Gubow
Rob Kolker
Ayn Lauren
Martin Lesak
Robert McCarthy
Nina Pakula
Joseph Rice
Nathan Schwam
Ruth Anne Secunda

BRET ADAMS, LTD.
448 West 44th St.
New York, NY 10036
212/765-5630
Fax: 212/265-2212

Bret Adams
Nancy Curtis
Mary Harden
Margi Rountree

**ADDIS-WECHSLER &
ASSOCIATES**
955 S. Carrillo Dr., 3rd Floor
Los Angeles, CA 90048
310/954-9000
Fax: 310/954-9009

Keith Addis
Steven Fargnoli
Gerald Harrington
Danny Heaps
Eli Seldon
Julie Silverman
John Tarnoff
Nick Wechsler

THE ADLER AGENCY
12725 Ventura Blvd., #B
Studio City, CA 91604
818/761-9850

Jerry Adler
Jeffrey Leonardi
Scott Penney

THE AGENCY
10351 Santa Monica Blvd., Suite 211
Los Angeles, CA 90025
310/551-3000
Fax: 310/551-1424

Ed Adler
Caron Champoux
Carolyn Kessler
David List
Sharon Mitchell
Michael Packingham
Laurence Roth
Laura Sutten
Michael Van Dyck
Jerry Zeitman

**AGENCY FOR THE
PERFORMING ARTS**
9000 Sunset Blvd., 12th Floor
Los Angeles, CA 90069
310/273-0744
Fax: 310/275-9401

888 Seventh Ave.
New York, NY 10016
212/582-1500
Fax: 212/245-1647

Ed Betz (NY)
Jon Brown
Lee Dintsman
Diana Doussant (NY)
John Gaines
Hal Gefsky
Jeff Goldberg
David Kalodner (NY)

Lee Kappelman
Jim Kellem
Marty Klein
Tom Korman
Richard Krawetz (NY)
Rick Leed
Harvey Litwin (NY)
Larry Masser
Stuart Miller
Mark Scroggs
Brett Steinberg
Burt Taylor
Steve Tellez

ALL-STAR TALENT AGENCY
21416 Chase St., Suite 2
Canoga Park, CA 91304
818/346-4313

Robert Allred

**BUDDY ALTONI TALENT
AGENCY**
P.O. Box 1022
Newport Beach, CA 92660
714/851-1711

Buddy Altoni

CARLOS ALVARADO AGENCY
8150 Beverly Blvd., Suite 308
Los Angeles, CA 90048
213/655-7978

Carlos Alvarado
Monalee Schilling

AMERICAN ARTISTS, INC.
6994 El Camino Real, Suite 208
Carlsbad, CA 92009
619/744-3456

Ronald E. Matonak

**FRED AMSEL &
ASSOCIATES, INC.**
6310 San Vicente Blvd., Suite 407
Los Angeles, CA 90048
213/939-1188
Fax: 213/939-0630

Fred Amsel
Mike Eisenstadt
John Frazier
Sara Margoshes

Ar-Be

FILM
PRODUCERS,
STUDIOS,
AGENTS AND
CASTING
DIRECTORS
GUIDE

I
N
D
E
X

O
F

A
G
E
N
T
S

&

M
A
N
A
G
E
R
S

IRVIN ARTHUR ASSOCIATES, LTD.
9363 Wilshire Blvd., Suite 212
Beverly Hills, CA 90210
310/278-5934
Fax: 310/276-7493

Irvin Arthur
Seth Feldman
Michael Green
Anne McDermott
Richard Super

THE ARTISTS AGENCY
10000 Santa Monica Blvd., Suite 305
Los Angeles, CA 90067
310/277-7779
Fax: 310/785-9338

Jim Cota
Mickey Freiberg
Merrily Kane
Carrie Kirshman
Ginger Lawrence
Michael Livingston
Andy Patman
Denny Sevier
Richard A. Shepherd
Bruce Tufeld
Don Wolff

ARTISTS AGENCY, INC.
(In Association with Favored Artists)
230 West 55th St., Suite 29D
New York, NY 10019
212/245-6960
Fax: 212/333-7420

David Herter
Jonathan Russo
Barry Weiner

ARTISTS ALLIANCE
(In Association with the Anne Geddes Agency)
8457 Melrose Pl., Suite 200
Los Angeles, CA 90069
213/651-2401

Audrey Caan
Karen Frank
Jack Panell
Rodney Sheldon

THE ARTISTS GROUP
1930 Century Park West, Suite 403
Los Angeles, CA 90067
310/552-1100
Fax: 310/277-9513

Conan Carroll
Ed Goldstone
Susan Grant
Nancy Moon-Broadstreet
Barry Saloman
Arnold Soloway
Hal Stalmaster

PETER ASHER MANAGEMENT
(Music)
644 N. Doheny Dr.
Los Angeles, CA 90069
310/273-9433

Peter Asher

HOWARD J. ASKENASE
6217 Glen Airy Dr.
Los Angeles, CA 90068
213/464-4114

Howard J. Askenase

ASSOCIATED TALENT INTERNATIONAL
9744 Wilshire Blvd., Suite 312
Los Angeles, CA 90212
310/271-4662

Bud Kenneally
Patrick White
Martin Zitter

B

BARRETT BENSON McCARTT & WESTON
9320 Wilshire Blvd., 3rd Floor
Beverly Hills, CA 90212
310/247-5500
Fax: 310/247-5599

Christopher Barrett
Jeff Benson
Randi Caplan
Dianne Fraser
Joel Gotler
Russ Lyster
Bettye McCartt
Stephen Rose
Howard Sanders
Sara Schedeen
Mark Schumacher
Irv Schwartz
Richard Weston
Tory Whipple

THE BARSKIN AGENCY
120 S. Victory Blvd., Suite 204
Burbank, CA 91502
818/848-5536

Beverly Barskin

BAUMAN, HILLER & ASSOCIATES
5750 Wilshire Blvd., Suite 512
Los Angeles, CA 90036
213/857-6666
Fax: 213/857-0368

250 West 57th St.
New York, NY 10019
212/757-0098

Richard H. Bauman
Walter N. Hiller
Victor Latino
Kay Liberman
Mark Redanty
Chris Schmidt
Lenore Zerman

BDP & ASSOCIATES
10637 Burbank Blvd.
North Hollywood, CA 91601
818/506-7615
Fax: 818/506-4983

Sharon DeBord
Dan Gebert
Samuel Gelfman
Morgan Paull

GEORGES BEAUME
3 Quai Malaquais
Paris, 75006 France
1.43.25.28.31

Georges Beaume

BENNETT AGENCY
150 S. Barrington Ave., Suite 1
Los Angeles, CA 90049
310/471-2251
Fax: 310/471-2254

Carole Bennett

LOIS BERMAN
240 West 44th St.
New York, NY 10036
212/575-5114

Lois Berman

J. MICHAEL BLOOM
233 Park Avenue South, 10th Floor
New York, NY 10003
212/529-6500
Fax: 212/529-5838

9200 Sunset Blvd., Suite 710
Los Angeles, CA 90069
310/275-6800
Fax: 310/275-6941

Ric Beddingfield
J. Michael Bloom
Peter Levine
Robert Risher
Marilyn Szatmary

BORINSTEIN ORECK BOGART
8271 Melrose Av., Suite 110
Los Angeles, CA 90046
213/658-7500
Fax: 213/658-8866

Mark Borinstein
Mary Oreck
Bari Bogart

BORMAN ENTERTAINMENT
9220 Sunset Blvd., Suite 320
Los Angeles, CA 90069
310/859-9292

Gary Borman

BRANDON & ASSOCIATES
200 North Robertson Blvd., Suite 223
Beverly Hills, CA 90211
310/273-6173

Eric Anders
Paul Brandon

THE BRANDT COMPANY
12700 Ventura Blvd., Suite 340
Studio City, CA 91604
818/506-7747
Fax: 818/509-7897

Geoff Brandt

BRESLER • KELLY • KIPPERMAN
15760 Ventura Blvd., Suite 1730
Encino, CA 91436
818/905-1155

111 West 57th St., Suite 1409
New York, NY 10019
212/265-1980

Sandy Bresler
Robbie Conrad
John Kelly
Perri Kipperman

THE BRILLSTEIN COMPANY
9200 Sunset Blvd., Suite 428
Los Angeles, CA 90069
310/275-6135
Fax: 310/275-6180

Bernie Brillstein
Brad Grey
Marc Gurvitz
Ray Reo
Sandy Wernick

BRODER-KURLAND-WEBB-UFFNER AGENCY
9242 Beverly Blvd., Suite 200
Beverly Hills, CA 90210
310/281-3400
Fax: 310/276-3207

Bob Broder
Norman Kurland
Beth Uffner
Elliot Webb
Gayla Nethercott
Tammy Stockfish

CURTIS BROWN, LTD.
10 Astor Place
New York, NY 10003
212/473-5400

606 N. Larchmont, Suite 309
Los Angeles, CA 90004
213/461-0148

162/168 Regent Street
London W1 England
071/872-0331
Fax: 071/872-0332

Laura Blake (NY)
Jeannine Edmunds
Peter Ginsberg (NY)
Emilie Jacobson (NY)
Timothy Knowlton (NY)
Virginia Knowlton (NY)
Marilyn Marlowe (NY)
Leah Schmidt (UK)
Irene Skolnick (NY)
Clyde Taylor (NY)
Jess Taylor (NY)
Maureen Walters (NY)
Walter Wood

DON BUCHWALD & ASSOCIATES INC.
10 East 44th St.
New York, NY 10017
212/867-1200
Fax: 212/972-3209

Richard Basch
Don Buchwald
David Elliott
Renee Jennett
Michael Katz
Steven Kaye
Scott Linder
Joanne Nici
Ricki Olshan
Michael Raymen
Randi Ross
Michael Traum
Jonn Wasser
David Williams

C

BRETT CALDER AGENCY
17420 Ventura Blvd., Suite 4
Encino, CA 91316
818/906-2825

Maury Calder

CAMDEN • ITG
822 S. Robertson Blvd., Suite 200
Los Angeles, CA 90035
310/289-2700
Fax: 310/289-2718

729 Seventh Avenue
New York, NY 10019
212/221-7878
Fax: 212/302-0335

Merritt Blake
Joel Dean
Michael Farrell
Wayne Forte (NY)
Paul Kelmenson
Nancy Schmidt
Danielle Thomas
John Ufland
David Wardlow

CAMERON'S MANAGEMENT
163 Brougham Street
Sydney NSW Australia
61/2/356-2155

Ca-Cr

FILM
PRODUCERS,
STUDIOS,
AGENTS AND
CASTING
DIRECTORS
GUIDE

I
N
D
E
X

O
F

A
G
E
N
T
S

&

M
A
N
A
G
E
R
S

JUNE CANN MANAGEMENT
85 Ridge
North Sydney NSW Australia
61/2/922-3066

CARLYLE MANAGEMENT
639 N. Larchmont Dr., 2nd Floor
Los Angeles, CA 90038
213/469-3086

Spencer Baumgarten
Eric Kritzer
Phyllis Carlyle

WILLIAM CARROLL AGENCY
120 S. Victory Blvd.
Burbank, CA 91502
818/845-3791
Fax: 213/849-2553

CASAROTTO COMPANY, LTD.
60-66 Wardour Street
London W1 England
071/287-4450
Fax: 071/287-9128

Jenne Casarotto
Greg Hunt

CENTURY ARTISTS, LTD.
9744 Wilshire Blvd., Suite 308
Beverly Hills, CA 90212
310/273-4366
Fax: 310/273-1423

Louis Bershad

CHARTER MANAGEMENT
8200 Wilshire Blvd., Suite 218
Beverly Hills, CA 90211
213/278-1690

Toni Cosentino
Michael Greenfield

THE CHASIN AGENCY
190 N. Canon Drive, Suite 201
Beverly Hills, CA 90210
310/278-7505
Fax: 310/275-6685

Laurie Apelian
Tom Chasin

CHATTO & LINNIT LTD.
Prince of Wales Theatre
Coventry Street
London, W1 England
071/930-6677
Fax: 071/930-0091

CINEMA TALENT INTERNATIONAL
8033 Sunset Blvd., Suite 808
West Hollywood, CA 90046
213/656-1937

George Rumanes

CIRCLE TALENT ASSOCIATES
433 North Camden Drive, Suite 400
Beverly Hills, CA 90210
310/285-1585

Siegfried Hodel
Jon Klane
Donna Lee

CNA & ASSOCIATES
1801 Avenue of the Stars, Suite 1250
Los Angeles, CA 90067
310/556-4343
Fax: 310/556-4633

Marty Barkan
Ellen Drantch
Stuart Jacobs
Christopher Nassif
Adrienne Spitzer

KINGSLEY COLTON & ASSOCIATES
16661 Ventura Blvd., Suite 400
Encino, CA 91436
818/788-6043

Kingsley Colton

CONTEMPORARY ARTISTS, LTD.
132 S. Lasky Drive
Beverly Hills, CA 90212
310/278-8250
Fax: 310/278-0415

Gary Fuchs
Carmella Gallien
Bill Hart
Ronnie Leif
Al Melnick
Christopher Schiffrin
Sara Wallach

THE COOPER AGENCY
10100 Santa Monica Blvd., Suite 310
Los Angeles, CA 90067
310/277-8422

Brian Cooper
Frank Cooper
Jeff Cooper
Christine D'Angelo

THE COPPAGE COMPANY
11501 Chandler Blvd.
North Hollywood, CA 91601
818/980-1106
Fax: 818/509-1474

Judy Coppage

CREATIVE ARTISTS AGENCY (CAA)
9830 Wilshire Blvd.
Beverly Hills, CA 90212
310/288-4545
Fax: 310/288-4800

Abbie Adams
Dan Adler
Johanna Baldwin
Marty Baum
Jane Berliner
Glen Bickel
Carol Bodie
Amy Bookman
Bob Bookman
Eric Carlson
Leslie Castanuela
Donna Chavous
Sandy Climan
Joe Cohen
Justin Connolly
Kevin Cooper
Al Duncan
Lee Gabler
Bill Haber
Ken Hardy
Rand Holston
Kevin Huvane
Phil Kent
Tony Krantz
Adam Krentzman
Richard Kurtzman
John Levin
Josh Lieberman
Brian Loucks
Brian Lourd
Richard Lovett
Mike Marcus
Michael Menchel
Ron Meyer
Ted Miller
Jay Moloney
Rick Nicita
Tina Nides
David O'Connor
Michael Ovitz
Marc Pariser
Rowland Perkins
Michael Piranian
Pam Prince
Rob Prinz

Jack Rapke
Melanie Ray
Mitch Rose
Sonia Rosenfeld
Tom Ross
Rob Scheidlinger
Jane Sindell
Bradford Smith
Todd Smith
Fred Specktor
Rosalie Swedlin
Adam Venit
Bruce Vinokur
Paula Wagner
Jonathan Weisgal
Fred Whitehead
Sally Willcox
Michael Wimer

CREATIVE TECHNIQUE, INC.
Box 311, Station F
Toronto, Ontario M4Y 2L7
Canada
416/466-4173

Suzanne De Poe

CROUCH ASSOCIATES
59 Frith St.
London, W1 England
071/734-2167
Fax: 071/494-0315

D

DADE/SCHULTZ ASSOCIATES
11846 Ventura Blvd., Suite 100
Studio City, CA 91604
818/760-3100
Fax: 818/760-1395

Ernie Dade
Kathleen Schultz

JUDY DAISH ASSOCIATES LTD.
83 Eastbourne Mews
London, W2 England
071/262-1101
Fax: 071/262-1101

LARRY DALZELL ASSOCIATES LTD.
17 Broad Court, Suite 12
St. Martin's Lane
London, WC2 England
071/379-0875
Fax: 071/240-1466

DIAMOND ARTISTS, LTD.
215 North Barrington Ave.
Los Angeles, CA 90049
310/278-8146
Fax: 310/705-1850

Abby Greshler
Guy Steiner

DYTMAN & ASSOCIATES
433 North Camden Dr., Suite 600
Beverly Hills, CA 90210
310/288-1827

Jack Dytman

E

ROBERT EISENBACH AGENCY
6072 Franklin, Suite 203
Los Angeles, CA 90028
213/962-5809

Robert Eisenbach

E.M.A.
(See Curtis Brown Ltd.)

EMERALD ARTISTS, INC.
6565 Sunset Blvd., Suite 312
Los Angeles, CA 90028
213/465-2974
Fax: 213/465-2923

Lisa Everett
Ida Fisher

EPSTEIN-WYCKOFF & ASSOCIATES, INC.
280 S. Beverly Dr., Suite 400
Beverly Hills, CA 90212
310/278-7222
Fax: 310/278-4640

Brooke Bundy
Larry Corsa
Gary Epstein
Stephen LaManna
Stephen Rice
William Veloric
Karin Wakefield
Craig Wyckoff

F

CAROL FAITH AGENCY
(Music)
280 S. Beverly Dr., Suite 411
Beverly Hills, CA 90212
310/274-0776
Fax: 310/274-2670

Carol Faith
Wayne Burgos

FAVORED ARTISTS
8150 Beverly Blvd., Suite 201
Los Angeles, CA 90048
213/653-3191
Fax: 213/653-3816

George Goldey
Scott Henderson
Paul Yamamoto

MAGGIE FIELD AGENCY
12725 Ventura Blvd., Suite D
Studio City, CA 91604
818/980-2001
Fax: 818/980-0754

FILM ARTISTS ASSOCIATES
7080 Hollywood Blvd., Suite 704
Hollywood, CA 90028
213/463-1010
Fax: 213/463-0702

Chris Dennis
Penrod Dennis

SY FISHER COMPANY
10590 Wilshire Blvd., Suite 1602
Los Angeles, CA 90024
310/470-0917

FLICK EAST WEST TALENTS, INC.
1608 N. Las Palmas
Hollywood, CA 90028
213/463-6333
Fax: 213/462-3674

881 Seventh Ave., Rm. 1110
New York, NY 10019
212/307-1850

Peg Donegan (NY)
Alan Mindel
Denise Shaw
Hilary Shor

Fr-Go

FILM
PRODUCERS,
STUDIOS,
AGENTS AND
CASTING
DIRECTORS
GUIDE

I
N
D
E
X

O
F

A
G
E
N
T
S

&

M
A
N
A
G
E
R
S

PETERS FRASER & DUNLOP
5th Floor, The Chambers
Chelsea Harbour
London, SW10 England
071/376-7676
Fax: 071/352-7356

Tim Corrie
Ken Ewing
Anthony Jones
Mark Lucas
Richard Wakeley
Charles Walker

KURT FRINGS AGENCY, INC.
139 S. Beverly Dr., Suite 328
Beverly Hills, CA 90210
310/277-1103

G

THE GAGE GROUP
9255 Sunset Blvd., Suite 515
Los Angeles, CA 90069
310/859-8777
Fax: 310/859-8166

315 West 57th Street, Suite 4H
New York, NY 10019
212/541-5250
Fax: 212/956-7466

Rick Ax
Martin Gage
Jerry Koch
Jonathan Westover
David Windsor

GALLIN-MOREY ASSOCIATES
8730 Sunset Blvd.
Penthouse West
Los Angeles, CA 90069
310/659-5593

Sandy Gallin
Jim Morey

CLIFF GARDNER AGENCY
1024 Ocean Drive, Suite 301
Miami Beach, FL 33139
305/532-5600
Fax: 305/673-5009

HELEN GARRETT AGENCY
P.O. Box 889
Hollywood, CA 90028
213/871-8707
Fax: 213/871-0485

Helen Garrett
James Garrett

THE GEDDES AGENCY
8457 Melrose Pl., Suite 200
Los Angeles, CA 90069
213/651-2401
Fax: 213/653-0901

Ann Geddes

GELFAND, RENNERT & FELDMAN
1880 Century Park East, Suite 900
Los Angeles, CA 90067
310/553-1707

PAUL GERARD TALENT AGENCY
2918 Alta Vista Dr.
Newport Beach, CA 92660
714/644-7950
Fax: 714/852-1819

Steve England
Helen Ruth

ROY GERBER & ASSOCIATES
9046 Sunset Blvd., Suite 208
Los Angeles, CA 90069
310/550-0100

Roy Gerber

THE GERSH AGENCY
232 N. Canon Dr.
Beverly Hills, CA 90210
310/274-6611
Fax: 310/274-3926

130 West 42nd St., Suite 2400
New York, NY 10036
212/997-1818
Fax: 212/391-8459

Richard Arlook
Lorrie Bartlett
Ron Bernstein
Ellen Curren (NY)
David DeCamillo
Bob Duva (NY)
Bob Gersh
Dave Gersh
Phil Gersh

David Guc (NY)
Barbara Halprin
Raelle Koota
Leslie Latkin
Jennifer Lyne (NY)
Mary Meagher (NY)
Susan Morris (NY)
Nancy Nigrosh
Diane Roberts
Scott Yoselow (NY)
Peter Young

JAY GILBERT TALENT AGENCY
8400 Sunset Blvd., Suite 2A
Los Angeles, CA 90069
213/656-5906

PHILLIP B. GITTELMAN
1221 N. Kings Rd., PH-405
Los Angeles, CA 90059
213/656-9215
Fax: 213/656-9184

Phillip B. Gittelman

HARRY GOLD & ASSOCIATES
3500 West Olive Ave.
Burbank, CA 91505
818/972-4300
Fax: 818/955-6411

Adena Aedna
Missy Eusterman
Francine Gersh
Harry Gold
Ruth Hansen
Cricket Haskell
Bonnie Liedtke
Darryl Marshak
Jeff Melnick
Mike Rosen
Sue Wolh

THE GOLDSTEIN COMPANY
864 S. Robertson Blvd., Suite 304
Los Angeles, CA 90035
310/659-9511
Fax: 310/659-8779

Gary Goldstein

GORES/FIELDS AGENCY
10100 Santa Monica Blvd., Suite 700
Los Angeles, CA 90067
310/277-4400
Fax: 310/277-7820

Linda Berke
Suzanne Costello
Jack Fields

Sam Gores
Dee Dee Jacobson
Trice Koopman
Michael Levine
Judith Moss
Arthur Toretzky

THE GORFAINE/ SCHWARTZ AGENCY

3301 Barham Blvd., Suite 201
Los Angeles, CA 90068
213/969-1011
Fax: 213/969-1022

Michael Gorfaine
Samuel Schwartz
Vasi Vangelos

GRAY/GOODMAN, INC.

211 S. Beverly Dr., Suite 100
Beverly Hills, CA 90212
310/276-7070
Fax: 310/276-6049

James Briggeman
Mark Goodman
Stephen Gray
Darrell Kern
S. Charles Lenhoff
Geri Prentiss

ARTHUR B. GREENE

101 Park Av., 43rd Floor
New York, NY 10178
212/661-8200

HAROLD R. GREENE, INC.

13900 Marquesas Way
Building C, Suite 83
Marina Del Rey, CA 90292
310/823-5393

Harold R. Greene

LARRY GROSSMAN & ASSOCIATES

211 S. Beverly Drive, Suite 206
Beverly Hills, CA 90212
310/550-8127

Janet Grossman
Larry Grossman

THE GURIAN AGENCY

9450 Cherokee Lane
Beverly Hills, CA 90210
310/550-0400

Naomi Gurian

H

REECE HALSEY AGENCY

8733 Sunset Blvd., Suite 101
Los Angeles, CA 90069
310/652-2409

Dorris Halsey

THE MITCHELL J. HAMILBURG AGENCY

292 S. La Cienega Blvd., Suite 312
Beverly Hills, CA 90211
310/657-1501

Michael Hamilburg

HARRIS & GOLDBERG TALENT AND LITERARY AGENCY

1999 Avenue of the Stars, Suite 2850
Los Angeles, CA 90067
310/553-5200
Fax: 310/557-2211

130 West 57th Street, Suite 5B
New York, NY 10019
212/315-4455
Fax: 212/315-4688

Nevin Dolcefino
Howard Goldberg
Michelle Grant
Deborah Haeusler
Scott Harris
Kenneth Kaplan (NY)
David Rose
Emily Gerson Saines (NY)
Sandy Weinberg
Frank Wuliger

RICK HASHAGEN & ASSOCIATES

157 West 57th St.
New York, NY 10019
212/315-3130

HEACOCK LITERARY AGENCY

1523 Sixth St., Suite 14
Los Angeles, CA 90401
310/393-6227
Fax: 310/394-0629

Jim Heacock
Rosalie Heacock

DUNCAN HEATH ASSOCIATES LTD
(In Association With ICM)

162-170 Wardour Street
London, W1 England
071/439-1471
Fax: 071/439-7274

Ian Amos
Steve Baile
Duncan Heath
Paul Lyons-Maris
Sue Rodgers

THE HELLER/ MITROVICH COMPANY

5757 Wilshire Blvd., Suite 459
Los Angeles, CA 90036
213/937-1251

Seymour Heller
Dan Mitrovich

HENDERSON/HOGAN AGENCY, INC.

247 S. Beverly Drive, Suite 102
Beverly Hills, CA 90212
310/274-7815
Fax: 310/274-0751

850 7th Avenue
New York, NY 10019
212/765-5190
Fax: 212/586-2855

Andrew Greenman (NY)
Margaret Henderson
Jerry Hogan (NY)
Karen Kirsch (NY)
Richard Lewis
Melanie Sharp
Fran Tolstonog
Jean Walton (NY)

THE RICHARD HERMAN TALENT AGENCY

9601 Wilshire Blvd., Suite 333
Beverly Hills, CA 90210
310/550-8913

Richard Herman

HOLLY AGENCY

890 Biddle Rd., Suite 343
Medford, OR 97504
503/776-3032

Go-Ho

FILM
PRODUCERS,
STUDIOS,
AGENTS AND
CASTING
DIRECTORS
GUIDE

I
N
D
E
X

O
F

A
G
E
N
T
S

&

M
A
N
A
G
E
R
S

Hu-Ka

FILM
PRODUCERS,
STUDIOS,
AGENTS AND
CASTING
DIRECTORS
GUIDE

I
N
D
E
X

O
F

A
G
E
N
T
S

&

M
A
N
A
G
E
R
S

ROBERT G. HUSSONG AGENCY
721 N. La Brea Ave., Suite 201
Los Angeles, CA 90038
213/652-2893

Robert Hussong

I

MICHAEL IMISON PLAYWRIGHTS LTD.
28 Almeida Street
London N1 England
071/354-3174
Fax: 071/359-6273

Michael Imison

INTERNATIONAL CREATIVE MANAGEMENT (ICM)
8899 Beverly Blvd.
Los Angeles, CA 90048
310/550-4000
Fax: 310/550-4108

40 West 57th Street
New York, NY 10019
212/556-5600
Fax: 212/556-5665

38 Via Siacci
Rome, Italy
806-041

Oxford House
76 Oxford Street
London, W1R 1RB England
071/636-6565
Fax: 071/323-0101

Duncan Heath Associates Ltd.
162-170 Wardour Street
London, W1 England
071/439-1471
Fax: 071/439-7274

Ian Amos (UK)
Bridget Aschenberg (NY)
Steve Baile (UK)
Jordan Bayer
Leigh Beeks
Jeff Berg
Alan Berger
Michael Black
Steve Carbone
Diane Cairns
Sam Cohn (NY)
Patty Detroit

Arlene Donovan (NY)
Bill Douglas
Steve Doutanville
Sandi Dudek
Andrea Eastman (NY)
Richard Feldman
George Freeman
Joe Funicello
Jack Gilardi
Sylvia Gold
David Goldman
Elaine Goldsmith
Alan Greenspan
Iris Grossman
Bob Gumer
Duncan Heath (UK)
Toni Howard
Nancy Josephson
Jodi Levine
Robert Levinson
David Lewis (NY)
Ed Limato
David Lonner
Lisa Loosemore (NY)
Martha Luttrell
Paul Lyons-Maris (UK)
Paul Martino (NY)
Guy McElwaine
Robert Newman
Lou Pitt
Steve Rabineau
Sylvie Rabineau
Lynn Radmin
Peter Rawley
Bill Robinson
Sheila Robinson
Sue Rodgers (UK)
Amy Rosen
Joe Rosenberg
Bob Sanitsky
Richard Saperstein
Scott Schwartz
Risa Shapiro
Jim Wiatt
David Wirtschafter
Eddie Yablans (NY)

INTERTALENT AGENCY, INC.
131 S. Rodeo Dr., Suite 300
Beverly Hills, CA 90212
310/858-6200
Fax: 310/858-6222

Scott Arnovitz
Bill Block
Michael Chesler
Ian Copeland
Barbara Dreyfus
Ariel Emanuel
David Greenblatt
J. J. Harris
Judy Hofflund

Adam Isaacs
Chris Moore
Mark Rossen
Robin Russell
David Schiff
Lloyd Segan
Danny Sexton
Tom Strickler
Jeanne Williams

J

JANKLOW & ASSOCIATES
1900 Avenue of the Stars, Suite 770
Los Angeles, CA 90067
310/785-9550

JANKLOW & NESBITT ASSOCIATES
598 Madison Avenue
New York, NY 10022
212/421-1700

Morton Janklow
Lynn Nesbitt

THOMAS JENNINGS & ASSOCIATES
28035 Dorothy St.
Agoura, CA 91301
818/879-1260

Tom Jennings

K

BEN F. KAMSLER LTD.
5501 Noble Ave.
Sherman Oaks, CA 91411
818/785-4167

Ben F. Kamsler
Irene Kamsler

KAPLAN-STAHLER AGENCY
8383 Wilshire Blvd., Suite 923
Beverly Hills, CA 90211
213/653-4483
Fax: 213/653-4506

Mitch Kaplan
Elliot Stahler

PATRICIA KARLAN AGENCY
4425 Riverside Dr., Suite 102
Burbank, CA 91505
818/846-8666

THE KEENER ORGANIZATION
9121 Sunset Blvd.
Los Angeles, CA 90069
310/273-9876

Matt Keener

WILLIAM KERWIN AGENCY
1605 N. Cahuenga Blvd., Suite 202
Los Angeles, CA 90028
213/469-5155
Fax: 213/871-0234

PAUL KOHNER AGENCY
9169 Sunset Blvd.
Los Angeles, CA 90069
310/550-1060
Fax: 310/276-1083

Liz Danzig
Gary Salt
Lori Rothman
Robert A. Schwartz
Pearl Wexler

KOPALOFF COMPANY
1930 Century Park West, Suite 403
Los Angeles, CA 90067
310/203-8430
Fax: 310/277-9513

Don Kopaloff

THE KRAFT AGENCY, INC.
(Music)
6525 Sunset Blvd., Suite 407
Hollywood, CA 90028
213/962-4716
Fax: 213/962-4903

Richard Kraft

LUCY KROLL
390 West End Ave.
New York, NY 10024
212/877-0556
Fax: 212/769-2832

Barbara Hogenson
Lucy Kroll
Holly Lebed

HELEN KUSHNICK
330 Bob Hope Dr., Room C-209
Burbank, CA 91523
818/840-7550

Helen Kushnick

L

THE CANDACE LAKE AGENCY
(In Association with Camden·ITG)
822 S. Robertson Blvd., Suite 200
Los Angeles, CA 90035
310/289-0600
Fax: 310/289-0619

Candace Lake

THE LANTZ OFFICE
(In Association with The Roberts Company)
888 7th Ave., 25th Floor
New York, NY 10106
212/586-0200
Fax: 212/262-6659

Joy Harris
Robert Lantz

IRVING PAUL LAZAR AGENCY
120 El Camino Dr., Suite 206
Beverly Hills, CA 90212
310/275-6153
Fax: 310/275-8668

One East 66th Street
New York, NY 10021
212/355-1177

Irving Paul Lazar
Alan Nevins

LEMON UNNA & DUBRIDGE LTD.
24 Pottery Lane
London W11 England
071/727-1346
Fax: 071/727-9037

Stephen Durebridge

JACK LENNY ASSOCIATES
9454 Wilshire Blvd., Suite 614
Beverly Hills, CA 90212
310/271-2174

100 West 57th St., Suite 3-I
New York, NY 10019
212/582-0270

Jim Lenny

LITKE/GALE/MADDEN
10390 Santa Monica Blvd., Suite 300
Los Angeles, CA 90025
310/785-9200

Barbara Gale
Marty Litke
Molly Madden

LONDON MANAGEMENT
235/241 Regent Street
London, W1 England
071/493-1610
Fax: 071/408-0065

STERLING LORD LITERISTIC
One Madison Ave.
New York, NY 10010
212/696-2800

Philippa Brophy
Lizzie Grossman
Jody Hotchkiss
Elizabeth Kaplan
Stuart Krichevsky
Sterling Lord
Peter Matson

GRACE LYONS AGENCY
8380 Melrose Blvd., Suite 202
Los Angeles, CA 90069
213/655-5100

Grace Lyons

M

MACNAUGHTON LOWE REPRESENTATION
200 Fulham Rd.
London SW10, England
071/351-5442
FAX: 071/351-4560

CHRISTOPHER MANN, LTD.
39 Davies Street
London, W1 England
071/493-2810

Christopher Mann

SHERI MANN AGENCY
8228 West Sunset Blvd., Suite 303
Los Angeles, CA 90046
213/655-6266
Fax: 213/655-9312

Ma-Mo

FILM
PRODUCERS,
STUDIOS,
AGENTS AND
CASTING
DIRECTORS
GUIDE

I
N
D
E
X

O
F

A
G
E
N
T
S

&

M
A
N
A
G
E
R
S

STEPHANIE MANN AGENCY
8323 Blackburn Ave., Suite 5
Los Angeles, CA 90048
213/653-7130

Stephanie Mann

**SANDRA MARSH
MANAGEMENT**
9150 Wilshire Blvd., Suite 220
Beverly Hills, CA 90212
310/285-0303
Fax: 310/285-0218

Lee International Studios,
Studio Number 37, Studios Road,
Shepperton
Middlesex TW17 0QD England
0932/568148
Fax: 0932/569452

Linda Koulisis
Sandra Marsh

**HAROLD MATSON
COMPANY, INC.**
276 Fifth Avenue
New York, NY 10001
212/679-4490

M.C.E.G. MANAGEMENT
11355 Olympic Blvd., Suite 500
Los Angeles, CA 90064
310/208-3262

JAMES McHUGH AGENCY
8150 Beverly Blvd., Suite 303
Los Angeles, CA 90048
213/651-2770

James McHugh

MEDIA ARTISTS GROUP
6255 Sunset Blvd., Suite 627
Hollywood, CA 90028
213/463-5610
Fax: 213/463-2766

Barbara Alexander
Raphael Berko
Steve Cohn
Keith Driscoll
Debra Lavere
Jon Samsel
Heidi Schwartz
Carolyn Thompson

HELEN MERRILL, LTD.
435 West 23rd St., Suite 1-A
New York, NY 10011
212/691-5326

**MILANDER SCHLEUSSNER
KAUFMAN AGENCY INC.**
4146 Lankershim Blvd., Suite 401
North Hollywood, CA 91602
818/761-4040
Fax: 818/985-0881

Michael Horner
Jeff H. Kaufman
Stan Milander
Cathy Schleussner

THE MILLER AGENCY
23560 Lyons Ave., Suite 209
Santa Clarita, CA 91321
805/255-7173

Tom Miller

THE MISHKIN AGENCY
2355 Benedict Canyon
Beverly Hills, CA 90210
310/274-5261

Meyer Mishkin

MONTEIRO ROSE AGENCY
17514 Ventura Blvd., Suite 205
Encino, CA 91316
818/501-1177
Fax: 818/501-1194

Keri Kelsey
Candy Monteiro
Fredda Rose

WILLIAM MORRIS AGENCY
151 El Camino Drive
Beverly Hills, CA 90212
310/274-7451
Fax: 310/859-4462

1350 Avenue of the Americas
New York, NY 10019
212/586-5100
Fax: 212/246-3583

2325 Crestmoore Rd.
Nashville, TN 37215
615/385-0310

31-32 Soho Square
London W1, England
071/434-2191
Fax: 071/437-0238

Via Giosue Carducci, 10
Rome, Italy
011-48-608-1234

Lamonstrasse 9
Munich 27, West Germany
011-47-608-1234

Jeff Alpern
Larry Auerbach
Arthur Axelman
Mel Berger (NY)
Adam Berkowitz (NY)
Pam Bernstein (NY)
Nan Blitman
Boaty Boatwright (NY)
Leo Bookman (NY)
Norman Brokaw
Bruce Brown
John Burnham
Michael Carlisle (NY)
Rob Carlson
Lee Cohen
James Crabbe
Bob Crestani
Ames Cushing
Roger Davis
Brian Dubin (NY)
Tony Fantozzi
Jeff Field
Peter Franklin (NY)
Alan Gasmer
Steve Glick
Christopher Godsick
Dodie Gold
Michael Gruber
Jeff Haar
Peter Hagan (NY)
Sam Haskell
Leonard Hirshan
Andrew Howard
Joan Hyler
Alan Iezman
Mark Itkin
Peter Kelley (NY)
Lora Kennedy
Ernest Kerns
Steven H. Kran
Debbie Kotick
George Lane (NY)
Owen Laster (NY)
Ned Leavitt (NY)
Sol Leon
Walter Lifkin
Greg Lipstone
Gary Loder
Ron Mardigian
Gayle Nachlis
Lanny Noveck
Gilbert Parker (NY)
Michael Peretzian
David Petrizzi
Gary Rado
Glenn Rigberg
Elizabeth Robinson

Leonard Rosenberg
Hal Ross
Katy Rothacker (NY)
Amy Schiffman
Marc Schwartz
Esther Sherman (NY)
Chris Simonian
Mike Simpson
Erica Silverman (NY)
Jim Stein (NY)
Lee Stollman
Daniel Sussman
Beth Swofford
Bobbi Thompson
Irene Webb
Steve Weiss
Irv Weintraub
Fred Westheimer
Jeff Witjas
Carol Yumkas
Scott Zimmerman

THE MORTON AGENCY
1620 Westwood Blvd., Suite 201
Los Angeles, CA 90024
310/824-4089

Michael Werner

O

OMNI ARTISTS
9465 Wilshire Blvd., Suite 530
Beverly Hills, CA 90212
310/858-9686
Fax: 310/858-9687

Ed Barnes
Robert Majeski
Curry Walls

FIFI OSCARD AGENCY
24 West 40th Street, 17th Floor
New York, NY 10018
212/764-1100

Elizabeth Ames
Vincent Crapelli
Francis Del Duca
Ivy Fischer-Stone
Hillary King
Carmen LaVia
Kevin McShane
John Medeiros
Nancy Murray
Fifi Oscard
Peter Sawyer

THE DANIEL OSTROFF AGENCY
9200 Sunset Blvd., Suite 402
Los Angeles, CA 90069
310/278-2020

Dan Ostroff

P

PARAMUSE ARTISTS ASSOCIATION
1414 6th Av.
New York, NY 10011
212/758-5055

BARRY PERELMAN AGENCY
9200 Sunset Blvd., Suite 531
Los Angeles, CA 90069
310/274-5999

Barry Perelman

PHOENIX LITERARY AGENCY
315 South F St.
Livingston, MT 59047
406/222-2848

Bob Datilla

THE PIMLICO AGENCY
155 East 77th Street, Suite 1A
New York, NY 10021
212/628-9729

Kirby McCauley
Kay McCauley

PLESHETTE & GREEN AGENCY
2700 N. Beachwood Dr.
Los Angeles, CA 90068
213/465-0428

Lynn Pleshette
Richard Green

BARRY POLLACK
9255 Sunset Blvd., Suite 404
Los Angeles, CA 90069
310/550-4525

PREFERRED ARTISTS
16633 Ventura Blvd., Suite 1421
Encino, CA 91436
818/990-0305

Sylvia Hirsch
Randall Skolnik

Roger Strull
Michele Wallerstein
Sussie Weissman
Lew Weitzman

JIM PREMINGER AGENCY
1650 Westwood Blvd., Suite 201
Los Angeles, CA 90024
310/475-9491

Harvey Harrison
Jim Preminger
Monica Riordan

PROGRESSIVE ARTISTS AGENCY
400 S. Beverly Dr., Suite 216
Beverly Hills, CA 90212
310/553-8561
Fax: 310/553-4726

Bernie Carneol
Belle Zwerdling

R

DOUGLAS RAE MANAGEMENT
28 Charing Cross Road
London WC2, England
071/836-3903
Fax: 071/497-2536

Douglas Rae

DAN REDLER
3474 Laurelvale Dr.
Studio City, CA 91604
818/985-8590
Fax: 818/985-2577

JOHN REDWAY ASSOCIATES
5 Denmark Street
London, W1 England
071/836-2001
Fax: 071/379-0848

THE RICHLAND-WUNSCH-HOHMAN AGENCY
9220 Sunset Blvd., Suite 311
Los Angeles, CA 90069
310/278-1955
Fax: 310/278-1156

Robert Hohman
Daniel A. Richland
Joseph Richland
Robert J. Wunsch

Ri-Se

FILM
PRODUCERS,
STUDIOS,
AGENTS AND
CASTING
DIRECTORS
GUIDE

**RISKY BUSINESS
MANAGEMENT**
10966 Le Conte Ave., Suite A
Los Angeles, CA 90024
310/478-7609

Ronnie Kaye
Jim Rissmiller
Pat Walsh
Victor Roccki

FLORA ROBERTS, INC.
157 West 57th St.
New York, NY 10019
212/355-4165

Flora Roberts

**ROBINSON, WEINTRAUB,
GROSS & ASSOCIATES, INC.**
*(In Association with The Marion
Rosenberg Office)*
8428 Melrose Pl., Suite C
Los Angeles, CA 90069
213/653-5802
Fax: 213/653-9268

Judith Everett
Ken Gross
Kerry Jones
Gary Pearl
Stuart Robinson
Bernie Weintraub
Fred Welch

ROGERS & ASSOCIATES
3855 Lankershim Blvd., Suite 218
North Hollywood, CA 91604
818/509-1010

Stephanie Rogers

ROLLINS & JOFFE INC.
130 West 57th St., Suite 11-D
New York, NY 10019
212/582-1940

Lorimar Productions
Building 137, Suite 1016
300 South Lorimar Plaza
Burbank, CA 91505
818/954-7035

Charles Joffe
Jack Rollins (NY)

JACK ROSE AGENCY
9255 Sunset Blvd., Suite 603
Los Angeles, CA 90069
310/274-4673

Dave Baratta
Carol DeTanna-Dean
Eddie Keyes
Karen Rae
Jack Rose
Bette Schwartz

**THE MARION
ROSENBERG OFFICE**
*(In Association with Robinson,
Weintraub, Gross & Associates)*
8428 Melrose Pl., Suite C
Los Angeles, CA 90069
213/653-5802
Fax: 213/653-9268

Mathew Lesher
Greg Malier
Marion Rosenberg

ROSENSTONE/WENDER
3 East 48th St.
New York, NY 10017
212/832-8330

Howard Rosenstone
Phyllis Wender

S

**SANFORD-SKOURAS-
GROSS & ASSOCIATES**
1015 Gayley Ave., 3rd Floor
Los Angeles, CA 90024
310/208-2100
Fax: 310/208-6704

Rick Berg
Brad Gross
Julia Kole
Geoffrey Sanford
Spyros Skouras

THE SARNOFF COMPANY
12001 Ventura Pl., Suite 300
Studio City, CA 91604
818/761-4495
Fax: 818/508-6857

**THE IRV SCHECHTER
COMPANY**
9300 Wilshire Blvd., Suite 410
Beverly Hills, CA 90212
310/278-8070
Fax: 310/278-6058

Elinor Berger
Joannie Burstein

Merrill Jonas
Debbie Klein
Don Klein
Cynthia Land
Michael Margules
Victorya Michaels
Anya Mitchell
Nancy Rainford
Charlotte Safavi
Irv Schechter
Andrea Simon

**SCHIOWITZ &
ASSOCIATES, INC.**
8228 Sunset Blvd., Suite 212
Los Angeles, CA 90046
213/650-7300

Charles Clay
Josh Schiowitz

**SUSAN SCHULMAN
LITERARY AGENCY, INC.**
454 West 44th St.
New York, NY 10036
212/713-1633
Fax: 212/581-8830

Susan Schulman

**DON SCHWARTZ
ASSOCIATES, INC.**
8749 Sunset Blvd., Suite 200
Los Angeles, CA 90069
310/657-8910
Fax: 310/657-8940

Al Criado
Suzanne Doran
Carey Gosa

SELECT ARTISTS
337 West 43rd St.
New York, NY 10036
212/586-4300

Cindy Alexander
Alan Willig

SELECTED ARTISTS AGENCY
3575 Cahuenga Blvd. West,
2nd Floor
Los Angeles, CA 90068
818/905-5744

Flo Joseph
David Kainer

DAVID SHAPIRA & ASSOCIATES

15301 Ventura Blvd., Suite 345
Sherman Oaks, CA 91403
818/906-0322
Fax: 818/783-2562

Lesley Bader
Dede Binder
Dick Bloch
Allison Brush
Doug Brodax
Peter Giagni
Jim Hess
Kathryn Knowlton
Jeff Leavitt
David Shapira

SHAPIRO-LICHTMAN, INC.

8827 Beverly Blvd.
Los Angeles, CA 90048
310/859-8877
Fax: 310/859-7153

Christine Foster
Michael Lewis
Mark Lichtman
Mike Robins
Bob Shapiro
Marty Shapiro
Mitchel E. Stein

SHAPIRO/WEST & ASSOCIATES

141 El Camino Dr., Suite 205
Beverly Hills, CA 90212
310/278-8896

Diane Barnett
George Shapiro
Howard West

SHARR ENTERPRISES

P.O. Box 69453
Los Angeles, CA 90069
213/278-1981

Ina Bernstein Sharr

SHEIL LAND ASSOCIATES, LTD.

43 Doughty Street
London WC1 England
071/405-9351
Fax: 071/831-2127

LEW SHERRELL AGENCY, LTD.

1354 Los Robles Rd.
Palm Springs, CA 92262
619/323-9514

Jo Martin
Lew Sherrell

SHORR/STILLE & ASSOCIATES

800 S. Robertson Blvd, Suite 6
Los Angeles, CA 90035
310/659-6160

Lucy Stille
Lucy Stutz

LINDA SIEFERT ASSOCIATES

18 Ladbroke Grove Terrace
London W11 England
071/229-5163
Fax: 071/221-0637

GERALD K. SMITH & ASSOCIATES

P.O. Box 7430
Burbank, CA 91510
213/849-5388

Gerald K. Smith

SUSAN SMITH & ASSOCIATES

121 N. San Vicente Blvd.
Beverly Hills, CA 90211
310/852-4777
Fax: 310/658-7170

192 Lexington Avenue
New York, NY 10016
212/545-0500
Fax: 212/545-7143

Jonathan Baruch
Jim Carnahan
Justen Dardis
Patricia Hacker
Scott Landis (NY)
Sandra Lucchessi
Marsha McManus (NY)
Judy Page
Susan Smith
Michael Stubbs

SMITH • GOSNELL • NICHOLSON & ASSOCIATES

1515 Palisades Dr., Suite N
P.O. Box 1166
Pacific Palisades, CA 90272
310/459-0307
Fax: 310/454-7987

Cecilia Banck
Ray Gosnell
Patty Mack
Skip Nicholson
Crayton Smith

STE REPRESENTATION, LTD.

9301 Wilshire Blvd., Suite 312
Beverly Hills, CA 90210
310/550-3982
Fax: 310/550-5991

888 Seventh Ave.
New York, NY 10109
212/246-1030
Fax: 212/246-1521

Alisa Adler
Tex Bena (NY)
Susan Calogerakis
JoAnne Colonna
Joel Rudnick
Jerilyn Scott
Clifford Stevens

CHARLES H. STERN AGENCY, INC.

11755 Wilshire Blvd., Suite 2320
Los Angeles, CA 90025
310/479-1788

Charles H. Stern

ROCHELLE STEVENS & COMPANY

2 Terretts Place
Upper Street
London N1 England
071/359-3900
Fax: 071/354-5729

STONE MANNERS TALENT AGENCY

9113 Sunset Blvd.
Los Angeles, CA 90069
310/275-9599
Fax: 310/274-8384

Scott Manners
Clark Moffat
Dan Pietragallo
Lynn Rawlins
Tim Stone
Christopher Wright

THE SHIRLEY STRICK AGENCY

1901 Avenue of the Stars, Suite 385
Los Angeles, CA 90067
310/551-0899

Silvio Narizzano
Shirley Strick

Sh-St

FILM
PRODUCERS,
STUDIOS,
AGENTS AND
CASTING
DIRECTORS
GUIDE

I
N
D
E
X

O
F

A
G
E
N
T
S

&

M
A
N
A
G
E
R
S

Sw-Wa

FILM
PRODUCERS,
STUDIOS,
AGENTS AND
CASTING
DIRECTORS
GUIDE

I
N
D
E
X

O
F

A
G
E
N
T
S

&

M
A
N
A
G
E
R
S

H.N. SWANSON, INC. AGENCY
8523 Sunset Blvd.
Los Angeles, CA 90069
310/652-5385
Fax: 310/652-6390

Michael Siegel
Annette Van Duren

T

TALENT GROUP, INC.
9250 Wilshire Blvd.
Beverly Hills, CA 90212
310/273-9559
Fax: 310/273-5142

David Brady
Pat Brannon
Carole Fields
Charles Massey
Mark Measures
Judy Rich

TRIAD ARTISTS
10100 Santa Monica Blvd.,
16th Floor
Los Angeles, CA 90067
310/556-2727
Fax: 310/557-0501

888 Seventh Ave.
New York, NY 10106
212/489-8100
Fax: 212/245-2316

Tim Angle (NY)
Ben Bernstein
Judy Clain (NY)
Nicole David
Jenny Delaney (NY)
Arlene Forster
Frank Frattaroli (NY)
Brian Gersh
Ian Greenstein
Peter Grosslight
Todd Harris
Scott Henderson
Steve Himber
Cindy Horowitz
Sarah Horowitz (NY)
Jonathan Howard
Jeff Hunter (NY)
Diane Kamp (NY)
Bruce Kaufman
John Kimble
Tracy Kramer
Rob Lee
Jennifer Lewis

Devra Lieb
Bayard Maybank
Joel Millner
Lawrence Mirisch
Geoff Nagle
Ken Neisser
Gene Parseghian
Hylda Queally
Ronda Gomez Quinones
Marshall Resnick
Arnold Rifkin
Frank Riley
Lee Rosenberg
Richard Rosenberg
Joanna Ross (NY)
Wally Saukersom (NY)
Paul Schwartzman
J. Rick Shipp (NY)
Michelle Stern
James Suskin
Brian Swardstrom
David Westberg
Ted Wilkins (NY)
James Yelich (NY)
David Yocum

PETER TURNER AGENCY
3000 W. Olympic Blvd., Suite 1438
Santa Monica, CA 90404
310/315-4772

Peter Turner

THE TURTLE AGENCY
12456 Ventura Blvd., Suite 1
Studio City, CA 91604
818/506-6898
Fax: 818/506-8440

Beth Bohn
Cindy Turtle

TWENTIETH CENTURY ARTISTS
3800 Barham Blvd., Suite 303
Los Angeles, CA 90068
213/850-5516
Fax: 213/850-1418

Jerry Davidson
Diane Davis
Estelle Hertzberg
Vivian Hollander
Stan Jacob

U

UNITED TALENT AGENCY
9560 Wilshire Blvd.
Beverly Hills, CA 90212
310/273-6700
Fax: 310/247-1111

Marty Bauer
Peter Benedek
Jim Berkus
Gary Cosay
Ilene Feldman
Risa Gertner
Chris Harbert
Jill Holwager
Toby Jaffe
Nancy Jones
David J. Kanter
John Lesher
Missy Malkin
Tory Metzger
Wendy Murphey
Gavin Palone
Cynthia Shelton
Nick Stevens
Robert Stein
Jeremy Zimmer

V

VANGUARD ASSOCIATES
2730 Wilshire Blvd., Suite 500
Santa Monica, CA 90403
310/829-5000
Fax: 310/829-9929

Jay Feldman
Howard Rothberg

W

WARDEN, WHITE & ASSOCIATES
8444 Wilshire Blvd., 4th Floor
Beverly Hills, CA 90211
213/852-1028

David Warden
Steve White

A. P. WATT, LTD.
20 John Street
London WC1 England
071/405-6774
071/831-2154

SANDRA WATT & ASSOCIATES
8033 Sunset Blvd., Suite 4053
Los Angeles, CA 90046
213/653-2339

Sandra Watt

ELLIOT WAX & ASSOCIATES
9255 Sunset Blvd., Suite 612
Los Angeles, CA 90069
310/273-8217

Elliot Wax
Marc A. Wax

SOLOMON WEINGARTEN & ASSOCIATES
11110 Ohio Ave., Suite 108
Los Angeles, CA 90025
310/479-4706
Fax: 310/478-7339

THE WELTMAN COMPANY
425 S. Beverly Dr.
Beverly Hills, CA 90212
310/556-2801

Philip Weltman

WILE ENTERPRISES, INC.
2730 Wilshire Blvd., Suite 500
Santa Monica, CA 90403
310/828-9768

Shelly Wile

THE WRIGHT CONCEPT TALENT AGENCY
1015 N. Cahuenga Blvd.
Hollywood, CA 90038
213/461-3844
Fax: 213/461-2958

Tali Nesher
Marcie Wright

WRITERS & ARTISTS AGENCY
11726 San Vicente Blvd., Suite 300
Los Angeles, CA 90049
310/820-2240
Fax: 310/207-3781

19 West 44th Street, Suite 1000
New York, NY 10036
212/391-1112
Fax: 212/398-9877

John Barkworth
Marti Blumenthal
Philip Carlson (NY)
William Craver (NY)
Karen Friedman (NY)
Robert Golenberg
Rima Greer
Sarah Horowitz (NY)
Scott Hudson (NY)
Michael Lazo
Jeff Robinov
Joan Scott
Donald Spradlin
Jeanne St. Calbre
Michael Stipanich
Hilary Wayne

Z

ZIEGLER & ASSOCIATES
606 Wilshire Blvd., Suite 304
Santa Monica, CA 90401
310/278-0070

★ ★ ★ ★

TAKE A FEW MINUTES TO GO THROUGH YOUR GARBAGE.

Every Sunday, more than 500,000 trees are used to produce the 88% of newspapers that are never recycled.

We throw away enough glass bottles and jars to fill the 1,350-foot twin towers of New York's World Trade Center *every two weeks.*

Americans go through 2.5 million plastic bottles *every hour,* only a small percentage of which are now recycled.

American consumers and industry throw away enough aluminum to rebuild our entire commercial airfleet *every three months.*

Every year we dispose of *24 million tons* of leaves and grass clippings, which could be composted to conserve landfill space.

We throw away enough iron and steel to *continuously* supply all the nation's automakers.

The ordinary bag of trash you throw away is slowly becoming a serious problem for everybody.

Because the fact is, not only are we running out of resources to make the products we need, we're running out of places to put what's left over.

Write the Environmental Defense Fund at: 257 Park Avenue South, New York, NY 10010, for a free brochure that will tell you virtually everything you'll need to know about recycling.

One thing's for certain, the few minutes you take to learn how to recycle will spare us all a lot of garbage later.

IF YOU'RE NOT RECYCLING SM **YOU'RE THROWING IT ALL AWAY.**

© 1988 EDF

CASTING DIRECTORS

LISTINGS

A

* Casting Society of America

CECILY ADAMS
Ulrich/Dawson Casting
100 Universal City Plaza, Bldg. 466
Universal City, CA 91608
818/777-7802
Fax: 818/777-4987

PAUL ADLER
Manager of Casting
Disney/Touchtone Pictures
500 S. Buena Vista St., Casting Bldg., #7
Burbank, CA 91521
818/560-7509
Fax: 818/563-3719

DOUG AIBEL
FIVE CORNERS   1988

STUART AIKENS
A NEW LIFE   1988

JANE ALDERMAN CASTING
c/o WLS-TV
190 N. State St.
Chicago, IL 60601
312/899-4250
Fax: 312/899-4245

*Jane Alderman**
*Susan Weider**

ENDLESS LOVE   1981
FOUR FRIENDS   1981
BAD BOYS   1983
DR. DETROIT   1983
THE COLOR OF MONEY   1986
FERRIS BUELLER'S DAY OFF   1986
NOTHING IN COMMON   1986
NO MERCY   1986
LUCAS   1986
WEEDS   1987
A NIGHT IN THE LIFE OF JIMMY REARDON   1988
SHE'S HAVING A BABY   1988
CHILD'S PLAY   1988
MIDNIGHT RUN   1988
BETRAYED   1988
POLTERGEIST III   1988
MUSIC BOX   1989
NEXT OF KIN   1989
MAJOR LEAGUE   1989
FIELD OF DREAMS   1989
THE LONG WALK HOME   1990
MEET THE APPLEGATES   1991
BACKDRAFT   1991
THE BABE   1992
HEAVEN IS A PLAYGROUND   1992
THE GO BETWEEN   1992

ROBIN JOY ALLAN*
Landsburg/Allan Casting
Raleigh Studios
5358 Melrose Avenue, West Bldg., #203-W
Los Angeles, CA 90038
213/960-4063
Fax: 213/460-3971

SANDY ALLISON
1759 Orchid
Los Angeles, CA 90028
213/874-3631

CAST A GIANT SHADOW   1959
DOCTOR ZHIVAGO   1965
OPERATION CROSSBOW   1965
THE DIRTY DOZEN   1967
THE FIXER   1968
HOT MILLIONS   1968
MRS. BROWN, YOU'VE GOT A LOVELY DAUGHTER   1968
GOODBYE, MR. CHIPS   1969
MY LOVER, MY SON   1970
RYAN'S DAUGHTER   1970
THE GETTING OF WISDOM   1977
THE GREEK TYCOON   1978
THE RIDDLE OF THE SANDS   1979

JULIE ALTER*
Julie Alter Casting
8721 Sunset Blvd., #210
West Hollywood, CA 90069
310/652-7373

HONOR BRIGHT   1988
THE LAST TEMPTATION OF CHRIST   1988

ALAN AMTZIS
THE PRINCE OF PENNSYLVANIA   1988

DONNA ANDERSON*
c/o C.S.A.
6565 Sunset Blvd., Suite 306
Los Angeles, CA 90028
213/463-1925
Fax: 213/463-5753

ANDERSON/McCOOK/WHITE CASTING
3855 Lankershim Blvd.
North Hollywood, CA 91614
818/760-3934
Fax: 818/505-8101

Catherine White
Nancy McCook

DEBORAH AQUILA*
Deborah Aquila Casting
333 West 52nd Street
New York, NY 10019
212/664-5049
Fax: 212/664-3429

STICKY FINGERS   1988
sex, lies and videotape   1989
LAST EXIT TO BROOKLYN   1990
HANGIN' WITH THE HOMEBOYS   1990
THE RAPTURE   1991
DECEIVED   1991

Aq

FILM
PRODUCERS,
STUDIOS,
AGENTS AND
CASTING
DIRECTORS
GUIDE

C
A
S
T
I
N
G

D
I
R
E
C
T
O
R
S

MAUREEN A. ARATA*
100 Universal City Plaza
Building 466, Rear Entrance
Universal City, CA 91608
818/777-3036
Fax: 818/777-4987

MARIA ARMSTRONG
DEAD OF WINTER   1987

JEANNE ASHBY
Barbara Remsen & Associates
Raleigh Studios
650 North Bronson Avenue, Suite 124
Los Angeles, CA 90004
213/464-7968
Fax: 213/464-7970

LOVING LULU   1992

ALYCIA AUMULLER*
330 W. 89th St.
New York, NY 10024
212/877-0225

NINA AXELROD
8439 Sunset Blvd., #200
Los Angeles, CA 90069
213/656-9130

NIGHTFLYERS   1987
DUDES   1987
MAID TO ORDER   1987
THREE FOR THE ROAD   1987
PASS THE AMMO   1988
TRADING HEARTS   1988
REMOTE CONTROL   1988
RENTED LIPS   1988
THE BIG PICTURE   1989
FRIGHT NIGHT PART II   1989

B

LINDA BACA
6557 Bellaire Ave.
North Hollywood, CA 91606
818/762-1230

BARBARA BALDAVIN*
c/o C.S.A.
6565 Sunset Blvd., Suite 306
Los Angeles, CA 90028
213/463-1925
Fax: 213/463-5753

NANCY BANKS
BAT 21   1988

MARY ANN BARTON
930 N. Westbourne
Los Angeles, CA 90069
818/905-7005

FRAN BASCOM*
Studio Plaza
3400 Riverside Drive, #1075
Burbank, CA 91505
818/972-8332
Fax: 818/972-0523

PAMELA BASKER*
7266 Franklin Avenue
Suite 213
Los Angeles, CA 90046
213/851-6475
Fax: 213/851-5424

Warner Bros.
4000 Warner Blvd.
Producers Bldg. 4, Room 16
Burbank, CA 91522
818/954-3107
Fax: 818/954-4396

POLICE ACADEMY   1984
POLICE ACADEMY 4: CITIZENS ON PATROL   1987
STEEL DAWN   1987
THE NAKED GUN: From the Files of Police Squad!   1988
TROOP BEVERLY HILLS   1989
PET SEMATARY   1989
OUT FOR JUSTICE   1990
DREADNOUGHT   1992

CHERYL BAYER*
12001 Ventura Place, 2nd Floor
Studio City, CA 91604
818/760-5278
Fax: 818/760-5163

LISA BEACH*
Parkway Productions
Sony Pictures Entertainment
10202 W. Washington Blvd., Metro Bldg., #113
Culver City, CA 90232
310/280-4470

JUDY BELSHE
4731 Laurel Canyon, #3
North Hollywood, CA 91607
818/760-1380

BENSON/PERRY CASTING
Lantana Center
3000 W. Olympic Blvd., Bldg. 2, #2416
Santa Monica, CA 90404
310/315-4865
Fax: 310/315-4797

*Annette Benson**
Penny Perry

A NIGHTMARE ON ELM STREET 3: DREAM
   WARRIORS   1987
MY DEMON LOVER   1987
UNIVERSAL SOLDIER   1992

STUART BESSER
THE MODERNS   1988

SHARON BIALY*
Pagano/Bialy/Manwiller Casting
1680 N. Vine St., Suite 904
Los Angeles, CA 90028
213/871-0051
Fax: 213/871-0509

EXTREMETIES 1986
CHILD'S PLAY 1988
BLOODHOUNDS OF BROADWAY 1989
DRUGSTORE COWBOY 1989
GRAVEYARD SHIFT 1990
POINT BREAK 1991
DON'T TELL MOM THE BABYSITTER'S DEAD 1991
THE BRIDGE 1992
DIGGS TOWN 1992
RINGERS 1992
RULES OF THE GAME 1992
GAS FOOD AND LODGING 1992
BLOOD IN BLOOD OUT 1992

TAMMY BILLIK*
Sunset Gower Studios
1438 N. Gower St. #2407
Los Angeles, CA 90028
213/460-7266
Fax: 213/460-7670

JAY BINDER*
513 W. 54Th St.
New York, NY 10019
212/586-6777
Fax: 212/977-5686

PHALIA BLASSINGAME
SQUARE DANCE 1987

SUSAN BLUESTEIN*
4063 Radford Ave., Suite 105
Studio City, CA 91604
818/505-6636
Fax: 818/505-6635

Marsha Shoenman

EUGENE BLYTHE*
Vice President of Television Talent
Walt Disney Studios
500 S. Buena Vista St., Team Disney Bldg., #417-E
Burbank, CA 91521
818/560-7625
Fax: 818/562-1661

REBECCA BOSS
WITCHBOARD 1987

DEE DEE BRADLEY*
Warner Bros.
4000 Warner Blvd.
Burbank, CA 91522
818/954-2015

RISA BRAMON CASTING
Ixtlan
3110 Main Street
Santa Monica, CA 90405
310/450-1333

*Risa Bramon**

MEGAN BRANMAN*
100 Universal City Plaza
Bldg. 463, Rm. 112
Universal City, CA 91608
818/777-1744

IN THE MOOD 1987

JACKIE BRISKEY*
Briskey Chamian Casting
Warner Hollywood Studios
1041 N. Formosa
Santa Monica Bldg., #115
Los Angeles, CA 90046
213/850-3599
Fax: 213/850-3596

TOUCH AND GO 1987

JAKI BROWN
213/856-6155

STAND AND DELIVER 1988
FIVE HEARTBEATS 1991
BOYZ N THE HOOD 1991
JUICE 1992

BROWN/WEST CASTING
7319 Beverly Blvd., Suite 10
Los Angeles, CA 90036
213/938-2575

Ross Brown
*Mary West**

BUCK/EDELMAN CASTING
4051 Radford Ave.
Bungalow B
Studio City, CA 91604
818/506-7328
Fax: 818/761-2356

*Mary Buck**
*Susan Edelman**

STAR TREK II: THE WRATH OF KHAN 1982
OLIVER & COMPANY 1988
THE LITTLE MERMAID 1989
THE RESCUERS DOWN UNDER 1990

PERRY BULLINGTON*
MacDonald/Bullington Casting
6930 Sunset Blvd., Second Floor
Los Angeles, CA 90028
213/957-0091
Fax: 213/957-0092

ASSASSINATION 1987
NUMBER ONE WITH A BULLET 1987
MESSENGER OF DEATH 1988
KINJITE (FORBIDDEN SUBJECTS) 1989

Bu

**FILM
PRODUCERS,
STUDIOS,
AGENTS AND
CASTING
DIRECTORS
GUIDE**

C
A
S
T
I
N
G

D
I
R
E
C
T
O
R
S

JACKIE BURCH*
c/o C.S.A.
6565 Sunset Blvd. #306
Los Angeles, CA 90028
213/463-1925
Fax: 213/463-5753

PROJECT X   1987
PREDATOR   1987
THE RUNNING MAN   1987
COMING TO AMERICA   1988
RED HEAT   1988
DIE HARD   1988
PUNCHLINE   1988
SKIN DEEP   1989

TOM BURKE
Director of Casting
CBS Entertainment
7800 Beverly Blvd., Suite 284
Los Angeles, CA 90036
213/852-2835
Fax: 213/655-2368

WHITNEY BURNETT-VOSS*
c/o C.S.A.
311 W. 43rd St.
New York, NY 10036
212/333-4552

VICTORIA BURROWS*
Green/Epstein Productions
4400 Coldwater Canyon, #300
Studio City, CA 91604
818/753-9086
Fax: 818/753-9481

BUSTLES CASTING
11634 Moorpark Ave.
Studio City, CA 91604
818/980-2924

C

IRENE CAGEN*
Liberman/Hirschfeld Casting
Sunset-Gower Studios
1438 N. Gower St., Suite 1410
Los Angeles, CA 90028
213/460-7258
Fax: 213/460-7547

REUBEN CANNON & ASSOCIATES
1041 N. Formosa Ave., Bldg. G, #201
Los Angeles, CA 90046
213/850-3528

*Reuben Cannon
Carol Dudley**

A SOLDIER'S STORY   1984
THE COLOR PURPLE   1985
WHO FRAMED ROGER RABBIT   1988

MARGOT CAPELIER
THE UNBEARABLE LIGHTNESS OF BEING   1988
FRANTIC   1988

ANNE CAPIZZI*
Bob Booker Productions
6605 Eleanor Avenue
Hollywood, CA 90038
213/465-7877

KEN CARLSON
CLARA'S HEART   1988
HER ALIBI   1989

LYNNE CARROW
HOUSEKEEPING   1987

MAGGIE CARTIER
INDIANA JONES AND THE LAST CRUSADE   1989

MATT CASELLA
Disney Studios
500 S. Buena Vista St.
Western Bldg. 3, Suite 4
Burbank, CA 91521
818/560-1159
Fax: 818/560-5132

ALICE CASSIDY*
20th Century-Fox Studios
10201 W. Pico Blvd.
Pico Apartments, #5
Los Angeles, CA 90035
310/203-1127
Fax: 310/203-1623

THE CASTING COMPANY
8925 Venice Blvd.
Los Angeles, CA 90034
310/842-7551
Fax: 310/842-7566

*Janet Hirshenson**
*Jane Jenkins**

CASTING SOCIETY OF AMERICA
6565 Sunset Blvd.
Suite 306
Los Angeles, CA 90028
213/463-1925
Fax: 213/463-5753

311 W. 43rd St.
New York, NY 10036
212/333-4552

FRANCESCO CENIERI
DANCERS   1987

CENTRAL CASTING
2600 W. Olive St., 5th Floor
Burbank, CA 91505
818/569-5200
Fax: 818/563-6275

Co

FILM
PRODUCERS,
STUDIOS,
AGENTS AND
CASTING
DIRECTORS
GUIDE

C
A
S
T
I
N
G

D
I
R
E
C
T
O
R
S

DENISE CHAMIAN*
Briskey/Chamian Casting
Warner Hollywood Studios
1041 N. Formosa, Santa Monica Bldg., #115
Los Angeles, CA 90046
213/850-3599
Fax: 213/850-3596

BACK TO THE BEACH   1987

FERN CHAMPION CASTING
7060 Hollywood Blvd., Suite 808
Hollywood, CA 90028
213/466-1884
Fax: 213/466-2719

*Fern Champion**
Mark Paladini

SERGEANT PEPPER'S LONELY HEARTS
   CLUB BAND   1978
CHEECH & CHONG'S NEXT MOVIE   1980
FADE TO BLACK   1980
CHEECH & CHONG'S NICE DREAMS   1981
THINGS ARE TOUGH ALL OVER   1982
POLICE ACADEMY   1984
POLICE ACADEMY 2: THEIR FIRST
   ASSIGNMENT   1985
MOVERS AND SHAKERS   1985
APRIL FOOL'S DAY   1986
POLICE ACADEMY 3: BACK IN TRAINING   1986
POLICE ACADEMY 4: CITIZENS ON PATROL   1987
DATE WITH AN ANGEL   1987
STEEL DAWN   1987
POLICE ACADEMY 5: ASSIGNMENT MIAMI
   BEACH   1988
THE NAKED GUN: From the Files of Police Squad!   1988
TROOP BEVERLY HILLS   1989
PET SEMATARY   1989
SKI PATROL   1990
MARKED FOR DEATH   1990
SUBURBAN COMMANDO   1991
HIGHLANDER II, THE QUICKENING   1991
BODY PARTS   1992
GRAND ISLE   1992

ALETA CHAPPELLE*
c/o C.S.A.
311 W. 43rd St.
New York, NY 10036
212/333-4552

GARDENS OF STONE   1987
NEW YORK STORIES: "Life Without Zoe"   1989

NAN CHARBONNEAU
THE PACKAGE   1989

NGUYEN THI MY CHAU
FULL METAL JACKET   1987

BRIAN CHAVANNE*
c/o C.S.A.
6565 Sunset Blvd., Suite 306
Los Angeles, CA 90028
213/463-1925
Fax: 213/463-5753

ELLEN CHENOWETH*
c/o Werthemer, Armstrong & Hirsch
1888 Century Park East
Suite 1888
Los Angeles, CA 90067
310/333-4552

BROADCAST NEWS   1987
MOON OVER PARADOR   1988
COOKIE   1989
SHE-DEVIL   1989
ENEMIES, A LOVE STORY   1989
BUGSY   1991

MICHAEL CHINICH
TWINS   1988
GHOSTBUSTERS II   1989

BARBARA CLAMAN*
Barbara Claman, Inc.
6565 Sunset Blvd., Suite 412
Los Angeles, CA 90028
213/466-3400
Fax: 213/466-3943

DAYS OF HEAVEN   1978
DEFENDING YOUR LIFE   1991
BURDEN OF PROOF   1992

LISA CLARKSON
Studio Plaza
3400 Riverside Drive, #747
Burbank, CA 91505
818/972-8561

TIN MEN   1987

ROSS CLYDESDALE
DEAD OF WINTER   1987

LORI COBE*
10351 Santa Monica Blvd., #410
Los Angeles, CA 90025
310/277-5777
Fax: 310/556-3821

NIGHT EYES   1990
LAST CALL   1990
COMMON GROUND   1990
TOTAL EXPOSURE   1990
WAKE, RATTLE & ROLL   1990
TWOGETHER   1992
SECRET GAMES   1992
SEXUAL RESPONSE   1992
THE OTHER WOMAN   1992
THE PAMELA PRINCIPLE   1992
NIGHT EYES II   1991

ANDREA COHEN*
Warner Bros.
4000 Warner Blvd.
N. Administration Bldg., #27
Burbank, CA 91522
818/954-1621

Co

**FILM
PRODUCERS,
STUDIOS,
AGENTS** and
**CASTING
DIRECTORS**
GUIDE

C
A
S
T
I
N
G

D
I
R
E
C
T
O
R
S

DAVID COHN*
6565 Sunset Blvd., Suite 306
Los Angeles, CA 90028
818/377-9677

HUNK 1987
IT TAKES TWO 1988

RICHARD COLE*
Mccorkle Casting
264 W. 40th St., 9th Floor
New York, NY 10024
212/840-0992

PATRICIA COLLINGE*
Collinge/Pickman Casting
138 Mt. Auburn Street
Cambridge, MA 02138
617/492-4212
Fax: 617/492-1306

ANNELISE COLLINS*
Centre Films
1103 El Centro Avenue
Los Angeles, CA 90038
213/962-9562
Fax: 213/465-6657

MARY COLQUHOUN*
c/o C.S.A.
311 W. 43rd St.
New York, NY 10036
212/333-4552

THE BEDROOM WINDOW 1987
THE SECRET OF MY SUCCESS 1987
HAMBURGER HILL 1987
HAIRSPRAY 1988
A NEW LIFE 1988
BRIGHT LIGHTS, BIG CITY 1988
LEAN ON ME 1989
SEA OF LOVE 1989
GLORY 1989
MY GIRL 1991
LEAVING NORMAL 1992

RUTH CONFORTE*
5300 Laurel Canyon Blvd., Suite 168
North Hollywood, CA 91607
818/760-8220

PRIME TARGET 1992
IN EXILE 1992
GIANT OF THUNDER MOUNTAIN 1992

JUDY COURTNEY
84 CHARING CROSS ROAD 1987
JACKNIFE 1989

ALLISON COWITT
Fenton & Associates
Universal Studios
100 Universal City Plaza, Trailer 78
Universal City, CA 91608
818/777-4610
Fax: 818/777-8284

ELAINE CRAIG VOICE CASTING
6565 Sunset Blvd., Suite 418
Hollywood, CA 90028
213/469-8773
Fax: 213/469-6990

MARGUERITE CRAVATT
Creative Casting
1680 N. Vine St., Suite 709
Hollywood, CA 90028
213/466-7319
Fax: 213/463-3375

DIANNE CRITTENDEN
THREE MEN AND A BABY 1987
THE UNBEARABLE LIGHTNESS OF BEING 1988
THE SERPENT AND THE RAINBOW 1988
BLACK RAIN 1989

D

GLENN DANIELS*
Paramount Studios
5555 Melrose Ave.
Y. Frank Freeman Bldg., #226
Los Angeles, CA 90038
213/956-8259

WHO'S THAT GIRL 1987
CLEAN AND SOBER 1988
TANGO AND CASH 1989
CHILD'S PLAY 3 1991

ANITA DANN*
P.O. Box 2041
Beverly Hills, CA 90213
310/278-7765
Fax: 310/652-7663

DAVID & ZIMMERMAN
WILLOW 1988

AMY DAVIS*
CBS
51 W. 52nd, 23rd Floor
New York, NY 10019
212/975-3851

NOEL DAVIS
SUPERMAN IV: THE QUEST FOR PEACE 1987
CRUSOE 1989

ERIC DAWSON
Ulrich/Dawson Casting
100 Universal City Plaza, Bldg. 466
Universal City, CA 91608
818/777-7802
Fax: 818/777-4987

PAUL DECKER
NBC
3000 W. Alameda Ave.
Burbank, CA 91523
818/840-3500
Fax: 818/840-4412

DENNISON/SELZER/RUSH CASTING
3000 Olympic Blvd.
Santa Monica, CA 90404
310/652-7528
Fax: 310/306-9753

Sally Dennison*
Justine Jacoby*
Julie Selzer*

ROBOCOP   1987
AMAZON WOMEN ON THE MOON   1987
THROW MOMMA FROM THE TRAIN   1987
THE ACCUSED   1988
HEATHERS   1989
IMMEDIATE FAMILY   1989
HERO WANTED   1992

PATRICIA de OLIVEIRA*
c/o C.S.A.
6565 Sunset Blvd., Suite 306
Los Angeles, CA 90028
213/463-1925
Fax: 213/463-5753

LOUIS DiGIAIMO
513 West 54th Street, 3rd Floor
New York, NY 10019
212/713-1884
Fax: 212/977-9509

TIN MEN   1987
DEADLY ILLUSION   1987
GOOD MORNING, VIETNAM   1987
RAIN MAN   1988
THE PACKAGE   1989
THELMA AND LOUISE   1991
29TH STREET   1991
COLUMBUS   1992

DIANE DIMEO*
12725 Ventura Blvd., Suite H
Studio City, CA 91604
818/505-0945
Fax: 818/505-0078

JOAN D'INCECCO*
ABC Entertainment
101 W. 67th St.
New York, NY 10023
212/887-3844

DICK DINMAN*
213/469-2283

c/o C.S.A.
6565 Sunset Blvd., Suite 306
Los Angeles, CA 90028
213/463-1925
Fax: 213/463-5753

BARBARA DIPRIMA*
Di Prima Casting
7200 Lake Ellenor Drive #135
Orlando, FL 32809
407/240-4718

3390 Mary Street, PH-J
Coconut Grove, FL 33133
305/445-7630
Fax: 305/445-2147

PAM DIXON*
P.O. Box 672
Beverly Hills, CA 90213
310/271-8064

BABY BOOM   1987
MADE IN HEAVEN   1987
THE MODERNS   1988
MUSIC BOX   1989
CITY SLICKERS   1991
FREEJACK   1992
WATERDANCE   1992
PLAYBOYS   1992
RAISING CAIN   1992
MR. SATURDAY NIGHT   1992
EQUINOX   1992
BEYOND SUSPICION   1992
YEAR OF THE COMET   1992

DONNA DOCKSTADER*
Universal Studios
100 Universal Plaza #463-110
Universal City, CA 91608
818/777-1961

CHRISTIE DOOLEY
Bell Phillips Productions
7800 Beverly Blvd., Suite 3371
Los Angeles, CA 90036
213/852-4501
Fax: 213/655-8760

KIM DORR*
The Arthur Company
100 Universal City Plaza, Bldg. 447
Universal City, CA 91608
818/505-1200
Fax: 818/505-1900

JO DOSTER*
P.O. Box 120641
Nashville, TN 37212-0641
615/385-3850

MARION DOUGHERTY
Vice President - Talent
Warner Bros.
4000 Warner Blvd.
Burbank, CA 91522
818/954-3021
Fax: 818/954-3021

ESCAPE FROM ALCATRAZ   1979
URBAN COWBOY   1980
FULL METAL JACKET   1987
THE LOST BOYS   1987
NUTS   1987

Do
FILM PRODUCERS, STUDIOS, AGENTS and CASTING DIRECTORS GUIDE

CASTING DIRECTORS

331

Du

FILM
PRODUCERS,
STUDIOS,
AGENTS AND
CASTING
DIRECTORS
GUIDE

C
A
S
T
I
N
G

D
I
R
E
C
T
O
R
S

FUNNY FARM   1988
CLEAN AND SOBER   1988
GORILLAS IN THE MIST   1988
BATMAN   1989
LETHAL WEAPON 2   1989
THE LAST BOY SCOUT   1991
MEMOIRS OF AN INVISIBLE MAN   1992
SINGLES   1992

CAROL DUDLEY*
Reuben Cannon & Associates
1041 N. Formosa Ave., Bldg. G, #201
Los Angeles, CA 90046
213/850-2500

c/o C.S.A.
6565 Sunset Blvd., Suite 306
Los Angeles, CA 90028
213/463-1925
Fax: 213/463-5753

PENNIE du PONT
ROXANNE   1987

NAN DUTTON*
12001 Ventura Place, #305
Studio City, CA 91604
818/508-9683

OUT COLD   1989

E

SUSAN EDELMAN*
Buck/Edelman Casting
4051 Radford Avenue, Bungalow B
Studio City, CA 91604
818/506-7328
Fax: 818/761-2356

ELITE CASTING
CRIMINAL LAW   1989

PENNY ELLERS*
Penny Ellers Casting
8285 Sunset Blvd., Suite 1
Los Angeles, CA 90046
213/656-9511
Fax: 213/656-5976

CODY MICHAEL EWELL*
c/o C.S.A.
311 West 43rd Street
New York, NY 10036
212/333-4552

F

RACHELLE FARBERMAN*
The Kushner-Locke Company
11601 Wilshire Blvd., 21st Floor
Los Angeles, CA 90025
310/445-1111
Fax: 310/445-1191

FIRE IN THE DARK   1991

BETTY FARROW
13338 McCormick
Van Nuys, CA 91401
818/986-7113

JANE FEINBERG
THE STEPFATHER   1987
FROM THE HIP   1987
FULL METAL JACKET   1987
HARRY AND THE HENDERSONS   1987
INNERSPACE   1987
STAKEOUT   1987
EMPIRE OF THE SUN   1987
ARTHUR 2 ON THE ROCKS   1988
LEVIATHAN   1989

MIKE FENTON & ASSOCIATES
100 Universal City Plaza, Trailer 78
Universal City, CA 91608
818/777-4610
Fax: 818/777-8284

Allison Cowitt
*Mike Fenton**
Valorie Massalas

AMERICAN GRAFFITI   1973
CHINATOWN   1974
ONE FLEW OVER THE CUCKOO'S NEST   1975
RAIDERS OF THE LOST ARK   1981
E.T. THE EXTRA-TERRESTRIAL   1982
BACK TO THE FUTURE   1985
THE STEPFATHER   1987
FROM THE HIP   1987
FULL METAL JACKET   1987
HARRY AND THE HENDERSONS   1987
INNERSPACE   1987
STAKEOUT   1987
EMPIRE OF THE SUN   1987
ARTHUR 2 ON THE ROCKS   1988
BEACHES   1988
THE 'BURBS   1989
FAREWELL TO THE KING   1989
CHANCES ARE   1989
LEVIATHAN   1989
INDIANA JONES AND THE LAST CRUSADE   1989
HONEY, I SHRUNK THE KIDS   1989
TURNER AND HOOCH   1989
BACK TO THE FUTURE PART II   1989
BACK TO THE FUTURE PART III   1990
NOISES OFF   1992

STEVEN FERTIG
205 Canon Drive
Beverly Hills, CA 90210
310/276-6267

HOWARD FEUER*
3619 Motor Avenue, #280
Los Angeles, CA 90034
310/204-2242
Fax: 310/280-1811

ALL THAT JAZZ   1979
HAIR   1979
ARTHUR   1981
STAR 80   1983
PLACES IN THE HEART   1984
NADINE   1987
SUSPECT   1987
MOONSTRUCK   1987
ISHTAR   1987
BIG BUSINESS   1988
THE HOUSE ON CARROLL STREET   1988
BIG BUSINESS   1988
MISSISSIPPI BURNING   1988
MARRIED TO THE MOB   1988
DANGEROUS LIAISONS   1988
SLAVES OF NEW YORK   1989
DEAD POETS SOCIETY   1989
IN COUNTRY   1989
AN INNOCENT MAN   1989
SLAVES OF NEW YORK   1989
THE ABYSS   1989
BASIC INSTINCT   1992

SUSIE FIGGIS
CRUSOE   1989

LEONARD FINGER*
1501 Broadway, Suite 1511
New York, NY 10036
212/944-8611

SPIKE OF BENSONHURST   1988

DON FINN
1807 Courtney Avenue
Los Angeles, CA 90046
213/969-8743

THAT NIGHT   1992
THE SUPER MARIO BROTHERS   1992
THE CROWDED ROOM   1992

MALI FINN
1807 Courtney Avenue
Los Angeles, CA 90046
213/969-8743

BIG SHOTS   1987
OUTRAGEOUS FORTUNE   1987
AMAZING GRACE AND CHUCK   1987
THE UNTOUCHABLES   1987
LADY IN WHITE   1988
SPLIT DECISIONS   1988
THE WIZARD   1989
WELCOME HOME, ROXY CARMICHAEL   1990
FLATLINERS   1990
PACIFIC HEIGHTS   1990
SHADOW OF CHINA   1990
TERMINATOR 2: JUDGEMENT DAY   1991

HOT SHOTS   1992
HOUSE OF CARDS   1992
THAT NIGHT   1992
THE SUPER MARIO BROTHERS   1992
THE CROWDED ROOM

BONNIE FINNEGAN*
Paramount Pictures
Gulf & Western Plaza
New York, NY 10036
212/316-2863

ALEXA L. FOGEL*
ABC
40 W. 66th St., 3rd Floor
New York, NY 10023
212/887-3631
Fax: 212/887-3023

NANCY FOY*
VP of Casting
Paramount
5555 Melrose Avenue, Dressing Room Bldg., #330
Los Angeles, CA 90038
213/956-5444

D.O.A.   1988
THE MILAGRO BEANFIELD WAR   1988
LOST ANGELS   1989
FAT MAN AND LITTLE BOY   1989

LINDA FRANCIS
1645 N. Vine St., #706
Los Angeles, CA 90028
213/467-3838

SISTER, SISTER   1988

JERRY FRANKS*
Onorato/Franks Casting
1717 N. Highland Ave., Suite 904
Los Angeles, CA 90028
213/468-8833
Fax: 213/468-9172

FRAZIER/GINSBERG CASTING
335 N. Maple Drive, #356
Beverly Hills, CA 90210
310/247-0370

*Carrie Frazier**
*Shani Ginsberg**

RIVER'S EDGE   1987
EIGHT MEN OUT   1988
THREE FUGITIVES   1989

LISA FREIBERGER
Vice President - Talent & Casting
CBS Entertainment
7800 Beverly Blvd.
Los Angeles, CA 90036
213/852-2335
Fax: 213/655-2368

JEAN FROST*
3900 W. Alameda Ave., #2010
Burbank, CA 91505
818/567-5684

Fr

FILM
PRODUCERS,
STUDIOS,
AGENTS AND
CASTING
DIRECTORS
GUIDE

C
A
S
T
I
N
G

D
I
R
E
C
T
O
R
S

FILM
PRODUCERS,
STUDIOS,
AGENTS AND
CASTING
DIRECTORS
GUIDE

G

MELINDA GARTZMAN*
Paramount Studios
5555 Melrose Avenue
Clara Bow Bldg., #219
Los Angeles, CA 90038
213/956-4373
Fax: 213/956-0056

JEFF GERRARD
10661 Whipple St.
Toluca Lake, CA 91602
818/508-8665

BONNIE GINNEGAN
HIDING OUT   1987

SHANI GINSBERG*
Frazier/Ginsberg Casting
335 N. Maple Drive, #356
Beverly Hills, CA 90210
310/247-0370

RIVER'S EDGE   1987
EIGHT MEN OUT   1988
THREE FUGITIVES   1989

JAN GLASER*
10100 W. Washington Blvd., #7118
Culver City, CA 90232
310/280-6238
Fax: 310/558-5859

LAURA GLEASON*
c/o C.S.A.
311 W. 43rd St., Suite 700
New York, NY 10036
212/333-4552

SUSAN GLICKSMAN*
5433 Beethoven
Los Angeles, CA 90066
213/302-9149
Fax: 213/302-9189

VICKI GOGGIN
Barbara Claman, Inc.
6565 Sunset Blvd., Suite 412
Los Angeles, CA 90028
213/466-3400
Fax: 213/466-3943

MARY GOLDBERG
11811 W. Olympic Blvd.
Los Angeles, CA 90067
310/477-9972

BETRAYED   1988
MUSIC BOX   1989

PAT GOLDEN*
c/o C.S.A.
6565 Sunset Blvd.
Suite 306
Los Angeles, CA 90028
213/463-1925
Fax: 213/463-5753

EDDIE MURPHY "RAW"   1987

PETER GOLDEN*
Vice President of Talent & Casting
Stephen J. Cannell Productions, Inc.
7083 Hollywood Blvd.
Los Angeles, CA 90028
213/856-7576
Fax: 213/463-4987

DANNY GOLDMAN
1006 N. Cole Ave.
Los Angeles, CA 90038
213/463-1600
Fax: 213/463-3139

ELISA GOODMAN*
P.O. Box 67217
Los Angeles, CA 90067
310/317-1299

DELUSION   1992
UNDER THE CAR   1992

ALIXE GORDIN*
129 W. 12th St.
New York, NY 10011
212/627-0472

SUMMER OF '42   1971
KLUTE   1971
THE SEDUCTION OF JOE TYNAN   1979
SOPHIE'S CHOICE   1982
SCARFACE   1983
PRIZZI'S HONOR   1985
SEE YOU IN THE MORNING   1989
PRESUMED INNOCENT   1990

LYNDA GORDON*
Taylor/Gordon Casting
P.O. Box 461198
Los Angeles, CA 90048
818/501-3160

500 S. Buena Vista St.
Zorro Bldg. 5, #6
Burbank, CA 91521
818/560-2700

BEACHES   1988
LEVIATHAN   1989
HONEY, I SHRUNK THE KIDS   1989
TURNER AND HOOCH   1989

CHRISTOPHER GORMAN*
Senior Director of Casting
CBS Entertainment
51 West 52nd Street
33rd Floor
New York, NY 10019
212/975-2263
Fax: 212/975-5945

DAVID GRAHAM*
590 N. Rossmore Ave.
Suite 2
Los Angeles, CA 90004
213/871-2012

MARILYN GRANAS
220 S. Palm Drive
Beverly Hills, CA 90212
310/278-3773

JEFF GREENBERG*
Paramount Studios
5555 Melrose Ave.,
Marx Bros. 102
Los Angeles, CA 90038
213/956-4886
Fax: 213/956-1368

LOOK WHO'S TALKING 1989

LAURIE GROSSMAN
PATTI ROCKS 1988

DAN GUERRERO
625 N. Flores St.
Los Angeles, CA 90048
213/655-2417

H

JILL HABERMAN*
c/o C.S.A.
311 W. 43rd St., Suite 700
New York, NY 10036
212/333-4552

PEG HALLIGAN*
c/o C.S.A.
6565 Sunset Blvd., Suite 306
Los Angeles, CA 90028
818/840-7628

YONIT HAMER-TUMAROFF*
Unique Casting
540 NW 165th St., #110
Miami, FL 33169
305/947-9339
Fax: 305/947-0713

MILT HAMERMAN*
c/o C.S.A.
6565 Sunset Blvd., Suite 306
Los Angeles, CA 90028
213/463-1925
Fax: 213/463-5753

BARBARA HANLEY
WEEDS 1987

TED HANN*
Lorimar Casting
300 S. Lorimar Plaza
Bldg. 140, First Floor
Burbank, CA 91505
818/954-7642
Fax: 818/954-7678

ROBERT HARBIN*
Vice President - Talent and Casting
20th Century Fox
10201 W. Pico Blvd.
Executive Bldg., Suite 325
Los Angeles, CA 90035
310/203-3847
Fax: 310/203-2954

NATALIE HART*
c/o C.S.A.
311 W. 43rd St., Suite 700
New York, NY 10036
212/333-4552

PRELUDE TO A KISS 1992

CYRENE HAUSMAN
c/o Cinehaus
245 W. 55th St.
New York, NY 10010
212/245-9060
Fax: 212/265-9831

HOUSE OF GAMES 1987
THINGS CHANGE 1988

GENO HAVENS
1323 11th St., #3
Santa Monica, CA 90401
310/394-1495

PATTI HAYES
419 N. Larchmont Ave., Suite 249
Los Angeles, CA 90004
213/933-0116

KAREN HENDEL*
2049 Century Park East
Suite 4100
Los Angeles, CA 90067
310/201-9309
Fax: 310/201-9293

TURNER AND HOOCH 1989

He

FILM
PRODUCERS,
STUDIOS,
AGENTS AND
CASTING
DIRECTORS
GUIDE

**C
A
S
T
I
N
G

D
I
R
E
C
T
O
R
S**

He

FILM
PRODUCERS,
STUDIOS,
AGENTS AND
CASTING
DIRECTORS
GUIDE

C
A
S
T
I
N
G

D
I
R
E
C
T
O
R
S

CATHY HENDERSON*
4307 Coldwater Canyon
Studio City, CA 91604
818/763-6649

WEEDS   1987

JUDY HENDERSON*
330 W. 89th St.
New York, NY 10024
212/877-0225
Fax: 212/724-1620

PAULA HEROLD*
c/o Gracie Films
20th Century Fox, Bung. 9
10201 W. Pico Blvd.
Los Angeles, CA 90035
310/203-3845

THE LEGEND OF BILLIE JEAN   1985
"CROCODILE" DUNDEE   1986
PRETTY IN PINK   1986
BROADCAST NEWS   1987
BIG   1988
ROOFTOPS   1989
CRY BABY   1989
IN THE SPIRIT   1990

MARC HIRSCHFELD*
Liberman-Hirschfeld Casting
Sunset-Gower Studios
1438 N. Gower St.
Suite 1410
Los Angeles, CA 90028
213/460-7258
Fax: 213/460-7547

ALIEN NATION   1988
NIGHT WALK   1989

JANET HIRSHENSON*
The Casting Company
8925 Venice Blvd.
Los Angeles, CA 90034
310/842-7551
Fax: 310/842-7566

ARMED AND DANGEROUS   1986
GARDENS OF STONE   1987
ADVENTURES IN BABYSITTING   1987
BACK TO THE BEACH   1987
THE PRINCESS BRIDE   1987
PLANES, TRAINS AND AUTOMOBILES   1987
SHE'S HAVING A BABY   1988
BEETLEJUICE   1988
MYSTIC PIZZA   1988
WILLOW   1988
THE PRESIDIO   1988
TUCKER: THE MAN AND HIS DREAM   1988
WHEN HARRY MET SALLY...   1989
PARENTHOOD   1989
GHOST   1990
HOOK   1991

HOFFMAN/FISHBAUGH CASTING
1020 N. Cole Ave., Suite 4370
Hollywood, CA 90038
213/463-7986

*Bobby Hoffman**

JUDITH HOLSTRA*
Judith Holstra Casting
4043 Radford Avenue
Studio City, CA 91604
818/761-9420

48 HRS   1982
EXTREME PREJUDICE   1987
NO MAN'S LAND   1987
GREAT BALLS OF FIRE!   1989
PUNP UP THE VOLUME   1990

HOPKINS & BRAMON CASTING
Lincoln Theatre Center
150 W, 65th St.
New York, NY 10013
212/362-7600
Fax: 212/873-0761

*Risa Bramon**
*Billy Hopkins**

DESPERATELY SEEKING SUSAN   1985
AT CLOSE RANGE   1986
SOMETHING WILD   1986
FATAL ATTRACTION   1987
WALL STREET   1987
MAKING MR. RIGHT   1987
ANGEL HEART   1987
CANDY MOUNTAIN   1987
TALK RADIO   1988
MR. NORTH   1988
THE JANUARY MAN   1989
UNCLE BUCK   1989
BORN ON THE FOURTH OF JULY   1989
NATIONAL LAMPOON'S CHRISTMAS VACATION   1989
BLUE STEEL   1990
JFK   1991

STUART HOWARD*
c/o C.S.A.
311 W. 43rd St., Suite 700
New York, NY 10036
212/333-4552

VICKI HUFF*
962 N. La Cienaga Blvd.
West Hollywood, CA 90069
310/659-8557
Fax: 310/659-8923

PHYLLIS HUFFMAN*
Warner Bros.
75 Rockefeller Plaza, 23rd Floor
New York, NY 10019
212/484-6371

BIRD   1988
PINK CADILLAC   1989

Jo

FILM
PRODUCERS,
STUDIOS,
AGENTS AND
CASTING
DIRECTORS
GUIDE

C
A
S
T
I
N
G

D
I
R
E
C
T
O
R
S

HUGHES/MOSS CASTING
c/o C.S.A.
311 W. 43rd St., Suite 700
New York, NY 10036
212/333-4552

Julie Hughes*
Barry Moss*

DOMINICK AND EUGENE 1988

ANDREW HURTZ
Director of Casting
Concorde/New Horizons
11600 San Vicente Blvd.
Los Angeles, CA 90049
310/820-6733
Fax: 310/207-6816

AFTERSHOCK 1992
FIRE HAWK 1992
KILLER INSTINCT 1992
MUNCHIES II 1992
BLACK BELT 1992
INNOCENT BLOOD 1992
BODY WAVES 1992

BETH HYMSON*
Warner/Hollywood Studios
1041 N. Formosa Blvd.
Santa Monica South Bldg., #193
Los Angeles, CA 90046
213/850-2607
Fax: 213/850-2605

I

DONNA ISAACSON*
Isaacson Casting
453 W. 16th St., 2nd Floor
New York, NY 10011
212/691-8555

RAISING ARIZONA 1987
THE BELIEVERS 1987
HELLO AGAIN 1987
COCKTAIL 1988
ROCKET GIBRALTAR 1988
DIRTY ROTTEN SCOUNDRELS 1988

J

RICK JACOBS*
Senior Vice President of Talent & Casting
Columbia Pictures Television
Studio Plaza
3400 Riverside Dr., Suite 8-56
Burbank, CA 91505
818/972-8591

Sunset/Gower Studios
1438 N. Gordon St.
Los Angeles, CA 90028
213/460-7245
Fax: 213/460-7603

STEVE JACOBS
SOME KIND OF WONDERFUL 1987
HIDING OUT 1987

ELLEN JACOBY*
Ellen Jacoby Casting, International
420 Lincoln Rd.
Miami, FL 33139
305/531-5300
Fax: 305/531-4748

JUSTINE JACOBY*
Dennison/Selzer Casting
11500 Tennessee Ave.
Los Angeles, CA 90064
310/444-7542
Fax: 310/312-2085

JANE JENKINS*
The Casting Company
8925 Venice Blvd.
Los Angeles, CA 90034
310/842-7551
Fax: 310/842-7566

ARMED AND DANGEROUS 1986
GARDENS OF STONE 1987
ADVENTURES IN BABYSITTING 1987
BACK TO THE BEACH 1987
THE PRINCESS BRIDE 1987
PLANES, TRAINS AND AUTOMOBILES 1987
SHE'S HAVING A BABY 1988
BEETLEJUICE 1988
WILLOW 1988
THE PRESIDIO 1988
MYSTIC PIZZA 1988
TUCKER: THE MAN AND HIS DREAM 1988
WHEN HARRY MET SALLY... 1989
PARENTHOOD 1989
GHOST 1990
HOOK 1991

PRISCILLA JOHN
WHO FRAMED ROGER RABBIT 1988

Jo

FILM
PRODUCERS,
STUDIOS,
AGENTS AND
CASTING
DIRECTORS
GUIDE

C
A
S
T
I
N
G

D
I
R
E
C
T
O
R
S

JOHNSON/LIFF CASTING
1501 Broadway, Suite 1400
New York, NY 10036
212/391-2680

Geoffrey Johnson*
Vincent G. Liff*
Tara Jayne Rubin*
Andrew M. Zerman*

MARILYN JOHNSON
84 CHARING CROSS ROAD 1987

MELVIN JOHNSON*
Universal Studios
100 Universal City Plaza
P.O. Box 8640
Universal City, CA 91608
818/760-3012

1000 Universal Studios Plaza, Bldg. 22
Orlando, FL 32819
407/363-8582

7061 Grand National Drive, #131
Orlando, FL 32819
407/352-4857

PSYCHO IV: THE BEGINNING 1990
PROBLEM CHILD II 1991

ED JOHNSTON
FULL MOON IN BLUE WATER 1988

ALLISON JONES
1420 N. Beachwood, Bldg. 62
Los Angeles, CA 90028
213/468-3225
Fax: 213/468-3414

CARO JONES*
5858 Hollywood Blvd., Suite 220
Los Angeles, CA 90028
213/464-9216
Fax: 213/962-9866

ROCKY 1976
THE KARATE KID 1984
THE KARATE KID PART II 1986
CAN'T BUY ME LOVE 1987
FOR KEEPS? 1988
THE KARATE KID PART III 1989
ROCKY V 1990
THE POWER OF ONE 1992

JACK JONES
5858 Hollywood Blvd., Suite 220
Los Angeles, CA 90028
213/464-9216
Fax: 213/962-9866

WAXWORK II: LOST IN TIME 1991
INTO THE SUN 1992

ROSALIE JOSEPH*
165 W. 46th St.
New York, NY 10003
212/921-5781

K

PATTI KALLES*
Patti Kalles Casting
506 2nd Ave., Smith Tower #1525
Seattle, WA 98104
206/447-9318

DARLENE KAPLAN*
P.O. Box 261160
Encino, CA 91426
818/981-3527
Fax: 818/981-9339

AVY KAUFMAN*
c/o C.S.A
311 West 43rd Street
New York, NY 10036
212/333-4552

EIGHT MEN OUT 1988
MISS FIRECRACKER 1989

ELIZABETH H. KEIGLEY*
713/895-5100

c/o C.S.A.
6565 Sunset Blvd., Suite 306
Los Angeles, CA 90028
213/463-1925
Fax: 213/463-5753

SQUARE DANCE 1987

KELLY CASTING
Chelsea Studios
3859 Lankershim Blvd.
Studio City, CA 91604
818/762-0500
Fax: 818/762-8449

LORA KENNEDY
SLAMDANCE 1987
SWEET HEARTS DANCE 1988
DISORGANIZED CRIME 1989
ALWAYS 1989

MALLORY KENNEDY
6815 Willoughby, Suite 105
Los Angeles, CA 90038
818/562-3329
Fax: 818/562-3223

RODY KENT*
5422 Vickery Blvd.
Dallas, TX 75206
214/827-3418

La

FILM
PRODUCERS,
STUDIOS,
AGENTS AND
CASTING
DIRECTORS
GUIDE

C
A
S
T
I
N
G

D
I
R
E
C
T
O
R
S

SUSIE KITTLESON
1302 N. Sweetzer, Suite 503
Los Angeles, CA 90069
213/652-7011

BETH KLEIN
Viacom
10 Universal City Plaza, 32nd Floor
Universal City, CA 91608
818/505-7661

MARSHA KLEINMAN*
704 N. Gardner St., Suite 2
Los Angeles, CA 90046
213/852-1521
Fax: 213/852-1936

NANCY KLOPPER
Paramount Studios
5555 Melrose Ave.
Trailer 10, #1
Los Angeles, CA 90038

BLIND DATE   1987
THE BIG TOWN   1987
SUNSET   1988
EVERYBODY'S ALL-AMERICAN   1988

EILEEN KNIGHT*
CBS-MTM Studios
4024 Radford, 5th Floor
Studio City, CA 91604
818/760-5855
Fax: 818/760-5497

KATHY KNOWLES
Baker-Nisbet
451 N. La Cienaga Blvd.
Los Angeles, CA 90048
310/657-5687
Fax: 310/657-7943

JOANNE KOEHLER
Lorimar Casting
300 S. Lorimar Plaza
Bldg 140, First Floor
Burbank, CA 91505
818/954-7636
Fax: 818/954-7678

SARAH KOEPPE
THE UNBEARABLE LIGHTNESS OF BEING   1988

KORDOS & CHARBONNEAU CASTING
c/o C.S.A.
6565 Sunset Blvd., Suite 306
Los Angeles, CA 90028
213/463-1925
Fax: 213/463-5753

*Nan Charbonneau**
Richard Kordos

THE PACKAGE   1989

ANNAMARIE KOSTURA*
NBC Entertainment
Director of Daytime Casting
3000 W. Alameda Ave., Suite 233
Burbank, CA 91523
818/840-4410
Fax: 818/840-4412

SID KOZAK
THE STEPFATHER   1987
LOOK WHO'S TALKING   1989

LYNN KRESSEL*
c/o C.S.A.
311 W. 43rd St.
New York, NY 10036
212/333-4552

ANDY WARHOL'S BAD   1971
TWINS   1988
CALL ME   1988
APPRENTICE TO MURDER   1988
TEENAGE MUTANT NINJA TURTLES   1990

FRAN KUMIN
CROSSING DELANCEY   1988
LOVERBOY   1989
FAMILY BUSINESS   1989

DEBORAH KURTZ
1600 N. Highland Ave., Suite 4
Los Angeles, CA 90028
213/461-3800

WENDY KURTZMAN*
c/o C.S.A.
6565 Sunset Blvd. #306
Los Angeles, CA 90028
213/463-1925

L

RUTH LAMBERT
Emshell Productions
2600 W. Olive Ave., #941
Burbank, CA 91505
818/972-3450

SOME KIND OF WONDERFUL   1987

JUDY LANDAU
1018 N. Cole Ave.
Los Angeles, CA 90038
213/464-0437

SHANA LANDSBURG*
Landsburg/Allan Casting
Raleigh Studios
5358 Melrose Avenue, West Bldg., #203-W
Los Angeles, CA 90038
213/960-4063
Fax: 213/460-3971

La

FILM
PRODUCERS,
STUDIOS,
AGENTS AND
CASTING
DIRECTORS
GUIDE

C
A
S
T
I
N
G

D
I
R
E
C
T
O
R
S

JASON LA PADURA*
39 W. 19th St., 12th Floor
New York, NY 10011
212/206-6420

Occidental Studios
201 N. Occidental Blvd., Bldg. 3
Los Angeles, CA 90026
213/384-3331
Fax: 213/384-2684

PRELUDE TO A KISS   1992

NANCY LARA-HANSCH
Cannon Pictures, Inc.
8200 Wilshire Blvd., #206
Beverly Hills, CA 90212
213/966-5651
Fax: 213/653-5485

BARFLY   1987
ALIEN FROM L.A.   1987
SALSA   1988
KINJITE (FORBIDDEN SUBJECTS)   1989
CYBORG   1988
ROCKULA   1989
THE SECRET OF THE ICE CAVES   1989
A MAN CALLED SARGE   1989
PHANTOM OF THE OPERA   1989
DELTA FORCE 2   1989
I'LL BE HOME FOR CHRISTMAS   1990
NINJA: THE AMERICAN SAMAURI   1990
THE HUMAN SHIELD   1992
RESCUE ME   1992
50/50   1992
NO RETURN   1992

ELIZABETH LARROQUETTE*
4000 Warner Blvd.
Burbank, CA 91522
818/954-2605
Fax: 818/954-4060

BARBARA LAUREN
11684 Ventura Blvd., #911
Studio City, CA 91604
818/506-6111
Fax: 818/506-1461

JUDIE LAWSON
Bergeron/Lawson Casting
P.O. Box 1489
La Canada, CA 91011
818/790-9832

SALLY LEAR*
121 Washington St.
Reno, NV 89503
702/322-8187

GERALDINE LEDER
Lorimar Casting
300 S. Lorimar Plaza, Bldg. 140, First Floor
Burbank, CA 91505
818/954-7635
Fax: 818/954-7678

KATHLEEN LETTERIE*
761 N. Cahuenga Blvd.
Los Angeles, CA 90038
213/465-7132
Fax: 213/957-0846

ERNEST SAVES CHRISTMAS   1988
ENCINO MAN   1992

ELIZABETH LEUSTIG*
1173 N. Ardmore, Suite 1
Los Angeles, CA 90029
213/667-2103

Warner Bros.
4000 Warner Blvd.
Producers Bldg. 6, Room B
Burbank, CA 91522
818/954-2188

A NIGHT IN THE LIFE OF
   JIMMY REARDON   1988
SCENES FROM THE CLASS STRUGGLE IN
   BEVERLY HILLS   1989
CHECKING OUT   1989
GLEAMING THE CUBE   1989
SHAG   1989
THE BEAR   1989
NEWSIES   1992

JOHN LEVEY*
Director of Talent
Warner Bros. Television
4000 Warner Blvd.
N. Administration Bldg., #17
Burbank, CA 91522
818/954-4080
Fax: 818/954-6709

GAIL LEVIN
1800 N. Highland Ave., #406
Los Angeles, CA 90028
213/957-4171

TORCH SONG TRILOGY   1988
LETHAL WEAPON 2   1989

MARION LEVINE
Manager of Casting
NBC Entertainment
3000 West Alameda Avenue
Burbank, CA 91523
818/840-4729
Fax: 818/840-4412

HEIDI LEVITT*
310/450-1333

NATIONAL LAMPOON'S CHRISTMAS
   VACATION   1989
JACOB'S LADDER   1990
BRIGHT ANGEL   1990
ONE GOOD COP   1990
MR. DESTINY   1990
JFK   1991

Lo

**FILM
PRODUCERS,
STUDIOS,
AGENTS AND
CASTING
DIRECTORS
GUIDE**

**C
A
S
T
I
N
G

D
I
R
E
C
T
O
R
S**

ELLEN LEWIS
Universal Studios
100 Universal City Plaza, Bldg. 506, #157
Universal City, CA 91608
818/777-9602

WORKING GIRL   1988
NEW YORK STORIES: "Life Lessons"   1989
CAPE FEAR   1991

MEG LEIBERMAN*
Liberman/Hirschfeld Casting
Sunset-Gower Studios
1438 N. Gower St., Suite 1410
Los Angeles, CA 90028
213/460-7258
Fax: 213/460-7547

ALIEN NATION   1988
NIGHT WALK   1989

LIBERMAN/HIRSCHFELD CASTING
Sunset-Gower Studios
1438 N. Gower St., Suite 1410
Los Angeles, CA 90028
213/460-7258
Fax: 213/460-7547

Sony Pictures
10202 W. Washington Blvd., #321
Culver City, CA 90232
310/280-6692

*Irene Cagen**
*Marc Hirschfeld**
*Meg Liberman**

ALIEN NATION   1988
NIGHT WALK   1989

AMY LIBERMAN
Viacom
100 Universal City Plaza, Bldg. 157
Universal City, CA 91608
818/777-4820

VINCE LIEBHART*
524 W. 57th St., Suite 5330
New York, NY 10019
212/757-4350

TERRY LIEBLING*
8407 Coreyell Place
Los Angeles, CA 90046
213/957-7510

BLACK WIDOW   1987
TWO JAKES   1990
MAN TROUBLE   1992

MICHAEL LIEN
Michael Lien Casting
7461 Beverly Blvd., Suite 203
Los Angeles, CA 90036
213/937-0411
Fax: 213/937-2070

VINCENT LIFF*
Johnson/Liff Casting
1501 Broadway, Suite 1400
New York, NY 10036
212/391-2680

TRACY LILIENFIELD*
c/o C.S.A.
6565 Sunset Blvd., #306
Los Angeles, CA 90028
213/463-1925

SHAWN LINAHAN*
c/o C.S.A.
6565 Sunset Blvd., #306
Los Angeles, CA 90028
213/463-1925

ROBIN LIPPIN*
NBC Productions
330 Bob Hope Drive, #107
Burbank, CA 91523
818/840-7643
Fax: 818/840-4412

RICOCHET   1991

MARCI LIROFF
P.O. Box 48498
Los Angeles, CA 90048
213/850-4581

COUSINS   1989

TONI LIVINGSTON
P.O. Box 2472
Toluca Lake, CA 91610
213/969-1673

STAND AND DELIVER   1988

LAUREN LLOYD
Paramount Studios
5555 Melrose Ave., Dressing Room Bldg. #227
Los Angeles, CA 90038
213/956-8565
Fax: 213/956-2007

COLORS   1988
TORCH SONG TRILOGY   1988

LISA LONDON*
818/506-0692

c/o C.S.A.
6565 Sunset Blvd., #306
Los Angeles, CA 90028
213/463-1925

LEPRECHAUN   1992
THE SEVENTH COIN   1992

BEVERLY LONG
Crossroads of the World
6671 Sunset Blvd., Suite 1584-A
Los Angeles, CA 90028
213/466-0770

Lo

FILM
PRODUCERS,
STUDIOS,
AGENTS AND
CASTING
DIRECTORS
GUIDE

C
A
S
T
I
N
G

D
I
R
E
C
T
O
R
S

MOLLY LOPATA*
4043 Radford Ave.
Studio City, CA 91604
818/753-8086
Fax: 818/753-5029

LEESA LORD
7058 Worster Ave.
North Hollywood, CA 91605
818/765-8080

CHERYL A. LOUDEN-KUBIN*
The Casting Crew, Inc.
1948 Tyler St.
Hollywood, FL 33020
305/927-2329

JUNIE LOWRY-JOHNSON*
20th Century-Fox
10201. W. Pico Blvd., Bldg. 26, Stage 2
Los Angeles, CA 90035
310/203-1296

SUMMER HEAT   1987
LA BAMBA   1987
BORN IN EAST L.A.   1987
THE HAND THAT ROCKS THE CRADLE   1992

M

MacDONALD/BULLINGTON CASTING
6930 Sunset Blvd., Second Floor
Los Angeles, CA 90028
213/957-0091

*Perry Bullington**
*Bob MacDonald**

NUMBER ONE WITH A BULLET   1987
BARFLY   1987
SHY PEOPLE   1987

AMANDA MACKEY
Mackey/Sandrich Casting
9155 Sunset Blvd.
Los Angeles, CA 90069
310/278-8858

Paramount Studios
5555 Melrose Ave., Dressing Room Bldg., #321
Los Angeles, CA 90038
213/956-5751

STACKING   1987
GLADIATOR   1992

MAGIC CASTING AGENCY
439 S. La Cienega Blvd., Suite 215
Los Angeles, CA 90048
310/276-8024

FRANCINE MAISLER*
New World Entertainment
1440 S. Sepulveda, First Floor
Los Angeles, CA 90025
310/444-8190

ANN REMSEN MANNERS
Barbara Remsen & Associates
Raleigh Studios
650 N. Bronson Ave.
Los Angeles, CA 90004
213/464-7968
Fax: 213/464-7970

SHEILA MANNING
508 S. San Vicente, Suite 101
Los Angeles, CA 90048
213/852-1046
Fax: 213/655-1044

DEBI MANWILLER
Pagano/Bialy/Manwiller Casting
1680 N. Vine St. #904
Los Angeles, CA 90028
213/871-0051
Fax: 213/871-0509

THE BRIDGE   1992
DIGGS TOWN   1992
RINGERS   1992
RULES OF THE GAME   1992
GAS FOOD AND LODGING   1992

SUSAN MARGARETTE-HAVINS
437 S. Fairview
Burbank, CA 91505
818/562-3329

IRENE MARIANO*
Vice President, Lorimar Casting
300 S. Lorimar Plaza, Bldg. 140, First Floor
Burbank, CA 91505
818/954-7643
Fax: 818/954-7678

MINDY MARIN*
Casting Artists, Inc.
P.O. Box 1731
Pacific Palisades, CA 90272
310/454-1065

MISS FIRECRACKER   1989
NEXT OF KIN   1989
L.A. STORY   1990
NECESSARY ROUGHNESS   1991
NAKED GUN 2 1/2   1991
CLIFF HANGER   1992

VALORIE MASSALAS
Fenton & Associates
100 Universal City Plaza, Trailer 78
Universal City, CA 91608
818/777-4610
Fax: 818/777-8284

ARTHUR 2 ON THE ROCKS   1988
INDIANA JONES AND THE LAST CRUSADE   1989
BACK TO THE FUTURE PART II   1989
TRIUMPH OF THE SPIRIT   1989

Mi

FILM
PRODUCERS,
STUDIOS,
AGENTS AND
CASTING
DIRECTORS
GUIDE

C
A
S
T
I
N
G

D
I
R
E
C
T
O
R
S

VALERIE McCAFFREY
Director of Feature Casting
Universal Studios
100 Universal City Plaza, Bldg. 508, First Floor
Universal City, CA 91608
818/777-7581
Fax: 818/777-7159

DARKMAN 1990
PROBLEM CHILD 1990
PROBLEM CHILD 2 1991
AN AMERICAN TAIL: FIEVEL GOES WEST 1991
WE'RE BACK 1992
THE BABE 1992

HANK McCANN
P.O. Box 6020
Beverly Hills, CA 90212
310/654-7217

THE SECRET OF MY SUCCESS 1987
STEEL MAGNOLIAS 1989

NANCY McCOOK
Anderson/McCook/White Casting
3855 Lankershim Blvd.
North Hollywood, CA 91604
818/760-3934

PAT McCORKLE*
264 W. 40th St.
New York, NY 10018
212/840-0992

END OF THE LINE 1987
FOR KEEPS? 1988
THE WIZARD OF LONELINESS 1988

BEVERLY McDERMOTT*
923 N. Golf Drive
Hollywood, FL 33021
305/625-5111

COCOON: THE RETURN 1988

PHILIP WILLIAM McKINLEY*
c/o C.S.A.
6565 Sunset Blvd. #306
Los Angeles, CA 90028

VIVIAN McRAE*
P.O. Box 1351
Burbank, CA 91507
818/848-9590

MARGARET McSHARRY
Director of Casting
CBS Entertainment
7800 Beverly Blvd., Suite 284
Los Angeles, CA 90036
213/852-2862
Fax: 213/655-2368

VIRGINIA McSWAIN
11909 Weddington St., Suite 202,
North Hollywood, CA 91607
213/463-1925

JOAN MELLINI
8281 Melrose Ave., Suite 201
Los Angeles, CA 90046
213/653-9240

JOANNA MERLIN*
440 West End Ave.
New York, NY 10024
212/724-8575

JEFF MESHEL*
Driector of Casting
NBC Entertainment
3000 W. Alameda Ave.
Burbank, CA 91523
818/840-4729
Fax: 818/840-4412

ELLEN MEYER*
The Landsburg Building
11811 W. Olympic Blvd.
Los Angeles, CA 90064
310/444-1818
Fax: 310/444-4918

ADRIANA MICHEL*
Saban Entertainment
4000 W. Alameda, 5th Floor
Burbank, CA 91505
818/972-4800

BARBARA MILLER*
Senior VP of Talent, Lorimar Casting
300 S. Lorimar Plaza, Bldg. 140, First Floor
Burbank, CA 91505
818/954-7645
Fax: 818/954-7678

DEE MILLER*
1524 N.E. 147th St.
North Miami, FL 33161
305/944-8559
Fax: 305/948-3298

VERA MILLER
CRIMINAL LAW 1989

RICK MILLIKAN*
Director of Talent
Columbia Pictures TV
3400 Riverside Dr. #853
Burbank, CA 91505
818/972-8344

ED MITCHELL
23901 Civic Center Way, #348
Malibu, CA 90265
310/456-2095

FULL MOON IN BLUE WATER 1988
KANSAS 1988
NIGHT GAME 1989
SKETCH ARTIST 1992

PATRICIA MOCK*
8489 W. Third St.
Los Angeles, CA 90048

THE COUCH TRIP 1988
FLETCH LIVES 1989

NUALA MOISELLE
THE DEAD 1987
DA 1988

PAT MORAN
HAIRSPRAY 1988

BOB MORONES*
733 N. Seward St.
Hollywood, CA 90038
213/467-2834

EL NORTE 1984
SALVADOR 1986
PLATOON 1986
PUMPKINHEAD 1988
ROMERO 1989
AMERICAN ME 1992
SHADOW OF THE WOLF 1992

BOBBI MORRIS
8150 Beverly Blvd., Suite 204
Los Angeles, CA 90048
213/653-4031

BARRY MOSS*
Hughes Moss Casting
311 W. 43rd St., #700
New York, NY 10036
212/307-6690

DOMINICK AND EUGENE 1988

JULIE MOSSBERG CASTING
1501 Broadway, Suite 2605
New York, NY 10036
212/921-4745
Fax: 212/921-5793

HELEN MOSSLER*
Vice President - Talent
Paramount Television
5555 Melrose Ave., Bluhdorn 128
Los Angeles, CA 90038
213/956-5578

DREW MURPHY
Ahmanson Theatre
135 N. Grand Ave.
Los Angeles, CA 90012
213/972-7401

WENDY MURRAY
SUPERMAN IV: THE QUEST FOR PEACE 1987

ROGER MUSSENDEN*
The Casting Company
8925 Venice Blvd.
Los Angeies, CA 90034
310/842-7551
Fax: 310/842-7566

ELISSA MYERS*
333 W. 52nd St., #1008
New York, NY 10024
212/315-4777

N

ROBIN STOLTZ NASSIF*
Director of Casting
ABC Entertainment
2040 Avenue of the Stars, 5th Floor
Los Angeles, CA 90067
310/557-6423
Fax: 310/557-7160

NANCY NAYOR*
Vice President - Feature Film Casting
100 Universal City Plaza, Bldg. 500, 10th Floor
Universal City, CA 91608
818/777-3566

THE LAND BEFORE TIME 1988
DARKMAN 1990
PROBLEM CHILD 1990
WHITE PALACE 1990
MOBSTERS 1991
SHOUT 1991
THE BABE 1992
PURE LUCK 1992

DEBRA NEATHERY
4820 N. Cleon Ave.
North Hollywood, CA 91601
818/506-5524

D.L. NEWTON
84 CHARING CROSS ROAD 1987
JACKNIFE 1989

WALLIS NICITA*
Paramount Studios
5555 Melrose Ave., Dressing Room Bldg. #201
Los Angeles, CA 90038
213/956-8514
Fax: 213/956-2007

ESCAPE FROM ALCATRAZ 1979
PRIVATE BENJAMIN 1980
CADDYSHACK 1980
DIE LAUGHING 1980
GOING APE! 1981
WHOSE LIFE IS IT ANYWAY? 1981
BODY HEAT 1981
MISSING 1982
LOVE CHILD 1982
THE BIG CHILL 1983
WARGAMES 1983
THE RIGHT STUFF 1983
UNDER FIRE 1983
DR. DETROIT 1983
AMERICAN DREAMER 1984
ELECTRIC DREAMS 1984
RACING WITH THE MOON 1984

MIKE'S MURDER 1984
BLAME IT ON RIO 1984
PEE WEE'S BIG ADVENTURE 1985
AMERICAN FLYERS 1985
SILVERADO 1985
THE FALCON AND THE SNOWMAN 1985
CLUB PARADISE 1986
CROSS MY HEART 1987
THE WITCHES OF EASTWICK 1987
OVERBOARD 1987
A TIME OF DESTINY 1988
MASQUERADE 1988
THE ACCIDENTAL TOURIST 1988
THE MIGHTY QUINN 1989
MAJOR LEAGUE 1989
EARTH GIRLS ARE EASY 1989
A DRY WHITE SEASON 1989
OLD GRINGO 1989
THE FABULOUS BAKER BOYS 1989
WE'RE NO ANGELS 1989

ELLEN NOVACK*
20 Jay St., Suite 9B
New York, NY 10013
212/431-3939

PATRICIA O'BRIEN
3701 W. Oak Street
Burbank, CA 91505
818/954-3000

PAULINE O'CON
Director of Casting
ABC Entertainment
2040 Avenue of the Stars, 5th Floor
Los Angeles, CA 90067
310/557-6425
Fax: 310/557-7160

MERYL O'LOUGHLIN*
New World Pictures
1440 S. Sepulveda Blvd., #110
Los Angeles, CA 90025
310/444-8189

AL ONORATO*
Onorato/Franks Casting
1717 N. Highland Ave., Suite 904
Los Angeles, CA 90028
213/468-8833
Fax: 213/468-9172

ONORATO/FRANKS CASTING
1717 N. Highland Ave., Suite 904
Los Angeles, CA 90028
213/468-8833
Fax: 213/468-9172

Jerry Franks*
Al Onorato*

LORI OPENDEN*
Vice President - Talent & Casting
NBC Entertainment
3000 W. Alameda Ave., Suite 233
Burbank, CA 91523
818/840-3774
Fax: 818/840-4412

FERN ORENSTEIN*
Susan Glicksman Casting
5433 Beethoven
Los Angeles, CA 90066
213/302-9149

PAT ORSETH*
c/o C.S.A.
6565 Sunset Blvd., Suite 306
Los Angeles, CA 90028
213/372-8411

BARFLY 1987

GREGORY ORSON
Vickie Rosenberg & Associates
Sunset/Gower Studios
1438 North Gower Street
Casting Apartments #1406
Los Angeles, CA 90028
213/460-7593

JEFF OSHEN*
Disney Studios
500 S. Buena Vista St., Zorro Bldg. 1
Burbank, CA 91521
818/560-6930

JESSICA OVERWISE*
17250 Sunset Blvd., Suite 304
Pacific Palisades, CA 90272
310/459-2686

RICHARD PAGANO
Pagano/Bialy/Manwiller Casting
1680 N. Vine St., Suite 904
Los Angeles, CA 90028
213/871-0051
Fax: 213/871-0509

EXTREMITIES 1986
CHILD'S PLAY 1988
BLOODHOUNDS OF BROADWAY 1989
DRUGSTORE COWBOY 1989
GRAVEYARD SHIFT 1990
POINT BREAK 1991
DON'T TELL MOM THE BABYSITTER'S DEAD 1991
THE BRIDGE 1992
DIGGS TOWN 1992
RINGERS 1992
RULES OF THE GAME 1992
GAS FOOD AND LODGING 1992
BLOOD IN BLOOD OUT 1992

Pa

FILM
PRODUCERS,
STUDIOS,
AGENTS AND
CASTING
DIRECTORS
GUIDE

C
A
S
T
I
N
G

D
I
R
E
C
T
O
R
S

PAGANO/BIALY/MANWILLER CASTING
1680 N. Vine St.
Suite 904
Los Angeles, CA 90028
213/871-0051
Fax: 213/871-0509

Richard Pagano
*Sharon Bialy**
Debi Manwiller
Anne Mongan

EXTREMITIES   1986
CHILD'S PLAY   1988
BLOODHOUNDS OF BROADWAY   1989
DRUGSTORE COWBOY   1989
GRAVEYARD SHIFT   1990
POINT BREAK   1991
DON'T TELL MOM THE BABYSITTER'S
    DEAD   1991
THE BRIDGE   1992
DIGGS TOWN   1992
RINGERS   1992
RULES OF THE GAME   1992
GAS FOOD AND LODGING   1992
BLOOD IN BLOOD OUT   1992

MARVIN PAIGE*
P.O. Box 69964
West Hollywood, CA 90069
213/760-3040

RASSAMI PAOLUENGTONG
GOOD MORNING, VIETNAM   1987

PARADOXE CASTING
7441 Sunset Blvd., Suite 205
Los Angeles, CA 90046
213/851-6110

JENNIFER J. PART*
100 Universal City Plaza
Bldg. 507, Suite 4-F
Universal City, CA 91608
818/777-5013

CAMI PATTON*
Sunset/Gower Studios
1438 N. Gower St.
Casting Apartments, #2410
Los Angeles, CA 90028
213/460-7676

DONALD PAUL PEMRICK*
Director of Casting, Feature Films & TV
IRS Media
3939 Lankershim Blvd.
Universal City, CA 91604
818/505-0555
Fax: 818/505-1318

MERCEDES PENNEY
5000 Lankershim Blvd., Suite 3
North Hollywood, CA 91601
818/509-1026

NANCY PERKINS
Director pf Talent & Casting
Columbia Pictures Television
1438 N. Gower St.
Los Angeles, CA 90028
213/460-7254
213/460-7603

SALLY PERLE & ASSOCIATES
12178 Ventura Blvd., Suite 201
Studio City, CA 91604
818/762-8752

PENNY PERRY
Benson/Perry Casting
Lantana Center
3000 W. Olympic Blvd., Bldg. 2, #2416
Santa Monica, CA 90404
310/315-4865
Fax: 310/315-4797

*Annette Benson**
Penny Perry

MIDNIGHT EXPRESS   1978
THE JERK   1979
WHEN A STRANGER CALLS   1979
FOXES   1980
THE IDOLMAKER   1980
ORDINARY PEOPLE   1980
CATTLE ANNIE AND LITTLE BRITCHES   1980
DEAD MEN DON'T WEAR PLAID   1982
REUBEN, REUBEN   1983
THE STAR CHAMBER   1983
LOCAL HERO   1983
THE GOLDEN SEAL   1983
NATE AND HAYES   1983
THE STING II   1983
THE NEVERENDING STORY   1984
THE STONE BOY   1984
2010   1984
ALL OF ME   1984
THE LIGHTSHIP   1985
SUMMER RENTAL   1985
THAT WAS THEN, THIS IS NOW   1985
COCOON   1985
THE HITCHER   1986
WHERE THE RIVER RUNS BLACK   1986
WISDOM   1986
YOUNGBLOOD   1986
RUNNING SCARED   1986
SUMMER SCHOOL   1987
TOUCH AND GO   1987
THE MONSTER SQUAD   1987
IN THE MOOD   1987
THE PRINCIPAL   1987
FLOWERS IN THE ATTIC   1987
BATTERIES NOT INCLUDED   1987
SHOOT TO KILL   1988
VICE VERSA   1988
YOUNG GUNS   1988
VICE VERSA   1988
TAP   1989
BERT RIGBY, YOU'RE A FOOL   1989

Re

FILM
PRODUCERS,
STUDIOS,
AGENTS AND
CASTING
DIRECTORS
GUIDE

C
A
S
T
I
N
G

D
I
R
E
C
T
O
R
S

CAROLYN PICKMAN
Collinge/Pickman Casting
138 Mt. Auburn Street
Cambridge, MA 02138
617/492-4212
Fax: 617/492-1306

BONNIE PIETILA
20th Century-Fox Studios
10201 W. Pico Blvd., Trailer 716
Los Angeles, CA 90035
310/203-3632

SURRENDER 1987

LOIS PLANCO*
c/o C.S.A.
311 W. 43rd St.
New York, NY 10036
212/333-4552

PAM POLIFRONI*
3000 W. Alameda Ave., Studio 11, 2nd Floor
Burbank, CA 91523
818/840-4641
Fax: 818/840-3441

HOLLY POWELL*
c/o C.S.A.
6565 Sunset Blvd., #306
Los Angeles, CA 90028
213/655-2970

JAN POWELL
3000 W. Alameda Ave., Studio 11, 2nd Floor
Burbank, CA 91523
818/840-4641

SALLY POWERS*
c/o C.S.A.
6565 Sunset Blvd., Suite 306
Los Angeles, CA 90028
213/463-1925

R

STEVEN RABINER
ULTRAVIOLET 1992
HEAT OF PASSION 1992
FINAL EMBRACE 1992

PAMELA RACK
PATTY HEARST 1988

JOHANNA RAY*
940 N. Mansfield Ave.
Los Angeles, CA 90038
213/463-9451

GABY—A TRUE STORY 1987
THE BLOB 1988
PARADISE 1991
STORYVILLE 1992

BETTY REA*
222 E. 44th St.
New York, NY 10017
212/983-1610

KAREN REA*
c/o C.S.A.
6565 Sunset Blvd., Suite 306
Los Angeles, CA 90028
213/372-8411
Fax: 213/463-5753

NEAR DARK 1987
ALIEN NATION 1988
TRUE BELIEVER 1989
BILL & TED'S BOGUS JOURNEY 1989

ROBI REED*
8306 Wilshire Blvd., #429
Beverly Hills, CA 90211

NBC Productions
330 Bob Hope Drive, #C-107
Burbank, CA 91523
818/840-7540
Fax: 818/840-4412

Raleigh Studios
5300 Melrose Ave.
Office Bldg. East, 4th Floor
Los Angeles, CA 90038
213/871-4440

SCHOOL DAZE 1988
DO THE RIGHT THING 1989
HARLEM NIGHTS 1989

JOE REICH*
c/o C.S.A.
6565 Sunset Blvd., Suite 306
Los Angeles, CA 90028
213/463-1925
Fax: 213/463-5753

BARBARA REMSEN & ASSOCIATES
Raleigh Studios
650 N. Bronson Ave., Suite 124
Los Angeles, CA 90004
213/464-7968
Fax: 213/464-7970

Jeanne Ashby
Ann Remsen Manners
*Barbara Remsen**

SOUTH OF RENO 1988
LOVING LULU 1991

GRETCHEN RENNELL*
Accent Entertainment
8282 Sunset Blvd., Suite C
Los Angeles, CA 90046
213/654-0231

347

SHARI RHODES*
Casting Association
1154 1/2 North Orange Grove
Los Angeles, CA 90046
213/913-9608
Fax: 213/653-9250

CRITICAL CONDITION 1987
SQUARE DANCE 1987
RETURN OF THE LIVING DEAD II 1990
LONG WALK HOME 1991
THE MAN IN THE MOON 1991
RUSH 1991
WATCH IT! 1992
BIG BAD JOHN 1992
A DOG OF FLANDERS 1992
RICH IN LOVE 1992
PASSENGER 57 1992

SHIRLEY RICH*
200 E. 66th St., Suite E-1202
New York, NY 10021
212/688-9540

JEFF ROSEN
1600 N. Highland Ave., Suite 1
Los Angeles, CA 90028
213/461-3800

STU ROSEN*
7631 Lexington Avenue
Los Angeles, CA 90046
213/851-1661

VICKI ROSENBERG & ASSOCIATES
Sunset/Gower Studios
1438 N. Gower St.
Casting Apartments, #1406
Los Angeles, CA 90028
213/460-7593

*Vicki Rosenberg**
Gregory Orson

DONNA ROSENSTEIN*
Vice President - Casting
ABC Entertainment
2040 Avenue of the Stars
Los Angeles, CA 90067
310/557-6532
Fax: 310/557-7160

CAROL ROSENTHAL
SLAMDANCE 1987

MARCIA ROSS*
Vice President - Talent & Casting
Warner Bros. Television
4000 Warner Blvd.
Burbank, CA 91522
818/954-1123

EXTREME PREJUDICE 1987
NO MAN'S LAND 1987

RENEE ROUSSELOT*
3815 Hughes Avenue
Culver City, CA 90232
310/841-4365

MARIE ROW
GOOD MORNING, VIETNAM 1987

BEN RUBIN*
5455 Wilshire Blvd., Suite 700
Los Angeles, CA 90036
213/937-4607

5750 Wilshire Blvd., #222
Los Angeles, CA 90036
213/965-1500

DAVID RUBIN*
Aaron Spelling Productions
5700 Wilshire Blvd., #575
Los Angeles, CA 90036
213/965-5951

DRAGNET 1987
SPACEBALLS 1987
THE BIG EASY 1987
LESS THAN ZERO 1987
SCROOGED 1988
THE WAR OF THE ROSES 1989
THE BIG EASY 1989
MEN DON'T LEAVE 1990
AFTER DARK, MY SWEET 1990
THE ADDAMS FAMILY 1991
FRIED GREEN TOMATOES 1991
FINAL ANALYSIS 1992

TARA JAYNE RUBIN*
Johnson/Liff Casting
1501 Broadway, Suite 1400
New York, NY 10036
212/391-2680

DEBRA RUBINSTEIN*
ABC Productions
2020 Avenue of the Stars, #400
Los Angeles, CA 90067
310/557-6942
Fax: 310/557-7160

S

DORIS SABBAGH
Columbia Pictures Television
Studio Plaza
3400 Riverside Drive, #1071
Burbank, CA 91505
818/972-8339

MARK SAKS*
Lorimar Casting
300 S. Lorimar Plaza, Bldg. 140, First Floor
Burbank, CA 91505
818/954-7326

MIGUEL SANDOVAL
Together Brother Productions
9505 W. Washington Blvd.
Culver City, CA 90230
310/841-2301

WALKER   1987

CATHY SANDRICH
Mackey/Sandrich Casting
9155 Sunset Blvd.
Los Angeles, CA 90069
310/278-8858

Paramount Studios
5555 Melrose Ave., Dressing Room Bldg., #321
Los Angeles, CA 90038
213/956-5751

AMY SCHECTER*
Stuart Howard Associates
22 W. 27th St., 10th Floor
New York, NY 10001
212/725-7770

GUS SCHIRMER
1403 N. Orange Grove Ave.
Los Angeles, CA 90046
213/876-5044

JEAN SCOCCIMARO*
Warner Hollywood Studios
1041 N. Formosa Ave.
Santa Monica Bldg., #108
West Hollywood, CA 90046
213/850-2455

SUSAN SCUDDER*
7083 Hollywood Blvd.
Los Angeles, CA 90028
213/856-7574

JOE SCULLY*
5642 Etiwanda Ave., Suite 8
Tarzana, CA 91356
818/763-2028

LILA SELIK
1551 S. Robertson, #202
Los Angeles, CA 90035
310/556-2444

MARY SELWAY
GORILLAS IN THE MIST   1988
A DRY WHITE SEASON   1989

JULIE SELZER*
Dennison/Selzer/Rush Casting
11500 Tennessee Ave.
Los Angeles, CA 90064
310/652-7528

ROBOCOP   1987
AMAZON WOMEN ON THE MOON   1987
THROW MOMMA FROM THE TRAIN   1987
THE ACCUSED   1988
HEATHERS   1989
IMMEDIATE FAMILY   1989
HERO WANTED   1992

GARY SHAFFER*
1502 Queens Road
Los Angeles, CA 90069
213/934-1800

BARBARA SHAPIRO
MATEWAN   1987
ZELLY AND ME   1988
EIGHT MEN OUT   1988
THE GOOD MOTHER   1988

SARI SHAPIRO
P.O. Box 69277
Los Angeles, CA 90069
213/874-1719

KIYO GLENN SHARP
4567 Nagle Ave.
Sherman Oaks, CA 91423
818/789-7842

ROSE TOBIAS SHAW
BERT RIGBY, YOU'RE A FOOL   1989

SUSAN SHAW*
c/o C.S.A.
6565 Sunset Blvd., Suite 306
Los Angeles, CA 90028
213/372-8411
Fax: 213/463-5753

VALENTINO RETURNS   1989

BILL SHEPARD*
c/o C.S.A.
6565 Sunset Blvd., Suite 306
Los Angeles, CA 90028
818/789-4776

SPACEBALLS   1987
STAR TREK V: THE FINAL FRONTIER   1989
THE VAGRANT   1992

Sh

FILM
PRODUCERS,
STUDIOS,
AGENTS AND
CASTING
DIRECTORS
GUIDE

CASTING DIRECTORS

TONY SHEPHERD*
Vice President - Talent & Casting
Aaron Spelling Productions
5700 Wilshire Blvd., #575
Los Angeles, CA 90036
213/965-5718

MELANIE SHERWOOD
6305 Yucca, #600
Los Angeles, CA 90028
213/462-6817

JENNIFER SHULL*
c/o C.S.A.
6565 Sunset Blvd., Suite 306
Los Angeles, CA 90028
213/463-1925

FUNNY LADY   1975
THE GOODBYE GIRL   1977
CALIFORNIA SUITE   1978
THE HUNTER   1979
THE ELECTRIC HORSEMAN   1980
GRAND CANYON   1991

MARGERY SIMKIN*
c/o C.S.A.
311 W. 43rd St., Suite 700
New York, NY 10036
213/203-1530

CRITICAL CONDITION   1987
HOUSEKEEPING   1987
FIELD OF DREAMS   1989

JOAN SIMMONS
4841 Fir Avenue
Seal Beach, CA 90740
310/430-7392

MEG SIMON CASTING
1600 Broadway, Suite 1005
New York, NY 10019
212/245-7670
Fax: 212/765-8499

*Meg Simon**

CROSSING DELANCEY   1988
FAMILY BUSINESS   1989
ONCE AROUND   1990

MELISSA SKOFF*
11684 Ventura Blvd., Suite 5141
Studio City, CA 91604
818/760-2058

THE EMERALD FOREST   1985
BACK TO SCHOOL   1986
HAMBURGER...THE MOTION PICTURE   1986
HOUSE   1986
MIRACLES   1986
SOUL MAN   1986
THE GOLDEN CHILD   1986
HOUSE II: THE SECOND STORY   1987
DISORDERLIES   1987
18 AGAIN!   1988
HOT TO TROT   1988

DEEPSTAR SIX   1989
THE HORROR SHOW   1989
THE PUNISHER   1990
WARLOCK   1991

KATHY SMITH
12001 Valleyheart Drive
Studio City, CA 91604
818/508-2058

STANLEY SOBLE*
Head of Casting
Mark Taper Forum/Ahmanson at the Doolittle Theatre
601 W. Temple Ave.
Los Angeles, CA 90012
213/972-7374

LEAN ON ME   1988
AMERICAN BLUE NOTE   1988
TAILSPIN   1988

CAROL SOSKIN CASTING
P.O. Box 480106
Los Angeles, CA 90048
213/473-7044

PAM SPARKS*
6126 Glen Alder
Los Angeles, CA 90068

AUSTEN SPRIGGS
HAMBURGER HILL   1987

LYNN STALMASTER
9911 W. Pico Blvd., Suite 1580
Los Angeles, CA 90035
310/552-0983
Fax: 310/552-0435

OUTRAGEOUS FORTUNE   1987
AMAZING GRACE AND CHUCK   1987
DRAGNET   1987
SPACEBALLS   1987
THE UNTOUCHABLES   1987
THE BIG EASY   1987
SWITCHING CHANNELS   1988
LADY IN WHITE   1988
PHYSICAL EVIDENCE   1989
DEAD-BANG   1989
SEE NO EVIL, HEAR NO EVIL   1989
WEEKEND AT BERNIE'S   1989
CASUALTIES OF WAR   1989
FRANKIE AND JOHNNY   1991
FOR THE BOYS   1991

ILENE STARGER
Vice President of Casting
Disney/Touchtone Pictures
500 S. Buena Vista St., Casting Bldg., #7
Burbank, CA 91521
818/560-7510
Fax: 818/563-3719

NO WAY OUT   1987
THE BEAST   1988
THE DREAM TEAM   1989
THREE MEN AND A LITTLE LADY   1990
ROBIN HOOD: PRINCE OF THIEVES   1991

Ta

FILM
PRODUCERS,
STUDIOS,
AGENTS AND
CASTING
DIRECTORS
GUIDE

C
A
S
T
I
N
G

D
I
R
E
C
T
O
R
S

JANE STAUGUS CASTING, INC.
10153 1/2 Riverside Dr., Suite 108
Toluca Lake, CA 91602
818/508-8868

DAWN STEINBERG*
c/o C.S.A.
6565 Sunset Blvd., Suite 306
Los Angeles, CA 90028
213/463-1925

RON STEPHENSON*
Director of Casting
Universal Television
100 Universal City Plaza, Bldg. 463, Suite 100
Universal City, CA 91608
818/777-3498

SALLY STINER*
12228 Venice Blvd., Suite 503
Los Angeles, CA 90066
310/827-9796

20th Century-Fox
10201 W. Pico Blvd., Bldg. 26, #125
Los Angeles, CA 90035
310/203-1545

1420 N. Beachwood, Bldg. 62
Los Angeles, CA 90028
213/468-3225

STANZI STOKES*
Universal Studios
100 Universal City Plaza, Bldg. 133
Universal City, CA 91608
818/777-3446

BILL AND TED'S EXCELLENT ADVENTURE   1989

RANDY STONE*
9336 W. Washington Blvd.
Above Stage 4, #200
Culver City, CA 90232
310/202-3393
818/762-4578
Fax: 310/202-3204

SAY ANYTHING...   1989

STUART STONE
1600 North Highland Avenue, Suite 4
Los Angeles, CA 90028
818/955-6567

GILDA STRATTON*
Warner Studios
4000 Warner Blvd., Bldg. 3A, #18
Burbank, CA 91522
818/954-2843

ROGER STURTEVANT*
BSB
405 Lexington Avenue
New York, NY 10174
212/297-7498

RON SURMA
OVER THE TOP   1987

SUE SWAN
Champion/Basker Casting
7060 Hollywood Blvd., Suite 808
Hollywood, CA 90028
213/466-1884

MONICA SWANN*
5300 Melrose Ave., Suite 309E
Los Angeles, CA 90038
213/856-1702

Paramount Studios
5555 Melrose Avenue, Bob Hope Bldg., #101
Los Angeles, CA 90038
213/956-4703

DANIEL SWEE*
Playwrights Horizons
416 W. 42nd St.
New York, NY 10036
212/564-1235

T

JUDY TAYLOR*
Taylor/Gordon Casting
P.O. Box 461198
Los Angeles, CA 90046
213/656-9971

500 S. Buena Vista St.
Zorro Bldg. 5, #6
Burbank, CA 91521
818/560-2700

THE STEPFATHER   1987
HARRY AND THE HENDERSONS   1987
INNERSPACE   1987
STAKEOUT   1987
EMPIRE OF THE SUN   1987
BEACHES   1988
THE 'BURBS   1989
FAREWELL TO THE KING   1989
CHANCES ARE   1989
HONEY, I SHRUNK THE KIDS   1989
TURNER AND HOOCH   1989
BACK TO THE FUTURE PART II   1989
TRIUMPH OF THE SPIRIT   1989
INDIANA JONES AND THE LAST CRUSADE   1989

JULIET TAYLOR*
130 W. 57th St., Suite 12E
New York, NY 10019
212/245-4635

HEARTBURN   1986
RADIO DAYS   1987
SEPTEMBER   1987
BILOXI BLUES   1988
MISSISSIPPI BURNING   1988

Te

FILM
PRODUCERS,
STUDIOS,
AGENTS AND
CASTING
DIRECTORS
GUIDE

**C
A
S
T
I
N
G
D
I
R
E
C
T
O
R
S**

BIG   1988
ANOTHER WOMAN   1988
WORKING GIRL   1988
DANGEROUS LIAISONS   1988
NEW YORK STORIES: "Oedipus Wrecks"   1989
CRIMES AND MISDEMEANORS   1989
THIS IS MY LIFE   1992

TEITLBAUM/HEIT
2000 W. Magnolia Blvd., Suite 209
Burbank, CA 91506
818/845-9041

TEPPER/GALLEGOS CASTING
7033 Sunset Blvd., Suite 208
Los Angeles, CA 90028
213/469-3577

Dennis Gallegos
Estelle Tepper

MARK TESCHNER*
ABC Prospect
4151 Prospect Ave., Stage 54
Hollywood, CA 90027
213/557-5542

TODD M. THALER
RUNNING ON EMPTY   1988

CAROLINE THOMAS
ANNA   1987

VICKIE THOMAS
Paramount Studios
5555 Melrose Avenue, Bob Hope Bldg., #105
Los Angeles, CA 90038
213/956-8204

REPO MAN   1983
TRUE STORIES   1985
SID AND NANCY   1985
BEVERLY HILLS COP II   1987
MASTERS OF THE UNIVERSE   1987
WALKER   1987
BIG TOP PEE-WEE   1989
TAPEHEADS   1989
BREAKING IN   1989
BLAZE   1989
K-2   1990
ROADSIDE PROPHETS   1990
THE PIANO LESSON   1990
THE GRIFTERS   1990
EDWARD SCISSORHANDS   1990
WHITE MEN CAN'T JUMP   1992
DRACULA   1992
INDECENT PROPOSAL   1992

JOEL THURM
THE ROCKY HORROR PICTURE SHOW   1975
GREASE   1978
ALTERED STATES   1980
AIRPLANE!   1980

ROSEMARIE TICHLER*
New York Shakespeare Festival
425 Lafayette St.
New York, NY 10003
212/598-7100

BONNIE TIMMERMAN*
c/o C.S.A.
311 W. 43rd St.
New York, NY 10036
212/333-4552

LIGHT OF DAY   1987
BEVERLY HILLS COP II   1987
GARDENS OF STONE   1987
DIRTY DANCING   1987
HAPPY NEW YEAR   1987
IRONWEED   1987
FRANTIC   1988
BULL DURHAM   1988
STEALING HOME   1988
MILES FROM HOME   1988
TEQUILA SUNRISE   1988
JOHNNY HANDSOME   1989
MOBSTERS   1991
PAST MIDNIGHT   1992
THE LAST DAYS OF EDEN   1992

TLC/BOOTH
6521 Homewood Ave.
Los Angeles, CA 90028
213/464-2788

JOY TODD*
Carolco Pictures
8800 Sunset Blvd.
Los Angeles, CA 90069
310/855-7300

STREET SMART   1987
SOMEONE TO WATCH OVER ME   1987
RAMBO III   1988
LOCK UP   1989
RUDE AWAKENING   1989

DAN TRAN
FULL METAL JACKET   1987

SUSAN TYLER
Chelsea Studios
3859 Lankershim Blvd.
Studio City, CA 91604
818/506-0400

U

ULRICH/DAWSON CASTING
100 Universal City Plaza, Bldg. 466
Universal City, CA 91608
818/777-7802
Fax: 818/777-4987

Cecily Adams
Eric Dawson
*Robert Ulrich**

UNIQUE CASTING
540 NW 165th St. Road
Miami, FL 33169
305/947-9339

Ed Arenas
*Yonit Hamer-Tumaroff**

KAREN VICE*
12001 Ventura Place, 2nd Floor
Studio City, CA 91604
818/760-5263

JOSE VILLAVERDE*
c/o C.S.A.
6565 Sunset Blvd., Suite 306
Los Angeles, CA 90028
213/463-1925

LEON VITALI
FULL METAL JACKET 1987

APRIL WEBSTER*
c/o C.S.A.
6565 Sunset Blvd., Suite 306
Los Angeles, CA 90028
213/285-8631

JUDITH WEINER
Paramount Studios
5555 Melrose Ave., Dietrich Bldg., #204
Los Angeles, CA 90038
213/956-4822

SOME KIND OF WONDERFUL 1987
LIKE FATHER, LIKE SON 1987
THE GREAT OUTDOORS 1988
K-9 1989
GROSS ANATOMY 1989
DAD 1989

MARY WEST
Brown/West Casting
7319 Beverly Blvd., Suite 10
Los Angeles, CA 90036
213/938-2575

CATHERINE WHITE
Anderson/McCook/White Casting
3855 Lankershim Blvd.
North Hollywood, CA 91604
818/760-3934

NICK WILKINSON*
Director of Casting
ABC Entertainment
2040 Avenue of the Stars, 5th Floor
Los Angeles, CA 90067
310/557-6547
Fax: 310/557-7160

SUSAN F. WILLETT*
Susan Willett Casting Associates
1170 Broadway #1008
New York, NY 10001
212/725-3588

PRANCER 1989

TAMMY WINDSOR
14001 Peach Grove
Sherman Oaks, CA 91423
818/501-3510

GERI WINDSOR-FISCHER*
4500 Forman Ave., #1
Toluca Lake, CA 91602
818/509-9993

LIZ WOODMAN*
c/o C.S.A.
311 W. 43rd St., Suite 700
New York, NY 10036
212/787-3782

GERRIE WORMSER
P.O. Box 6449
Beverly Hills, CA 90210
310/277-3281

DARLENE WYATT*
1138 E. Highland
Phoenix, AZ 85014
602/263-8650

THE VAGRANT 1992

LORI WYMAN*
16499 N.E. 19th Avenue, Suite 203
North Miami Beach, FL 33162
305/354-3901

RONNIE YESKEL*
20th Century-Fox Studios
10201 W. Pico Blvd., Pico Apts. #6
Los Angeles, CA 90035
310/203-2662

DIANNE YOUNG*
14955 Calvert St.
Van Nuys, CA 91411
818/778-2324

Yo

FILM PRODUCERS, STUDIOS, AGENTS AND CASTING DIRECTORS GUIDE

SUSAN YOUNG*
c/o C.S.A.
6565 Sunset Blvd., Suite 306
Los Angeles, CA 90028
213/463-1925

Z

JOANNE ZALUSKI*
9348 Civic Center Dr., Suite 407
Beverly Hills, CA 90210
310/456-5160

OVERBOARD   1987
MAJOR LEAGUE   1989
CAROLINE ZELDER
HERO AND THE TERROR   1988

ANDREW ZERMAN*
Johnson-Liff Casting
1501 Broadway #1400
New York, NY 10036
212/391-2680

JEREMY ZIMMERMAN
SUPERMAN IV: THE QUEST FOR PEACE   1987

GARY M. ZUCKERBROD*
3961 Landmark St., 2nd Floor
Culver City, CA 90232
310/202-0873

SHOCKER   1989
A MIDNIGHT CLEAR   1992

★ ★ ★ ★

CASTING DIRECTORS

INDEX BY FILM TITLE

HIS JOB, HIS HOME, HIS FAMILY. SOME PEOPLE WILL PAY ANYTHING FOR COCAINE.

Cocaine really is expensive. Look what it almost cost this man.

He's getting help at a Drug Rehabilitation Center. They got help from the United Way. All because the United Way got help from you.

Your single contribution helps provide therapy for a child with a learning disability, a program that sends a volunteer to do the shopping for a 79 year-old woman, and a place for a 12 year-old to toss a basketball around after school.

Or, in this case, rehabilitation for a cocaine abuser. A man who, without your help, could very well have ended up paying the ultimate price.

United Way ® Ad Council

It brings out the best in all of us.™

INDEX OF FILM TITLES
CASTING DIRECTORS

3-Bu

FILM
PRODUCERS,
STUDIOS,
AGENTS AND
CASTING
DIRECTORS
GUIDE

I
N
D
E
X

O
F

F
I
L
M

T
I
T
L
E
S

Note: This is not a list of all film titles,
only those listed in the casting directors section.

Ca-Fr

FILM
PRODUCERS,
STUDIOS,
AGENTS AND
CASTING
DIRECTORS
GUIDE

I N D E X   O F   F I L M   T I T L E S

C

CADDYSHACK .... WALLIS NICITA
CALL ME .... LYNN KRESSEL
CAN'T BUY ME LOVE .... CARO JONES
CANDY MOUNTAIN .... HOPKINS & BRAMON CASTING
CAPE FEAR .... ELLEN LEWIS
CAST A GIANT SHADOW .... SANDY ALLISON
CASUALTIES OF WAR .... LYNN STALMASTER
CATTLE ANNIE AND LITTLE BRITCHES .... PENNY PERRY
CHANCES ARE .... JUDY TAYLOR
CHANCES ARE .... MIKE FENTON & ASSOCIATES
CHECKING OUT .... ELIZABETH LEUSTIG
CHEECH & CHONG'S NEXT MOVIE .... FERN CHAMPION CASTING
CHEECH & CHONG'S NICE DREAMS .... FERN CHAMPION CASTING
CHILD'S PLAY .... JANE ALDERMAN
CHILD'S PLAY .... PAGANO/BIALY CASTING
CHILD'S PLAY .... SHARON BIALY
CHILD'S PLAY 3 .... GLENN DANIELS
CHINATOWN .... MIKE FENTON & ASSOCIATES
CITY SLICKERS .... PAM DIXON
CLARA'S HEART .... KEN CARLSON
CLEAN AND SOBER .... GLENN DANIELS
CLEAN AND SOBER .... MARION DOUGHERTY
CLIFF HANGER .... MINDY MARIN
CLUB PARADISE .... WALLIS NICITA
COCKTAIL .... DONNA ISAACSON
COCKTAIL .... LYONS/ISAACSON CASTING
COCOON .... PENNY PERRY
COCOON: THE RETURN .... BEVERLY McDERMOTT
COLOR OF MONEY, THE .... JANE ALDERMAN
COLOR PURPLE, THE .... REUBEN CANNON & ASSOCIATES
COLORS .... LAUREN LLOYD
COLUMBUS .... LOUIS DiGIAIMO
COMING TO AMERICA .... JACKIE BURCH
COOKIE .... ELLEN CHENOWETH
COUCH TRIP, THE .... PATRICIA MOCK
COUSINS .... MARCI LIROFF
CRIMES AND MISDEMEANORS .... JULIET TAYLOR
CRIMINAL LAW .... ELITE CASTING
CRIMINAL LAW .... VERA MILLER
CRITICAL CONDITION .... MARGERY SIMKIN
CRITICAL CONDITION .... SHARI RHODES
CROCODILE DUNDEE .... PAULA HEROLD
CROSS MY HEART .... WALLIS NICITA
CROSSING DELANCEY .... FRAN KUMIN
CROSSING DELANCEY .... SIMON & KUMIN CASTING
CROWDED ROOM, THE .... MALI FINN
CROWDED ROOM, THE .... DONN FINN
CRUSOE .... NOEL DAVIS
CRUSOE .... SUSIE FIGGIS
CRY BABY .... PAULA HEROLD
CYBORG .... NANCY LARA-HANSCH

D

D.O.A. .... NANCY FOY
DA .... NUALA MOISELLE
DAD .... JUDITH WEINER
DANCERS .... FRANCESCO CENIERI
DANGEROUS LIAISONS .... HOWARD FEUER
DANGEROUS LIAISONS .... JULIET TAYLOR
DARKMAN .... NANCY NAYOR
DARKMAN .... VALERIE McCAFFREY
DATE WITH AN ANGEL .... FERN CHAMPION CASTING
DAYS OF HEAVEN .... BABARA CLAMAN
DEAD MEN DON'T WEAR PLAID .... PENNY PERRY
DEAD OF WINTER .... MARIA ARMSTRONG
DEAD OF WINTER .... ROSS CLYDESDALE
DEAD POETS SOCIETY .... HOWARD FEUER
DEAD, THE .... NUALA MOISELLE
DEAD-BANG .... LYNN STALMASTER
DEADLY ILLUSION .... LOUIS DiGIAIMO
DECEIVED .... DEBORAH AQUILA
DEEP SIX .... MELISSA SKOFF
DEFENDING YOUR LIFE .... BABARA CLAMAN
DELTA FORCE 2 .... NANCY LARA-HANSCH
DELUSION .... ELISA GOODMAN
DESPERATELY SEEKING SUSAN .... HOPKINS & BRAMON CASTING
DIE HARD .... JACKIE BURCH
DIE LAUGHING .... WALLIS NICITA
DIGGS TOWN .... DEBI MANWILLER
DIGGS TOWN .... RICHARD PAGANO
DIGGS TOWN .... SHARON BIALY
DIRTY DANCING .... BONNIE TIMMERMAN
DIRTY DOZEN, THE .... SANDY ALLISON
DIRTY ROTTEN SCOUNDRELS .... DONNA ISAACSON

DIRTY ROTTEN SCOUNDRELS .... LYONS/ISAACSON CASTING
DISORDERLIES .... MELISSA SKOFF
DISORGANIZED CRIME .... LORA KENNEDY
DO THE RIGHT THING .... ROBI REED
DOCTOR ZHIVAGO .... SANDY ALLISON
DOG OF FLANDERS, A .... SHARI RHODES
DOMINICK AND EUGENE .... BARRY MOSS
DOMINICK AND EUGENE .... HUGHES/MOSS CASTING
DON'T TELL MOM THE BABYSITTER'S DEAD .... PAGANO/BIALY CASTING
DR. DETROIT .... JANE ALDERMAN
DR. DETROIT .... WALLIS NICITA
DRACULA .... VICKIE THOMAS
DRAGNET .... DAVID RUBIN
DRAGNET .... LYNN STALMASTER
DREADNOUGHT .... PAMELA BASKER
DREAM TEAM, THE .... ILENE STARGER
DRUGSTORE COWBOY .... PAGANO/BIALY CASTING
DRUGSTORE COWBOY .... SHARON BIALY
DRY WHITE SEASON, A .... MARY SELWAY
DRY WHITE SEASON, A .... WALLIS NICITA
DUDES .... NINA AXELROD

E

E.T. THE EXTRA-TERRESTRIAL .... MIKE FENTON & ASSOCIATES
EARTH GIRLS ARE EASY .... WALLIS NICITA
EDDIE MURPHY "RAW" .... PAT GOLDEN
EDWARD SCISSORHANDS .... VICKIE THOMAS
EIGHT MEN OUT .... AVY KAUFMAN
EIGHT MEN OUT .... BARBARA SHAPIRO
EIGHT MEN OUT .... FRAZIER/GINSBERG CASTING
EIGHT MEN OUT .... SHANI GINSBERG
EL NORTE .... BOB MORONES
ELECTRIC DREAMS .... WALLIS NICITA
EMERALD FOREST, THE .... MELISSA SKOFF
EMPIRE OF THE SUN .... JANE FEINBERG
EMPIRE OF THE SUN .... JUDY TAYLOR
EMPIRE OF THE SUN .... MIKE FENTON & ASSOCIATES
ENCINO MAN .... KATHLEEN LETTERIE
END OF THE LINE .... PAT McCORKLE
ENDLESS LOVE .... JANE ALDERMAN
ENEMIES, A LOVE STORY .... ELLEN CHENOWETH
EQUINOX .... PAM DIXON
ERNEST SAVES CHRISTMAS .... KATHLEEN LETTERIE
ESCAPE FROM ALCATRAZ .... MARION DOUGHERTY
ESCAPE FROM ALCATRAZ .... WALLIS NICITA
EVERYBODY'S ALL-AMERICAN .... NANCY KLOPPER
EXTREME PREJUDICE .... JUDITH HOLSTRA
EXTREME PREJUDICE .... MARCIA ROSS
EXTREMITIES .... PAGANO/BIALY CASTING

F

FABULOUS BAKER BOYS, THE .... WALLIS NICITA
FADE TO BLACK .... FERN CHAMPION CASTING
FALCON AND THE SNOWMAN, THE .... WALLIS NICITA
FAMILY BUSINESS .... FRAN KUMIN
FAMILY BUSINESS .... MEG SIMON
FAREWELL TO THE KING .... JUDY TAYLOR
FAREWELL TO THE KING .... MIKE FENTON & ASSOCIATES
FAT MAN AND LITTLE BOY .... NANCY FOY
FATAL ATTRACTION .... HOPKINS & BRAMON CASTING
FERRIS BUELLER'S DAY OFF .... JANE ALDERMAN
FIELD OF DREAMS .... JANE ALDERMAN
FIELD OF DREAMS .... MARGERY SIMKIN
FINAL ANALYSIS .... DAVID RUBIN
FINAL EMBRACE .... STEVEN RABINER
FIRE IN THE DARK .... RACHELLE FARBERMAN
FIREHAWK .... ANDREW HERTZ
FIVE CORNERS .... DOUG AIBEL
FIVE HEARTBEATS .... JAKI BROWN
FIXER, THE .... SANDY ALLISON
FLATLINERS .... MALI FINN
FLETCH LIVES .... PATRICIA MOCK
FLOWERS IN THE ATTIC .... PENNY PERRY
FOR KEEPS? .... CARO JONES
FOR KEEPS? .... PAT McCORKLE
FOR THE BOYS .... LYNN STALMASTER
FOUR FRIENDS .... JANE ALDERMAN
FOXES .... PENNY PERRY
FRANKIE AND JOHNNY .... LYNN STALMASTER
FRANTIC .... BONNIE TIMMERMAN
FRANTIC .... MARGOT CAPELIER
FREEJACK .... PAM DIXON
FRIED GREEN TOMATOES .... DAVID RUBIN
FRIGHT NIGHT PART II .... NINA AXELROD

FILM
PRODUCERS,
STUDIOS,
AGENTS AND
CASTING
DIRECTORS
GUIDE

FROM THE HIP ..... JANE FEINBERG
FROM THE HIP ..... MIKE FENTON & ASSOCIATES
FULL METAL JACKET ..... DAN TRAN
FULL METAL JACKET ..... JANE FEINBERG
FULL METAL JACKET ..... LEON VITALI
FULL METAL JACKET ..... MARION DOUGHERTY
FULL METAL JACKET ..... MIKE FENTON & ASSOCIATES
FULL METAL JACKET ..... NGUYEN THI MY CHAU
FULL MOON IN BLUE WATER ..... ED JOHNSTON
FULL MOON IN BLUE WATER ..... ED MITCHELL
FUNNY FARM ..... MARION DOUGHERTY

G

GABY—A TRUE STORY ..... JOHANNA RAY
GARDENS OF STONE ..... ALETA CHAPPELLE
GARDENS OF STONE ..... BONNIE TIMMERMAN
GARDENS OF STONE ..... JANE JENKINS
GARDENS OF STONE ..... JANET HIRSHENSON
GAS FOOD & LODGING ..... DEBI MANWILLER
GAS FOOD & LODGING ..... RICHARD PAGANO
GAS FOOD & LODGING ..... SHARON BIALY
GETTING OF WISDOM, THE ..... SANDY ALLISON
GHOST ..... JANE JENKINS
GHOST ..... JANET HIRSHENSON
GHOSTBUSTERS II ..... MICHAEL CHINICH
GIANT OF THUNDER MOUNTAIN ..... RUTH CONFORTE
GLADIATOR ..... AMANDA MACKEY
GLEAMING THE CUBE ..... ELIZABETH LEUSTIG
GLORY ..... MARY COLQUHOUN
GO BETWEEN, THE ..... JANE ALDERMAN
GO BETWEEN, THE ..... SUSAN WEIDER
GOING APE! ..... WALLIS NICITA
GOLDEN CHILD, THE ..... MELISSA SKOFF
GOLDEN SEAL, THE ..... PENNY PERRY
GOOD MORNING, VIETNAM ..... LOUIS DiGIAIMO
GOOD MORNING, VIETNAM ..... MARIE ROW
GOOD MORNING, VIETNAM ..... RASSAMI PAOLUENGTONG
GOOD MOTHER, THE ..... BARBARA SHAPIRO
GOODBYE, MR. CHIPS ..... SANDY ALLISON
GORILLAS IN THE MIST ..... MARION DOUGHERTY
GORILLAS IN THE MIST ..... MARY SELWAY
GRAND CANYON ..... JENNIFER SHULL
GRAND ISLE ..... FERN CHAMPION
GRAND ISLE ..... MARK PALADINI
GRAVEYARD SHIFT ..... PAGANO/BIALY CASTING
GREASE ..... JOEL THURM
GREAT BALLS OF FIRE! ..... JUDITH HOLSTRA
GREAT OUTDOORS, THE ..... JUDITH WEINER
GREEK TYCOON, THE ..... SANDY ALLISON
GRIFTERS, THE ..... VICKIE THOMAS
GROSS ANATOMY ..... JUDITH WEINER

H

HAIR ..... HOWARD FEUER
HAIRSPRAY ..... MARY COLQUHOUN
HAIRSPRAY ..... PAT MORAN
HAMBURGER HILL ..... AUSTEN SPRIGGS
HAMBURGER HILL ..... MARY COLQUHOUN
HAMBURGER...THE MOTION PICTURE ..... MELISSA SKOFF
HAND THAT ROCKS THE CRADLE, THE ..... JUNIE LOWRY-JOHNSON
HANGIN' WITH THE HOMEBOYS ..... DEBORAH AQUILA
HAPPY NEW YEAR ..... BONNIE TIMMERMAN
HARLEM NIGHTS ..... ROBI REED
HARRY AND THE HENDERSONS ..... JANE FEINBERG
HARRY AND THE HENDERSONS ..... JUDY TAYLOR
HARRY AND THE HENDERSONS ..... MIKE FENTON & ASSOCIATES
HEARTBURN ..... JULIET TAYLOR
HEAT OF PASSION ..... STEVEN RABINER
HEATHERS ..... DENNISON/SELZER/RUSH CASTING
HEATHERS ..... JULIE SELZER
HEAVEN IS A PLAYGROUND ..... JANE ALDERMAN
HELLO AGAIN ..... DONNA ISAACSON
HELLO AGAIN ..... LYONS/ISAACSON CASTING
HER ALIBI ..... KEN CARLSON
HERO AND THE TERROR ..... CAROLINE ZELDER
HERO WANTED ..... DENNISON/SELZER/RUSH CASTING
HERO WANTED ..... JULIE SELZER
HIDING OUT ..... BONNIE GINNEGAN
HIDING OUT ..... STEVE JACOBS
HIGHLANDER, THE QUICKENING ..... FERN CHAMPION CASTING
HITCHER, THE ..... PENNY PERRY
HONEY, I SHRUNK THE KIDS ..... JUDY TAYLOR

HONEY, I SHRUNK THE KIDS ..... LYNDA GORDON
HONEY, I SHRUNK THE KIDS ..... MIKE FENTON & ASSOCIATES
HOOK ..... JANE JENKINS
HOOK ..... JANET HIRSHENSON
HORROR SHOW, THE ..... MELISSA SKOFF
HOT MILLIONS ..... 68SANDY ALLISON
HOT SHOTS ..... MALI FINN
HOT TO TROT ..... MELISSA SKOFF
HOUSE ..... MELISSA SKOFF
HOUSE II: THE SECOND STORY ..... MELISSA SKOFF
HOUSE OF CARDS ..... MALI FINN
HOUSE OF GAMES ..... CYRENE HAUSMAN
HOUSE ON CARROLL STREET, THE ..... HOWARD FEUER
HOUSEKEEPING ..... LYNNE CARROW
HOUSEKEEPING ..... MARGERY SIMKIN
HUMAN SHIELD, THE ..... NANCY LARA-HANSCH
HUNK ..... DAVID COHN
HUNK ..... PAUL BENGSTON

I

I'LL BE HOME FOR CHRISTMAS ..... NANCY LARA-HANSCH
IDOLMAKER, THE ..... PENNY PERRY
IMMEDIATE FAMILY ..... DENNISON/SELZER/RUSH CASTING
IMMEDIATE FAMILY ..... JULIE SELZER
IN COUNTRY ..... HOWARD FEUER
IN EXILE ..... RUTH CONFORTE
IN THE MOOD ..... MEGAN BRANMAN
IN THE MOOD ..... PENNY PERRY
IN THE SPIRIT ..... PAULA HEROLD
INDECENT PROPOSAL ..... VICKIE THOMAS
INDIANA JONES AND THE LAST CRUSADE ..... JUDY TAYLOR
INDIANA JONES AND THE LAST CRUSADE ..... MAGGIE CARTIER
INDIANA JONES AND THE LAST CRUSADE ..... MIKE FENTON & ASSOCIATES
INDIANA JONES AND THE LAST CRUSADE ..... VALORIE MASSALAS
INNERSPACE ..... JANE FEINBERG
INNERSPACE ..... JUDY TAYLOR
INNERSPACE ..... MIKE FENTON & ASSOCIATES
INNOCENT BLOOD ..... ANDREW HERTZ
INNOCENT MAN, AN ..... HOWARD FEUER
INTO THE SUN ..... JACK JONES
IRONWEED ..... BONNIE TIMMERMAN
ISHTAR ..... HOWARD FEUER
IT TAKES TWO ..... DAVID COHN
IT TAKES TWO ..... PAUL BENGSTON

J

JACKNIFE ..... D.L. NEWTON
JACKNIFE ..... JUDY COURTNEY
JACOB'S LADDER ..... HEIDI LEVITT
JANUARY MAN, THE ..... HOPKINS & BRAMON CASTING
JERK, THE ..... PENNY PERRY
JFK ..... HEIDI LEVITT
JFK ..... HOPKINS & BRAMON CASTING
JOHNNY HANDSOME ..... BONNIE TIMMERMAN
JUICE ..... JAKI BROWN

K

K-2 ..... VICKIE THOMAS
K-9 ..... JUDITH WEINER
KANSAS ..... ED MITCHELL
KARATE KID, THE ..... CARO JONES
KARATE KID PART II, THE ..... CARO JONES
KARATE KID PART III, THE ..... CARO JONES
KILLER INSTINCT ..... ANDREW HERTZ
KINJITE (FORBIDDEN SUBJECTS) ..... NANCY LARA-HANSCH
KINJITE (FORBIDDEN SUBJECTS) ..... PERRY BULLINGTON
KLUTE ..... ALIXE GORDIN

INDEX OF FILM TITLES

La-Pa

FILM
PRODUCERS,
STUDIOS,
AGENTS AND
CASTING
DIRECTORS
GUIDE

I
N
D
E
X

O
F

F
I
L
M

T
I
T
L
E
S

360

L

M

N

O

P

FILM
PRODUCERS,
STUDIOS,
AGENTS AND
CASTING
DIRECTORS
GUIDE

I
N
D
E
X

O
F

F
I
L
M

T
I
T
L
E
S

R

S

FILM
PRODUCERS,
STUDIOS,
AGENTS AND
CASTING
DIRECTORS
GUIDE

T

U

V

W

Y

Z

★ ★ ★ ★

ENTERTAINMENT BANKS

BANK OF AMERICA
Entertainment Industries Division
555 South Flower Street
Los Angeles, CA 90071
213/228-2875

Mr. Gary Matus

BANK OF CALIFORNIA
Entertainment Division
9401 Wilshire Blvd.
Beverly Hills, CA 90212
310/273-7200

Mr. Michael Caponnetto

CALIFORNIA UNITED BANK
Entertainment Industries Group
250 N. Canon Drive
Beverly Hills, CA 90210
310/205-0444

Ms. Yaffa Koresh

CHEMICAL BANK
333 South Grand Avenue
Los Angeles, CA 90071
213/253-5057

Mr. John Miller

CITY NATIONAL BANK
Entertainment Division
400 North Roxbury Drive, Suite 400
Beverly Hills, CA 90210
310/550-5696

Ms. Martha Henderson

DAIWA BANK
800 West 6th Street, Suite 950
Los Angeles, CA 90017
213/623-0060

Mr. Chris Ball
Mr. Will Tyrer

DRESDNER BANK
725 Figueroa Blvd., Suite 3950
Los Angeles, CA 90017
213/489-5720

Mr. Jon Bland

CREDIT DU NORD
520 Madison Avenue
New York, NY 10022
212/308-5300

Mr. Ron England

FIRST LOS ANGELES BANK
Entertainment Industries Division
2049 Century Park East, 36th Floor
Los Angeles, CA 90067
310/557-1211

Ms. Maryann Lovatelli

LEWIS HORWITZ ORGANIZATION
A Division of Imperial Bank
1840 Century Park East
Los Angeles, Ca. 90067
310/275-7171

Mr. Charles Avis

IMPERIAL BANK
Entertainment Banking
9777 Wilshire Blvd., 4th Floor
Beverly Hills, CA 90212
310/338-3139

Mr. Steven J. Leibovitz

MERCANTILE NATIONAL BANK
Entertainment Industries Division
1840 Century Park East
Los Angeles, CA 90067
310/282-6716

Ms. Irene Romero

BANQUE PARIBAS
2029 Century Park East, #3900
Los Angeles, CA 90067
310/556-8759

Mr. David Burdge

UNION BANK
445 South Figueroa Street, 15th Floor
Los Angeles, CA 90071
213/236-5791

Ms. Julie Beghold

The FOURTH EDITION of
FILM PRODUCERS, STUDIOS, AGENTS
AND CASTING DIRECTORS GUIDE

ALL LISTINGS ARE FREE.

DON'T BE LEFT OUT!!! Guarantee your *FREE* listing (please read the introduction for qualifications) by filling out and returning this form to us *IMMEDIATELY*. *(Photocopy as many times as necessary).*

PERSONAL INFORMATION

Name _____

Company _____

Address _____

City/State/Zip _____

Area Code/Phone _____

Birth Date & Place _____

Home ❑   Business ❑

PLEASE PRINT OR TYPE

REPRESENTATIVE'S INFORMATION

Agent ❑   Personal Manager ❑   Attorney ❑
Business Manager ❑   Other ❑   AFM ❑
(List as many representatives as you would like. Continue listing on reverse, if necessary.)

Name _____

Company _____

Address _____

City/State/Zip _____

Area Code/Telephone _____

PLEASE PRINT OR TYPE

CREDITS

List your credits as follows: Please note alternate titles in parentheses. Please note Academy nominations/awards for your work. If you need more space, please continue on reverse side.

FEATURES: DRIVING MISS DAISY ★★   Warner Bros., 1989, w/Lili Fini Zanuck*
THE ROAD WARRIOR   *MAD MAX II*   Warner Bros., 1982, Australian, EP

_____

_____

_____

_____

_____

_____

_____

MAIL or FAX form *IMMEDIATELY* to
FILM PRODUCERS, STUDIOS, AGENTS AND
CASTING DIRECTORS GUIDE
Fourth Edition
950 South Flower Street, Suite 310
Los Angeles, CA 90015
310/471-8066 or 310/471-4969 (FAX)

Questions ???
Problems ???
Call 310/471-8066

FILM
PRODUCERS,
STUDIOS,
AGENTS AND
CASTING
DIRECTORS
GUIDE

INDEX OF ADVERTISERS

A special thanks to our advertisers whose support makes it possible to bring you the third edition of **FILM PRODUCERS, STUDIO AGENTS AND CASTING DIRECTORS GUIDE.**

★ ★ ★

FILM
PRODUCERS,
STUDIOS,
AGENTS AND
CASTING
DIRECTORS
GUIDE

ABOUT THE EDITORS

JACK LECHNER'S firmly held belief that no fact is too trivial has vexed his friends and family since childhood. Nonetheless, he has constructed crossword puzzles and word games for various publications; written the unfortunately titled *Ivy League Rock & Roll Quiz Book;* and set an unbreakable record for losing the most money on *Final Jeopardy.* He has also worked as a development executive for film and television production companies in New York, Los Angeles and London.

Jack lives in London with his wife Sam Maser and their transatlantic cat, Flora Turnpike.

★ ★ ★

DAVID KIPEN has written articles and reviews for *The Hollywood Reporter, Boxoffice, L.A. Style, and American Film.* He has also read aloud for the blind, captioned television for the deaf, and written coverages for several film companies. He is the author of a forthcoming Hollywood novel and a reticent screenplay.

David lives in downtown Los Angeles, and is not afraid to go out at night.